D1327578

BROWN'S
DICTIONARY OF
BIBLE CHARACTERS

A Preacher's Dictionary of Bible Characters

BY THE REV. DR. JOHN BROWN

EDITED BY GEOFFREY STONIER

CHRISTIAN HERITAGE

Engraved by Andrew Wilson

FROM AN ORIGINAL PAINTING

JOHN BROWN

LATE MINISTER OF THE GOSPEL, HADDINGTON, AND
PROFESSOR OF DIVINITY UNDER THE ASSOCIATE SYNOD

Copyright © Christian Focus Publcations 2007

ISBN 978-1-84550-266-9

10 9 8 7 6 5 4 3 2 1

Published in 2007
in the
Christian Heritage Imprint
by
Christian Focus Publications,
Geanies House, Fearn, Ross-shire,
IV20 1TW, Scotland

www.christianfocus.com

Cover design by Daniel Van Staaten

Printed and bound by WS Bookwell, Finland

CONTENTS

INTRODUCTION

BY GEOFFREY STONIER

J ohn Brown was born in 1722 and died in 1787. His Dictionary was first printed in 1769 when he was 47 years of age. He died after producing two further editions, which were enlarged into two volumes. A life of the author by his grandson was included in 1806, and a concordance was added in 1807. The last printing appeared in 1869, giving a useful life for the Dictionary, which never went out of print, of exactly 100 years.

As a frequent visitor to African and Asian countries, I can vouch for the fact that Pastors have nothing, or next to nothing, by way of biblical resources, in order to prepare themselves for preaching. For example, I could only find a tattered 2-volume Bible Dictionary in the Indian language of Telugu, and that was printed way back in the 1960's! There is little evidence that the situation among the vast number of rural pastors in the Third World developing countries is any better, when even Bible Dictionaries in English remain outside their financial grasp.

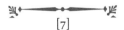

To remedy this situation, I was asked by the publishers to prepare a modern version of John Brown's Bible Dictionary. What I came to discover most valuable was not only the comprehensive information on Bible characters and Bible words, but also many valuable hints of application, looking, as the New Testament does on occasion, for types and antitypes, particularly with reference to our Lord Jesus Christ. These things are eminently useful for busy preachers.

Another fact must also be recognised: John Brown was, above all, a Biblical theologian. From the standpoint of his theological base, he could look at any point made in his dictionary, and fit any fact or application within a gospel context. Brown's Dictionary is eminently Christ-centred, making it entirely useful for gospel preachers. Other doctrines he emphasises over and over again are: God's redeeming purposes in history, the pitiful and helpless condition of sinners, justification by faith alone, and the exposure and final downfall of all of God's enemies. Thus, the reader of this dictionary becomes a theological preacher!

Brown's Dictionary covers practically everything. This present volume extracts from his Dictionary all the significant Bible names, giving salient facts, and providing many provocative thoughts by way of application. I can never forget Brown's summary after a long survey of the life of Christ, which provides a typical example of his inspirational preaching style:

"When we consider the relationship between Christ's Person as God-Man with his work in executing his offices, and his states of humiliation and glory, when we consider how God is in, and with, him, and how all his perfections are displayed, and his truths exemplified in him, when we consider his various relationships with the purposes, covenants, words, and ordinances of God, and with the Church, and with the privileges, duties, and worship of the saints, whether in time or eternity, we have a delightful view of him as *All, and In All.* (Col. 3:11)"

Neither will I ever forget his words describing the work of Antichrist, and his overthrow in the plain preaching of the gospel, and by the sovereign works of God:

"This antichrist began his work in the apostolic age, but was checked by the power of the Roman Empire till its destruction, when a fearful apostasy from the faith happened in the Church. His duration is 1260 years, during which he promotes idolatry, lies, and blasphemy; treads the church under foot; and persecutes the saints who, all along bear witness against his abominations. Nor do the terrible ravages of the Eastern angels loosed from the Euphrates in the east, make his subjects repent of their idolatries, murders, sorceries, fornications, and thefts. At the end of his reign, he will, with craft and fury, almost entirely cut off faithful witnessing for Christ. But, all of a sudden, by the pure preaching of the gospel, by the pouring out of sevenfold plagues, or vials of divine wrath, by the revolt and opposition of his own subjects, he will be terribly destroyed, to the consternation of his adherents and the great joy of the saints, both Jew and Gentile."

May this Dictionary of Bible names prove very useful in equipping gospel preachers, and in directing them to preach Christ, and him crucified! (1 Cor. 1:23)

Geoffrey Stonier
International Director Preachers' Help

A MEMOIR OF THE REV. JOHN BROWN

BY HIS GRANDSON THE
REV. JOHN BROWN PATTERSON

The Rev. Dr. John Brown, the author of the *Self-Interpreting Bible*, was born in the year 1722 at Carpow, a village in the parish of Abernethy and county of Perth. His parentage, in respect of external circumstances, was obscure, his father having, for most of his life, followed the humble occupation of a weaver, and was almost entirely lacking in the advantages of regular education. What was better, however, than fortune or learning, he seems to have been a man of superior intelligence and worth, and even to have possessed some portion of that zeal in pursuit of knowledge, and that facility in acquiring it, without the ordinary help that his son so largely inherited. The subject of this memoir writes of his deep obligations to the faithfulness with which his father discharged the duties of his domestic ministry in the midst of a remarkably spiritually careless neighbourhood. He rightly considered the need of the advantages of fortune was more than compensated by the privilege he enjoyed of joining

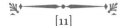

daily in the ordinances of family devotion, and the care that was taken by both his parents over his Christian education. "My parents' instructions", he said on his deathbed, "accompanied by God's dealings, early made such impressions on my heart as I trust will continue with me to all eternity."

Elementary education

His own opportunities for intellectual culture, as far as outward advantages were concerned, were not much greater than his father's. In consequence of the circumstances of his parents, he was able to spend only a very limited amount of time at school in achieving those things that constitute the ordinary education of the lower classes in Scotland - the elements of reading, writing, and arithmetic. "One month at school", he adds with much simplicity, "and without my parents' allowance, I bestowed upon the Latin." His thirst for knowledge was intense, which stimulated him even at this early period to extraordinary diligence in all departments of study. Yet even then the bent of his mind towards theology seems to have been decided. He has recorded the special pleasure he had when at school in committing to memory the catechisms of John Flavel and the Westminster Assembly, and the important benefits he considered himself to have derived from the exercise. His recollections of this part of his youthful training were most probably the occasion of the attention which, in future life, he bestowed on catechetical instruction, both in his pastoral care and in his published writings. The strong direction of his mind from the beginning to scholarship in general, and to that kind of it more closely connected with divinity in particular, seems to have early suggested to his mother the possibility of his one day finding scope for the indulgence of his tastes in the service of the church, and made her often picture, in her visions of maternal fondness, the day when she would, to use her own perhaps too homely expression, "see the crows flying over her bairn's kirk."

Meanwhile, personal piety, the first of all qualifications for the sacred office was lacking. He did not in later years feel himself justified in distinctly specifying any particular period as to the date of his conversion. In the fragment of his own life, however, which he left behind, he refers with much interest to the devotional impressions made on his mind when he was eight year of his age, at a sacramental occasion in the parish of Abernethy, when, having found his way into the church during the dispensing of the ordinance, and hearing the communion addresses of "a minister who spoke much to the commendation of Christ", he felt his young affections sweetly and delightfully captivated with the excellencies of the Saviour, and was led from his own experience to deny the practice, now happily discontinued, which then prevailed, of excluding all but intended communicants from witnessing a service so well calculated to impress and attract the heart.

When he was about eleven years of his age, he was deprived by death of his father, and, soon after, of his mother, and was himself reduced by four successive attacks of fever to a state that made it probable that he was speedily about to join his parents in the grave. But his Master had work for him on earth; and, having sanctified his sufferings to impress him with very solemn and affecting views of eternal things, at length raised him up from his bed of sickness, but an orphan, and without a home.

A shepherd

When his father and mother forsook him, his better Parent took him up, and provided him with a friend and protector. Among the mountains in the neighbourhood of Abernethy, John Ogilvie, a shepherd venerable for age, and eminent in piety, fed his flock. This worthy man was an elder of the parish of Abernethy; yet, though a person of intelligence and religion, he was so destitute of education as to be unable even to read - a circumstance that may appear strange to those accustomed to hear of the universal provision of elementary education among the Scottish peasantry, but which is to be accounted for in the case of the elder Brown by the disordered state of all the social institutions in Scotland up to the end of the seventeenth century. The system of parochial schools in particular, which the wisdom of our ancestors (to employ a much abused expression in a case where it is well deserved) had connected with the ecclesiastical establishment of Scotland, and which, during the Episcopal domination, had fallen into complete neglect, was not restored by law till the year 1696. In these circumstances, the godly shepherd was glad to embrace the opportunity of supplying a need he must have felt so severely as his incapacity to read and study for himself the written Word of the God he served, by engaging young Brown to help him in tending his flock, and read to him during the intervals of comparative inaction and rest which that occupation affords, of the character and work of Him who feeds His flock like a shepherd, and who gave His life for his sheep. To screen themselves from the storm and the heat, they built a little lodge among the hills, and to this, their mountain tabernacle (long after pointed out by this name by the peasants), they frequently went to celebrate their pastoral devotions. Often "the wilderness and the solitary place were glad for them, and the desert rejoiced even with joy and singing."

Mr. Brown speaks of his spiritual experience during this period of sweet and edifying communion as having been specially lively and affecting. By the dealings of divine providence, as well as by the books he read, and the sermons he heard, he was brought and kept under very impressive knowledge of divine things; the frequency and the pleasantness of his secret devotions were greatly increased; and in the same proportion he felt his conscience becoming more lively and tender, and his external conduct more pure and blameless. He confesses, however, a strong taint of legality (to use the phrase of the time) running through his religious experience at this period, which may explain the sudden decay of its force and vividness that presently came about.

Before long, it happened that Ogilvie retired from his occupation as a shepherd, and settled in the town of Abernethy. In consequence of this change, young Brown entered the service of a neighbouring farmer, who maintained a larger establishment than his former friend. This step he laments as having been followed by much practical apostasy from God, which showed itself in a sensible decline of religious attainments, and a general lukewarm-ness in religious duty, Still, however, during this season of backsliding which he himself saw reason to deplore, his external character was remarkably distinguished by many virtues, and especially by the rare and truly Christian grace of meekness. Such was the impression produced by his patience under trying provocations, and his readiness to pardon gross insult and injury in the mind of a fellow shepherd who had previously taken a malicious pleasure in annoying the young saint, that he could find no rest in his mind till he had personally expressed his shame and regret for his conduct, and had received a hearty assurance of forgiveness. He afterwards showed the sincerity of his repentance by making it his study from that time forward to oblige and serve him whom formerly he had persecuted; and the same individual, on his death-bed, declared his obligation to Mr. Brown for the religious instruction and admonitions he had received from him during their time as fellow servants, saying that it was more than he could express.

In the year 1733, four ministers of the Church of Scotland, among whom was Mr. Moncrieff of Abernethy, declared a secession from its authorities, alleging as their reasons for taking this step the following list of grievances: "The sufferance of error without adequate censure; the infringement of the rights of the Christian people in the choice and settlement of ministers under the law of patronage; the neglect or relaxation of discipline; the restraint of ministerial freedom in opposing mal-administration, and the refusal of the prevailing party to be reclaimed." To this body, our young shepherd early attached himself, and ventured to conceive the idea of one day becoming a shepherd of souls in that connexion. Accordingly, he prosecuted his studies with increasing ardour and diligence, and began to attain considerable knowledge of Latin and Greek. These acquisitions he made entirely without aid from others, except that he was able occasionally to snatch an hour when the flocks were folded at noon, in order to seek the solution of such difficulties as his unaided efforts could not master from two neighbouring clergymen, one, Mr. Moncrieff of Abernethy, whom we have just mentioned as one of the founders of the Secession, and the other, Mr. Johnston of Arngask, father of the late venerable Dr. Johnston of North Leith; both of whom were very obliging and communicative, and took great interest in promoting the progress of the studious shepherd-boy. An anecdote has been preserved of this part of his life and studies, which deserves to be mentioned. He had now acquired so much knowledge of Greek that it encouraged him to hope that he might at length be prepared to reap the richest of all rewards which classical learning could confer on him, the capacity of reading in the original tongue the blessed New Testament of our Lord and Saviour Jesus Christ. Full of this hope, he became anxious to possess a copy of the invaluable volume. One night, accordingly, having folded his flocks in safety, and his fellow shepherd, whose sentiments towards him were now those of friendship and veneration, having undertaken to discharge his pastoral duties for the succeeding day, he set out on a midnight journey to St. Andrews, a distance of twenty-four miles. Having reached his destination in the morning, he went straight to the nearest bookseller, and asked for a copy of the Greek New Testament. The owner of the shop, though, situated as he was in a provincial Scottish University, he must have been accustomed to hear such books asked for by youths whose appearance and dress were none of the most civilized, was nevertheless somewhat astonished at such an application from so unlikely a young man, and was rather disposed to taunt him for his presumption. Meanwhile, a party of gentlemen, said to have been professors in the University, entered the shop, and having understood the matter, questioned the lad about his employment and his studies. After hearing his tale, one of them asked the bookseller to bring the volume, who, accordingly, produced it, and threw it down upon the table. "Boy", said he, "read that book, and you shall have it for nothing." The offer was too good to be true, and young Brown, having acquitted himself to the admiration of his judges, carried off his cheaply-purchased Testament in triumph, and, before the next evening, was studying it among his flock on the hills of Abernethy.

Circumstances connected with his conversion

While pursuing these occupations, and having now reached the age of nineteenth, he was again visited in his person with a severe attack of fever, and, in his mind with bitter repentance for his late spiritual decline. This feeling was increased to agony by a sermon he heard soon after his recovery on John 6:64 - "*There are some of you which believe not.*" Although afterwards he saw the rashness of such a judgement, at this period, he felt like giving up all his past spiritual experiences as delusions, or at best the effects of that influence of the Holy Spirit in which the unconverted may participate. This depression was not allowed to continue long. The following day, he heard another sermon by the Reverend Adam Gib on Isaiah 53:4 - "*Surely he hath borne our griefs, and carried our sorrows*", which brought sudden relief to his wounded spirit, and led him into much "*peace and joy in believing.*" For more than a year after this memorable day, he went on his way rejoicing, and seems always to have looked back on those happy months as the brightest of his spiritual life on earth.

Persecution

A new trial, however, awaited him, and that of a very extraordinary kind. His remarkable acquirements he had been able to make in the Latin, Greek, and Hebrew languages, by his diligent and persevering hard work, stirred up against him that malign spirit of envy against which superior excellence, however combined with an unassuming conduct, is never secure. The way in which this feeling was expressed was in the circulation of a tale, which, though it now sounds ridiculous, was, in those days, very serious. It began to be whispered that the young scholar had acquired his knowledge in a sinful way by dealings with that Evil Spirit who, with the bait of knowledge, ensnared our original mother, and to whom tradition has always ascribed special advantages to the diligent and solitary student. This malicious suggestion was eagerly caught up by the ignorant, and, circulated far and wide, haunting his steps for five further years almost like the consciousness of guilt, producing a degree of suffering in his mind which, with our way of thinking these days, we find it hard to understand. The days of sending to trial before judges the dealers in the dark arts had happily passed away; but in those days this spirit, to a great degree, still survived, and was still able to inflict on its victims painful persecution. It is sorrowful to think that this absurd and wicked attack on his reputation should have had enough influence on a respectable minister to make him withdraw for a time his presence and support from the meritorious and gifted young man whom he had so far patronised. That gentleman, it is fair to say, afterwards regretted and repented of his rash judgement; but it must have been especially painful to the feelings of our young scholar and Christian that one who knew him so well should so easily have listened to such slander.

He was comforted, however, during this attack and desertion by the sympathy and good opinion of many steadfast friends, especially the members of a prayer group with whom he was connected, and the support of others among the leaders of the Secession, such as the brothers Erskine and Mr. Fisher. "But my chief support", he writes, "was the word of truth, which the Lord enabled me to believe. Meanwhile, by the reproach that was cast upon me, he led me out to ponder my own heart and ways, and to question myself before Him whether I was a devil. This made me submit to my lot, and kept me from naming my slanderers. Then, and ever since, I have found that the Lord has most plainly vindicated me when I have made not the least carnal struggle for my own honour. I am bound to say also that the sting I had found in my learning tended to keep me humble, and the false reproaches I then met with made me all along less naïve in what I heard about other people. On these and other accounts, I have since looked on affliction as a kind providence to my soul."

A peddler
Soon after the start of this malicious report, and probably as a result of the annoyance to which it exposed him, he gave up the occupation of a shepherd and undertook that of a peddler (a travelling merchant). This way of life was once of much greater importance and higher esteem in Scotland than at present,

when such people acted as the means of communication between all parts of the country, and such commerce was highly valued, and was often pursued by people of great intelligence and respectability. Its pursuit specially trained the mind to love nature, and to form in it a knowledge of the world, as is seen in a great poet of our day. It will not, however, be considered very surprising when we say that young Brown did not shine much in his new profession. During his mercantile wanderings, which lay chiefly in the rural areas of Fife and Kinross-shire, he made it a rule to call at no house where the family did not have the reputation of being religious and given to reading. When he was received into any such home, his first care was to have all the books it could furnish collected together, among which, if he found a new one, he fell with greediness on the literary feast, finding in the appetite to feed his soul a forgetfulness of the hunger of his body, and, in the traffic of knowledge, he forgot to sell his peddlers' wares. It is told, and we may well believe it, that the contents of his pack on his return to headquarters from one of his expeditions used to present a lively image of chaos, and that he was very glad to express his obligations to any neat-handed housewife who would take the arrangement of them on herself. Many a time, and often, he was prudently reminded of the need to attend more to his business, and not waste his time on what did not concern him, till his supervisors at last gave up his case in despair, and, wisely shaking their heads, pronounced him "good for nothing but to be a scholar."

While he was engaged in this thankless profession, the young adventurer Charles Edward (Bonny Prince Charlie) made his bold attempt to regain for his family the forfeited British crown. One day, as young Brown was going his rounds, he observed at a distance a troop of Highlanders approaching, and, aware that their "lifting" habits made the mountain warriors poor customers, he took refuge behind a cairn of stones that happened to be at hand, till the blue bonnets were out of sight. Thus warned that these were not times for the exercise of his peaceful calling, he determined to retire from it, at least for a time; and, sharing the feelings of the great body of the Presbyterian interest, among whom the Seceders were at this crisis honourably distinguished for their loyalty, he decided to devote himself to the defence of those civil and religious liberties which were then in danger from the ambitious daring of the Popish Pretender. Accordingly, having safely deposited his wares in the heart of a peat-stack, he enlisted in a volunteer corps that was then raised in Fife for the defence of the established government. Although he does not appear to have been at any time actually engaged with the enemy, he exercised his military capacity for some time in the fort of Blackness, and in Edinburgh castle. The pay, which he received during his term of service, went chiefly to the bookseller's shop; so when his regiment was disbanded after the putting down of the rebellion at the decisive battle of Culloden, he left his quarters in Edinburgh castle with a sum in his pocket amounting to three pence. This money carried him across the Queen's Ferry into the scenes of his former wandering, and the vicinity of the peat stack that contained his stock in trade, where he found it perfectly safe and in good condition.

His teaching

He was soon, however, persuaded to abandon this unsettled and uncongenial life, and, on the advice of some of his friends, he took himself to the more suitable employment of teaching school. For this purpose, he established himself in the year 1747 at Gairney Bridge, a village in the neighbourhood of Kinross, and there laid the foundation of a school which went on for a long time afterwards, and which, fifteen years later, was taught by another individual whose name has also become well-known in the world. During Mr Brown's incumbency, which lasted for two years, this school became remarkably successful, and attracted scholars from considerable distances. Afterwards, he taught for a year and a half at another school at Spittal, in the congregation of Linton under Mr James Mair. The practical character of his talents, the accuracy of his learning, the tender experience in which, as a self-taught scholar, he must have experienced elementary difficulties, and the best means of solving them, and the conscientiousness and perseverance that always were the distinguishing features of his character, must have specially qualified him in the discharge of his duties, and laid a solid foundation for his general acceptance as an instructor of youth. It can readily be believed that he did not neglect the opportunities that were afforded him of filling his pupils' minds with the most important of all sorts of knowledge - the practical knowledge of religion. It was his custom every Saturday to address them on this subject with all that warning energy and pathos he always displayed in dealing with the young on the matter of their eternal interest. These instructions, there is reason to believe, were in many cases attended with the best results; and it is perhaps in a great measure to their influence that the striking fact can be traced, that not fewer than eight or nine of his pupils ultimately became ministers of the gospel.

While active in superintending the studies of others, he did not relax in learning on his own account. On the contrary, his ardour seems to have led him into unwise extremes of working. He would commit to memory fifteen chapters of the Bible as an evening exercise after the labours of the day, and, after such killing efforts, allow himself just four hours of sleep. To this excess of exertion, he was probably stimulated by the near approach of the period to which he had long looked forward with trembling hope - the day that would reward the toils and trials of his youthful days - by investing him with the solemn function of an ambassador of Christ. During the school holidays, he was now engaged in the regular study of philosophy and divinity under the inspection of the Associate late Synod, and under the superintendence of the Rev. Ebenezer Erskine and James Fisher, two of the original founders and principal lights of the Secession church. At length, in the year 1751, having completed his preparatory course of study, and proved himself in his trial before the Associate Presbytery of Edinburgh, he received his licence from this august body at Dalkeith to preach the gospel in their society. He entered upon the sacred work with deep impressions of its solemnity and awesomeness. He has himself mentioned that his mind, immediately before his receiving authority to preach, was very vividly affected by that awe-inspiring text in Isaiah 6:9-10 - "*He said, Go and tell this people, Hear ye indeed, but understand not; see ye indeed, but perceive not; make the heart of this people fat, and make their ears heavy, and shut their eyes; lest they see with their eyes, and hear with their ears, and understand with their hearts, and convert and be healed.*" Nor could he help remarking, with a reverential sense of the goodness and severity of God, that the leading author and propagator of those lies from which he had suffered so severely, had been excommunicated by his own supporters at the very time that he was sent out in vindicated innocence as the acknowledged and commissioned messenger of Christ.

Pastoral life

He had not long been a probationer, when he received two nearly simultaneous calls to the settled discharge of ministerial duty; one from the congregation of Stow, a village in the Shire of Edinburgh, and the other from Haddington, the principal town in the county of that name. The Presbytery of Edinburgh, within whose bounds both congregations were included, and which had therefore, according to the Presbyterian constitution, the right of deciding between their competing claims, submitted the matter to his own discretion. His choice was set on Haddington, partly by his feelings of sympathy with that congregation for disappointments it had already experienced, and partly by his modest estimate of his own qualifications, to which he felt the smaller of the two charges more suitable. Over this congregation, therefore, he was finally ordained pastor in the month of June 1751. It deserves mention, however, that he continued regularly to visit and examine the congregation of Stow until it was supplied with a regular minister.

The life of Mr. Brown during this period was full of the usual monotony that characterises that of a minister in a quiet country town; and his biography from now on must consist of the account of habits rather than of incidents.

To the duties of the sacred office, he devoted himself with the most zealous and laborious industry. The smallness of his congregation enabled him at once to undertake the widest range of ministerial duty, and to execute it with the greatest diligence and exactness. Besides regularly preaching four sermons every Lord's day during the summer, and there during winter in his own place of worship, and occasionally in the country during the week, he visited all his people annually in his pastoral capacity, and took them twice in the same period through a course of public catechetical examinations. He was very quick to visit the sick and afflicted, and not just to members of his own congregation, but to all of every denomination who asked for his services. The peculiar characteristic of his manner of address on all these occasions, both public and private, was an intense solemnity and earnestness, which demanded attention even from the scorner, and was obviously the genuine expression of his own overwhelming sense of the reality and importance of his message. "His grave appearance", says an English divine who attended his ministry for some time, "his solemn, weighty, and energetic manner of speaking, used to affect me very much. Certainly his preaching was personal, and his address to the conscience pungent. Like his Lord and Master, he spoke with authority and in hallowed tones, having tasted the sweetness and felt the power of what he delivered."

To the same effect, the celebrated David Hume, having been led to hear him preach on one occasion at North Berwick, remarked, "That old man preaches as if Christ were at his elbow." Except for this overawing seriousness, and occasionally a melting sweetness in his voice, it does not appear that his delivery was by any means attractive. "It was my mercy", he says, with characteristic modesty, "that the Lord, who had given me some other talents, withheld from me a popular delivery, so, though my sermons were not unpalatable to the serious, so far as I have heard, they were not so agreeable to many hearts as to those of my brothers, whom it was a pleasure to me see possessed of that talent which the Lord, to restrain my pride, denied me."

The diction he used of in his public speaking was chiefly and carefully scriptural. In the earlier part of his ministry, like most young preachers, he was tempted to indulge in a wordy and fanciful style, which he afterwards saw reason to repent of and discard. "I had made an observation", he says, "in the days of my youth, that what touched my conscience and my heart were not airy flights or well-turned phrases, but express scriptural expressions, or whatever came close to them. The older I grew, it was more and more my aim to preach Scriptural truths in Scriptural language."

His choice of subjects was very varied and extensive. His mind was thoroughly versed, and his faith firmly established, in that system of Christianity commonly known under the name of Calvinism, and explicitly declared in the standard books of the Scottish Church. He made it his object to declare, in the course of his preaching, the whole counsel of God, and to exhibit and enforce all the parts of the Christian scheme in their proper proportion and connection. The sermons to which he refers as having been preached with most pleasure to his own soul are chiefly on subjects connected with the consolations and the joys of experimental religion. Those again of his published writings, which give us best idea of his power as a preacher, are his addresses to various classes of individuals, especially the young, on the necessity of personal reconciliation with God, which are characterised by a point, with a sense of urgency and fervour of earnest application that Richard Baxter himself could hardly have exceeded.

In the general conduct of divine service and pastoral duty, Mr. Brown kept close to the established order of the Presbyterian churches, although he showed his good sense in being brief and varied, to relieve as much as possible the tedium with which that routine occasionally produces. His sermons, and even more his prayers, were remarkably to the point, except on days of humiliation and thanksgiving, when prayer was the characteristic service. "Be short", he used to tell his students, "in the pulpit and the family; in secret you may be as long as you like."

In one part of the established order of worship, Mr. Brown saw a great deficiency, which he attempted in some measure to correct. There is no portion of religious service in which the

Presbyterian churches in Scotland have so grossly departed from the acknowledged example of the early Christians, as in the infrequent dispensation of the Lord's Supper. In the period when Mr. Brown began his ministry, this holy ordinance was nowhere in Scotland administered more than once year.

Mr. Brown, soon after his arrival in Haddington, attempted to introduce some improvement of the system into his congregation, and, after the year 1756, had the Lord's Supper regularly dispensed twice a year; though so strong were the prejudices against this measure that he could find only one of his brothers who would assist him in carrying it into effect. He drew up a letter at this period, which was printed after his death, urging a reform in this matter over Scotland in general - a reform that has since taken place in the Secession churches to such an extent, that, in a considerable number of churches connected with that association, the sacrament in question is administered once every three months.

While thus diligent in the discharge of his own more direct and official duties for promoting the spiritual improvement of his people, he was eager to support every means by which they might become fellow-labourers with him in advancing each other's spiritual interests. Among these means, he extended special help to those periodic conferences among a few individual Christians, connected by friendship or acquaintance, which formerly, under the name of Fellowship-meetings, were much more general among the godly than at present, and which, like the best institutions of earth, are liable to abuse through human frailty and imprudence, were certainly in their own nature eminently Christian, and calculated to be edifying. Such institutions, both among the young and old, he made an effort to support to the utmost of his power, by earnestly recommending them from the pulpit, by giving them all facilities for assembling in his house, and by regularly visiting their meetings, wisely superintending their procedure, and generously partaking in their exercises. He was especially concerned for the spiritual interests of the young, and used every means for promoting them.

His labours were not vain in the Lord. The members of his congregation, the smallness of which he often spoke of as a mercy, seem to have been enabled to walk, in a great measure, suitably to their profession and their privileges; and he had less experience than most ministers of that bitterest of all trials attached to a conscientious pastor's situation - scandalous irregularities of practice among those in regard to whom he can have no greater joy than to see them walking in the truth. Nor were his exertions without success for the great end of converting sinners from the error of their ways. He was often overwhelmed with awful impressions, like those under which he began the work of preaching, of the effects of a gospel ministry abused in emphasising the guilt and condemnation of those who sat beneath its sound. "Frequently", he says, "have I had an anxious desire to be removed by death from being a curse to my poor congregation." He often, however, saw occasion to check these distrustful and descending thoughts; and there is reason to suppose that the cases were much more numerous than he knew, in which he was an instrument of saving souls from death, and covering a multitude of sins.

In ecclesiastical policy he was a staunch Presbyterian and Seceder in the original sense of the term, as denoting an individual separated, not from the constitution of the Established Church either as a church or as an establishment, but from the policy and control of the predominant party in her authority. In general, however, he was an advocate of strict communion, though far from the uncharitableness of unchurching all other denominations. His public prayers were liberal and catholic, and he always showed the strongest affection for gospel ministers and true Christians of every name. In an unpublished letter to a noble lady of the Episcopal Communion, he expressed his hope "that it will afford her a delightful satisfaction to observe how extensive and important the agreement, and how small the difference of religious sentiments, between a professedly staunch Presbyterian and a truly conscientious Episcopalian, if they both cordially believe the doctrine of God's free grace reigning in men's eternal life, through the imputed righteousness of Jesus Christ our Lord." He made a point of regularly attending and acting in the church courts, though he avoided taking any leading part in the management of ecclesiastical business. His own account and judgement of his conduct in this matter are given in the following words:

> "In public things, I have been rather inclined to act up to my own views, than to push others into a conformity with me. I had little relish for making ecclesiastical rules without great harmony. I had found no small difficulty in fixing my own sentiments on some things; and this made me averse to urge my opinions on others, unless I had plain Scripture to support them. I laid it down as a rule never to be very zealous in favour of anything in which my own self-interest or honour was in any respect concerned. I found it was dangerous, even in the lawful defence of self, to go too far. My sense of the forwardness of my temper, and that several of my brothers saw more quickly or farther than I did, restrained me from obstinacy in judgement. My knowledge of the miserable effects of clerical contentions in the Christian church, and my strong inclination to peace, sometimes, I believe, led me to undue yielding or silence."

Such are the outlines of his professional conduct and character. As a private believer, he was distinguished by a remarkable saintliness of thought, feeling, and bearing. His characteristic traits as a Christian were profoundly low views of himself as a sinner, and highly exalted views of Christ as his Saviour. The emphatic expressions of humiliation and self-abasement, which occur in all his private papers, cannot but appear overstrained and almost in bad taste to those who do not apprehend so vividly as he the majesty of holiness that invests the great Creator, or the malignity and vileness of sin, even in what men would call its most venial forms, in the creatures of His hand. But this feeling of his own worthlessness only served to enhance in his opinion the worth of the Redeemer, and to call forth in regard to Him an intenser flame of admiration and love. His chief delight was to lose himself amid the height and depth, the length and breadth, of this immeasurable subject; and the knowledge that he panted for most earnestly was that of which he most readily confessed that the subject passes knowledge, the love of God in Christ Jesus our Lord.

The uniformity and universality of his habits of personal devotion were remarkable. Of him it might well be said that he walked with God, and that in God he, as it were in his own consciousness, moved, and lived, and had his being. He acquired a holy skill in deriving from every scene of nature, and every incident of life, occasions of Christian thought, impulses of Christian feeling, and motives for Christian duty. His *Christian Journal* seems to have been literally the picture of his daily course and association of ideas, and the beautiful motto he prefixed to it, to have been the expression of his own experience: "The ear that is ever attentive to God never hears a voice that speaks not of Him; the soul, whose eye is intent on Him, never sees an atom in which she doth not discern her Best Beloved."

He could hold sweet communion with his heavenly Father in the most terrible displays of His majesty, not less than in the softer manifestations of His blessings. One day, hearing a tremendous crash of thunder, he smilingly exclaimed to those around, "That is the low whisper of my God." His seasons of prayer, stated and special, secret and domestic, were frequent beyond the rules of any prescribed routine. Often he was overheard, in the nightly and the morning watches, talking with his God in prayer and praise, remembering his Maker upon his bed, and having his song with him in the night. Amid the ordinary details of life, the devout aspirations of his heart were continually breaking forth in prayers and expressions of thanksgiving and holy desire. His conversation habitually dwelt on heavenly things; or, if secular subjects were introduced, he would turn them with sanctifying ingenuity into divine emblems and spiritual analogies. His whole mind and life seemed full of devotion, and all his days formed, as it were, one Sabbath.

Towards his fellow men, he displayed an ardent benevolence and charity. The chief of Christian graces he had frequent opportunities of exhibiting under all its various forms - whether of a tender and active gratitude exercised on behalf of the benefactors of his youth, or an imperturbable forbearance and cordial forgiveness towards those who had slandered and reviled him, or an alert and extensive grace in relieving the needs around him whether spiritual or temporal. The extent of his generous liberality was surprising. He considered it a binding duty on every Christian to devote at least one tenth of his income to pious uses; and, out of an income which, during most of his life, amounted to only forty pounds a year, and never exceeded fifty, and from which he had a family to support, he generally exceeded that proportion. He distributed his benevolence with strict attention to the Saviour's command, "Let not thy left hand know what thy right hand doeth." His charities were accounted, not through the ostentation of the giver, but from the gratitude of the receiver; and often he took great care that those whom he obliged should not have it in their power to give thanks to anyone.

In the highest work of Christian benevolence, that of propagating the gospel among the heathen, he never had the same opportunities of joining in as it is our privilege to enjoy. The resolve, however, that would have led him to embrace these opportunities with delight was strong within him. He was accustomed often to act as a home missionary, preaching the true gospel in destitute places of the country, at a great expense of time and labour; and no news from foreign parts was received with so much rapture as that of the apostolic labours and success of the illustrious David Brainerd, and like-minded men. Towards the end of his life, in his public discourses, he used to dwell with special interest on the subject of missions to the heathen.

He was aware of the importance of conversation amongst those to whom he wished to do good, and, though he laments his own "sinful weakness and lack of skill in advancing religious discourse", he was too conscientious to neglect any opportunity that presented itself to promoting, in this way, the glory of God and the best interests of men. He made it a distinct principle never to leave any company in which he might be placed without saying something which, by the blessing of God, might promote their spiritual good. It is related that, having accidentally met Ferguson the poet walking in Haddington churchyard, and being struck with his pensive appearance, he modestly addressed him, and offered him certain serious advice concerning things that were deeply afflicting him at the time, and doubtless had their share in exciting and promoting those terrible convictions which later overwhelmed the poet's mind, and in which it may perhaps be hoped he knew something better than "the sorrow which worketh death."

He knew, however, that there is a certain discretion that should be used in such cases, and a selection to be made of the "*mollia tempora fandi*" (the seasons when words are fitly spoken). Of this, the following anecdote is an example: Having occasion to cross the ferry between Leith and King Horn with a Highland gentleman as a fellow passenger, he was much grieved to hear his companion frequently take the name of God in vain, but restrained himself from taking any action over it in the presence of the rest of the company. On making land, however, and observing the same gentleman walking alone along the beach, he stepped up and calmly reminded him of the offence he had been guilty of, and the law of God that forbade and condemned it. The gentleman received the reproof with expressions of thanks, and declared his resolution to attend to it in future. "But", added the choleric Celt, "had you spoken to me in this way in the boat, I believe I would have run you through."

Correspondence

Mr. Brown's letters, by his own choice, were not very extensive. Besides his more immediate friends, however, and in his own country and communion, he corresponded with Mr. Mason of New York, Mr. Anna of Boston, Mr Phillips of Serum, Mr. Charles Simeon of Cambridge, and the celebrated Selina, Countess dowager of Huntingdon. These letters of his that have been preserved show great depth of Christian feeling, and great experience in the Christian life. His general manner was very grave and serious. When occasionally in the society of those friends who most resembled him, he relaxed into cheerfulness and an innocent pleasantry. The normal tone and colour of his social deportment was an intense and uniform solemnity; all the personal feelings of humanity were in him kept under strict control by a clear judgement, and continually assessed with a vivid perception of eternal realities. So neither did the successes of ordinary life greatly elevate, nor its calamities greatly depress him, and his whole train of thought and feeling seemed to glide on in one even and uniform tenor of almost passionless serenity.

It will not be supposed that, after having given himself with such ardour to study in circumstances of comparative disadvantage, he neglected to avail himself of the more favourable opportunities he now enjoyed of extending and consolidating his knowledge. By a diligent use of the morning hours, and a studious economy of time throughout the day, he rarely spent fewer than twelve hours of the twenty-four in his study. He possessed extraordinary patience with the physical labour connected with such hard study. No degree of toil in the way of reading, or even of writing, seemed to daunt or tire him. Though he never enjoyed the assistance of a secretary, he transcribed most of his works several times in his own hand, and even without a view to the press, he more than once undertook the same fatigue for the convenience of private individuals. In this way, at the request of the Countess of Huntingdon, he copied out his System of Divinity before its publication for the use of her Ladyship's Theological Seminary in Wales. He had a remarkable facility in his acquisition of languages; and of this species of knowledge - the key to every other - he possessed an extraordinary flair. Besides the three commonly called the scholarly tongues, he was acquainted with Arabic, Syrian, Persian, and Ethiopian; and of modern languages, French, Spanish, Italian, Dutch, and German.

In the various departments of real, as distinct from, verbal knowledge, his reading was very wide-ranging and varied in subject. His favourite pursuits were history and divinity; but every subject, that more nearly or more remotely bore on the literature of his profession, he considered worthy of his attention.

"Through desire, having separated himself, he sought out and intermeddled with all knowledge." He afterwards saw reason to repent of the wideness of his aims in this respect, and to regret "the precious time and talents which", to use his own words, "he had vainly squandered in the mad attempt to become a universal scholar." His reading, though extensive, was at the same time very exact and accurate. In order to render it so, he, in many cases, adopted the tedious and laborious method of compiling regular abridgements of important and voluminous books. Among the works he thus summarised were Judge Blackstone's *Commentaries*, and the *Ancient Universal History*. The general results of his experience in literary study that he put on record are the following:

> "From experience I have found that it is vain to attempt to be a universal scholar; that a few books, well chosen and carefully used, are better than a multitude. Many books are not worth the reading, and if read once, we had better extract their useful hints into a notebook, and never look into them any more; that abridging more important books, especially if they are large, is very useful; that few plays or romances are safely read, as they are apt to pollute the heart, and even those that are most pure, as of Young, Addison, Thomson, Richardson, bewitch the soul, and are apt to indispose for holy meditation and other religious exercises, and so should be read at most but very sparingly. In reading histories, the Lord often made me not only take up the facts as his doing, and as verifications of some part of his Word, but also made them to suggest some useful, and sometimes very sweet thoughts respecting the redemption-scheme."

In another place, he says:

> "None who know how long and how eagerly I have hunted after human literature, as my circumstances permitted, will easily suspect me of being an enthusiastic condemner of it; but, as on the brink of eternity, I dare boldly pronounce it all to be but vanity and vexation of spirit when compared with, and not

subordinated to, the experimental knowledge of Christ as made of God to us wisdom and righteousness, and sanctification and redemption. There is no language, ancient or modern, like that of the gospel of the grace of God, pronounced by the Holy Spirit to the heart, and by heaven-born souls to God under His influence - no history like that of Jesus Christ, redemption through His blood, and the effective application of His grace - no science like that of beholding the Word made flesh, and contemplating the infinite perfections of Jehovah, in Him, and through Him, in every creature, as from eternity manifested, and for ever to be manifested, in our inconceivable happiness, to the praise of the glory of his grace."

Marriage and the home

In the month of September 1753, about two years after his ordination, Mr. Brown entered the married state. The lady who was to become his partner in life was Miss Janet Thomson, daughter of Mr. John Thomson, merchant at Musselburgh. For eighteen years, he enjoyed her as a "helpmeet" for himself in his Christian course, and, at the end of that period, he surrendered her, as he himself expresses it, "to her first and better Husband." They had several children, of whom only two survived their mother, John and Ebenezer, both of whom their father before his death had the satisfaction of introducing as ministers into the church of Christ, the former at Whitburn, and the latter at Inverkeithing, and both of whom received grace to continue faithful unto this day. Two years after the death of his first wife, which took place in 1771, he was married a second time to Miss Violet Crombie, daughter of Mr William Crombie, merchant in Stenton, East Lothian, who survived him for more than thirty years, and by whom he left at his death four sons and two daughters, of whom only half are still now alive. In his domestic economy and discipline, Mr. Brown laboured after a strict fidelity to his ordination vow, by which he promised to rule well his own home. His notions in regard to the authority of a husband and a father were very high, and all his authority, which, as such, he thought himself to possess, was faithfully employed in maintaining both the form and the power of godliness. "He commanded his children and his household after him, that they should fear the Lord, and walk in his ways." He was not content with keeping up the more ordinary routine of family religion, but was accustomed frequently to appoint extraordinary periods of domestic devotion, and from time to time to call his household to the exercise of fasting and thanksgiving, according to the different frames of their own spirits, and the varying aspects of divine providence. In the case of domestic trials and bereavements, which he had not infrequently to endure, he felt deeply, but not ostentatiously. His external demeanour on such occasions of domestic affliction was remarkable only for a more than ordinary quietness, and an apparently deeper retirement into his own thoughts. Like Aaron, "he held his peace."

Literary output

In the year 1758, Mr Brown, for the first time, appeared as an author. His first publication was entitled "*A Help for the Ignorant, being an Essay towards an Easy Explication of the Westminster Confession of Faith and Catechisms, compiled for the use of the young ones of his own congregation.*" In addition to this, he published, six years later two short catechisms: one introductory to, and the other explanatory of, the Shorter Catechism. All these publications have been very extensively used, though with our improved ideas of elementary education, it might perhaps be felt an objection to them, as intended for this purpose, that they are rather expansions than simplifications of the works they profess to illustrate, and that they rather aim at explaining the particular applications and mutual relations of the doctrines taught in the standard, than at putting their meaning into simpler words and more popular expressions.

At the same time, we must regard as worthy of all praise and imitation, the care shown by our author and the good men of his age, to make their people thoroughly conversant with the evangelical system taught in the standards of the Church. Without them, such preliminary acquaintance with the general scheme of Christianity, the religious instructions which are afterward received from the pulpit and the press, are apt to lose half their value by being taken up as a mass of loose disjointed fragments, of which that precise tendency and necessary limitations are either misconceived or not conceived at all. We know no better means of preventing this, or of giving solidity and consistency to a man's religious knowledge, than an intelligent familiarity with those admirable forms of sound words which the Presbyterian churches acknowledge as the exhibition of their creed. If it is only an intelligent familiarity, let the too common practice of acquiring them just by rote be resisted and discouraged, and let the catechumens be taught to answer not merely with their lips, but with their understanding also.

Now, to return to our author, the publication of his *Larger Catechism* was the means of involving him in a very unexpected theological controversy. A statement contained in it, that the obedience or active righteousness of Christ is imputed to believers only, so far as to answer the demands which the Law of God has of them as individuals, and not in all the infinitude of merit which it intrinsically possesses as rendered by the Eternal Word, was represented by several of his Christian brothers, at the head of whom appeared Mr. Dalzell of Earlston, as heretical, impious, blasphemous, and so on and so forth, according to the usual vocabulary of the *odium theologicum*. In consequence of these attacks, Mr Brown published, in 1759, a *"Brief Dissertation on Christ's Righteousness, showing to what extent it is imputed to us in Justification, together with the sentiments of orthodox divines on this important question."* The argument on this subject, both from the principles of that divinity which both parties professed, and from the authority of those divines, whom both respected as most orthodox, seems quite conclusive, and is not unskilfully managed. We cannot help introducing here a short extract from the preface, beautifully illustrative of a true Christian spirit in the conduct of religious controversy. Our author says:

> "Had those who differ from me, signified their scruples to me in a Christian manner, either by word or writing, I do

not doubt that I would have offered them such replies and solutions as might have prevented that conduct which (though charity obliges me to hope it was entirely an inadvertent and well-designed mistake) some will readily reckon a wounding of truth, a dishonouring of Christ, an instructing of their people to revile, and in the injuring of their own reputation among impartial men. But now that the fact is committed, though I reckon it my duty to contribute to the support of injured truth, and to restore to the scriptures, and the most eminent Protestant divines, their due honour of being my instructors in this point; yet instead of intending to resent with similar conduct the injury which these reverend brothers have done me, I reckon myself on account thereof so much the more effectually obliged by the Christian law, Matt. 5:44; Luke 6:27-28; Rom. 12:14, 20-21; 1 Pet. 2:23 and 3:9) to contribute my utmost endeavours towards the advancement of their welfare, spiritual or temporal, and am resolved, through grace, to discharge these obligations as providence shall give opportunity for the same. Let them wish or do to me what they will, may their portion be redemption through the blood of Jesus, even the forgiveness of sins according to the riches of His grace; and call me what they please, may the Lord call them the holy ones, the redeemed of the Lord, sought out and not forsaken."

In 1765, Mr. Brown published what was at the time by far the most popular and successful of his works, entitled, *"The Christian Journal, or Common Incidents Spiritual Instructors."* This work, though it has some of the literary defects which, on such a subject might have been expected from an author so circumstanced, such as the occasional indulgence of unrefined images, the excess of detail in tracing the analogies, and a certain monotonous rhythm of style, in many cases scarcely distinguishable from blank verse, nevertheless, it displays an extraordinary richness and ingenuity of fancy, and in many instances rises into a most impressive and heart-warming eloquence. It breathes throughout a high tone of Christian devotion, and is altogether well adapted to answer its end of training its readers in the holy art of imbuing all their associations with the ideas of God and of eternity, of abiding with God in their daily callings, and continuing in the fear of the Lord all day long.

In 1766, Mr Brown published a *History of the Rise and Progress of the Secession*, and the year following, a series of *Letters on the Constitution, Discipline, and Government of the Christian Church*. These two works contain an elaborate vindication of his principles as a Presbyterian and a Seceder though it may perhaps he felt that he has occasionally taken up higher ground in their defence than is altogether tenable. These tracts were followed by his *Sacred Topology*, the first of a series of works, the object of which is thus explained by the author: "The advantage of a clear, comprehensive, and regular view of the *Figures, Types, and Predictions of Scripture* is obvious. In the first we observe the surprising eloquence of heaven, and discern, in almost every form of nature, a guide to, and illustrator of inspired truth. By the second we perceive the whole substance of the gospel of Christ truly exhibited in ancient shadows, in laws apparently carnal and trifling. In the third we observe how astonishingly inspired predictions, properly arranged, and compared with the history of nations and churches, do illustrate each other, and modern events, as with the evidence of miracles, and confirm our faith in the oracles of God."

Of the Trilogy here mentioned, the first part was published in 1766, the second and third not till 1781. These works are almost entirely arbitrary in the form of their statements, containing merely results without the evidence from which they are deduced. In his treatment of the *Figures and Types*, he was often led by the spirit of the age, and the school of divinity to which he belonged, to strain the analogy, and introduce mixed and multiplied meanings; yet the volumes in question contain many fine and pleasing views, and are all imbued with a pervading spirit of ardent devotion, and extraordinary richness of Scriptural knowledge. The *Harmony of Prophecy*, in particular, is a very judicious and well-written manual.

Professor of Divinity

In the year 1768, in consequence of the death of the Rev. John Swanson of Kinross, Professor of Divinity under the Associate Synod, Mr. Brown was elected to the vacant chair. The duties of this important office he discharged with great ability and exemplary diligence and success. His public lecture was directed towards two main objects: first, of instructing his pupils in the science of Christianity, and, secondly, of impressing their hearts with its power. The system of Divinity which, in the course of his professional duties, he was led to compile, and which was afterwards published, is perhaps the one of all his works that exhibits most striking proofs of precision, discrimination, and enlargement of thought; and is altogether one of the most dense, and at the same time far-reaching reviews that has yet appeared concerning the theology of the Westminster Confession. This compilation served as a textbook in the classroom for the examination of his students, and included additional expositions by their Professor. Each student was required to make a transcript of the whole book for his own use in the course of his five years' attendance at the Hall, as well as to commit to memory fully the texts referred to at the end of each paragraph as proof of the doctrine it contains.

As the characteristic peculiarity of his own preaching was its Scriptural richness, so the great object he seemed to have at heart in training others for similar work "was to render them mighty in the Scriptures, readily able to support the several articles of our holy religion by the self-evidencing and conscience-commanding testimony of the Holy Spirit, and to express the things of God in his own divine language." We cannot help mentioning the practice of accustoming theological students to the thorough acquisition and public repetition of the Scriptures as a thing of the best example to every Theological Seminary. In addition to his course of systematic theology, Mr Brown was accustomed to deliver to his class a few lectures in Casuistic Divinity (Christian Ethics), which likewise were afterwards given to the world, and are generally marked with strong good sense, and a rare freedom from exaggeration.

In the other, and still more important part of his duty as an instructor of candidates for the holy ministry, was that of reminding them of their own concern in the doctrines they were preparing to teach to others, and urging on them the necessity of cultivating personal piety and pastoral faithfulness. In this, he was particularly eminent. "Whilst I have been occupied in instructing you", he could confidently appeal to them towards the close of his labours, "your consciences must bear me witness that my principal concern was to impress your own minds with the great things of God." A specimen of the exhortation, which he was accustomed with this view to address to them, was contained in the dedication of his system to his pupils, and is remarkably solemn and impressive, and its warning note in the delivery seldom failed to melt both speaker and hearers into sympathetic tears.

To each of his students, when called to undertake the care of souls, he was accustomed to send a letter of serious advice. The two series of letters that he composed for the use of his pupils on the best way of preaching the gospel, and on the exemplary behaviour required of ministers, and which have been published among his *Posthumous Works*, are highly judicious and weighty.

The charge, however, which he took of those committed to his care, was not entirely of the "ex cathedra" description. The situation of the Hall in a small provincial town, and the manners of his age, combined with his just sense of the importance of the students' private exertions and personal habits, enabled him to exercise a much more minute and household superintendence over the young men under his direction. Frequently in the morning, he was accustomed to go his rounds among their lodgings, to assure himself that they were usefully employing "the golden hours of prime." The personal contact between professor and pupils was thus remarkably close and unbroken, and hence we find that among those who can recollect their attendance at the Divinity Hall at Haddington, the interest with which every mind looks back to the scenes and seasons of early study has a greater character of individuality, and is associated with minute recollections than we generally meet with after so long a lapse of years.

The same year in which he was elected to the Theological Chair, he preached and published a very powerful sermon on *Religious Steadfastness*, in which he dwells at considerable length on the religious state of the nation, and expresses violent apprehension at the visible spread of what he called latitudinarianism, and what we of this tolerant age would call liberality of religious sentiment. He, likewise, this year gave to the world one of the most elaborate, and certainly one of the most valuable of all his writings, his Dictionary of the Holy Bible. For popular use, it is unquestionably the most suitable work of the kind that ever existed, containing the results of most extensive and various reading both in science and in the literature of Christianity, given without pretension or parade, and with a uniform reference to practical usefulness.

In 1771, the year of his first wife's death, the Honourable and Reverend Mr. Shirley, by command of the Countess of Huntingdon, applied to Mr. Brown for his opinion on the great subject of justification, in view of a conference to he held on this question with Mr. Wesley and his preachers. This application gave occasion to a long and animated correspondence with that noble and elect lady (a correspondence which, in consequence of our author's modesty, remained a secret till after his death), and to a series of articles from his pen on the doctrine of justification, which appeared from time to time in the *Gospel Magazine* and *Theological Miscellany*, between the years 1770 and 1776. In the same year, he was led by a desire to contribute to the yet better instruction of his students, to form a plan to compose a manual of *Church History* on a general and comprehensive plan. It would consist of three parts: "the first comprehending a general view of transactions relating to the Church from the birth of our Saviour to the present time, the second containing more fully the histories of the Reformed British Churches in England, Scotland, Ireland, and America; the third to comprehend the histories of the Waldenses and the Protestant Churches of Switzerland, France, Holland, Germany, Denmark, Sweden,

Poland, and Hungary." Of these, he completed the first two, when his *General History* was published in 1771, and his *History of the British Churches* at the beginning of 1784. These form very useful popular texts, though destitute of much historical authority. The history of the British Churches, as a work of original research, is more superior to the more general compilation, which is little more than an abridgment of Mosheim, written in a more fervent spirit than the latter used to display.

Mr Brown's next publication appeared in 1775, and was an edition of the"Metrical Psalms, with notes, exhibiting the connexion, explaining the sense, and for directing and animating the devotion." This work rests on the same principles as the old custom of prefacing the Psalms sung in public worship, with some account of their scope and tendency, and exhortation to exercise appropriate feeling, a custom very useful and almost absolutely necessary while the not very rational fashion was in use, of singing right through the Psalter from beginning to end in the weekly service of the Church. Viewed in this light, the plan of the work is very well conceived, and well executed. The general substance of each Psalm is neatly extracted, its devotional spirit happily caught, and the whole work is wonderfully free of that arbitrary typical interpretation for which the Psalms gives ample opportunity.

In 1778, he gave to the world the great work on which his reputation is mainly based, his *"The Self-interpreting Bible."* The object of this work is to condense within a manageable limit all the information that an ordinary reader might find necessary for attaining an intelligent and practical knowledge of the sacred Oracles. The apparatus which he collected for this purpose consisted of: first, an introduction, containing a section on the Divine authority of the Scriptures; rules for acquiring an experimental acquaintance with their contents; a general view of the typical system on which he considered a great part of the Bible to be constructed; and a very complete summary and rationale of the history contained in it, or connected with it. Secondly, illustrations accompanying the text, containing an accurate notice of the general aim of each separate book, and the contents of each individual chapter; a vast collection of illustrative and parallel passages in respect of both the sense and expression; a paraphrase of the most obscure or important parts, and a continued series of evangelical and devotional reflections. Thirdly, illustrations given, containing a great variety of tables, such as of the names given in the Bible to Christ and his Church, of Scripture metaphors and synonyms, of prophecies and promises, proper names and offices of men, times, weights, measures, etc. The general execution of the work in its various departments is not less creditable than the conception of its plan. Considering the circumstances of the writer, and the general state of Biblical literature at the period it was composed, even its critical merit may be pronounced remarkable, while its devotional worth has been acknowledged and ratified by the extraordinary popularity it has enjoyed with the religious public since its publication. The growing demand for it has produced this present edition. Its first publication was attended with considerable difficulties in consequence of the claim of the King's printers to the exclusive right to print the Authorized Version of the Scriptures, whether accompanied or not with illustrative matter. This claim, however, was set aside, so the work was at length given to the world in 1778, and received with a high and gradually increasing, and still inexhaustible, applause.

The same year, he published a small tract entitled "*The Oracles of Christ, Abominations of Antichrist*", and four years later, his "*Letters on Toleration*", strenuously maintaining, in the spirit of the times, the unlawfulness of tolerating by authority a false religion in a professedly Christian country. These publications originated in the universal sentiment of alarm entertained by the evangelical Presbyterians of Scotland, both within and without the Establishment, in consequence of the proposed abolition of the penal code against the Roman Catholics. At this time, a worthy brother in the ministry having died very suddenly, he did what he could to provide for the best interests of those with whom the deceased was most closely connected, that is, his family and congregation, by drawing up for their use respectively two letters of most solemn and heart-warming advice, which he addressed to them as from the dead, and bequeathed to them as the best legacy of a dying father and minister. These letters were later published.

In 1781, beside his work on the types and prophecies formerly referred to, he published a sermon on the *Duty of Raising up Spiritual Children unto Christ*, preached partly at Whitburn, and partly after his son Ebenezer's ordination at Inverkeithing. The text of this sermon is selected quite in the spirit of his lately published book on the *Types*, the passage on which he chose to build a most powerful exhortation to ministers to labour for the conversion of sinners, being none other than the ordinance in Deuteronomy 25:5-10 about loosing the shoe of him who refuses to raise up seed to his deceased elder brother by marrying his widow. Likewise, in the course of the same year, he wrote a pamphlet in defence of the *Re-exhibition of the Testimony*, and a collection of the biographies of *Eminent Divines* under the name of the *Christian Student and Pastor*. This was the first of a series of similar compilations, intended as illustrations and examples of practical religion, and was followed in 1781 by the *Young Christian*, and in 1783 by the *Lives of Thirteen Eminent Private Christians*.

These memoirs abound in the habitual scrutiny of the heart, and that minute anatomy of religious feeling, that distinguished the Christians of a former age; and the general tone of spiritual experience that pervades them is very similar to that which characterises most of the religious Diaries and Memoirs published about that time.

In 1782, during which the *View of Natural and Revealed Religion* appeared in print, he presided at the moderation of a call in Edinburgh, and preached a sermon on that occasion that gave considerable offence, some of its allusions having been understood as pointing to a particular candidate. This sermon, which, taken apart from the personal question, is a remarkably sound and judicious discourse, he published for the sake of truth and justice, accompanied with an elaborate appendix in which he argues strongly against the propriety of translating ministers from one charge to another without the very highest need.

In 1783, he published a small *Concordance of the Bible*. The following year, he received an invitation from the Reformed Dutch Church in America to become their Professor of Divinity, which he declined, and modestly kept secret. In 1785, he concluded his career as an author with a pamphlet against the *Travelling of the Mail on the Lord's Day*, a day for the observance of which, in the strictest degree of sanctity, he always showed himself peculiarly jealous, not only abstaining himself, but prohibiting his family from speaking on that day on any worldly affair, even on those that related to what may be called the secularities of religion and the church. The tracts published by him in periodical works, along with his *Letters on Gospel Preaching* and his *Behaviour of Minister*s, were collected together after his death, and published under the title of "*Remains*."

Throughout his writings, Mr Brown's uniform aim was general usefulness. Personal payment formed no part of his object, and certainly very little of his attainment, as the whole profit accruing to himself from his voluminous, and, in many cases, successful works, amounted to only £10. Judging of his intellectual character from his works, we can say that he was characterised more by the knowing than by the inventive faculties. "I look upon it as my mercy", he himself remarks, "that, considering the dreadful pride of my heart, God did not make my talent to lie so properly in a quick and extensive view of things at first, but rather in a close, persevering, and unwearied application to that in which I engaged. In the former respect I was always much inferior to many of my brothers." Without possessing much original genius, but, on the other hand, too ready, it may be said, to submit the freedom of his mind to system and authority, he was endowed with a strong aptitude for acquisition, and great power of arrangement, a sound and generally sober judgement, and a rich and vivid fancy, though united with a defective, or perhaps, an uncultivated taste. From his exclusively popular aims in the composition of most of his works, there are few of them suitable as being appealed to as books of authority. They exhibit the results to which his own researches led him, but they contain no view of the researches themselves, no exposition of evidence, and not much deduction of argument. Hence, while the mass of facts and sentiments they contain will prove a most valuable acquisition to those whom the author contemplated as his readers, that great body of people who are not in a situation to engage in deep and learned investigations for themselves, but who will take much for granted, both from the pulpit and the press, trusting in the strength and confidence and worth of their instructors. Those, on the contrary, whose duty or wish it is to take their study deeply into the evidence of the subject, must seek the materials of their researches elsewhere.

Keeping this idea of the plan and object of our author's writings in view, we find in them a great deal to applaud. The selection of subjects, and general conception of almost every one of them, is very happy, and, in many cases, the execution proves his high endowments for the task he undertook. Of his superior abilities as an interpreter and illustrator of Scripture, his edition of the *Sacred Word*, taken along with his *Dictionary of the Bible*, makes a distinguished monument. To his extensive knowledge, clear conception, and power of accurate arrangement as a theologian, ample testimony is borne by his *System of Divinity*; while of his high attainments as a private Christian, his delight in communion with God, and his holy skill and ingenuity in its cultivation, the *Christian Journal* is a very characteristic and pleasing specimen. These three works taken in combination convey the best idea of his elevated character as a Christian, a scholar, a minister, and a professor, and supply the best vindication of his claim to the praise of an able (and what was his one object in assuming the character) and useful, and edifying author.

With regard to diction and style, he was abundantly aware of his own deficiencies. Alluding to the subject in a letter to the Countess of Huntingdon, he apologises, on the ground of his having been destitute of a natural perception of melody, and of the advantages of regular education, for his "poverty of diction, and incapacity of expressing himself handsomely to an English ear." And it must be admitted, that a fastidious taste in the perusal of his works, must make considerable allowance for occasional uncouthness of expression, as well as for frequent abruptness of transition, and a peculiarly awkward use of the connective particles. A devout mind, however, whenever our author gets fairly warmed with his subject, will soon lose the sense of all minor deficiencies, in sympathy with the kindling raptures of his soaring devotion, or the force and poignancy of his emotional outpourings.

During the interval of two years that elapsed between the last of his publications and the author's death, he seems, from his private papers, to have been much employed in humble and grateful recollection of the dealings of God's providence towards him throughout his life. During this interval, at the request of some intimate friends and connections, he wrote the brief notice of his own character and history, to which we have frequently referred, and a short extract of which we shall now introduce, as a fitting conclusion to the history of his active life, and as beautifully illustrative of the Christian feeling with which, from the borders of the grave, he looked back on all "the way by which the Lord his God had led him."

A written testimony

"Now, after near forty years' preaching of Christ and his sweet and great salvation, I think that I would rather beg my bread all the labouring days of the week for an opportunity of publishing the gospel on the Sabbath to an assembly of sinful men, than, without such a privilege, to enjoy the richest possessions on earth. By the gospel do men live, and in it is the life of my soul. Oh the kindness of God! Despite He left me a poor orphan, without any relations on earth who were able to help me to any purpose - many whose parents have been spared with them far longer than I had mine, who are now in deep poverty, or what is infinitely worse, are abandoned to all manner of wickedness, while by strange means the Lord hath restrained and preserved me. From low circumstances, God hath by his mere grace exalted the orphan to the highest station in the church, and I hope hath given me some success, not only in preaching and in writing, but in training up many for the ministry, whom I trust the Lord hath made, or will make, far more useful in winning souls to Christ than ever I have been. In this how plainly hath the Lord appeared as the father of the fatherless, and the orphan's stay. He chose me to be his servant, and took me from the sheepfold; from following the ewes with young he brought me to feed Jacob, his people, and Israel his inheritance. Lord, what am I, and what is my father's house, that thou hast brought me hitherto!"

The time now drew near for him to die. For some years previous he had been greatly annoyed with a gradual failure, at once in his power of digestion and then his mental faculty of memory, symptoms of a constitution nearly worn out by the intense and incessant labours to which it had been subjected. In the beginning of 1787, his complaints increased to an alarming degree, accompanied by a general and extreme tiredness. Feeling in himself the irremediable exhaustion of nature, he calmly disposed himself to "resign the earthly load of death called life, which him from life did sever." On the 25th of February, with difficulty and supporting himself in the pulpit, he preached from Luke 2:26 - "Unto him it was revealed, that he should not taste of death till he had seen the Lord's Christ." At the close of his sermon, he intimated to his own flock that, in that place, they would see his face no more, and bade them a solemn and affectionate adieu. In the evening, he took a similar farewell of the miscellaneous congregation, consisting chiefly of members of the established church, who were in the habit of attending his evening service. With even more than usual earnestness, he made his parting declaration of the embassy entrusted to him, from Acts 13:26 - "To you is the word of this salvation sent" - and then, amid the tears of all his audience, he went down to die in the hope of that gospel of which, through life, he had proclaimed the grace, and exemplified the holiness.

Throughout his last illness, he was remarkably filled with the consolations of the Holy Spirit. During life, he had been always remarkably reserved in talking about his private religious experience; but as he drew near to the end of his course, and came into more immediate view of heaven, his reserve entirely vanished, and his language to all with whom he came in contact was, "Come and see what God hath done for my soul." The intense self-abasement and self-distrust which had characterised him throughout life, continued with him to the end; but his confidence of salvation through Jesus Christ was brightened into the full assurance of hope, and quickened with unspeakable ardour and desire. It is at the close of a life like his, in which faith has proved its reality by active and persevering obedience, that this triumphant assurance is entertained, and most reasonably, and most gracefully, expressed.

It was in these circumstances that the Apostle gloried with such exulting confidence in the prospect of the crown of righteousness; and it was in these circumstances that our dying saint at length felt justified in declaring, that he knew "his own calling and sure election." The lingering and gradual character of his disorder, gave him an opportunity not only of calmly composing his own mind for departure, but of setting his house in order in every respect. During this period also, he employed himself in revising and improving his *Christian Journal*, finding probably the devotional and spiritual character of that work more in keeping with his feelings when about to depart, than that of any other of his writings. A large collection of his sayings during his last illness has been preserved, from which we can select a few specimens:

"Oh to be with God", he exclaimed, "to see Him as He is; to know Him even as He is known; it is worth dying to see a smiling God!"

Again, "I desire to depart and be with Christ, which is far better; and though I have lived sixty years very comfortably in the world, yet I would gladly turn my back upon you all to be with Christ. I am sure Christ may say of me, 'These sixty years this wretch hath grieved me.'"

Addressing himself to his two sons in the ministry, he said with peculiar earnestness, "Oh, labour, labour for Christ while ye have strength! I now repent I have been so slothful in his service. Oh, I commend Jesus; there is none like Christ, there is none like Christ, there is none like Christ! I have been looking at Him these many years, and never yet could find a fault in Him but what was of my own making, though He has seen ten thousand-thousand faults in me. Many a comely person I have seen, but none so comely as Christ; many a kind friend I have had, but none like Him in loving kindness and tender mercies."

On March 22nd, he had no sooner sat down to breakfast, than, like a man enraptured, he broke into the following lines, which he repeated three times with increasing ardour:

> We with the fatness of thy house
> Shall be well satisfied;
> From rivers of thy pleasures thou
> Wilt drink to us provide.

Some days after, a friend inquired of his welfare. "I am weak", he answered, "but it is delightful to feel oneself weak in the everlasting arms." And, "Oh, what must Christ be in Himself," he exclaimed, "when it is He that sweetens heaven, sweetens scriptures, sweetens ordinances, sweetens earth, and even sweetens trials, oh, what must Christ be in Himself!"

On the 29th of March, a friend happened to say, "I suppose you do not make your labours for the good of the church the ground of your comfort." He replied with an uncommon emphasis, "No! No! No! It is the finished righteousness of Christ that is the only foundation of my hopes. I have no more dependence on my labours than on my sins."

On the 5th of April, taking a walk in a field attached to his house, he pointed to several spots where he had been ravished with views of God's grace. "Yes," he added, "my soul hath been so transported here, that, as the Apostle speaks, whether I was in the body or out of the body I could scarce tell; and perhaps it is superstition in me, but I confess that I have a peculiar love for those very spots."

Some days after, having sat down in the same field, and feeling dazzled with the bright shining of the sun, he exclaimed, "Oh, how pleasant to be in that place where they are so overcome with the glory of the Sun of righteousness, that they cover their faces with their wings!"

On the 5th of June, after family worship in the evening, he remarked, "Oh, it would be pleasant if our experience in ordinances were such here as that they would fit us for the exercises of heaven! Our prayers here are a stretching forth of our desires for the enjoyment of God and the Lamb; and our praises here are a tuning of our hearts for the songs above."

On the 18th, a friend observed that he suffered much, and said, "I hope, Sir, the Lord is not forsaking you now." "No", he answered, "God is an unchanging rock."

Fixing his eyes on two or three of his relations who stood at his bedside, he addressed them with extreme pathos, "Oh, sirs, dying work is serious, serious work indeed, and that you will soon find!"

On the 19th of June, his lips moved much, but from the feebleness of his speech, few of his words were understood. The last he was heard to utter were these, "My Christ!" About four hours later, he slept in Jesus.

On the 24th, there followed his remains to their place of rest in Haddington churchyard and nearly the whole inhabitants of the town, and a large concourse of his friends and brothers at a distance. On the succeeding Sabbath, the Rev. John Henderson of Dunbar preached a funeral sermon in Mr. Brown's own church, but there were few ministers in that connection, which he had done so much to edify and adorn, who did not embrace the opportunity of rendering in their own churches a similar tribute of respect to his memory. At the first meeting of the Associate Synod after his decease, "The Synod", as their own minutes bears, "unanimously agreed to take this opportunity of testifying their respect to the memory of the Rev. John Brown, their late Professor, whose eminent piety, fervent zeal, extensive charity, and unwearied diligence in promoting the interests of religion, will be long remembered by this court, especially by those members of it who had the happiness of studying divinity under his inspection."

"He restest from his labours, and his works do follow him." (Rev. 14:13)

BROWN'S
DICTIONARY
OF BIBLE
CHARACTERS

AARON, *a strong mountain.*

A Levite, the son of Amram, and brother of Moses and Miriam, born in BC 1575, about a year before Pharaoh ordered the male infants of the Hebrews to be slain.

When he was grown up, he married Elisheba the daughter of Amminadab, a chief prince of the tribe of Judah, and had four sons by her: Nadab, Abihu, Eleazar, and Ithamar. (Exod. 6:20, 23) He was a holy and compassionate man, an excellent speaker, and appointed by God to be the spokesman for his brother Moses to Pharaoh and the Hebrews. (Exod. 4:14-16) Along with his brother, he spoke of God's gracious purpose, and of their speedy deliverance, to his distressed kinsmen; and, in the name of God, demanded of Pharaoh immediate permission for them to go into the wilderness of Arabia to serve the Lord their God. Pharaoh ordered Aaron and Moses to be gone from his presence, and increased the Hebrews' servitude, denying them straw with which to make their bricks. Aaron and Moses were then reproved and cursed by their brothers for asking for their dismissal, so occasioning their extra labour and misery. (Exod. 5)

About two months later, when the Hebrews, newly delivered from Egypt, fought with Amalek in Rephidim, Aaron and Hur went with Moses to the top of an adjacent hill, and held up his hands while he continued encouraging the struggling Hebrews, and praying for their victory. (Exod. 17:10-13) At Sinai, he, with his two older sons, and seventy of the Elders of Israel, accompanied Moses part of the way up the Mount, and, without coming to any harm, they received very immediate and distinct views of the glorious symbols of the divine presence when the Lord spoke to Moses. (Exod. 24:1-2, 9-11) Almost immediately after, he and his posterity were divinely chosen to execute the office of priesthood among the Jews till the coming and death of the promised Messiah. (Exod. 28-29). Hardly had this distinguished honour been assigned to him, when, to mark his personal insufficiency in recommending others to the favour of God, he himself fell into the most grievous sin. The Hebrews solicited him to make them gods, to be their directors instead of Moses, who still remained in the Mount. He ordered them to bring him all their pendants and earrings; and

these were brought, perhaps more readily than he expected. Having collected them into a bag, he caused them to be melted down into a golden calf in imitation of the ox Apis, which the natives, and probably too many of the Hebrews, had adored in Egypt. This idol he ordered them to place on a pedestal to make it more conspicuous. He called a solemn feast to be observed in its honour, and had proclaimed before it, "*These be thy gods, O Israel, which brought thee out of the land of Egypt.*" While he was thus occupied, Moses descended from Mount Sinai, and sharply reproved him for this horrible offence. Amid the deepest confusion, Aaron attempted to excuse himself by laying the blame on the wickedness of the people, and by a false and stupid pretence that he had just cast the earrings into the fire, and a golden calf had been formed from them by mere chance. (Exod. 32)

Aaron heartily repented of this scandalous crime, and, with his four sons, after about two months, he was solemnly invested with the sacred robes, and consecrated by solemn washing, anointing, and sacrifices, to the office of priesthood. (Lev. 8). He immediately offered sacrifice for the congregation of Israel; and while he and his brother Moses blessed the people, the sacred fire descended from heaven and consumed what lay on the brazen altar. (Exod. 29) His two oldest sons, perhaps intoxicated with wine drunk at their consecration, instead of taking sacred fire from the *brazen* altar, took common fire to burn the incense on the *golden* altar. Provoked by their inattention and disobedience, God immediately consumed them with a flash of lightning, and ordered that, from now on, no priest should taste wine when he was going to officiate in holy things. Aaron was resigned entirely to this just, but awful stroke; nor did he and his surviving sons make any lamentation over them, except in abstaining from the flesh of the people's sin offering that day. (Lev. 10:19)

Hardly a year passed before Aaron and Miriam, envying the authority of Moses, rudely reproved him for his marriage to Zipporah the Midianitess, and for overlooking them in the constituting of the seventy elders. Aaron, whose priestly performances were daily necessary, was spared, but Miriam was smitten all over with leprosy. Aaron immediately discerned his guilt, acknowledged his fault, and begged forgiveness for himself and his sister, that she might speedily be restored to health. (Num. 12) It was not long after when Korah and his company, envying the honours of Aaron, thought to thrust themselves

into the priestly office. These rebels were miraculously destroyed by God, yet the Hebrews accused Moses and Aaron of murdering them! The Lord, provoked by this, sent a destructive plague among the people that threatened to consume the whole congregation. Aaron, who had lately by his prayers prevented their being totally ruined along with Korah, now generously risked his own life for the deliverance of his ungrateful and injurious brothers. He ran in between the living and the dead, and, by offering up the incense, atoned for their trespass; and so the plague was stopped. To reward this benevolent deed, and prevent future contention about the priesthood, God confirmed it to Aaron by making his rod all of a sudden, when laid before the mercyseat, to blossom and bear almonds, while the rods of the other Hebrew tribes continued in their withered state. (Num. 16-17)

We hear no more of Aaron till at Meribah, when he and his brother Moses sinned in not sufficiently expressing their confidence in God in providing water for the congregation. To punish this, and to mark the insufficiency of the Aaronic priesthood in bringing men into the heavenly inheritance, Aaron was debarred from entering Canaan. About a year before the Hebrews entered that country, and while they were encamped at Mosera, he, at the command of the Lord, went up to Mount Hor, and his sacred robes were stripped off him by Moses and put on Eleazar his son and successor. He suddenly expired before the Lord, aged 123 years, in BC 1452. His own sons and brother buried him in a cave, and all the Israelites mourned for him thirty days. (Num. 20:2, 6, 8, 10, 12, 23-26, 28-29; Deut. 10:6) His offspring were called Aaronites, and so numerous were they that they had to have thirteen cities assigned to them from the tribes of Judah and Benjamin. (Josh. 21:13-19; 1 Chron. 6:54-65)

Some reputable authors think that the story of the heathen Mercury was hammered out of Aaron's. But may we not, with far more edification, consider him as a personal type of Jesus Christ? (Heb. 5:4-5) Christ's call to his office of priesthood was timely, and divinely solemn. An unmeasurable unction of the Holy Spirit, and perfect purity of nature, prepared him for the execution of the office. His miracles were unnumbered. The destruction of his Jewish and other enemies, the budding of his gospel rod in the conversion and sanctification of men, all abundantly confirm his office. He is the leader of his people from their spiritual bondage; and he guides, justifies, and sanctifies them in their wilderness journey. He is their great prophet who can speak well to their respective cases and doubts. He is their distinguished *High Priest,* and the spiritual Father of all the innumerable company of men who are made priests unto God. With unequalled purity, patience, pity, courage, and labour, he, amid inconceivable injuries and temptations, faithfully executed his work. At the expense of his life, he averted the burning plague of endless vengeance from his unreasonable foes; and, having finished his work of obedience, he publicly and willingly, on Calvary, surrendered himself unto death, bequeathing his robes of finished righteousness to his spiritual seed.

Extra note

We are indebted to our alphabetical order for opening our Dictionary with a character among the most interesting to guilty man in any in the Sacred Oracles. *Aaron* means *a strong mountain*; in this sense, it must refer to him as the founder of God's worship in his holy *mountain* of old. But others, seeming to be correct, derive it from the root *to teach*; and is thus a teacher. The personal history and office of Aaron is left on record as one of the clearest illustrations of the Person and office of the Great High Priest over the house of God (Heb. 10:21), ordained not by the law of a fleshly commandment, but by the power of an endless life.

1. In reviewing the life of Aaron, the first subject worthy of notice is the manner of his introduction into the history. He appears first as a kind of assistant, and is thus inferior to his brother Moses. Yet Aaron had some advantages that seemed to entitle him to prior consideration. He was the elder brother, was an eloquent speaker, and was favoured by divine inspiration. Why he was not preferred to Moses in respect of authority, we do not understand. We can only say that it was due to the divine good pleasure.

2. Among the most confirming signs given by God to Moses was his interview with his brother Aaron, which, being predicted by God, and happening *directly*, was a very convincing proof to Moses. We see something similar in the case of Jeremiah. (Jer. 32:8) It would seem also that Aaron would not have undertaken a journey of two months from Egypt to Mount Sinai (according to Thomas Shaw in his *Travels into Egypt*) at great risk and at much expense, unless he had been well assured of the authority that sent him. Neither could he

have expected to find Moses where he did unless by divine direction, since the place afterwards called the *Mount of God* was then secluded and unfrequented. Inasmuch, then, as Aaron was a sign to Moses by meeting him there, so Moses was a sign to Aaron. Aaron seemed to have joined Moses after the affair of Zipporah. No doubt he narrated to Moses the events in Egypt, and the death of the former Pharaoh, etc.

3. It would seem that Aaron lived in Egypt in circumstances superior to those of the lower order of people, as one from among those kept to their daily bondage could hardly have spared time and money for such a journey to Horeb; his family; and his work would have cost him too much. It is probable that, though the family of these two brothers had no pretension to sovereign authority by descent, they were considerably well-off in their property, or their office, or in some other way.

It seems probable in every way that Aaron was a governor over the Israelites while they were building the pyramids. Whether he was the chief ruler, or whether subordinate, we cannot determine; perhaps it was the former. He was certainly under the authority of Pharaoh's officers, yet he might have been the head of his own people, for it is customary in the east for all societies, trades, etc., to have a head who is responsible to the government. And we rather think that this was the case here, because we do not read of any intrusion of Aaron into office, or any election by the people, or any charge of such *assumption* brought against him by Pharaoh; for both Moses and Aaron seemed to be acknowledged by Pharaoh himself, and evidently by many of his servants, as apparently the right people to speak on behalf of the Israelites to the King.

Aaron performed miracles before Pharaoh, such as the changing of his rod into a serpent, etc., without any (recorded) wonder expressed by Pharaoh, as to how a person kept to his daily labour could acquire such skill in eloquence, etc. (Exod. 7:19ff) Had Moses and Aaron been just private persons in the estimation of Pharaoh, jail would have punished their impertinence.

4. Aaron was left in charge of Israel in conjunction with Hur, while Moses was in the Mount receiving the Law; and, to his shame, we find him guilty of a crime that certainly his authority should have been used to prevent. This violation of his duty cannot be excused; yet, it was not so gross as is usually presented. We may well ask as to

Aaron's personal concern in this matter. Was his own faith or patience exhausted? If so, and he also supposed Moses to be dead, then there could be no agreement between them. Would Aaron have dared to do as he did had he expected the return of Moses very soon? It is true that he put the fault on the people; but if he had had any recent information respecting Moses (by Joshua, or otherwise), would he have ventured on something he knew would certainly be punished? The activity of Aaron in building the altar for the calf, and his later submission to Moses, are utterly inexplicable had not a divine conviction been employed on this occasion. A whole revolting nation, obedient to a single returning ruler! Nevertheless, though he was actively blameworthy, Aaron seems more to have allowed and tolerated the evil, rather than promoted it. The expression is remarkable - *"The Lord plagued the people because they made the calf, which Aaron made."* (Exod. 32:35)

Nothing is said of Hur, the coadjutor of Aaron in the government of the people, respecting any interference in this affair. Perhaps he thought it was not his business; but Aaron should have engaged Hur's (and the elders') authority also, had he been wholehearted in his refusal of the people's request. He seemed to have flinched from his duty of resistance to the proceedings of the people, fearing their mischievous plan and set purpose, which he pleaded in his excuse.

5. The quarrel and treachery of Aaron and Miriam against Moses (Num. 12:1) provides another argument against the supposition of any agreement between Moses and his brother. It is true that Aaron assumed at first a high tone, and made no great pretensions to better gifts than his brother; but afterwards he owned his folly, and, with Miriam, submitted. Aaron was not visited with leprosy, but he could well judge its reality in his sister. It was his duty to exclude her from the camp for seven days; and, by his expression *flesh half consumed*, it would seem this exclusion was of a very severe kind, and therefore all the more grave. Aaron's feelings, interest, and passion, all concurred to harden him against anything less than the full conviction that this case was an interposition from above, as he must have known well that it was not in the personal power of Moses to produce this disease in Miriam.

6. The departure of Aaron at his death has something very impressive about it, and was altogether singular. In the sight of all the congregation, he quit the camp for the mountain where he was to die. On

the way there, his brother Moses, and Eleazar his son, took off his priestly garments. Attending him to the last, they buried him there, and that so privately that his tomb remains unknown. We view, in our imagination, this feeble old man ascending the Mount to a convenient height, there transferring the insignia of his office to his son, going out of the sight of the people, and giving up his spirit with that faith, that resignation, that meekness, which suited one who had been honoured with the Holy Spirit, and was a typical representation of the great High Priest himself.

7. The general character of Aaron has in it much of the meekness of his brother Moses. He seemed an easy good-natured man, willing to serve his brothers, but too easily persuaded against his own judgement, as appeared when the people urged him to make the golden calf, and when Miriam urged him to rival his brother; for it should be put down mainly to Miriam's intermeddling, as well as – a not uncommon characteristic of her sex – her dislike of foreign women, as well as her being named before Aaron (*Miriam and Aaron spoke against Moses, and here contemptuously dismissed Zipporah as an Ethiopian*), and from the disease that afflicted her, while Aaron was least punished, probably because he was less guilty, and because he was punished by deep feelings for his sister, as well as on the commonly suggested reason, the importance of his priestly office.

The Apostle Paul, in writing to the Hebrews (see ch. 5), assures us that no one takes the honour of the priesthood to himself unless called by God, as Aaron was. The Father said to his well-Beloved, "*Thou art my Son, this day have I begotten thee; he consecrated him a priest forever, after the order of Melchisedec.*" (Ps. 110:4; Heb. 4:4, 6, 7:17, 21) Was not Aaron anointed with the sacred oil that was not to be touched by any other? Christ, the Lord's anointed, was filled with the Holy Spirit above his fellows. He officiates in the presence of God for his guilty people in all things pertaining to God. All the concerns of his Church are on his shoulder; and, if Korah and his company were punished with destruction from the presence of the Lord for presuming to officiate in the sacred functions of an earthly Priest, how dreadful will be the judgement of God when it is executed on all who presume to draw near to God other than by the great High Priest's offering and incense! The heavenly Father, in a decided manner, gave his sanction to his authority as priest on the throne by the effusion of the Holy

Spirit on the day of Pentecost. Then his rod of power blossomed: *The same day were added to the Lord three thousand souls.* (Acts 2:41) Now has the true High Priest consulted with the Urim and Thummim. He answers all the questions and fears and doubts of his congregation. When he died, it was not to lay down his office, for, on the third day, he rose from the grave and entered the heavenly temple dressed in all the divine robes of his office, there to appear in the presence of God for us. He abides a merciful and faithful Priest who has compassion on the ignorant, and those who are out of the way.

ABADDON, *destruction*
Apollyon the *destroyer* is the name of the king and head of the apocalyptic locusts under the fifth trumpet. (Rev. 9:10-11) His name is set apart both in Hebrew and Greek to indicate that he is a destroyer both of Jews and Gentiles. But who he is, is not so well known. Some think he is the devil, who goes about *seeking whom he may devour.* (1 Pet. 5:8) Without excluding Satan, *who was a murderer from the beginning* (John 8:44), we suppose the Spirit of God points directly to the popes as this king of the locusts, *this angel of the bottomless pit* (found only in Rev. 9:11 – *And they had a king over them, which is the angel of the bottomless pit, whose name in the Hebrew tongue is Abaddon, but in the Greek tongue hath his name Apollyon*), these *sons of perdition*, who, at the head of unnumbered clergy and other agents, ruin the souls and murder the bodies of inconceivable multitudes of men. He points also to Mahomet and his inferior agents who, partly under a delusion, and partly with ravage and murder, have destroyed countless numbers. It would be shocking to relate the thousands and millions murdered by Hejajus and Abu Moslem the Saracens, and Tamerlane the Tartar (1336-1405), Bajazet (1389-1403) and Mahomet II (1429?–1481), the Turks, Shah Abbas (1571-1629) the Persian, and other heads of the Mahometan party. See also Antichrist.

ABBA, *father*
A Syriac word. It is the same whether read backwards or forwards, which may perhaps hint to us that God's fatherly affection for his people is the same, whether he smiles on them in prosperity or chastens them with heavy crosses and sore adversity. The Spirit of adoption, making the saints cry *ABBA, FATHER*, shows that by his influence, both Jews and Gentiles in one united body have the most assured faith

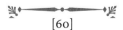

in their love for God, and in close fellowship with him. (Found only in Mark 14:36, Rom. 8:15; Gal 4:6)

ABDON, *servant of judgement*
(1) The son of Hillel to an Ephraimite. He succeeded Elon in BC 1164, and judged the Israelites eight years; after which he died and was buried at Pirathon in the land of Ephraim. He left forty sons and thirty grandsons who rode on the colts of asses according to the manner of the great men of their age. (Judg. 12:14)

(2) The son of Micah, one of Josiah's messengers, sent to consult Huldah the prophetess. (2 Chron. 34:20)

ABEDNEGO, *servant of light.* See Shadrach
See Daniel 1:7, 2:49, 3:12-14, 16, 19-20, 22-23, 26, 28-30

ABEL, *vanity*
The second son of Adam and Eve, born BC 4002-4003. It seems that his parents by this time were sufficiently convinced of the vanity of all created enjoyments, and hoped little from him, and therefore called his name *vanity*. When he was grown up, he began to shepherd his father's flock. *At the end of days* (Gen. 4:3); that is, he offered to God the best of his flock on the Sabbath, or, at the beginning of the year, by faith in the divine institution of sacrifices, and in the promised Messiah prefigured by it. By consuming his offering with a flash of fire from heaven, or by some other visible token, God showed his regard for Abel by accepting his sacrifice. When no such honour was given to Cain, who, at the same time, offered the fruits of the field, his brother held a relentless grudge against Abel on account of his holy behaviour, and the special regard that was shown him by God. He had no rest until he had murdered him in the field, and, it seems, secretly buried him in the earth. His murder was divinely taken exception to, so distinguished vengeance was heaped on the head of Cain who, together with his seed, was cast out of the Church of God. (Gen. 4:2-16; Heb. 11:4). Abel *being dead yet speaketh* (Heb. 12:14); his example teaches us to live by faith in a crucified Redeemer, and to behave soberly, righteously, and godly in this present world, whatever persecution we may be exposed to. His blood cried out for vengeance on Cain, his murderer, a prayer among many prayers referred to in Rev. 6:9-10.

Extra note

It may be observed that among the *divers manners* in which *God spoke unto the fathers by the prophets* (Heb. 1:1), the prophetic inspiration by which names were conferred was very remarkable. Abel was the first on whom the divine curse was executed, *dust thou art and unto dust thou shalt return*, illustrating the first instance of the Psalmist's statement, *Behold, thou hast made my days as an handbreadth; and mine age is as nothing before thee: verily every man at his best state is altogether vanity.* (Ps. 39:5) Abel was a keeper of sheep, but Cain was a tiller of the ground. Thus, in another way, the curse appeared accomplished when we read, *in the sweat of thy face shalt thou eat bread.* (Gen. 3:19) Though heirs of empires, they must labour for their subsistence. The nature of their worship is briefly, but strikingly, described by the inspired penman in Genesis 4:3-4.

Was not our adored Jesus prefigured in this first martyr? He grew as a root out of dry ground, appeared in the likeness of sinful flesh, and had his name smeared with the worst, the vilest, reproach. He is the great Shepherd of his Father's flock of ransomed men. By faith in his Father's call and assistance, he offered the infinitely excellent sacrifice of himself. His horrible murder by his malicious brothers the Jews resulted in terrible judgements from heaven upon them and their seed. And he still speaks to men by his example, oracles, and ordinances.

ABIATHAR, *excellent father*

The tenth High Priest of the Jews, and fourth in descent from Eli. When Saul murdered Ahimelech his father, and the other priests at Nob, Abiathar escaped to David in the wilderness, and joined his party. Through him, David consulted the Lord at Keilah and Ziklag. (1 Sam. 22:20-22, 23:6,9, 30:7) Saul placed Zadok, a descendant of Eleazar, in the office of High Priest instead of Abiathar, but, when David came to the throne, he appointed Abiathar, with Zadok next to him, as chief priests. And thus matters remained while David reigned. (2 Sam. 20:25) Abiathar and Zadok wanted to come to David with the ark as he fled from Absalom, but he advised them to return with it and obtain for him true intelligence. (2 Sam. 15:24-29) Just before the death of King David, Abiathar treasonably conspired to make David's son Adonijah successor. The result was that Solomon forbade him to remain in office. Instead, he was confined to his city of Anathoth, and Zadok was put in his place. (1 Kings 1-2) Thus was the family of Eli forever put out of the high priesthood. (1 Sam. 2:29-36) It was not Abiathar, but his son, that was called Ahimelech (or Abimelech). Nor is it Abiathar's father, but himself, that is mentioned in Mark 2:26, for it is certain that, had he lived, he might have had a great hand in procuring the showbread for David. Nor does that text indicate that Abiathar then executed the office of High Priest.

ABIGAIL
(1) The sister of King David, wife of Jether, and mother of Amasa. (1 Chron. 2:16-17)

(2) The wife of Nabal. She was a woman of great discretion and wisdom; but, perhaps, through the covetousness of her parents, was married to a rich drunkard. When his rude behaviour to David's messengers brought him and his family into the utmost danger, Abigail, hearing of it from some of her servants, loaded several asses with provisions, and went to meet David. In a most polite and discreet manner, she brought him her present. Her address not only disarmed his rage, but gained his highest esteem for her virtue. Returning to her husband, she told him the danger they had been in by his folly, and how she had prevented their ruin. He shortly died of deep depression, and she, not long after, was married to David. She bore him two sons, Daniel and Chileab, if these two names do not refer to the same person. She was taken captive by the Amalekites when Ziklag was burnt; but, in a few days, was rescued by her husband David. (1 Sam. 25 and 30; 2 Sam. 3:3; 1 Chron. 3:1)

ABIHU, *my father himself*
The son of Aaron the High Priest and Elisbeba, who was consumed together with his brother Nadab by fire sent from God because he had offered incense with strange fire. (Lev. 10:1; Num. 3:4, 26:21)

ABIJAH, ABIJAM, or ABIA
(1) The son of Rehoboam and his wife Maacah. He succeeded his father to the throne of Judah in BC 948. He married fourteen wives, by whom he had twenty sons and sixteen daughters. He reigned only three years, and imitated the impiety of his father. He was almost constantly at war with Jeroboam, King of Israel, once taking the field with 400,000

against him, and then 800,000. Their armies being drawn up very near to one another, Abijah climbed to the top of Mount Zemaraim and harangued the troops of the enemy to persuade them to return to their usual subjection to the house of David, and to the true worship of God. Meanwhile, Jeroboam detached a part of his army round the hill to attack the rear of Abijah's troops. Abijah and his army, seeing themselves surrounded, cried to the Lord for help, and the priests sounded the silver trumpets. Such a sudden panic seized the host of Jeroboam that Abijah's army cut off 500,000 of them on the spot, and, following up the victory, took Bethel Jeshanah, Ephraim, and many other places from the ten tribes. (1 Kings 15:1-8; 2 Chron. 11:20, 22, 13:1-4, 15, 17, 19-22)

(2) The only gracious son of Jeroboam. When he fell sick, the prophet Abiajah told his mother that he would certainly die, and that he would be the only one of Jeroboam's family to die a natural death and be dignified with funeral honours. He died the very moment of his mother's return to her house, and was greatly lamented by the people. (1 Kings 14:1-18)

ABIMELECH, *my father the king*
(1) King of the Philistines, who lived in Gerar. Captivated with the beauty of Sarah, and informed by Abraham that she was his sister, he took her into his palace intending to make her his wife. God did not allow him to take her to bed, but appeared to him in a dream, and threatened him with sudden death if he did not immediately restore her to her husband. Indeed, God had already smitten him and the women of his family with a condition that made them incapable of procreation or childbirth. Abimelech excused himself to his Maker because of Abraham's pretence that Sarah was only his sister. He quickly restored her the next day, severely reproving the Patriarch for deceiving him. Abraham confessed that she was indeed his wife, but was likewise his sister, born to a different mother. Abimelech gave Abraham a number of valuable presents, and offered him a resting place in any part of his kingdom. He, too, begged his prayers for the healing of his family, and cautioned him to beware of such a deception in the future. He also gave Sarah a thousand pieces of silver, or about £115, to purchase a veil to cover her face, which still, at 90 years of age, was beautiful and sparkling. Thus publicly instructed and reproved,

Abraham prayed for Abimelech's family, and they were cured of their condition. About fourteen years later, Abimelech, dreading danger to himself or his posterity from the increase of Abraham's power, came with Phichol his chief captain, and begged him to enter into a covenant of friendship, which was readily granted. (Gen. 20:2-4, 8-10, 14-15, 17-18, 21:22, 25-27, 29, 32)

(2) The son and successor of the former, was also deceived by Isaac in the same way that his father had been by Abraham. Happening from his window to see some sportive familiarity between Isaac and Rebekah, he immediately concluded that she was his wife, not his sister, as they had pretended. He immediately sent for Isaac and reproved him for involving him and his subjects in guilt and punishment. The fear of losing his life for the sake of his beautiful wife was the only thing that Isaac pleaded on his own behalf. Abimelech, therefore, immediately issued orders that none of his subjects, under pain of death, should in the least injure Isaac or Rebekah. Abimelech, finding that his subjects were terrified by, and envied mightily, the great prosperity and power of Isaac, politely asked him to leave his territories *because he was become mightier than they; or much increased at their expense.* Sometime later, Abimelech, mindful of the covenant his father had made with Abraham, and dreading danger from the increase of Isaac's power and wealth, took with him Ahuzzath his friend, and Phichol his chief captain, and, coming to Isaac, solemnly renewed the covenant with him at Beersheba, and were there entertained by him at a splendid feast. (Gen. 26:1, 8-11, 16, 26)

(3) As King of Israel, he was the illegitimate son of Gideon by his concubine at Shechem. He was a most wicked, ambitious, and bloody wretch. To take the government for himself, he hinted to the people of Shechem how much better it would be for them to have him, their own citizen and blood relation, to be their governor, than to have all the 70 sons of his father to rule over them. His Shechemite friends took out for him seventy shekels of silver from the temple of their idol Baalberith (a little more than £8 pounds). With this, he hired a band of vagabonds that assisted him to murder at one spot in Ophrah all his seventy brothers, only Jotham the youngest escaping. The Shechemites then proclaimed him king. It was on the occasion of his coronation, or soon after, that Jotham, from the top of Mount Gerazim, an adjacent hill, announced his parable to the men of Shechem, meaning that their

bestowal of the government on the only wicked man in Gideon's family, and the ungrateful murderer of the rest, would result in the speedy ruin of all concerned. The event quickly verified his prediction. Abimelech had not reigned more than three years when there was a dispute between him and the men of Shechem. While, it seems, Abimelech removed his residence to Arumah, a place near Shechem, and left Zebuel to inspect the city, Gaal the son of Ebed, and his friends, urged on and headed the conspiracy. At one of their idolatrous feasts, in a most outrageous way, they mocked and cursed Abimelech. Informed of this by Zebuel his officer, he marched the troops by night in four companies against the Shechemites. Gaal and his friends, having no time to prepare themselves, were easily routed. On the following morning, when the men of Shechem came out to the field, perhaps to bring in the harvest, Abimelech and his troops fell on them and murdered them. He next took the city in an assault, murdered the inhabitants, and demolished the buildings. A thousand of the Shechemites fled to the temple of Baalberith hoping to defend themselves, or expecting the sanctity of the place to protect them. Abimelech and his troops carried fuel from an adjacent wood and set fire to the temple, consuming it and all that were in it. He next marched to Thebez, a place about nine miles to the east. The inhabitants fled to a strong tower built in the middle of their city. Abimelech assaulted the tower with the utmost fury, and was just about to set fire to it when a woman from the top of it struck him with a piece of a millstone and broke his skull. He ordered his armour-bearer to thrust him through with his sword that it might not be said that he had been killed by a woman. His order was executed. He died BC 1206, and his troops were dispersed. (Judg. 9:1, 3-4, 6, 16, 18-25, 27-29, 31, 34-35, 38-42, 45, 47-50, 52, 55-56)

ABINADAB, *a father of a vow*, or *a free mind*
(1) The son of Jesse. (1 Sam. 16:8)
  (2) The son of Saul. (1 Sam. 31:2)
  (3) The son-in-law of Solomon. (1 Kings 4:11)

ABIRAM
(1) The son of Eliab the Reubenite. He, with his brother Dothan, and Korah, conspired to wrest from Moses and Aaron the powers

conferred on them by God. On this account, he, with his whole family and property, were swallowed up alive in the earth. (See Num. 16)

(2) The oldest son of Hiel the Bethelite. He lost his life when his father rebuilt the walls of Jericho. (1 Kings 16:34)

ABISHAG, *the error of my father*
A young woman, a native of Shunam, in the tribe of Issachar. David, at the age of about seventy, finding no warmth in his bed, was advised by his physicians to obtain some woman who might give him the heat he wanted. To this end, Abishag was presented to him as one of the most beautiful young women in all Israel. She was put in his bed (See 1 Kings 1:1-5)

ABISHAI, *the reward of my father*
The son of Zeruiah the sister of David. He was a notable warrior, and an early assistant and steady friend of his uncle. Entering Saul's tent along with David, he insisted on despatching the tyrant, but was not allowed to. (1 Sam. 26:7-11) He served in David's wars with Ishbosheth, and vigorously pursued the fleeing enemy. In the war with the Edomites, he cut off 18,000 of them in the Valley of Salt. In the war with the Syrians and Ammonites, he commanded the troops which engaged with, and routed, the latter. In the war with the Philistines, he killed Ishbibenob, a famous giant who was just about to murder his uncle and king. At another time, he alone attacked a body of three hundred, and killed them to a man. Highly provoked with Shimei's bluster, he begged his uncle leave to cut down the insolent wretch; but he was not permitted. He commanded a third part of the army that defeated Absalom, and headed the household troops that pursued Sheba the son of Bichri.

ABNER, *my father's lamp*
The son of Ner. He was the uncle of King Saul, and general of his army. Being mostly in the camp, and in a high station, it is not surprising that he did not know David at Ephes-dammim. He was more culpable when he guarded his master so badly in the camp at Hachilah, when David and Abishai entered and went off without being seen. (1 Sam. 14:50-51, 17:55-57, 26:5, 7, 14-15) After Saul's death, he proclaimed Ishbosheth king, and, for seven years, supported the family of Saul in opposition to David. But, in most of his skirmishes, he came off with loss. While

Ishbosheth and David's troops rested near one another, just outside Gibeon, Abner barbarically challenged Joab to advance twelve of David's warriors to fight with an equal number of his. Joab consented. The twenty-four engaged; and, taking each other by the beard, and thrusting his sword into his side, they fell down together dead on the spot. A fierce battle ensued, and Abner and his troops were routed. Abner himself was hotly pursued by Apsahel. When he begged him to stop the pursuit, he was refused, but Apsahel was killed by a back stroke of his spear. He was, however, still pursued by Joab and Abishai, till he, who, in the morning sported with murder, was obliged at night to beg that Joab would stop his troops from their hostile pursuit. (2 Sam. 2)

Not long after, Abner, taking it highly amiss when Ishbosheth charged him with immoral behaviour with Rizpah, Saul's concubine, he vowed that he would quickly betray the whole kingdom into the hands of David. He had scarcely threatened it, when he heard from David, and had an interview with him at Hebron to that effect. Abner had just left the splendid feast where David had entertained him, when Joab, informed of the matter, warmly complained to his uncle that Abner had come as a spy. At his own hand, he sent a messenger to invite him back to have some further communication with the King. Abner had just come into Joab's presence, when partly from jealousy that Abner might become his superior, and partly to revenge his brother Asahel's death, he mortally stabbed him as he pretended to salute him. Informed of this, David heartily detested the fact, protested to Joab, and honoured Abner with a splendid funeral and a mournful elegy. (2 Samuel 3)

THE ABOMINATION THAT MAKES DESOLATE
(1) The image of a pig on the brazen altar, and that of Jupiter Olympius in the Jewish Temple, which Antiochus Epiphanes erected to prevent the worship of God. (Dan. 11:31)

(2) The Roman armies, composed of heathen idolaters, who had the image of idols and Emperors painted on their banners, and who, highly hated by the Jews, entered, and burnt their Temple, and spread ravage and desolation throughout their country (Dan. 9:27; Matt. 24:15), mainly by the *abomination of desolation*, seen at Jerusalem during the last siege of that city by the Romans under Titus. This referred

to the ensigns of the Roman army, with the images of their gods and Emperors on them, as they surrounded the city, and which were lodged in the Temple when city and Temple were taken. The Evangelists add, *"...whoso readeth, let him understand"* (Matt. 24:15 and Mark 13:14), indicating that this event was about to take place, and that the reader would do well to leave the city as quickly as possible, which was thus threatened with the execution of the divine anger. Certainly, the passages were written before Jerusalem was destroyed, and, no doubt, were instrumental in warning many believers, and perhaps unbelievers also, to escape the coming wrath.

(3) Antichrist, who horribly defiles and wastes the Church of God. (Dan. 12:11)

ABRAM, ABRAHAM, *high and mighty father*

A son of Terah. Though mentioned before his brothers Nahor and Haran, he appears to have been the youngest in his family, born in the 130th year of his father's life, BC 1996. For the first seventy years of his life, he resided with his father's family in Ur of the Chaldees, and no doubt concurred with them in their idolatrous worship. (Josh. 24:2) After the death of his brother Haran, God appeared to him, doubtless hinting at the detestable nature of idolatry, and, it is certain, ordering him to leave his native country. He and his father's household removed to the northwest of Mesopotamia and settled in Haran (or Charran), a place so-called perhaps, to commemorate his deceased brother. After about five years residence there, Terah died, and God appeared to Abram again, assuring him of a numerous seed that would be a blessing to all the nations. He ordered him to leave his father's family and travel to a land to which he would direct him. All obedient, Abram took with him Sarai his wife, and Lot his brother Haran's son, and all their possessions, and went towards Canaan, neither knowing the country nor the place he was to go. (Gen. 11:26-32, 12:1-5; Deut. 26:5; Josh. 24:2-3; Isa. 41:8; Acts 7:2-4; Heb. 11:8)

Coming into Canaan and visiting Egypt

In BC 1921, he entered Canaan, crossing the Jordan south of the Galilean Sea. There, he pitched his tent at Shechem, and there, he erected an altar to the Lord. God again appeared to him, confirming his former promises, and assuring him that Canaan would one day be the property of his seed. He had scarcely received this promise when a famine obliged him to leave the country. Without consulting his Maker, he went south towards Egypt. Sarai was now sixty-five years of age, but retained enough of her beauty to endanger the man's life who passed for her husband, especially in Egypt where the women were not very pretty. Abram, therefore, and Sarai agreed that both should pretend she was his sister when they arrived. They had not been there long when her beauty charmed the Egyptians, and at last captivated Pharaoh himself. Abram received vast numbers of sheep, oxen, camels, asses, men-servants, and maid-servants, besides gold, silver, and other precious things, as presents for the sake of his pretended sister, and Sarai was in imminent danger of being taken to Pharaoh's bed. To prevent this, God inflicted on him and his family plagues that clearly pointed to their cause. Pharaoh sent for Abram, sharply rebuked him for his dangerous deception, and returned to him his wife untouched, giving orders for their safe departure from his dominions. (Gen. 12; Ps. 105:14-15)

Separation from Lot, and its consequences

The famine in Canaan being over, Abram returned greatly enriched by Pharaoh's presents, and by the silver and gold he had got from the sale of his cattle. On the altar he had built near Bethel and Hai, he offered a sacrifice of thanksgiving for his safe return. Contention between his herdsmen and those of his nephew Lot obliged them to separate. Abram made a peaceful proposal, and gave his nephew the choice of where he would like to go. Lot had just departed for the plain of Sodom when God reassured Abram that his seed would possess as much of the country as he could see. Abram removed south from near Bethel, and pitched his tent in the plain of Mamre, which is in Hebron. There, he erected an altar to God, and contracted a friendship with Mamre, Aner, and Eshcol, the chief men of that place. Before he had long enjoyed this agreeable situation, news was brought to him that Chedorlaomer and his allies had ravaged the country of Sodom and Gomorrah and carried away Lot as prisoner. Abram armed 318 of his own servants; and, with these and a few allies, and headed by his friends Mamre, Aner, and Eshcol, he pursued the conquering potentates. He surprised them at night at the springs of Jordan, and routed and pursued them as far as Hobah, north of Damascus. There, he rescued Lot with all his family

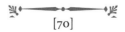

and possessions, together with the rest of the captives, and the plunder of Sodom. On his return, Melchizedek met him at Salem, entertained him with provisions, blessed him, and received from his hand a tithe of all the spoil. The young King of Sodom generously offered him all that he had recovered except the men and women. Abram, even more generously, refused the least share of it. (Gen. 13-14)

Further promises

To reward Abram's generosity, and dependence upon God, the Lord graciously and immediately assured him that he was his *shield* and his *exceeding great reward*, and repeated the promise of a numerous seed, and of Canaan as his inheritance. In a terrifying darkness, and with a fiery meteor passing between the pieces of the heifer, the she-goat, the ram, the turtledove, and the pigeon, he confirmed the covenant, prophesied their affliction, and hinted that, at last, their salvation would go forth *as a lamp that burneth*. (Compare Gen. 15:17 with Isa. 62:1) At the same time, he assured him that his seed would remain for four hundred years in a land not their own, and part of that time be terribly oppressed; but, in the fourth generation, they would be brought from the land of their bondage with great wealth, and take possession of Canaan, from the Euphrates on the northeast to the borders of Egypt on the southeast. (Gen. 15)

The tragedy of Hagar

Hearing that a child of Abram's own body would be heir of Canaan, Sarai, imagining it impossible for one of her age and circumstance to be a joyful mother, advised her husband to make Hagar her maid his concubine and get children by her. Without consulting God, Abram agreed too rashly. Hagar no sooner found herself pregnant than she behaved towards her mistress in a haughty and insolent manner. This occasioned bitter, but unjust, reproaches on Abram from his wife, as if he had encouraged his maid in her pride. Harsh treatment from her mistress provoked Hagar to flee the family. But, being advised by God, she returned and submitted herself. She produced a son whose name was Ishmael. For thirteen years after his folly with Hagar, God appeared to have denied Abram the more notable tokens of his favour and presence. However, in BC 1987, he repeated the promise of numerous seed, and the land of Canaan for their possession. To confirm this covenant, and to separate Abram and his family from the rest of the world, and to seal to them the blessings of grace, he ordered Abram and all the males of his family and seed to have their foreskins cut off. He changed his name to Abraham, which means *the father of a multitude.* Sarai's he changed to Sarah, which means *the lady* or *mistress.* He assured him that Ishmael would live and have numerous descendants, and Sarah, now ninety years of age, would bear a son, in whose *seed all the nations of the earth would be blessed.* Immediately after this vision, Abraham and all the males were circumcised. (Gen. 16-17)

The promise of an heir

Not long after, the Son of God, accompanied by two angels in human form, passed by Abraham's tent on their way to destroy Sodom and the cities nearby. Upon Abraham's kind entreaty, they entered his tent and were entertained by him as travellers. The angel Jehovah, asking for Sarah, assured her and her husband that after nine months she would have a son called Isaac. Abraham accompanied his guests part of the way towards Sodom. To reward him for the pious upbringing of his family, the Lord disclosed to him his intention of destroying these wicked cities. Moved with compassion, chiefly towards Lot, Abraham interceded for their preservation. God granted him whatever he asked. He offered to save them if fifty, or forty, or twenty, or even ten gracious souls could be found there. But, as there were none except Lot, only he and his two daughters were preserved. (Gen. 18-19) Scarcely had Sarah conceived, when her own and her husband's deception at Gerar issued in her being forced from his side by King Abimelech. She was, however, quickly restored, without receiving any stain of disloyalty to her marriage bed. (Gen. 20)

In BC 1896, Isaac was born to the great joy of Abraham and Sarah. At first, he was circumcised, and then suckled. When Isaac was weaned, Abraham threw a splendid feast for his household. On that occasion, Ishmael showed his contempt for Isaac. Sarah observed it, and begged her husband to expel Hagar and her son from the family, as she would never allow him to inherit Canaan alongside Isaac. This request was extremely disagreeable to Abraham, but, being reproved by God, he readily agreed. Abraham now dwelt at Beersheba where Abimelech, King of Gerar, came to make a covenant of friendship with him, moved perhaps by the report of the promise of Canaan as his seed. Abraham reproved the king concerning a well that his servants had taken by force. That being restored, a covenant was made between them, and was ratified with an oath. Abraham also built an altar there to the Lord. (Gen. 21)

Jehovah-Jireh

Isaac was now 25, or perhaps 33, years of age, when God ordered his father to offer him up as a burnt sacrifice on a distant hill. All obedient, Abraham rose early next morning, and set off with Isaac and some servants with a knife, fire and wood for the offering. After travelling three days, he came to Moriah, the appointed Mount. The servants and asses being left behind, Isaac carried the wood, and his father the knife and fire. On the way, Isaac asked where the sacrifice was. Abraham replied that God would provide it. They came to the appointed spot where an altar was built. Isaac was bound and stretched out upon it. Abraham had just lifted up his hand with the knife to plunge it into the throat of his son when the Lord himself stopped the blow, and told Abraham that he had now sufficiently discovered his fixed faith in his promise, and his respect for his precepts. Meanwhile, the Patriarch, looking behind him, saw a ram caught by its horns in a thick bush. This, he caught, and offered up in place of his son. He called the place *Jehovah-Jireh*, indicating that God had chiefly manifested his favours in perplexing circumstances, and would *provide* for his people whatever they needed. After God had renewed his promises, and confirmed them with an oath, Abraham rejoined his servants, and returned home to Beersheba. He was there informed that his brother Nahor now had numerous children. (Gen. 22)

The death of Sarah

Abraham's next work was the burial of his beloved Sarah. She died at Hebron where her husband, it seems, was then living. He requested from the Hittites of that place to sell him a burial place. They offered him the pick of any of their sepulchres; but he desired the cave of Machpelah. Ephron, the owner, begged him to take it as a present, but Abraham insisted on giving the full value, and paid 400 shekels for it, which amounted to £46, or, according to Prideaux, £60. There, he buried his wife Sarah.

Isaac and Rebekah

Three years later, he resolved to provide a wife for his son Isaac. He called in Eliezer his chief servant, and, after giving him instructions, and binding him by a solemn oath to take for his son a wife from among his own family members, and to avoid every inducement to make Isaac return to Mesopotamia, he sent him away with a suitable caravan, and a number of presents. Rebekah was then obtained for Isaac. Next year, Abraham himself married his concubine Keturah (1 Chron. 1:32); and, his body, being invigorated under the influence of God, he had six sons by her, their names being: Zimran, Jokshan, Medan, Midian, Ishbak, and Shuab. These, Abraham, in his lifetime, set up, and sent them east into the desert of Arabia, where they became heads of tribes numerous and powerful. In BC 1841, Abraham died in the 175th year of his age. His sons Isaac and Ishmael, who now lived at a small distance from one another, buried him in the cave of Machpelah, beside his wife Sarah. (Gen. 33-35)

Abraham also appears famous in the stories of the ancient heathen, and of the Mahometans, Indians, and Jews, as a king of Damascus, and as a teacher of arithmetic and astronomy to the Egyptians, etc. It is probable that human sacrifices arose among the Canaanites from his intended offering of Isaac. Severus, the Roman Emperor, reckoned him one of his deities, alongside Jesus Christ. The sacred Scriptures present him as the *friend of God* (James 2:23), as the father and pattern of the faithful, as one who, with joy unspeakable, foresaw the coming of the promised Messiah, and as a notable professor of the heavenly glory (hence, a share of it is represented as *lying in his bosom*) (See Matt. 8:11; Luke 16:22; John 8:56-58; Rom. 4; Heb. 11)

Abraham a type

Was not Jesus Christ typified in this venerable patriarch? Astonishing was his meekness, his love and kindness to men, his intimacy with, fear of, obedience to, and trust in, his God. He is the chosen favourite of heaven, the father and covenant-head of innumerable millions of the saved. To him were all the promises relative to the evangelical and eternal state of his church originally made. All obedient, and at his Father's call, he left his native abode of bliss and became a stranger and wanderer on the earth, not having anywhere *to lay his head*. (Matt. 8:20; Luke 9:58) At his Father's call, he offered himself as

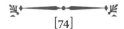

an acceptable sacrifice to God. By his prevalent intercession, and supernatural influence, he delivers all his too ungrateful friends from the hand of their foes. After long patience, he obtains a numerous seed in the Jewish and gospel Church. In his visible family are many claimants, children of the bond-woman, relying on the covenant of works, who, in the issue, are like the modern Jews, rejected and cast out into a state of wickedness and misery. The true children are those of the freewoman, who, like Isaac, are, by the powerful influence of the promise, born again unto God. (Gal 4:22-23, 30)

Extra note

The person and character of Abraham is among the most distinguished to which the Scriptures call our attention, whether we view him in his own personal history, or rather his place in the Church of God. If we are ultimately saved, it is as *Abraham's seed* (Rom. 4:16); if we are blessed with the knowledge and belief of the truth, it is the blessing of *Abraham* come down to us; for, according to the sacred oracles, in Abraham *all nations are blessed.* (Gen. 12:3, 18:18, 22:18, 26:4)

He appears to have been the younger son of Terah, but was born when his father had reached the advanced age of 130 years. In whatever light it may be viewed, it is an undoubted fact that every millennium of the duration of the world is connected with some extraordinary event related to the state of the Church. The birth of Abraham brought in a new and important era. That blessing which, in the very first promise, was generally expressed concerning the seed of the woman, is now conveyed by a particular channel; for from Abraham's loins was to proceed the blessed Saviour, who could say, *"Before Abraham was, I am."* (John 8:58) For a considerable part of Abraham's early life, we have no other account of him except that he resided with his father, and was an idolater. (Josh. 24:2) How remarkable does Divine sovereignty appear in the selection of the most eminent worthies, whose histories are recorded in the Word of God! The same power that brought Moses from attending Jethro's flock, David from his father's flock, Paul from his mad and persecuting zeal against the followers of Jesus, also brought Abraham from his idols, *that the excellency of the power might be of God, and not of men.* (2 Cor. 4:7)

An assessment of Abraham

Biographers generally take delight in tracing remarkable and inviting circumstances, even in childhood or early youth, to show his fitness for future elevation. The inspired biographer only says, *"Now the Lord had said to Abraham, get thee out of the country."* (Gen. 12:1) With respect to the mode in which divine revelation was communicated in the Patriarchal age, we cannot now determine. It is sufficient for our present purpose to say that it was enough to convince Abraham that it was the Lord who spoke to him. The gospel now, similar to what was preached to Abraham, calls on us to forsake the idolatry of our father's house, our native lusts and hopes, and to follow Jesus wherever he commands us. Abraham, obedient to the heavenly call (Heb. 11:8), proceeded on his journey to Canaan; and, on his arrival there, he pitched his tent at Shechem where he established the worship of the God who had appeared to him. The place where this altar was built later became famous as a place of worship in Israel. Here was a sacred oak or grove (see Gen. 33:18). God made a visible appearance to him at this place, confirming his former promises. From what has already been mentioned, the reader will be able to judge or form some idea of the nature of patriarchal worship: how nearly allied it was to that of the Tabernacle in the wilderness, and how much it was designed to be a shadow of good things to come.

In the 18th chapter of Genesis, we find related there a most interesting portion of the eventful history of Abraham, from which we may infer the following:

(1) The direct and immediate communication that existed between Abraham and the Lord.

(2) Abraham's hospitality, as referred to by the Apostle in Hebrews 13:2.

(3) The importance of the subject revealed in the birth of Isaac, when such great pains were taken to renew and enforce it, clearly proving that a more important matter than the birth of Isaac was in view.

(4) Sarah's unbelief; the natural operation of the mind from the circumstances of her time of life; and the way in which her unbelief was overcome.

(5) The overthrow of Sodom and Gomorrah.

(6) Abraham's intercession, and God's reply *I will not destroy for ten's sake* are a token that everlasting destruction will not be executed

against the ungodly until the iniquity of mankind is full, and faith becomes rare on the earth. It may easily be seen that the gospel is the salt of the earth, and that this world is only preserved from that judgement for which it is ripe till the last elect vessel of mercy is converted to the knowledge of the truth. On Genesis 18:17-19, we observe that it was to reward him for the religious education of his family that the Lord disclosed to him his intention of destroying these wicked cities; but it is more than probable that there was also another object in view, that is, to teach Abraham the punishment due to sin, and the grand design of executing judgement on the wicked. The destruction of Sodom was one of the clearest displays of the Last Judgement exhibited in the sacred pages.

We now turn our attention to consider what may rightly be entitled the most memorable event in Abraham's history, by referring to the offering up of his son Isaac. The circumstances attending this trans-action are so numerous and important that it would require extensive limits to investigate them, however slightly. We take note of the following particulars briefly:

1. Abraham's faith was remarkably tested in the promise of the birth of Isaac, when he was called to believe, hope against hope. He had received this son, in whom all the promises centred, yet he was called upon to sacrifice him. That this was a severe trial to his natural feelings, all acknowledge; but the Christian will perceive something far more important - the trial of his *faith*, for if Isaac died, what would happen to all the promises of God? And thus, as the Apostle says, he could only offer him up by believing that God was able to raise him from the dead. (Heb. 11:19)

2. Abraham was called upon to go to the land of *Moriah*; that is, the *fear* (or rather, the *worship*) *of Jehovah*. How apparent in such a circumstance was the plan of God, who would, in the fullness of time, establish his worship in that very land, and sacrifice his well-beloved, perhaps on the very spot of ground where Isaac was bound! We are certain of this, that Jerusalem and its vicinity was called *the land of Moriah*. On one of these mountains, the Temple was built. And as Abraham named the place *Jehovah-Jireh*, there cannot exist any doubt that in that very place the Lord was seen.

3. We observe further, that on *the third day* Abraham saw the place afar off. (Gen. 22:4) From the period of leaving home, Isaac travelled

under sentence of death from his father; and, on the third day, he received him from the dead in a figure. In the same way, Isaac's great antitype, Jesus Christ, lay under sentence of death. Christ's burnt offering was acceptable to God the Father, who, on *the third day* received him from the dead. The various circumstances recorded by the Spirit of God bear such a striking analogy to the sufferings and death of Christ that *he that runs may read* without the details being spelt out.

4. Abraham was next called to witness the death of his beloved Sarah, who, of the two, first paid the tribute of nature. He mourned and wept over his loss for the partner of his cares, who had long been his comforter during his pilgrimage. Shortly after that, he adopted a plan for the marriage of his son Isaac; and, having accomplished it, the next year he himself married Keturah by whom he had six sons, who later became the heads of numerous tribes. Being sent to the east country, they carried with them the knowledge of the true God. The remains of true worship are still to he traced among their descendants. Abraham died at an advanced age. The taper of his life burned out, rather than being extinguished, and he was gathered to his fathers. This then is a brief tracing out of the outlines of an important history.

ABSALOM

The third son of King David. His mother was Maachah, the daughter of Talmai, King of Geshur. He became one of the most handsome men that ever breathed. Every year, he cut the hair of his head, with it weighing 200 shekels, or about six pounds in English weight, or perhaps it was valued at the rate of 200 shekels of silver, which, at least, is about £23, or according to Humphrey Prideaux, £30. He had three sons, all of whom died in their childhood, and a beautiful daughter named Tamar. (2 Sam. 3:3, 14:25-27, 18:18)

When Tamar was raped by her half-brother Amnon, she complained to Absolom of the injury Amnon had done her. Absalom resolved on a thorough revenge. Planning to execute it, he entirely concealed his resentment. After two years, he invited his brothers to a shearing feast at Baalhazor. When Amnon had drunk deeply, Absalom ordered his servants to kill him, and fled to his grandfather at Geshur in Syria. He continued three years in exile, when Joab, observing David's desire for a reconciliation, prompted an artful widow of Tekoah, with a pretended speech concerning the danger of her son, who, she said, had, in a passion, killed his brother, to bring it about. Absalom was recalled; but he lived two years at Jerusalem without entering his father's presence. Stung with grief and indignation, he sent for Joab with a view to engaging him to be his advocate with the King. At first, Joab refused, but Absalom, by burning his corn, forced him to go. On coming to the King, Joab understood his feelings, went directly to David, and secured Absolom's admission to court. Scarcely had this reconciliation been effected, when Absalom made preparations to usurp his father's throne. He got himself a number of horses and chariots, and 50 men to run before him. By treating kindly those who came to his father for judgement, and by indirect hints that their causes were good, but his father was neglecting to do them justice, and by wishing that it was in his power to give them justice, he won the hearts of the people over.

About Pentecost, BC 1024, in the 40th year after David had been anointed by Samuel, and in the 4th year after Absalom's return from Syria under the pretence of fulfilling a vow, he asked his father's permission to go to Hebron, a city south of Jerusalem. Two hundred notable pople accompanied him without suspecting his designs. He immediately opened his mind to them, and caused it to be proclaimed in all the cities of Israel that he was ruling in Hebron. Ahithophel, David's principle counsellor, upon invitation, immediately went over to him. Then the body of the Israelites followed his example. David, with a handful of those friends he could depend on, fled from Jerusalem. Ahithophel, after publicly raping ten of David's concubines, advised Absalom without delay to give him the command of 12,000 chosen troops, and he would directly pursue his father and arrest him before he had time to recover from his fright. This advice was certainly to the point. But Hushai was also consulted. He pretended that Ahithophel's counsel was not timely, as David and his friends were brave and desperate fellows, and would readily spring from pits, or similar hiding places, and, all of a sudden, cut off some of Absalom's forces, and so dispirit the whole alliance before it was firmly established. To flatter Absalom's vanity, and give David time to put himself into a position of defence, he advised Absalom to assemble every man of Israel capable of bearing arms; and that he should command them in person. He pretended that, with this huge army, they could not fail in ruining David and his party, whether they found him in city or field.

Hushai's advice was approved and followed. Absalom collected his troops, and marched over the Jordan to attack his father. A battle was fought in the wood of Ephraim, where his raw undisciplined host was easily defeated in the providence of God by his father's veteran troops. The wood tore vast numbers of them to pieces, or otherwise led to their ruin. David ordered his warriors to spare the life of his rebellious son; but, while riding through the wood, an oak branch caught hold of Absolom's highly prized hair, and hung him from it like a halter, while his mule went on its way. Informed of this, Joab hastened to the place and put an end to his life. Absolom had erected a proud monument to perpetuate his name, but did not receive the honour of being buried there. His corpse was thrown into a pit like the carcass of an ass, and a great heap of stones was thrown over him. Whether his father, who so lamented his death, removed it to a more honourable place, we do not know. (2 Sam. 13-17)

ACHAN, or ACHAR

He was a descendant of Judah by Zerah, Zabdi, and Carmi. At the taking of Jericho, contrary to the direct command of Joshua, he coveted part of the spoil that had been put under a curse. Having seized a Babylonish garment, a wedge of gold, and two hundred shekels of silver, he concealed them in his tent. Offended by his crime, and to deter others from secret wickedness, God showed his indignation in the defeat of three thousand Hebrews at Ai, with the slaughter of thirty-six. Pained with grief, Joshia and the elders of Israel tore their clothes and cried to the Lord for help. The Lord informed Joshua that someone had taken the accursed spoil and hidden it among his possessions. Until they discovered and punished this crime, they should not expect any further assistance from him.

Under the direction of God, the whole assembly of Israel sanctified themselves, and prepared themselves for a solemn search the next day. The search was referred to the determination of the lot: first the tribe of Judah, next the family of Zerah, next the family of Zabdi, and lastly, Achan was taken. Reproved by Joshua, he openly confessed his offence, and, it is hoped, truly repented of it. The stolen goods were brought out and publicly exposed before the assembly. Then he and

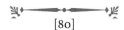

his children, who probably concurred in the theft, and all his cattle, were publicly stoned to death to the terror of others, and their dead bodies, with the household furniture, were burnt to ashes in the valley of Gilgal, called from that time on *Achor* (trouble); and a great heap of stones was raised up on the site. (1 Chron. 2:5-7; Josh. 7:1, 18-20, 24, 22:20)

ACHISH, or ABIMELECH

King or lord of the Philistines at Gath. To avoid Saul's persecution, David retired to Gath. The courtiers represented to Achish that this David had killed Goliath, and was celebrated as a notable destroyer of their nation. Informed of these insinuations, David saved his life by pretending to go mad. Achish hinted to his servants that they had no reason to be afraid, and he needed no one to make sport to him, so he ordered them to expel him from the city. About four years later, David returned to Gath. Achish, the same king who had formerly driven him away, or perhaps his son, gave him a friendly reception. He assigned him and his warriors Ziklag, one of his cities to dwell in. Almost two years later, he asked David and his warriors to assist him and the Philistines against Saul and the Hebrews, and promised to make them his lifeguard. The other lords of the Philistines absolutely refused to allow David and his men to serve in their army. Achish, therefore, discreetly dismissed them to go to their homes. (Ps. 34:1; 1 Sam. 21, 27-28 and 24)

ACHSAH

The daughter of Caleb the son of Jephunneh. (1 Chron. 2:49) To encourage some brave warrior to gain by force Kirjathsepher from the Canaanitish giants, Caleb offered his daughter Achsah as a reward. On these terms, Othniel, her cousin, quickly won her. On her way home to her husband's residence, she got off her ass, threw herself at her father's feet, and begged him for springs in the dry southland, where she would have a moist field abounding in watersprings. He gave her one, perhaps two fields, thoroughly moist. (Josh. 15:16-19; Judg. 1:12-15)

ADAM, *from the earth*

This name was divinely imposed on both of the original parents of the human race, indicating their earthly origin, their beauty, and their

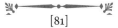

affectionate union. (Gen. 4:1-2, 5:1-5) It is a name extraordinarily appropriate for man. On the sixth day of the creation, when God had made the earth as a residence, he formed man's body from the dust of the ground. He breathed into his nostrils the breath of life, and endued him with a rational soul, so that he might resemble God in knowledge, righteousness, and holiness. For exercise and refreshment, he placed him in the garden of Eden to keep and cultivate it. Though perfect obedience was due to his Maker, and needed no valuable reward, God, in rich condescension and grace, made a covenant with him, declaring that, upon condition of his perfect obedience to every precept of the divine law, he and all his posterity would be rewarded with happiness and life, both natural, spiritual, and eternal. However, in case of failure, he would be subjected to the opposite, death. This, Adam agreed to. To be sure, it was the shortest, easiest, and most probable method of securing happiness for mankind. Adam too, was perfectly able, and lay under the strongest obligation to keep this condition. To render him the more attentive, and to keep him mindful of his fallible nature, and to remind him that his happiness consisted only in the enjoyment of God, and to test his obedience, he was prohibited under pain of immediate death to eat the fruit of the *tree of the knowledge of good and evil.*

That same day, God made him lord over the fish, birds, cattle, creeping things, vegetables, and other things on the earth. The birds, cattle, and creeping things he brought before Adam as his servants, and Adam showed his wisdom and authority in assigning to each its proper name. None of these animals was a fit companion for Adam, so God put him into a deep sleep, took a piece of his body (a rib from his side) without the least pain, and formed it into the body of a most beautiful woman. She too he endued with a rational soul, and brought her to Adam, who received her as his wife with the utmost affection. As the weather was perfect, and there was no irregularity in their nature, they both went naked, with no harm nor shame to themselves. (Gen. 1:26-31, and ch. 2; Ps. 8:4-7; Rom. 5:12-19)

That very day, or soon after, Satan, just expelled from his heavenly abode, conceived the strongest envy at the happiness of mankind, and decided to bring about their ruin. Considering nothing too wicked, he entered into a serpent, the most simple and subtle of the animals. Then, finding the woman all alone, he conferred with her, tempting her to suspect the meaning and certainty of the divine prohibition, and to eat of the forbidden fruit. Requested by her, Adam followed his wife's example and received part of the fruit from her hand and ate it. No doubt, he hoped for happiness, and at least impunity from punishment in doing so. However, it is quite absurd to imagine that he was willing to throw himself into endless woe because of his affection for her. Guilt immediately seized their consciences, and strange passions awoke in their souls. They were ashamed of their nakedness and used fig leaves as a covering. In the cool, or late afternoon, of the day, they heard the voice, the Word, or the Son of God, walking in the Garden, and fled to hide themselves among the thick bushes or trees. God called for Adam, and inquired why he had fled, how he had became ashamed of his nakedness, and why he had eaten the forbidden fruit? Adam laid the whole blame on Eve whom, he said, God had given him as an assistant and comfort. Eve blamed the serpent as her deceiver. After passing a sentence of ruin on Satan and his agents by means of the seed of the woman, and of affliction on the serpent, the instrument of his deceit, he spoke to the woman and her female offspring of her sorrow, painful childbirth, and subjection to her husband. God threatened Adam and his whole posterity with a curse on their fields, with diminished crops, and sorrow, and toil. Finally, he spoke of his death and return to the dust.

God's threatening of Satan implied a promise of mercy and redemption to mankind through the blood of God's Son. Therefore, God now instructed Adam and his wife in the manner and meaning of typical sacrifices. To mark their degrading of themselves to the level of beasts by sin, and promising their recovery by the imputed righteousness of the great atonement, God clothed them with the skins of sacrificed animals. To testify his displeasure with sin, and prevent their vain attempts to gain happiness and immortality by eating from the tree of life, God expelled them from Eden to cultivate the fields to the east. The symbols of the divine presence hovered over the east of the Garden where some angels, and perhaps some fiery meteors, were placed, rendering it impossible for mankind to re-enter. Just before his expulsion, Adam called his wife *Eve* because she was to be the universal mother of mankind, particularly of those appointed to everlasting life. Then he took her, and she conceived and bore Cain, and, soon after, Abel. These turned out to be a source of great grief to their parents. Soon after the murder of Abel, Adam, in his 130th year, had Seth. Beside that, he had a great many other children. After he had lived 930 years, he died. A number of fanciful stories concerning him are reported in heathen and Jewish writers; but he is presented in Scripture as a covenant-breaker, as a coverer of his transgressions, as a source of guilt and death to his posterity, and as a type or figure of the promised Messiah. (Gen. 3-5; Hosea 7:6; Job 31 and 33; Rom. 5:12-19; 1 Cor. 15:21-22, 45-49)

Jesus Christ is called the *last Adam* because of his similarity with the first. He is, in a special way, the *Son of God*, the *express image of his Person*, and the *brightness of his glory*. (Heb. 1:3) He is a new thing created in the earth by the overshadowing influence of the Holy Spirit. He is the glorious fruit of the earth, the product of the chief counsels of God, and the ornament and centre of all his works. He is the Head and representative of his people in the second and last covenant, He is their common parent who communicates to them his spiritual image, entitling them to all the fullness of God. He is their great prophet, priest and king. All things, without reserve, are subjected to him for their sake. Having, by his blood, regained the heavenly paradise, he resides in it, and cultivates the whole garden of his Church, having given men the power to eat of the tree of life. By the determinate counsel of God, he was cast into the deep sleep of debasement and death, and his Church, as her true members, was formed out of his broken body and pierced side. Divinely, she is espoused to him; and to her he cleaves at the expense of once leaving his Father in heaven, and now leaving his mother, the church and nation of Judah. (1 Cor. 15:22, 43-49)

ADONIBEZEK, *the king of Bezek*

Just before Joshua entered the land of Canaan, Adonibezek waged a furious war with his neighbouring kings. Seventy of them he took captive; and, after cutting off their thumbs and great toes, caused them, like dogs, to feed on the crumbs that fell from his table. After Joshua's death, the tribes of Judah and Simeon, finding themselves restricted by the Canaanites, resolved to clear their cantons of these accursed nations. Among others, they fell on Adonibezek, took his capital, and made him prisoner. They also cut off his thumbs and great toes. At that, he acknowledged the just vengeance of heaven on him for his

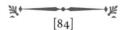

cruelty toward his fellow princes. They brought him along with them to Jerusalem, where he died about BC 1434. (Judg. 1:4-7)

ADONIJAH

The 4th son of King David, born at Hebron. When his two older brothers, Amnon and Absalom, were dead, and Chileab had perhaps become weak and inactive, and his father was languishing under the infirmities of old age, Adonijah attempted to seize the kingdom for himself. He prepared for his own use a magnificent equipage of horses and horsemen, and 50 men to run before him. This did not please his father. His interest at court became powerful, such that Joab, the general of the forces, Abiathar the High Priest, and others, joined his party, although Benaiah, Zadok, and Nathan the prophet, and most of the mighty men, did not. To introduce himself to the throne, he prepared a splendid entertainment at Enrogel; to this he invited all his brothers except Solomon, whom he knew his father had proclaimed successor to the throne, and all the great men of Judah, except who supported Solomon.

While they caroused at their cups, and wished Adonijah a happy reign, Nathan the prophet got wind of their design. He and Bathsheba immediately informed King David, and applied in favour of Solomon. Those who opposed Adonijah were stricly ordered to anoint Solomon with the utmost solemnity. Adonijah's party became alarmed with the shouts of applause, and being fully informed by Jonathan the son of Abiathar, they dispersed in great terror and amazement. Deserted by his friends, and conscious of his crime, Adonijah fled for protection to the horns of the altar, probably the one on the threshing-floor of Arauna. Solomon sent him word that his life would be safe provided he behaved himself in the future. He came and presented himself on his knees before Solomon; and then, at his order, returned to his own house. Soon after his father's death, he made Bathsheba his agent to request Abishag the Shunammite as his wife, who had been his father's concubine. Solomon suspected this was a plot to obtain the kingdom, and, perhaps informed by others of his treacherous designs, ordered Benaiah his general to kill him. His death occurred about a year after his attempt to usurp the kingdom. (1 Kings 1:5, 7-9, 11, 13, 18, 24-25, 41-43, 49-51)

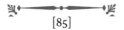

ADONIRAM
The principal receiver of Solomon's tribute, and director of the 30,000 sent to cut timber in Lebanon for the building of the Temple and other magnificent structures. (1 Kings 4:6; 5:14)

ADORAM
(1) King David's general receiver of the tribute. (2 Sam. 20:24) Whether he was the same as Adoniram, we do not know.

(2) Adoram, or, Hadoram, King Rehoboam's chief treasurer, and overseer of his works. His master sent him to deal with the ten revolting tribes to ensure their allegiance. Suspecting him of encouraging their oppressive taxes, or from fury at his master, they stoned him to death on the spot. (1 Kings 12:18; 2 Chron. 10:18)

ADRAMMELECH and SHAREZER
Sons of Sennacherib. It is possible the former was named after an idol of the same name. Dreading their father's intention to sacrifice them, or having some strong prejudice against him, they murdered him as he worshipped his idol Nisroch, and then fled to the country of Armenia. (Isa. 37:88; 2 Kings 19:37)

AGABUS
A prophet who foretold the famine that came in AD 44, in the days of Claudius Caesar. (Acts 11:28) About AD 60, he visited Paul at Caesarea and foretold his being bound in Jerusalem. (Acts 21:10-11) It is said that he suffered martyrdom at Antioch.

AGAG
It appears to have been a name common to the kings of Amalek. Indeed, they had a mighty king of this name as early as the time of Moses. (Num. 24:7) One of this name governed them in the days of Saul, who was extremely cruel and bloody, and his sword bereaved many mothers of their children. Saul, when divinely ordered to cut off that whole nation, spared him with the best of the flocks. He appeared before Samuel the prophet with the most delicate airs, expressing his hope that he had no reason to fear a violent and tormenting death. But the prophet, with his own hand, or another under his orders, cut him to pieces before the Lord at Gilgal. (1 Sam. 15:8-9, 20, 32-33) Haman

was called an Agagite probably because he was an Amalekite, and of the blood-royal. (Esther 3:1)

AGRIPPA

The grandson of Herod the Great, and son of Aristobulus and Bernice. He was at Rome in the company of the Emperor Claudius when his father died in AD 44. The Emperor was inclined to bestow on him the whole dominions possessed by his father, but his courtiers dissuaded him from it. The next year, the governor of Syria thought to compel the Jews to lodge the ornaments of their high priest in the tower of Antonia, under custody of the Roman guard, but, through the influence of Agrippa, they were allowed by the Emperor to guard them themselves. In AD 49, Herod, King of Chalcis, his uncle, died, and he was constituted his successor by the Emperor Caligula. But four years later, that kingdom was taken from him, and the provinces of Gaulonites and Trachonites were given him in its place. To these, soon after, Nero added Julius in Perea, and a part of Galilee on the west of the Sea of Tiberias.

When Festus was made governor of Judea in AD 60, Agrippa, and his sister Bernice, with whom he was thought to be living in incest, came to Caesarea to congratulate him. In the course of their conversation, Festus mentioned the affair of Paul's trial, and his appeal to Caesar. Agrippa was extremely curious to hear what Paul had to say for himself. The next day, Festus granted their request to hear him in the public hall. When Paul knew that Agrippa wanted to hear his defence, he declared how he had been converted from a furious persecutor into a zealous preacher, and how he had, according to the ancient prophets, preached the resurrection of the dead. Agrippa was so charmed with the good sense and majesty of the discourse, and the Apostle's polite address to himself, that he declared he was *almost persuaded to be a Christian*. Paul, expressed his earnest wish that King Agrippa and all his audience, might be as himself except for his bonds and trouble. Agrippa indicated to Festus that Paul might have been set at liberty if he had not appealed to Caesar. (Acts 25-26)

About two years later, Agrippa deposed Joseph Cabei, the Jewish High Priest, for the great offence he had given to the people in murdering James, the brother of John, whose distinguished meekness and sanctity was universally respected, and appointed Jesus, the son of Damneus, High Priest in his place. It was not long after that he allowed the Temple singers to wear linen robes like the common priests. He restrained for a while the rebellion of the Jews against their Roman superiors. When, at last, made desperate by the oppression and insolence of their governors, the Jews openly revolted, and Agrippa was obliged to side with the Romans. After the destruction of Jerusalem, he and his sister Bernice retired to Rome where he died, aged 70, in AD 90.

AGUR

The son of Jakeh, is thought by some to be Solomon himself. But Solomon had no reason to disguise his name; nor would he pray against riches; nor was his style and manner of writing similar to Agur's, who, under inspiration, uttered the 30th chapter of Proverbs to his two friends Ithiel and Ucal. In it, he professed his great ignorance of the unsearchable greatness, and marvellous works of God, his esteem of God's Word, and his desire for a moderate share of worldly things. He mentions four kinds of very wicked people, four things insatiable, four things wonderful, four small but wise, and four beautiful in appearance.

AHAB

(1) The son and successor of Omri. He began his reign over Israel in BC 918, and reigned 22 years. In impiety, he far exceeded all the kings of Israel. He married Jezebel, the daughter of Ethbaal, King of Zidon, who introduced the whole abominations and idols of her country, such as Baal and Ashtaroth, and vigorously prompted her husband to do everything horrible. To punish their wickedness, God, by the prophet Elijah, first threatened, and then sent, more than three years of continuous drought. A terrible famine resulted. Charging this to the account of the prophet, Ahab sought him out in his own country and the kingdoms adjacent in order to murder him. At last, Elijah, by means of Obadiah, a courtier, informed Ahab where he was. Ahab hastened to the spot, and rudely charged him as a *troubler of Israel*. (1 Kings 18:17-18) The prophet replied that he himself and his family, in forsaking the true God, and in following the Baals, had brought these judgements on the people. He required Ahab to assemble the Israelites, and all the prophets of Baal, on Mount Carmel. This was done; and

Elijah, having, by the descent of fire from heaven in order to consume his sacrifice, demonstrated Jehovah, not Baal, to be the true God, ordered the people to slay the prophets of Baal to the number of 450. Quickly afterwards, by his prayers, he brought about an abundance of rain. (1 Kings 16:29-34; 17-18)

About BC 901, Benhadad, King of Syria, who besieged Samaria with a powerful army, sent Ahab a message stating that all his silver, gold, wives, and children were his property. Ahab immediately agreed. In a second messsage, Benhadad ordered him to deliver up his silver, gold, wives, and children, and threatened that the next day he would send his servants to strip the city and palace of everything valuable. The elders and people dissuaded Ahab from listening to this. Hearing of his refusal, Benhadad outrageously swore that his troops, before long, would demolish Samaria till not a trace remained. Offended by the Syrian pride, God, through a prophet, instructed Ahab in his measures, and assured him of victory. Ahab ordered his small army of 7000, with 232 pages (young noblemen) at their head, to march out of the city at noon. Benhadad ordered his troops to bring the young commanders directly to him, whatever they intended. But the Hebrew troops still advanced, and killed all that opposed them. Benhadad and his army were entirely routed, leaving behind much booty. This victory was gained by raw, inexperienced commanders, that it might appear wholly of God.

The prophet informed Ahab that Benhadad would invade his kingdom next spring, and advised him to take precautions. This invasion took place with a powerful army. Ahab, assured of victory by the prophet, drew up his small army before the Syrians seven days successively, and, on the last day, gave them battle. A hundred thousand Syrians were killed on the spot. The rest fled to Aphek where the walls, brought down by an earthquake, killed 27,000 more. Benhadad threw himself on the mercy of Ahab, and was kindly received. An agreement was drawn up on condition that Ahab should have all the cities restored that had been taken from him and his father, and that Ahab should be allowed to set up for his own use *market places*, or rather, *citadels* or *streets*, for Israelites to dwell in, enjoying the privileges of the city under their own king and their own laws in Damascus. This kindness shown to a horrible blasphemer and murderer, whom providence had put into Ahab's power to slay, greatly provoked the Lord. As he returned home, a prophet assured him that since he had allowed Benhadad to escape, his life would be forfeit for his life, and his people for his. Ahab was at first considerably anxious, but the impression of the prophet's words soon wore off. (1 Kings 20)

Intending to make himself a kitchen garden next to his palace in Jezreel, Ahab demanded that Naboth sell him his vineyard, or exchange it for a better one. Naboth absolutely refused to violate the divine law in giving up the inheritance of his fathers. Stung by this refusal, Ahab went home greatly displeased, threw himself on his bed, and would eat nothing. Informed of the cause of his distress, to comfort him, Jezebel assured him that she would quickly put him into possession of Naboth's vineyard. By issuing orders to the elders of the city, and suborning (bribing) false witnesses against Naboth, she had him murdered after being charged with blasphemy and treason. Informed of his death, Ahab went and took possession of the vineyard. On his return home to Samaria, Elijah met him, and divinely assured him that for his murder of Naboth, and for seizing his vineyard, dogs would lick his blood on the spot where they had licked Naboth's. His wife Jezebel, would be eaten up by dogs beside the wall of Jezreel, and the rest of his family would have their carcasses devoured by dogs in the city, or by wild beasts and birds outside. Terrified at this prediction, Ahab tore his clothes, put on sackcloth, and mourned for his conduct. To reward his repentance, even though it was not of an evangelical kind, God deferred the full execution of the stroke till after his death in the reign of Jehoram his son, and perhaps altered some of its particulars. (1 Kings 21)

In BC 897, Benhadad failing to fulfill his treaty in restoring to Israel their property, Ahab prepared to retake by force Ramothgilead, a fortified city near the southeast border of Syria. Just then, Jehoshaphat happened to pay a visit to Ahab, and agreed to assist him; but he wanted some prophet to be consulted first whether the Lord would favour the attempt. Four hundred prophets of Baal were consulted. With one voice, they assured the kings that the Lord would deliver the city into their hands. Suspecting their lies, Jehoshaphat inquired for a prophet of the true God. Ahab informed him of one Micaiah: *But*, said he, *I hate him; for he doth not prophesy good concerning me, but evil.* (1 Kings 22:8) Being sent for at Jehoshaphat's insistance, and then consulted, he bid Ahab go up to Ramothgilead and prosper.

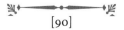

Ahab, discerning the irony in his voice, commanded him to tell him nothing but the truth. Micaiah then seriously assured him that his army would be scattered, and return without him at their head; and that, by divine permission, a lying spirit had seduced his false prophets to entice him to go up and perish in the attempt. Enraged at this, Ahab ordered Micaiah to prison, there to be half-starved till he himself returned in peace. Micaiah replied that, if ever the Lord had spoken by him, he would never return in peace. To avoid the prophecy, Ahab treacherously persuaded Jehoshaphat to put on his royal clothes, while he went to the battlefield in disguise. Consequently, all the Syrian captains, as directed by their master, set upon Jehoshaphat, suspecting him to be Ahab. At last, God delivered Jehoshaphat; but Ahab, despite his precautions, met with his fate. A Syrian arrow shot at random, and entering by the joints of his harness, pierced him to the heart, and Ahab ordered his charioteer to carry him away from the battle for he was severely wounded. The battle continued, and Ahab, bleeding in his chariot, faced the enemy till night and then died. His army was immediately warned to disperse and shift for themselves. Ahab was carried to Samaria in his chariot and buried there. When his chariot and armour were washed in the pool, the dogs licked up his blood, and his son Ahaziah reigned in his place. (1 Kings 22)

2. Ahab, the son of Kolaiah, and also Zedekiah, the son of Maaseiah, were two false prophets who, about BC 598, seduced the Jewish captives at Babylon with the hope of a speedy deliverance, and stirred them up against Jeremiah. The Lord threatened them with a public and ignominious death before the ones they had deceived, and that their names would become a curse, men wishing that their foes might be made like Ahab and Zedekiah, whom Nebuchadnezzar King of Babylon roasted in the fire. (Jer. 29:21-22)

AHASUERUS

(1) The Mede. (Dan. 9:1) He was the son of the brave Cyaxares, who assisted Nebuchadnezzar in overturning the Assyrian Empire and in the ruination of the city of Nineveh. He succeeded his father to the Median throne and reigned 35 years, but did nothing of importance except repulsing an inroad into his territories by Evilmerodach, King of Babylon. He died in BC 560, leaving children, including Darius the Mede his successor, and Mandane the mother of Cyrus.

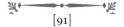

(2) Ahasuerus (or Cambyses), King of Persia. He succeeded his father Cyrus in BC 529, and reigned seven years and five months. He had scarcely mounted the throne, when the Samaritans requested him to put a stop to the rebuilding of the Temple in Jerusalem. He did not, and perhaps could not, formally revoke the decree of his father. The building work, however, was stopped during his reign.

He was noted for nothing but violence, foolishness, and cruelty. His fits of passion often hurried him into downright madness. In the second year of his reign, he entered Egypt, reduced the revolters, wasted their country, killed their sacred ox, and carried off thousands of their idols. Here, he continued five years, and ruined a greater part of his army in the dry deserts of Libya in a mad attempt to invade Ethiopia. Daily, he sacrificed some important Persians in his fury, his own brother and sister not excepted. Informed that Patizithes the Magus, whom he had left to govern Persia in his absence, had placed his own brother Smerdis on the throne, pretending he was Smerdis the brother of Cambyses, he hastened back to his kingdom. It is said that he wreaked his fury on the Jewish nation as he passed by their territories. Near Mount Carmel, he mounted his horse with such precipitate rage that his sword fell out of its scabbard and severely wounded his thigh. The wound appearing to be mortal, Cambyses called his principal nobles, and informed them that his brother Smerdis had been murdered on his orders, and begged them not to allow the Magian impostor to transfer the government to Medea. Soon after that, he expired.

It is sufficiently clear that Cambyses is the Ahasuerus, and Smerdis Magus the Artaxerxes of Scripture, who hindered the rebuilding of the Temple, None but these ruled in Persia between Cyrus (who gave the edict for building) and Darius (who renewed it). (Ezra 4:6-7)

(3) Ahasuerus, the husband of Esther. Who he was, is not universally agreed. Joseph Juste Scaliger, John Gill, and others, identify him with Xerxes, the fourth King of Persia after Cyrus. His wife Amestris they suppose to have been the very same as Esther; and that the report of her cruelty arose from her involvement in the execution of Haman and his sons, and the death of the 70,000 opposers who were slain by the Jews in their own defence. The authors of the *Universal History* (Humphrey Prideaux, and others) identify him with Artaxerxes Longimanus, the son of Xerxes, who greatly favoured the Jews, particularly in the seventh year of his reign, etc. (Ezra 7; Neh. 1:2; Esther 2:16);

and, indeed, Flavius Josephus called him by this name. The seventy interpreters, and the apocryphal additions to Esther, constantly call him Artaxerxes. According to Herodotus, Atossa, the beloved wife of Darius Hystaspes, was never divorced, but lived with him till his death. Both she and Aristone, his next beloved wife, were the daughters of Cyrus. These hints should effectively command our assent if we did not remember that Artaxerxes began his reign in BC 456. His seventh year, when Esther was taken to his bed, would have been BC 449, between which and BC 599, when Mordecai was carried captive to Babylon with King Jehoiachin (Esther 2:5), is an interval of 155 years. How incredible he should still be alive, or be capable of managing the affairs of a large Empire! How improbable that his cousin Esther could be so young as to attract the king's affection, above all the fine beauties of Persia! We are therefore obliged to agree with the sentiments of the great James Ussher, Augustine Calmet, etc., that this Ahasuerus was *Darius Hystaspes*. He, first of the Persian kings, reigned from India to Ethiopia below Egypt, and was notable for his imposition of taxes and his hoarding of money. (Esther 1:1, 10:1) We should even reckon him too late, could we possibly be certain of those before him. Atossa, the name of his beloved wife, is easily formed from Hadassah, the Hebrew designation of Esther. Herodotus might very easily be mistaken concerning her lineage, as she long concealed it herself; and the Persians could hardly fail to challenge her as one of their royal blood rather than count her among the contemptible Jews.

Ahasuerus, if Darius Hystaspes, was a Persian of royal blood, a descendant of Achtaemenes, and an attendant of Cyrus in his warlike expeditions. Soon after the death of Cambyses, he and six other Persian lords, killed Smerdis the usurper. They agreed to meet next morning on horseback at an appointed place before sunrise, and that he whose horse should neigh first would be acknowledged king by the rest. Hearing of this agreement, Darius' groom caused his master's horse to cover a mare in the palace by night. The conspirators no sooner met next morning, than Darius' stallion neighed for his mate. The rest immediately alighted and acknowledged Darius as their sovereign. This took place in BC 521. To strengthen his royal claim, he, according to Herodotus, married Atossa, the daughter of Cyrus, who had first been married to his brother Cambyses, and afterward to Smerdis the usurper, and then Aristone her sister.

In the second year of his reign, the Jews, encouraged by the prophets Haggai and Zechariah, resumed the rebuilding of their Temple. The Samaritan governors, who were the means by which the work had suffered more than nine years' interruption, demanded their authority. The Jews referred them to the edict of Cyrus. The governors informed Darius of this, and begged him to inquire if such an edict had been granted, and send them his orders. After a search, the edict was found at Achmeta among other ancient records. Darius confirmed it, and ordered his Samaritan governors to assist the Jews, if necessary, and provide them with everything they needed for sacrifice. He also dedicated to an ignominious death and destruction anyone who refused to obey. (Ezra 5)

When his Empire, containing 127 provinces extending from India to African Ethiopia, was fully established, and his new palace of Shushan finished, he put on a very splendid entertainment for his noblemen which lasted six months, at the end of which he provided a feast lasting seven days for all the people of Shushan. His Queen Vashti, at the same time, gave a feast for the ladies at court and other women in the same splendid fashion. On the seventh day, Ahasuerus, warmed with wine, and brighter than usual, ordered his principal eunuchs Mehuman, Biztha, Harbona, Bigthan, Abagtha, Zethar, and Carcas to bring Queen Vashti to the assembly of the men to display her charms. She refused to obey. Enraged at this, Ahasuerus, on the advice of Memucan, and his other six counsellors, gave Vashti an irrevocable divorce. A war with the revolting Babylonians, which issued in the ruin of most of them, and the reduction of their walls, employed his thoughts for more than two years. He now thoroughly repented of his rash divorce from Vashti. His servants advised him to seek out all the beautiful virgins of his vast Empire, and choose whomever he pleased to be her successor. The maidens were brought together at Shushan, and, after a year's preparation, and with fine spices, they in their turn were admitted to his bed. None of them pleased him as much as Esther the Jew. She was made queen in the seventh year of his reign. Whether his fruitless expedition into Scythia happened during the purification of the women, or even afterwards, we do not know.

No sooner was Esther made queen, than Bigthan and Teresh, two of his chamberlains, plotted to murder the king, disgusted perhaps with his treatment of Vashti. Mordecai informed against them, the

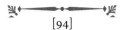

crime was proved, and the traitors were hanged. Just afterwards, Ahasuerus appointed Haman his chief minister of state, who, enraged that Mordecai denied him all the honours he desired, obtained an edict to have the whole Jewish people cut off in one day, and their estates confiscated to the king. To prevent the execution, Esther, advised by Mordecai, risked her life by approaching the royal presence uncalled for. Melted with affection, Ahasuerus held out his golden sceptre to her as a token that her life was not in danger, and asked her request. She invited him and Haman to a splendid feast. At the banquet, he again offered her whatever she asked, up to a half his kingdom. She only begged that they would come again tomorrow to a second entertainment. That very night, the king could not sleep. He therefore ordered the records of the Empire to be read to him. The reader happened on the passage of Mordecai's information against the treacherous chamberlains. Finding that Mordecai had been neglected, the King resolved how to reward him. Haman, who had just entered the palace to ask permission to hang Mordecai on the gallows that he had prepared, was called in and asked what was the right thing to do to for the man the King delighted to honour. Haman, expecting the honour to be conferred on him, advised that the man should be dressed in the royal robes, crowned with the royal diadem, and mounted on the King's horse, while one of the chief courtiers should lead his horse through the streets, proclaiming along the way, *Thus shall it be done to the man whom the king delighteth to honour.* (Esther 6:9) The king immediately ordered Haman to treat Mordecai the Jew in the way he had suggested.

That very day, at Esther's banquet for the third time, the king offered to grant her whatever she requested, up to the half of his kingdom. She then begged that he would intervene for the life of herself and her people. If they were given over to be murdered, this would only harm the King's reputation. Informed that Haman was the manager of this horrible plot, Ahasuerus flew into a rage and went into his garden. Returning in a little while, he found Haman at the feet of Queen Esther begging for his life. It seems that in his passion for his queen, he imagined that Haman was trying to rape her on the bed where she was sitting at the banquet. He therefore ordered his face to be covered as a sign of death. One of the pages present informed Ahasuerus that Haman had in his house a gallows prepared to hang Mordecai, the preserver of the King's life. Ahasuerus ordered Haman to be hanged on it, and gave Haman's whole power and honours to Mordecai. Now, though, according to Persian law, he could not revoke the decree against the Jews; so he allowed Mordecai and Esther to write to all the provinces that the Jews should stand up in their own defence, and, in such a way, discourage the heathen from attempting to massacre them. (Esther 1 and 9)

Soon after Mordecai became his chief minister, Ahasuerus levied a tax on his inland territories, and on that part of Asia Minor and the islands that belonged to him. About BC 509, he invaded India and obliged the inhabitants to pay him 365 talents of silver annually. He suffered a great deal of bickering among the Greeks in Asia Minor, and with the Athenians, and others in Europe, which resulted in his loss and disgrace. A little before his death, the Egyptians also revolted from his yoke. He died in BC 485 after a reign of 36 years, and was succeeded by his son Xerxes.

AHAZ

Son of Jotham, King of Judah. At about ten years of age, he was married to Abijah, the daughter of Zechariah, by whom he had a son, Hezekiah, about a year later. At twenty years of age, Ahaz became heir to the crown in BC 739, and reigned sixteen years. In imitation of the kings of Israel, he abandoned himself to the most abominable idolatries. One of his sons he sacrificed to the idol Moloch, and, perhaps caused the rest to pass through the fire as an offering. He did not merely connive at the people's offering sacrifices in high places, as many of his predecessors had done, but he himself ordered sacrifice and incense to be offered in high places, hills, groves, and under green trees. Towards the end of his father's reign, the Syrians under Rezin, and the Israelites under Pekah, began to harass Judah. Observing Ahaz to be a weak prince, they agreed to dethrone him and make a son of Tabeel their deputy king in his place. Their armies invaded his kingdom all at once. He and his people were seized amid utmost consternation. The prophet Isaiah assured him that none of their projects would prosper, and that, since the Messiah had not yet come, there was no reason to fear the departure of the sceptre from Judah. (Isa. 7-8)

This stroke was diverted; but Ahaz, proceeding from bad to worse, the two kings made a further attack on him. Rezin marched to Elath, a notable seaport on the Red Sea, and populated it with Syrians. Pekah attacked Ahaz's army and killed 120,000 of them in one day, together with Maaseiah his son, and carried off 200,000 prisoners, men, women, and children. Moved by the protest of Oded the prophet, the princes of Israel, Asariah, Berechiah, Jehizkiah, and Amasa, persuaded the troops to dismiss their prisoners; and they returned them with tokens of humanity. Meanwhile, the Edomites from the south ravaged the country, and carried off a number of people as slaves. The Philistines from the west invaded the low country adjacent to their territories, and to the south, and took Bethshemesh, Ajalon, Gederoth, Shocho, Timnah, and Gimzo, and populated them with a colony of their nation.

In his distress, Ahaz grew more and more wicked. He did not seek the Lord, but, stripping the Temple and city of all the gold he could find, he sent it as a present to Tiglathpileser, King of Assyria, to whom he surrendered himself as his vassal, and begged his assistance against his enemies. By cutting off the Syrians that were a barrier against the eastern powers, and by imposing on his kingdom a tribute, Tiglathpileser harmed rather than helped him. Ahaz went to Damascus to congratulate the Assyrian monarch on his victory over Syria, and there he noticed an idolatrous altar that mightily suited his taste. He sent off a plan of it to Urijah the High Priest to make one similar, and Urijah had it finished before Ahaz returned to Jerusalem. Ahaz ordered it to put in the place of the brazen altar erected by Solomon, and to offer all the sacrifices on it. To gratify the King of Assyria, who, it seems, returned his visit, he converted the royal entrance to the court of the Temple, taking away the *covert for the Sabbath* (2 Kings 16:18), where, it seems, the priests stood to read the Law, with the royal family in attendance. He downgraded the brazen lavers and sea by removing their pedestals, and rested them on the ground, or on a pavement of stone. Proceeding in his wickedness, he sacrificed to the idols of Syria, who, he imagined, were the authors of his calamities, in order to render them more favourable. He broke in pieces the sacred vessels, shut the gates of the Temple, and erected altars in every corner of Jerusalem and in every city of Judah for the burning of incense. He died in the sixteenth year of his reign. He was buried in Jerusalem, but was not given the honour of interment in the royal tombs. (2 Kings 15:37-38, and 16; 2 Chron. 28; Isa. 8)

AHAZIAH

(1) The son of Ahab. He was made his father's associate in power when he went off to war at Ramothgilead, and came to the throne about a year after his father's death. He imitated his parents in the worship of Baal and Ashtaroth, and in every other crime. He and Jehoshaphat fitted out a fleet at Eziongeber to trade with Ophir for gold, but a storm broke their ships to pieces almost as soon as they left the harbour. Ahaziah intended to fit out a second fleet, but Jehoshaphat refused to have anything to do with it. The Moabites, who, till now, had remained tributary to the ten tribes, revolted, and refused to pay their annual tribute of sheep. Ahaziah was made incapable of reducing them because, falling from one of his windows, or from the balcony of his house, he was seriously hurt and became very ill. He sent messengers to Baalzebub, the idol god of Ekron, to inquire if he would recover. Elijah met the messengers, and asked them if it was for lack of a God in Israel that their master had sent them to inquire of Baalzebub. Moreover, he assured them that, for this reason, the king would certainly die of his illness. They returned, and reported to the king what they had heard. By the description they gave, he quickly perceived it had been Elijah who had met them. He ordered a troop of his forces to fetch him immediately. The captain of the band addressed Elijah too roughly; and, as he made his request, fire from heaven consumed him and his troop. A second troop was sent on the same errand. Their captain, putting on the same haughty airs as his predecessor, he and his company of fifty were consumed in the same way. As both companies were idolaters, they deserved this treatment. A third troop was sent. The captain, warned by the fate of the others, addressed the prophet with reverence and awe, and begged him to spare the life of himself and his soldiers. It was done, and Elijah went along with them. Entering the chamber of Ahaziah, he boldly assured him that, because he had issued orders to consult Baalzebub the idol of Ekron, he would certainly die of his illness. Nor was it long before he expired, and his brother Jehoram reigned in his place. (1 Kings 22:49; 2 Chron. 20:36, 37; 2 Kings 1)

(2) AHAZIAH. See Azariah, or Jehoahaz

He was the grandson of Jehoshaphat, and son of Jehoram and Athaliah the daughter of Ahab. When he was 22 years old, and in the 42nd year of the royal house of his mother's family, he succeeded his father to

the throne of Judah. On the advice of his mother Athaliah, he walked after the pattern of Ahab his grandfather, worshipping the Baals and Ashtaroth, and commanding his subjects to follow his example. He had reigned just one year when he went to Jezreel to visit his uncle Jehoram, King of Israel, who had returned there from Ramothgilead to be healed of his wounds. At that very time, Jehu, the destroyer of the house of Ahab, came out to cut down Jehoram. Knowing nothing of his intentions, Jehoram and Ahaziah went out to meet him. Jehoram was immediately struck dead with an arrow, and Ahaziah fled to Samaria to hide himself. During a search, he was found by a party that Jehu had despatched after him. It seems that they brought him back part of the way to Jezreel, but at Gur, near Ibleam a city of the Manassites, under Jehu's orders, they inflicted deadly wounds on him. His own servants took him away with them in his chariot till they came to Megiddo where he died, and his corpse was taken from there and carried away to be interred in the royal sepulchres of Jerusalem. About the same time, 42 of his brothers (or rather nephews, for his brothers had all been slain by the Arabians) went to visit Jehoram. With these, Jehu was involved in the total ruin of the house of Ahab. Whatever children or friends remained to Ahaziah were all (except Joash) murdered by his mother about the same time.

Ahaziah, his son Joash, and his grandson Amaziah, are excluded from Matthew's genealogy of Christ. Such was the ruin and shame that resulted from Jehoshaphat marrying his son into the wicked family of Ahab and Jezebel. Let parents and others take note! (2 Kings 8:24-29, 9:16, 21, 23, 27-29, 10:12-14, 11:1-2; 2 Chron. 22)

AHIJAH

A prophet of the Lord who lived at Shiloh. Perhaps he was the one who encouraged Solomon while building the Temple, and who threatened him with the division of his kingdom after his shameful fall. (1 Kings 6:11, 11:6) Meeting with Jeroboam, the son of Nebat, in a field, he tore his garment into twelve pieces, and gave him ten of them as a token that he would be king over ten tribes of Israel. About twenty years later, Jeroboam's only pious son fell sick. Fearing to visit the prophet himself, Jeroboam sent his wife in disguise to consult Ahijah whether he would recover. She, according to the custom of the times, carried to the prophet a present of ten loaves, some biscuits,

and a jar of honey. Though blind in his old age, Ahijah, instructed by God, told the queen at her entrance that he knew who she was. He assured her that her distressed son would die on her return, and the rest of her family would meet a miserable and ignominious end. (1 Kings 11 and 14) Ahijah wrote part of the history of Solomon's reign. (2 Chron. 9:29)

AHIKAM

The son of Shaphan and father of Gedaliah. He was one of the princes of Judah sent by Josiah to consult Huldah concerning the threatening of God against the nation for their wickedness. (2 Kings 22:12, 14) He exerted himself greatly to protect Jeremiah's life. (Jer. 26:24)

AHIMAAZ

The son and successor of Zadok the High Priest. He and Jonathan, the son of Abiathar, performed a very important service for David during the progress of Absalom's rebellion. Their parents and Hushai, all fast friends of David, continued living in Jerusalem unsuspected by Absalom. The two young men waited near Enrogel, outside the city, to send intelligence to the King. Informed from Hushai by means of a maid what had passed in Absalom's privy council, they sent the information off to David. Informed of this by a young man, who had seen them, Absalom detached a party to pursue and apprehend them. To avoid these pursuers, Ahimaaz and Jonathan retired to a friend's house in Bathurim. The man had a deep well in his court; so down they went while the mistress spread a cover over the well's mouth, and laid ground corn on it. Her work was just complete when the pursuers came up in hot pursuit. The mistress affirmed that they had gone. The pursuers, not finding them, returned to Jerusalem. The young priests then finished their journey to King David, and informed him of the counsel of the rebels; and that Hushai advised him to pass over the Jordan with the utmost speed to put himself beyond their reach.

Not long after this, Absalom's troops were entirely routed. Ahimaaz strongly begged Joab to allow him to run with the news to David. Coming by the way of the plain, he caught up with Cushi, whom Joab had sent off before him. When the sentinel of Mahanaim warned David of the approach of a single runner, the king immediately concluded that he was bringing news, for if the army had been broken, the people

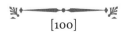

would have come fleeing in crowds. When Cushi came in sight, and Ahimaaz was recognised, David suggested that, as he was a good man, he hoped he was bringing good news. Ahimaaz came up and informed the King that all was well, and, falling down at his feet, blessed the Lord who had cut off his enemies. David asked if Absalom was safe. Ahimaaz prudently, if not truthfully, replied that just before he and Cushi were sent off he saw a great tumult, but he did not know what it meant. He stood by till Cushi came up and plainly informed the king of Absalom's death. Some years later, Ahimaaz succeeded his father in the high priesthood, and, in his turn, was succeeded by his son Azariah. (2 Sam. 15:27, 36, 17:17-22, 18:19-32; 1 Chron. 6:8, 9, 53)

AHIMELECH

(1) Son of Ahitub, great grandson of Eli, and brother of Abiah, whom he succeeded in the office of High Priest. During the government of Saul, he, together with a number of other priests, resided at Nob beside the Tabernacle. To him, David repaired in his flight from Saul's court, saying that Saul had sent him and his attendants on a most pressing errand which required the utmost despatch. He then begged that he would grant them some food. Ahimelech assured him that he had nothing but the showbread, which was allowed only to the priests. But, said he, he believed that David and his servants might eat if, for any reasonable time, they had abstained from women. David assured him that they had not had any relations for at least three days, so Ahimelech gave them some loaves. David further asked him for a sword or spear. Ahimelech gave him the sword of Goliath that had been hung up in the Tabernacle as a trophy.

Doeg the Edomite, the chief of Saul's herdsmen, happened to be at the Tabernacle for some purification, and witnessed the scene. When Saul was afterwards complaining to his servants that none of them were affected by his misfortunes, nor disposed to inform him of David's treasonable plots, Doeg related what he had seen and heard at Nob. Ahimelech and 84 other priests were immediately ordered to appear before Saul. He rudely questioned them why they had conspired with David against him, had given him provisions and arms, and had inquired of the Lord in his favour. Ahimelech humbly replied that he always took David, the king's son-in-law, to be one of his best friends; that he had all along prayed for him, and knew nothing of any division between them. Regardless of this sufficient vindication, Saul sentenced Ahimelech and all his relatives to death. He immediately ordered his guards to butcher the 85 priests that were present, but they declined this horrible and murderous task. However, Doeg, in reponse to the call, slew them to a man. A party was immediately sent, probably under the direction of Doeg, to murder every man, woman, and child, and the very cattle of Nob, the city of the priests. These devilish orders were so punctually executed that none but Abiathar, Ahimelech's son, escaped and fled to David. This happened about BC 1060, and was part of the terrible vengeance that pursued the family of Eli for indulging his sons in their profane behaviour. (1 Sam. 21-22)

(2) Ahimelech (or Abimelech), the son of Abiathar. He and Zadok, whom Saul appointed as High Priest after the murder of the former Ahimelech, were second priests about the latter end of the reign of King David. Before him, and many other notable people, Shemaiah the scribe wrote down the orders and divisions of the priests, singers, and Levites; and they cast lots for their turn to serve in the Temple of God. (1 Chron. 24:3, 6, 31, 18:16; 2 Sam. 8:17)

AHITHOPHEL

A native of Giloh, in the tribe of Judah. He was so renowned a statesman and counsellor that his advice was usually received as an oracle of God. Disgusted with David for his defilement of Bathsheba, who is said to have been his granddaughter, or rather, for some other reason unknown to us, he, to the no small displeasure of David, early revolted and joined Absalom's party. David begged God in prayer to confound his counsels, and advised Hushai to join Absalom, but only outwardly, and to oppose Ahithophel's advice. Ahithophel first advised Absalom to rape ten of his father's concubines that had been left to look after the house. This, he was sure, would prove that the breach between him and his father was irreconcilable, and so attach his party more firmly to Absolom's interest. In compliance with this horrible and shameful advice, Absalom, with a tent spread over the top of the house, raped the women in the sight of his followers. Next, Ahithophel advised that 12,000 chosen forces should be given him that very night, and he would pursue David and slay him before he recovered from his fright. Then all David's party would be scattered, and never more amount to anything.

Absalom and his princes were greatly taken with this proposal, and, indeed, nothing could more effectively further their ends.

When Hushai was asked, he replied that, however sensible and wise Ahithophel's proposal might be in itself, it did not fit the present occasion. To persuade them of this, he displayed in the most striking way what mighty heroes David and his followers were; that he was too wily to lodge all night with his friends, but would hide himself in some pit; that he and his party, being so valiant, and furthermore enraged and desperate, it was hard to say what slaughter they might have made of Ahithophel's 12,000 men in the night, and what terror might have seized Ahithophel himself. So a small loss at first, magnified by a report, might discourage the whole party and ruin it before it was firmly established. Hushai, therefore, proposed that every Hebrew able to bear arms, should be assembled, and that Absalom himself should take the honour of commanding this great army, and fall on his father as the dew falls on the ground. He would quite overwhelm him with numbers, and even draw the city which he might chase with ropes into the adjacent river. This humorous proposal, designed for their ruin, so gratified the pride of Absalom and his nobles that they preferred it to that of Ahithophel. Ahithophel, partly from a proud indignation that his advice was not followed, and perhaps partly from foresight that Hushai's measures effectively tended to reinstate David, saddled his ass, rode home to Giloh, set in order the affairs of his family, and then hanged himself. (2 Sam. 15:12, 31, 16:20-21, 23, and ch. 17)

AHITUB

The son of Phinehas, and brother of Ichabod. When his father was slain in that unhappy engagement in which the ark of God was taken by the Philistines, he succeeded Eli his grandfather in the high priesthood, executed his office under Samuel, and was succeeded by his two sons: first Ahiah and then Ahimelech. (1 Sam. 14:3) Beside this, there were two Abitubs, both fathers of Zadoks, and descended from Eleazar. But it does not appear that the first of them could execute the office of High Priest. (1 Chron. 6:8, 11)

AHOLAH and AHOLIBAH

Two made-up names by which the prophet Ezekiel represented the kingdoms of Israel and Judah. The first means a *tent*, signifying Samaria

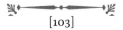

and the ten tribes; the second means *my tent is in her*, signifying Jerusalem and her subjects. Both were presented as of Egyptian extraction because of the Hebrews living in Egypt, and prostituting themselves to the Egyptians and Assyrians, imitating their idolatries, and relying on their help. For this reason, the Lord threatened to make these very people their oppressors, and the means of their captivity and cruel slavery. (Ezek. 23:4-5, 36, 44)

AHOLIBAMAH, *my tent,* or, *famous mansion*
Originally called Judith, the daughter of Beeri (Anah) (Gen. 26:34). She became the wife of Esau. (Gen. 36:2, 5, 14, 18)

AIJELETH. *A hind.*
This title was applied to Christ. (Song 2:9, 17, 8:14) Psalm 22 is entitled *Aijeleth Shahar*, which is translated in the KJV margin as the *hind of the morning*. Some suppose this to refer to some musical instrument, others that this was one of the Psalms with which the morning service commenced. But a more important meaning may be found in the 20th verse of this Psalm. The hind was not only an emblem of *agility*, but *strength and prowess*. The *morning* which this Psalm celebrates is the *morning* of the resurrection. The *hind of the morning* is perhaps one of the most striking characteristics of the resurrection of the dead that language can give.

ALEXANDER, and **RUFUS**
(1) Alexander and Rufus were two notable Christians, the sons of Simon the Cyrenian who assisted our Saviour in carrying his cross. (Mark 15:21; possibly Rom. 16:13)

(2) Alexander Lysimachus, the brother of the famous Jewish philosopher Philo. He was Alabarch (Magistrate) of Alexandria, and was reckoned to be the richest Jew of his time, for he made a great number of valuable presents to the Temple. He was thrown into prison by Caligula probably for refusing to worship that mad monarch, and continued there till the Emperor Claudius set him free. He is thought to have been the Alexander who was in company with the chief priests and elders when they imprisoned the Apostles for healing the impotent man. (Acts 4:6)

(3) Alexander the coppersmith. For a time, he accepted the Christian faith; but when he started to blaspheme, Paul delivered him over to Satan. This enraged him even more, and he did the Apostle all the harm that lay within his power. (1 Tim. 1:20; 2 Tim. 4:14-15)

(4) It is uncertain whether he was the one who was in some danger of his life by attempting to quell the mob that Demetrius the silversmith aroused at Ephesus: nor is it so certain that Alexander was a Christian. (Acts 19:33)

ALPHEUS

(1) The father of the Apostles James and Jude. Some think that Mary his wife was the sister of the holy Virgin; and hence his sons are called the brothers of our Lord. (For example, *James* in Gal. 1:19; Mark 6:3) He may be reckoned to be the same as Cleophas. (Matt. 10:3; John 19:25)

(2) The father of Matthew (Levi) the Evangelist. (Mark 2:14)

AMALEK

Eliphaz, the son of Esau, had a son by this name by his concubine Timna, a son that succeeded Gatam in the government of the Edomites. (Gen. 36:16; 1 Chron. 1:36) He is supposed by many to be the father of the Amalekites, a powerful nation that lived in Arabia the Rocky, between Havilah and Shur, which is much the same as between the Dead and Red Seas, and is supposed to have been separated from the other Edomites on account of his spurious birth, and to have hated the Israelites because of Jacob depriving their ancestor of his birthright and blessing. But consider that Moses represented the Amalekites as living in the days of Chedorlaomer, perhaps 200 years before this Amalek was born, that Balaam represented them as the *first or beginning of the nations* (Gen. 14:7; Num. 24:20), that the immediate children of Amalek were probably alive when the Hebrews came out of Egypt, and so were very unlikely to be numerous enough to attack that huge multitude. Furthermore, the Amalekites' attack on the Israelites is never presented as done to brothers, nor do the Edomites ever seem to have assisted the Amalekites; so we are persuaded that they were not the descendants of Esau, but a far more ancient tribe, probably descended from Ham, as Arabic writers suggest.

About BC 1913, Chedorlaomer terribly ravaged the country of the Amalekites. (Gen. 14:7) It was then, I suppose, that vast numbers of

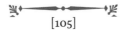

them left, and poured into Egypt, becoming the shepherds whom Manetho mentions as terrible ravagers and oppressors of Egypt. About 420 years after that, they, perhaps in league with the Egyptians, or rather greedy for booty, attacked the Hebrews at Rephidim near the northeastern point of the Red Sea, and killed those who were weary and unguarded among them. But, by means of Moses' prayer and Joshua's bravery, they were repulsed. This ungenerous attack provoked God to swear that he would gradually waste the Amalekites till they were utterly ruined; and he charged the Hebrews to revenge themselves on them. (Exod. 17; Deut. 9:14, 25:19) About two years later, they assisted the Canaanites in cutting off a number of the rebellious Hebrews at Hormah. (Num. 14:29-30) Long after that, they assisted Eglon, King of Moab, and then the Midianites, in oppressing and murdering the Israelites. (Judg. 3:13, 6:6)

Their continual wickedness rendered them ripe for destruction. About BC 1074, God charged Saul to invade their country with the whole power of Israel, and destroy them utterly with all their possessions. He ravaged their territories, and killed vast numbers of them; but, contrary to the commandment of the Lord, he spared Agag their King, and the best of their cattle and moveables. (1 Sam. 15) Never after this did the Amalekites come to anything. While David was in exile at Ziklag, he and his warriors invaded their country and slew as many as he could, seeking revenge for when they, in David's absence, had burnt Ziklag, and carried off his and his servants' wives and children and wealth. He pursued them, slew part of them, dispersed the rest, and recovered the booty to considerable advantage. (1 Sam. 27, 30) About 160 years later, they joined in the grand alliance against Jehoshaphat; but it did them great harm. (Ps. 83:7) In the days of Hezekiah, 500 Simeonites routed the remnant of them, and lived in their territory. (1 Chron. 4:48) About BC 506, Haman, an Amalekite, plotted the genocide of the Jews. This plot resulted in the ruin of himself and his friends. Since which, the name *Amalekites* does not appear in history, but perished forever. (Exod. 17:14, 16; Num. 24:20-22; Esther 3 and 9)

Extra note

The Amalekites were a nation much spoken of in the earlier part of Scripture, and particularly as enemies of the Church of God. When God said, *I will put enmity between the seed of the woman and the*

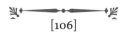

seed of the serpent, he intimated what has been clearly seen ever since. How much earlier we read of the sons of God and the daughters of men! Egypt was the first persecutor of Israel; then came Amalek, the Philistines, the Syrians, the Chaldeans, the Babylonians, etc., each, in their turn, proving to be enemies of the Church of Christ. And, in the latter days, the antichristian kingdom, that *mystery of iniquity* (2 Thess. 2:7), has vented her utmost rage on the despised followers of the Lamb.

Thomas Paine, author of *The Age of Reason*, attacked revelation on account of the way in which the destruction of Amalek, and the other nations of Canaan, were recorded. Ignorant of the Scriptures, he attempted to blaspheme them. Immediately on Israel leaving Egypt, Amalek opposed them and God was aware that he would utterly expunge the memory of Amalek from under heaven. (Exod. 17:14, 16) By expelling these nations when their iniquity was full, God punished the one and made room for the other. Behold the goodness and severity of God! Little do the propagators of infidelity in these days consider the awful side they are taking in blinding and deceiving the nations that the measure of their iniquity might be complete! The character and moral justice of God does not require infidelity to support it. His goodness and forbearance is now evident without question. He *commandeth all men everywhere to repent.* (Acts 17:30) The destruction of Amalek is just a faint picture of the awful vengeance that will be poured out on the nations which do not recognise God when he arises to shake terribly the earth.

AMASA

The son, perhaps the bastard, of Jether (or Ithra), and Abigail the sister of David. He was general of the rebels under Absalom; but David, displeased with Joab for killing Absalom, easily pardoned Amasa, and made him general of his army in Joab's place. When Sheba the son of Bichri induced the Israelites to a new revolt, Amasa was ordered to assemble the men of Judah and pursue the rebels with all expedition. Amasa took more time than was assigned him. Abishai was therefore despatched with the household troops to pursue the rebels before the rest came up. Joab went along with his brother as a volunteer. They had just marched north to the great stone of Gibeon, when Amasa came up to them with his army. At the meeting, Joab, with seeming

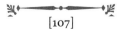

kindness, inquired about his cousin's health, and took him by the beard to kiss him. Meanwhile, he treacherously stabbed him under the fifth rib, shed out his bowels, and covered his body with a cloth because the army was stopping, as they passed, to look at his body. (2 Sam. 17:25, ch. 18, 19:13, ch. 20)

AMASAI

The son of Elkanah. It was probably he who was chief of the captains of Judah and Benjamin under Saul, who came to David in his exile, along with a number of his friends. Informed of their approach, David went to meet them, assuring them that if they came in peace his heart would be knit to them, and wishing God's rebuke on them if they intended to betray him into the hand of Saul. Prompted by God, Amasai replied in their name, "*Thine are we, David, and on thy side, thou son of Jesse; peace be unto thee, and to thine helpers.*" David immediately received them, and gave them the command of some of his troops. (1 Chron. 12:16-19)

AMAZIAH

(1) The eighth king of Judah, the son and successor of Joash. In his 25th year, he began his reign in BC 839, and reigned 29 years. At the beginning of his reign, he behaved well, but not with an upright heart. He quickly executed just punishment on the murderers of his father; but, according to the Law of Moses, and contrary to the then bloody custom of many countries, he did not harm their innocent children. Intending to reduce the Edomites, who, about 54 years before, had revolted from King Jehoram, he levied 300,000 of his own subjects, and, with a hundred talents of silver (£34,218) hired 100,000 men of Israel. A prophet remonstrated with him that the idolatrous Israelites would bring a curse on his undertaking unless he dismissed them. Bearing a grudge for the loss of his 100 talents, he sent them home. He then proceeded against the Edomites, tackling their army in the Valley of Salt, and killing ten thousand on the spot. Next, he made himself master of Selah, their metropolis. He barbarously threw ten thousand of his prisoners from the top of the rock on which their city was built, dashing them to pieces. After that, he changed the name of the place to Joktheel, which, it seems, was its ancient name before the Edomites took it from Judah. He also carried off their idols, and quickly became

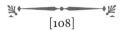

a fond worshipper of them. A prophet rebuked him for worshipping such idols, as he had seen that they did not deliver their devotees out of his hand. He threatened to punish the prophet, but he desisted. The prophet bore all this, but told him that for his obstinacy in his idolatry the Lord was determined to destroy him.

Taking it as a high affront, and perhaps disappointed at the expected booty from Edom, the Israelitish troops he had dismissed on their return home fell upon the cities of Judah and burnt a great many of them north of Bethlehem. They slew 3000 of the inhabitants, and carried off much spoil. Proud of his victory over Edom, Amaziah demanded satisfaction for the injury done. That not being granted, he haughtily challenged Joash (or Jehoash) King of Israel, to war. Joash gave an answer in the form of a parable of a wild beast treading down a proud thistle that demanded the daughter of a strong and stately cedar in marriage. (2 Kings 14:9; 2 Chron. 25:18) He advised him to forswear going to war if he was to consider the welfare of himself or his subjects. Despising this outspoken but sensible answer, Amaziah immediately marched his troops to Bethshemesh. There, Joash gave him battle, defeated his forces, and took him prisoner. He carried him off to Jerusalem, broke down the wall of the city to the extent of 240 yards, and carried off all the wealth of the Temple and palace, and a number of hostages to secure the peace.

After this, Amaziah reigned fifteen years, but he never returned to the Lord. His own servants formed a conspiracy against him. Informed of this, he fled to Lachish; but they despatched a party after him and slew him. His corpse was brought back and interred in the royal tombs, while Azariah (or Uzziah) his son reigned in his place. (2 Kings 14; 2 Chron. 25)

(2) The idolatrous high priest of the golden calf at Bethel. When Amos the prophet predicted the ruin of the high places of Israel, and the utter rooting out of the family of Jeroboam, the son of Joash, Amaziah accused the prophet before the King as a traitor who was discouraging and troubling the people. He advised the prophet to go home to his own country if he was concerned about his safety, and prophesy no more at Bethel where King Jeroboam had his chapel and court. The prophet boldly assured him that his persecution of him would be resented by God; that his own wife, for wickedness or want, would become a common prostitute, his sons and daughters would be

murdered, his inheritance would go into the possession of his enemies, and he himself would die in exile, for Israel would certainly go into captivity. (Amos 7:10, 12, 14)

AMMI, *my people.*
The imposing of this name on the ten tribes after their rejection points to the fact that, in the latter days, or in the millennium, God will redeem them from their misery and bondage, and bring them into a special covenantal relationship with himself. (Only found in Hosea 2:1)

AMMON
The son that Lot, sadly, had by his younger daughter. (Gen. 19:30-38) He became the ancestor of the Ammonites, who lived in the southeast of Gilead, and north of the country of Moab. (Gen. 19:38) The Ammonites destroyed an ancient race of giants called Zamzummims, and dwelt in their place, with their capital at Rabbah. They were notable idolaters, their chief idol being Moloch, which might be the same as Baal, Milcom, Adrammelech, Anammelech, and Chemosh. They were dispossessed of part of their territories by Sihon, King of the Amorites; but God not allowing the Hebrews to seize any part, they continued to live there.

The Ammonites were, however, barred forever from ruling over Israel because they hired Balaam to curse the people. (Deut. 2:19, 23:4) They joined Eglon, King of Moab, in opposing the Israelites, and shared in the success of that war. (Judg. 3). About 150 years later, they invaded the land of Israel, and, for 18 years, greatly oppressed them, mainly those on the east of Jordan. At last, Jephthah, being chosen as general by the Gileadites, sent a strong message to the King of the children of Ammon about his conduct. That monarch replied that he insisted the Israelites restored what they had seized as they came out of Egypt. Jephthah replied that the Hebrews took no territory from the Ammonites on that occasion; and that if they had taken any, the Ammonites had had sufficient time (about 300 years) to settle these claims! The Ammonitish King was bent on war, so Jephthah fell on him near Aroer, routed his army, and took twenty cities away from him. (Judg. 10-11) About BC 995, Nahash, the King of the Ammonites, revived the old claim to the land of Gilead. He ravaged a great part of the country, and the inhabitants of Jabeshgilead defended themselves against him. But when he laid siege to their city, they offered to acknowledge his authority. He refused to

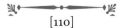

grant them any terms unless they consented to have their right eyes gouged out as a reproach to their nation. However, he allowed them seven days to consider his terms. On the eighth day, when he expected them to come to him, Saul, with a powerful army, attacked him in his camp and entirely routed his army, so that hardly two soldiers could be seen together. (1 Sam. 11) This Nahash, or rather his son, had shown some favours to David when he was in exile from Saul. David, therefore, on the occasion of Nahash's death, sent messengers with his compliments of condolence to his son Hanun. At the instigation of his servants, Hanun took them for spies, and rudely assaulted them. Resenting this abuse, David attacked the Ammonites in war. It turned out that he defeated them and their Syrian allies, conquered the whole country, and treated their chief men severely. They continued tributaries to David and Solomon, and probably the Kings of Israel, till the death of Ahab. (2 Sam. 10-12; 1 Chron. 19-20) They were part of the grand alliance against Jehoshaphat, but God caused them to slaughter one another. (2 Chron. 20:1, 10, 22-23)

While the Syrians were terribly oppressing the ten northern tribes, the Ammonites made the most inhuman ravages on Gilead, ripping up women with child. (Amos 1:13, 15) Uzziah, King of Judah, made them pay tribute. Under his son Jotham, they rebelled, but were again obliged to submit, and for three years paid a tribute of a hundred talents, and about 40,000 pods of wheat and barley. (2 Chron. 26-27) When Tiglath-pileser carried most of the Reubenites and Gadites into the east of Assyria, the Ammonites seized that part of the country; but probably, along with their neighbours the Moabites, they felt the full fury of the Assyrians. Long after, Baalis, their last king, entered into a treaty with Zedekiah against the Chaldeans; but when Jerusalem was destroyed, they rejoiced over the ruination of the unhappy Jews. For this and earlier injuries to that nation, the prophets threatened them with judgement and destruction. About five years after the destruction of Jerusalem, Nebuchadnezzar's troops ravaged their whole country, burnt Rabbah their capital, and carried the remnant into captivity, leaving the land desolate. It seems Cyrus allowed them to return and re-inhabit their land. In Nehemiah's time, Tobiah became their chief. During the contests between the Greek kings of Egypt and Syria, they became subject sometimes to the one, and sometimes to the other. Antiochus the Great took Rabbah their capital, demolished its walls, and put a garrison into it. During the persecution of Antiochus Epiphanes, the Ammonites cruelly treated the Jews in their neighbourhood. To avenge this, Judas Maccabeus attacked them, routed their forces, burnt their cities, and took their wives and children captive. In the second century of the Christian era, Justin Martyr, maybe by mistake, called the Ammonites a numerous nation. It is certain that, soon after, their poor remains so blended with the Arabs that their remembrance ceased from among men. (Amos 1:11-14; Jer. 11:25-26, 25:21, 27, 49:1-6; Ezek. 21:28-32, 25:1-7; Zeph. 2:8-11)

AMNON

The oldest son of David by Ahinoam, his second wife. Consumed by a violent passion for Tamar (his half-sister) he grew thin on account of her. On the advice of Jonadab his cousin, a crafty fellow, he pretended he was sick, and begged his father to allow Tamar to come and make him cakes, and give him something to eat. His request was granted. Tamar prepared the cakes, and brought them to him, but he refused to eat them until everyone except Tamar had left the room. He then made his lustful thoughts plain. Tamar protested against it as foolish and wicked; and either ignorant of the law forbidding the marriage of brothers and sisters, or stupified with fear and perplexity, she proposed that he should ask her father for her in marriage. Deaf to all her entreaties, he raped her. His violent passion at last satisfied, it immediately changed into a violent hatred. He ordered her to be gone from his presence, but she appeared reluctant to expose herself to public view. Amid tokens of grief and confusion, Amnon ordered his servant to throw her out by force, and bolt the door after her.

When David heard of this affair, he was extremely upset; but a sinful tolerance of his children made him quite reluctant to take strong measures against his oldest son. Absalom, the full brother of Tamar, saw her in tears as she was driven out by Amnon, and he advised her to keep quiet about the rape. He himself appeared as kind to Amnon as ever, but was planning revenge. After two years, he got his chance. Preparing a feast at sheep-shearing time, Absalom invited his father and brothers. David excused himself, but allowed his sons to be present. Beforehand, Absalom ordered his servants to murder Amnon when they saw him merry with wine. These orders were punctually executed, and Amnon died about BC 1030. (2 Sam. 13)

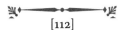

AMON

(1) A governor of Samaria, whom Ahab ordered to imprison the prophet Micaiah till he got back safely from the war at Ramothgilead. (1 Kings 22:26)

(2) The son of Manasseh by Meshullemeth, the daughter of Haruz. He was the 14th king of Judah. He began his reign at the age of 22, and ruled two years. He was a very monster of wickedness; nor did he, like his father Manasseh, repent, but went from bad to worse. His own servants murdered him in his house, and, it seems, were, in their turn, murdered by the mob. Amon was buried in the garden of Uzza, and Josiah his son succeeded him. (2 Kings 21:18-25; 2 Chron. 33:20-25)

(3) Ami (Amon), a notable chief of the returning captives. (Ezra 2:57; Neh. 7:59)

AMOS

The 4th of the minor prophets. He was originally a herdsman of Tekoah, a city of Judah, and a lowly gatherer of sycamore fruit (figs). God sent him to prophesy to the ten northern tribes during their great prosperity under Jeroboam II, son of Joash, two years before the earthquake, and therefore in the latter part of Jeroboam's reign. He began with a series of predictions of ruin to the Syrians, Philistines, Tyrians, Edomites, Ammonites, and Moabites. (Chapters 1-2) He next denounced the idolatry, oppression, worldly confidence, immorality, selfishness, and obstinacy of Israel and Judah, and threatened them with distress, ravage, captivity, and desolation on that account, but particularly because the family of Jeroboam, however prosperous, would quickly be wiped out by the sword. By representing him as a traitor to the government, and a troubler of the people, and by threatening him if he remained at Bethel, Amaziah, that idolatrous priest, thought to intimidate him and close his mouth. Amos boldly declared to the priest that sudden ruin would seize the family of Jeroboam, and the kingdom of the ten tribes, and added one further prediction of woe on Amaziah's own family. (Amos 2-7) He proceeded to threaten them with unavoidable ruin and captivity for their oppression, their fraud, and their breaking of the Sabbath, etc. He concluded his message and work with a prophecy of the Jewish return from Babylon, of the gathering of the Gentiles to Christ, of the conversion of Israel and Judah, and the return to their land at the beginning of the glorious millennium. (Chapters 8-9)

Amos lived to see many of his predictions fulfilled in the civil wars, and the beginning of the captivity of the ten tribes. It has been thought that the style of this prophet was of a rough and common kind, and that he was coarse in speech. But hardly any language can be more lofty than his description of God: *Lo, he that formeth the mountains, and createth the wind, and declareth unto man what is his thought, that maketh the morning darkness, and treadeth on the high places of the earth, the Lord the God of hosts is his name.* (Amos 4:13) How pitiful are the raptures of Homer compared with those of this husbandman!

AMRAM

The son of Kohath, the second son of Levi. He married Jochebed his cousin, or possibly his aunt, the daughter of Levi, and had three children by her: Aaron, Moses, and Miriam. He died in Egypt, aged 137 years old. (Exod. 6:18, 20; Num 3:19, 26:58-59)

ANAK

The son of Arbah, and father (or chief) of the gigantic Anakim. His sons were Sheshai, Ahiman, and Talmai. These Anakim (or children of Anak) were considerably numerous, living in Hebron, Debir, Ahab, and other places. (Josh. 21:11) Their fierce looks and extraordinary height quite terrified those unbelieving spies that Moses sent out to view the Promised Land. (Num. 13:22, 28, 33) About 45 years later, Caleb begged to have their residence allotted to him in Canaan that he might have the honour of rooting them out. Obtaining his desire, and assisted by his brothers of the tribe of Judah, he cut them off from Hebron, and Othniel, his nephew and son-in-law, expelled them from Debir. (Josh. 15:14; Judg. 1:20) Samuel Bochart thinks that the remains of the Bene-Anak (or children of Anak) retired north towards the territories of Tyre and Zidon, and gave them the name of Phoenicia.

ANANIAS and SAPPHIRA

Found among the first professors of Christianity at Jerusalem. This married couple sold their estate, and pretended to give the whole price into the common treasury of the believers, but actually kept back part of it for their own use. Though Ananias knew the Apostles were qualified by the Holy Spirit with the gift of discerning secrets, he affirmed to Peter that he had brought the whole price. Peter rebuked him sharply

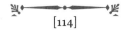

for his lying, in that, while he might lawfully have kept the whole, he had pretended to devote all to the service of Christ, and kept back part for himself. As he was speaking, Ananias was struck dead by the immediate vengeance of heaven, and was carried to his grave. About three hours later, Sapphira came in, and, being questioned whether their land was sold for as much as her husband had said, she affirmed that it was so. Peter rebuked her for agreeing with her husband to tempt the Lord, and put him to the test as to whether he could discern and punish their fraud. He told her that those who had just interred her husband would immediately carry her to her grave. While he was speaking, she was struck dead in his presence. This happened in AD 33 or 34, a little after Christ's Ascension, and made a deep impression on both friends and foes of the Christian faith. (Acts 5:1-11)

ANANIAS

(1) A disciple of Jesus Christ, perhaps one of the Seventy. (Mentioned in Luke 10:1, 17) He preached the gospel at Damascus, and, being directed in a vision to enquire at the house of Judas for Saul of Tarsus, who had just arrived, Ananias begged to be excused as he was informed that Saul was an outrageous persecutor, and had come with orders from Jerusalem to imprison all the Christians he could find in that city. The Lord assured him that he was in no danger; for, whatever Saul had been, he was divinely chosen to be a preacher of Christ to the Gentiles, and an eminent sufferer for his sake. Encouraged by these words, Ananias went to the house in Straight Street, found Saul blind, put his hands on him, and in Jesus' name bid him receive his sight and be filled with the Holy Spirit. Immediately, scales fell from his eyes and he recovered his sight. He was baptised, and received the Holy Spirit. (Acts 9:1-18)

(2) The son of Nebedeus, born about AD 48. He succeeded Joseph, the son of Camith, in the Jewish high priesthood. Quadratus, the Roman governor of Syria, having put down some disturbances caused by the Jews and Samaritans in Judea, sent Ananias to Rome to give an account of his behaviour during these commotions. The High Priest, having cleared himself to the satisfaction of Claudius the Emperor, was sent back to his country. Some years later, Paul was arrested and brought before this High Priest. He began in a most discreet manner to speak in his own defence, affirming that he had lived in all good

conscience before God to that day. Ananias, in a fury, ordered some of the bystanders to strike him across the mouth. Not knowing that he was the high priest, or not acknowledging him as such, Paul replied, *"God shall smite thee thou whited wall* (that is, thou hypocritical person); *for sittest thou to judge me according to the law, and yet commandest me to be smitten contrary to the law?"* (Acts 23:1-5) Ananias, and others also, encouraged a number of assassins to murder Paul secretly; but this was prevented by the Apostle's transportation to Caesarea, where Ananias went to prosecute him. Paul's appeal to Caesar put the affair under the jurisdiction of Rome.

When Albinus succeeded Festus in the government of Judea, Ananias, to ingratiate himself into his favour, asked for amnesty for a number of his friends who had plundered the countryside. At the same time, vast numbers of outrageous assassins were infesting Judea. Whenever any of their party fell into the hands of the governor, they made this known to the High Priest's friends. Once, Eleazar his son, in order to obtain the rescue of his friends with the help of the governor, he enlarged the number of their associates. At last, Eleazar, putting himself at the head of a body of mutineers that seized the Temple to stop the offering of sacrifices to the Emperor, the assassins joined with him. The Romans pulled down Ananias' house, and, finding him and one of his sons hidden in an aqueduct, they killed them both.

ANDREW

The brother of Simon Peter, a native of Bethsaida, and an Apostle of Jesus Christ. He was originally a fisherman. When John the Baptist began preaching, Andrew became one of his followers. Seeing him one day point to Jesus Christ as *the Lamb of God which taketh away the sin of the world* (John 1:35-44), he, together with another of John's disciples, followed Jesus and stayed with him all that night. Next day, he met with his brother Simon, and introduced him to Jesus. After passing a day with him, they returned to their ordinary employment of fishing. Some months after that, Jesus found them busy on the Sea of Galilee. He called them to be his followers, and promised to make them *fishers* (or gainers) of the souls *of men*. They immediately left their nets and followed him; nor did they ever leave him again, except on one occasion when they went back briefly to fishing. (Matt. 4:18-20; John 21:2-8)

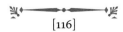

About a year after their call, when Jesus asked his disciples how he could find bread for the 5000 people who were with him for three days, Andrew replied that a lad of the company had five barley loaves and two small fish. *"But what,"* said he, *"are they among so many?"* (John 6:8-9) Just before our Saviour's passion, some Greeks applied to Philip to obtain an audience with him. Philip and Andrew together informed Jesus, and the Greeks were doubtless admitted. (John 12:22) Two or three days later, Andrew and some others asked Jesus concerning the time of the destruction of the second Temple, and the sign of his coming. (Mark 13:3-4) After Christ's Ascension, Andrew preached for some years at Jerusalem. It is said that, at last, he preached the gospel in Scythia, and was crucified at Patna of Achaia.

ANDRONICUS, *a victorious man*
A relative of Paul, and a fellow-prisoner with him. (Rom. 16:7)

ANER, ESHCOL, and **MAMRE**
Three Canaanite princes that assisted Abraham in his pursuit and defeat of Chedorlaomer and his allies. Not imitating the generosity of that Patriarch, they took their share of the booty that had been taken from the Sodomites, and recovered. (Gen. 14:13-24)

ANGEL, *messenger*
A name commonly given to those spiritual and intelligent beings by whom God partly executes his providential work, and who are most ready and active to do his work. The light of nature gives strong reason to suppose the existence of such beings; but Scripture alone puts the question beyond doubt. In vain, a great many of the Fathers, the Socinians, and other modern authors, assert that they were created long before the foundation of the world. Moses (indeed, God) assures us that the hosts of heaven were created during the first six days. (Gen. 2:1; Exod. 20:11) When God founded the earth on the first or second day, they sang together, and shouted for joy. (Job 38:6-7) They were created with eminent wisdom, holiness, and purity, and were placed in a most happy and honourable estate. But they were capable of change. Their knowledge is great, but not infinite. They *desire to look into* the mystery of our salvation, and learn from the Church the manifold wisdom of God. Nor can they search the hearts of men, nor

know future events, unless particularly instructed by God. (Jer. 17:10; Matt. 24:31, 33; Eph. 3:10; 1 Pet. 1:12) Nor do we understand their way of knowing things corporeal and visible, nor the way they reveal themselves in human form, nor their method of communication among themselves.

Their power, too, is very extensive, but reaches to nothing strictly miraculous. Their number is very great, amounting to vast millions. (Ps. 68:17; Dan. 7:10; Matt. 26:53; Rev. 5:11) The names of archangels, thrones, dominions, principalities, and powers, suggest an order among them, though of what kind we do not know. The elect angels kept their first estate; these, besides their honorary attendance on God, are, to their great satisfaction, subject to Christ as Mediator, and, by him, are reconciled to the saints, and are sent out *to minister, to teach,* reprove, comfort, direct, and protect those who are the heirs of salvation, and to transport their souls to heaven at death. How useful they are to the saints in suggesting good thoughts, in restraining Satan, in averting danger, and in assisting and providing for them; such things we can hardly conceive. (Matt. 18:10; Ps. 34:7; Heb. 2:14)

Angels were stationed so as to prevent fallen man approaching the tree of life. (Gen. 3:24) Two of them appeared to Abraham in his tent, and ate and drank with him, consuming the food in a way we do not know. Two of them were courteously invited by Lot to stay with him. They smote the depraved Sodomites with blindness, as they threatened to abuse them, and warned Lot of the approaching overthrow of Sodom, prompting and assisting him to escape. Two companies of angels accompanied Jacob on his return from Mesopotamia, to protect him from the fury of Laban and Esau. An angel smote the firstborn of Egypt, and assisted the Hebrews in their exodus from that country, and in their marching through the wilderness. Thousands of them attended Jehovah as he gave the Law at Sinai, and perhaps formed the audible voice in the air by which it was expressed. (Gen. 18-19, 22; Exod. 12, 33:2; Num. 20:16; Ps. 68:17; Acts 7:53; Gal 3:19; Heb. 2:2:2, 5, 7, 9, 16)

When God offered the Hebrews an angel to be their great guide, Moses refused, knowing that nothing less than the patience of God was able to endure such perverseness that was found in Israel. An angel of the Lord fed Elijah in the wilderness of Judah; and afterwards angels carried him soul and body to heaven. Troops of them protected Elisha at Dotham. To punish David's numbering of the people, an angel slew 70,000 of them in one day. An angel, in one night, cut off 185,000 of Sennacherib's army, and delivered Jerusalem from his fury. Angels frequently spoke to Daniel, Zechariah, and John the Apostle. (Exod. 33-34; 1 Kings 19; 2 Kings 2:11, 6:17, 19:35; 2 Sam. 24:16-17; Rev. 10:8-9) An angel at times troubled the waters of the pool of Bethesda. (John 5:4)

An angel foretold the birth of Jesus Christ and of John the Baptist. In great numbers they attended our Saviour's birth, and proclaimed it to the shepherds near Bethlehem. An angel warned Joseph and Mary to flee into Egypt with the divine Babe, and return back to Judea when it was safe. Angels ministered to Jesus in the wilderness when the devil had left him. An angel assisted him in his bloody agony in the garden. Two of them rolled away the stone from the mouth of his tomb, and informed the women that he had risen from the dead. Many of them accompanied him in his Ascension, some of whom informed the gazing disciples that they would see him return from heaven in the same way and form he had left. An angel freed the Apostles at Jerusalem, brought Peter out of Herod's prison, and set Paul and Silas free in Philippi. An angel assured Paul of his safe landing, and of those that were with him in the ship. (Matt. 1:20-21, 2:13, 19, 4:11, 28:2; Luke 1:11, 22:43, 24:45; Acts 1:10-11, 5:19, 12:7, 10, 16:26, 27:23)

Some believe that every person has an angel in attendance, and every kingdom its particular guardian angel. But none of these opinions are sufficiently warranted from Scripture. One angel is sometimes presented as acting for many, and multitudes of angels are presented as protecting one. What solemn conventions they hold for giving an account of their work I dare not imagine. It is, however, certain that their ministrations to men in no way interfere with their enjoyment of the beatific vision of God. All of them are inexpressibly delighted with the work of our redemption, and celebrate the same in their highest anthems of praise. On the Last Day, all their unnumbered millions will attend our Redeemer in the judgement, will gather the elect from the four winds of heaven to his right hand, and drive the damned into their horrible regions of eternal misery. (Gen. 32:1; Job 1:6, 2:1; Ps. 34:7; Isa. 37:36; Dan. 10:20; Matt. 13:39, 49, 18:10, 25:31; Acts 12:15; Rev. 14:18, 16:5)

Vast numbers of angels, soon after their creation, fell from their happy estate; but whether pride, envy of man's happiness, or some other crime was the cause, we are not directly informed. These are usually called *devils, unclean spirits, Satan,* etc. When they sinned, they were immediately excluded from the heavenly mansions, and irrevocably condemned to endless misery. They were not, however, confined to the prison of hell, for God allowed them to rove about in our world to test and punish mankind. Such is their desperate malice that, knowing every injury to mankind would certainly increase their eternal torment, and knowing that every temptation of saints will result in their welfare, and in their own aggravated unhappiness they never cease going about seeking whom they may devour. (John 8:44; 1 Tim. 3:16; 1 Pet. 5:8; 2 Pet. 2:4, 11; Jude v. 6)

These apostate spirits appear to have one chief, with whom, perhaps, their apostasy began, who was probably once an archangel in his happy estate. The rest are presented as his servants. He is called *the Devil, Satan, Beelzebub, prince of the power of the air, prince and god of this world.* It was probably he who, in the form of a serpent, seduced our first parents, and received an additional curse on that account, to be effected chiefly through our redemption by Christ. It was probably he who attacked our Saviour in the desert and elsewhere, and tempted him to the vilest of sins. (Gen. 3; Matt. 4, 25:41; Luke 4; John 14:30)

These evil angels perpetually deceive or harass the children of men, and have, through different idols, been worshipped by most of them. They often enter into familiar correspondence with numbers of diviners, wizards, witches, etc, deceiving them, and enabling them to control, or injure, their fellows. These evil angels often assume the appearance of holiness, and warmly urge men to take up the semblance of pious religion; but it is always to promote some wicked and sinful end. God ordered a number of these angels to harass the Egyptians. One or more of them was permitted by God, by means of robbers, and by lightning and storms, and other things, to destroy the substance and family of Job, and to strike his body all over with boils. Permitted by God, they tempted King David to number the Hebrews, and seduced the prophets of Baal to mislead Ahab who went up and fell at Ramothgilead. Vast numbers of them were permitted to take possession of the bodies of men in our Saviour's time, that his power might be made more conspicuous when he cast them out. All along, these spirits have, by means of the heathen and other persecutors, and subtle heretics, terribly harassed the Christian Church. During

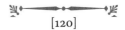

the glorious millennium, their power will be greatly restrained. At the end of it, they will again deceive the nations, and, soon after, be publicly condemned and shut up in everlasting perdition. (Deut. 32:17; 1 Kings 22; 2 Kings 21:6; 1 Chron. 21:1; Job 1:2; Ps. 78:49; Acts 10:38; 1 Cor. 10:20; 2 Cor. 11:14; Eph. 2:2; 1 Pet. 5:8; Rev. 2:10; 12, 20) The holy angels, in their disputes with devils, refuse to bring any ranting accusation against them, but act with mildness and meekness, as we should, even with the worst of men. (2 Pet. 2:11; Jude v. 9) The angels, for whose sake the Corinthian women ought to remain covered in worshipping assemblies, are the good angels, in whose presence nothing immodest is proper. Such women give to the evil angels no handle of temptation to frivolity, especially in the worship of God. (1 Cor. 11:10)

Jesus Christ is called an Angel. He was sent by his Father to publish and fulfil the work of our redemption; and, to him, he has committed all judgement. He appeared to Hagar, to Abraham, to Jacob, to Moses, to Balaam, to Joshua, to the Hebrews at Bochim, to Gideon and Manoah, to Daniel, and to Zechariah the prophet, all under the form of an angel. (Gen. 16-17, 32; Exod. 3; Num. 22; Josh. 5; Judg. 2:6; Dan. 10; Zech. 1-6) Whenever an angel is presented as speaking from God, or as sovereign of the Church, we are to understand that it was our Redeemer. He is called *the angel* (Messenger) *of the covenant* (Mal. 3:1): he publishes the plan, fulfils the condition, and executes the promise, of the covenant of grace. He is the *angel of* God's *presence* (or *face*) (Isa. 63:9). He is the Son of his love, the delight of his eyes, and the mirror in which his glory is displayed. He came from his bosom, is always near him, sits at his right hand, and appears before his throne interceding for us.

Extra note

Ministers are also called Angels. The evidence for this comes from Scripture, and chiefly rests on this, that the Epistles to the seven churches in Revelation 2-3 are addressed to the *angels* of those different churches, which, some say, means their bishops, others, the presiding rulers, and others, ministers in general. Dr. Joseph Mede throws considerable light on this subject in his account of the ministration of angels. It is very evident, as we have already mentioned, that angels are employed in ministering to the heirs of salvation; so the churches of the saints, or Bethels, are places where they are particularly resident. When Jacob saw the house of God at Bethel, he saw the angels ascending and descending. (Gen. 28) Solomon enforced his exhortation to be watchful over our lips in the house of God *before the angel* (Eccles. 5-6). Indeed, Paul supports his direction for necessary decorum when he desires the women to be covered in their assemblies *because of the angels.* (1 Cor. 11:10) If these invisible spirits minister to the saints individually, much more then collectively; and their guardian care over the churches is frequently hinted at.

They have a commission from God to publish his messages, and execute his work in bringing men to his Son; and, as the angels in heaven, so they ought to excel in knowledge, humility, holiness, harmony, zeal, and readiness to serve Jesus Christ and his people, in prying into the mysteries of our redemption, in praising God, and rejoicing over the conversion of sinners. (Rev. 1:20, 14:6-8) A plurality of ministers is represented as one Angel to denote their union and harmony, and their having someone to preside at their judicial assemblies. (Rev. 2:1, 8, 12, 18, 3:1, 7, 14) They are perhaps the angels that come from the temple and altar having power over fire. They serve in God's Church, and worship. They pronounce God's fiery judgements, the fall of antichrist, and, by their prayers and preaching, accelerate his ruin. (Rev. 14:16, 18) The angels that gather Christ's elect are either ministers who gather them to Christ on their conversion, or proper angels who will gather them to his right hand on the Last Day. (Matt. 24:31) The ministers of God's judgements against his enemies are called Angels. The Eastern powers are presented as four angels loosed from the River Euphrates, appointed for a year, a month, a day, and an hour, to slay a third part of mankind. Though the Turks had, in the 11th century, established four sultanates, or kingdoms, near the River Euphrates, yet the invasion of the Tartars, the sacred war of the Franks, or papist Crusades, and their own civil arguments, restrained them for a long time. At length, about AD 1281, or according to others, 1302, Ortogrul, and his three sons, passed the Euphrates to the west, and began their ravages on much of the Roman Empire, cutting off great numbers of Saracens, but chiefly nominal Christians, in Asia, Europe, and Africa for 391 years, from 1281 to 1672, or 396 years, from 1302 onwards till the the Peace of Carlowitz in 1698. (Rev. 9:14) The instruments of God's vengeance against the pagans and Mahometans, whether proper angels, ministers, magistrates, or armies, are presented as seven angels, pouring vials of wrath on the earth, waters, rivers, sun, air, etc. Appointed by God, they sufficiently execute his vengeance, and, with great activity and success, entirely, but gradually, ruin the enemies of Christ. (Rev. 15:6, 8, ch. 16)

ANNA
The daughter of Phanuel, of the tribe of Asher. She was married early, and lived seven years with her husband. After his death, she devoted herself to the service of God, and she attended every morning and evening sacrifice in order to pour out her prayers. When she was 80 years of age, she found the blessed Virgin with her divine babe in the Temple, and Simeon blessing God for him. Inspired by the Holy Spirit, she praised the Lord, and commended the babe as the promised Messiah to those that were waiting for, and expecting, the redemption of Israel by him. (Only found in Luke 2:36-37)

ANNAS
Also called Ananus, the son of one Seth. He enjoyed the office of High Priest for 11 years, and is reckoned the only one, having five sons, that successively exercised that office. When he was turned out, he still retained a great share in the public management of the office. When Christ was arrested, he was first brought to Annas, and then to Caiaphas his son-in-law, who was High Priest, or perhaps no more than deputy to Annas that year. (Luke 3:2; John 18:13, 24) Both these two became malicious persecutors of the Apostles on account of their preaching of Christ. (Acts 4:6)

ANTICHRIST
An adversary of Jesus Christ. Heretics who deny the doctrine of the Trinity, or the divinity or incarnation of Christ, etc., are called antichrist. Of this sort, there were many in the time of the Apostle John. (1 John 2:18, 23, 4:3; 2 John 7) But one particular system of wicked persons, principles, and practices, is chiefly referred to, in the daily fear of which the early Christians lived. The Scripture presents this Antichrist as a very *man of sin*, and *son of perdition*, as a strong delusion overspreading the whole Roman Empire like a terrible judgement introduced by ignorance and hatred of the truth, and apostasy from it. He springs from the bottomless pit amid the terrible smoke of superstition and error; as sitting in the Temple or Church of

God; as exalting himself above magistrates, angels, and everything to do with God; as a despiser of the gods of the idolatrous heathen, and the God of his professed fathers in the early Church, and setting up a new class of *Mahuzzim*, deities to protect his different dominions, giving them over to the vilest blasphemy, error, cruelty, and persecution; as possessing civil and ecclesiastical power over the ten parts of the Roman Empire, and seizing upon three of them as his rightful domain; as establishing his abominations unnumbered with false miracles and lying wonders; as excluding from civil commerce those who do not more or less solemnly acknowledge, and submit to, his power.

United under one head - the *destructive angel of the bottomless pit -* the promoters of this delusion are many and mischievous, like locusts and scorpions, ruinous to those who know nothing of the true grace of God, having their conscience seared as with a hot iron, speaking lies in hypocrisy, propagating the doctrines of devils, forbidding to marry, or, on occasion, to use lawful and wholesome meats, while their hearers had itching ears, heaping up teachers, and giving attention to their fables. They are lovers of themselves, covetous, proud, blasphemers, disobedient to parents, unthankful, unholy, without natural affection, breaking their word, false accusers, despisers of those that are good, treacherous, headstrong, high-minded, lovers of pleasure more than lovers of God, creeping into houses and leading captive silly women burdened with sins. The chief residence of this monster would be Rome; his name, *Mystery, Babylon the great, the mother of harlots, and abominations of the earth.* The number of his name is 666, whose numeral letters constitute Latinus or Romiith, denying the articles of faith, and upholding many other things in the Romish church.

This antichrist began his work in the apostolic age, but was checked by the power of the Roman Empire till its destruction, when a fearful apostasy from the faith happened in the Church. His duration is 1260 years, during which he promotes idolatry, lies, and blasphemy; treads the church under foot; and persecutes the saints who, all along bear witness against his abominations. Nor do the terrible ravages of the Eastern angels loosed from the Euphrates in the least make his subjects repent of their idolatries, murders, sorceries, fornications, and thefts. At the end of his reign, he will, with craft and fury, almost entirely cut off faithful witnessing for Christ. But, all of a sudden, by the pure preaching of the gospel, by the pouring out of sevenfold plagues, or vials of divine wrath, by the revolt and opposition of his own subjects, he will be terribly destroyed, to the consternation of his adherents and the great joy of the saints, both Jew and Gentile. (Dan. 7:8-12, 20-26, 11:36-40; 2 Thess. 2:3-12; 1 Tim. 4:1-3; 2 Tim. 3:1-7, 4:3-4; Rev. 9:1-11, 20-21 and chs. 11, 13-19)

The above characteristics drawn from Scripture cannot be wholly found in the heathen Emperors of Rome, much less in the fanciful Danitish-Antichrist of popish writers, or the Armillus of the Jews, or the Daggial of the Mahometans. The Mahometan system may indeed be considered as a lesser antichrist, but neither contain *all* the characteristics applicable to it. It does not sit in the Church, nor appear to men to have a power equal to God's. It allows no idolatry, nor is it notable for the persecution of the saints, nor was it established by lying wonders, but by the power of the sword. Actually, every characteristic is clearly found in the papacy.

If with the two great Newtons (Isaac and Thomas), and Moses Lowman, we date the rise of antichrist from the pope becoming a civil prince in AD 750 or 756. I rather incline to date the rise of Antichrist from his claim to universal headship over the Christian Church in AD 606, or 608, for in this, I suppose, his character of *Antichrist* chiefly consists. (See *Antichrist*: in 1 John 2:18, 22, 4:3; 2 John 1:7; and *Antichrists* in 1 John 2:18)

APOLLOS

A Jew of Alexandria, who came to Ephesus just as Paul set off on his third missionary journey to Jerusalem. He was a very eloquent man, and had a great knowledge of the Scriptures. With distinguished fervour and diligence, he taught the things of the Lord Jesus, knowing only the baptism of John. Aquila and Priscilla, hearing him preach boldly in the synagogue that Jesus was the promised Messiah and Saviour, took him home with them and instructed him more fully in the Christian faith. He departed from there with letters of recommendation to Achaia, where he was very useful in strengthening new converts, and demonstrating to the Jews from Scripture that Jesus of Nazareth was indeed the Messiah promised to their fathers. Here, as at Ephesus, he watered the churches that Paul had planted. His fine address, and obliging behaviour nearly led to a split at Corinth, when some pretended to be of Paul's party, others of Apollos', others of Cephas', and others to the higher grade of Christ's. Vexed at this, Apollos left Achaia, and, along with Zenas the lawyer, sailed for Crete. From there, he went to Ephesus, and was present when Paul wrote his first Epistle to the Corinthians. He could hardly be prevailed upon to return. (Acts 18:24-28, 19:1; 1 Cor. 1:12, 3:4-6, 22, 4:6, 16:12; Titus 3:13)

APOLLYON. See Abaddon

APOSTLE, *sent*

A messenger, sent on a special and important errand. Jesus Christ is called the *Apostle of our profession.* (Heb. 3:1) God sent him to declare his will and build his Church; and he is the author, subject, and end of those divine truths that we are required to believe and profess.

Corresponding to the twelve patriarchs, or twelve tribes of Israel, our Saviour, in the second or third year of his public ministry, first appointed, and then sent out twelve of his disciples, whom he named *Apostles.* These, he sent out in pairs: Simon Peter and Andrew his brother, James the son of Zebedee and John his brother, Philip and Bartholomew, Thomas and Matthew, James the son of Alpheus, and Jude his brother, Simon the Canaanite and Judas Iscariot. (Matt. 10:2) Of these Apostles, Matthew was a tax-collector; the other four, if not nearly all the rest, were Galilean fishermen. The New Testament Church was not founded till after our Saviour's resurrection, so their first mission was only temporary, confined to the cities of Israel, and was not superior to that of the seventy disciples, afterwards sent out on the same errand. Their work was to preach that *the kingdom of heaven*, or gospel dispensation, *was at hand*, and to confirm their doctrine by the miraculous healing of diseases and the casting out of devils. They were to provide no food or money for their journey, but to expect it from their hearers. Nor were they to use any fawning politeness to curry favour, but were to shake off the dust from their feet as a testimony against any city or family that rejected them. In the execution of their mission, they had great success. When Jesus travelled, they were his ordinary attendants, and when he multiplied the loaves, they, like his servants, distributed the bread to the multitude.

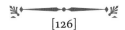

At their request, he set them a pattern on which to model their prayers. What he publicly preached to the multitude, he privately explained to them. He often discussed with them his sufferings, and committed to them the keys of the kingdom of heaven. When James and John marked their ambition for high places in his government, the rest were greatly offended, for as yet they did not know the nature of his kingdom. Earlier, it seems that most of them agreed with Judas in taking offence at Mary's expensive anointing of their Master. Just before his death, Jesus informed them of the approaching destruction of the Jewish church and state, and of his own coming to judgement. He assured them that, in a few days, one of them would betray him into the hands of his enemies to be crucified. He celebrated his last Passover with all of them, except perhaps Judas, and observed his first sacred supper. On that occasion, he delivered to them a great number of suitable exhortations and consolatory promises, particularly concerning the Holy Spirit who was to be poured out on them. They were so taken with this teaching that, whatever impertinent questions they had formerly asked, they now agreed that he *spoke plainly*. (John 16:29) When Jesus was arrested, he desired his persecutors not to lay hands on them. However, ungenerously, they forsook him and fled. His crucifixion threw them into tremendous perplexity as they had all along dreamed of his bringing in a worldwide kingdom. Judas Iscariot being dead, and Thomas absent, on the evening after his resurrection, he appeared to ten of them in their perplexity. He renewed their mission, and breathed on them as a sign of his sending the Holy Spirit. (Luke 11; Matt. 16, 20, 24-26; John 12-18, 20)

After providing them with repeated proofs of his resurrection, just before his Ascension, he gave them a formal commission to *go into all the world and preach the gospel to every creature* (Mark 16:15), and assured them of his presence and protection, and that he would confirm their teaching by miraculous proofs. He told them to *tarry at Jerusalem* for the outpouring of the Holy Spirit, which would happen in a few days. (Luke 24:49) After they had witnessed their Master's departure to the heavenly mansions, they chose Matthias in place of Judas. On the day of Pentecost, a feast appointed to commemorate the giving of the Law, the Holy Spirit, in the shape of divided tongues of fire, descended on each of them, making them bold and infallible in preaching the gospel, and qualifying them to speak with power in every language, to discern men's thoughts, and to confer the miraculous influence of speaking with tongues on others by the laying on of hands. They preached to the crowds, and thousands were converted. They went daily to the court of the Temple, where, amid vast numbers, they proved Jesus to be the true Messiah, who had risen from the dead and ascended to glory. They confirmed their mission with innumerable miracles. Stung with indignation at their extolling one they had put to death as a criminal, and at their bold charges concerning the guilt of his murder, the Jewish Sanhedrin imprisoned them. An angel liberated them, and they returned to their preaching work. They were again arrested, and angrily prohibited from preaching in their Master's name. With amazing joy, they endured their sufferings, and went on with their work, both in public and private. When they were next arrested, the Sanhedrin almost agreed to put them to death; but, advised by Gamaliel, they dismissed them with a solemn charge to never again preach in our Saviour's name. Soon after this, they ordained a number of deacons to manage the alms of the church. A furious storm of persecution arose that scattered the other preachers, but the Apostles remained in Jerusalem. When they had continued in Judea about 18 years, the Eleven (for James, the brother of John, was murdered by Herod) called a solemn synod, where it was decided *that no observance of the Mosaic ceremonies ought to be imposed on the (Gentile) Christian converts*; but, to avoid giving offence to weaker brothers, they should *abstain from meats offered to idols, and from things strangled, and blood.* (Matt. 28; Mark 16; John 21; Acts 1-7, 15)

Not long after, it seems that the Apostles dispersed themselves into other countries, going their various ways, so is said, by lot. Peter went into Pontus, Galatia, and places adjacent, Andrew into Scythia and Sogdiana, John into Asia Minor, Philip into Armenia, Media, and Colchis, Bartholomew into Arabia Felix, Matthew into Chaldea, Persia, and Parthia, Thomas into Hircania, Bacteria, and India, Jude into Syria, and Mesopotamia, Simon the Canaanite into Egypt, Cyrene, Libya, and Mauritania, Matthias into Cappadocia and Colchis, while James, the brother of Jude, remained in Judea. Meanwhile, Paul, who more than sufficiently took the place of James the brother of John, flew like a seraph almost everywhere to win souls for Christ.

Without a shadow of proof, our *common creed* is ascribed to the Apostles as it authors. Nobody can tell us when or where they met to

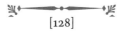

draw it up, or show us how a creed written by inspired men could fall short of divine authority. None of the fathers in the first three centuries state that it was written by the Apostles; nor, in the early years, did it have the same wording in all churches, or was the same as what we now possess. Far less ought the canons and constitutions called by their name pass for *apostolic*. Besides a variety of other blunders, they refer to general letters and other things not found in the Christian Church till after the Apostles were long buried in their graves. It is probable that they were collected, or forged, in the fifth century, when impostors were becoming bold, and the people credulous. Vast numbers of false and pretended apostles very early pestered the churches, particularly those of Syria, Galatia, Corinth, Colosse, etc. (Acts 15; Gal 1:7-9; 2 Cor. 10-11; Col. 2)

AQUILA, and PRISCILLA
A Jew, born in Pontus. He, with his wife Prisca (or Priscilla) ran their business making make leather tents for the Roman troops. They were early converted to the Christian faith, perhaps by Peter's Pentecostal sermon. After they had resided some time at Rome, the edict of Claudius banished all Jews from that city, obliging them to leave and return to Corinth. Involved in their business, and probably to please the Gentiles, they went and lodged with Justus. They befriended Paul in Ephesus, and there exposed their necks to protect him. Here, they instructed Apollos more perfectly in the way of the Lord. They returned to Rome; and, in their house, a meeting of Christians was held. There, they were greeted by Paul in his Epistle to that church. They returned to Asia, and resided in or near Ephesus, and were there when Paul wrote his second Epistle to Timothy. (Acts 18:2, 18, 26; Rom. 16:3; 1 Cor. 16:19; 2 Tim. 4:19)

ARAM
(1) The fifth son of Shem. (Gen. 10:22)

(2) The grandson of Nahor, father of the Aramites, or Syrians. (Gen. 10:22, 22:21) It is observable that Hesiod and Homer, those ancient Greek authors, called the Syrians Aramaeans. Aram is the Hebrew name for Syria; and hence we read of *Aram-Naharaim* (or Mesopotamia), *Aram-Zobah* (or Syria of Zobah), *Aram-Damascus* (or Syria of Damascus), and *Aram-Bethrehob* (or Syria of Bethrehob), etc.

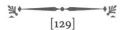

(3) Aram, or Ram, the great-grandson of Judah, and father of Amminadab. (Ruth 4:19; 1 Chron. 2:23; Luke 3:33)

ARAUNAH
Also called Oman the Jebusite, who had a threshing floor on Mount Moriah. When David perceived the angel of the Lord over and above Jerusalem preparing to destroy its inhabitants as a punishment for his numbering the people, he was warned by Nathan the prophet to build an altar and offer sacrifice to stop the plague. Instructed by God to build a Temple on that spot, David hastened to Araunah. The good Jebusite and his sons hid themselves in a hole for fear of the destroying angel, but, when he saw David coming, he ran to meet him, fell at his feet, and asked what he wanted. Informed that he needed to purchase his threshing floor for the erection of an altar and the offering of a sacrifice, that the destructive plague might be stopped, Araunah offered the King a free gift of the floor, and wood and oxen sufficient for the sacrifice. Hating to serve the Lord at the expense of another, David refused to accept these things till the price was fixed. For the floor and the oxen, he gave him 50 shekels of silver, and for the whole field, about 600 shekels of gold. (2 Sam. 24:16, 18, 20-24)

ARCHANGEL
A chief angel. But whether this word in Scripture ever refers to a created angel, or always Christ, the Lord of angels, is hard to determine. (Only found in 1 Thess. 4:16 and Jude v. 9)

ARCHELAUS
A son of Herod the Great by Malthace, his fifth wife. He was regarded as the most cruel and bloody of his father's children. Herod murdered his sons Alexander, Aristobulus, and Antipater, and stripped Herod Antipas of his claim to the kingdom. Later, he wrote a will naming Archelaus his successor on condition the Roman Emperor agreed. The people and soldiery appeared very well pleased when this will was read, and promised allegiance and fidelity. Archelaus interred his father with great ceremony, and, returning to Jerusalem, called a solemn mourning of seven days. He provided the people with splendid entertainment; and, having convened them in the court of the Temple, he assured

them of a mild government, and that he would not assume the royal title before the Emperor confirmed it.

Just afterwards, in AD 1, the rabble assembled, and required him to execute the men who had advised his father to kill a notable zealot who had pulled down the golden eagle from the gate of the Temple. They demanded that Joazas should be divested of the high priesthood, and loaded the memory of Herod with the bitterest curses and reproaches. To revenge this insult, Archelaus ordered his troops to fall on the mob, which killed 3000 of the rioters on the spot just beside the Temple. He next went off to Rome for the confirmation of his father's will; but his brother Herod Antipas insisted on the ratification of his father's former will, constituting him Herod's successor, alleging that this will was made when his judgement was more sound. After hearing both parties, Augustus delayed in giving sentence. The Jewish nation petitioned the Emperor to lay aside the whole family of Herod, and make them into a Roman province subject to the governor of Syria. Naturally, Archelaus opposed this petition. The Emperor heard both, but delayed giving judgement. A few days later, Augustus called Archelaus, assigned to him a part of his father's kingdom, with the title of Ethnarch, and promised him the crown if his future conduct deserved it.

Returning to Judea, Archelaus deposed Joazas the High Priest, pretending that he had stirred up the rebellion against him, and appointed Eleazar his brother High Priest in his place. When Archelaus had governed about seven years with the utmost violence and tyranny, the Jews and Samaritans jointly accused him to the Emperor. His agent at Rome was ordered to bring him there where his cause was heard. He was banished to Vienne in France, and lived there in exile till his death. It was the cruel temper of this monster that made Joseph and Mary fear to live in Judea with their blessed babe. (Only mentioned in Matt. 2:22-23)

ARCHIPPUS

A notable preacher of the gospel at Colossae. The church members there were requested to stir him up to diligence, care, and courage, in the work of his ministry. (Col. 4:17) Paul salutes him in Philemon verse 2.

ARETAS

Many kings of this name, or, as the natives express it, Hareth, reigned in the Arabian kingdom of Ghassan, east of Canaan; but only the successor of Obodas, and father-in-law of Herod-Antipas, is mentioned in Scripture. His name is only found in 2 Corinthians 11:32. One Sylleus, thought to have ruined himself before the Emperor Augustus, pretended that he had usurped the Arabian throne by his own hand. When his treachery was discovered, Aretas was solemnly confirmed in his government. Offended with Herod for divorcing his daughter to make way for Herodias, Aretas declared war against him under pretence of adjusting their territory in Galilee. Herod was often defeated, and begged the assistance of the Emperor Tiberius, who ordered his lieutenant in Syria to bring him Aretas dead or alive. Vitellius immediately marched to attack the Arabian king; but, hearing of Tiberius' death, he returned without joining in battle. Not long after, Aretas' deputy at Damascus joined the Jews in their persecution of Paul, and kept the gates shut night and day in order to catch him. (Acts 9:23-24) See also 2 Corinthians 11:32

ARIMATHAEA. See Joseph (3)
For Joseph of Arimathaea, see Matthew 27:57; Mark 15:43; John 19:38.

ARIOCH
(1) A king of El-Lassar, one of Chedorlaomer's allies. (Gen. 14:1, 9)

(2) A captain of Nebuchadnezzar's guard, who was appointed to kill all the wise men of Babylon. At Daniel's request, he delayed the execution of this order, and introduced that prophet to the King to describe and interpret his dream. (Dan. 2:14-15, 24-25)

ARISTARCHUS

A native of Thessalonica. He became a zealous Christian, and accompanied Paul during the Apostle's stay in Ephesus, where, amid the tumult raised by Demetrius the silversmith, he barely escaped with his life. He met up with Paul on his return to Greece and on his journey to Asia. Having gone with him from Jerusalem to Rome, it is said that he was beheaded along with Paul. (Acts 19:29, 20:4, 27:2; Col. 4:10; Philem verse 24)

ARISTOBULUS

He is supposed to have been the brother of Barnabas, and one of our Saviour's Seventy disciples, and to have preached with great success in Britain. But it is really uncertain if he was so great a Christian, since not he, but his family, were greeted by Paul. (Mentioned only in Rom. 16:10)

ARTAXERXES, Smerdis, Mardus, Sphendadates, Oropastes.

Ahasuerus Cambyses, while he was ravaging Egypt, left Patizithes the Magus to govern the Persian state. Hearing that Cambyses had murdered his only brother Smerdis, Patizithes, considering how much his own brother Smerdis resembled the murdered prince, put him on the throne in Cambyses' absence, and made out that he was the real brother of the king. Informed of this, Cambyses marched homeward to dethrone him; but, dying on the way, he begged his nobles to pull down Smerdis, who, he swore, was not his brother, but a Magian impostor. To clear the matter up with certainty, Ostanes, a nobleman who knew that the ears of the Magus had been cut off by Cyrus or Cambyses, got information by his own daughter, a concubine of Smerdis, that his ears were still intact. He, Darius Hystaspia, Gobrias, and four other princes, after binding themselves with an oath to slay the Magus, or perish in the attempt, rushed into the palace and killed him and his brother. During the impostor's short reign of five months, Bishlam, Mithredath, Tabeel, Rehum the chancellor, Shimshai, and their Samaritan tribes, wrote him a letter, bearing the news that Jerusalem had once been a very powerful and rebellious city, and that if it was rebuilt, he might expect the Jews to revolt quickly and deprive him of all his tribute to the west of the Euphrates. His reply to this letter said that, upon inspection of the ancient histories, he found it to be as they had suggested, and ordered them to stop the Jews rebuilding either the city or Temple till they had received further orders from him. (Ezra 4:7-24)

ARTAXERXES LONGIMANUS

The youngest son of Xerxes, and grandson of Darius Hystaspes. Artibanus, captain of the guards, intending to seize the Persian throne for himself, privately murdered Xerxes his father, and persuaded Artaxerxes that Darius his elder brother had done it, and intended to murder him as well. On this information, Artaxerxes flew directly to the apartment of his brother Darius, and, with the assistance of Artibanus and the guards, killed him on the spot. His second brother, Hystaspes, being in Scythia, Artibanus placed Artaxerxes on the throne, intending to pull him down at pleasure and seize it for himself. But his murder and treason coming to light, he was quickly punished with the loss of his life. His friends raised an army to revenge his death but were totally crushed. After a war of two years, Hystaspes and his party were irrecoverably ruined. Artaxerxes, then, to the joy of his subjects, applied himself to put right their disorders.

In the 7th year of his reign, in which, perhaps, he made Esther his Queen (Esther 2:16), he authorized Ezra, with as many Jewish attendants as he could find, to return to Judea. He allowed him to collect what money he could in Chaldea for the use of the Temple; he presented him with a variety of sacred vessels; he ordered his collectors on the west of the Euphrates to pay to him from the public revenue 100 talents of silver, 100 measures of wheat, 800 gallons of wine, and as much oil, and whatever salt, was necessary for the use of the Temple. He exempted from tribute all the priests, Levites, and Nethinim; he authorised Ezra to promote to his utmost the service of his God and the welfare of his nation; and he empowered him to fine, imprison, or kill, anyone that dared to oppose the laws of God or the King. (Ezra 7) In the 20th year of his reign, he, perhaps urged on by Esther, empowered Nehemiah to go and rebuild the city of Jerusalem, and ordered Asaph, the keeper of the royal forest, to allow him to use whatever timber he needed. (Neh. 2)

The Egyptians, weary of the Persian yoke, revolted about the 5th year of his reign, and made Inarus, King of Lydia, their sovereign, entering into a treaty with the Athenians. An army of 300,000, commanded by Achemenides, the brother or son of the King's mother, was sent to reduce them. Inarus and his allies defeated this powerful host, and killed the general and 100,000 of his troops. The rest fled to Memphis, and there defended themselves for three years till Megabysus and Artabasus, with another Persian army, relieved them. They defeated the Egyptians, and reduced them to their usual slavery, and took prisoner Inarus, and many others of the chief men. About the same time, the Athenians so badly harassed the Persian Empire that Artaxerxes was obliged to make peace with them on these terms: that all the Greek cities of Asia should enjoy full liberty; that no Persian ships of war should enter the sea between the Euxine and the Pamphylian coast; that not any of their land forces approach nearer the shore than three days' journey; and that the Athenians should attack no place belonging to the Persians. After five years' of begging, Artaxerxes gave up Inarus and the other Egyptian princes to the will of his mother. To revenge the blood of Achemenides, she put them to a cruel death. Megabysus, who had taken them prisoner, and promised them safety, became very angry, retired to Syria, and raised an army to take revenge on the King and his mother. Twice he routed the royal army of 200,000, and obliged Artaxerxes to pardon and recall him to court.

ARTEMAS
Seems to have been a notable preacher. Paul intended to send him, or Tychicus, to Crete, probably to take the place of Titus, while he came to visit the Apostle at Nicopolis. (Titus 3:12)

ASA
He succeeded his father Abijah on the throne of Judah in BC 955, and reigned 41 years. He was educated by Maachah, the daughter of Abishalom, a notable idolater; but was pious himself. For the first ten years of his reign, he had no war, and applied himself to reforming his kingdom. He did not pull down the high places where his subjects, contrary to orders, worshipped the true God, but he did abolish the idols, altars, high places, and the groves belonging to them, and commanded his subjects to worship only the true God. Those abominable creatures, the Sodomites, he entirely exterminated. Meanwhile, he fortified the main cities on his frontiers, and took great care in training his subjects in war, so that soon he had a militia of 300,000 Jews armed with shields and spears, and 280,000 Benjamites armed with bows and shields. He had scarcely reigned 12-14 years when Zerah, King of Ethiopia, invaded Judah with a million soldiers on foot, and 300 scythed chariots. After prayer to God, Asa attacked them at Mareshah, and, with an army vastly inferior in numbers, routed them, pursued them as far as Gerar on the southwest of Canaan, smote the cities round about in alliance with them, and returned home loaded down with booty.

In gratitude to God, and in obedience to his prophet Azariah, Asa employed himself further in reforming his kingdom. He and his

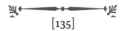

subjects engaged themselves by covenant to serve the Lord, and agreed that it should be held, according to law, a capital crime to worship an idol. He deprived his grandmother Maachah of what authority she held because she was a worshipper, if not priestess, of some idol, perhaps a very obscene one. Her idol and its grove he trampled under foot, and burnt with fire in the Valley of Hinnom, and cast the ashes into the brook Kidron to mingle with the filth of the city. The dedicated things of his father, with much of his late spoils, he devoted to the service of God; and, having repaired the altar of burnt offering, he sacrificed on it 700 oxen and 5,000 sheep of his Ethiopian booty.

The fame of his reformation, and the blessings that came from it, encouraged vast numbers of pious Israelites to enter his kingdom. To prevent the loss of his subjects, Baasha, King of Israel, in the 16th year of Asa, and the 36th from the *division* of the tribes, engaged in a war with Judah. He took Ramah, and began to fortify it as a means of preventing all communication between the two kingdoms. On this occasion, Asa dug a remarkable pit, but for what purpose, whether to hide himself, or more probably to hide his wealth, or to entrap Baasha, we are not told. (Jer. 41:9) To thwart Baasha's designs, Asa took all the silver and gold he could find in his own exchequer, or in the Temple, and sent it to Benhadad, King of Syria, begging him to break his pact with Baasha and enter into one with him. Excited by this valuable present, and with hopes of extending his power, Benhadad fell on the north parts of Baasha's kingdom and took several cities there. Meanwhile, Asa, from the south, retook Ramah, carried off the materials prepared for its fortifications, and fortified Geba and western Mizpah with them.

Asa's distrust of the divine power and goodness that had so lately rendered him victorious over a more formidable enemy, and his treacherous application for heathen aid, highly displeased the Lord. Under divine direction, Hanani the prophet sharply reproved him, and assured him that, henceforth, he would have war. Instead of thankfully receiving the admonitions of God, he outrageously imprisoned the prophet, and oppressed those of his subjects, who, it seems, marked their displeasure at his conduct. He and Baasha continued in a state of war. In the last part of his life, he appears to have become extremely irritable, and, in the 39th year of his reign, he suffered from gout, or some other ailment in his feet. He applied to his physicians rather than to God for relief. After two years' illness, he died. We are tempted to

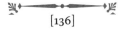

think that the awful smell of his corpse obliged them to fill his funeral bed with odours and spices; nor can we say whether his body was first burnt to ashes, and these alone interred. (1 Kings 15; 2 Chron. 14-16)

ASAHEL

The son of Zeruiah, and brother of Joab. He was one of David's thirty heroes, and was extremely swift of foot. After the battle of Gibeon, he pursued Abner so relentlessly that the general was obliged to kill him. Joab later resented this slaughter, with Abner murdering his brother. (2 Sam. 2:18-19, 3:26-27)

ASAPH

Reckoning them up, his ancestors were Berachiah, Shimea, Michael, Baaseiah, Malchiah, Ethni, Zerah, Adaiah, Ethan, Zimmah, Shimei, Jahath, Gershom, Levi. His sons were Zaccur, Joseph, Nethaniah, and Asarelah. He was one of the three senior singers, and his children constituted the 1st, 3rd, 5th, and 7th class of the Temple musicians. (1 Chron. 6:39-43, 25:2, 9:15) It seems that their station was on the south side of the brazen altar. The 50th and 73rd Psalms, and the ten following them (12 in all) are ascribed to Asaph. But we know that he could not have composed them all, as some of them relate to later times. Perhaps their title means no more than that they were chiefly sung by his posterity.

ASENATH

The daughter of Potipherah, and wife of Joseph. Some have imagined that she was the daughter of Potiphar, and that her discovery of her father and mother's wicked behaviour towards Joseph endeared her to the young patriarch. (The name is found only in Gen. 41:45, 50, 46:20) However, Potipherah was a priest of On. See also Potiphar and Potipherah.

ASHER

The son of Jacob by Zilpah his maid, and father of one of the Hebrew tribes. His children were Jimnah, Ishua, Issui, and Beriah (from whom sprang the Jimnites, Jesuites, Berites), and Serah their sister. Amazingly, 41,500 of this tribe fit for war came out of Egypt under the command of Pagie, the son of Ocran. Their spy for searching the

Promised Land was Sethur the son of Michael, and the prince for their division was Ahihud, the son of Shelomi. (Gen. 46:17; 1 Chron. 7:30-40; Num. 26:44, 1:13, 40-41, 13:13) They increased in the wilderness to 53,400. (Num. 26:47) Their inheritance fell by lot in the northwest of Canaan, where the soil was extremely fertile and the mines plentiful; but, through faintness and cowardice, they allowed the Canaanites to retain the cities of Zidon, Ahiab, Achzib, Helbon, Aphek, and Rehob. (Gen. 49:20; Deut. 33:24-25; Josh. 19:24-31, 34; Judg. 1:31-32)

This tribe was one of six that echoed AMEN to the curses from Mount Ebal. (Deut. 27:12, 13) They tamely submitted to the oppression of Jabin, King of Canaan, and sometime later assisted Gideon in his pursuit of the Midianites. (Judg. 5:17, 7:16, 23) Forty thousand of them, all expert warriors, accompanied David's coronation as King over Israel. Baanah, the son of Hushai, was their deputy-governor under Solomon; and many of them joined in Hezekiah's reformation. (1 Kings 4:16; 1 Chron. 12:36; 2 Chron. 30:11)

ASHPENAZ

The governor of Nebuchadnezzar's eunuchs. He changed the name of Daniel and his three companions into something that was related to Chaldean idols. He was afraid to allow these Jews to live on pulse (a mixture of beans and peas), lest their leanness should show and offend the king. But Melzar, his inferior steward, allowed them. (Dan. 1:3-17)

ASHTAROTH, ASHTORETH (ASTARTE)

A famous goddess of the Zidonians. Her name in the Syrian language means *ewes whose teats are full of milk*; or it may come from Asherah, a *grove, a blessed one*. It could be in the plural because the Phoenicians had many female deities.

The Phoenicians round about Carthage reckoned Ashtaroth the equivalent of the Roman Juno. Others honour her as the wife of Ham, the father of the Canaanites. Lucian thinks - and, I suppose, very rightly - that the moon or queen of heaven was worshipped under this name. Cicero called her the fourth Venus of Syria. The Phoenician priests affirmed to Lucian that she was Europa, the daughter of their King Agenor, whom Jupiter carried off by force, and who was deified by her father's subjects to comfort him for his loss. Perhaps she is the

Aester (or Eostre) of the Saxons, from whom our term Easter is derived, thus not too far distant from the British goddess Andraste. She is variously represented: sometimes in a long, sometimes a short, dress, sometimes holding a long stick with a cross on the top, sometimes crowned with rays; at other times, with a bull's head, whose horns, according to Sanchoniatho (Johann Conradus Orellius), were emblems of the new moon. Her temple at Aphek in Lebanon was a horrible sink of the most bestial iniquity, because there, it was pretended, Venus first had intercourse with her beloved Adonis, or Tammuz.

She was probably worshipped by the Amorites in the days of Abraham, and who gave her name to Ashtarothkarnaim, that is, the Ashtaroth with two horns. (Only found in Gen. 14:5) Soon after the death of Joshua, the Israelites began to adore her; and, in all their relapses into idolatry, as under Jephthah, Eli, and Solomon, etc., she was one of their idols. Jezebel, the wife of Ahab, propagated her worship, with all its shocking abominations, among the ten northern tribes, and appointed four hundred priests for her service. Under Manasseh and Amon, she was adored with great ceremony and care in Judah, where the women wove hangings for her residence. The remnant of the Jews left with Gedaliah obstinately forwarded her worship, pretending that their forsaking of it under Josiah had been the cause of all their subsequent disasters. (Judg. 2:13, 10:6; 1 Kings 11:5, 18:19; 2 Kings 23:4, 13; Jer. 44) For Ashtoreth, see 1 Kings 11:5, 33.

ASHUR, ASSHUR

(1) The son of Shem, and father of the Assyrians. (Gen. 10:11, 22; 1 Chron. 1:17)

(2) Asshur sometimes means *Assyria* (Num. 24:22-24; Hosea 14:3 = Asshur). When I consider what Eupolemus (circa BC 158) said, that David conquered the Assyrians in Galadene (or Gilead), that Ishbosheth was made King over the Ashurites in Gilead, that Ashur joined the alliance with the Ammonites and Moabites against Jehoshaphat, that the Ashurim made benches of ivory for the Tyrians (2 Sam. 2:9; Ps. 83:8; Ezek. 27:6, 23, 32:22), I can only conclude that a colony of Assyrians settled in Arabia Deserta perhaps about the time of Cushanrishathaim.

(3) The father of Tekoa. (1 Chron. 2:24, 4:5)

ATHALIAH
The granddaughter of Omri, daughter of Ahab, and wife of Jehoram, King of Judah. She was extremely wicked, and seduced her husband and her son Ahaziah into following the idolatrous course of her father. (2 Kings 8:18-26) Informed that Jehu had slain her son and 70 other members of the royal family of Judah, many of them probably her grandchildren, she assumed the government, and, to secure it for herself, killed off all the remainder of the royal family except Joash, her infant grandchild, who was carried off by his aunt and was hidden six years in some apartment in the Temple, during which time Athaliah governed the Jews, and promoted the vilest idolatry with all her might.

In the seventh year, Jehoiada the High Priest, engaging the leading men of the kingdom in his interest, produced the young prince at a public assembly in the court of the Temple. He caused the people to take an oath of fidelity to him, and charged both them and their King to serve the Lord. Arming the Levites and other friends with weapons deposited in the Temple, he commanded one section of them to guard the royal prince, the rest to secure the gates of the sacred courts. Next, he produced the young man, put a crown on his head, anointed him with oil, and, with the sound of a trumpet, acompanied by the shouts of the populace, proclaimed him king. Alarmed at the noise, Athaliah ran to the Temple to see what was happening. Shocked at the sight of the king on his throne, she tore her clothes, and cried out, *Treason, Treason*. At Jehoiada's orders, the guard immediately carried her out of the courts and killed her at the stable gate of the palace, BC 878. (2 Kings 11; 2 Chron. 23)

AUGUSTUS CAESAR
The second Emperor of Rome. He succeeded his uncle Julius in BC 29. After being partner with Mark Antony, he defeated him at the battle of Actium in his first year, and assumed sole sovereignty. No sooner had he established universal peace and order throughout his vast Empire, than he appointed all his subjects, and the value of their property, to be entered into the public records, that he might know exactly how many subjects he had that were fit for war, or for other reasons, and whatever tax could be reasonably raised. He made three such enrolments: the second began about seven years before our Saviour's birth, and was

not then over, being the occasion of his mother and adoptive father's journey to Bethlehem at the very time of his nativity (Luke 2:1-6), although no tax was levied till some years later.

The purpose of this book is not to set out in detail this Emperor's wars with Brutus, Cassius, and other enemies of his uncle, his wars with Anthony, then with the Spaniards, Retians, and Arabs, not to mention his friendship with Herod the Great, and his relations with the Jews of Egypt and Cyrene, nor his sorting out of the Sybilline books, and destroying whatever he thought was forged and corrupted. His moderate government brought happiness to most of the known world, and almost destroyed Roman prejudice against absolute monarchy. But the sexual behaviour of his daughter Julia and her children, and other family disorders, rendered his life a burden to himself.

At last, after declaring Tiberius his successor, and giving him a number of excellent instructions, he dressed himself up as a stage player and asked his friends if he had acted his part well. He had no sooner heard that he had, than he died in the arms of his beloved wife Livia, at the age of 75 in the 56th of his reign, and 15 years after our Saviour's birth. The Apostle Paul made his appeal to this Caesar. (Acts 25:21, 25)

AZARIAH.

(1) See Ahaziah.

(2) UZZIAH, King of Judah. At the age of 16, he succeeded his father Amaziah in BC 810, and reigned 52 years. His mother's name was Jecholiah. His personal behaviour was right before God, but he neglected to demolish the high places, or restrain the people from sacrificing on them. During the first part of his reign, politically, he was extremely successful. He terribly mauled the Philistines, breaking down the walls of Gath, Jabneh, and Ashdod, and built his forts in their country. He routed the Arabs of Gurbaal, and the Mehunim, both of which, I suppose, dwelt on the southwest of Canaan, and spread his terror all the way down to Egypt. The Ammonites, though at a considerable distance in the east, were glad to court his favour with presents. His army amounted to 310,000, of which 2,600 were valiant commanders, Jeiel, Maaseiah, and Hananiah being its chief generals. He built a great number of forts; he fortified his cities; and he furnished his army with shields, spears, helmets, coats of chain mail, bows, and slings. He intructed his artificers

to make for him special engines to throw huge stones at a great distance, and to shoot arrows with unusual force. Meanwhile, by his example, he encouraged every kind of husbandry.

While the pious Zechariah continued to be his counsellor, Uzziah's conduct was regular; but, after his death, his prosperity made him so proud that he used to rush into the Temple to burn incense. Azariah the High Priest checked him boldly, and told him that his unholy attempts to burn incense would bring about his shame. While Uzziah stood enraged at these words, leprosy broke out on his forehead. The priests directly thrust him out of the Temple; indeed, he was in a hurry to get out. He continued as a leper till the day he died, living in a separate house, while his son Jotham managed the affairs of the kingdom. (2 Kings 15; 2 Chron. 26) Josephus writes of a great earthquake occurring the moment Uzziah was struck with the leprosy, but nothing could be more demonstrably untrue. The earthquake happened two years after Amos began to prophesy, and consequently during the reign of Jeroboam, thus in, or before, the 15th year of Uzziah, 12 years at least before Jotham was born, and about 36 years before he was capable of governing the state. (Compare Amos 1:1 with 2 Kings 14:23 and 15:32-34).

(3) The son of Oded, a prophet, who, after the defeat of the Cushites, remonstrated with Asa on the low state of religion, declaring that happiness could only be expected by the way they served God. He encouraged him to proceed further in reforming the kingdom; and his admonition was obeyed. (2 Chron. 15)

(4) Jehoshaphat had two sons of this name. They, and their brothers Jehiel, Zechariah, Michael, and Shephatiah were portioned out before their father's death; but soon afterwards, were murdered by Jehoram their older brother. (2 Chron. 21:2-4, 13) We find four other princes of this name: two under Solomon, another the son of Nathan the prophet. (1 Kings 4:2, 5, 15) Another one, along with Berechiah, Jehizkiah, and Amasa the son of Hadlai, at the instigation of Oded the prophet, opposed the bringing back of the Jewish captives taken by Ahaz into Samaria. They believed the guilt of the ten tribes was already too great, and that the retaining of these captives of their brothers would add to it. The Jews looked after those of the captives who needed to be clothed and shod, and all of them were sufficiently supplied with food. For those who were weak, they provided asses. And thus, in a most generous manner, they brought them back to Jericho. (2 Chron. 38:11-16) Another prince of

this name, and son of Hushaiah, along with Johanan the son of Kareah, accused Jeremiah of telling lies; and, contrary to the warning of God, went down into Egypt, carrying Jeremiah along with them. (Jer. 43:2)

(5) We find six priests of this name, a son and a grandson of Zadok, the last of whom is, by some, thought to be the same as Amariah the High Priest under Jehoshaphat. (1 Kings 4:2; 1 Chron. 6:9; 2 Chron. 19:11) The third was a grandson of the last mentioned; the next withstood in the way I have already described; the fifth was high priest under Hezekiah; and the sixth under Josiah. (1 Chron. 6:1-14; 2 Chron. 31:10) There were others of this name after the captivity, one of whom accompanied Ezra from Babylon, and another repaired part of the wall of Jerusalem under Nehemiah. (Ezra 7:3; Neh. 3:23)

The frequency of this name, which means *the help of the Lord*, tempts me to think that the pious Hebrews lived a great deal under a sense of their dependence on God, and the favours he showed them.

AZAZEL, *scapegoat*

Our KJV translation rightly makes the Hebrew word *scapegoat*, which was driven into the wilderness on the great day of the Fast of Expiation. Some think, it refers to a horrible precipice, over which the female goat was thrown headlong. Herman Witsius, Johannes Cocceius, and others, think this signifies Satan, for, they say, this goat was abandoned in the wilderness, or as a type of Christ led by the Spirit into the desert to be tempted by the devil, or led by Pilate and the Jews to have his heel bruised, and his life taken away outside the gate. (Lev. 16:8, 10, 26 compare with Heb. 13:12-13)

B

BAAL, *lord* or *husband*

Perhaps, in the earliest ages, it signified the true God. It is certain, that it was a very common name for the principal male idols of the east, just as Ashtaroth was a common name for their female deities. The Moabites, Phoenicians, Assyrians, Chaldeans, and often the Hebrews, had their Baal, and which, from his place of worship, or supposed office, often had distinguishing epithets added, such as Baal-berith, Baal-peor, Baal-zebub, etc. The name *Baal* was often part of

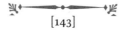

the names of people and cities, perhaps to signify that most of them were dedicated to his service. This, the pious Hebrews sometimes turned it into *Bosheth*, which means *shame*. Thus Jerubbaal is turned into Jerubbesheth, Eshbaal into Ishbosheth, and Meribaal into Mephibosheth. (Judg. 6:31-32; 2 Sam. 9:6; 1 Chron. 1:32, 34) This idol is sometimes represented as a female deity. (Rom. 11:4) On the other hand, Ashtaroth is sometimes presented as a male. Perhaps Baal is often called *Baalim* (in the plural) because there were many Baals, at least many images of him.

Who the first Baal was, whether the Chaldean Nimrod, or Belus, or the Syrian Hercules, etc., is not too clear, except that the Phoenicians adored the sun under that name, though perhaps their idolatry, described to us by secular writers, was not the most ancient, but a more recent form introduced by the Assyrians. Every sort of abomination was committed at the festivals of this idol and Ashtaroth his mate. In his *chamanim* (or temple) was kept a perpetual fire. Altars were erected to him in groves, high places, and on the tops of houses. (2 Kings 17:16, 23:4-12; Jer. 32:29, 35; Hosea 4:14)

The Moabites began their worship of Baal before the days of Moses, and the Hebrews began theirs during this time. (Num. 22:41; Ps. 106:28) They relapsed into that idolatry after the death of Joshua, and under the Judges Ehud, Gideon, and Jephthah. (Judg. 2:11, 13, 3:7-8, 13, 7:25, 10:6, 10) Samuel seems to have quite abolished the worship of this idol from Israel (1 Sam. 7:4), but Ahab and Jezebel, more than 200 years later, re-imported it from Zidon with all its abominations. There were 350 priests appointed to attend his service, and nearly as many for Ashtaroth. These priests of Baal were extremely humiliated at Mount Carmel; their God appeared quite regardless of their cries and the slashing of their flesh to move him to pity. When the impotence of their idol was exposed, they were, by Elijah's orders, arrested and slain. Jehoiada the son of Ahab did not worship Baal himself, but his subjects continued to do so. After his death, Jehu, pretending a superlative regard for Baal, convened his prophets and priests in his temple, and there put them all to the sword. Not long after, Jehoiada abolished the worship of Baal from Judah, but Ahaz and Manasseh re-introduced it. Josiah re-abolished it, but it was restored by his sons. (1 Kings 16:31-32, 18:18-19, 21, 25-26, 40; 2 Kings 3:1-2, chs.10-11, 16:16, 17, 21:34, 23:3-5; Jer. 19:5)

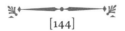

BAALZEBUB, BEELZEBUB

The idol god of Ekron. This name, meaning *lord of the flies*, does not seem to have been given him in contempt, since Ahaziah his adorer called him by it. But either because he was painted as a fly, though others say he was figured as a king on his throne, or because he was supposed to chase off the harmful swarms of flies, he could be the same as the god Achor at Cyrene, who was reckoned a preserver from flies. As the prince of devils in the New Testament is called by the name *Beelzebub*, one is tempted to suspect that he might be Pluto, or god of hell, of the Greeks. (These names are only found in the following verses: 2 Kings 1:2-3, 6, 16 = Baalzebub; Matt. 10:25, 12:24, 27; Mark 3:22; Luke 11:15, 18-19 = Beelzebub)

BALAAM

The son of Beor (or Bosor), a notable prophet or diviner of the city of Pethor on the Euphrates. Observing the vast numbers of the Hebrew nation as they passed his territories on their way to Canaan, and fearing they might fall on his country and forcibly take it from him, as they had done with the Amorites, Balak, the son of Zippor, King of Moab, in conjunction with the princes of Midian, sent messengers to this famous enchanter, promising him a valuable reward if he came and cursed the Hebrews, which they hoped would render them easily conquered. Readily, the noble messengers executed their commission. Greedy of the unholy reward, Balaam earnestly desired to comply; but, for some divine impression on his mind, he did not dare to give them an answer till, in the night, God (he possibly meant the devil) would direct him. But during that night, the true God forbade him to curse the Israelites. Vexed at this, he informed the messengers that he was divinely forbidden to go with them. On their return, Balak, supposing his messengers, presents, or promised reward, had not been to the taste of the enchanter, sent other even greater princes with very large presents, and promises of the highest advancement. To their message, Balaam replied that he could not, for a house full of gold and silver, go one inch beyond the commandment of the Lord. Longing to earn the wages of unrighteousness, he desired the messengers to wait till he had found out whether the Deity had changed his mind. During the night, God appeared and permitted him to go if the messengers insisted; but he assured him that he must curse or bless the people just as he directed him.

Without waiting for any further light, next morning, Balaam rose early and rode off with the messengers. To punish his raging avarice, the Angel of Jehovah placed himself in his way with a drawn sword in his hand. The enchanter did not perceive the Angel, but the ass did, and turned aside; so Balaam beat her back again into the road. The Angel then moved into a place between two vineyards where the ass, in fear, ran against the wall and crushed her master's foot. The angel next placed himself in a still narrower passage, when the ass fell down in fear, and dare not go forward. Enraged at that, the enchanter beat her unmercifully. Meanwhile, the Lord miraculously enabled the ass to reprove him vocally for his madness and cruelty, when he might easily have guessed there was some unusual reason for her conduct. Accustomed to speaking with devils in the form of beasts, or maddened with rage, Balaam, unaffected, talked with the ass. Jehovah immediately made himself visible with his drawn sword, rebuked him for his abuse of the beast, and assured him that, had it not been her turning aside, he would have now perished in his wicked course. Balaam confessed his guilt, and unwillingly offered to return. He was permitted to proceed on his journey provided he was careful to say nothing except as God directed him.

Informed of his approach, Balak met him on the frontiers of his kingdom, and tactfully blamed him for not coming at the first invitation. The enchanter excused himself due to the divine restraint he was under. Balak conducted him to Kirjathhazoth, his capital, and entertained him with a splendid feast. Next day, he conducted him to an adjacent hill sacred to the idol Baal that he might view the Hebrew camp from there. To obtain divine permission to curse them, Balaam desired seven altars to be reared, and a bullock and ram offered on each. His orders were directly obeyed. While Balak stood by his sacrifices, Balaam retired to meet with enchantments, or perhaps with serpents as instruments of divination. He was divinely inspired with this unwelcome message, that in vain he had been brought from the east to curse the Israelites whom God had not cursed; and that they would be the numerous and special favourites of heaven. In delivering this message, Balaam wished his death, and that his posterity might resemble that of Jacob.

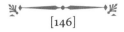

Balak was heartily vexed, but hoped that change of place, or alteration of prospect, might bring him better luck. He carried Balaam to the top of Pisgah where he saw just a section of the Hebrew camp. With seven altars erected, and a bullock and a ram offered on each, he again retired to think up some enchantment against them. God met him, and ordered him back to tell Balak that the unchangeable and almighty Jehovah had blessed the Hebrews, had forgiven their iniquities, took delight in them, and had, by miracles, brought them out of Egypt, and would enable them like lions to devour the nations and seize on their property. Offended at this, Balak begged that he would at least refrain from blessing them. The enchanter assured him that he was divinely constrained to act as he did.

Still intent to have Israel cursed, both agreed to make a third trial. On the top of Peor, seven other altars were reared, and a bullock and a ram offered on each. Determined by God, Balaam forbore to seek for enchantments, but, turning his face to the Hebrew tents, after a haughty preface, he extolled the beautiful arrangement of their encampment. He foretold that they would become a flourishing and mighty nation, far superior to every foe, and that those who blessed and favoured them would be blessed, and those who cursed and hated them would be cursed and ruined. Transported with rage, Balak charged him to get himself home to his country, since, by adhering to divine suggestions, he had abused him, and deprived himself of honour and wealth. Balaam replied that, from the very first, he had told his messengers he could do nothing except what God permitted. He added that, in aftertimes, a Hebrew prince would subdue the country of Moab; that a Hebrew Messiah, marked at his birth by a star, would subdue the world to the obedience of faith; that Idumea and Seir would be ruined, while the Hebrews would do valiantly; that Amalek, however powerful at present, would, for their injuries to that people, perish for ever; that the Kenites, despite their advantageous habitation among the rocks, would, after a variety of distresses, be carried captive to Assyria; that the Greeks from Macedonia, and the Romans from Italy, would seize on Assyria and its conquests, and, at last, perish themselves.

Some have thought Balak, in his earnestness to have Israel cursed, asked Balaam whether, by offering thousands of rams, and ten thousand rivers of oil, or sacrificing his firstborn, he might obtain his desire; but he replied that the only way to find favour with God was to *do justly, and love mercy, and walk humbly with God.* But that question and its answer seem plainly to refer to the Jews and the prophet Micah. (Micah 6:7-8) It is certain that Balaam advised Balak to cause the most beautiful women of his country to frequent the Hebrew camp, and entice the people into prostitution and idolatry, and thereby deprive them of God's favour. This infernal suggestion issued in the death of 1000 Hebrews by public execution, and 23,000 more by plague. Not long after, God appointed Israel to resist these enticements by the Midianites. Balaam was killed in that war, and fell into the pit he had dug for others. (Num. chs.12-16, 24-25, and 32; Deut. 23:4-5; Josh. 24:9; Neh. 13:2; Micah 6:5) Balaam is called a prophet not merely because he pretended to foretell things by enchantments, but because God inspired him against his will to foresee and declare a variety of future events. (2 Pet. 2:15) Some false teachers of the apostolic age were compared to Balaam, as they, like him, loved the wages of unrighteousness, and taught the doctrine of sexual immorality and idolatry. (Jude v. 11; Rev. 2:14)

Extra note

The history of Balaam has occasioned much controversy, and the question whether he was a prophet of the Lord, or merely an enchanter whose powers originated from Satan, yet remains undecided among the scholars. On the one hand, it is observed that he is called *a prophet* (2 Pet. 2:16), and that he calls the God of Israel *The Lord my God.* (Num. 22:18) Those who were prophets in the apostolic age, and were seduced from the truth by covetousness and ambition, are presented as Balaam's followers, *cursed children who have forsaken the right way,* which seems to imply that he, like them, had once assumed the character of a prophet of the Lord. That he was not an Israelite is no solid objection to this, for it is evident that the knowledge of the true God was not confined to the Jews: he revealed himself to Abimelech (Gen. 20), to Pharaoh (Gen. 41), and to Nebuchadnezzar (Dan. 2). And in what striking language do Job and his friends speak of the true God!

On the other hand, it is remarked that he came from Aram or Mesopotamia, out of the mountains of the East, a country famous for soothsayers and diviners (Isa. 2:6), that his mode of worship was contrary to the Law of Moses (Num. 23:1-2), that he went after

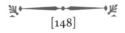

enchantments (Num. 24:1), and that he is expressly called a *soothsayer* (Josh. 13:22). Let the reader judge for himself. It may, however, be proper to add that if Balaam was merely an enchanter, how did God speak through him? The magicians did their utmost in Egypt, and in Babylon, but heaven never employed them to prophesy; and if merely an *enchante*r, how does his love of the wages of unrighteousness become a beacon to the Church of God? The speaking of the ass has been a fund of mockery for unbelievers. We have a solid reply: Balaam was rebuked for his iniquity; the dumb ass, speaking with man's mouth, forbade the madness of the prophet. Says Bishop Thomas Newton, "The miracle was not superfluous; it evidenced that the same divine power that caused the dumb ass to speak compelled Balaam to utter blessings contrary to his inclination."

BAPTIST

John, the son of Zacharias, was so-called because he was the first to administer baptism as an ordinance of God. (Matt. 3:1) See JOHN THE BAPTIST

BARABBAS

This was the name of a notorious robber, guilty of treason and murder. He happened to be imprisoned for his crimes when Christ's trial was in progress. As it was normal to release some prisoner to the Jews at their feast of Passover, Pilate put Jesus and Barabbas in competition that the Jews might choose one of them for release. Contrary to his expectation and wishes, they warmly begged for the release of the notorious criminal and the crucifixion of the blessed Jesus. (Matt. 27:16-26; Mark 15:7-15; Luke 23:18; John 18:40)

BARAK, *lightning.* See DEBORAH

See Judges 4:6, 8-10, 12, 14-16, 22, 5:1, 12, 15; Hebrews 11:32.

BARJESUS

In the Arabic language, his name was Elymas, or *the sorcerer*. He was a notable Jewish magician in the island of Cyprus. When Sergius Paulus, the prudent deputy or proconsul of that place under the Roman Emperor, sent for Paul and Barnabas to hear from them the teachings of Christianity, this sorcerer tried to hinder the deputy's conversion.

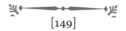

With holy indignation, Paul looked at him, pronounced him full of all subtilty and mischief, an enemy of all righteousness, and an unceasing perverter of the right ways of the Lord, and foretold that his opposition to the light of gospel truth would quickly be punished with the loss of his natural sight. The threat took effect immediately, and the sorcerer was obliged to ask someone to lead him along the way. In view of this miracle, the deputy determined to embrace the Christian faith at once; and it is likely he conferred his own name *Paulus* on Saul, the honoured instrument of his conversion. (Only found in Acts 13:8-12)

BARJONA
A designation of Peter, indicating that he was *the son of Jona*, or *Jonas*. (Only found in Matt. 16:1; compare John 1:42, 21:17)

BARNABAS
His ancestors were Levites, and he had retired to Cyprus perhaps to shun the ravages of the Syrians, Romans, or others in Judea. Here he was born, and was at first called Joses. But after his conversion to the Christian faith, he was called Barnabas, *the son of prophecy*, from his eminent gifts and foresight of future things, or *the son of consolation* because his large estate, and affectionate preaching, greatly comforted the early believers. (Acts 4:36-37) That he was one of the Seventy disciples of our Saviour, or was educated by Gamaliel along with Paul, we have no certain evidence; but it was he who introduced Paul to the Christians of Jerusalem, and assured them of his conversion. (Acts 9:26-27) He was sent to order the affairs of the church newly planted at Antioch in Syria; and, finding the work too heavy for him, he went to Tarsus and engaged Paul to be his companion. Sometime later, he and Paul carried a large contribution from Antioch to their starving brothers in Judea. (Acts 11:22-30)

Not long after, he and Paul were divinely appointed to leave Antioch and plant new churches among the Gentiles. After three years, they returned. At Lystra, during their second journey into Asia Minor, Barnabas was taken for Jupiter, probably because of his attractive appearance and serious manner. Some time later, he and Paul were delegates from the Syrian church to the Council at Jerusalem, and were then appointed to carry the decrees to the Gentile churches. At Antioch, Barnabas was led astray into Judaistic Christianity by Peter.

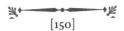

On their return to Asia Minor, he and Paul had a sharp argument about taking Mark, Barnabas' nephew, along with them; so they separated, and Barnabas and Mark went to Cyprus. (Acts chs.13-15; Gal 2:13) What became of him afterward, whether, as some suggest, he preached in Italy, and was stoned to death at Salamis near Athens, we do not know. A spurious Gospel and Epistle are ascribed to him.

BARSABAS

(1) Joseph Justus was perhaps one of Christ's Seventy disciples. It is certain that he was an eyewitness of Christ's public work and ministry. He stood as candidate, along with Matthias, for the apostleship in place of Judas, but was not chosen by God. (Found only in Acts 1:21-26)

(2) Barsabas Judas. He was a member of the Council of Jerusalem, and was sent along with Paul, Barnabas, and Silas, to publish its decrees among the Gentile churches. After preaching a while at Antioch, he returned to Jerusalem. (Found only in Acts 15:22-34)

BARTHOLOMEW

He was one of our Lord's twelve Apostles. As John never mentions Bartholomew, but refers only to Nathanael, and the other Evangelists never mention Nathanael but Bartholomew, and as John couples Philip with Nathanael as the others do Philip and Bartholomew, and as Nathanael is mentioned with the other Apostles that met with their risen Saviour at the Sea of Tiberias, and as Bartholomew is not a proper name, but only signifies *the son of Tolmai* (just as Peter was called Barjona), so we suppose Bartholomew and Nathanael were one and the same person. Informed by Philip concerning our Saviour as the true Messiah, Nathanael doubted how anything good could come out of a place so notoriously obscure or wicked as Nazareth. Philip desired him to satisfy himself concerning Jesus' excellence by conversing with him; so he agreed. At the sight of him, Jesus declared him *an Israelite indeed,* without any fraud and guile. Nathanael asked how he knew him? Jesus replied that he knew what had passed under a certain fig tree where he used to retire to his most private devotions. Struck with this discovery of Christ's omniscience, Nathanael, all in a rapture, acknowledged him as the Son of God, and the promised Messiah or King of Israel. Jesus assured him that his ready faith would be quickly rewarded with further proof of his Messiahship. He would see the angels of God attend him (as the angels on Jacob's ladder), and serve him as their high and sovereign Lord. Sometime later, he was sent along with Philip to preach and work miracles in the land of Israel. And, with the other Apostles, he received frequent visits from his risen Redeemer. (Matt. 10:3; Mark 3:18; Luke 6:14; John 1:45-51, chs.20-21; Acts 1:13)

After teaching in Jerusalem for about 18 years, he is said to have preached to the East Indians, and committed to them *the Gospel according to Matthew*. From there, it is said, he travelled to Lycaonia; and, at last, was flayed alive by the Albanians on the Caspian Sea, and crucified with his head downwards. A spurious Gospel is attributed to him.

BARTIMEUS, *son of Timeus*

A blind man, who sat begging by the wayside as Jesus passed by with a great crowd from Jericho to Jerusalem. Informed that Jesus was among this crowd, he cried out, *Jesus, thou Son of David, have mercy on me.* Jesus stopped, and ordered him to he brought near. This was done. Jesus asked him what he desired from his hand? He begged for the recovery of his sight. Jesus bade him go his way, for his faith had saved him. Immediately, he received his sight, and followed his divine Physician. Mark 10:46-52 is the only time his name is mentioned. Matthew mentions two blind men cured on this occasion (Matt. 20:30-34), but, as Bartimeus was most outstanding, or expressed the greatest earnestness and the strongest faith, Mark mentions him and omits the other. It is Luke who relates the cure of another blind man by Christ on his going to Jericho. (Luke 18:35-43) Oh, how fast, how cheerfully, would our Redeemer heal our spiritual maladies, if asked!

BARUCH

(1) A Jewish prince, son of Neriah, grandson of Maaseiah, and brother of Seraiah one of Zedekiah's courtiers, who attached himself to the prophet Jeremiah, and was, for some time, his secretary or scribe. When King Jehoiakim imprisoned that prophet, Baruch, according to the direction of God, wrote the prophecies from his mouth, and read them to the people as they assembled at some special fast. The courtiers, informed of this by Michaiah, one of his hearers, sent for him, and he read them again in their hearing. Affected with what they had heard,

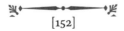

the courtiers advised Baruch and Jeremiah to bide their time, for it was their duty to lay the matter before the king. Having laid up the writing in the chamber of Elishama the scribe, they waited on the King, and informed him of its contents. On his order, Jehudi fetched and read it before him and his princes. Hardly had four or five pages been read, when Jehoiakim, in a rage, and contrary to the intercession of several princes, took the manuscript, cut it in pieces, and threw it into the fire. He gave orders to arrest Jeremiah and Baruch, but they could not be found. Soon after, Baruch wrote another copy, more enlarged, from the mouth of the prophet. Baruch, having lost all probable aspiration to honour and wealth, and being in danger of his life, grew extremely depressed. Inspired by God, Jeremiah reproved him for his ambition after *great things*, when the ruination of Judah was at hand, and assured him of divine protection in every circumstance. (Jer. 36, 45)

In the 10th year of Zedekiah, Baruch, under Jeremiah's direction, carried his deeds of the field of Hanameel, and put them in an earthen vessel, that they might remain safe till after the Captivity. After Jerusalem was taken, Nebuzaradan allowed Jeremiah and Baruch to remain in Judea with Gedaliah. After the murder of that good deputy, Johanan, and other principal men, falsely blamed Baruch for enviously exciting Jeremiah to forbid their going to Egypt, and carried them both into that country. Whether Baruch, after the death of Jeremiah, removed from Egypt to Babylon, we do not know. An Apocryphal book is falsely ascribed to him. (Jer. 32:12-16, 43:3, 6)

(2) The son of Zabbai. Under the direction of Nehemiah, he earnestly repaired a part of the wall of Jerusalem. Perhaps, too, he sealed the covenant of reformation, and was the father of Maaseiah. (Neh. 3:20, 10:6, 11:5)

BARZILLAI, *hard as iron*

(1) A Simeonite of Meholah, and father of Adriel, the husband of Merah, the daughter of Saul. (1 Sam. 18:19; 2 Sam. 21:8)

(2) A Gileadite of Rogelim, who plentifully supplied David and his small army with provisions as they lay at Mahanaim during the revolt of Absalom. On David's return to his capital, and to take possession of his royal dignity, Barzillai accompanied him to the passage of Jordan. David insisted that he should go and dwell with him at Jerusalem, but Barzillai pleaded old age and unfitness for the court. His excuse

was allowed, and David dismissed him to go home with the warmest embraces; but, with his permission, he retained at court Chimham his son. (2 Sam. 17:27-29; 19:31, 40)

(3) A priest descended from the daughter of the former Barzillai, and head of a number of priests that returned from the Babylonian captivity. (Ezra 2:61; Neh. 7:63)

BATHSHEBA, *the seventh daughter*

Or Bathshua (1 Chron. 3:5), the daughter of Eliam (see 2 Sam. 11:3, 23:34), (or Ammiel), perhaps granddaughter of Ahithophel, and wife of Uriah the Hittite. While her husband was employed in the siege of Rabbah, she happened to be bathing, it seems, in her garden. David spied her from the top of his adjacent palace, and, being informed who she was, sent for her and seduced her. Falling pregnant, she informed King David of it, that he might devise how to conceal their guilt. He sent directly for Uriah, as if intending to learn the affairs of the siege; but his real design was to give him an opportunity of being with his wife, and so become the reputed father of the child. Uriah came, and, after a few trifling questions concerning the state and progress of the army, David ordered him home to his house, and sent food from his own table after him. Determined by providence and his self control and bravery, Uriah thought it beneath himself to enjoy sexual pleasures while his fellow-soldiers were encamped in the field of battle; so he slept with the guards at the palace gate. Informed of this, next day, David called him to his table, and, to inflame his appetite, made him drink heartily, and then ordered him home. Uriah again slept with the guards, and excused himself to the King by alleging that it was improper for him to enjoy the embraces of his wife while Joab and the army, indeed, the ark of God, were encamped in the open field of battle. Vexed with this disappointment, David sent him back to the army with a letter, directing Joab how to accomplish his murder. Bathsheba, hearing quickly of her husband's death, and having mourned in the usual way, David sent for her and married her. The child conceived in adultery had only just been born when it fell sick; and, despite David's repentance and fasting, died as was threatened by Nathan in the name of the Lord. Bathsheba, however, was honoured to bear David four more sons, including Solomon, and another Nathan, both ancestors of Jesus Christ. (2 Sam. 11-12; Matt. 1:6)

Bathsheba, it seems, was extremely careful in the upbringing of her children, particularly Solomon, concerning whom many promises were made. The last chapter of Proverbs, perhaps, contains some of her instructions. David, having promised to her that Solomon her son would be his successor, a warm public declaration from her and Nathan the prophet prevented Adonijah from seizing the throne, and procured the coronation of Solomon. When, on Adonijah's instigation, she petitioned for his being allowed to marry Abishag, his father's concubine, Solomon, however honourably he received her, with no small spirit, and with marks of displeasure, he rejected her petition. (1 Kings 1:11.15-16, 28, 31, 2:13, 18-19)

BELIAL

A name given to Satan, presenting him *without yoke, profit,* or *ascent.* To mark out people who are worthless, wicked, and unruly, or things most horrible and abominable, they were called children, men, or things, of *Belial.* (Deut. 13:13; 1 Sam. 1:16, 2:12, 25:17, 25, 30:22; 2 Sam. 20:1, 23:62; 2 Cor. 6:15)

BELOVED

Christ is the *beloved* of God, who infinitely esteems, loves, and delights in him as his Son and mediatorial servant. (Matt. 3:17) He is the *beloved* of the saints, and is highly esteemed, desired, praised, and delighted in with their whole heart, mind, and strength. (Song 4:16) Saints are the *beloved* of God and Christ, and the Church a *beloved* city. In infinite love for them, God devised their salvation, and Jesus laid down his life, and now intercedes for them. All the divine Persons concur to save and delight in them. (Song 5:1-2; Rev. 20:9)

BELSHAZZAR. Nabonedus, or Labynitus.

The son of Evilmerodach and Nitocris, and grandson of Nebuchadnezzar, and King of Babylon. He was a most worthless and inactive wretch; but his famous mother exerted herself greatly for the support of the kingdom. About the 17th year of his reign, in BC 538, and just when Cyrus the famous conqueror was laying siege to his capital, Belshazzar, probably during a festival sacred to the idol Sheshach, put on a splendid feast for a thousand of his lords. Heated with wine, he ordered the sacred vessels taken from the Temple of God at Jerusalem to be brought in. These, he, his wives, concubines, and lords, drank from in a drunken and idolatrous manner, singing songs in honour of their idols. An angel, taking the form of a hand, wrote the king's condemnation on the wall, checking their mirth, and filling them with terror. Belshazzar was in such a panic that the joints of his thighs loosed, and he trembled greatly. None present could either read or explain the writing. The magicians, astrologers, and others famous for their wisdom, were called, and a scarlet suit of apparel, a gold chain for his neck, and the office of third ruler in the kingdom, was the reward promised to whoever could read and interpret it. Ignorant of the characters, or struck with a panic, none of them could pretend to read or interpret the writing. The wise Nitocris, hearing of the perplexity of her son and his courtiers, wanted Daniel, who, it seems, had long been a stranger to the court, to be sent for, whom she hoped would read and interpret it.

Daniel was immediately brought in, and a reward offered him, which he modestly refused. After a faithful reproof of the king for his idolatry, and his ungrateful abuse of the sacred vessels of the Jewish Temple, he read the writing, which went like this: *Mene, mene, tekel, upharsin.* MENE, said he to the king, means that God has numbered the days of your royalty, and is just finishing it. TEKEL, you are weighed in the balances of God's purpose and law, and are found wanting in goodness, and you will suddenly be cut off. PERES, your kingdom is divided, forced away from you, and given to the Medes and Persians. Daniel immediately received the promised reward; and it seems the king and his courtiers returned to their drinking. Cyrus, the general of the Persian troops, and his uncle, Darius the Mede, had already besieged Babylon for two years without success. Foreseeing this feast, he diverted the Euphrates from its channel, and, that very night, he marched his troops along its channel. The brazen gates on the river had been left open by the drunken Chaldeans, so the soldiers rushed in and filled the city with terrible bloodshed and confusion. Gobrias and Gadata, two Babylonian deserters, with some choice Persian warriors, rushed into the palace, killed the guards, plunged their swords into the bowels of King Belshazzar and his nobles while they were scarcely awake from their sleep and drunkenness. It seems the king's corpse had not so much as a decent burial.

Christian historians sufficiently agree that Babylon was taken by the Persians, Medes, and Armenians, with the Empire given over to the Medes, and thus to the Persians. All agree that, after Belshazzar, no Chaldean reigned in Babylon; but, as Herodotus relates, quite differently from the Scriptural account, not all are agreed that Belshazzar was Nabonedus, or if he was Nebuchadnezzar's grandson. Joseph Juste Scaliger identifies him with the infant Laboroschard, the son of Neriglissar by Nebuchadnezzar's daughter. Marcham identifies him as Evilmerodach. But it is certain that God promised the service of the nations to Nebuchadnezzar, and his *son*, and his *son's son*. It is plain then, that Belshazzar could not be Evilmerodach, who was only the son of Nebuchadnezzar. Nor could he be Laboroschard, who was only Nebuchadnezzar's daughter's son, and, besides, reigned just a few months, and died an infant, whereas Belshazzar reigned several years, and had wives and concubines. (Isa. 13-14; Jer. 1, 51; Dan. 5 and 8)

BELTESHAZZAR, *keeping Bel's treasures*
A name given to Daniel. (Dan. 1:7) See Daniel

BENAIAH, *the son of Jah*
This son of Jehoiada was one of David's valiant men, and captain of his guard. He killed the two famous Ariels of Moab. He killed a lion that had slipped into a pit in the time of snow. Armed with a staff, he attacked an Egyptian champion carrying a spear, plucked the spear out of his hand, and slew him immediately. Having adhered to Solomon against Adonijah, and assisted at his coronation, he was made general in the place of Joab; and, on Solomon's orders, he put Joab and Adonijah to death. (2 Sam. 23:20, 23, 30; 1 Kings 1-2)

BENAMMI, *the son of my people*
Sadly, the son of Lot by his second daughter. (Only found in Gen. 19:38)

BENHADAD, *son of noise*
(1) The son of Tabrimon, and King of Syria. Prompted by Asa's presents, he broke his league with Baasha, King of Israel, and ravaged the northern parts of his kingdom. In the reign of Omri or Ahab, he

constructed streets, marketplaces, or rather citadels for himself in Samaria. (1 Kings 15:18, 20, 20:34)

(2) Benhadad, the son and successor of the former, was a still more terrible scourge to the kingdom of Israel. In the reign of Ahab, he ravaged the country, laid siege to Samaria the capital, insolently claimed his wives, children, and wealth, and everything valuable in the city. The Israelites rejected his absurd conditions, and were miraculously enabled, with a few troops, to rout his powerful army. Remembering that God gave the Law from a mountain, and had his Temple on another, his servants persuaded Benhadad that the Hebrew God was only the *God of the hills*, and that, had they fought them in a plain, they would have certainly gained the victory. This silly superstition he readily believed; and, displacing his thirty-two tributary kings from their place in his army, he filled it with captains, who, he hoped, were more skilful or trustworthy in war. The next year, he returned to make a full conquest of the kingdom of Israel. To chastise his wickedness, God, with a handful of Israelites, inflicted on him a terrible defeat. A hundred thousand of his forces were slain on the spot. An earthquake tumbled the wall of Aphek upon 27,000 more, crushing them to death. Reduced to the brink of despair, Benhadad, on his servant's advice, threw himself on Ahab's mercy. The insolent blasphemer had not only his life granted him, but liberty to return to his kingdom on the easiest of terms. Contrary even to these, he detained Ramothgilead, a city of Israel in his hands; and, when Ahab attempted to wrest it from him, he most ungratefully ordered his troops to aim their strokes chiefly at him, who, by a sinful excess of pity, had so lately granted him his life and kingdom. (1 Kings 20, 22)

Soon after, he made war on Jehoram, Ahab's successor, and carried off a number of Hebrew captives. Informed by one of these that a Hebrew prophet could cure Naaman his general of leprosy, he sent him to King Jehoram for that purpose. The general had just returned home, cured of his loathsome disease, when Benhadad poured his ravaging troops into the kingdom of Israel, chiefly aiming at cutting off Jehoram himself. Informed that Elisha had revealed his designs to Jehoram, he sent a party to arrest the prophet. At Elisha's request, God smote them with partial blindness, and he led them to Samaria where King Jehoram would have killed them. But, advised by Elisha, he gave them refreshment, and dismissed them in safety. Terrified at Elisha's power, or moved by Jehoram's generosity, for about four years, Benhadad withdrew his plundering bands. At last, he invaded the country, and besieged Samaria till the famine grew excessive. The head of an ass was sold for almost £10, about 3 gills (¾ of a pint) of "doves' dung" (coarse pulse) cost 12 shillings, and women ate their own infants. Elisha foretold that next day a bushel of fine flour and two bushels of barley would be sold for about half a crown (12½ pence). That very night, the Lord terrified the Syrian host. They imagined and heard a terrible noise, and concluded that Jehoram had hired a huge army of Egyptians, Hittites, and others, to swallow them up. In great consternation, they fled from their camp, leaving it just as it was. On the way, they flung off their garments, and threw away what they had taken with them. Four lepers, whom hunger had forced to cast themselves on the Syrians' mercy, finding the camp deserted, informed King Jehoram. After some precautions, and taken to see if the Syrians had really fled, the Hebrews plundered the camp, and the "plenty" fulfilled the prophet's prediction. (2 Kings 5-7) Next year, Benhadad fell ill and, being informed that Elisha was somewhere near Damascus, he sent to him Hazael his general with a present of forty camel loads of the most precious things of Syria, to inquire if he would recover. Elisha replied that there was nothing mortal in his illness, but, however, he would certainly die. Hazael informed his master that the prophet foretold his recovery. But, to prevent it, he took a thick cloth, dipped it in water, spread it on his master's face, and so suffocated him to death; he then seized his throne. (2 Kings 8)

(3) Benhadad, the son of Hazael, also became King of Syria. Under him, the kingdom was brought to the brink of ruin. Jehoash and Jeroboam, kings of Israel, beat his troops in a variety of pitched battles, and forced him to restore to the Israelites whatever his predecessors had seized. (2 Kings 12:3)

BENJAMIN

The youngest son of Jacob and Rachel, born in BC 1732. His mother, dying in childbirth, called him Benoni, *the son of my sorrow*; but, unwilling to have the name as a constant reminder of his beloved Rachel's death, Jacob called him Benjamin, the *son of the right hand*. He married young, and was scarcely 32 years of age when he had ten sons: Belah, Becher, Ashbel, Gera, Naaman, Eli (or Ahiram), Rosh,

Muppim (Shupham), Huppim (Hupham), and Ard, five of whom died childless. (Gen. 35:18, 24, 46:19, 21) When a famine obliged Jacob to send his other ten sons to Egypt for corn, he kept Benjamin at home, in consideration of the only surviving child of his beloved wife. Joseph ordered them to bring Benjamin down with them at their return, or they would be arrested as spies. With no small reluctance, Jacob was at last persuaded to let him go. To test his brothers' affection for him, Joseph, after giving him superior honours at his feast, soon brought him into great danger when his silver cup was found in his sack, as if stolen by him. Soon afterwards, he gave him five suits of clothing, and about £53 in money.

In his last benediction, Jacob foretold that the tribe of Benjamin would, at the beginning and end of the Jewish state, be remarkable for valour and ravage, and Moses said that it would have safe residence among the people of God. (Gen. 42-45, 49:27; Deut. 33:12) When this tribe came out of Egypt, it consisted of five families: the Belaites, Ashbellites, Ahiramites, Shuphamites, and Huphamites. Their chief prince was Abidan, the son of Gideoni; the number of armed men under him was 35,400. In the wilderness, they increased to 45,600. They marched in the camp of Ephraim, and pitched their tents behind the Tabernacle. Their spy to search the Promised Land was Palti, the son of Raphu; their prince to divide it was Elided the son of Chislon. Their inheritance lay to the north and northeast of the lot of Judah. (Num. 1:11, 36-37, 2:18-22, 13:9, 26:38-41, 34:21; Josh. 18) Not long after the death of Joshua, this tribe patronised the sexually coarse wretches of Gibeon, and drew a war upon themselves. They were then famous warriors, especially in the use of the bow. With 25,000, they twice defeated about 368,000 of the other tribes, and slew 40,000. In the third battle, they were defeated, and, except for 600 who fled to the rock Rimmon, their whole tribe was cut off. The extermination of this tribe brought great grief to their brothers as soon as they had leisure to think about it. They, therefore, from the virgins of Jabeshgilead and Shiloh, procured wives for the 600 that remained. (Judg. 20-21, It was perhaps hardly 60 years later, when Ehud, one of this tribe, judged Israel, and delivered them from the Moabites. Saul and Ishbosheth, the first kings of Israel, were of this tribe. About 20 of the most valiant of this tribe came over to David before Saul's death (1 Chron. 12:2, 16, 29), and 3000 more after the death of Ishbosheth.

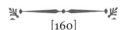

When David numbered them a little before his death, there were of the Belaites 22,034 warriors, of the Becherites 20,200, of the Jediaelites 17,200, besides others. (1 Chron. 7:6-12) The captain of their 24,000 trained bands was Abiezer the Anetothite, and their chief prince was Jasiel the son of Abner. (1 Chron. 27:12, 21) When the other ten tribes revolted in favour of Jeroboam, the Benjamites remained faithful to Judah and the house of David; and, all along, shared in the religion and fate of that tribe. Under Jehoshaphat, their militia amounted to 38,000. After the Captivity, a vast number of them lived in Jerusalem. (1 Chron. 8-9; 2 Chron. 11-12)

But the great honour of this tribe was the Apostle Paul, who, in the morning of his life, ravaged the Christians as a persecutor, but who, in the latter half, converted multitudes to Christ. (Gen. 49:27 compare Rom. 11:1 and Phil. 3:5)

BERA

A King of Sodom who saw his country severely ravaged by Chedor-laomer and his allies. When Abraham defeated the conquerors, and recovered the spoil, Bera offered him the whole booty, the captives excepted. But Abraham refused any part of it, lest it should be said that not Jehovah, but the King of Sodom, had made him rich. (Only found in Gen. 14:1-24)

BERNICE, *a sage victory*

The daughter of Agrippa the Great. She was first betrothed to Mark, the son of Alexander, governor of the Jews at Alexandria. She next married her own uncle, Herod, King of Chalcis. After his death, she married Polemon, King of Pontus, on condition that he was circumcised. She very quickly abandoned him, and returned to Agrippa, her brother, with whom, it is believed, she lived in habitual incest. They both appeared with great pomp to hear Paul's defence at Caesarea. (Only found in Acts 25:13, 23 and 26:30)

BEULAH, *married*

A name given to the Jewish nation, and the Church of God in the latter days, speaking of their marriage to Christ as their husband and sovereign Lord. (Only found in Isa. 62:4)

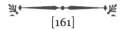

BEZALEEL, *in the shadow of God*
The son of Uri, of the tribe of Judah. He and Aholiab the son of Ahisamach, of the tribe of Dan, were two notable artificers (craftsmen), called by God, and eminently qualified with wisdom and skill. Their main task was to form the various things connected with the Mosaic Tabernacle, and perform everything with perfect exactness. Were they not in this *figures* of Jesus Christ who, being called of God, and qualified with the spirit of wisdom and understanding, rears up his Church in exact agreement with his Father's purpose and will? (Exod. 31, 36, 39)

BILDAD
A descendant of Shuah, the son of Abraham by Keturah. He was one of Job's four visitors in his distress. In his first two replies to Job, he attempted to prove that God only punishes notable transgressors with severe affliction, and insinuated that Job's severe calamities were a proof of his being a hypocrite. In his last, he celebrated the greatness and infinite purity of God in contrast with man's sinfulness (Job 8:1-7), and asked how a man can be justified before God (25:1-6).

BILHAH
The handmaid of Rachel, concubine of Jacob, and mother of Dan and Naphtali. She committed adultery with Reuben, thus losing him his birthright. (Gen. 35:22)

BOANERGES, *sons of thunder*
See James and John, sons of Zebedee. (Found only in Mark 3:17)

BOAZ, *in strength*
Or *Booz*, a noble and wealthy Jew, the son of Salmon and Rahab, who lived in Bethlehem; and, after much kindness to Ruth, a poor Moabitish widow, he married her, and had a son by her called Obed. Since roughly 360 years passed between the marriage of Salmon and the birth of David, some have put forward two or three who went by the name of Boaz; but a threefold genealogy concurs to overthrow such a supposition; nor is it necessary. Boaz could have been born about 60 years after the death of Moses. In the 100th year of his life, he married Ruth and had Obed. In the 100th year of his life, Obed had Jesse. About the same age, Jesse had David the youngest of his sons.

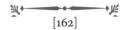

Was not Boaz a figure of our blessed Redeemer who, though great and wealthy, thought kindly of us sinners among the Gentiles, and, after many tokens of kindness, espoused us to himself as his Church and people? (Ruth 2-4, compare with Isa. 54:1-6)

BRANCH

Christ is called the *Branch*, and the *Branch of righteousness*. As regards his human nature, he sprang from the root of Jesse. His human nature has no personality of its own, but exists as an engrafted branch into his divine Person. He flourishes and protects his people with his shadow, and brings forth the highest honour to God, and the greatest happiness to men. He is infinitely righteous in himself and in his acts, and is made of God to us righteousness. (Isa. 4:2; 11:1, 53:2; Jer. 23:5, 33:15; Zech. 3:8, 6:12) When he is compared with a tree, his boughs are his ordinances, and his protecting and supportive power and grace. (Ezek. 17:23) The saints are compared with *branches*; they are united to Jesus, and derive their nourishing influence from him as their root. They refresh and protect the world with their shadow, and produce the fruit of holiness. (John 15:2-6) And when they are compared with trees, their boughs are like the top of the palm trees, and their heavenly graces and exercises, which are many, are closely and beautifully connected, and stand out in a fleshly world. (Song 7:8)

BUZ, *despising*

The son of Nahor by Milcah, and the ancestor of Elihu, the companion of Job. His posterity dwelt in Arabia the Desert, and were terribly distressed and enslaved by Nebuchadnezzar. (Gen. 22:21; Job 32:2, 6; Jer. 25:23)

C

CAIAPHAS

The High Priest of the Jews who succeeded Simon, the son of Camith about AD 16, or 25 (as Augustine Calmet thinks), and married the daughter of Annas. It is certain that he was High Priest the year in which our Saviour was crucified. When the priests and Pharisees, heartily vexed at the raising of Lazarus from the dead, consulted together whether they should arrest Jesus or not and put him to death, Caiaphas rebuked them for their stupidity, and told them it was necessary for Jesus to die for the people that the whole nation might not perish. Doubtless, he meant that his death was necessary to prevent the Romans destroying their nation; but the Spirit of God, who directed his lips in this sentence, signified that Jesus' death was necessary for the salvation of the children of God, whether Jew or Gentile. (John 11:49-50)

When Jesus was arrested by the servants of Caiaphas and other rascals, he was first brought to Annas and examined by him. Next, he was taken to Caiaphas' hall, where the priests and elders were convened to judge him. After nothing could be proved against him by their bribed witnesses, Caiaphas, in order to find a charge against him, commanded him by the living God to declare whether he was the Christ, the true Messiah, or not. Jesus acknowledged that he was, and would later appear gloriously in the clouds. Caiaphas, as if shocked, tore his clothes, and, warning the company to witness that they had heard his blasphemy, and asked what they thought he deserved? They all agreed that he deserved death. No doubt Caiaphas attended the Council next day when they delivered up Jesus to Pilate, and begged that he might be crucified. (Matt. 26:3, 76; Luke 22:54; John 18:13-28) Soon after that, at a meeting of the Sanhedrin, he asked the Apostles why, contrary to orders, they dared to preach Jesus as the Messiah. They replied that they were obliged to obey God rather than men. (Acts 5:27-32) In AD 35, both Caiaphas and Pilate were deposed by Vitellius, the Roman Governor of Syria; and Jonathan, a son of Annas, was appointed High Priest.

CAIN, *possession*
The oldest son of Adam. When his mother Eve bore him, she imagined him to be the divine Man who would destroy the serpent's head, and the power of the devil. This is implied in these words from Gen. 4:1, *A man from the Lord*, or literally, "a man, the Lord". When grown up, he applied himself to cultivating the earth, as his brother Abel did in feeding the flocks. On the Sabbatical last day of the week, or at the end of the year, Cain offered his firstfruits, and Abel the best firstling of his flock. Cain, having made his offering with an unbelieving and wicked heart, God did not show any respect for it in the descent of

fire from heaven, or any such similar sign, as he did with Abel's. Cain was enraged to see his brother the darling of heaven, and took note of it with a sullen countenance and a surly temper. God reproved him, and told him that the refusal of his offering was owing solely to his own wickedness; that if he speedily believed and repented, he would be accepted, but if not, his sin that already lay on his conscience, would quickly bring ruin on his head. He hinted that Cain had no right to be angry with Abel as he still continued in his usual subjection to his brother as his superior in age.

Despising his Maker's admonition, Cain decoyed his brother into a field and murdered him, and, it seems, buried him in the ground. The Lord quickly called him to account, and asked him what had become of his brother Abel? Cain replied angrily that he did not know, and had no business being his brother's keeper. God charged him with the murder, warning him of its horrible nature and consequence; that Abel's blood, however hidden, cried out for vengeance against him, and that the earth, which covered it over, would never more yield him a plentiful crop or a settled abode. Cain complained of God's divine severity, that his crime had not been forgiven, and that he would be unbearably punished, and everyone who found him would kill him. God assured him that a sevenfold vengeance would come on his murderer; and either by some present token assured him of preservation, or by some visible mark of continual trembling, sullenness of countenance, or suchlike, marked him out to others for his safety. Driven from the east of Eden where the symbols of the divine presence were often visible, and from the Church of God, he retired to a country called Nod, away from his unsettled condition, and there built a city called Enoch after the name of his son. There, his family increased and spread throughout a large part of the world. They continued till the Flood up to seven generations, famous for the invention of the arts, and for their godlessness. By intermarriage with them, the posterity of Seth corrupted itself, and provoked God to bring on the general deluge. See Lamech. (Gen. 4 and 6)

CALEB, *as a hart*
(1) The son of Jephunneh, brother of Kenaz, and descendant of Judah. When the spies returned from their search of the Promised Land, Caleb and Joshua, endued by the Spirit of the Lord, opposed the rest,

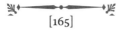

and presented Canaan as a good land, tearing their clothes for grief that the congregation, believing the majority, were about to return to Egypt, yet might be fully persuaded that, with the assistance of God, they could easily conquer it. To reward their piety, they, alone of the twelve spies, survived the wilderness wanderings, for they, of all the armed men that came out of Egypt, actually entered Canaan, as Moses promised Caleb the possession of the area around Hebron where, without being dismayed, he had seen the monstrous giants. (Josh. 14:6-15, 15:13-15, 21:10-12, 1 Sam. 25:2, 3, 30:14) Forty-five years later, Caleb's strength and courage being in no way abated, be begged Joshua, who was going to divide the land, to give him the country of the giants as Moses had predicted, that, depending on the assistance of heaven, he might have the honour of expelling them. Joshua blessed him, and granted him his request. Assisted by some of his brothers from Judah, he marched against Hebron, and slew there the children of Anak. From there, he marched on to Debir. As the place was extremely well guarded, he offered his daughter Achsah to any hero who would take it. Othniel his nephew took it, and obtained Achsah, plus a considerable portion of ground. When, or how Caleb died, we are not told by his three sons, Iru, Elah, and Naam, leaving behind a numerous and honoured posterity. (Num. 13-14; Josh. 14:6, 24, 30, 38, Num. 15:13-19; Judg. 1:12, 14-15, 20; 1 Chron. 4:15-20)

(2) CALEB, or CHELUBAI, the son of Hezron, and brother of Jerahmeel. His wives, perhaps in succession, were Azubahjerioth and Ephrath, with Ephah and Maachah, his concubines. His sons were Jesher, Shobab, Ardon, Hur, Mesha, Haran, Moza, Gazez, Sheber, Tirhanah, Shaaph, Sheva, and a daughter also called Achsah, and perhaps others. His posterity was very numerous. (1 Chron. 2:18-19, 42, 49-50)

(3) Caleb, the son of Hur, and grandson of the former Caleb. His sons were Shobal, Salina, Hareph. His descendants populated the whole country around Bethlehem, Kirjathjearim, Bethgader, etc. (1 Chron. 2:50-55)

CANAAN, *a merchant*; CANAANITES
The youngest son of Ham. When Ham made light of his father's nakedness, Noah denounced him with a curse of the most humbling servitude, and especially against Canaan. Whether Canaan joined in

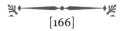

the crime, and informed his father of the shameful sight, or whether Noah could not pronounce the curse against Ham himself, who had been formerly blessed of God, or whether the words *"father of"* ought to be supplied before Canaan (as *son* is in Matt. 4:21, and *wife* in John 19:25), and *father* in Acts 7:16), or whether the curse was chiefly directed against Ham's posterity in Canaan, where they would be mostly exterminated by the Hebrews, is not agreed by scholars. It is certain that the Lord is righteous in all his ways, and it is certain that parents are punished in the misery of their offspring. And, from subsequent history, it appears that the Canaanites were made slaves of the posterity of Shem and of Japheth, just as the curse said. It is probable that Canaan lived and died in the land of promise, as well as giving his name to it. His posterity were numerous: Sidonians, Tyrians, Hittites, Jebusites, Amorites, Girgashites, Hivites, Arkites, Sinites, Arvadites, Zemarites, Hamathites, Perizzites, and another tribe that was called the Canaanites, though how they got this name more than the rest we do not know. Seven of these tribes (the Canaanites, Hittites, Jebusites, Amorites, Girgashites, Perizzites, and Hivites) populated Canaan. The other tribes went on to populate Phoenicia and parts of Syria.

CANDACE (The Kandake)
The Queen of Ethiopia, probably a country to the south of Egypt. It is said that the name means *royal authority*, and was commonly given to the queens of Meroe. It is certain that *Kanidak* in the Abyssinian language means a *governor of children*. Pliny (the Elder = Gaius Plinius Secundus) in his *Natural History* says that the government of Ethiopia rested for several generations in the hands of queens named Candace. It is said that by the preaching of her Eunuch, she was converted to the Christian faith. (Only found in Acts 8:27)

CEPHAS. See PETER.
See John 1:42; 1 Corinthians 1:12, 3:22, 9:5, 15:5; Galatians 2:9.

CAESAR
The Emperors of Rome, such as Augustus, Tiberius, Claudius, Nero, etc. (Matt. 22:17, 21; Mark 12:14, 17; Luke 2:1 = *Augustus* 3:1, 20:22, 25, 23:2; John 19:12, 15; Acts 11:28, 17:7, 25:8, 11-12, 21, 26:32, 27:24, 28:19;

Caesar's: Matt. 22:21; Mark 12:16-17; Luke 20:24-25; John 19:12; Acts 25:10; Phil. 4:22)

CHEDORLAOMER, *a generation of bondage*

King of Elam, about BC 1926, who subdued the kingdoms of Sodom, Gomorrah, Admah, Zeboim, and Zoar. After they had served him for twelve years, they rebelled. In the 14th year, he decided to reduce them. Assisted by Amraphel, King of Shinar, Arioch, King of Ellassar, and Tidal, King of Goiim - four nations - he marched against them. To deprive them of all possible aid, he first attacked the neighbouring powers. Marching south on their east, he smote the Rephaim near the source of the River Arnon, and pillaged Ashterothkarnaim. He routed the Zuzim at Ham, the Emim in Shavehkirjathaim, and the Horites in Mount Seir. Having proceeded on the south side till he came to Elparan, he returned, and directed his course to the northeast. On his way, he ravaged the country of the Amalekites, and smote the Amorites who lived around Hazezontamar. At last, he attacked the allied troops of the revolting kingdoms, where the field of battle was full of slime pits. The army of the revolters was routed, and those who escaped the slaughter fled to the mountains, possibly those on the northeast, which later fell to the lot of the Reubenites. Chedorlaomer and his allies, after ravaging the country, and carrying off captives and great booty, directed their march north, intending to return home by the southeast of Syria. Informed that Lot his nephew, and his family, were among the captives, Abraham, with a handful of servants, and a few Canaanite allies, pursued the conquerors, overtook them at Dan, and routed them. Then he pursued them to Hobah, a little to the north of Damascus, and re-took their captives and booty. Samuel Shuckford believes Chedorlaomer was the Assyrian Ninyas. Arthur Bedford thought him to be a deputy of Zameis, King of Assyria; but to me his reasoning does not appear conclusive. (Gen. 14:1, 4-5, 9, 17)

CHERUB, CHERUBIM

Angels are so-called because they often appeared as young men, mighty in power and knowledge. (Ps. 18:10) Cherubim, or angels, with the appearance of a flaming sword, were placed at the east entrance of the Garden of Eden after Adam's expulsion, to prevent his return; or God dwelt in the cherubim as a flaming sword. (Gen. 3:24) The cherubim, or winged figures, that covered the sacred ark in the Holy of Holies, and those painted on the wall or hangings of the sanctuary, who seemed each to have had the four faces of a man, a lion, an ox, and an eagle, might represent angels and ministers who, with great activity, wisdom, boldness, patience, and knowledge, view and admire the work of our redemption, and are employed in ministering to the Church and people of God. (Exod. 25:19-20, 22, 25, 26:1, 31) The cherubim that attended the wheels, or mingled with the palm trees in Ezekiel's vision, may mean either angels or ministers as subservient to the operations of providence, joined with, and ministering to, the saints. (Ezek. 10:1-3, 6-9, 15-16, 18-20, 41:18) God's riding on the cherubim indicates his majestic use of angels in his dispensations of providence. (Ps. 18:10) His *dwelling between the cherubim* means his particular presence in the Jewish Holy of Holies, but mainly his special satisfaction and pleasure in our Mediator, his law-magnifying righteousness, and his readiness to be found by those who seek him through him. (Ps. 80:1) The King of Tyre is called a covering cherub: he afforded his subjects an agreeable and glorious protection, while his fine apparel made him shine like an angel, or glitter like the golden cherubim over the ark. (Ezek. 28:14-16).

CHRIST. See Jesus

He is the Lord and Saviour of mankind, called Christ (or Messiah) because he was anointed, sent, and equipped by God to execute his mediatorial office, and called Jesus because, by his righteousness, power, and Spirit, he was qualified to save to the uttermost those who come to God through him. He is appointed by God for that end, and is freely given in the offer of the gospel. (Isa. 61:1-3; Matt. 1:21) He is the eternal Son of God, equal with his adored Father in all unbounded perfection. No one who doubts his being the only true and most high God can be, in consistency with common sense, a Christian. If Jesus is not the supreme God, he was a setter up of idolatry, encouraging men to worship himself; and Mohammed, who zealously opposed such worship, must be a valued reformer! If Christ is not God, the Jews did well to crucify him as a notorious blasphemer, for he made himself equal with God. (John 5:18) They did well to persecute his Apostles who represented him as the object of worship. If Christ is not God, the whole of the mystery of our redemption is erroneous or misleading.

Where is the divine love in sending a false God to redeem us? Or what can his death avail when our sins are not false, but we are real transgressors against the infinite Majesty? If Christ is not the supreme God, how obscure, absurd, and impious, must be the language of the Holy Spirit, particularly in the prophesies about him! If Christ is not God, what is the whole Christian religion but a mere comedy and farce, where one appears in the character of God who is not really so? What are its miracles, predictions, and mysteries but a system of magic, invented or effected by Satan to promote the blasphemous adoration of a creature?

The divine nature of Christ
Nor is his eternal generation and divine Sonship less clearly marked out in Scripture. What a number of texts there present him as God's proper and only begotten Son prior to the donation of him to the world! (John 1:14, 3:16; Rom. 8:3, 32) How often things proper to God are ascribed to him when he is declared to be God's Son! (Matt. 11:27, 14:33, 27:54; Luke 1:32, 35 with 16, 17, 46, 47; John 3:31, 35, 36, 1:18, 6:46, 9:35-38) How often his character as Son is plainly distinguished from his official character as Christ! (Matt. 16:15-16; John 1:49, 6:66-67, 7:29) How often by his silence he plainly granted to his enemies that his claim to be *Son of God* meant that he was asserting himself equal with God! (John 5:17-19, 10:31-39, 19:7) To pretend that he is called *the proper, the only begotten Son of God* because God sent him as Mediator, or because of his miraculous conception by the Virgin, is not only groundless and absurd, but equally blasphemous; for if the personal properties of Father, Son, and Holy Spirit are given up, there must be three distinct Gods, or one Person manifested in three different characters. From eternity, God foresaw men's destruction of themselves, and intended to recover them in part. It was impossible for any but a divine person to be a Mediator, Redeemer, Surety, Priest, Prophet, or King, to answer their rebellious, lustful, guilty, ignorant, condition. Nor was it less necessary that this divine Person should assume the nature of transgressors, and thus execute the whole work of their redemption. (Rom. 8:3-4; Gal 4:4-5) Nothing is more delightful than to observe in what respects the personal union of the divine nature and human was necessary for the execution of every office, the sustaining of every relation, and his standing as our blessed Redeemer. God set him up

in his purpose as the head of an elect world, chose them in him for everlasting life under the New Covenant, and settled with him all the conditions of their salvation, and every circumstance associated with it. (Ps. 40:6-8, 89:3-4, etc.) Thus our remedy was prepared long before we were ruined; and for uncountable ages, our Redeemer took delight in the sons of men before they were formed.

The human nature of Christ

It was not right that the Son of God should assume our nature and suffer immediately after the Fall. The absolute insufficiency of other means for reforming the world had not yet been fully revealed: the stupendous power of sin was not yet sufficiently known; men were not sufficiently warned of his appearance, nor were there enough people to witness the facts, or be agents of them, nor was there enough opposition to be conquered by the doctrines of his cross. Preparation, however, was made daily for this astonishing event. By many typical and verbal predictions, every circumstance of his future life was marked out, that the world might be qualified to give his character a thorough examination whenever he should appear. To show his readiness to invest himself with our nature, he often appeared in the form of a man; and almost every metaphorical representation of God was taken from things to do with men.

When the government was just departing from the tribe of Judah, and when the 490 years mentioned by the angel to Daniel was drawing to an end, and when the nations had been sufficiently shaken by the overthrow of the Persian and Greek Empires by the erection of the Roman, and while the second Temple remained in its glory, and when an alarming rumour of the sudden rise of a Jew to govern the world had spread throughout most of the earth, and just six months after the conception of the blessed Baptist, our Saviour's forerunner, the angel Gabriel told the Virgin Mary that, by the influence of the Holy Spirit, she would conceive and bear the promised Messiah. (Gen. 3:15, 49:10; Ezek. 21:27; Dan. 11:24-25; Hag. 2:6-9, 21-23; Mal. 3:1; Luke 1:32-35) This virgin was betrothed to Joseph, a carpenter. Both were humble in circumstances, despite being descendants of the now debased royal family of David. According to the genealogy of Matthew (and we must add three names that are omitted there), Joseph was the 32nd in line from David, in the royal line of Solomon. According to Luke, Mary, by whose marriage Joseph was the son-in-law of Heli, was the 41st from David by Nathan, and the 74th from Adam. The two lines of Solomon and Nathan, both sons of David, appear to meet in the persons of Salathiel and Zerubbabel; but Joseph sprang from Abiud, an elder son of Zerubbabel, and Mary from Rhesa, a younger son. Before Joseph had taken her to bed, he, with great unease, observed her with child. He might have insisted on putting her to death according to the law, but, being a good man, and perhaps hoping that she might have been raped, he decided to conceal the matter, and give her a private bill of divorce. But while he was thinking over these things, an angel warned him to take her home to him as his wife, as she was pure, and, by the power of the Holy Spirit, she had conceived, and would bear the Messiah and Saviour of the world. Joseph then cheerfully accepted her, but did not have sex with her till she brought forth her illustrious Child. By this marriage, the virgin's honour was protected; she had a husband ready to assist and provide for her in her difficulties, and her divine Son had ready access to the congregation, and every ordinance of the Jewish church. (Matt. 1; Luke 3:23-38)

Joseph and Mary lived in Nazareth, but, as this was not the place appointed for the birth of the Messiah, an enrolment of Roman subjects took place while Cyrenius was governor of Syria, for taxation purposes, which obliged the Jews at this very time to go to the places and families to which they originally belonged. Joseph, with Mary now heavy with child, was obliged to travel about 82 miles south to Bethlehem, and there, they and probably their Son, were registered in the public records of the Empire as descendants of David. Every inn in Bethlehem was so crowded with strangers that Joseph and Mary were only able to lodge in a stable. There, she gave birth to her divine Babe, and, for lack of a cradle, laid him to rest in a manger. That very night, an angel solemnly informed the shepherds, who were watching their flocks on an adjacent field, of Jesus' birth, and a host of other angels sang an anthem of praise for God's grace and mercy towards men. The shepherds hastened to Bethlehem, and found the Babe in the lowly condition the angel had said. To honour the ordinance of God, and to avow himself a member of the Jewish church, and a debtor to fulfil the whole Law, and to receive his Father's seal of the New Covenant made with him, and to begin his shedding of blood for his people, this divine Babe was circumcised on the 8th day of his life, and was called

Jesus (the Saviour), as the angel had directed before his birth. About 33 days later, his mother presented herself and her Babe at the Temple. Simeon, a notable saint, took the Child in his arms, blessed God for his appearance, and wished to die immediately as he had seen the incarnate Saviour. He warned Mary that her Son would be a sign for the fall and rise of many of the Jews, and would, by the treatment he would suffer, bring her much grief. (Luke 2:25-35) At that very instant, Anna, an aged prophetess, discerned him to be the Messiah, and told her pious friends of his greatness. (Luke 2:36-38)

The visit of the Wisemen

After going to Nazareth and settling their affairs, it seems that Joseph and Mary returned to Bethlehem, intending, no doubt, to comply with the ancient prediction of the place of the Messiah's appearance. Warned by the ancient oracle of Balaam, and other predictions in Scripture, and warned by the widespread rumour of the Messiah's immediate appearance, and alarmed at the appearance of an uncommon star, certain Magi (Wisemen) came from Persia, Chaldea, or Eastern Arabia to see and worship the newborn King of the Jews. At Jerusalem, they inquired for him. Herod and his subjects were greatly troubled at the news of the Messiah's birth. A council was called, which agreed that Bethlehem was to be the place. After a private inquiry as to when the star had appeared, and giving them orders to return and inform him of the Babe, Herod sent them on their way to Bethlehem. They had just left Jerusalem, when the star appeared to them in the lower region of the sky, and conducted them to the very place where Joseph and Mary were. With joy, they completed their journey, and, having found the Babe, worshipped him, and gave him presents of gold, frankincense, and myrrh. As Herod intended to murder the holy Child, an angel warned the Wisemen to return home without re-visiting him. He also warned Joseph, now ready for his journey by the presents they had been given, to carry the Child and his mother to Egypt, and stay there till further orders. Joseph immediately obeyed. Herod, enraged that the wisemen had not returned to inform him of the Child's whereabouts, sent out his troops, and murdered all the children under two years old in Bethlehem and its neighbourhood that he might make sure that Jesus was among them. After Herod's death, an angel warned Joseph and his family to return to Canaan. They did so. However, Archelaus' cruelty made them afraid of settling in Judea, so, under the direction of God, they went north and settled back in Nazareth, which, unknown to them, fulfilled the ancient predictions of Christ's being the *Notzer, the Preserver,* or the *Netzer, the Branch.* (Matt. 2:23; Job 7:20; Isa. 11:1)

Jesus in the Temple
At twelve years of age, Jesus went up to celebrate the Passover along with his mother and adoptive father. After the festival was over, they returned; but he remained behind and conferred with the Jewish rabbis, to the surprise of all that heard him. His parents, at last missing him, returned to search for him. On the third day, they found him. His mother asked him why he had caused her and her husband to search for him so long with sorrowing hearts? He replied that they should have known that he was the object of his divine Father's care, and be employed in his business. He, in the most submissive manner, returned with them to Nazareth, and, no doubt, laboured as a carpenter with Joseph, meanwhile increasing in wisdom and grace, and behaving in such a way that recommended him to the favour of God and men. (Luke 2:52)

The ministry of John the Baptist
His forerunner, John the Baptist, now began his public ministry. When Jesus was about 30 years of age, he visited him at Bethabara, and asked for baptism that he might, according to covenant engagement, *fulfil all righteousness.* His baptism sealed his and his Father's will, and excited and encouraged the graces of his human nature. On this occasion, the heavens were opened, and the Holy Spirit descended on him in the form of a peaceful dove, and the Father proclaimed him his *beloved Son, in whom he was well pleased.* The Holy Spirit, by his powerful influence, led him into the wilderness, perhaps that horrible area in the mountains of Quarantana, north of Jericho, or that of Mount Pisgah on the east of the Jordan. There, he spent 40 days in fasting and prayer to fit himself for his public ministry. Here too, he was greatly tempted by Satan, especially at the end of those days. When he was hungry, Satan tempted him to doubt his Sonship, and work a miracle for his own preservation. He then carried him away to Jerusalem, and placed him on a pinnacle of the Temple, tempting him to throw himself down in the hope of divine preservation. He next carried him to a high

mountain where he showed him all the kingdoms of the world and their glory, and offered to give him them all if he would fall down and worship him. With detestation, and with Scriptural arguments, Jesus baffled these horrible enticements. Satan then left him for a time, and holy angels came and ministered to him, comforted him, and gave him provision. (Matt. 3-4; Luke 4) Jesus left the wilderness, and went to the place where John was baptising. John pointed him out to his hearers as the *Lamb of God* that had come to make atonement for the sins of the world - Gentiles as well as Jews. Next day, he pointed him out in the same way to Andrew, and perhaps John, two of his disciples. They went after Jesus, and inquired where he was staying. He took them along with him, and they remained with him all that day. Informed by Andrew that they had found the Messiah, Peter went along with his brother to see him. It was then that Jesus gave him the name *Cephas* (or *Peter*), to signify that he would be constant and fixed as a rock in his religious profession and work. Next day, on his return to Galilee, Jesus found Philip, and desired him to go along with him. Philip, finding Nathanael, informed him that they had found the promised Messiah, Jesus of Nazareth. Nathanael thought it impossible such a blessing could come out of Nazareth, but, when Jesus reminded him of his very secret devotions, he acknowledged him as the Son of God and expected Redeemer. (John 1:28-51)

The beginning of Christ's work

Three days later, he, his mother, and his disciples, attended a marriage of some friend at Cana of Galilee. When the wine ran out, Jesus' mother hinted the need for him to do a miracle for their extra supply. He respectfully replied that it was not proper for her to direct his miraculous operations, but ordered the servants to fill with water some pots that stood by for washing. This water, he turned into the most excellent wine; and thus began the display of his divine power, that his disciples might believe in him. Quickly afterwards, he went up to Jerusalem to keep the Passover, and, finding the outer court polluted by a market of sheep, cattle, and doves for the sacrifices, and tables for the exchange of money, with a scourge of small cords, he drove out the animals and overturned the tables of the money-changers, telling them that the place ought to be used for prayer, not for robbery and deceit. Some of the Jewish rulers present asked for his warrant for this action. He replied that the resurrection of his body on the third day, after they had murdered him, would show it. He performed a great many miracles at this feast, and many believed that he was the Messiah; but as he was aware of their deceit and inconstancy, he did not trust himself to them. Nicodemus was one of these believers, so he came to him by night for instruction. Jesus finding him grossly ignorant of spiritual things, informed him of the need for regeneration, and of the cause, nature and end of his coming into the world. (John 2:1-3:21)

Jesus then left Jerusalem, perhaps to the country around Jericho. Here, he began to baptise (not personally) by his disciples. Multitudes resorted to him. Some Jews argued with John's disciples that the baptism of Jesus was more effective for the purifying of the soul than that of their master, whereupon they complained to John that everybody was going to desert him, preferring Jesus and his baptism. John replied that this was right, and that it gave him much pleasure that Jesus' fame was growing and his decreasing. After John was imprisoned, and the Pharisees became alarmed at the great number of Jesus' followers, he left Judea and retired north to Galilee. Ardent concern for the salvation of lost sinners determined him to visit Samaria on the way. Tired with his journey, he rested at Jacob's well close to Sychar, while his disciples went on to the town to buy some food. Here, he spoke with a Samaritan prostitute, and, despite her many arguments, showed himself as the all-refreshing and life-giving gift of God, convincing her of her immorality and wickedness, and, informing her of the spiritual nature of divine worship, he assured her that he was the Messiah. Alarmed at her commendation of him, her neighbours came and received instruction, and many of them believed in him. This, he informed his disciples, was a sign of the conversion of the Gentiles. (John 3:22-36, 4:1-42)

When he returned to Galilee, many who had seen his miracles at Jerusalem listened to his instructions with wonder. When he was at Cana, a nobleman of Capernaum, hearing of his fame, came and begged that he would come and cure his son who was on the point of death. Jesus replied that it was not reasonable that they would not accept his heavenly doctrines without miraculous signs. He bid the nobleman go, and he would find his son recovered. The nobleman's servants met him by the way and informed him that the child's fever had left him at the exact time Jesus had promised his recovery. The nobleman and his whole family believed in Jesus as the promised Messiah. On his journey through Galilee, Jesus came to Nazareth, his native town. Accordingly, as usual, he stood up on the Sabbath, and read and expounded the Scripture in the synagogue. The passage he read was Isaiah chapter 61, which spoke of his mission, and the qualifications for his work. His sermon astonished his audience, but his lowly birth and lack of liberal education prejudiced them against him. He told them it was common for prophets to be despised in their own country. He showed them, from the case of Elijah and Elisha, that they had small reason to expect to be much blessed with his miracles. In a rage, they dragged him to the top of the hill on which their city was built, intending to throw him down headlong; but, by his divine power, he rescued himself, and left the place. (Luke 4:14-30; John 4:43-53)

Next, we find him at Capernaum, on the borders of the land of Zebulun and Naphtali. There, as was foretold of old, he instructed the inhabitants, and called them to change their erroneous feelings and evil course of life since the New Testament dispensation of the gospel was at hand. Here, he called Peter and Andrew, James and John, to leave their employment of fishing, and go with him to preach the gospel for the salvation of men. The first two he rewarded with a miraculous draught of fish for the use of their boat to preach in. As he was teaching one day in a synagogue, an evil spirit cried out from a possessed person, *Why do you disturb us? Have you come to torment us before the time?* Jesus ordered him to leave the man, which, after a hideous roaring and a terrible distortion of the man, he was obliged to do. Soon after, by a touch and a word of command, he healed Peter's mother-in-law of her fever, and she rose directly and gave him some food. That evening, he healed a number of possessed and diseased people with a touch of his hand. Next morning, he employed himself in solemn prayer; and, despite the entreaties of his disciples and others, he departed from there to preach in other synagogues in Galilee. The fame of his miracles spread throughout Canaan and part of Syria, so they brought multitudes of distressed sufferers, mainly those who were pronounced incurable by physicians, and he healed them all. (Matt. 4:12-25; Mark 1:15-40; Luke 5:1-11; 4:34-44)

Great crowds accompanied him, so he went up to a mountain and instructed them concerning the blessedness of those who were truly religious. He showed the excellence and usefulness of good works and declared that the divine Law was unalterable in its moral precepts, and its prohibition of malice, angry words, lustful looks, toleration of beloved evil desires, and profane swearing of every kind. He called for the most humble and peaceful behaviour towards others, love of one's enemies, and the universal imitation of the gracious God in all that we do. He taught them the matter and manner of prayer, and the way to practise almsgiving and fasting. He showed them the duty of heavenly thoughts and affections, and of confident trusting in God with respect to outward concerns, and of the prime need to seek out a saving interest in his kingdom and God's righteousness. He prohibited the rash judging of others, and showed them that they should do to others what they wanted other to do to themselves. He called for earnest prayer, and diligent endeavours to receive the Lord Jesus, and to walk in him. He warned them to avoid false teachers, and be wary of resting on outward shadows of godliness. The important themes, and the affectionate and solemn delivery of his sermon, astonished his audience. (Matt. 5-7)

Leaving that mountain, he went towards Capernaum. In a village nearby, he healed a supplicant leper, ordering him to conceal the miracle of his cure, and to make an offering for his cleansing. The leper blazed the matter abroad, and many, hearing of it, came for cures. Jesus retired, and spent some time in solemn and secret prayer. He had just entered Capernaum, when a centurion, very friendly to their nation, and who had built them a synagogue, sent some respectable Jews to beg him to come and heal his servant who lay at the point of death. At their earnest invitation, Jesus went along with them. On the way, other messengers met him, and told him that the centurion thought himself unworthy of his presence, and begged that he would command a cure at a distance, and it would be so. Jesus signified his great pleasure in the strong faith of this Gentile soldier, and observed that it was another sign that many of the heathen nations would be quickly converted to the Church and brought into the heavenly mansions, while the body of the Jewish nation would be excluded, and plunged into temporal or eternal misery. He ordered the disease to leave the servant, as his master believed he could. (Mark 1:40-46; Matt. 8:1-18; Luke 7:1-10)

To avoid the crowds, Jesus intended to cross the Sea of Tiberias to the east. As he travelled to the shore, a scribe, expecting outward honour, offered to become his disciple. Jesus, knowing his heart, told him he need expect no earthly profits or honour in following him, as he himself had not so much as any settled abode. About the same time, one of his disciples begged leave to go and bury his father. Jesus exhorted him to leave worldly cares to worldly men dead in sin, and attend to the preaching of the gospel. Another one begged him to let him go and take farewell of his relatives. Jesus told him that if he was weary of his work, he was unfit to be a chief founder of the New Testament Church. While Jesus and his disciples crossed the sea, a terrible storm blew up. Being very tired, and to test his disciples' faith, he fell asleep. They woke him up, and begged him to rescue them from destruction. After reproving them for the weakness of their faith, he ordered the storm to cease. A calm ensued. The seamen were astonished, and the ship quickly reached the eastern shore. They had scarcely landed in the territory of the Gadarenes (or, Gergasenes), when two possessed men met him, the one so very angry that he could not be confined, nor kept from tearing his own flesh, among the tombs and rocks. From these, Jesus ejected some thousands of devils that, at his permission, entered a herd of swine, which rushed furiously into the lake and were drowned. Thus, at once he exposed the reality of the possession and its terrible effects. He also manifested his own power, and punished the Jews for breeding pigs contrary to their Law. The owners begged him to leave their country. The man who had been most mad begged that he and his companion might follow him. But when Jesus ordered them to go home and tell their friends about the deliverance that had been granted them, they readily obeyed. (Matt. 8:18; Mark 5:1-20; Luke 8:22-40, 9:57-62) Jesus returned to Capernaum where many, plus the Pharisees and doctors of the Law, assembled around him, and were instructed. Miracles again confirmed his teaching. One afflicted with paralysis was let down through the roof in front of Jesus, as the crowd were hindering his friends bringing him in through the door. He healed him, and, to the fury of the Pharisees, declared his sins forgiven. Matthew, a publican, he called to be one of his Apostles. At a feast in his house, he vindicated his eating with publicans and sinners, and indicated that it was such people, not the righteous who had no consciousness of sin, that he had come to call to repentance. He vindicated his not imposing fasting, or other severe duties of religion, on his disciples, since they were no more able to bear them than old bottles were to preserve new wine, or new cloth was to mend an old garment, or a wineskin used for old wine was no good for holding the new. Meanwhile, Jairus, a ruler of the synagogue, came and begged him to come and cure his daughter, who appeared to be in a dangerous condition. As he went along, a woman distressed for twelve years with a bloody emission, and who had spent all that she had on physicians without being made one bit better, depending on his miraculous virtue by touching the hem of his garment, she was made perfectly well. Finding she could not conceal the matter, she confessed the whole to his honour, and was dismissed with a blessing. Meanwhile, the ruler's daughter died, but Jesus restored her to life. On his return from the ruler's house, he cured two blind men, and dislodged the devil from one who was struck dumb. Though the Pharisees ascribed these miracles to magic and collusion with Satan, he went on preaching, and healing the distressed. (Matt. 9; Mark 2:21; Luke 5:27, 8:41-56)

Moved with compassion towards the multitudes that crowded to hear his instructions, he commanded his disciples to pray that the Holy Spirit, the Lord of the spiritual harvest, would speedily provide a suitable number of preachers. After spending a whole night in prayer, he set apart Peter and Andrew, James and John, Philip and Bartholomew, Thomas and Matthew, James and Jude, Simeon the Zealot, and Judas Iscariot, for this work. He ordered them to go out in pairs into all the cities of Israel, preach the gospel, and work miracles for the relief of the distressed. He directed them to rely on the care of heaven for provision to lodge with good people; to give a solemn testimony against the rejecters of their message; to behave with meekness, innocence, and wisdom; and to persevere in their work, despite the most fiery persecutions. After descending from the mountain, he gave the multitude present a shorter version of his former Sermon on the Mount. As he travelled along from that place, he raised to life the only son of a widow of Nain as he was being carried to his grave. (Matt. 9:36-38, 10; Mark 3:13-19; Luke 6:13, 7:11-16, 9:1-6)

To confirm his own or his disciples' faith, from his prison, John the Baptist sent two of them to ask Jesus whether he was the true Messiah. Jesus ordered them to inform John of the miracles they had seen performed, and the gospel they had heard preached to the poor, and let him judge for himself. He commended John to the crowd present, and remarked that neither the severe behaviour of John, nor his own more social lifestyle, was capable of gaining that hardened generation to the faith and obedience of the truth. About this time, the Twelve returned and informed him of their success. He rejoiced in spirit, and thankfully adored his Father's sovereignty in revealing his truth to the poor and weak, while concealing it from the wise and far-sighted. He reproved Chorazin, Bethsaida, and Capernaum for their inattention to his instructions and miracles, and threatened their ruin; but he invited sinners, weary and heavy burdened with sin or distress, to come to him for spiritual rest. (Matt. 11; Luke 7:16-35) Returning to Capernaum, he was entertained by Simon, a wealthy Pharisee. A woman who had been notoriously wicked, probably Mary Magdalene, washed his feet with her tears and wiped them with her hair, which was the occasion for an excellent discourse on the forgiveness of sin as the reason for such evangelical love. Soon after, he went up to Jerusalem to keep the Passover with his disciples, together with Mary Magdalene, Joanna the wife of Chuza, Herod's steward, and Susanna and others who ministered to his needs. At Jerusalem, he cured the impotent man who had lain there 38 years to no purpose at the pool of Bethesda, and ordered him to mark the perfection of his cure by carrying his bed. As it was the Sabbath day, the Jewish leaders, being informed that Jesus was his adviser, decided to have him punished. In his own defence, he remarked that as his Father continued his work of providence every day, it was proper he should follow his pattern of doing so on the Sabbath. His affirming God as his Father, caused them to charge him with blasphemy, in reply to which, he largely vindicated his divine sonship and mission. (Luke 7:36-50, 8:1-3; John 5) The next Sabbath, being the second after the first day of Unleavened Bread, he and his disciples were walking through some cornfields. In their hunger, the disciples plucked and ate some ears of corn. The Pharisees were offended. Jesus excused his disciples for their hunger and necessity, remarking that in a similar case, David and his servants had eaten the hallowed showbread, and that on the Sabbath, the priests in offering their sacrifices, did things otherwise unlawful on the Sabbath day; and that in any case he was Lord of the Sabbath, and had made it for the real welfare of mankind. Next Sabbath, he healed a man who had a withered hand. To vindicate himself, he remarked that it was usual to draw a sheep or ox out of a ditch on that day, and so it was certainly lawful to cure a man. The Pharisees were mad with rage, and, along with the Herodians, plotted to put him to death.

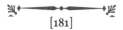

The omniscient Saviour, knowing of their plotting, retired to Capernaum. Here, vast crowds from Jerusalem, Idumea, Perea, or the country east of Jordan, and from Tyre, Sidon, and Galilee, came to him. He healed many diseases, and cast out many evil spirits. On his return from the seaside to his lodgings, so many came to him for cures or instruction that his friends almost forcibly carried him away to take some food, saying, he was *beside himself, or would certainly faint, though he seemed insensible of it*. Not long after, he cured one whom a satanic possession had rendered both blind and dumb. The crowd was amazed, but the Pharisees ascribed his cures to hellish influence. Knowing their thoughts, Jesus remarked on their absurdity in imagining that Satan would cast out Satan, and their self-contradiction in attributing his own case to Satan, that, in the case of their own children, they ascribed to the Spirit of God. He assured them that the ascription of his or his Apostles' miracles to Satan, contrary to the clearest evidence, would never be forgiven them. Unaffected by this awakening discourse, they demanded that he would confirm his mission by a visible sign from heaven. Referring to the typical fate of Jonah, he told them that no new kind of sign would be allowed them except his resurrection from the dead on the third day. He assured them that the Ninevites, who repented at the preaching of Jonah, and the Queen of Sheba, who so admired the wisdom of Solomon, would, in the last judgement, bear witness against the impenitence and unbelief of the Jewish nation; and by the parable of an evil spirit going out and returning of its own accord, suggested that the means used to reform them were likely to bring them into a most wretched condition. A woman present, and affected by his discourse, cried out that she was blessed who had born such a son. Jesus replied that it was not a natural relationship to him or any other, but faith and obedience to God's word, that marked one truly blessed. Meanwhile, his mother and other friends wanted to speak to him. He suggested to the crowd that he esteemed his disciples, and others who obeyed his heavenly Father, his nearest and dearest relatives. (Matt. 12; Mark 2:23, 3; Luke 6:6-12, 11:14-32)

Various parables
When a great crowd assembled to hear him, Jesus retired from the city to the shore, and taught the people from a ship. By the parable

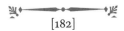

of the seed falling on the wayside, and on the stony, thorny, and good soil, he represented the different effects of the gospel on careless, hard-hearted, worldly, and serious souls. By that of the tares among the wheat, he showed that hypocrites and wicked men will continue among the saints till the end of the world, and then be fully separated, and wrathfully cast into hell-fire. By the gradual growth of corn, he represented the slow, but imperceptible growth of his Church, and of the graces of his people. By the parable of a grain of mustard-seed, he showed that from the smallest beginnings, and by the weakest means, his Church would gradually enlarge, fill the whole earth, and afford spiritual rest and refuge to the heathen world. By that of the leaven, he suggested that the gospel dispensation, in all its doctrines and influence, would gradually affect multitudes, and bring them to the obedience of faith. By that of the treasure hidden in the field, he meant that himself and his truth, found in the field of his Word by every wise man, would far outweigh every other consideration. By that of the pearl of great price, he suggested that men ought to possess themselves of him and the blessings of the gospel, at whatever the cost. By that of the net cast into the sea, he taught that, by means of the gospel dispensation, many different tribes and nations would be brought into the Church, and, that at the last day, the good would be separated from the bad, these going into everlasting punishment, but the righteous into life eternal. Returning to his lodgings, he privately explained these parables to his disciples, and required them to ponder his instructions: that as lights in the world, they might be qualified to teach others. (Matt. 13; Mark 4; Luke 8:4-19)

Further miracles

Leaving Capernaum, he went to Nazareth, the inhabitants still imagining that his low pedigree and education were a sufficient proof that he was an impostor. Their unbelief rendered it improper to favour them with many instructions or miracles, so he only healed a few diseased people, and, retiring from them, taught in neighbouring villages. He sent out the twelve Apostles with the same orders and powers as before, or, perhaps, it was now that they were sent out, though they had been formerly called to that work. Hearing of his fame, Herod strongly suspected that he might be John the Baptist, whom he had murdered, raised from the dead. To prevent every murderous attempt, Jesus left the area. The Twelve returned, and gave him an account of their success. He thanked God, and, along with them, retired from the crowds. They crossed the Lake of Tiberias to the east and came to the desert of Bethsaida. Many quickly assembled there, where he taught them and healed their sick. With five loaves and two small fish, he feasted five thousand men, besides women and children; and twelve baskets full of fragments were left over. This miraculous multiplication of their food, having convinced the crowd that he was the promised Messiah, they resolved to make him their king. To prevent this worldly attempt, he sent off his disciples to Bethsaida, on the other side of a creek, and retired to a hill for his secret devotions. A violent storm almost drowned the disciples, though they sailed on their Master's orders. When morning came, they had advanced only about three or four miles, when Jesus came to them, walking on the tempestuous sea. Fearing it was an evil spirit come to destroy them, they cried out in fear. Jesus comforted them, and told them who he was. On this occasion, Peter, through his rashness and unbelief, would have drowned as he walked on the water had not Jesus supported him. Upon our Saviour's entrance into the boat, the storm ceased, and they quickly reached the land in the country of Gennesaret, a little to the south of Capernaum. Here, he instructed the multitudes who came, and healed their sick. The people whom he had left on the east side of the lake came over in boats to Capernaum in quest of him. Jesus earnestly called them to labour for spiritual and eternal blessings rather than for outward provision; and he represented himself as the true bread that satisfies and forever renders happy the receivers. Offended by these convicting remarks, and the spiritual nature of his discourse, many of these followers completely forsook him. He asked the Twelve if they intended to desert him also. Peter replied that they could safely go nowhere else, as he alone *had the words of eternal life*, and the power to confer it. Jesus replied that one of them – meaning Judas Iscariot - was a devil. (Matt. 13:53-58, 14; Mark 6; Luke 9:1-17; John 6)

Growing opposition

Jesus had attended the Passover at Jerusalem, but repeated attempts against his life determined him to leave Judea and return to Galilee. A number of Scribes and Pharisees followed him to Capernaum to find something to accuse him of. They and other Jews were greatly

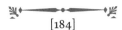

offended that he and his disciples did not observe their superstitious custom of washing their hands, indeed their cups, pots, and even the couches on which they sat, before they took a meal. He replied that their superstitious traditions rendered their religious worship unprofitable, and contradicted the indispensable laws of heaven, particularly in pretending to consecrate to the Lord what ought to be given for the relief of aged parents. He told them that it was not the food that a man ate that defiled him in God's sight, but the many evils of his wicked heart and life. To avoid the effects of their rage, he retired to the coasts of Tyre and Sidon. Here, after a severe trial of a Syro-Phoenician woman, who urgently and often begged relief for her possessed daughter, he graciously healed the maid and extolled the faith of the mother. Returning from this heathen country, he crossed the Jordan to the east, and continued for some time in Decapolis. Here, after curing a deaf man, and a number of others who were diseased, he spent a night in solemn prayer. He then proceeded to instruct the assembling crowds. After they had accompanied him three days, he fed four thousand men, besides women and children, with seven loaves and a few small fish; and seven baskets full of fragments remained. To prevent an insurrection in his favour, he crossed the Sea of Galilee to the west, and, landing near Dalmanutha, he passed through it and Magdala on his way to Capernaum. Here, the Pharisees tempted him with ensnaring questions, insisting that he should confirm his pretence to Messiahship with signs from heaven. He rebuked their hypocrisy, and told them that no new sign would be given them but that of his resurrection, which had been so long ago typified by the deliverance of Jonah from the belly of the whale. Finding that the truths he spoke made no impression on the Pharisees, he and his disciples again crossed the Sea of Galilee towards the east; and, during their passage, he exhorted them to beware of the leaven, the corrupting doctrines, of the Pharisees, Sadducees, and Herodians.

On their landing at Bethsaida, he gradually cured a blind man, anointing his eyes with his spittle. After a short stay in Decapolis, he went north to Caesarea Philippi and taught there, and in other places nearby. His disciples told him that some took him for John the Baptist, others for Elijah, others for Jeremiah, or some ancient prophet raised from the dead. He asked them for their own feelings. Peter replied that they were fully persuaded that he was the *Christ* (or *Messiah*), *the Son of the living God.* Jesus, after signifying that Peter had not gained this knowledge by human instruction, but by the special teaching of God, he assured him that, upon his own immoveable person and office, and the truth just confessed concerning it, he would build his New Testament Church, and make him and his fellow Apostles its honoured preachers and governors. He had hardly proceeded to inform them of his approaching death, when Peter begged him to spare himself, and desired that such things should never happen. Jesus sharply rebuked him as one acting Satan's part in tempting him to lay aside his work, and was influenced by worldly views, not from a regard for the honour of God. He exhorted all present to study self-denial, and a cheerful acceptance of trouble as a necessary preparation for eternal life. He assured them that no worldly gain could balance the eternal ruin of their soul, and, that if they were ashamed to own him and his truths among wicked men, he would disdain them at his glorious appearance. He added that it would not be long before he entered his glory, and that some of them present would live to see it displayed in the erection of his gospel Church, and the terrible ruin of his Jewish opposers. (Matt. 15-16; Mark 7-8; Luke 9:18-27)

The Transfiguration

After six free days, and on the eighth day after the time of the last discourse, as he and his disciples were by themselves at the foot of a mountain, probably not Tabor, but one nearer Caesarea Philippi, he took Peter, James, and John along with him to the top of the mount. As he was praying there, his external appearance was changed, marked with inconceivable brightness and brilliance. To represent him as the scope and substance of the Law and the Prophets, Moses and Elijah descended from heaven to converse with him on the great topic of his suffering and death. The disciples, awakening from their sleep, saw the vision. Peter rashly begged leave to build three tabernacles, one for his Master, and one for each of the prophets, imagining they were to stay a considerable time. He had scarcely uttered this hasty request, when a bright cloud received the prophets to heaven, and the voice of God proclaimed from it, *This is my beloved Son, in whom I am well pleased; hear him,* implying that Jesus was above every prophet. The three disciples were frightened; but Jesus encouraged them, and commanded them to tell nobody what they had seen till after his resurrection. He too informed them that *John the Baptist* was the New Testament *Elijah*, and had suffered already. When he came down from the mount next morning, he found the Scribes scolding his disciples because they could not cast out a stubborn devil from a tortured child. The child's father related the case to Jesus himself, and begged that, if possible, he would relieve his son. After hinting the necessity of faith, and rebuking the father and others present for their lack of, or weakness in, it, he ordered the devil to go out of the child. After terribly distorting the youth, he came out, and the child was healed. Soon after, Jesus privately assured his disciples that strong faith, and much fervent prayer and fasting, were necessary to dislodge so stubborn a fiend.

On his way to Capernaum, Jesus reminded his disciples of his future sufferings. When he entered the city, the Roman tax collectors asked Peter whether his Master would pay the common tribute. To prevent all suspicion of his being of the Galilean party, who refused to acknowledge Roman authority, or of his being a despiser of the Temple, he ordered Peter to cast his hook into the sea and open the mouth of the fish he caught first, and he would find there a shekel of silver to pay tribute for them both. On the way, his disciples had been arguing about which of them would have the highest offices in the temporal kingdom, which they imagined he would quickly bring in. To rebuke them, Jesus presented a little child to them, and told them that it was absolutely necessary that they should be like him in humility and self-denial. John replied that they had been so zealous for his honour that, seeing someone, not of his society, casting out devils, they forbade him. Jesus told him that was wrong; that it was extremely sinful and dangerous to discourage the very weakest of his sincere followers. He showed the danger of giving or taking, offence, and the sin of despising the least saint, since not only his angels attended them, but he thought it so worthy of him to seek out the lost sheep of sinful men. He directed them how to deal with offending brothers, and how to secure the maintenance of their own grace. By the parable of a master forgiving 10,000 talents (about £3,481,875), and that very debtor refusing to forgive his fellow-servant one hundred pence, which is just over £3, he showed the absurdity and danger of neglecting or refusing to forgive injuries. (Matt. 17-18; Mark 9; Luke 9:28-48)

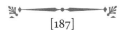

At the Feast of Tabernacles

When the Feast of Tabernacles drew near, Jesus' family, who indeed did not believe in him, urged him to go up to Jerusalem, and there make a name for himself. He reproved their worldly views, and declined going up with them without telling them if he intended to go at all. After a few days, he went up privately. About the middle of the festival, he taught publicly in the Temple, cleared himself of selfish intentions, vindicated his performing a miracle on the Sabbath day, and foretold that he would quickly be beyond the reach of his enemies. On the last day, while the people drew water to pour out in the sacred court, he solemnly invited the crowds to believe in him, that they might abundantly receive the influences and fruits of his Spirit. The Jewish rulers sent their officers to arrest him, but these, touched by his words, returned and told their superiors that *never man spoke like this*. That evening, as was his way, Jesus returned to Mount Olivet and spent the night in meditation and prayer. Next morning, he returned to the Temple Court and taught the crowds. The Scribes and Pharisees presented to him a woman taken in the very act of adultery, and, to trap him, asked what should be done with her? After appearing for a time quite regardless, he advised an accuser who was outwardly innocent of such a crime to cast the first stone at her. Conscious of their guilt, and worried that he might expose them, they all hastily slipped off, beginning with the oldest. None of them stayed to condemn her, so Jesus dismissed her with a solemn charge to avoid such a sin in the future. To his numerous audience, he showed himself as the light of the world, and he vindicated the truth and effectiveness of his teaching, and declared that unless, by means of his word, they were freed from the bondage of sin, and brought out of the family of their father the devil, their descent from Abraham would be of no use to them. He assured them that he existed before Abraham, and that his foreseen appearance in the flesh was the joy of that patriarch's heart. Enraged at that, the Jews, who had just before reproached him as wicked and satanic, took up stones to kill him; but he slipped away out of their company. In his going off, or perhaps some time later, he cured a man born blind by anointing his eyes with clay, and ordered him to wash them in the pool of Siloam. The Jewish rulers arrested the poor man, and severely examined him concerning his cure and physician; and, because he avowed that certainly he who could perform such a miracle

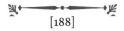

must be a good man and a prophet, they excommunicated him from their synagogues. (John 7-8, 9:1-34)

Leaving Jerusalem, Jesus retired to Galilee where he taught for about six weeks till the Feast of Dedication was near. Although he knew there were plots against his life, he resolved to take the opportunity of this human festival to instruct the people. On his way through the country of the Samaritans, he sent James and John before him to find lodgings for himself and his disciples. When that malicious people knew he was going to the feast at Jerusalem, they refused to receive him. The two disciples were eager to command fire from heaven to burn them up quickly, but Jesus rebuked them for their furious zeal, and told them that his mission on earth was not to destroy, but to save. On his way to Jerusalem, he sent out seventy of his disciples with much the same powers and instructions as he had twice before given to the Twelve. After executing their orders, they returned to him with great joy because of their success, probably after he was at Jerusalem. He told them it was just a prelude to the fall of Satan's kingdom, and advised them not to make their success, but their saving interest in the redeeming kindness of God, the chief ground of their joy. When he was within a few miles of Jerusalem, a lawyer asked him what he should do to inherit eternal life. Jesus hinted that the fulfilment of the whole law of love to God and our neighbour was necessary. The lawyer, wanting to justify himself, asked who was his neighbour whom he ought to love as himself, and whether it meant just the Jews? By the parable of the tender hearted Samaritan, Jesus made him confess that no national prejudice should hinder our love to anyone. At Bethany, the two sisters Martha and Mary looked after his needs. The former he reproved for her anxious care in getting the meal ready, and the latter he commended for chiefly minding her eternal concerns. (Luke 10)

At Jerusalem, in the Temple Court, he found the man who had recently been cured of his blindness, and asked him if he believed in the Son of God. He assured him that he Himself was the one; then the man immediately worshipped him. Jesus then remarked to the audience that by his coming, those who were sensible of their blindness would see, but those who were insensible of their spiritual blindness would have it increased and be exposed. Some Pharisees present asked if he took them to be blind and ignorant? He told them that they improved what knowledge they had chiefly to aggravate their sin. He entertained

his audience with a long and delightful discourse concerning himself as the true shepherd of his people, who would give his life for their redemption, and would preserve every one of them safely for eternal life. On his avowing himself EQUAL to, and ONE with his Father, and stating that his miracles testified such, the Jews considered arresting him; but he escaped out of their hands and went to Bethabara beyond the Jordan. (John 9:35, 10:42)

While he continued there, at his disciples' request, he gave them a pattern of prayer much the same as he had done in his Sermon on the Mount. He recommended the utmost earnestness in their addresses to God as a proper way to succeed. He showed that his casting out of devils was no effect of collusion with Satan. He foretold that the punishment of those who misapplied his instructions and miracles would be heavier than that of the heathen world. A Pharisee, who had invited him to dinner, taking offence at his sitting down without washing his hands, was sharply rebuked (and his sect) by Jesus for his superstitious scruples in avoiding external impurity, while they were so unconcerned for that of their heart; and that while they scrupulously paid tithes of their anise, mint, and rue, they neglected justice, mercy, and faith. He compared them to graves, where decomposition is concealed. He reproved the lawyers for burdening others with their imposed ceremonies, and for their pretence of deep respect for the ancient prophets, while they hated the messengers of God who lived in their own times. He assured them that that generation had approved, or would approve by their conduct, all the murders of righteous men, from Abel to Zacharias, and be punished accordingly. (Luke 11)

The conclusion of Christ's ministry in Galilee

From Perea, he went north towards Galilee. Great numbers attended his instruction. He directed his disciples to be always frank and open in their conduct, to stand in due awe of their God, to trust themselves to his care, and depend upon his immediate direction what they should answer to their persecutors. After refusing to act the part of a civil judge in the division of an inheritance between two brothers, he warned his hearers to beware of covetousness and earthly-mindedness. By the parable of a rich man cut off by death just after his plentiful crop, and while he comforted his soul with the hope of a luxurious life for many years, he enforced his injunctions. He warned them to make it their

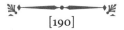

chief concern to secure happiness above, and to be always ready for an entrance into that eternal state. He told them that he himself was shortly to be baptised with painful sufferings and a bloody death, and that, as they might expect their share of trouble in adhering to the gospel, it would be wise to speedily ensure their saving interest in, and peace with, God. (Luke 12)

About this time, he was informed of Pilate's murdering some Galileans while they were offering their sacrifices in the Temple. He told his audience that they were not to consider these men, or the 18 Jews on whom the tower of Siloam had lately fallen, sinners above others, but that God, by their fate, was warning the nation to repent, otherwise they would also perish in a wrathful manner. By the parable of a long-barren fig tree, he taught that unless the present dispensation of the gospel to the Jewish nation brought them speedily to repentance and holiness, they would soon be terribly punished, and their church and state altogether ruined. On a Sabbath day, he cured a woman who, for 18 years, had suffered with her disease, and vindicated his conduct by remarking that even oxen and asses were taken out to be watered on the Sabbath; so much more might a Jewess, and a good woman, be healed on the day.

On his way south, as he taught, someone asked him if only few were to be saved? He earnestly admonished those present to secure their own entrance into a new covenant state, as many who had a form of religion would be eternally ruined, and the Gentiles, though last invited, would come from every quarter, and sit down with Abraham, Isaac, and Jacob, while the Jews, who had the first invitation, and were a kind of *heirs of the kingdom of heaven*, would be cast out. Some Pharisees, informing him that it was necessary for him to leave Galilee, as Herod intended to kill him, he told them, "Go tell that fox, that cruel and crafty tetrarch, that it was beyond his power to touch him till his work was perfected, and that he would go up and die at Jerusalem." On mentioning this, he broke out into a mournful lament over the wickedness and ruin of that city. (Luke 13)

While he dined in the house of a Pharisee on the Sabbath, a man came to him for a cure of his chronic dropsy. Jesus asked those present whether he might heal on the Sabbath. None offered to reply, so he, with a touch, restored the man to perfect health. To vindicate his conduct, he observed that an ox or ass could be drawn out of a pit on the Sabbath day. Observing how the guests picked out the best seats for themselves, he advised them to be humble if they had a mind to be truly honoured, and to bestow their liberality on the poor rather than in feasting their rich friends. By the parable of a Great Supper, he taught that the Jews, and afterward the Gentiles, should, in the gospel dispensation, be solemnly invited and urged to come and enjoy the fullness of God. In his later travels, he advised the attending crowd to ponder seriously what trouble and expense it might cost them to follow him faithfully. From his intimate eating with publicans and some notable transgressors, the Pharisees inferred that he was a bad man himself. To vindicate himself, he, by the parables of *the lost sheep*, *the lost piece of money*, and *the prodigal son*, taught with what infinite pains, mercy, and pleasure, God recovers and saves self-destroyed, polluted, lost, and prodigal sinners, chiefly among the Gentiles. To stimulate his audience to wisely improve their spiritual advantages, he told the parable of the unjust steward. He reproved the Pharisees' pride, and their ill-grounded divorces. To warn them against trusting in riches, and indulging themselves in sensual pleasures, he, by the parable of Lazarus and the *rich glutton*, showed them that these things often corrupt men's hearts, and ripen them for eternal misery. He warned them to avoid offences, readily to forgive injuries, and to entertain a just awe of the divine authority, and a sense of the unworthiness of their most perfect obedience. About this time, he healed ten lepers, one of which, being a Samaritan, returned to give him thanks. (Luke 14-16, 17:1-19)

Christ's final ministry in Judea

Probably after crossing the Jordan south of Tiberias, Jesus went south along the east side of the river till he was over against Judea. He assured his Pharisaic audience that his kingdom would not come in the earthly and outward way they expected, and that many fearful plagues would quickly fall on the Jewish nation. By the parable of the *importunate widow*, he showed the advantage of earnestness and perseverance in prayer. To reprove the Pharisees' pride, and remark on the harmfulness of a self-righteous attitude, he declared the parable of the *Pharisee and Publican* praying in the Temple. He then pointed out the true causes of divorce. He blessed the babies that were brought to him. He directed the young ruler how to attain eternal happiness, and showed the difficulty

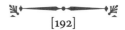

of rich men being truly religious, and the happiness of those who, at any age or period, forsake all to follow him and his truth. This last point he illustrated by the parable of *the labourers*, hired at different hours to work in a vineyard, and yet, through the liberality of the master, receiving an equal reward. He again foretold his sufferings. He checked James and John who, at their mother's instigation, ambitiously desired the highest civil offices in the worldly kingdom that they expected him to begin soon, and solemnly prohibited all lordly dominion or rule in his Church. (Matt. 19-20; Mark 10; Luke 17:20, and ch. 18)

When Lazarus, the brother of Martha and Mary fell ill, they sent for Jesus to heal him. After continuing where he was two days longer, till he knew Lazarus was dead, Jesus set off with his disciples for Bethany. Before he reached that place, Lazarus had been dead for four days, and was buried; nevertheless, after some conversation with his sisters, Jesus restored him to life. This notable public miracle convinced a number of Jews who were there from Jerusalem that he was the Messiah. Others, being hardened in their unbelief, went and informed the Sanhedrin, which resolved to kill him, and issued orders that whoever knew where he was, should let them know. To lessen the evidence of the miracle, they also agreed to put Lazarus to death. Great inquiry and talk concerning him ensued; but Jesus retired to a village called Ephraim, near the wilderness between Bethel and Jericho. To the last of these places, he soon went, and healed three blind beggars, one as he entered the city, and two as he left. Here, he converted Zaccheus the publican. At a feast in his house, Jesus, by the parable of the *pounds distributed* by a great man to his servants, to trade with till he returned from a far country, taught them that he himself would quickly ascend into heaven to receive his glorious kingdom, and would return to judge the world on the last day: and that it was only those who improved their gifts and endowments that might expect a happy reward, while the Jewish nation would be destroyed by the Roman troops for rejecting him. (Matt. 20:29; Mark 10:46; Luke 18:35-43, 19:1-29; John 11)

On the 6th day before the Passover, Jesus, amid a crowd of attendants, returned to Bethany, and was kindly entertained by Lazarus and his sisters. The day after, he sent his disciples to fetch him an ass, and rode on it into Jerusalem, while a huge crowd laid branches, and even their clothes, on the road, and echoed loud acclamations of praise, signifying that he was the Royal Messiah. Enraged at this, some Pharisees wanted

him to silence the noise, but he replied that God had determined to honour him, and, if these children and others were silent, the very stones would praise him. As he passed the Mount of Olives, and had a full view of Jerusalem below, he lamented with tears, and foretold its approaching siege and destruction by the Romans. The inhabitants were greatly moved at his entrance, and asked what this concourse and these acclamations meant? When he entered the Temple Court, he, for the second time, cleared out the money-changers, and the merchants of animals for sacrifice, and commanded the people to make it a place of prayer, not of fraud and deceit. The rest of that day, he taught in the Temple, while the youths and others, imagining he was just about to set up an earthly kingdom, made the whole court resound with loud acclamations of his praise. In the evening, he retired to Bethany, and, returning next morning, he observed a fig tree covered with leaves. Though the time of gathering figs had not yet come, he hoped this forward tree might have some ripe ones; but finding it had none, he cursed it into future barrenness, with withering as an emblem of what would befall the Jewish nation, which, despite their general running after John the Baptist or himself, continued in her barrenness and lack of good works. Hearing that some Greeks wanted to see him, and whom doubtless he admitted, he spoke about his death and resurrection, and of its blessed fruit among the Gentiles, while the Jews would continue hardened in their unbelief; and he exhorted his audience to take hold of the gospel while they had it, as it would quickly be taken from them. (John 12; Matt. 21:1-23; Mark 11:1-27; Luke 19:29-46)

As he taught in the Temple, some priests, elders, and scribes demanded his authority. By offering to inform them if they would first tell him whether the baptism of John was of human or divine authority, he checked their impudence. By the parable of *two sons*, appointed to labour in their father's vineyard, he suggested that despite the Jews' professed readiness in the service of God, the long rebellious Gentiles would soon yield to the obedience of faith. By the parable of a *husbandman farming a vineyard*, and abusing the owner's servants and son, he hinted that, for the Jews' abuse of God's prophets, and the murder of his Son, their church-state would be taken from them, and they would be miserably destroyed by the Romans. By the parable of *a marriage-feast for a king's son*, he spoke of God's earnestness in calling sinners, both Jews and Gentiles; and the fearful vengeance that would overtake the despisers of the gospel, and hypocritical embracers of it. (Matt. 21:23, 22:1-14; Mark 11-12; Luke 20:1-19) He lodged that night in Bethany. On his return to Jerusalem next morning, Peter remarked that the cursed fig tree was already withered; so Jesus took occasion to point out the power of faith in prayer, and the necessity of forgiving injuries.

During the night, the Pharisees resolved to carry out his murder, and, if possible, draw in the Roman governor. To make Jesus obnoxious, under pretence of friendship and scruples of conscience, they asked him if it was lawful to pay tribute to Caesar. From their use of money bearing Caesar's superscription and image, he inferred they were Caesar's subjects, and owed him his tax, but in such a way that God would not be wronged. Next, the Sadducees attempted to puzzle him with a question concerning the resurrection of the dead. He showed them that the error sprang from their ignorance of the Scripture and of the power of God, and that the truth of the resurrection was plainly implied in God calling himself the God of Abraham, Isaac, and Jacob after they were dead. Next, the Pharisees attempted to puzzle him by asking which was the greatest commandment? He replied that our whole duty lay in first loving God with all our heart, soul, mind, and strength, and in loving our neighbour as ourselves. As they acquiesced in the correctness of his answer, he, in his turn, asked them how the Messiah could at once be David's Son and Lord. To this, they were unable to make any reply. While the people stood astonished at his wisdom, he warned them to avoid imitating the Scribes and Pharisees in their professing much and doing little, in their hiding the vilest practices under a religious disguise, and in a proud affectation of honorary titles. Turning himself to the Scribes and Pharisees, he pronounced a number of woes against them for their wickedness and deceit, and assured them of the approaching ruin of their city and Temple for the contempt and murder of God's messengers and Son. Observing the people casting their offerings into the sacred treasury, be remarked that a poor widow's two mites were a most notable donation, as they were all she had. (Matt. 22:15, 23; Mark 12:14; Luke 20:20) As he was retiring from the Temple, one of his disciples remarked what a fine structure it was. He told him that, in a while, not one stone would be left upon another. When he had passed the Valley of Jehoshaphat, and had sat down on the Mount of Olives, Peter and Andrew, James and

John, asked him when the destruction of the Jewish Temple and the end of the world would happen, and what would be the signs of it. In his reply, he connected both together, and told them that false christs and prophets would arise; terrible wars, famines, pestilences, and persecutions would happen; Jerusalem would be besieged; the Jewish church and nation overturned; the capital and other cities razed; and they themselves for many ages would become wretched exiles in almost every nation of the world. He warned them to prepare for it, as they did not know how suddenly it might come; and God, on that occasion, would show singular favour to the godly, and execute terrible vengeance on the wicked, particularly on those that knew their duty and did not do it. This point he illustrated by the parables of a *householder* coming unawares upon his servants, and of a *bridegroom* coming at midnight to *virgins foolish and wise*, and of a nobleman calling his servants to account for the talents he had delivered to them before his setting off on a long journey. He concluded with a plain prediction of his own awful procedure in the Last Judgement of the world. (Matt. 24-25; Mark 13; Luke 21)

Next day, he stayed at Bethany, and told his friends that, after two more days, his sufferings and death would take place; and even then the Jewish rulers consulted how to put him to death, though they feared to do it on the feast-day for fear of the people taking his side. In the evening, he dined in the house of one Simon, whom he had healed of leprosy. Lazarus and his sisters were present, and Martha superintended the meal. Mary, to the no small grief of Judas Iscariot, and it seems of other disciples, poured a box of precious ointment, worth over £9, on Jesus' head, as he sat at table. He gently vindicated her conduct, alleging that they would have opportunities later to show benevolence to the poor when they would not have his bodily presence to honour. Fired with indignation, Judas sent a message to the Sanhedrin, and agreed to betray his divine Master into their hands for the price of a slave, a sorry rate of over £3. This treachery Jesus perceived, but seemed to take no notice of it. It was after this entertainment, or after the Passover Supper next night, that Jesus washed his disciples' feet, to teach them humility and brotherly affection. (Matt. 26:1-16; Mark 14:1-11; Luke 22:1-6; John 13)

The Last Supper and teaching

Next day, being the first day of Unleavened Bread, Jesus sent Peter and John to go to Jerusalem where they would meet a man carrying a jug of water, who, when asked, would give them a furnished room prepared for celebrating the Passover. In the evening, he and they, on the very day observed by other Jews, observed the Passover. As they were eating the supper of bitter herbs, Jesus told them that one of them would betray him. Filled with perplexity, they asked him one by one, "Lord, is it I?" Jesus replied that it would be one of them, and his fate would be terrible. Instigated by Peter, John, who was reclining on the couch next to Jesus, secretly asked who the person was? By giving a sop dipped in the sauce to Judas Iscariot, Jesus hinted that it would be HIM. Judas, suspecting the act, said, "Lord, am I the traitor?" Jesus told him that he had hit on the very person, and added, *What thou doest, do quickly."* Confounded by this discovery, Judas immediately went out. Jesus then observed that now God would glorify his Son in making him an atoning sacrifice, and would be glorified in him. The mention of his future glory started a new argument among the Eleven as to which of them would be greatest in his kingdom. He rebuked them sharply, and advised them to follow humility and perseverance in his service if they desired a glorious reward. While they continued their supper, Jesus, consecrating the bread and wine, instituted and dispensed the sacrament of his body and blood. This over, he told them he would quickly leave them as to his bodily presence, and charged them to manifest themselves as his disciples by loving one another. He warned them that they would all desert him that very night, and Peter would deny him three times, though his faith would not utterly fail. He warned them to prepare themselves with spiritual strength for their approaching trials. This, they foolishly imagined to mean their providing themselves with weapons of war. After he had instructed them with a long consolatory discourse concerning the heavenly mansions, which he was going to prepare for them; concerning the Father's love to them, and the coming of the Holy Spirit to instruct and comfort them; and concerning their union with, and service to, himself, then he concluded with a solemn prayer, mainly on behalf of his disciples and people; and, after singing a hymn, they left the house at nearly midnight. (Matt. 26:15 38; Mark 14; Luke 22:6-38; John 13-17)

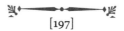

Christ's arrest, trials, and crucifixion

Crossing the brook Kidron, they came to the Mount of Olives, to the Garden of Gethsemane. Jesus, along with Peter, James, and John, retired to a corner there. Going a little from them, he prayed three times with the utmost fervour, that if it was possible, and consistent with his Father's will, his sufferings might be prevented. At every turn, his disciples fell asleep. Meanwhile, the impressions and fears of his Father's wrath threw him into such an agony of soul-trouble that he sweat great drops of blood, though the night was cold, and he was lying on the ground. At length, Judas, coming with a band of ruffians from the High Priest, pointed out to them with a kiss which was he, that they might arrest him. To show his power to withstand them, he, with a word caused them to fall backward; and after they had recovered themselves, he desired them to let his disciples go if they wanted him. Peter drew his sword, and cut off the ear of Malchus, one of the high priest's servants. Jesus rebuked him, and told him that it was right for him to endure what sufferings his Father had appointed him; and that if it were not so, he could easily obtain bands of angels to protect him; and, with a touch, he healed Malchus' ear. Meanwhile the disciples fled, and Judas, with his band, carried Jesus before Annas, the former High Priest. Annas interrogated him concerning his disciples and doctrines. Jesus replied that, as he had taught nothing privately, the Jews could bear witness to his teaching. Enraged with this mild and just reply, one of the High Priest's servants struck him in the face. Jesus meekly asked him if it was right to strike him for no reason.

Jesus, was then brought to the palace of Caiaphas the High Priest, and was stood before a convention of priests and elders. Great pains were used to find false witnesses, but none *sufficient* could be found. Those they had bribed did not agree in their depositions. At last, two presented themselves who claimed that they heard him say that he would destroy the Temple and build another in three days. This testimony was neither true of itself, nor was the thing declared worthy of punishment, nor did they swear to the very same words. Jesus, meanwhile, remained completely silent. Caiaphas, therefore, adjured him by God to tell them whether he was the true Messiah or not. Jesus acknowledged that he was, and would later, with great power and glory, judge the world.

Caiaphas immediately tore his clothes, and cried out that they had no need of further witnesses, having heard him blaspheme. The whole court declared him worthy of death. They were dismissed, and Jesus was committed to a band of soldiers who, during the night, threw him a thousand insults. Peter, having followed Jesus into the judgement-hall to see the end, with very slight provocations three times wickedly, and at last with horrible oaths, denied in his presence that he had ever known him. At the second crowing of the cock, Jesus graciously looked at him, which, being attended with a powerful conviction of his conscience, he went out and wept bitterly. (Matt. 26:35-75; Mark 14:30-72; Luke 22:38-71; John 18:1-27) Next morning, the Council assembled early in their ordinary place in the Temple, and Jesus was brought before their bar. They interrogated him if he was the *Messiah, the Son of God*. He replied that it was needless to tell them, as they were determined not to believe what he said; but they would afterwards be obliged to acknowledge his power when they saw him at the right hand of God inflicting punishment on his enemies. They again demanded if he was the *Son of God*. He replied that he was. The judges cried out that he deserved death for his blasphemy. They then carried him bound to Pontius Pilate the Roman Governor, that he might ratify their sentence, and give orders for his execution. Judas the traitor, stung with guilt, came and asserted his Master's innocence, and threw down the reward of his treachery. Unmoved at that, they proceeded to Pilate's judgement-hall; but would not enter it, for fear of defiling themselves in a heathen's house during their feast of Unleavened Bread. Pilate, therefore, came out to a balcony and asked their charge against Jesus. They told him that he was certainly an evildoer who deserved death, which they had no power to inflict. Pilate insisted on a particular charge and proof. They claimed he had perverted the nation, forbidding the payment of tribute to Caesar, and calling himself the Messiah. After Pilate had examined Jesus concerning his royalty, he told the Jews that he could find no fault in him. The priests and elders all the more vehemently accused him, alleging he had begun at Galilee, and stirred up the people to rebellion against the Emperor. To these accusations, Jesus, to the governor's surprise, never answered a word. Hearing that he had been in Galilee, Pilate sent him to Herod the Tetrarch of that country, who was then at Jerusalem, and was pleased to have such

respect shown to his authority, and to have an opportunity of meeting Jesus.

To the questions of Herod, and the continued charges of the Scribes and elders, Jesus answered nothing. To express his contempt of him, and of the charges laid against him, Herod, after mocking him a while, sent him back to Pilate dressed as a mock king. Once and again, Pilate remonstrated with the Jews that, in his view, Jesus was innocent; and, warned by his wife's dream, he washed his hands in water, protesting that he had no hand in his death. The Jewish crowd cried for his crucifixion, and wished that his blood might fall on them and their children. Pilate, after permitting the soldiers to clothe him in purple, and crown him with thorns as a mock sovereign, caused him to be scourged in order to move them to pity, and employed some further means to obtain his rescue. Finding the mob was mad on the release of Barabbas and the crucifixion of Jesus, and fearing they might cause an uproar in the city and accuse him of being unfaithful to Caesar, he, against his conscience, released Barabbas, a notorious murderer, and condemned Jesus to be crucified.

The Jews and the Roman guard roughly hurried him to Golgotha, the place of execution. All the way, they insulted and abused him, and forced him to carry his own cross. When he almost fainted under its pressure, they compelled Simon a Cyrenian to assist him. Some pious women attended Jesus, weeping over his treatment. He told them to weep for themselves and their children; for if he, though *innocent*, suffered in this way, what terrible vengeance would overtake their *guilty* nation, so ripe for the judgement of heaven! After offering him vinegar and myrrh mingled with gall, and stripping off his clothes, the soldiers nailed him to his cross, with a thief on each side, and then divided his clothing. On the top of his cross, Pilate set an inscription in Hebrew, Greek, and Latin: *This is Jesus of Nazareth, King of the Jews.* Nor would he alter the inscription to make it carry the least charge against him. The Jewish rulers and others ridiculed Jesus as he hung on the cross, and he begged his Father to forgive these outrageous murderers. At first, it seems, both the thieves that were crucified along with him, ridiculed him. At last, one of them rebuked his fellow, asserted Jesus' innocence, and begged him to save him from ruin. Jesus told him that on that very day, he would be with him in the heavenly paradise. Jesus next recommended his sorrowful mother to the care of John, the son of Zebedee. About noon, when he had hung perhaps for three hours on the cross, the sun was supernaturally darkened, and continued like that until three o'clock in the afternoon. Jesus cried out in the Hebrew or Syriac, *My God, my God, why hast thou forsaken me?* Some mocked him, and thought that he was calling for Elijah. Jesus, quickly after that, cried out, *I thirst.* Someone held up to him a sponge full of vinegar, which, when he had tasted, he cried out that his suffering work was finished; and, recommending his soul to God, he bowed his head and gave up his spirit. (Matt. 27:1-50; Mark 15:1-38; Luke 22:68, 23:46; Luke 23:28, 19:1-30)

When Jesus breathed his last, the veil of the Temple between the sanctuary and Most Holy Place was torn in two from the top to the bottom, to show that the ceremonial distinction between Jews and Gentiles was now abolished, and our access to the heavenly mansions obtained. The earth shook, the rocks split, and the graves were opened; and now, or rather at his resurrection, a number of saints arose, and appeared to many in Jerusalem. The spectators were struck with awe. The centurion who commanded the guard of soldiers cried out, certain that Jesus was a *righteous man*, indeed, the *Son of God*. The soldiers beat their breasts for terror and in grief for their hand in his death. The pious women who had accompanied Jesus from Galilee were deeply afflicted. That the body of Jesus and his fellow-sufferers might not remain on the cross during the Passover Sabbath, the Jewish rulers begged Pilate's permission to have their death hastened by breaking their legs. The legs of the thieves were broken; but Jesus, being dead, not a leg or a bone was broken; only a soldier thrust his spear into his side, and there issued from his heart blood and water. Joseph of Arimathea, having the disposal of Jesus' corpse allotted to him by Pilate, he and Nicodemus, after perfuming and wrapping it in fine linen, laid it in Joseph's new grave, which he had cut out in a rock in his garden. Under pretence of fear that his cowardly disciples might steal away the corpse and say he had risen, the Jewish leaders got the sepulchre sealed, and a guard of soldiers to watch it till the third day was over, the day in which he said he would rise. (Matt. 27:51-66; Mark 15:38-47; Luke 23:47-54; John 19:31) Their precautions to detain him in his grave contributed to render his resurrection more mighty and manifest.

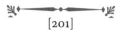

The Resurrection

Early on the third day, the first of the week, a terrible earthquake occurred. Angels, appearing in a glorious form, made the soldiers flee in astonishment as they rolled away the stone from the door of the grave. Jesus, the prisoner of divine justice, was solemnly released, and immediately resumed his natural life by the influence of the Holy Spirit. He came out of the tomb, leaving his grave clothes behind, a token that he would visit the grave no more. Mary Magdalene, and other holy women, who, on the Friday, had prepared spices for a further perfuming of his body, came early to his grave. They were astonished to find it open and the body gone, especially as they saw two angels in the glorious appearance of men, one at the head of the niche where the corpse had been lain, and the other at the foot. One of them kindly addressed them, and told them their Saviour had risen as he had foretold. The women ran to inform the disciples. However badly they judged the report, Peter and John ran to the grave to see for themselves. They saw the grave clothes, were persuaded he had gone, and hastened to inform the brothers. Mary Magdalene ran back a second time and wept at the grave. One of the angels comforted her and asked why she was crying. She had just turned round to go home when Jesus himself appeared to her. As soon as she knew it was he, she was going to embrace him, but he told her to desist for the present, but to go, run, and tell his disciples, particularly Peter, who had so recently denied him, that he had risen from the dead, and would shortly ascend into heaven. On her way, she met with the other women; and Jesus visited them. Meanwhile, the guard of soldiers informed the Jewish rulers of what they had witnessed, and were bribed to say that his disciples had come and stolen him away while they slept. What a farce! How deeply flawed this most glaring falsehood! That very night, Jesus appeared to two of his disciples as they went to Emmaus, speaking mostly about his sufferings and glory; and he made himself known in the breaking of bread. By this time also, he had graciously appeared to Peter, who had so shamefully denied him. At night, he visited some of his disciples while they were meeting in an upstairs room, and desired them to handle him to make sure he was really there, and not a spirit. Eating a part of their meal with them, he breathed upon them as a sign of their receiving the Holy Spirit, and authorised them to be officers in his Church. Thomas, being absent, swore he would not believe in

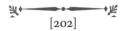

his Master's resurrection until he felt the wounds that had been made on his body. A week later, Jesus appeared to the Eleven, and offered Thomas the proof he had asked for. Soon after, when Peter, James and John, Thomas and Nathaniel, were fishing on the Sea of Tiberias, Jesus appeared to them; and, under his direction, they caught a great many fish as a sign that many would speedily be converted to Christ. Here, he shared fellowship with them, and interrogated Peter concerning his love for him, and predicted his future afflictions.

Soon after, on a mountain in Galilee, he appeared to James, to the Eleven, and, in all, to more than 500 of his followers. Forty days after his resurrection, he appeared to his Apostles at Jerusalem, ordered them to wait there till they were endued with the miraculous powers of the Holy Spirit, and then commanded them go and *preach the gospel to every person and nation, baptising them in the name of the Father, Son, and Holy Spirit.* He assured them of his extensive power, and of his gracious presence with them and their successors, to protect them and bring success on their labours. Thus talking to them, he led them out to the Mount of Olives near Bethany, perhaps the very spot where he had experienced his bitter agony, and, while he blessed them, he was conveyed up to heaven amid multitudes of angels, and sat down at the right hand of God. There, in inconceivable happiness and honour, he now employs himself in ruling his Church, interceding, and preparing the heavenly mansions for his people. By his Word and Spirit, and providence on earth, he is preparing them for above. About 40 years after his death, his terrible vengeance fell on, and ruined, the Jewish church and nation. At the last day, in a glorious way, he will judge the world of devils and men, put an end to every earthly form of government, and present all his chosen before the Father. Through eternity, he will continue in our human nature, the everlasting means of fellowship between God and ransomed men. (Ps. 110:4; Isa. 9:7, 60:19; Matt. 25:31-46, and 28; Mark 14; Luke 24; John 20-21; Acts 1:12, 3:20-21; 1 Cor. 15:24-28; Rev. 21:23)

An assessment of the life and ministry of Christ

Whatever astonishing mysteries are implied in the incarnation, obedience, and death of the Son of God, it is still more inconceivable how any deceiver, unlearned or learned, could, with such honesty, present a character so grand and amiable. When the birth, life,

death, resurrection, and glory of Jesus of Nazareth, and the various circumstances surrounding it, are compared with the ancient types and predictions, the agreement is so clear and complete that it is surprising how anyone can doubt his Messiahship. His doctrines, miracles, and resurrection, attested by friends and foes, the success of his gospel, even the unbelief of the Jews, and the terrible ruin of their church and nation, yet their miraculous preservation as a distinct race in their dispersion and distress, and all the false christs or messiahs that have appeared among them, at once fulfil his predictions and demonstrate his Messiahship. Nothing, therefore, but ignorance of the ancient prophecies and ceremonies, pride, and the mad desire for an earthly deliverer and sovereign Messiah, could, or can, influence the Jews to accept him. The stupid attitude in which they confirm themselves in their unbelief, how low and pitiful it is! For a while, being ignorant of chronology, they foreshortened the time between their return from Babylon and Jesus' birth, and pretended that the time of the Messiah's appearance predicted by the prophets had not yet come. Next, they became perplexed and divided in their feelings. Some pretended that his coming was delayed because of their sins; but how sin could be a reason for delaying a *deliverer from sin*, they do not know! Others pretend that he was born about the time their sceptre departed, and their city and Temple were ruined by Titus; but that he was concealed among the lepers at Rome, or in an earthly paradise, till Elijah should come and reveal him to men. For many ages past, they used to curse the man who pretends to calculate the time of the Messiah's appearance. Instead of justly applying the many different prophecies to the twofold state of the Messiah, they have stupidly split him into two: as a descendant of Ephraim who, amid terrible distress, will, with the troops of Ephraim, Manasseh, Benjamin, and Gad, attempt to deliver the Jews, and will perish in this work; or of the family of David, who will raise the former from the dead, revive the dead Jews, rebuild their Temple at Jerusalem, and conquer and rule the whole earth.

When we consider the relationship between Christ's Person as God-Man with his work in executing his offices, and his states of humiliation and glory, when we consider how God is in, and with, him, and how all his perfections are displayed, and his truths exemplified in him, when we consider his various relationships with the purposes, covenants, words, and ordinances of God, and with the Church, and with the privileges, duties, and worship of the saints, whether in time or eternity, we have a delightful view of him as *All, and In All.* (Col. 3:11)

False Christs
False Christs are those that pretend to be the Messiah. What a number of these have appeared among the Jews, as a punishment for rejecting Jesus, can be seen in their history! (Matt. 24:24)

CREATOR
The creation of all things from nothing happened about 4004 years before our common account (according to Bishop James Ussher). To give us an example of working six days, and resting on the seventh, and to make the order of his operation obvious to us, God used six days to bring his work of creation to perfection. On the **first** day, he formed the general system of earth, and probably the angels. The earth was at first a rough mass, without form and beauty, inhabitants, or product. The divine Spirit, in his actuating influence, hovered over the dark surface of this deep chaos. By the Word, and the will of the eternal Son of God (Col. 1:15-16), light was formed and separated from the darkness, to make a succession of day and night. On the **second** day, God made a firmament, expansion, or atmosphere, to support the water in the clouds, and separate it from what was below. On the **third** day, he drained the water from the earthy parts of our system, and gathered it into seas, either in the bowels of the earth, or in beds on the surface specially made for the purpose. On the **fourth** day, he further collected the light, and formed the sun, moon, and stars, and appointed them their circuits and use. On the **fifth** day, he formed the fish from water, and the birds from a mixture of water and earth. On the **sixth** day, he formed cattle, creeping things, and the body of Adam, out of the dust of the ground, and the body of Eve out of a rib taken from Adam's side: both Adam and Eve were, in their formation, given rational and immortal souls.

Louis Cappellus and others believed that the creation came about in the spring, the first day being about the 11th of April. But as many of the most ancient secular writers reckoned the beginning of their year from the harvest, nor do we know of any other reckoning till the Jews' departure from Egypt, and as the trees and herbs bore seed on the day of their creation, we are inclined, with the great Ussher and others, to think that the world was created in the harvest time; but whether on the 22nd day of October as Ussher suggested, or about the 1st of September as Joseph Juste Scaliger and Friedrich Spanheim, we leave undetermined, though the latter opinion appears the most probable. As Moses' account of the creation is very short, René Descartes, Thomas Burnet, Walston, Buffon, and others have attempted a philosophical explanation, if not a confutation of other opinions. But, as we believe, Moses' informant knew better how it was done than any of these learned gentlemen, we shall not burden serious readers with any of their fancies! And, as you know, what the scholars put out as solid ideas are really only opinions.

CHRISTIANS

The saints are so-called because they belong to, obey, and imitate Jesus Christ, and are anointed with the same Spirit of God. To constitute someone a true, mature Christian, he must be united to Christ as his head and husband, have Christ and his Spirit dwelling in his heart, have Christ's grace implanted in all the faculties of his soul, and must believe, profess, and practise Christ's truths in conformity with his example and commands. Probably, by divine direction, his disciples were *first called Christians at Antioch* in the apostolic age, and they still retain this title. (Acts 12:26, 26:28; 1 Pet. 4:16)

To have *Christ formed in us* is to have our persons united to him by spiritual union, that he and his Spirit of grace may dwell in our hearts by faith. (Gal 4:19; Eph. 3:17) Jesus and his people, considered as united in one mystical body of which he is Head, under whom they are members, are called Christ. (1 Cor. 12:12)

CLAUDIA

A Roman lady, who, it is thought, was converted to Christianity through Paul (2 Tim. 4:21), possibly the wife of Pudens.

CLAUDIUS CAESAR

The 5th Roman Emperor. He succeeded the mad Caligula in AD 41, and reigned 13 years. The Senate wanted to assert its ancient liberty, but, by the army and populace, and the craftiness of Herod Agrippa, Claudius obtained the imperial throne. To mark his gratitude to

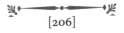

Agrippa, he gave him the sovereignty of Judea, and the kingdom of Chalcis to his brother Herod. He also confirmed the Alexandrian Jews in their privileges, but prohibited those in Rome to hold any public meetings. Some time later, he reduced Judea to a Roman province, and ordered all the Jews to depart from Rome. His reign was notable for almost nothing but a terrible famine, for his own timidity, and for the abominable and disorderly lives of Messalina and Agrippina, his wives. (Acts 11:28, 18:2)

CLAUDIUS LYSIAS
A tribune of the Roman guard at Jerusalem. With a great price, he had obtained his freedom as a Roman citizen. (Acts 22:28) When the Jewish mob wanted to murder Paul, Lysias rescued him out of their hands, bound him with chains, and carried him off to the garrison's fort of Antonia. He then ordered Paul to be scourged, hoping to extort a confession out of him; but, upon information that he was a Roman citizen, he cancelled his orders, and, next day, brought him before the Council. Finding Paul's life in danger among them, he again by force carried him back to the fort. Soon after, he was informed that more than 40 Jews had sworn neither to eat nor drink till they had murdered Paul. Lysias, therefore, sent him off to Felix at Caesarea under the protection of a strong guard. (Acts 21-23)

CLEMENT
A notable Christian who preached the gospel along with Paul at Philippi. He wrote an excellent personal letter to the Corinthians, and is thought by many to have been the fourth Bishop of Rome. (Only found in Phil. 4:3)

CLEOPHAS
Probably the same as Alpheus, and is said to have been the brother of Joseph, our Lord's adoptive father, and the husband of Mary, the sister of the blessed Virgin (see John 19:25), and father of Simon and James the Less, and of Jude and Joseph (or Joses), the cousins-germane of Christ.

Though Cleophas and his family were followers of our Saviour, he remained very ignorant of the mystery of his death; and, when it happened, he greatly doubted his Messiahship. On the evening after the resurrection, while Cleophas and another disciple (possibly his wife) travelled to Emmaus, and were talking about Jesus, he himself joined them in the form of a traveller, and, from the Scriptures, showed them the necessity of the Messiah's sufferings to enter into his glory. Cleophas invited him to dine with them; and, while they were eating, they discerned that it was the Lord; but he disappeared by going off suddenly. Cleophas and his companion hastened back to Jerusalem and informed the disciples, who, in their turn, observed that he had also appeared to Peter. Just as they were speaking, Jesus presented himself among them. (Luke 24:13-35) It is probable that Cleophas was an inhabitant of Galilee rather than of Emmaus.

CORNELIUS

A centurion, belonging to the Italian Band. He was a Gentile by birth, probably of the *Cornelii* at Rome, but a devout proselyte at the gate of the Jewish religion, living in Caesarea. While be was employed in solemn prayer and fasting, an angel appeared to him, assuring him that God had accepted his prayers and alms, and he was to send to Joppa for Simon Peter, that he might receive further directions from him in his religious concerns. He immediately sent off two of his servants to bring Peter. Peter was prepared for this invitation by a vision of mixed beasts, both clean and unclean, which meant to him that God had chosen for himself a people from among the Gentiles also; therefore he ought to have no scruple in preaching the gospel to the Gentiles or admitting them as members of the Christian Church. Therefore, directed by the Holy Spirit, he went along with the servants. On the next day, about mid-afternoon, he arrived at Cornelius' house where, with a number of his friends, he was awaiting his arrival. It seems that Cornelius mistook Peter for the Messiah, and so fell at his feet to worship him, but was quickly checked by Peter, who raised him up and informed him that he was a mere man. After Cornelius had told Peter how he came to send for him, and that he and his friends were assembled to hear the Word of God, Peter preached them a sermon concerning Jesus the Messiah, about his miracles, sufferings, and glorious resurrection, and of his sufficiency to save them from sin. Meanwhile, to the surprise of Peter's Jewish attendants, the Holy Spirit in his miraculous power fell upon Cornelius and his Gentile friends, and they spoke in tongues. At Peter's command, they were

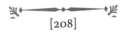

immediately baptised. Cornelius detained Peter so that he might stay with him for a few days. At first, the believers at Jerusalem were offended with Peter for baptising Gentiles; but, on hearing the whole story, they glorified God for granting the Gentiles faith and repentance. This was the first notable gathering of Gentiles to Christ; and, perhaps, at this very time, the sceptre entirely departed from Judah. (Gen. 49:10; Acts 10-11)

COZBI

A daughter of Evi, prince of Midian. She, and a number of her countrywomen, came into the camp of the Israelites to seduce them into sex and idolatry; but being taken in the very act of adultery with Zimri the son of Sallu, a prince of the Simeonites, Phinehas the High Priest thrust them both through the belly in the middle of their infamous embrace. (Num. 25:6-15) She is the first of a long line of idolatrous seducers and enemies of the people of God, such as Jezebel (1 Kings 16:31, 18:4; Rev. 2:20), and the great whore (Rev. 17:16, 19:2).

CYRENIUS, Quirinus

The Roman deputy in Syria, some years after our Saviour's birth. He obliged the Jews to pay the tax they had been enrolled for, at the same time. (Only found in Luke 2:1-2)

CYRUS, *the womb*

The son of Cambyses, King of Persia, by Mandane the daughter of Ahasuerus, King of the Medes. The story of his grandfather's appointing him to death when an infant, and of his exposure and education by a shepherd, and of his violent death on the orders of the Scythian queen, we pass over as unworthy of him. His parents were extremely careful of his education, and he showed early an unusual sprightliness, wisdom, and courage. About 12 years of age, his mother carried him to her father's court. His generous, obliging, and heroic behaviour, quickly gained him the affection of the Medes. After five years, he returned to Persia. Aged about 40, he assisted Darius the Mede, his uncle, with 30,000 Persian troops. He reduced the revolting Armenians. Neriglissar, the king of Babylon, then intended to reduce the kingdom of Media. His huge army of Babylonians, Lydians, Cappadocians, Carians, Phrygians, Cilicians, and Paphlagonians, bid fair to swallow up Cyrus and his uncle, but his host

was routed, and Neriglissar himself was slain. Soon afterwards, Cyrus and his uncle, encouraged by Gobrias and Gadates, two revolting Babylonian lords, carried the war almost up to the very gates of Babylon, filling the country with terror, ravage, and bloodshed. To oppose him, Belshazzar entered into an alliance with Egypt, Thrace, and all the nations of Asia Minor, and raised an army of 420,000 men, of which Croesus, king of Lydia, had the command. Cyrus, with less than half the number, totally defeated them. He pursued Croesus to Sardus his capital, and, having taken it, ordered the inhabitants to bring him their gold and silver to save the place from being plundered. Croesus was the first to obey. Either his ready compliance, or his repeating a saying of Solon the Athenian sage indicating that no one was happy till his death, so touched the generous heart of Cyrus, that he ever after honoured Croesus, restored to him almost the whole power of his kingdom, and carried him about with him in all his later expeditions as a counsellor and friend. He then reduced the various nations of Asia Minor, Syria, and part of Arabia Deserta, took Babylon, and put an end to the Chaldean Empire. After settling their new form of government, and dividing their territories into 120 provinces, the command was handed over to those who had distinguished themselves in the war. Cyrus left Darius his uncle and father-in-law to govern the Empire, and marched to the conquest of Egypt.

Two years after the reduction of Babylon, Darius died, and Cyrus, having married his only daughter, became heir to the crown. Having perhaps read the Jewish prophecies concerning himself, or only determined by the providence of God, he, of his own accord in the first year of his reign, issued a warrant for the Hebrew captives to return to their country and rebuild the Temple of their God. About seven years later, in the 30th year of his reign over Persia, and the 70th of his life, he died in BC 529. (Dan. 2:39, 7:5, 8:3, 20; Isa. 41:2-3, 25, 44:26-28, 45:1-4, 13, 47:11; Ezra 1-3)

Extra note

The history of Cyrus is no less remarkable than it is important. He was the subject of prophecy long before his birth. His name is expressly mentioned in Isaiah; and, although a stranger to the commonwealth of Israel, he appears as an illustrious type of Messiah. It was he who fulfilled *"all the divine pleasure, saying to Jerusalem, thou shalt be built, and to the temple, thy foundation shall be laid."* (Isa. 44:28-29)

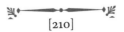

D

DAN, *judgement*

The fifth son of Jacob, and the oldest son of Bilhah. He had only one son, Hushim (or Shuham, see Gen. 46:23) yet, when his tribe came out of Egypt about 210 years later, they amounted to 62,700 under the command of Ahiezer, the son of Amishaddai. In the wilderness, they increased to 64,400. Their spy to search the Promised Land was Ammiel, the son of Gemalli, and their prince to divide it was Bukki, the son of Jogli. They, with the tribes of Asher and Naphtali, formed the fourth division of the Hebrew camp, and marched last. (Num. 1:12, 39, 8:25, 13:12, 26:43, 34:22) They had their inheritance on the northwest of Judah; but the Amorites retained a great part of the low country, particularly Ajalon and Shaalabin, till the neighbouring tribe of Ephraim obliged them to become tributaries. (Josh. 19; Judg. 1:34-35) Some of the Danites, informed of a city on the north of Bashan which might easily be taken from the Canaanites, 600 of them went and seized it and called it Dan. On the way, they robbed Micah the Ephraimite of his idol, and at Dan they set it up, and continued to worship it till they were carried captive by Tiglath-pileser. (Deut. 23:2; Judg. 18) During the oppression of King Jabin, the Danites, unconcerned at the misery of their brothers, applied themselves to their sea-trade, or shipped off their possessions to some other country. (Judg. 5:17) Samson, who came from this tribe, when judge of Israel, privately, and in no open war, terribly mauled the Philistines. (Judg. 15-16) There were 28,600 Danites at David's coronation. (1 Chron. 12:35) As this tribe lay so close to the Philistines, it was no doubt specially harassed by them.

DANIEL, *the judgement of God*

(1) A son of David by Abigail, perhaps identical with Chileab. (2 Sam. 3:3; 1 Chron. 3:1)

(2) A priest of Ithamar's family who returned with Ezra to Judea in BC 454, and who, about 20 years later, probably sealed Nehemiah's covenant of reformation. (Ezra 8:2; Neh. 10:6)

(3) Daniel the prophet was of the royal family of Judah, and, along with others, was carried captive to Babylon in BC 606. By Nebuchadnezzar's order, he, and three other boys, were educated in the

learning of Chaldea. All four had new names imposed on them, each meaning something to do with the idols of Babylon. Daniel was called *Belteshazzar*, Hananiah *Shadrach*, Mishael *Meshach*, and Azariah *Abed-nego*. These, and other young men educated in the same way, were appointed a daily allowance of provision from the king's own table. But such provision was partly forbidden by the Jewish Law, or would pamper their flesh too much, and perhaps entice them to idolatry. As it was at least not suitable for the captive state, Daniel and his three companions begged the prince of the eunuchs to give them pulse (a soup made from beans and peas) instead. He refused, lest their feeding on pulse should make them thin, and endanger his life. But Melzar his deputy, after testing them for ten days with pulse, and finding that they looked better than those who had eaten the king's provision, allowed them pulse as their ordinary diet. All four quickly excelled their fellow students in beauty and learning, and were admitted to wait on the king. Their wisdom was found to be far superior to that of all the wisemen of Babylon. (Dan. 1) Daniel's renown for piety and wisdom was very great, even when he was a youth. (Ezek. 14:14, 20; 28:3) Repeated occasions gave him the opportunity to reveal his wisdom.

About BC 604, Nebuchadnezzar dreamed of a large image, whose head was of gold, its breast and arms of silver, its belly and thighs of brass, its legs of iron, and its feet partly of iron and partly of clay. It was broken in pieces by a small stone cut from a mountain without hands, and which gradually increased into a mountain that filled the whole earth. This dream greatly affected the king; but he quickly forgot it. He convened a vast number of his wisemen, and, because they could not tell him his dream, nor its interpretation, he gave orders to kill them, whether present or absent. Daniel and his three companions, though not called to test their skill, were also appointed to die. Hearing of this bloody mandate, Daniel begged Arioch, the captain appointed to oversee the execution, to delay it till he and his fellows tried to meet the wishes of the king. After Daniel and his companions had spent some hours in fasting and prayer, Daniel was conducted by Arioch into the king's presence. He related the dream of the image, explained the golden head as the Chaldean monarchy, the silver breast and arms as the Medo-Persian Empire, the brazen belly and thighs as the Greek Empire, which was soon after its erection divided into the Syro-

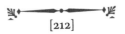

Grecian Empire and Egypto-Grecian Empire. The iron legs and feet were the Roman Empire, divided, in process of time, into the eastern and western Empires, and, at last, into ten sovereignties. These fourfold Empires would be overturned one after the other to make way for the glory of Christ and his Church to fill the whole earth. Nebuchadnezzar was so eminently satisfied with this speech and interpretation of his dream that he immediately constituted Daniel the chief of all his wisemen, and, at Daniel's request, promoted his three companions to places of authority in the province of Babylon. (Dan. 2)

About 16, or maybe 32, years later, when Nebuchadnezzar returned from his conquest of Judea, or Egypt, he set up a monstrous idol in the plain of Dura, and ordered everybody, as soon as they heard the sound of the orchestra on that occasion, to fall down and worship it. Daniel was then either absent from Babylon, or his high honoured position, and his large share of the king's favour made his enemies afraid to accuse him. But Shadrach, Meshach, and Abed-nego were accused, and made pannels (accused as criminals) before the king. At their interrogation, they declared their resolution not to worship the idol, and their firmest assurance of their God's ability to deliver them from the burning fiery furnace. Enraged at this uncompromising reply, Nebuchadnezzar ordered them to be cast bound into the furnace of fire, heated up sevenfold. The flame caught hold of those who cast them into the fire, and burnt them to ashes. But, at the interposal of the Son of God, who appeared walking with them in the furnace, the fire was only permitted to burn their bonds, but not so much as singe their garments or the hair of their heads. Nebuchadnezzar, observing this, commanded them to come out, which they did, and were advanced to even more honourable stations. And the king made this decree: That if anybody should speak reproachfully of the God of the Jews, whose power and majesty was so great, he would be put to death, and his house turned into a dunghill. (Dan. 3)

About the 35th year of his reign, Nebuchadnezzar dreamed of a large and flourishing tree cut down, and no more of it left except a stump fixed in the earth, wet with the dew of heaven till seven times passed over it. When none of the magicians, or other pretenders to wisdom, could interpret it, Daniel, after a handsome introduction and friendly advice, told the king that this dream meant that he would be deprived of his reason and royal dignity, and for seven years live as a beast in the field, after which, his reason and royal dominion would be returned to him. (Dan. 4)

About BC 553, Daniel himself had a vision of four beasts rising out of the sea: a lion, a bear, a leopard, and a monstrous beast. An angel informed him that they signified the Chaldean, Persian, Greek, and Roman Empires, the last of which, he was assured, would, at its fall, be divided into ten sovereignties, and give rise to Antichrist, whose duration would be 1260 years. (Dan. 7) Two years later, he had another vision of a pushing ram with two horns, and of a male goat that destroyed him. An angel informed him that the ram signified the Empire of the Medes and Persians, and the male goat, the Empire of the Greeks which, under Alexander, would destroy the Persians, and afterwards be divided into different kingdoms, one of which would, a little before its downfall, be governed by Antiochus Epiphanes, notable for his wickedness, conquests, and his persecution of the Jews, and abolition of their daily sacrifice for 1150 days, or 2300 evenings and mornings (Dan. 8) In BC 538, on the advice of Nitocris, Daniel was sent for, and he explained to Belshazzar and his courtiers the handwriting on the wall, and was made the third ruler in the kingdom.

Darius the Mede, that very night, planned his way for the establishment of his new Empire, and constituted Daniel the third ruler in it, and intended to make him deputy-governor next to himself. The heathen governors hated him for his religion, and were enraged at his promotion. Despairing of finding anything blameable in his conduct, except the practice of his religion, they craftily persuaded King Darius to enact an unalterable law: That whoever should for the space of 30 days ask any favour from either God or man, besides the king himself, would be cast into the den of lions to be torn in pieces. Informed that this wicked act was ratified, Daniel thought it his duty to avow his worship of God more publicly than before. Three times a day he prayed to his God, and opened his window toward Jerusalem. His enemies, who were watching him, quickly arrested him, and brought him before the king to be punished. Darius did what he could to deliver him; but all was in vain, as the royal laws of the Medes and Persians were unalterable. Daniel was thrown into a den of lions, but they were divinely restrained from attacking him. Darius, who could not sleep that night by reason of his grief, came early the next morning and, with a most mournful air, called to Daniel, and asked if his God had been able to deliver him from the lions? Finding him perfectly safe, he ordered him to be drawn up, and his accusers and their friends to be thrown into the den. These, the lions quickly tore to pieces and devoured, even before they hit the bottom. (Dan. 6)

About this very time, finding from Jeremiah's predictions that the captivity of the Jews would be just 70 years, and so their deliverance was at hand, Daniel applied himself to solemn fasting and prayer. While he was thus employed, the angel Gabriel came and informed him that his prayer was accepted, and that about the end of 70 weeks, or 490 years from Artaxerxes' edict to rebuild Jerusalem, the Messiah would appear, and, by his death, make atonement for sin, and fulfil a multitude of ancient prophecies; and that, soon after, the Jewish nation would be punished with lasting desolation and misery. (Dan. 9)

In BC 533, he next had a vision of Jesus Christ as a man of brass marked with glory, which almost killed him with terror had not another angel comforted him. This angel informed him how the kings of Persia had been divinely supported, and would be restrained from harming the Jews; that their Empire would, after the reign of a few kings, be seized by Alexander the Great; that his kingdom would be divided after his death, but not to his friends; that his successors in Egypt in the south and Syria in the north would have civil war; and of Antiochus' persecution of the Jews, and his miserable end; of the rise and fall of the Antichristian and Mahometan states; and of the deliverance of the Jews from their present dispersion, and the last judgement. (Dan. 10-12)

The style of Daniel is extremely simple; but his language from the 4th verse of the second Chapter to the end of the seventh is in Chaldee, and closely relates to the affairs of that Empire. Enraged at his fixing the time of the Messiah's coming, the Jews now deny Daniel the name of *prophet*; but our infallible Saviour called him one. (Matt. 24:15) The order of his predictions is very exact, and they serve as a key to those of the Revelation, together with many others, such as in Isaiah, Ezekiel, etc. The legendary stories of his affair with Susannah, and with Bel and the Dragon, we count beneath our notice.

DARIUS, *inquiring*, or CYAXARES the Mede

The son of Ahasuerus (or Astyages), and the brother of Mandane, mother of Cyrus, and of Amyit the mother of Evil-merodach, king

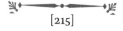

of Babylon. After a long war with the Babylonians, he got possession of their Empire on the death of Belshazzar, his grandnephew. He appointed 120 governors over his kingdom, and three chief ones to direct them, of which Daniel was one. On the occasion of Daniel's marvellous deliverance from the lions, he published an edict that all his subjects should have a reverential regard for the God of the Jews. (Dan. 5:31, chapter 6, 9:1, 11:1) He had scarcely reigned two years at Babylon when he died aged 64, and was succeeded by Cyrus, his nephew and son-in-law.

DARIUS Hystaspes. See Ahasuerus, the husband of Esther.

DAVID, *beloved*

The son of Jesse, and a descendant of Judah, was born at Bethlehem in BC 1085. No sooner had the Lord rejected Saul, than, to comfort Samuel, he sent him to anoint one of Jesse's sons to be king. David's seven older brothers were presented to that prophet, but he was instructed by God that none of them was the intended sovereign. David was brought home from the sheep, and, under the direction of God, was anointed to be king over Israel. After this, David returned to his flock, but the Spirit of God began to qualify him for his future office. Meanwhile, the spirit of government departed from Saul, and an evil spirit troubled him, producing a deep depression of spirit. David, who was an excellent musician, was brought to divert him with his music. His beauty, sober behaviour, and fine music, quickly gained him an interest in Saul's favour, and he became his armour-bearer. Saul's depression at length departed, and David returned to his flock.

The Philistines and Goliath

The Philistines then invaded the country. While they and the Hebrews encamped opposite one another for forty days, with the valley of Elah between them, Goliath presented himself, and offered to decide the fate of the war by a single combat with anyone they pleased, and defied them to produce the man that would engage him. The very sight of him terrified the Hebrews. At last, David came with provisions for his three older brothers who were serving in the army. Observing the proud Philistine defy the armies of the true God, and hearing that Saul's older daughter was offered to the man who would kill him, directed by God,

David showed his readiness to accept the challenge. Eliab, his elder brother, haughtily rebuked him, to which he gave a mild reply. Hearing of his offer, Saul sent for him to dissuade him from so one-sided a combat. David replied that he trusted in the Lord who had enabled him to slay a lion and a bear without any weapons, and who would give him the victory over this proud blasphemer. Pleased with this answer, Saul equipped him in armour similar to that of Goliath; but David, finding it a heavy burden, put it off, and met the giant with no arms at all but his staff, sling, and five small stones. Goliath disdained his appearance, and told him to come forward and he would give his flesh to the birds of the air and the beasts of the earth. David replied that he came against him armed with the protection and power of the God of Israel whom he had blasphemed, and whose armies he had defied. He slung a stone which, divinely directed, penetrated a hole in the giant's helmet, and, sinking into his forehead, brought him flat on the ground. David ran up to him, and, with Goliath's own sword, cut off his head. The Philistines' army fled, and the Hebrews pursued them with great slaughter to the very gates of Ekron. (1 Sam. 17)

The opposition of Saul

David's beard was now grown, and having his shepherd's dress on him, he was quite unknown to Saul and Abner his general till he informed them who he was. Jonathan had a very high regard for him. The Hebrew women, in their triumphal songs, having ascribed the slaughter of ten thousands to him, and of only thousands to Saul, that jealous monarch conceived an implacable resentment against him. He did indeed retain him in some post in the army, but treacherously gave away Merab his daughter to Adriel the Meholathite. When Saul returned to his house, and had no public affairs on hand, his depression returned, and David was called upon to divert him with music. Twice Saul attempted to murder him by throwing his javelin at him; but he escaped, and withdrew from his presence. Informed that his daughter Michal loved David, Saul planned to make this an occasion for murdering him. He proposed to David an offer of marriage with her, providing he would give a hundred foreskins of the Philistines as her dowry, hoping that he would perish in the attempt. David slew two hundred of these murderous enemies of his nation, and presented their foreskins to Saul who, on that account, was obliged to give him Michal as his wife. Just

DAVID

after, he directed Jonathan and other courtiers to kill David. Jonathan diverted this plot for the present. The Philistines then commenced a new war against Israel. David routed them with prodigious slaughter, and had hardly returned when, while he was diverting Saul with his harp, that malicious and unnatural wretch threw a javelin at him, and, because he escaped, ordered his guards to surround his house that night and murder him. Informed of her father's plan, Michal let David down by a window, and, laying an image in the bed, and pretending he was sick, spun out the time till he had got a good way off. (1 Sam. 17:55-58, chs. 18-19)

David fled to Najoth, where Samuel superintended a college of young men who were studying the divine Law, and preparing themselves to receive the gift of prophecy. Informed where he was, Saul sent two different parties to arrest him and bring him back. Whenever they came to the place, they were inspired, and fell to prophesying, or otherwise joined in the religious exercises of the college. Vexed that they did not return, Saul went there himself, and was so affected, that he lay on the ground almost naked before David and Samuel all that day and the following night. This might have taught him that God was David's protector. David, on invitation, returned, and entered into a solemn covenant of friendship with Jonathan, who undertook to discover whether his father was resolute in his determination to murder him or not. From his rage at David's absence on the feast of the new moon, he saw it evident that Saul was set on his murder; so, under pretence of shooting in the field, he went and informed David of his danger, and renewed their covenant of friendship. (1 Sam. 19:18-24, 20)

Ever after, David was in a state of exile from the court of his father-in-law. He, and a few of his servants went to Nob. Here, Ahimelech the High Priest, knowing nothing of the rupture between him and Saul, gave them showbread to relieve them in their absolute hunger, and gave David the sword of Goliath. This occasioned the murder of Ahimelech, and all the priests and inhabitants of Nob, Abiathar excepted. David fled to Achish, King of Gath, but finding that the Philistines knew and hated him for his killing of Goliath, he sinfully pretended to go out of his mind. Retiring from Gath, he went to Adullam, where his countrymen, and a number of malcontents, and people of desperate fortune, to the number of 400, came to him and promised to stand by him. His aged parents he carried off and put under the protection of the King of Moab, who might be an enemy of Saul. It was perhaps at this time that he went north to Mount Hermon, and married Maachah the daughter of Talmai, King of Geshur; and, on his return, he married Ahinoam the Jezreelitess. (2 Sam. 3:2-3) It is certain that the prophet Gad warned him not to return to the land of Judah. He obeyed, and remained in the forest of Hareth. Here, Abiathar came to him and told him of the destruction of Nob. Informed that the Philistines were ravaging Keilah, a city of Judah not far away, he marched to attack them, and took from them valuable booty. Saul, hearing that he was in Keilah, hastened, with some chosen troops to take him. Upon consulting the Lord whether the people of Keilah would ungratefully betray him to Saul if he remained in their city, he was informed that they would. He therefore retreated to the wilderness of Ziph; and that is where Jonathan came and renewed their covenant of friendship. The malicious Ziphites informed Saul where he was, so he came in quest of him. David retired to the wilderness of Maon, where he was at the point of being taken had not an invasion of the Philistines diverted Saul from his murderous pursuit. (1 Sam. 21, 23)

David retired eastward to the desert of En-gedi where he and his men lodged in a cave. Saul searched the countryside for him, and entered into this very cave to ease nature, or sleep during the heat of the day. Some of David's friends advised him to kill Saul when providence had delivered him into his hand; but he refused, and only cut off the skirt of his robe without being detected. When Saul had gone off some distance, David cried after him, and remonstrated how evident it was that he had no design on his life since he had only cut off his skirt when he might so easily have taken his life. Saul recognised the justice of what he had said, confessed his own guilt, and begged David not to destroy his family when he became king. After David had given him his word, he retired to his cave. David and his men had, till now, chiefly continued in the wilderness of Maon, in the southern part of the inheritance of Judah, and had protected Nabal's flocks from robbers and wild beasts. While Nabal kept his shearing-feast, David sent some of his servants to ask for small present of what he could best spare. Nabal abused the servants with foul language, calling David a base fellow that had outrun the king's service. Provoked by this, David furiously resolved to destroy him and his whole family had not Abigail intervened. (1 Sam. 24-25)

The Ziphites, eager to recommend themselves to the favour of Saul, informed him that David and his men had concealed themselves in the hill of Hachilah, close to Jeshimon. Saul, with 3000 chosen men, marched in quest of him. One night, David reconnoitred Saul's army, and, finding them all asleep, carried off Saul's spear and water pot. From a proper distance, be cried out and reproved Abner for guarding his master so badly, and how unjust it was to charge him with murderous designs against Saul when he had now, a second time, left him safe, while he had it so much in his power to slay him without being discovered. Saul readily acknowledged David's integrity, and, after receiving back his spear and cruse, went home. (1 Sam. 26)

Fearing that Saul might some time or other get him murdered, David too rashly decided to shelter in the country of the Philistines. Achish, King of Gath, having sufficient proof of the enmity between David and Saul, gave him the kindest reception, and allotted him and his men the city of Ziklag, which the Philistines had taken from the tribe of Judah as a dwelling place. While they stayed there, they made several attacks on the Amalekites, Geshurites, and Gezerites that lived in the west of the Arabian desert, and killed everybody they met, that no information might be given out against them. David made a present of the cattle to Achish, and pretended they had ravaged the country of the Kenites and the south of Judah. Achish believed this report, and placed his entire confidence in David. He even went with him to the war against Saul, and promised that he and his men would be his lifeguard. David pretended to he a hearty friend to Achish, but the opposition of the other lords of the Philistines obliged Achish to dismiss him and his men from the army as people not to be trusted. Had not providence thus interposed, David would have either sinfully fought against Israel, or proved treacherous to Achish. On his return to Ziklag, a number of valiant Manassites joined him, as some Gadites and Benjamites had done before; and it tuned out that the Amalekites, provoked by his late ravages, burnt Ziklag, and took his two wives Ahinoam and Abigail prisoners, and the rest of his people, and carried off what was valuable. His men were so enraged that they spoke of stoning him as the cause of this disaster, but he encouraged himself in the Lord, and consulted him whether he should pursue the plunderers, and if he could overtake them. Directed by God, he pursued them. An Egyptian slave of the enemy, who had been badly treated, and had fallen sick by the way, became his guide when he found the Amalekites spread abroad at a riotous feast in the field. He came on them unexpectedly, cut most of them to pieces, recovered the prisoners and booty, and took a rich spoil. Two hundred of his men had, by reason of fatigue, been obliged to halt at the brook Besor. The rest, who were engaged in the action, refused to give these anything but their wives and children; but David made them equal sharers of the booty with their brothers. His own share of the spoil he divided among his friends in Bethel, South Ramoth, Jattir, Aroer, Siphmoth, Eshtemoa, Rachal, Hormah, Chorashan, Athach, Hebron, and other cities on the south of Judah. By this means, he at once was able to express his gratitude for the kindness he had received; and, at this critical juncture, recommended himself to their favour. (1 Sam. 27-30)

Meanwhile, the Philistines defeated the Hebrews at Gilboa, and Saul and his three sons, with many in his army, were slain. On the third day after the battle, an Amalekite, expecting a reward, brought him Saul's crown, and pretended he had helped put him to death. David ordered him to be killed as a murderer of the king on his own confession. He and his warriors expressed great sorrow at the news of the defeat, and he composed a mournful elegy in honour of Saul and Jonathan. Finding the slaughter was entirely due to the Philistines' arrows, be ordered the men of Judah to be taught the use of the bow, that they might oppose the enemy on equal terms. (1 Sam. 31; 2 Sam. 1; 1 Chron. 10)

David made king of Judah and all Israel

Directed by God, David removed his family and warriors to Hebron. There, the princes of Judah came and made him their king; but Abner made Ishbosheth, Saul's son, king over the rest of the tribes. For some years, almost perpetual skirmishes took place between the troops of Ishbosheth and David, in which the latter always gained the advantage. At last, Abner, pretending to be offended at Ishbosheth, began to have dealings with David in order to make him king over all Israel, but he was murdered by Joab before he had fulfilled his purpose. David made it perfectly plain that he detested the murder, but Joab's reputation with the army saved him from deserved punishment. Baanah and Rechab, two Benjamites, murdered Ishbosheth, and brought his head to David expecting a reward; but he justly ordered them to be killed, and made them standing memorials of his detestation of their treachery and murder. (2 Sam. 2-4)

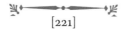

David had already governed the tribe of Judah seven years and six months when 339,822 armed men from the different tribes assembled to proclaim him king over all Israel. He therefore removed north to Jerusalem, and, with no small difficulty, reduced the proud Jebusites that had kept possession of it till now. Determined to overturn his government before it was established, the Philistines twice marched their troops almost up to the walls of Jerusalem, and camped in the Valley of Rephaim. It was probably about this time that they set up a garrison in Bethlehem. Adino, Eleazar, and Shammah, David's three main heroes, broke through their host, and brought David water from the well of Bethlehem, as that from Jerusalem was brackish (salty); but he would not drink it as they had endangered their lives in getting it, but poured it out as a drink-offering of thankfulness for their preservation. Attended by the direction of God, David gave these enemies two terrible defeats. He next removed the ark of God from Kirjath-jearim to bring it to a tent he had prepared for it at Jerusalem. Contrary to the Law, they brought it on a cart; but Uzzah, being struck dead for touching it when the oxen shook the cart, it was left in the house of Obed-edom. Three months later, with great solemnity, and according to order, it was carried up to Jerusalem on the shoulders of the Levites. David, dressed like a common priest, played on an organ before it. Michal reproved him for his behaviour as too lowly and base for a king. He replied that he thought no expression of gratitude to God, who had given him her father's throne, was too low, but honourable. (2 Sam. 5-6)

David now enjoyed profound peace, and resolved to build a house for the ark of God, as he thought it was not right that it should be more badly housed than himself. Nathan the prophet encouraged him in this project. But the Lord, through Nathan, quickly informed him that though he approved his good design, yet he had shed, and would go on shedding, too much blood, to be involved in such a sacred undertaking, but his son and successor would build it: and his family would be established on his throne, and the everlasting King, the Messiah, would spring from his loins. With the utmost thankfulness and wonder, David accepted the will of God, and contented himself with preparing a fund and materials for the erection of a Temple. (2 Sam. 7; 1 Chron. 17)

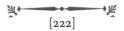

Subjugation of the Philistines

About BC 1044, he commenced a war with the Philistines, and made that troublesome nation his tributary. Provoked with the Moabites for the murder of his parents, or for some other reason, he subdued their country, dismantled their fortifications, and slew most of them, except those he needed to cultivate the fields. He next attacked the Syrians of Zobah, routed Hadadezer's army, and, just after, routed the allied army of Syrians from Zobah and Damascus, put garrisons in their cities, and rendered them tributary. About the same time, he attacked the Edomites; and, on the battlefield in the Valley of Salt, he cut off 11,000 of them, and 6000 more in the pursuit, or Abishai cut off 18,000, and Joab 12,000 more. (Ps. 6, title; 2 Sam. 7; 1 Chron. 18) It was about this time that he sought out Mephibosheth, and invited him to his table. (2 Sam. 9)

About BC 1037, his ambassadors were sent with compliments of condolence to Hanun, King of the Ammonites, and were badly treated as if they were spies, and were sent home with their clothes cut open in the middle of their buttocks, and their beards shaved. Fired with indignation, David commenced a war against them. Twice, he defeated their armies, though greatly reinforced by vast numbers of Syrians. Several petty kings of Syria submitted to him. (2 Sam. 10)

Adultery with Bathsheba

In the third year of this war, while Joab, after ravaging the countryside, invaded Rabbah the capital, in Jerusalem, after a sleep, David happened to take an evening walk on the flat roof of his house. He observed Bathsheba, the wife of Uriah, bathing in her garden. His sexual lust was inflamed, and he sent for her, and had sex with her. She became pregnant, and informed him of it. To prevent the discovery of their guilt, David called home Uriah from the army, and did what he could to make him go home and sleep with his wife, and so become the reputed father of the child. Neither the royal advice, nor the luxurious entertainment, could prevail on Uriah to approach his own house. David therefore sent back this worthy hero with a letter to Joab, ordering him to have him killed by the sword of the children of Ammon, while his bravery refused to yield to a shameful flight. Uriah, according to this directive, was deserted at the siege, and so slain by the Ammonites. Informed of his death, David just said that it was no more than the chance of war in the whole matter; and, soon after, he took Bathsheba as his wife.

This scene of wickedness highly provoked the Lord, offended the pious Hebrews, and tempted the very heathen to blaspheme God's way. On Joab's advice, David, with a strong reinforcement, marched to Rabbah, about 64 miles distant from Jerusalem, that he might have the honour of taking a place so noted for its strength. He took it by storm, gave it up to the ravage of his soldiers, and reserved only what belonged to the king for himself. The principal men, and most valiant that held out against him, he put to exquisite torture, tearing their flesh with harrows, saws, and axes of iron, burning them alive in their brick-kilns. Or, as some read the words, he obliged them to work at the saw, at the cutting of stones, the digging of iron mines, the hewing of wood, and the making of bricks. That is how he treated all the Ammonites that did not readily submit. Scarcely had David returned to Jerusalem in BC 1034, when Nathan the prophet, through a parable, brought him to condemn himself in the matter of Uriah, and to ask God for pardon of his sin. Nathan was soon after ordered by God to inform David that his crimes would not expose him to wrathful and eternal punishment, but to fearful chastisements in this life. His child of adultery would die in infancy, several of his family would come to an untimely end, one of his sons would rebel against him, and his wives would be raped in public. No less than four of his sons perished as a result. The child of adultery fell sick in its infancy, and, despite David's most earnest prayer and fasting for its life, was cut off. Next year, Bathsheba bore David a second son whom he called Solomon. God, by means of Nathan the prophet, called him Jedidiah, *beloved of the Lord*. (2 Sam. 11-12; 1 Chron. 20; Ps. 51)

Exile and Absalom

About BC 1030, his son Amnon raped Tamar his half-sister, and, after two years, was murdered by Absalom for his crime. About BC 981, Absalom drove his father from his throne, and raped in public ten of his concubines. David's lifeguard and principal friends fled along with him; but he persuaded Hushai, Abiathar, and Zadok, to serve his interest by staying in Jerusalem. He and his friends crossed the brook Kidron, weeping as they went. As they passed the Mount of Olives, Ziba met him with two ass-loads of provisions; and, by falsely

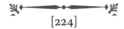

accusing Mephibosheth his master of intending to wrest the crown, he prompted David to make him a grant of Mephibosheth's estate. David had just advanced to Bahurim, when Shimei rudely insulted him, and bitterly cursed him as a most wicked and bloody monster. He endured all this with the utmost resignation and patience, taking it from the hands of his God; nor would he allow his attendants to take revenge on Shimei. Informed by Hushai of Absalom's plans, he fled beyond Jordan to Mahanaim, where Barzillai, Shobi, and Machir supplied him with plenty of provisions. During this rebellion, he composed a number of excellent Psalms, such as the 2nd perhaps to the 7th, the 41st to the 44th, and the 55th, etc. Absalom pursued him as quickly as possible with a formidable army. Absalom's troops were routed, and he, contrary to the command David had given to his warriors, was slain. David most bitterly lamented his death. Joab sharply reproved his behaviour for so discouraging his friends and troops that had saved his life at the risk of their own. David then stopped his mourning and spoke kindly to his friends. He next set out for Jerusalem, and sent word to the chief men of Judah to show their distinguished zeal on this occasion; and he promised Amasa his nephew the office of chief commander in the place of Joab, who had offended him by killing Absalom. The men of Judah, instigated by Amasa, immediately invited David back to his throne, and crowds turned out to escort him home.

Shimei, at the head of a thousand Benjamites, came with the first, and, at his frank confession of his recent behaviour, obtained a pardon, contrary to the protests of Abishai. Mephibosheth also met David, and cleared himself of the charge laid against him by Ziba. He continued in favour, but had no more than half his estate restored to him, while his treacherous servant was allowed the other half. To reward Barzillai the Gileadite for his recent generosity, David begged him to go and live with him in his palace; but when the old man declined this offer, David took Chimham his son with him. When the other tribes found that the men of Judah had gone before them to bring back their king, they were offended, and hot speeches were made on both sides, especially by Judah, as they reckoned themselves more deeply connected with David. Sheba, the son of Bichri, a Benjamite, instigated the ten tribes to a new revolt; but Joab, after murdering Amasa, who had perhaps not been very rightly invested with his office, pursued Sheba, and soon put an end to his life and rebellious attempt. (2 Sam. 13-20)

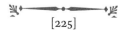

A serious famine

About BC 1021, God punished the Israelites with a famine for three years. Informed by God that it was for the punishment of Saul, and the people's sin, in murdering the Gibeonites, whom, by a solemn oath made about 430 years earlier, they were bound to keep safe, David sent for the remainder of that people and asked them what satisfaction they required for the injury done them? At their demand, Armoni and Mephibosheth, the sons of Saul by Rizpah, and the five sons of Adriel the son of Barzillai the Meholathite, born by Merab and brought up by Michal the daughter of Saul, were delivered up to the Gibeonites, and they hanged them before the Lord in Gibeah so that his anger was appeased. About this time, or perhaps before it, the Philistines, encouraged by a family of giants, made four attacks on the Israelites, in one of which David was almost slain if Abishai had not come to his assistance and killed the giant. After this, the Hebrews would no longer allow David to go to battle, lest his death should quench their light, glory, and comfort. (2 Sam. 21; 1 Chron. 20)

Numbering the people

The above famine had just ceased, when David, permitted by God, and tempted by Satan, proudly decided to number all his subjects capable of bearing arms; and Joab was appointed to take charge of the project. Joab protested against the task as not agreeable to the promise of God to make the Hebrews innumerable; but he was obliged to yield to the king's will. After nine months, he brought in the result. The men of Judah amounted to 470,000, which, together with the 24,000 of standing militia, made nearly 500,000. The men of Israel were 800,000, which, with several odd thousands, and the 264,000 of the eleven trained bands, came to nearly 1, 100,000. But Joab left out the Levites and Benjamites as he heartily detested the whole business. Offended by David's pride, God offered him a choice of three different punishments calculated to diminish the number of his subjects: he could have three years of famine added to the former three, three months flight before their enemies, or three days of pestilence. David chose the last, as it came immediately from the hand of a gracious God. It lasted about nine hours, and cut off 70,000 people, as David observed an angel brandishing his sword over Jerusalem, ready to destroy the inhabitants. With great earnestness, he implored mercy and forgiveness; and, having erected an altar on the threshing-floor of Araunah, and offered sacrifices there, the plague was stopped. (2 Sam. 24; 1 Chron. 21)

Abishag

About BC 1016, David's aged body was now so devoid of natural warmth, or smitten with a kind of paralysis, that he could not get warm in bed. They brought him Abishag the Shunamite, a beautiful young woman, to sleep with him and keep his body temperature up. He married her, but had no sexual relations with her. (1 Kings 1:3, 4, 15)

Solomon proclaimed King

Meanwhile, as David was too indulgent to his children, Adonijah attempted to proclaim himself his successor, but was prevented, and Solomon was proclaimed king as David had long ago promised to Bathsheba his mother. In the latter part of his reign, David made great preparations for the Temple of God, and he drew up rules for the priests, Levites, singers, and porters, concerning their respective orders and stations of service. His kingdom was put into excellent order. Of 288,000 standing militia, 24,000 served each month in turns, and leaders were assigned to the various tribes of Israel, and over the king's stores, vineyards, flocks, and herds. The history of the Mighties is a subject worthy of further study. (2 Sam. 16:6; 2 Sam. 23:8-9, 16-17, 22)

Perceiving that death was near, David confirmed Solomon's enthronement, gave him a model of the Temple which had been presented to him by God, with about 46,000 tons of gold and silver, besides an immense quantity of brass and other materials for its use. And having given him various solemn charges with respect to his religious and civil conduct, and commanding him to punish Joab for his double murder, and Shimei for his shameful conduct, then pouring out a prophetic prayer on his behalf, he breathed his last, expressing his firm assurance and full comfort in the everlasting covenant made with him and his seed. He reigned seven and a half years in Hebron, and thirty-three years in Jerusalem. He wrote a great number of Psalms, especially during his troubles.

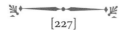

David a type of Christ

He was a notable type of our Saviour. God gave him the exalted character of his servant, and a man after his heart; but the Jewish rabbis, and other wicked men, rudely abused him. (2 Sam. 23:1; 1 Kings 1-2; 1 Chron. 22-29; Ps. 72)

Jesus Christ is frequently called David because he was the antitype of the former. He was the chosen one of God who sprang from Bethlehem, a man after his own heart who fulfilled all his counsels. How notable his faithfulness, meekness, and humility, and his love for God, his zeal for his honour, and his devout intimacy with him! Three times - at his conception, at his baptism, and at his ascension - he was plentifully anointed with the Holy Spirit above measure to be the Head of God's chosen people. He is the covenant-head of his spiritual seed, which are all kings unto God. (Rev. 1:6, 5:10) He is our sweet psalmist, who sings for God, composes our songs, and tunes our hearts to praise God. He is our great prophet and king who instructs, forms, and governs his Church, the Israel of God. Through what debasement, labour, reproach, temptation from the world, from his coming from heaven, from his descent into hell, from relatives, from friends, from foes, did he obtain his kingdom and glory! With what resignation, courage, and a steady eye to his Father's glory, and a sure hope of a good end, he endured the whole! How well he defeated and destroyed his lions and bears, and the giants of hell! He fulfilled the Law, destroyed death and the grave, and, by the gospel, he is conquering the nations to the obedience of faith, putting his chosen people into possession of the whole inheritance and dominion assigned them by God! How skilful, compassionate, and righteous is he in the government of his subjects! How active is he in preparing the temple above for his people, and in preparing them for it! His Mighties, who, by the word of the *gospel, do wondrous exploits*, are *prophets, apostles, evangelists, pastors, and teachers*, and his faithful warriors are those who, discontented with their natural state, poverty and debt, are obliged to enlist in his service. (Ps. 89; Ezek. 34, 37; Hosea 3:5)

DEBORAH, *a bee; the word of Jah (Jehovah)*
(1) Rebekah's nurse, who came along with her from Padan-aram. After her mistress's death, she continued with her countrywomen in Jacob's

family. She died near Bethel at a very advanced age, and was buried under an oak tree, called from that event *Alon-Bachuth, the oak of weeping.* (Gen. 24:59, 35:8)

(2) The prophetess and judge of Israel, and wife of Lapidoth. She lived under a palm tree between Ramah and Bethel. When Jabin, King of Canaan, grievously oppressed the Israelites for 20 years, she sent for Barak, the son of Abinoam, a man of Issachar, who lived in Kedeshnaphtali, and, from God, directed him to raise an army of 10,000 men from Naphtali and Zebulun, the tribes principally enslaved, and march them to Mount Tabor where the Lord would deliver Sisera and the mighty host of Jabin into his hand. He refused to attempt this unless she went along with him. She consented, but told him that his cowardice would be punished by the Lord, giving the chief honour of the victory, and the death of the general, into the hand of a woman. They had just raised their troops, and marched them from Kedesh to Tabor, when Sisera was at their heels with a huge army. It seems that hardly one of Barak's 10,000 had either sword or spear, but the Canaanites were struck with a panic when they saw the Hebrews coming down from the hill to attack them. The slaughter was so universal that few escaped. Barak and Deborah composed a song to commemorate their victory, and praised God on account of it, and, to celebrate the Hebrew princes, and Jael the wife of Heber the Kenite, for their instrumentality in the battle, and to condemn the tribes of Asher, Dan, and Reuben, for their inactivity. (Judg. 4-5)

DELILAH, *poverty*. See Samson
A Philistine woman who lived in the valley of Sorek. She is found only in Judges 16:4, 6, 10, 12-13, 18.

DEMAS, *of the people*, or *popular*
An early professor of Christianity, perhaps a preacher, who was, for a while, very serviceable to Paul in his imprisonment. (Col. 4:14; Philem. verse 24) However, about AD 65, he forsook Paul to follow a more profitable worldly business. (2 Tim. 4:10) It is said (in Epiphanius, *Refutation of all the Heresies*, 51) that he fell into the heresy of Ebion and Cerinthus, who held Christ to be a mere man.

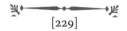

DEMETRIUS

A silversmith of Ephesus, who made little models of Diana's temple there with her image included. The tabernacles of Moloch (Acts 7:43) seem to have been similar to the shrines or representations in miniature of Diana, which were in great demand among the uncountable worshippers of this goddess, and consequently brought great profit to Demetrius and his associates. See Diana.

Angry at the success of the gospel, and the danger of his loss of business by the inhabitants turning their backs on idolatry, he convened a mob of his fellow tradesmen, and explained to them the danger to their craft and idolatrous work. They were immediately outraged, and, assisted by many rascals from amongst the inhabitants, they sent up for some hours a terrible outcry, *"Great is Diana of the Ephesians!"* They seized Aristarchus and Gaius, and hurried them into the theatre, no doubt with a view to having them condemned. Noticing Alexander (perhaps the coppersmith), they dragged him before the crowd. He begged that they would hear what he had to say for himself; but, understanding that he was a Jew, and so an enemy of their religion, they would not listen to him, and continued to bawl out, *"Great is Diana of the Ephesians!"*

Meanwhile, an officer of considerable influence in the city got the ear of the mob. He warmly warned them that the men whom they had seized could not be proved to be blasphemers of Diana, nor robbers of her temple, and that the honour of Diana was sufficiently established the world over, and the Ephesian zeal for her worship was well known. They were at the utmost risk of being called to account, and punished by their Roman superiors for their uproar, and that if Demetrius, or anybody else, had a plea, they should bring it before a lawful meeting of the magistrates, and not fill the city with confusion. With this soft and sensible advice, he quietened and dispersed the mob. Whether this Demetrius afterwards became a Christian convert, and had a good report by all, we do not know with certainty. (Acts 19:24-40; 3 John verse 12)

DEVIL. See Satan

A fallen angel, especially the so-called chief of them, who is a malicious accuser of God and his people. (Rev. 12:9, 12) Devils were (and are) worshipped in the idols of the heathen and false religions. (Lev. 17:7;

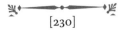

Deut. 32:17; Ps. 106:37; Rev. 9:20, 18:2). Devils themselves tremble at their view of the true God. (James 2:19) Wicked men are called *devils*; they resemble these evil spirits in malice and enmity against God and his people, and in reproach and slander of them, and are agents of Satan on earth. (John 6:70; 1 Tim. 3:11; Rev. 2:10)

Jesus was tempted over a period of 40 days and 40 nights by the devil. (Matt. 4:1-11, with parallels in other Gospels) He cast out devils. (Matt. 9:32-33, 12:22, 15:22, 17:18) He was accused of being possessed by the devil. (Matt. 9:32, 34; John 8:48) The Apostle Paul gives many warnings against the devil. (Eph. 4:27, 6:11; 1 Tim. 3:6-7; 2 Tim. 2:26) Exhortations about the devil are found in James 4:7 and 1 Pet. 5:8. Further facts about the devil are found in the book of Revelation: 12:9 (his fall from heaven), 12:12, 20:20 (his short time on the earth), 20:10 (his final and eternal end).

DIANA

A celebrated goddess of the heathen. She was especially renowned at Ephesus. She was one of the twelve superior deities, and was called by several names, such as Hebe, Trivia, Hecate, Diana, and Lucina. In the heavens, she was the *moon* or *queen of heaven*, and perhaps identical to *Meni* the numberer, or goddess of months. (Isa. 65:11; Jer. 7:18; Ezek. 16:25) On earth, she was Diana and Trivia, the goddess of hunting and highways. In hell, she was Hecate. In assisting women in childbirth, she was Lucina. She was said to be the daughter of Jupiter, and sister of Apollo, and was figured as a young huntress, with a crescent half-moon on her head; or as wholly covered with breasts, and her pedestal ornamented with the heads of stags, oxen, and dogs to mark her bounty, and power in hunting. She was worshipped with great solemnity at Ephesus. (Acts 19:24, 27-28, 34-35)

DINAH

Daughter of Jacob by Leah, and sister of Simeon and Levi. She was raped by Shechem, the son of Hamor, a Hivite chief. (Gen. 30:21; 34:1, 3, 5, 13, 26, 46:15.)

DIONYSIUS

The Areopagite, or judge in the court of the *Areopagus*. (Only found in Acts 17:34) In his youth, so it is said, he was brought up in all the famous learning of Athens, and went afterwards to Egypt to perfect himself in astronomy. Living in the Egyptian city of On when our Saviour died, he observed the miraculous darkness, and cried out, *Either the God of nature suffers himself, or sympathises with one that suffers.* He was converted at Athens by Paul, and, it is said, became an evangelist; and, according to Eusebius, he was burnt as a martyr in his own city in AD 95. Perhaps Damaris, the lady who was converted about the same time was his wife.

DIOTREPHES

A false Christian, whose ambition was to be preferred above everyone. He did all he could to oppose the reception of the messengers sent by the Apostle John, and said whatever he could to disparage that great Apostle. (Found only in 3 John verse 9)

DOEG

The accuser of Ahimelech the High Priest, and the murderer of him and eighty-four other priests. He probably came to some unhappy end. (1 Sam. 21-22; Ps. 52:1)

DRAGON

Satan is called a *dragon* because of his power, malice, and harmfulness. (Rev. 20:2) Cruel tyrants and conquerors, such as the kings of Assyria and Egypt, are compared with *dragons* (chiefly those that live in water), such as crocodiles, etc., for their terrible appearance, and destructive influence. (Ps. 74:13; Isa. 27:1, 51:9; Ezek. 29:3) The heathen Empire of Rome was compared with a great *red dragon*. In a most bloody manner, it wasted the nations, and persecuted the Church of God. (Rev. 12:3-4) The *dragon and his angels* were cast out to the earth when the power of these bloody persecutors was brought low, heathen idolatry and superstition were banished from cities to villages, and the power of Satan and his agents were trampled under foot. (Rev. 12:9) Antichrist *speaks as a dragon*; he teaches by diabolical and heathen authority, and, under the most terrible penalties, imposes devilish and pagan errors, superstitions, and idolatry. (Rev. 13:2) Wicked men are like *dragons*; they are the seed of the old serpent, full of sinful poison, and destruction and misery are in all their ways. (Isa. 25:7, 43:20) To *wail like dragons* is to mourn very bitterly, and in a hideous and hissing

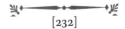

manner. But some think that whales and dolphins are meant here, who cry in the most pitiful way. (Job 30:28-31; Micah 1:8)

DRUSILLA

The youngest sister of Agrippa, Bernice, and Mariamne. Epiphanes, Prince of Comagena in Syria, was promised her in marriage if he would become circumcised; but as he declined that operation, she was given to Azizus, King of Emesa in Syria, who underwent the procedure to obtain her. It was not long after that she divorced him and married Felix, Governor of Judea, by whom she had a son called Agrippa. She was reckoned one of the most beautiful women of her age, but was far from being sexually pure. (Only found Acts 14:24)

E

EDOM, EDOMITES

The elder of the twin sons of Isaac, called *Esau* because, at his birth (he was born in BC 1831), he was as hairy as a grown man, and *Edom*, perhaps, because his hair and complexion were *red*. But he is chiefly remembered for the selling of his birthright for a meal of *red* pottage (lentil soup). When be grew up, he applied himself mainly to hunting. Because he supplied his father so often with venison, this made Isaac conceive a particular affection for him, while Jacob, being of a more gentle disposition, and staying much of the time at home in the tent, was the darling of Rebekah, their mother. One day, when Jacob had prepared for himself a little pottage of red lentils, Esau returned from his hunting starving to death. He begged Jacob to give him a little of his pottage, but Jacob refused unless Esau would immediately renounce his birthright in favour of him. Esau, despising the privileges connected with the birthright, renounced it, ate his pottage, and went on his way unconcerned. (Gen. 25:24-34)

When Esau was 40 years old, to the great grief of his parents, he married two wicked women of Canaan: one was Judith, the daughter of Beeri the Hittite, and the other Adah (or Bashemath), the daughter of Elon the Hittite. About 30 years later, Isaac feeling that he was near death, intended to give Esau his last blessing. To render the occasion the more tender, he ordered Esau to prepare him some venison just as he liked it. Esau took his weapons and went hunting. Rebekah, knowing from God that the blessing was divinely designed for Jacob, took some not very justifiable steps to get it for him.

When Esau returned, he found that Jacob had craftily counterfeited his appearance, and obtained his father's principle blessing. With tears and bitter outcries, he begged his father to bless him too. Moved by his pitiful outcry, Isaac told him that, though he had irrevocably bestowed his choicest blessings on Jacob, yet Esau would inherit a country refreshed with the dew, and, in some places, be fertile in its soil, and that he would live by the sword, as he and his posterity would be much employed in war, and that he would serve his brother and his posterity, but would sometimes throw off their yoke of subjection. Esau was keenly incensed with the deceitful way in which Jacob had taken away his birthright and blessing, and he resolved to be revenged on his brother by murdering him while the family were mourning for his father, whose death he daily expected. Meanwhile, finding his heathen marriages were very disagreeable to his parents, in order to please them, and to affirm his title to what had been promised to Abraham, he took as wife Mahalath (or Bashemath), a daughter of Ishmael, and removed himself from his parents to Mount Seir where the remnant of the Horites then lived. He also married Aholibamah, a daughter of Anah, a chief and prince of that tribe. (Gen. 26:34-35, ch. 32, 28:6-9, and ch. 36)

Jacob fled to Padanaram to avoid the fury of Esau. When he returned home twenty years later, he sent messengers with a present to conciliate him. With 400 armed men, Esau set out from Mount Seir to meet Jacob, probably with the intention of destroying him and all that he had. By the time they met on the southeast of the Sea of Galilee, providence had cooled Esau's temper, and he was all kindness. With some difficulty, he accepted the presents Jacob had prepared for him, as he thought that he possessed a great number of cattle already. He invited Jacob to Mount Seir, and offered his service to conduct him there; but Jacob, in the most obliging manner, declined the offer. About BC 1711, Jacob and Esau assisted together at their father's burial, and it seems that they were now both living in the south of Canaan; but as the country could not support their vast herds of cattle, Esau again retired to Mount Seir. (Gen. 32-33, 35:29, 36:6-7) Samuel Shuckford and others make out that Esau was a good man. They extol his hasty forgetfulness of the injuries done him by his brother, and his generous affection towards Jacob as marks of his goodness. They pass over God's *hatred* of him (Mal. 1:3) as amounting to nothing more than making him subordinate to Jacob with respect to the inheritance of Canaan, and the Holy Spirit calling him a *profane person* (Heb. 12:16) to mean nothing more than that he was too careless of the promise made to his father's family, and so was unfit to be the heir of the mercies that came with it. But with this kind of explanation, they may as well turn the Scripture upside down as they please!

Esau's descendants were called Edomites, and they were a people given to ravage and war. Esau had five sons: Eliphaz, the son of Adah; Reuel, the son of Mahalath; and Jeush, Jaalam, and Korah, the sons of Aholibamah. Eliphaz had seven sons, Teman, Omar, Zepho, Kenaz, Korah, Gatam, and Amalek. Reuel had four sons, Nahath, Zerah, Shammah, and Mizzah. These eleven, with the three sons of Aholibamah, were dukes in the land of Edom. The Edomites intermarried with the Horites, and, at last, swallowed up that people. Though the Edomites were divinely cursed to be the bond slaves of Satan, yet, in that early age, while the Hebrews endured the cruellest bondage, they were a powerful nation, and were governed by a race of eight kings: Bela, the son of Beer, Jobab, the son of Zerah of Bozrah, Husham, of the land of Temani, Hadad, who defeated the Midianites in the country of Moab, Samlah of Masrekah, Saul of Rehoboth, Baal-hanail, the son of Achbor, and Hadar of the city Pau. However, some think that these were rather kings of the ancient Horites. About the time of the Hebrews' travels in the wilderness, the Edomites had eleven dukes: Timnah, Alvah, Jetheth, Aholibamah, Elah, Pinon, Kenaz, Teman, Mibzar, Magdiel, and Iram. Perhaps the fear of that wandering multitude made them again unite under one king. It was probably that Moses sent messengers to this sovereign to beg a passage through his country. This was refused. When Moses sent a second request, intimating that they would pay for everything they asked, the king of Edom raised an army to stop them; but it seems that the Edomites changed their minds, and furnished them with provisions for money. (Gen. 36:1; Num. 20:14-21; Deut. 2:2-29; 1 Chron. 1)

For about 400 years after this, we hear nothing of the Edomites; but it is likely they applied themselves to commerce, both by sea and land. Elath and Eziongeber were their ports on the Red Sea. At the height of their prosperity, they gave some offence to David. So he turned his victorious army against them when 18,000 were slain in the Valley of Salt, and Joab ravaged the country till he scarcely left alive any of the males, bringing the whole kingdom under the Hebrew yoke. Numbers of them fled into other countries, particularly Phoenicia and Egypt, and no doubt took their skills along with them. Hadad their prince fled to Egypt (1 Kings 11:17, 19, 25), and, returning in the days of Solomon, built up a kingdom near the southeast of the land of Edom. But it seems his dominion was quickly reduced by the Jews, and Hadad, perhaps, was obliged to flee to Syria. (1 Kings 11:25) The Edomites were governed by deputies under the kings of Judah. Their troops assisted Jehoshaphat and Jehoram against the Moabites. It seems the Moabites soon after invaded their country and burnt the homes of their king to ashes. They joined in the grand alliance against Jehoshaphat, but were murdered by their allies, the Moabites and Ammonites. (2 Sam. 8:14; 1 Kings 11:14-25, 22:47; 2 Kings 3; 2 Chron. 20; Ps. 133; Amos 2:1)

After they had been subject to the Hebrews for 150 years, they threw off the yoke, and set up a king of their own in BC 889. Jehoram, king of Judah, attempted to reduce them, but could not do it, though he routed their troops with great slaughter. About BC 884, Amaziah, King of Judah, to revenge their buying up Hebrew slaves from the Philistines and Tyrians, or some such insult, invaded their country, took Selah their capital, killed 10,000 of them, cruelly cast another 10,000 from the rock on which their city was built, and carried off their idols. Uzziah his son again attacked them, and took Elath their chief sea trading city; but Rezin, King of Syria, retook it in the days of Ahaz, and either kept it for himself or restored it to the Edomites. (2 Kings 14:7, 16:6; 2 Chron. 21:8, ch. 26, 28:17; Amos 1:6-9)

The Assyrians under Sennacherib, or his son Esarhaddon, wasted the country of Edom terribly, and ruined Bozrah their capital. When the Chaldeans besieged Jerusalem, the Edomites joined them, and incited them to utterly raze the city and Temple. But scarcely five years elapsed, when the Chaldeans ravaged their own country, and this, or some other disaster about this time, rendered it a desolate wilderness. Those in the southern region joined with the Nebaioth (see 1 Chron. 1:29 and Isa. 60:7), and those in the northern region seized the southern area of the tribes of Simeon and Judah; since which, their own country has been cursed into perpetual barrenness and drought.

Darius Hystaspes ordered them to return to the Jews whatever of their country they had seized; but what effect this edict had, we do not know. About BC 164, Judas Maccabeus harassed them successfully, put about 40,000 of them to the sword, and sacked Hebron their capital. About BC 130, John Hyrcanus completely conquered them, obliging them to incorporate with the Jewish nation. Just before the taking of Jerusalem by Titus, a body of Edomites deserted the Jews, and went off laden with booty; since which time, their name has perished among men. (Ps. 137:7; Isa. 11:14, 21:11, ch. 34; Jer. 9:25-26, 25:9, 21, 27:3, 49:7-22; Lam. 4:21-22; Ezek. 25:12-14, 32:29, ch. 35, 36:2, 35; Joel 2:19; Amos 1:11-12, 9:12; Obad. verse 1; Mal. 1:3-4) *Edom, Moab, and the chief of the children of Ammon, shall escape out of his hand*; the Arabs, descended from Ishmael, and who dwelt in these countries, will not be subdued by the Turks. (Dan. 11:43) As the Edomites were cruel enemies of the Jews, so the enemies of the Church of whatever kind, subdued by Christ, are called *Edom* and *Bozrah*.

There is a remarkable Messianic prophecy in Isaiah 63:1: *Who is this that cometh from Edom, with dyed garments from Bozrah? this that is glorious in his apparel, travelling in the greatness of his strength? I that speak in righteousness am mighty to save.*

EHUD

The son of Gera, a Benjamite. He was left-handed, or probably paralysed in his right. Eglon, the King of Moab, together with the Ammonites and Amalekites, mightily oppressed the Israelites from BC 1343-1325, and made Jericho his main residence. As it was customary for the Hebrews to send their tribute or presents to Eglon, Ehud was appointed to deliver it. Directed by God, he considered the deliverance of his nation, and, for that purpose, concealed a two-edged dagger under his cloak. No sooner had he delivered his present, and sent away those that bore it, he returned to King Eglon and told him that he had a message from God to him.

All the Moabites present were ordered to withdraw, and Eglon, however fat and unwieldy, stood to his feet. Ehud plunged his dagger into his stomach, and, leaving him bleeding to death, locked the door of the parlour and carried off the key. Eglon's servants imagined their master was easing nature, or taking his afternoon sleep, so they waited a long time before they presumed to open the door with another key.

Meanwhile, Ehud had escaped to Mount Ephraim and collected a body of those Hebrews who were nearby. With these, he took the fords of Jordan to prevent the Moabites' return, and killed them to the number of 10,000 valiant men, and restored Israel to her liberty. (Judg. 3:15-30)

ELDAD (*God's beloved*) and MEDAD (*love*)
Divinely destined to be two of the 70 assistants of Moses, they modestly declined the office, and remained in the camp. There, the spirit of prophecy, which marked God's choice, seized them. Joshua, observing it, and fearing it might detract from Moses' honour, begged him to forbid them; but Moses replied that he would be glad if the whole assembly of Israel were made prophets. (Only found in Num. 11:24-30)

ELEAZAR, *the help of God*
(1) The third son of Aaron. Long after the death of his two older brothers, he succeeded his father Aaron in the high priesthood. After assisting Joshua in dividing the land of Canaan, and executing the office of High Priest for about 23 years at Shiloh, he died and was buried in a hill that belonged to Phinehas, his son and successor. Except the short time of about 120 years or upwards, to the honour of Eli's family, the high priesthood continued in the family of Eleazar till after the death of Christ. In David's time, 16 courses of priests were formed out of it, when only eight were formed of the family of Ithamar. (Num. 20:25-26, 28, 34:17; Josh. 14:1, 24:33; 1 Chron. 24:1-6, 28)

(2) The son of Dodo the Ahohite, and the second of David's mighty men. When, at Ephes-dammim, and deserted by his fellows, he stood his ground, and continued slaying the Philistines till his hand stuck to his sword. He made such a havoc of the enemy that the Hebrews, on their return, had nothing to do but to take the spoil. Along with Shammah, the son of Agee the Hararite, he defended a field full of lentils so well that the Philistines fled before them. (2 Sam. 23:9-12; 1 Chron. 11:12-14)

ELI, *my God*
A Jewish High Priest descended from Ithamar, who judged Israel after the death of Abdan. Why the high priesthood was transferred to him from the family of Eleazar, whether it was because of the high

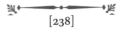

priest's offence in sacrificing Jephthah's daughter, or for some other reason, we do not know; but it is certain that the transfer was by the appointment of God. (1 Sam. 2:30) He was a good man in himself, but his sons Hophni and Phinehas were extremely wicked. They used to have sex with the women who assembled for devotion in the courts of the Tabernacle, they demanded their share of the peace or sin offerings before the fat was burnt, and they demanded more than their due in raw flesh instead of sodden. If anyone refused, the servants of the priests took it by force. Their profane behaviour provoked many of the Hebrews to withhold their offerings. Eli their father reproved them, but so gently that it made no difference. Through a prophet, the Lord charged Eli's sons with the most horrible abuse of his worship, and the father with honouring his sons above God. He prophesied that though he had conditionally promised the continuing of the high priesthood to his family, yet, since they had behaved so wickedly, their prosperity and power would quickly come to an end, and none of his sons would live to old age. Eli himself would see his country invaded by foreign enemies, the ark taken, his two sons die in one day, and the high priesthood given to another family that would be more faithful, to whom Eli's seed would abjectly crouch for a piece of bread, or the least pittance of provision.

Some years later, by young Samuel, the Lord further assured Eli of the approaching ruin of his family, and that it was in vain to attempt atonement for their sin by sacrifice. Eli received these denunciations with great submission to the divine will. (1 Sam. 2-3) These just and terrible threats came to a speedy end. The Philistines invaded the country, defeated the Hebrews, and killed 4000 of them. The Hebrew soldiers imagined that the ark of God would act like a charm in protecting them, and sent for it to the camp; but soon afterwards they received a most bloody defeat. Along with Hophni and Phinehas, 30,000 were killed, and the ark was taken and carried off. Informed of these things, Eli, with grief and astonishment, fell off his seat and broke his neck in the 98th year of his age, and the 40th year of his government. The wife of Phinehas, hearing of this, and former disasters, went into labour, and, in the stress of grief, was delivered of a son whom she called *Ichabod* to signify that the glory had *departed* from Israel, since the ark of God was taken. She then immediately died. Ahitub, the brother of Ichabod, succeeded his grandfather Eli, and, in his turn, was succeeded by his son Ahiah, and then by Ahimelech his brother, whose entire family, except Abiathar, was cruelly murdered by Saul. Thus Zadok, of the line of Eleazar, was made high priest in his place. About 50 years later, Solomon deposed Abiathar, and the poor remnants of the family lived in the most wretched conditions. *Let indulgent parents and connivers of sin take heed!* (1 Sam. 4, 14:3, 22; 1 Kings 2)

ELIAKIM, *the resurrection*, or, *God ariseth*
The son of Hilkiah. He succeeded Shebna as chief treasurer and master of the household to King Hezekiah. He, together with Shebna the Scribe, and Joah the son of Asaph, the Recorder, were sent as ambassadors to beg terms of peace from Sennacherib. They could obtain nothing but abusive language from his general, Rabshakeh, and so, without giving him a reply, they returned weeping and with their clothes ripped. Soon after, these two, and some of the elders of Judah, were sent to Isaiah to ask for his earnest prayers for the city. (2 Kings 19:2, 23:18-22; Isa. 33:7, 36:13, 37:12)

Was not Eliakim a type of Jesus, our great minister of state, who is over the whole household of God? Does He not succeed a treacherous Adam? Is He not the great messenger of Peace who, when he looked at Jerusalem, wept over it? Is He not the faithful manager, support, and glory of all things in the Church? (Isa. 22:20-25)

ELIEZER, *the help of God*
(1) His father was probably a Syrian from Damascus, but he himself was born in Abraham's family, and, it seems, was once designed his heir. (Gen. 15:2) When Abraham intended to seek a wife for his son Isaac, he bound Eliezer under a solemn oath that he would fetch him none of the Canaanites, but one of his relatives in Mesopotamia, and sent him off to Nahor, to a city there which might be about 460 miles northeast of Hebron. When he came near the city, he stopped at a well to which the young women of the place used to come morning and evening. There, he waited to refresh himself and his ten camels. Looking for divine direction, he lifted up his heart to God in prayer, and begged the Lord to find him a virgin suitable for Isaac by her offering to draw water for his camels, and do it only for himself. Rebekah came to the well. Eliezer had just asked her to draw a little water for him, when she

offered to draw water for his camels also. Pleased with her features, and finding that she was his master's grand-niece, he presented her with a pair of gold earrings, weighing about an ounce, and a pair of bracelets for her hands, which were five times as valuable, and inquired if he and his camels could be lodged at her father's house. She replied that they might. While she ran to inform her father's family, Eliezer returned his thankful acknowledgment to God for giving him his desired token. Laban, the brother of Rebekah, came down with haste, and kindly conducted him to the house. He had just sat down when he informed them who he was, what wealth his master had, and intended to bestow on Isaac, how he had charged him to find a suitable wife for Isaac, and what token he had received from God that Rebekah was that woman. In respect of whom, he requested a positive answer before he would eat or drink. Bethuel her father, and Laban her brother, replied that they saw that the matter was determined by God, and dare not oppose it. After a new lifting up of his heart to God in thanksgiving, Eliezer presented Rebekah with the fine jewels and rich clothing he had brought with him, and gave to her mother and brother a variety of valuable presents. Next morning, he insisted that Rebekah should be sent along with him. Her friends were not happy to see her going off so soon, but she was ready for immediate departure. They therefore got everything ready, and set off; and, in a few days, they arrived safely near Beersheba where Isaac was then living. (Gen. 24)

(2) The son of Moses. (Exod. 18:4, 8)

(3) The son of Becher. (1 Chron. 7:8)

(4) The son of Dodavah. He was the prophet that foretold Jehoshaphat that the trade-fleet he had built, in conjunction with impious Ahaziah, would be broken up by a tempest, and would be unfit for sailing to Tarshish. (2 Chron. 20:37)

ELIHU, *my God himself*

(1) The son of Barachel the Buzite, or a descendant of Nahor the brother of Abraham by Buz, his second son. When Job was in distress, Elihu paid him a visit. He gave close attention to the conference between him and his three friends Eliphaz, Bildad, and Zophar, and was highly offended at them. With the friends, he was offended by their strong insinuation that Job was a wicked hypocrite, when they had so little to say to support their charge. With Job, he was displeased

for throwing out in his defence a variety of offensive expressions that smacked of self-justification, and of his charges against the providence of God as rigorous and unjust. As he was younger than they, he waited patiently till the friends had nothing else to say. He then hinted that the matter urged him to speak on God's behalf. He left Job's state undetermined, but sharply reproved him for his faulty behaviour and rash speeches in his trouble; and, in a most grand and moving manner, he referred to the sovereign greatness, absolute purity, infinite justice, and wisdom of God, and how often he used affliction as the means of men's reformation, and earnestly called on Job to wait on him for deliverance. (Job 32:2, 4-6, 10; ch. 37)

(2) The great grandfather of Samuel, and an older brother of David, whom Samuel took for the divinely intended king of Israel, and who reproved David for talking of encountering Goliath. He later became a ruler of Judah. (1 Sam. 1:1, 16:6, 17:28; 1 Chron. 6:27, 34, 27:18)

ELIJAH, *my God Jehovah*

Elias (KJV, in the New Testament), the Tishbite, a native of Gilead, and a notable prophet.

The drought and its consequences

About BC 912, he assured King Ahab that for several years there would be neither dew nor rain until he was pleased to pray for it. The drought then began. Directed by God, Elijah concealed himself by the brook Cherith, near the east or west bank of the Jordan. There, he drank from the brook, and was miraculously fed with bread and flesh that ravens brought him every morning and evening, and which, no doubt, they fetched from someone's table. When the brook dried up, at the direction of God, he went and dwelt with a foreign widow of Zarephath. As he entered the city, he met this poor widow gathering a few sticks to cook a handful of flour and a little olive oil, for her and her son as their last meal, as she neither had, nor knew where to get, any more food. Elijah asked her to bring him a drink of water. As she went to fetch it, he called after her and told her bring him a little bread also. She explained the wretched case of herself and her son. Elijah told her to first cook a small cake for him, and then cook for herself and her child, for her handful of flour and small quantity of oil would never run out till plenty returned to the land. The Zidonian widow believed the prophet, obeyed his orders, and received him into her house. After he had stayed with her about two years, her only son died. Oppressed with grief, she complained that Elijah had come to call her sin to remembrance, and to slay her son. He took the child, put him on his own bed, stretched himself upon him, and earnestly begged the Lord to restore him to life. His request was quickly granted. (1 Kings 17)

When the drought and famine had continued for three and a half years, Elijah was divinely appointed to present himself before Ahab and inform him of the return of the rain. While Ahab's servants were dispersed throughout the country in quest of grass for the cattle that remained, Elijah met with Obadiah, one of the chief officers, and commanded him to go and inform his master that he wanted to see him. Obadiah replied that Ahab, with murderous designs, had scoured the whole kingdom and neighbouring kingdoms for him; and he feared that while he went to inform the king, the Spirit of the Lord would carry him off, and Ahab, in a rage, would murder him instead, which he begged might not be the case as he had been an useful protector of the Lord's prophets, having fed a hundred of them in two caves with bread and water. Elijah quickly assured him that he need not worry, as he firmly intended to show himself to Ahab. Obadiah believed him, and informed Ahab, who hastened to the place where Elijah was, and asked him if he was the one *that troubleth Israel*? (1 Kings 18:17) Elijah replied that it was not he, but the king himself and his family, who, by their idolatry and wickedness had brought these plagues on the nation. He further required that the people of Israel, with the 450 prophets of Baal, and 400 of the groves, should immediately be convened on Mount Carmel, that they might have a fair trial whether Jehovah or Baal was the true God. When they were assembled, Elijah rebuked the Israelites for *halting between the two opinions* (1 Kings 18:21-22), and begged that they would follow whichever of the two was truly God. The people remaining silent, he said that, though he was the only prophet of Jehovah present, he was willing to make a public trial of the power of his God in opposition to all of the 450 prophets of Baal. He proposed that each of the two parties should offer a bullock in sacrifice, and that whichever of the Gods, Jehovah or Baal, should burn up their sacrifice with fire from heaven, must be worshipped as the true God. The people agreed to this reasonable proposal.

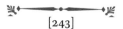

The prophets of Baal on Mount Carmel

The prophets of Baal erected their altar, sacrificed their bullock, and laid it on the altar, crying to their god for heavenly fire to consume it. As Baal continued deaf to their prayers, they leapt on the altar, slashed and stabbed their bodies to gain his pity, and, in a most earnest manner, begged him to grant their request. Elijah too insulted them, and told them to cry louder, for their God was certainly at a great distance, or was on some journey, or had fallen into a deep sleep. When the prophets of Baal had spent more than half a day in this mad manner, Elijah commanded the people to pay attention to him. With twelve stones, one for each tribe of Israel, he repaired a ruined altar of Jehovah. Having slain his bullock, he laid the flesh on it, but put no fire under it. He then ordered the people to bring water, and pour it on his sacrifice. They did so till the flesh, the wood under it, and the altar, were drenched with liquid, and even the trench round it was full to the brim. He next applied himself to requesting the Lord for a display of his power in consuming the sacrifice. He had just begun, when a flash of fire from heaven consumed the flesh, the wood, the stones, the water, and the earth around. Surprised by the miracle, the people cried out, *The Lord is God.* Elijah then ordered them to hold and kill the prophets of Baal. While Ahab looked on, they laid hold on them, and, dragging them to the foot of the hill, they slew them by the River Kishon.

The main cause of the famishing drought being removed, Elijah informed Ahab that now he might look for plenty of rain. He then returned, and on the Mount prostrated himself in prayer for it, and directed his servant (perhaps Gehazi) to observe what he saw rising out of the adjacent sea. At the seventh attempt, the servant told him that he saw a little cloud like a man's hand rising out of it. Elijah bade him tell Ahab to prepare his chariot, and ride post haste to Jezreel, lest rain should stop him. Elijah girded up his own loins and ran before the king to the entrance of the city. Meanwhile, there was a deluge of rain, attended, if we may believe the Greek dramatist Menander's *Annals of Tyre*, with terrible thunder. (1 Kings 18)

Flight from Jezebel

Jezebel the Queen had no sooner heard of the slaughter of her idolatrous priests than she sent Elijah a threatening message, suggesting that tomorrow he would pay for his conduct with the loss of his life. In

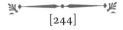

a cowardly manner, he fled away without halting to Beersheba, a place 84 miles, if not rather 110 miles, south of Jezreel. Here, he dismissed his servant, and pursued his course into the Arabian Desert. On the first night, being desperately tired, he lay down under a juniper tree and begged that since he was the only opposer of idolatry in Israel that had not already been murdered, God would take away his life that was now in danger. An angel touched him, and urged him eat the bread and drink the water he had brought to him. He did so; and after he had slept some hours, the next morning the angel invited him to eat a similar meal, as he had a long journey before him. He obeyed, and, without any more refreshment, travelled here and there for 40 days, till at last he came to Mount Horeb. Here, he lodged in a cave.

The Lord called to him, and asked him what he was doing there? Elijah replied that he had been very jealous for the honour of the true God, whose covenant the Israelites had forsaken, whose altars they had thrown down, and whose prophets they had murdered, all except himself, and now they were seeking to murder him. At the direction of God, he went out and stood in the mouth of the cave. A strong wind, an earthquake, and a flaming fire, succeeded one another, but the Lord again, in a still small voice, asked him what he was doing there? He repeated his former answer. The Lord assured him that there were still 7000 in Israel who had not bowed the knee to Baal. He commanded him to return home by the very roundabout and solitary way of the wilderness of Damascus, and anoint Hazael to be king over Syria, Jehu to be king over Israel, and Elisha prophet in his own place; by which three, God assured him, terrible havoc would be made of the Israelitish idolaters. He called Elisha to be his attendant, to whom he referred the anointing of the two kings. (1 Kings 19)

Elijah carried into heaven

About BC 899, directed by God, Elijah went to King Ahab and pronounced terrible judgements against him and his family for the murder of Naboth, and the unjust seizure of his vineyard. (1 Kings 21) In BC 896, both to Ahaziah's messengers, and to himself, he announced his approaching death, and consumed with fire from heaven two troops of 50 men each that came to arrest him. But at the humble request of the third, he spared him and his troop, and went along with them. Knowing that his translation to heaven was at hand, Elijah

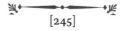

took various methods to get away from Elisha's company, that it might be entirely private. But the matter being divinely suggested to Elisha and other prophets around Bethel and Jericho, he would not leave him, and 50 young prophets followed them at a distance. When they came to the west bank of the Jordan, Elijah, with a stroke of his cloak, divided that deep river, and they went through on dry ground. Elijah then commanded Elisha to ask what might be done for him. He begged for a double, or a large portion, of his spirit. Elijah assured him that however great this request was, it would be granted him if he witnessed his translation. They had walked together only a little way, when a company of angels, in the form of a chariot and horses of fire, appeared, and Elijah, entering the chariot, was caught up in a whirlwind to heaven. Elisha cried after him, *"My father, my father, the chariot and horsemen of Israel!"* (2 Kings 2:12, 14) - that is, the strength and protection of heaven. He took up the cloak that fell from him as he entered the chariot, and, by striking the waters of the Jordan, he divided them, and returned to Jericho. Fifty strong men among the young prophets, contrary to Elisha's inclination, were permitted by him to go in quest of Elijah, as they imagined he might only have been carried into some desert place. After they had spent three days in this vain effort, they returned. (2 Kings 1-2)

About eight years later, a letter written by Elijah the prophet was brought to Jehoram, King of Judah, bearing on the theme that, on account of his forsaking the good example of his fathers, and since he had walked in the way of the house of Ahab and made his people do the same, and had murdered his brothers that were better than himself, therefore the Lord would strike his family and subjects with severe judgements, and his own bowels would burst and fall out by means of this terrible condition. Whether this letter was dropped from heaven, or rather was written before Elijah's translation and left with Elisha, or some other prophet, to be given to Jehoram at a proper season, is not clearly decided. (2 Chron. 21:12-15) About 930 years after his translation, Elijah descended from heaven and met and spoke with our Saviour on the Mount of Transfiguration. (Matt. 17:3, 4, 10-12)

Relation to John the Baptist

John the Baptist was called Elijah (or Elias). In his temperament, in his coarse and hairy clothing, in his austere method of living and holy

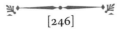

deportment, in his open and bold reproving of vice, and in his flaming zeal and useful gift of prophecy for the revival of religion, he resembled that ancient prophet. (Mal. 4:5-6; Matt. 17:10-13)

Elijah a type of Christ
And is not our Saviour the antitype of Elijah of old? He is the famous Prophet that announced the wrath of God, and restored the knowledge and worship of God upon earth. Solemn was his call, which was confirmed remarkably by miracles of mercy and judgement. His condition in life was lowly, afflicted, and persecuted. Forty days he fasted in the desert. Ardent was his zeal, and pungent his rebukes. With unquenchable love from within, and fierceness of wrath from above, his great sacrifice was inflamed. Powerfully, his intercession regulates the motions of providence, procures mercy to friends, and consuming vengeance on his foes. By him, kings are appointed to death or dominion, and prophets, apostles, and ministers to their office. How sovereign the bestowal of his presence! He removed his ordinances from the Jews that he might dwell with raven-like publicans and sinners, and with widowed Gentiles, and restore to life their dead in trespasses and sins. Passing through the waters of baptism in the River Jordan, and travelling through the Jordan of trouble and death, he ascended to heaven without seeing corruption. How vain, ever since, has been the laborious search of the Jews for their promised Messiah! How dreadful the vengeance that has overtaken these persecutors! And how lasting the misery of those who hate and oppose him!

ELIMELECH, *my God the king*
The husband of Naomi, from the tribe of Judah, formerly of Ephrathah, from Bethlehem, who died in the land of Moab. (Ruth 1:2-3, 2:1, 3) On the return of Naomi and Ruth the Moabitess to Bethlehem, a rich relative of Elimelech named Boaz married Ruth (Ruth 2:1, 3), thus becoming the ancestors of both King David and Jesus Christ.

ELIPHAZ, *the endeavour of God*
(1) The son of Esau by Adah. (Gen. 36:4, 10-12, 15-16; 1 Chron. 1:35-36)

(2) Probably the grandson of the former by Teman his son, who was the visitor to Job, and one of his comforters. As he spoke first in the conference, it is likely that he was older than Job's father. (Job 15:10)

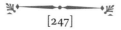

After acknowledging Job's former bright observances about religion, he insinuated his suspicion of Job's hypocrisy. From a vision that he had, and from experimental observation, he attempted to demonstrate that it was only those kinds of people that are punished in such an extraordinary manner. He urged Job to repent of his hypocrisy and wickedness, and look to God to deliver him. (Job 2:11, chs. 4-5, 15, 22, 42) God's anger was kindled at this false analysis: *My wrath is kindled against thee, and against thy two friends: for ye have not spoken of me the thing that is right, as my servant Job hath.* (Job 42:7)

ELISABETH
A descendant of Aaron the priest, the agèd wife of Zacharias, and mother of John the Baptist. She was long barren; but, at last, by supernatural influence, she conceived. After that, she concealed herself five months. When she met the blessed Virgin just after the conception of the Messiah, Elisabeth's baby leaped in her womb, and she herself broke out into a rapturous commendation of Mary, her cousin. (Found only in Luke 1:5, 7, 13, 24, 36, 40-41)

ELISHA, *the salvation of my God*
A native of Abelmeholah, the son of Shaphat, and the chosen disciple and successor of Elijah.

The call of Elisha
Directed by God, Elijah found him ploughing with twelve yoke of oxen, cast his cloak over him, thus intimating his call to follow and succeed him. After going home and saying farewell of his parents, Elisha returned; and, having slain a yoke of oxen, and provided a feast for the servants, he went after Elijah. (1 Kings 19:16-21) After witnessing the translation of that great man, he received a far larger share of his spiritual influence than the other prophets at that time. When he returned to Jericho after the translation of his master, he struck the waters of the Jordan with the cloak that had fallen from Elijah. But, to convince him that the cloak of the greatest of the prophets had no miraculous powers, the river did not divide. He struck the water a second time with the cloak, and cried out, *"Where is the God of Elijah?"* (2 Kings 2:14) The waters then divided, and he passed over on dry ground. When they saw this miracle, the young prophets at Jericho

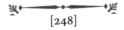

were assured of Elijah's spirit resting on Elisha, and they came and bowed low to him as their superior. (Verse15) It was these same men who, at their request, got his permission to search for Elijah, though he assured them it would be no use.

Miracles

When he came to Jericho, the inhabitants complained that, however agreeable the situation of their city was, the water was undrinkable and the ground barren; both of which, I suppose, were the result of Joshua's curse. (Josh. 6:26) Elisha called for a new bowl, and, filling it with salt, threw it into the springs and told them that, from now on, they would never have barren land or bad water. (19-21) And, it is said, that this very well provides to this day not only excellent water, but fertilises the ground around. When he went up to Bethel, the profane children of the place ridiculed him, and told him to go up to heaven, as he affirmed his master had done: *Go up, thou bald head; go up, thou bald-head!* (2 Kings 2:23-24) To punish these children, and the parents who had so badly trained them, he turned and cursed them in the name of the Lord. Whereupon, two female bears, came out of the adjacent forest and tore 42 of them to pieces.

He accompanied the combined army of Israel, Judah, and Edom that marched to put down the revolting Moabites. When these troops were almost dying of thirst, Kings Jehoram and Jehoshaphat came to him for relief. He angrily told Jehoram to apply to the (false) prophets of his idolatrous father and mother, and assured him that, were it not for the sake of Jehoshaphat, he would pay him no attention. After his passion was calmed by the music of a minstrel, and the Holy Spirit fell on his peaceful spirit, Elisha assured them that, without either wind or rain, the ditches he had ordered them to dig would be filled with water for their refreshment. That very night, the ditches were filled, and the people drank their fill. Soon after, a prophet's widow complained to him that her husband's creditor intended to sell her two sons to pay her debt. Elisha informed her that she had a small pot of oil in her house, and he miraculously multiplied the oil so that it filled all the vessels she could borrow. This, the prophet directed her to sell, pay off her debt, and live on the surplus. Being often at Shunem, a lady there kindly offered him hospitality and prepared a room for him. By prayer, he obtained a child for his barren hostess, and afterwards brought him back to life. When, during a famine, a young prophet at Gilgal made a soup of wild gourds, a herb bitter to the highest degree, his fellow prophets no sooner tasted it when they cried out that it was poisonous; but, with a little flour cast into the pot, Elisha removed the bitter taste, and the poisonous quality of the soup. Much about the same time, he miraculously so increased the power of 20 small barley loaves, that more than a hundred people ate to their satisfaction, with leftovers. (2 Kings 3-4)

About BC 894, Naaman the Syrian general came to him to be healed of his leprosy. To humble the proud captain, Elisha would not even speak to him, or allow him to speak to him, but sent him out orders to wash himself seven times in the River Jordan. Finding this prescription, however, too unpleasant to be effective at first, Naaman returned and offered him large presents. But Elisha would take nothing. When Gehazi, his covetous servant, ran after the Syrian, and took from him two talents of silver (about £684), and two changes of clothing, God disclosed the fraud to Elisha. He sharply rebuked Gehazi for it, and assured him that the leprosy would come on him and his family. Soon after, the young prophets were cutting wood on the banks of the Jordan. One of them let his axe head, which was borrowed, fall into the deep current. By putting a stick into the water near where it was, Elisha caused the axe head to float up, and so it was recovered. As the prophet informed Jehoram of the snares that the Syrians, who were then ravaging the country, had laid for him, that he might escape them, Benhadad, informed of this, sent a party to arrest him. But a company of angels surrounded and protected him and his terrified servant. At Elisha's request, the Lord smote the Syrian troops with partial blindness. Elisha then went up to them and told them that this was not the place where they would see the man they wanted, and offered to conduct them. He led them into the middle of Samaria where, at his request, God opened their eyes. When they saw where they were, they expected nothing but death, but Elisha told King Jehoram that it would be more inhumane to kill them than if they had surrendered themselves as prisoners. At the prophet's direction, he gave them refreshment, and sent them back to their master. This event deterred the Syrians from raiding the land of Israel with small parties. (1 Kings 5-6)

ELISHA

In times of war and threat of war

About BC 890, when Benhadad was besieging Samaria, the unclean head of an ass was sold for about £10, and a *very* small measure of *chick peas* ("dove's dung") for about twelve shillings, Jehoram, offended with Elisha, accused him of bringing this calamity upon them, or, at least, that he was doing nothing to relieve it, and sent a messenger to murder him. But the prophet, warned by God, ordered the door to be shut till the king himself came up. When he arrived and complained desperately of the distress of the city, Elisha assured him that before 24 hours were over, the plenty in Samaria would be such that a seah, which is more than an English peck (8 quarts) of fine flour, and two of barley, would be sold for less than 12½ pence. A certain lord present ridiculed the prophet, and declared that this was impossible unless God were to rain down corn from heaven. The prophet told him that he would see the harvest, but never taste of it. It so happened that the lord was trodden to death in the gate by the people who were bringing the spoil from the Syrian camp into the city. (2 Kings 6-7)

About BC 885, Elisha went to Damascus to declare Hazael King over Syria, as it seems Elijah had directed him. Hazael, then captain of the army, was sent to him with rich presents to ask if Benhadad, who was sick, would recover. According to our reading, Elisha told Hazael that Benhadad might recover in respect of his disease, as it was not mortal, but, nevertheless, would die by other means. But the textual reading of the Hebrew is: *He shall not certainly recover; the Lord hath showed me that he shall surely die.* (2 Kings 8:10) He then burst into tears as he looked on Hazael, and told him that it was because of his foreknowledge of the miseries the King would bring on the Israelites when he too held the throne of Syria. About the same time, he sent a young prophet to anoint Jehu to be King of Israel that he might cut off the idolatrous family of Ahab. About BC 839, Elisha fell sick. Jehoash, the King of Israel, came to visit him, and wept to see the prophetic protector and supporter of the kingdom dying. Elisha directed the king to take a bow and some arrows and shoot eastward, adding that this was a sign of deliverance from the Syrian yoke, and of a glorious victory at Aphek. He then asked the king to strike *against* the ground with the other arrows. He did so three times, then he stopped. The prophet reproved the King with great passion that, if he had struck the ground five or six times, he might as often have defeated the Syrian troops, whereas now, he would defeat them only three times. Sometime after Elisha died and was buried, a dead body, hastily thrown into his tomb, revived as soon as it touched his bones. (2 Kings 13:14-17, 20-21)

Elisha a type of Christ

Is not Jesus the great antitype of this ancient prophet? How solemn was his call to his work! How large his equipment! And by what numerous miracles was his mission confirmed! Coming after Elijah, Elisha was solemnly initiated into dividing the Jordan. In death, Jesus divided the floods of wrath and the Jordan of trouble. By his covenant *of salt*, he rectified the bitter water and barren soil of Law precepts and curses, and of multiplied afflictions. He makes streams of gospel grace break out in the wilderness to perishing sinners. This barren world he makes a joyful mother of Christians, and these he makes fruitful in good works. He multiplies their oil of grace till there is no more room to receive it. By his word, he often revived the physically dead, and, to many of them, his death brought them out of their graves. Thus it is with spiritual death. By his prayers and death, what a great number he makes alive who were once dead in trespasses and sins! What multitudes of Gentiles he cures of the leprosy of sin with a sevenfold washing in his blood! How he sweetens their bitter lot of temptation, raises their sinking spirits, and plentifully supplies them when they are famished! Is not he the strength, the *chariots and horsemen*, of his Church, giving them their victories, and overturning the nations around for the good of his people? How burning his zeal for God, and tender his compassion towards destitute, sorrowful, fainting, captives, and endangered men! How severe the resentment of heaven against his injuries! His mockers are torn to pieces while there is no deliverer. Ministers who, imitating Gehazi, preach for *filthy lucre* (1 Tim. 3:3, 8; Titus 1:7; 1 Pet. 5:2), infamously perish in their sin. Those who attend his ordinances for malicious purposes are smitten with spiritual blindness; those who despise his promised fullness will see it with their eyes, but will never partake of it. What vengeance to the uttermost came upon Judas who betrayed him, and upon the Jews who reviled, discredited, and persecuted him!

ELKANAH, *the zeal of God*
Various descendants of Korah, as well as others of this name. But the most famous was the son of Jehoram, the husband of Hannah and Peninnah, and the father of Samuel. (1 Sam. 1:1, 4, 8, 19, 21, 23; 1 Chron. 6:23-27, 35-36)

ELNATHAN, *God's gift*
The son of Achbor, and father of Nehushta the wife of Jehoiakim. He was sent to bring back the prophet Urijah from Egypt to murder him. Without succeeding, he beseeched Jehoiakim not to burn Jeremiah's roll. (2 Kings 24:8; Ezra 8:16; Jer. 26:22, 36:12, 25)

EMMANUEL, or **IMMANUEL**
A name given to our Saviour, signifying that he is *God with us*, coming in our nature, and on our side. (Only found in Isa. 7:14, 8:8 = *Immanuel*, and Matt. 1:23 = *Emmanuel*)

ENOCH
(1) A son of Cain, after whose name his father called the city that he built in the land of Nod, east of Eden, where we find the city Anuchtha, and where Pliny and Ptolemy placed the Henochii; but perhaps these names sprang from the others that follow them.

(2) The son of Jared, and father of Methuselah. While he was rearing his family, begetting and educating a vast number of children, he maintained a most holy life, living by faith, walking with God in sweet fellowship with him, and eminent conformity to him. To honour and reward such a spiritual walk, God not only testified to his delight in him while he lived, but, after he was 865 years of age, he translated him to heaven body and soul without tasting death. That he wrote anything cannot be proved; but he prophesied of the Last Judgement that *the Lord will come with ten thousands of his saints* (or angels) to convince the wicked of their hard speeches and ungodly deeds, and punish them on this account. This prophecy Jude might have had conveyed to him by tradition, but the Holy Spirit assures us that it was genuine. (Gen. 5:18-24; Heb. 11:5; Jude vv. 14-15)

The eastern writers, both Arabic and Persian, make a great deal of the prophet Enoch (or Edna, as they call him). They tell us that he received 30 volumes from heaven filled with mysterious science.

There is a book (actually, another two books have come to light since, Editor) ascribed to him, but it is certain that they did not come from his hand, but were written either by a fanciful Jew before the coming of Christ, or by a foolish Christian soon after. For about 1000 years, one was buried in oblivion till Joseph Juste Scaliger, about 200 years ago, discovered part of it. It foolishly maintains that, before the Flood, the angels, seeing the beautiful daughters of men, took them in marriage, had children by them, a race of ancient giants, and introduced idolatry, astrology, and other unlawful arts, into the world.

Was not our Saviour prefigured by Enoch, the son of Jared? He was *dedicated* in a special way to the service of God. He always did the things that pleased his Father, and twice was attested by God as his *Beloved Son* in whom he was *well pleased*. First in order of dignity and influence, he entered the heavenly mansions without tasting corruption. As our great Prophet, he foretold the Last Judgement and the ruin of the wicked generation of Judah. Scarcely was his Jewish seed, according to the spirit, removed by death, or fled from their country, when wrath came on that nation to the uttermost; nor will his whole chosen seed be sooner ripe for the mansions of eternal bliss than the floods of unmixed and endless woe that will overwhelm the world of the ungodly.

Here are all the references in the Bible to Enoch: Genesis 4:17-18, 5:18-19, 21-24; Luke 3:37; Hebrews 11:5; Jude verse 14.

ENOS, ENOSH, *man*

The son of Seth, and father of Cainan, was born BC 3769. His name indicates the sense his father had of the misery of mankind due to sin. In his day, men *began to call on the name of the Lord*; that is, those who detested the wicked offspring of Cain, and formed themselves into public worshipping societies. Perhaps, too, before his death in BC 2864, the descendants of Seth began *to profane the name of the Lord*, intermarrying with the offspring of Cain.

Here are all the references to Enos (Enosh): Genesis 4:26, 5:6-7, 9-11, 6:1-2; 1 Chron. 1:1; Luke 3:38.

EPAPHRAS

A native of Colosse, and a faithful and hard working preacher among the inhabitants there, by whose means many of them were converted

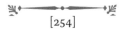

to Christ. When Paul was at Rome, Epaphras came from Phrygia to see him, and was, for some time, his fellow-prisoner. Understanding that, in his absence, false teachers had greatly corrupted and troubled his Colossian hearers, he put the case to Paul who, directed by God, wrote a letter to rectify these disorders. It is said that Epaphras suffered martyrdom at Colosse. (His name is only found in Col. 1:7, 4:12; Philem. v. 23)

EPAPHRODITUS
A notable preacher of the Christian faith at Philippi. He was sent to Paul by the believers there with a supply of money when he was a prisoner in Rome, and otherwise to assist him to the extent of their power. He executed his commission with such care and zeal that he brought on himself an indisposition that threatened his life; but, being mercifully recovered, he went home quickly, as he heard that the Philippians were extremely concerned about him, carrying along with him Paul's Epistle to the church. (His name is found only in Phil. 2:25, 4:18, 23)

EPHRAIM, *the fullness of the nations*
The younger son of Joseph, born about BC 1711. Joseph presented him and his brother Manasseh to his father Jacob when dying, that he might give them his blessing. To emphasise that Ephraim's tribe would be the most numerous and powerful, Jacob crossed his hands, laying the right hand on the head of Ephraim, and the left on the head of Manasseh; nor would the patriarch change his hands over, giving as his reason that, to his certain knowledge, Manasseh's tribe would be great and numerous, yet Ephraim's would be even more so. (Gen. 48:8-22) His sons Shuthelah, Becher, and Tahan (or, Tahath) were heads of large families. (Num. 26:35-36) He had other sons, namely, Zabad, Ezer, and Elead, Bered and Eladah, the first three of whom, together with Shutbelah, were murdered by the Philistines at Gath as they attempted to defend their herds of cattle from these robbers. He was extremely grieved at the loss of his children, and, happening to have a son born to him at that time, he called him *Beriah* (unfortunate), to indicate that it was not going well with his house. He also had a daughter, whose descendants built the two Bethhorons and Uzzensherah. (1 Chron. 7:20-27)

When the Ephraimites came out of Egypt, they amounted to 40,500; but they decreased to 8900 in the wilderness. Elishama the son of Ammihud was their chief prince and captain, Joshua the son of Nun their spy, and Kemuel the son of Shiphtan their agent for the division of the land. (Num. 2:18-19, 26:37, 13:8, 34:24) They, together with the Manassites and Benjamites, encamped behind the Tabernacle, and marched behind the ark; so God was said to lead Joseph like a flock, and to show himself in plain view of these tribes. (Num. 2:18-24, 10:21-24; Ps. 80:1-2) When Joshua became head of the Israelites, and conquered Canaan, he, according to the direction of God by lot, assigned his own tribe their inheritance in the very heart of the Promised Land, where that portion of ground lay which Jacob first bought from Hamor, and afterwards forcibly took from the Amorites. (Gen. 48:21) They and their brothers from Manasseh protested that their territory was too narrow; but he refused to add anything to it, and encouraged them to expel the Canaanites from their hill country. They took his advice, and, obliging a citizen to be their director, took Bethel, slew its inhabitants, and possessed it themselves. But they did not banish the inhabitants of Gezer and the villages around. (Judg. 1:22-29)

When Deborah, a prophetess of this tribe, judged Israel, and levied war against Jabin, a body of the Ephraimites was detached to attack the Amalekites who, it seems, were marching to ravage the south country of Israel or to join Sisera. When Gideon defeated the armies of Midian, the Ephraimites proudly reproved him because he had not arrived earlier to give them assistance; but he pacified them with soft words, making excuses by saying that their apprehending Oreb and Zeeb, the chief princes, and killing so vast a number of fugitives, was more important and honourable than his whole victory. When Jephthah raised an army against the Ammonites, he invited the Ephraimites to join him, but they declined. When, without their aid, he routed the enemy, vast numbers of them crossed the Jordan and rudely abused his troops like an army of vagabonds, and threatened to burn down his house upon him. Provoked by such ungenerous abuse, he and his troops fell on them and put them to flight; and, taking the passages of Jordan, they killed all they could discern to be Ephraimites by listening to them pronounce *Sibboleth* instead of *Shibboleth*. At this time, there fell 42,000 of them. Soon after this, Abdon an Ephraimite judged Israel eight years. (Judg. 5:12, 7:24-25, 8:1-3, ch. 12)

For about 300 years, the Tabernacle of God was lodged at Shiloh, in the tribe of Ephraim. In the war in which it was carried off by the Philistines, it seems the Ephraimites, though well armed, behaved with the utmost cowardice. (Josh. 18:1; 1 Sam. 4; Ps. 78:6) 20,800 valiant men of this tribe attended David's coronation. During his reign, Hoshea the son of Azaziah was their deputy-governor, and Helez the Pelonite their chief captain. (1 Chron. 12:30, 27:10, 20) Nothing remarkable happened to the tribe of Ephraim after this till Jeroboam, one of their tribe, decoyed it, and nine other tribes, to erect a separate kingdom for him, which continued for 254 years (BC 975-721). Most, if not all the kings came from this tribe, and the royal cities of Shechem and Samaria belonged to them. One of the golden calves was placed in Bethel, another one of their cities. As this tribe made so notable an appearance among the ten, they were often all called by its name. (2 Chron. 25:7; Isa. 28; Jer. 31:6, 1:19; Hosea 5-6, etc.)

EPICUREANS

A sect of heathen philosophers, followers of the doctrine of Epicurus the Athenian, who flourished about BC 304. They maintained that the world was formed not by God, nor by any design, but by the chance movement of atoms. They denied that God governs the world, or, at least, condescends to interfere with creatures below. They denied the immortality of the soul and the existence of angels. They maintained that happiness consisted in pleasure; but some of them placed this pleasure in a life of tranquillity and joy of the mind, arising from the practice of moral virtue, and this is thought by some to have been the true position of Epicurus. Others interpreted him in a gross sense, and looked for all their happiness in the bodily pleasures of eating, drinking, sex, etc.

When Paul preached in Athens, they called him a *babbler*, and a *setter forth of strange gods*. (Found only in Acts 17:18)

ERASTUS

The chamberlain, or city treasurer, of Corinth. (For other uses of *chamberlain*, see 2 Kings 23:11; Esther 2:3, 14-15; Acts 12:20) Having resigned his office, he accompanied Paul on his way to Ephesus, and was sent along with Timothy to Macedonia, probably to prepare the contribution for the poor Christians of Judea. When Paul wrote

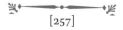

his Epistle to the Romans, we find Erastus in Corinth. (Acts 19:22; Rom. 16:23; 2 Tim. 4:20) Some make him out to be a bishop of Macedonia, and a martyr at Philippi, and others, just on slender grounds, Bishop of Paneas, at the springs of the Jordan.

ESARHADDON

The son and successor of Sennacherib. Finding his kingdom on the point of ruin at his accession in BC 708, he remained at home, establishing his power the best way he could. About the 29th year of his reign, either by force or by heirship, he obtained the Kingdom of Babylon, and took up his residence there. Grown powerful by this accession of dominion, he marched his army towards the west, took Jerusalem, and carried King Manasseh prisoner to Babylon. He also reduced the Egyptians and Ethiopians, and ravaged the country of Edom. Perhaps Tartan, his general, took Ashdod. The remains of the ten tribes and Syrians he transplanted to the eastern parts of his dominions, and brought men from Cuth, Avah, Sepharvaim, and other eastern provinces he had subdued, to populate the country in their place. See Samaritans.

After a glorious reign of 42 years, he died, and his son Saosduchin succeeded him. Probably Esarhaddon is the Sardanapalus of Clearchus, who died of old age. (2 Kings 17:24-28, 2 Kings 19:37; 2 Chron. 33:11; Ezra 4:2, 10; Isa. 37:38, 19:23, 20:1; Nahum 3:8, 10)

ESCAPE

To get away from danger or punishment. (Gen. 19:17, 19-20, 22; Heb. 2:3) Those who do escape are called an *escaping*. (2 Kings 19:30-31; Ezek. 6:8-9; Matt. 23:33; Luke 21:36; Acts 27:42; Rom. 2:3; 1 Cor. 10:13; 1 Thess. 5:3; Heb. 12:25)

ESHCOL, *grapes*

One of Abraham's allies that assisted him against Chedorlaomer. Perhaps the Valley of Eshcol in the southern territories of Judah was given this name by Abraham, though it is more probable that it was so called from the large *cluster of grapes* that Caleb and Joshua carried back with them after spying out the land. (Gen. 14:13, 24; Num. 13:23-24)

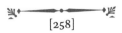

ESTHER, *secret*; or **HADASSAH**, *myrtle-tree*

From the tribe of Benjamin, she was the daughter of Abihail, the uncle of Mordecai. When her parents died when she was just a child, Mordecai, her cousin, brought her up. When Ahasuerus convened the beautiful young women of his Empire for him to select a queen from among them in the place of Vashti, Esther was brought among the rest of the women. A eunuch had charge of her, and provided her with everything she needed. Seven maids also attended and assisted her. After she had undergone a year's purification with sweet oils and perfumes, she was, in her turn, conducted to the king's bed. Superlatively delighted with her beauty and pleasing deportment, he put the royal crown on her head and declared her to be his queen. A splendid feast was arranged to honour the nuptials, and the king bestowed many valuable presents on the queen and the guests. He likewise released a vast number of prisoners, and forgave his subjects a considerable part of his revenue. Esther, on Mordecai's advice, entirely concealed her Jewish origin; but, informed by him of a plot against the king by two of his chamberlains, she notified the king. (Esther 2)

Upon Haman's obtaining the royal edict for the general destruction of the Jews, Mordecai, by Hatach, one of her attendants, informed Esther, and begged her to intercede with her husband the king. She replied that she had not been called into the king's presence for 30 days, and that to approach his presence unbidden was to run the risk of losing her life. Mordecai responded by begging that she would intercede, whatever the risk. He suggested that probably God had raised her to her high station for such an end, and that, if she continued to do nothing, deliverance would come to the Jews from some other quarter, and she and her friends would be destroyed. This message determined her to intercede, whatever the cost. After she and her ladies-in-waiting, and the rest of the Jews in Shushan, had spent three days in solemn fasting and prayer for a blessing on her attempt, on the third day, in a most splendid dress, she approached the king's presence without him summoning her.

He had no sooner seen her enter the inner court, when, all in raptures of affection, he stretched out the golden sceptre as a sign of his favour, and asked her request, for it would be granted up to half of his kingdom. That she might the more effectively insinuate herself into his favour when she mentioned her business, she only begged the King and Haman to honour her with their presence at a banquet she had prepared. She was granted what she desired; and while the entertainment lasted, Ahasuerus again asked her request. She only begged that he and Haman would vouchsafe her their presence at a second feast. Her request was readily granted. While they sat at this second banquet, the king, merry with wine, asked her once more what was her request, and it would be granted up to half of his kingdom. She begged that he would protect her life, and the lives of her people, which would seriously harm the public revenues. He immediately asked who had planned this thing, and was informed that it was Haman, there present. This discovery issued in the sudden ruin of Haman and his whole family, and his estate was given over to Esther, who appointed Mordecai its steward.

The edict against the Jews could not be revoked, according to the laws of the Medes and Persians, who considered royal edicts immutable; but Esther, and Mordecai, now prime minister in the place of Haman, wrote to the Jews in all the provinces of the Empire to defend themselves on the day appointed for their destruction. These letters discouraged the heathen from rising up; and of those who attempted to put the massacre into execution, the Jews killed about 75,800, but took no spoil from them. To commemorate this wonderful deliverance, Esther and Mordecai appointed the Jews to keep annually the Feast of Purim on the day they had been marked out for destruction.

These events are recorded in the book written in Esther's honour, and called by her name. Who the author was - whether Ezra, Mordecai, or someone else - is absolutely unknown. Never a Jew doubted its divine authority, despite the fact that the name of God is not mentioned anywhere, nor perhaps even a Christian, for though the canons of Melito and Athanasius do not mention it, it is probable they included it under Ezra. See Apocrypha.

ETHAN, *strength*

(1) A son of Zerah, the son of Judah. (1 Chron. 2:6, 8)

(2) The son of Kishi, and descendant of Merari, described as an Ezrahite. He was one of the wisest men of his age, Solomon excepted, and a chief musician of the Temple. He lived to a ripe old age, and penned the 89th Psalm on the occasion of the revolt of the ten tribes. (1 Kings 4:31; 1 Chron. 2:6, 8, 6:42, 44, 15:17, 19) If he is the same as

Jeduthun, he had six sons: Gedaliah, Zeri, Jeshaiah, Hashahiah, Mattithiah, and Shimei; all heads of many classes of the Temple singers. (1 Chron. 9:16; 16:38, 25:1, 3, 6, 17, 25:1, 3, 6; 2 Chron. 5:12) Many of the Psalms were given into his, and his descendants', hands to be sung by them. (1 Chron. 16: 41-42, Ps. 39, 62, 89:1, etc.)

EVE

The first woman, and the mother of us all. Having created the man, God presented before him the various animals of earth and air, but none of them were a helpmate for him. He therefore put him into a deep sleep, and, from his side, formed a most beautiful woman, and gave her to Adam as his wife. To mark their origin from the dust, and the oneness of affection between them, God called them both *Adam*, but Adam called her *Isshah* (woman) because she was taken out of the man (*Ish*), and bore a striking resemblance to him. They lived together in happiness only a few days, maybe for only one day, when Satan, envying their happiness, assumed the form of a serpent, or rather took possession of one, and, in this form, addressed the woman in the absence of her husband. In a crafty way, he insinuated that God had dealt badly with them in not allowing them to eat of every tree of the garden. She replied that they were only forbidden to eat or touch the tree of the knowledge of good and evil, and that under pain of death. Satan replied that there was no absolute certainty of their death if they ate it, for God knew that, after eating it, their eyes would be opened, and they would become as gods, knowing good and evil. Seeing the delightful appearance of the fruit, and ardently desiring higher degrees of wisdom, she took the fruit and ate it; and, being much taken with it, she gave it to her husband to eat. Their consciences quickly uncovered their guilt, and, with strange passions awakening in their soul, they became ashamed of their nakedness. When God called them to account, Adam threw the blame entirely on his wife. To mark his detestation of sin, God condemned her, and her female descendants, to many sorrows and painful labour in producing children, and to further degrees of subjection to their husbands.

After a revelation of man's recovery through Christ (see Gen. 3:15), Adam called her name *Havar,* (or Eve), because she was to be the mother of all the living. Quickly, after their expulsion from Paradise, she conceived and bore a son. Imagining she had got the promised *seed,* the Man, the Lord Redeemer, she called his name Cain, which means *possession*. Soon after, she bore a second son, and called his name Abel, or *vanity*. And long after, just after Abel had been murdered, she bore Seth, whom she accounted a *seed* given her in the place of Abel. See Adam, and Genesis chapters 2-4.

Here is a complete list of verses where Eve's name is mentioned: Genesis 3:20, 4:1; 2 Corinthians 11:3; 1 Timothy 2:13.

EVILMERODACH, or *Merodach the fool*

The son and successor of Nebuchadnezzar. It is said that he governed the Chaldean Empire during his father's madness, and was afterwards imprisoned for mismanagement, where be contracted a familiarity with Jehoiachin. On that account, he liberated and honoured him as soon as he came to the throne. (2 Kings 25:27; Jer. 52:31) He married Nitocris, the daughter of Astyages, King of Media, one of the most active and wise members of her sex, who advised Belshazzar her son to call in Daniel to read the handwriting on the wall. By a wanton ravage of part of the Median territories, he began a war between the two kingdoms that ended in the ruin of Chaldea. For about two years, after he had reigned, or rather wallowed, in sloth and wickedness, he was murdered by Neriglissar, his sister's husband, who succeeded him to the throne.

EUODIAS and SYNTYCHE

Two noted women of the Philippian church, who had, according to their status, greatly helped the Apostle Paul to propagate the Christian faith. Some argument blew up between them; so Paul warmly encouraged them to be reconciled, and live in perfect harmony. (Found only in Phil. 4:2)

EUTYCHUS

A young man of Troas, who, sitting in a window as Paul preached till late, fell asleep, tumbled from the third storey, and was taken up as dead. But Paul, taking him up in his arms, revived him, and returned him to the church until the break of day. (Found only in Acts 20:10)

EZEKIEL, *the strength of God*

The son of Buzi. He was a prophet and priest, carried captive to Babylon with Jehoiachin, King of Judah. In BC 595, in the 5th year of his captivity, and the 30th of his age, or from the 18th year of Josiah, when the great Passover was kept, as he was among the captives by the river Chebar in Chaldea, the Lord appeared to him on a throne, supported by Cherubim and wheels, signifying angels and changing providences, or ministers and churches, and directed him to go and declare his mind to the captive Jews. There appeared to him, about the same time, a roll, or book, filled with mournful threats of heavy judgements, which he was commanded to *eat*; that is seriously consider, and thoroughly understand. After he had continued another seven days with his fellow captives, the Lord made him a watchman, or prophet, to the house of Israel, assuring him that they would not listen to what he said, and that he would be seized and bound as a madman. (Ezek. 1-3)

When, by the direction of God, he shut himself up in his house, God commanded him to describe, or draw, the city of Jerusalem on a brick or tile, and to put a pan as a wall of iron between him and this plan of the city, then lie down before it on his left side 390 days, for the 390 years' sin of the ten tribes, and 40 days on his right side, for the 40 years provocation of Judah. This meant that, by the Chaldeans' furious and determined siege of Jerusalem, and the taking of it, the sins of Israel, from the setting up of the calves at Bethel and Dan, to that day, and the sins of Judah, during the wicked part of Manasseh's reign, with that of the years gone by since Josiah's death, would be avenged. Or might it not also mean that, after the Chaldeans had besieged it 390 days, they would again lay siege to it, and, after 40 days, make themselves masters of it? While he thus lay on his side, he was ordered to make himself bread from wheat, barley, beans, lentils, millet, and fitches (the *Nigella sativa*, a small annual of the order *Ranunculacece*, growing wild in the Mediterranean countries, and cultivated in Egypt and Syria for its seed), and either bake it, or rub it over with human excrement. But when he showed the greatest reluctance to do this last thing, he was allowed to use cows' dung instead. By this bread, and his manner of eating, it was prophesied that the Jews would be reduced to living on base and unclean food in small quantities, amid terrible fears of danger. (Chapter 4)

He was next directed to cut off his hair, divide it into three parts, burn one, cut another to pieces with a sword or knife, and scatter the rest to the wind, except that he should keep a few strands to burn with fire. This meant that the Jews would partly be destroyed with famine and pestilence, partly by the sword of the Chaldeans, and part of Judah would be carried into captivity and scattered among the heathen. Only a few of the survivors would be left in the land, and, by their folly, become a firebrand, a means of kindling the Chaldean resentment against the whole nation of the Jews. Soon after, he was employed to predict a variety of particular judgements against them. Next year, he was carried in spirit to Jerusalem, and had a vision of the abominable idolatries that prevailed there, and of five men, under the direction of Jesus Christ, who were appointed to slay the inhabitants, except those who were given to mourning and grief for the prevailing sins of the land. He also, in his vision, saw the Lord Jesus cast the fire of his vengeance from between the Cherubim onto the wicked city. At the same time, he was inspired to utter a variety of fearful threats concerning their destruction, and some promises of their merciful restoration. (Ch. 5-11)

After the Spirit had transported him back to Chaldea, he was ordered by God to dig through the wall of his house, and through the hole carry out his furniture in the evening when it was dark, and to eat his food with trembling. This prophesied Zedekiah's shameful flight from Jerusalem, and the calamities that were coming on the Jewish nation. After this, he declaimed against the false prophets and the hypocritical elders that were his fellow captives, and assured them that God's purpose in overturning the Jewish state was irrevocable, and the time of it was at hand. (Ch. 12-14) Using the metaphor of *a barren vine*, and *a wife* graciously married turning to prostitution, he foreshadowed the wickedness of the Jews, and the fairness of their approaching ruin; to which he added some promises of mercy. (Ch. 15-16) By the *parable of two eagles*, and their interference with the twigs of a cedar tree, he showed how justly the Chaldeans would punish Zedekiah and his subjects for their treacherous revolt by going over to the King of Egypt; and, after a prediction of the Messiah's incarnation and power, he vindicated the justness of all the calamities that were to come on them. (Ch. 17-18) By the taking of *young lions*, he was speaking of the unhappy end of the foul kings who succeeded Josiah. (Ch. 19) He rehearsed the crimes of the nation in former ages, and their abuse of the favours that God had heaped on them. He foretold the siege of Jerusalem as being near at hand; he rehearsed the horrible crimes of its inhabitants, and he told them that their sins,

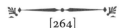

which had provoked God against them, were worse than those of Sodom and Israel. (Ch. 20-23)

In BC 590, though about 600 miles distant, he declared to his fellow captives that, that very day, Nebuchadnezzar had laid siege to Jerusalem, and the wicked inhabitants would be consumed in it, like flesh is boiled in a caldron, and the city itself would be melted as copper, that is, destroyed. That night, his wife died, and he was forbidden to weep for her. This meant that the Jews would quickly be deprived of their Temple, their civil and ecclesiastic constitution, and everything dear to them, without being so much as allowed to mourn over these things. (Ch. 24)

After he had predicted the overthrow of the kingdoms of Ammon, Moab, Edom, the Philistines, the Tyrians, and the Egyptians, by the hand of the Chaldeans, he was again solemnly admonished, as a spiritual watchman to the Jews. Hearing of the destruction of Jerusalem, his mouth fell agape. Then, in a most delightful manner, he foretold the coming of the Messiah as their spiritual King and Shepherd; their deliverance from Babylon, and from their present dispersion; the harmonious rejoining of their tribes; the purity of their worship; the destruction of their enemies, particularly Gog and Magog (or the Turks); and their happy and holy establishment in their country in the latter days; and, from the symbolic account of them, their land, Temple, and tribes, he projects the state of the gospel Church in the apostolic age, but chiefly in the millennial age. (Ch. 48)

Ezekiel began to prophesy six years before the destruction of Jerusalem by Nebuchadnezzar, and continued to at least 14 years after it. (Ch. 1:1, 40:1) In reproving sin, he is often abundantly clear, but he much more abounds in enigmatic visions than the rest of the prophets. Those in the first chapter, and in the last nine chapters, are reckoned so obscure by the Jews that they refrain from reading them till they are 30 years of age. The history of his death and burial, with many other things reported about him by Jews, Christian fathers, and Mahometan writers, are too uncertain and fabulous to have any place in this work. Perhaps Zoroaster (or Zerdusht), the great reformer of the Magian religion among the Persians, might have once been one of his disciples; but he apostatised to heathenism.

Ezekiel is referred to only twice, in Ezekiel 1:3 and 24:24.

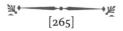

EZRA, *a helper*

The son of Seraiah, who was probably the High Priest slain at the burning of the Temple, a priest and ready scribe in the Law of his God. Whether he came to Judea with Zerubbabel, and then went back to Babylon, we are not certain, though we can hardly credit it. It is evident that Artaxerxes Longimanus, King of Persia, sent him to Judea in the seventh year of his reign, with a royal warrant to rectify the church and state of the Jews according to the Law of God. A great number followed him. At the River Ahava, he called a halt, and sent back for some more priests and Levites. After 258 had come up, they observed there a solemn fast to implore the guidance and protection of God, as Ezra did not choose to ask of the king an escort of troops. Here, he delivered into the hands of his main attendants an account of the gold and silver that the king had granted for the service of the Temple, to the value of about £800,000. In about the space of four months, to the number of 1,775, they arrived at Jerusalem. (Ezra 7-8) There, he found a vast numbers of Jews that had married heathen women of the accursed nations, or others. After a solemn confession of sin, and a deprecation of wrath, he issued a proclamation charging all the Jews in the country, under pain of excommunication, and confiscation of goods, to assemble and rectify this matter. After they had assembled, he made them sensible of their sin, and charged them by covenant to forsake it; but, on account of the great rain, commissioners were appointed to see the matter finished. In three months, they made a thorough inquiry, and about 113 priests, Levites, and other Jews, dismissed their strange wives, even though they had children by some of them. It does not appear that they put away the children, but carefully educated them in the Jewish religion. (Ezra 9-10) For 13 years, Ezra continued as director of the Jewish church and state. After Nehemiah came, and got the walls of Jerusalem rebuilt, Ezra, assisted by 26 Levites, read and expounded the Law to the people from morning to night as they assembled during the eight days of the Feast of Tabernacles. This was followed with a solemn confession of sin, and a renewal of their covenant with God. (Neh. 8-10)

It is probable that Ezra wrote the book called by his name, which, together with most of the facts related in this article, gives an account of the Jews' return from Babylon, and their founding and finishing the second Temple, despite the obstructions the Samaritans and others made to the work. (Chapters 1-6) As from 4:8-7:27, the book mostly relates to the affairs of the Empire, for the language is in Chaldee, while the rest is in Hebrew. It is generally supposed that he also wrote the two books of Chronicles, and those of Nehemiah and Esther. He received into the canon of authentic oracles whatever books he found deserved the honour, and sometimes changed the ancient names, and added expressions to render some places more intelligible. But whether he exchanged the Samaritan character for the Chaldee now used in our Hebrew Bibles, and whether he added the vowel points, is not so easily determined.

Ezra's name is found in 1 Chronicles 4:17; Ezra 7:1, 6, 10-12, 21, 25, 10:1-2, 5-6, 10, 16; Nehemiah 8:1-2, 4-6, 9, 13, 12:1, 13, 26, 33, 36.

F

FAMILIAR SPIRITS (DEMONS)

See *Familiar Spirit* in Leviticus 20:27; 1 Sam. 28:7-8; 1 Chronicles 10:13; Isaiah 29:4; and *Familiar Spirits* in Leviticus 19:31, Leviticus 20:6; Deuteronomy 18:11; 1 Sam. 28:3, 9; 2 Kings 21:6, 23:24; Isaiah 8:19, 19:3.

FATHER, MOTHER
FATHER

(1) The immediate male parent of a child (Gen. 9:18), but it is sometimes used for both parents. (Prov. 10:1)

(2) The grandfather, or any other progenitor, however remote, especially if any covenant was made with them, or granted to them. Thus Abraham, Isaac, Jacob, and others, were the fathers of the Jews at the time of Christ. (John 4:20, 8:53; Heb. 1:1)

(3) The inventor of an art, or method of living; an instructor of others in any science. (Judg. 17:10; 1 Sam. 10:12). So Jabal was the *father* of those who dwell in tents, and Jubal the *father* of musicians. (Gen. 4:20-21) Hiram the founder (foundry man) was a *father*, or chief director, of the artificers belonging to Hiram, King of Tyre, and Solomon. (2 Chron. 2:13) Elijah was a *father* to Elisha and the young prophets of Jericho. (2 Kings 2:12) Founders of cities, and progenitors of the inhabitants, are called *fathers* of those cities: so Salma was the father of Bethlehem, Hareph of Bethgadel, Joab of the

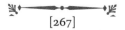

Valley of Charashim, and Jehiel the *father* of Gibeon. (1 Chron. 2:51, 4:14, 9:35)

(4) *Father* is a title of respect. Naaman's servants addressed him as their *father*. (2 Kings 5:13) Both Jehoram and Joash called Elisha their *father*. (2 Kings 6:21, 13:14)

(5) One who affectionately counsels, cares, and provides for another. So God is the *Father of the fatherless* (Ps. 68:5), Joseph a *father* to Pharaoh (Gen. 45:8), and Job a *father* to the poor. (Job 29:16) Among the Arabs, father, as well as son of such a thing, denotes qualities as *father of a belly*, *Father of eternity*, *Father of mercies*. (Isa. 9:6) God is called the *Father of Christ*, for in the first Person of the Godhead, he, from eternity, begot him. (John 1:14; Eph. 1:5)

God is called the *Father of Christ*; according to some intelligent and pious writers, it has reference to the great work of salvation in which the Godhead appeared to act as the Father, the Son, and the Holy Spirit. He is the *Father of spirits*, of *lights*, of *glory*, of *mercies*, of *all things*. He created angels and the souls of men, and preserves them in their nature and work. He is the origin and bestower of all light, glory, and merciful favours, and he is the former and preserver of all things. (Heb. 12:9; James 1:17; Eph. 1:17, 4:6; 2 Cor. 1:3) He is the *Father* and *mother* of the rain, dew, ice, and hoarfrost, as he forms and produces all these, and sends them on the earth. (Job 38:28-29) He was the *Father* of the Jews, and is so of all those who profess the true faith, as he marvellously raises them up, establishes them in their national and church state, and is their special Governor. (Gen. 6:2; Deut. 32:6)

He is the *Father* of the saints. He begets them again into his image by his Word and Spirit, adopts them into his family, makes them familiar with him, kindly cares, provides for, and protects them, and makes them joint heirs with Christ of his heavenly inheritance. (Rom. 8:15-16) He is the *Father* of all men by creation, by providential preservation, and by government. (Mal. 2:10) Christ is the *everlasting Father*: From eternity, the elect were chosen in him, and, by his obedience and suffering, by his Word and Spirit, he confers upon them their new state and nature, and gives them his kingdom, and everything needed. (Isa. 9:6, 53:10)

The Old Testament saints are called his *fathers*; the Apostles, and other New Testament believers, are called his *children*. (Ps. 45:16) Satan is called a father, for he introduced sin into the world, and makes men like him, directing and counselling them in their evil ways. (John 8:44) Abraham is the *father* of those who believe; he is an eminent pattern of their faith and obedience; and into his bosom they are gathered in the eternal state. (Rom. 4:11) Natural parents are called *fathers of our flesh*, as they only beget our body. (Heb. 12:9) We are to *call no man father*; we are to acknowledge none but Christ, and God in him, the Head of the Church, the author of our religion, or the Lord of our conscience. (Matt. 23:9) To call corruption *our father*, and the worms our mother and sister, is to acknowledge humbly that we sprang from the dust, and will, by corruption, return to it; and so, by way of lowliness, claim kindred with vermin. (Job 17:14) John the Baptist *turned the hearts of the fathers to the children* when he urged the Jews of his time to believe the principles, receive like endowments, and follow the practice of their godly ancestors. (Mal. 4:6) To *sleep with our fathers* is to go to them; or to be *gathered* to them is to die like our ancestors, and go with them to the grave into a separate state of souls. (Judg. 2:10; 1 Kings 2:10) Sometimes, the father-in-law, or father of one's wife, is called *father*; so Heli, the father-in-law of Joseph the carpenter, is called his *father*. (Luke 3:23)

MOTHER

(1) A woman who has given birth to a child. (Exod. 2:8)

(2) The female of an animal. (Exod. 23:19)

The character of a mother is applied:

(1) To the true Church. She is Christ's *mother*, as he assumed by her our nature, and was a member of her. (Song 3:11) She is the *mother* of all believers; in her, and by her ordinances, they are spiritually born again, nourished, protected, and directed. (Song 1:6, 4:4) She is now *free*, delivered from the bondage of ceremonies; and her true members are free from the broken Law, and the slavery of sin and Satan. She is *from above*; she is of a heavenly origin, constitution, and tendency, and her true members have their *conversation in heaven*. (Gal 4:26; Phil. 3:20)

(2) To the kingdom of Judah, or family of David, which produced such wicked oppressors as Jehoahaz, Jehoiakim, Jehoiachin, and Zedekiah. (Ezek. 19)

(3) To a metropolis, or capital city of a country or tribe; then the inhabitants, villages, or minor cities are called *daughters*. (2 Sam. 20:19; Jer. 1:12)

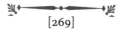

(4) To any female, superior in age, station, gifts, or graces, or who deals tenderly with others. Deborah was a *mother in Israel*. With tenderness and valour, she judged, instructed, and governed the people. (Judg. 5:7) The mother of Rufus was a mother to Paul; she kindly cared for him and provided for his needs. (Rom. 16:13)

(5) The saints are Christ's *mother, sisters, and brothers*; he is formed in their hearts by their spiritual union with him, and their receiving out of his fullness; and there is a dearer intimacy and relationship between him and them, than between their nearest relatives on earth. (Matt. 12:49-50)

(6) Rome is the *mother of harlots, and abominations of the earth*. The antichristian Papacy established there, produces multitudes of whoredoms (gross idolatries), and every other impiety. (Rev. 17:5)

All superiors are called *fathers and mothers*, or *parents*, to teach others to behave with tender affection towards their inferiors, and to teach their inferiors, whether children, wives, servants, people, subjects, pupils, etc., to behave with kindness and affection to them and their commands. (Exod. 20:12; Deut. 5:16) Kings are *nursing fathers*, and queens *nursing mothers*, to the Church, when civil rulers exert themselves to promote true religion, and see to the establishment, right government, and prosperity of the Church. (Isa. 49:23) To rebuke offenders as *fathers, mothers, brothers, or sisters*, must be done in a most humble, tender, and affectionate way. (1 Tim. 5:1-3)

FELIX, CLAUDIUS

He succeeded Cumanus as Roman deputy in the government of Judea. He enticed Drusilla to divorce Azizus, King of Emesa, and marry him. He sent prisoner to Rome someone called Eleazar, a notorious robber, who had committed great outrages in the country. He procured the death of Jonathan the High Priest for taking the liberty of admonishing him concerning his duty. He defeated about 4000 assassins, headed by an Egyptian impostor, who set up headquarters on the Mount of Olives. (Acts 21:38)

Paul was brought before Felix at Caesarea, where he resided, and, despite all that Tertullus and his assistants said, was treated by him with no little humanity. He refused to hear their accusations till Lysias the chief captain, who had sent him under guard, came down. He permitted Paul's friends to see him in prison, and do him what service they could. Hoping that they would purchase his release, he often sent for Paul to talk with him. On one of these occasions, Paul entertained Felix, and Drusilla his wife who was a hardened Jewish professor, with a discourse on self-control, righteousness, and the Last Judgement, till Felix's awakened conscience made him tremble. But, to avoid further conviction, he told Paul to leave off and go back to his prison; then he would call for him at a more convenient time. In AD 60, he was recalled to Rome, and Festus was sent as his replacement. To keep the Jews quiet, he left Paul bound. However, this did him no good, for numbers of them followed him to Rome and complained of his extortion and violence. He would have been punished with death had not his brother Pallas, due to his reputation at court, preserved his life. (Acts 24)

FESTUS, PORTIUS

He succeeded Felix in the government of Judea. When he first came to Jerusalem, some of the influential Jews solicited him to condemn Paul, whom Felix had left in prison, or, at least, given orders to send him to Jerusalem. Festus, perhaps, ignorant of their intention to murder him on the way, rejected their request, and told them that the Romans condemned nobody before they heard his defence. He bid them come down to Caesarea and he would consider their charges. They went down in a few days, and, after they had laid their charges against Paul, he was allowed to make his defence. Festus, perhaps influenced by a bribe, was inclined to send Paul to Jerusalem; but this was forestalled by Paul's appeal to Caesar. Sometime later, at the desire of Agrippa, Festus allowed Paul to make a further defence that he might write more accurately to the Emperor concerning the case. When Paul gave an account of his conversion and call to the apostleship, Festus, ignorant of these affairs, pronounced that Paul's *much learning had made him mad*, and, soon after, sent him to Rome. (Acts 25-26)

Festus was extremely active in suppressing the numerous bands of robbers and assassins infesting Judea at that time. He also suppressed a magician, who was drawing crowds after him into the desert. After Festus had enjoyed that office about two years, he died, and was succeeded by Nero Albinus.

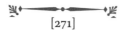

FOUNTAIN

God is called a *fountain of living waters*, and with him is the *fountain of living waters*. He is the unsearchable and unfading source of all our happiness and comfort. (Ps. 36:9; Jer. 2:13, 17:13) Jesus Christ is an open fountain, a *fountain of gardens*, a *well of living waters*, and *streams* from Lebanon. By his blood, righteousness, and spiritual influence, exhibited and offered in the gospel, our guilt and pollution are washed away, and all the churches and worshipping assemblies of his people are refreshed, made alive, and rendered fruitful in the works of righteousness. (Song 4:15; Zech. 13:1) The Holy Spirit, attending the preaching of the gospel, is a *fountain* coming forth from the house of the Lord, watering the Valley of Shittim. (Joel 3:18) Proceeding from, and sent by Jesus the residence of God, the Holy Spirit, by his gifts and graces, cools, refreshes, cleanses, and makes fruitful the barren souls of men, both Jews and Gentiles, and is a *well of water, springing up to eternal life* in growth of grace, and abounding in the practice of good works. (John 4:14, 7:38-39) The Church is a *spring shut up*, and *fountain sealed*; in her is lodged the fresh and ever-flowing fullness of Jesus' Word, blood, and Spirit, for the purification and refreshment of her members. None but Christ ought to rule or govern in her as her Head; and, by his providence and grace, her true members are safely and secretly secured in him alone. (Song 4:12; Isa. 58:11)

All the saints' *springs* are in the Church. In her, dwells God, the fountain of living waters. Jesus the smitten, the water-yielding Rock of Ages, the Holy Spirit, that *river of life* issuing from under the throne of God, and the Scriptures and ordinances - all these are subordinate wells of salvation, from where the saints draw their happiness and comfort, and which make them send forth rivers of edifying words and works in their lives. (Ps. 87:7; John 7:38) The saints are *fountains*; from their souls, replenished with the Spirit and the grace of Christ, flow out much edifying talk; and so their tongue or mouth is called a *well of life*, with much refreshing benevolence and many useful good works. But when they fall before the wicked by temptations and persecution, they are a *troubled fountain* and a *corrupt spring*, far less attractive and useful. (Prov. 10:11, 25:26) Spiritual knowledge and wisdom, and the fear of the Lord, are a *fountain*, or *wellspring of life*, a delightful means of promoting the temporal and spiritual happiness of ourselves and others. (Prov. 13:14, 14:27, 16:22, 18:4,) Wives are called *fountains and wells*; they bring forth children who, like streams, are dispersed in the streets, and are a notable means of happiness and comfort to their husbands. (Prov. 5:15-18) Children are *fountains*, as the offspring of Jacob were *his fountain*; they are a means of help and comfort to their parents, and, in due time, will produce children of their own. (Deut. 33:8; Prov. 5:18) But the *fountain of Israel* may either signify a well where the Israelites encamped on some noteworthy occasion, or Jacob's posterity, or Jesus, who sprang from him, or God, the source of all true comfort to Jacob and his seed. (Ps. 68:26) False teachers are *wells without water*; they promise men much instruction, edification, and comfort, yet afford nothing but fleshly errors, corrupt examples, and enticements. (2 Pet. 2:17) Whatever a thing proceeds from is called its *fountain* or *spring*. Thus the cause, or first rise of the circulation of the blood, is called its *fountain*. (Lev. 20:18; Mark 5:29) The right ventricle of the heart, from which comes the blood, and, with it, the life and vital spirits take their rise, is called a *fountain*. (Eccles. 12:6)

G

GABRIEL

A notable angel of God. For three weeks, he conflicted with the Prince of Persia, who was either some evil angel occupied with the Persian court, or rather the Persian king himself, whose counsels against the Jews he opposed and frustrated, meanwhile forwarding the ruin of Persia. (Dan. 10:13, 20) He explained to Daniel his visions of the four beasts, and of the ram and the he-goat. He declared the time of our Saviour's appearance on earth, his death, and the fearful consequences that would come upon the Jewish nation. He informed him of the ruin of the Persian Empire, and of the wars between the Greek kings of Egypt and Syria, of the distress of the Jews under Antiochus Epiphanes, of the rise and fall of antichrist, and of the present adversity and future restoration of the Jews. (Dan. 7-12)

He informed Zachariah of the birth of his son, John the Baptist, and of his punishment of dumbness till he was born. He afterwards informed the Virgin Mary of her conception, and the birth of the Messiah, and told her that her cousin Elisabeth was now in the sixth month of her pregnancy. He admonished Joseph not to divorce his wife,

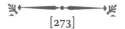

to flee into Egypt, and to return after the death of Herod. (Matt. 1-2; Luke 1:19, 26)

GAD

(1) The son of Zilpah, the handmaid of Leah, called Gad to signify that a *troop*, or *good fortune*, was coming. (Gen. 30:9-11) He had seven sons: Ziphion, Haggai, Shuni, Ebzon, Eri, Arodi, Areli, all of whom were fathers of numerous families. (Gen. 46:16; Num. 26:15-18) When this tribe came out of Egypt under their prince, Eliasaph the son of Deuel, it came to 45,650, but decreased to 5,150 in the wilderness. Their spy to search the Promised Land was Geuel, the son of Machi. (Num. 13:15) They, along with the Reubenites, petitioned for, and obtained, their inheritance from Moses on the east of Jordan, between the Reubenites on the south, and the Manassites on the north. (Deut. 32, 33:20-21) Their warriors assisted in conquering Canaan on the west of Jordan; and from Mount Ebal they gave their AMEN to the curses of the Law. (Josh. 1:12, 4:12; Deut. 27:13) After seven years, they returned to their homes. (Josh. 22) Eleven captains of this tribe, after swimming through the Jordan when highly swollen, came to David in the stronghold, and routed some Arabs, or Philistines, they found in the Valley of Jordan; and great numbers of them attended David's coronation as King of Israel. (1 Chron. 12:8-15, 37-38) The situation of the Gadites exposed them to terrible harassment from the Syrians and Arabians; but, as it turned out, they got the better of them. About the time of Jeroboam the second, they cut off a prodigious number of the Arabian Hagarites, and seized their cattle and country. (Gen. 49:19; Deut. 33:20) When Tiglath-pileser transported the Gadites and Reubenites to Assyria, the Ammonites and Moabites seized their country. (1 Chron. 6:18-26; Jer. 49:1, 48:18-24, 27-28)

(2) A prophet that accompanied David during his persecution by Saul, and afterwards. In the first year of David's exile, Gad divinely warned him to depart from the country of Moab to the land of Judah. (1 Sam. 22:5) When David numbered the people, Gad, in the name of the Lord, offered him a choice of three plagues: famine, pestilence, or war. When David chose pestilence, and, with humble prayer, obtained its shortening, Gad, by the Lord's direction, ordered him to build an

altar on the threshing-floor of Araunah. Gad wrote a history of David's life. (2 Sam. 24:11, 13-14, 18-19; 1 Chron. 21:9, 11, 13, 18-19, 29:29)

GAIUS

(1) A notable Christian, baptised by Paul at Corinth, and in whose house Paul lodged when he wrote his Letter to the Romans. He sent his greetings to them in Rome. He and Aristarchus, both originally Macedonians, accompanied Paul to Ephesus, where, by the mob raised by Demetrius, they were dragged from their lodgings to the theatre; but it seems came to no remarkable harm. (Acts 19:29, 20:4; Rom. 16:23; 1 Cor. 1:14)

(2) Whether he was the same as Gaius of Derbe we do not know. (Acts 20:4)

(3) A hospitable person, to whom John directed his third Epistle. (3 John 1)

GALLIO

The brother of Seneca a famous moralist, and the adopted son of Lucius Junius Gallio, from whom he received his name. Under the Emperors Claudius and Nero, he was proconsul, or deputy-governor, of Achaia, about AD 54, when the Jews, enraged at Paul's conversion of many of the Corinthians to Christianity, dragged him to Gallio's tribunal, guilty of teaching men to worship God contrary to Roman law. As Paul was about to answer for himself, Gallio, being of a temper extremely mild, calmly told the Jews that had their charges against Paul been of a criminal nature, he would have thought himself obliged to give them a hearing, but since they only related to vain disputes about their Law, he ordered them directly out of his presence. The heathen Greeks, glad of an opportunity of affronting the Jews, laid hold of Sosthenes, the chief ruler of their synagogue, and beat him in front of the tribunal, without Gallio concerning himself in the affair. (Only found in Acts 18:12-17) Not many years later, Gallio and his brother were murdered on the orders of Nero.

GAMALIEL

(1) The son of Pedahzur, a descendant of Joseph (Num. 1:10, 2:20, 7:54, 59, 10:23)

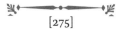

(2) A notable Pharisee, and doctor of the Jewish Law, at whose feet Paul was brought up. When, not long after our Saviour's Ascension, the Jewish Council was on the point of killing the Apostles, Gamaliel advised them to let them alone, for if they were impostors, their folly would quickly appear, and their project would come to nothing, as happened in the case of Judas and Theudas; but, if their cause was of God, all opposition to it amounted to fighting against God. With this speech, he persuaded the Council to spare their lives. (Acts 5:34-40, 22:3) It is said that Gamaliel was the son of the famous Hillel, and uncle of Nicodemus, and, for 32 years, President of the Jewish Sanhedrin. What is further rumoured, that he was converted to Christianity, and had a share in the honourable burial of Stephen, we pass as unworthy of notice.

GEDALIAH

The son of Ahikam, a Jewish prince, who went over to the Chaldeans a little before the destruction of Jerusalem. Nebelzaradan, the Chaldean general, made him governor of the poor people that were left in the land of Judah. Jeremiah and Baruch retired to him at western Mizpeh. Numbers of Jews, who fled into the land of Moab and Ammon, came and put themselves under his protection, and he assured them of safety, provided they lived peaceably. Ishmael, the son of Nethaniah, instigated by Baal, King of the Ammonites, came to murder him, and set himself up. Gedaliah was told in good time of this horrible plot, but would not believe it. He generously entertained Ishmael and his attendants, but the feast had hardly ended, when Ishmael and his party murdered Gedaliah, and all that were present with him at that time, whether Jews or Chaldeans. The remnant of the Jews that were under his protection, fearing that Nebuchadnezzar would blame them for the murder of his deputy, retired into Egypt, despite all that the prophet Jeremiah could say to stop them. (2 Kings 25:22; Jer. 40-43)

GEHAZI

Had possibly been the servant of Elijah. It is certain he accompanied Elisha for some time. He tried to recover the Shunamite's son by laying his master's staff on him. Some time later, his greed of money tempted him to run after Naaman the healed leper, whom his master had freely dismissed, and demand some money and clothes off him in

his master's name. He readily obtained more than he asked, but Elisha, highly displeased with his conduct, rebuked him, and, with a solemn curse, laid him and his posterity under the leprosy. He was immediately infected, and left his service. But it seems that about five or six years later, he conferred with Jehoram, King of Israel, concerning Elisha's miracles. (2 Kings 4-5, 8)

GENTILES, HEATHEN

All nations except the Jews. For many ages before Christ, these nations were destitute of true religion, and gave themselves up to the grossest ignorance, or most absurd idolatry, superstition, and horrible sins. Their most learned men that pretended to wisdom, as well as others, were absurd in the main, and complied with, or promoted, the absurd customs they found among their countrymen. They were *strangers to the covenants of promise, without God, and without hope in the world*, living in subjection to Satan, and in the most horrible and often unnatural lusts. (Rom. 1:19-32; 1 Cor. 6:1, 10; Eph. 2:2-3, 12, 5:8; 1 Pet. 5:8) It was, however, divinely foretold that, in Abraham's seed, all nations should be blessed; that to the Saviour they should gather, and become his inheritance, and rejoice with his people, be enlightened and saved by him, and seek after him. (Gen. 22:18, 49:10; Deut. 32:43; Ps. 2:8; Isa. 10, 11:10, 42:6-7, 49:5-8) Indeed, it was particularly predicted that the Chaldeans, Assyrians, Arabians, Philistines, Egyptians, Ethiopians, Tyrians, inhabitants of the isles, and the ends of the earth, should believe on him. (Ps. 87:4, 72:8, 11, 68:31, 45:12; Isa. 19:18, 25, 23:18, 60:5-7, 66:19) To prepare matters for the accomplishment of these and similar promises, vast numbers of the Jews after the Chaldean Captivity were left scattered among the heathen. The Old Testament was translated into Greek, which was the most common language of the heathen world. A rumour of the Saviour's appearance in the flesh was spread far and wide among them.

When Christ came, he preached mainly in Galilee where there were many Gentiles. He never praised the faith of anyone but Gentiles, nor did he ever prohibit them to publish his fame. To the Greeks desiring to see him, he hinted that, after his death and resurrection, vast numbers of Gentiles would be brought into the Church. (Matt. 4; John 12:20-24) For the last two centuries, the Jews have been generally rejected, and the Church of God has been composed mainly of Gentiles. (Rom. 11) Paul was the Apostle, or notable missionary of Christ, for promoting the conversion of the Gentiles, as Peter was of the Jews. (Gal 2:7; 1 Tim. 2:7) As the nations were of old destitute of the knowledge and worship of the true God, the word *heathen*, or *Gentile* was sometimes used for those who are outside the Church, and are ignorant, atheistic, idolatrous, etc. Thus, excommunicated persons are to be treated by us as the *heathen* and *publicans*; they must be secluded from the seals of the covenant, and we must keep at all possible distance from them in civil matters, that they may be ashamed of their wickedness. (Matt. 18:17) The *Gentiles* who tread the outer court of the Church for 1260 years are the Papists, who resemble the ancient heathen in ignorance, idolatry, and superstition. (Rev. 11:2)

GERSHOM, or GERSHON

The oldest son of Levi. At the Exodus from Egypt, his family consisted of 7500 males, 2630 of them fit for service. They were stationed at the west end of the Tabernacle in the wilderness, and were governed by Eliasaph, the son of Lael. Their work was to carry the veils and curtains of the Tabernacle, as Ithamar ordered. (Num. 3:21-25, 4:22-41) When they came to Canaan, they had 13 cities assigned to them: Golan and Beeshterah, from the eastern half tribe of Manasseh, from Issachar, Kishon, Dabareh, Jarmuth, and Engannim, from Asher, Mishal, Abdon, Helkath, and Rehob, from Naphtali, Kedesh, Hammoth-dor, and Kartan, with their suburbs, some of whose names were changed, or perhaps the cities exchanged for others. (Josh. 21:6, 27-33; 1 Chron. 6:16-17, 20, 43, 62, 71) The family of Gershon consisted of two branches, those of Laadan, for their heads in the days of David: Jehiel, Zetham, Joel, Shelomith, Haziel, and Haran, and those of Shimei: Jahath, Zinah, Jeush, and Beriah. (1 Chron. 23:7-11, 15-16) Jehiel's sons, Zetham and Joel, were overseers of the treasures in the house of the Lord. (1 Chron. 26:21-22)

HOLY GHOST (SPIRIT). See God.

GIANTS

People far exceeding the usual height. The Hebrews called them *Nephilim* because of their violent falling upon, and oppressing, others, and *Rephaim* because their terror and strokes rendered others incurable or dead. Many of the mixed posterity of Seth and Cain were *giants* before the Flood; and it is possibly, in allusion to these, that

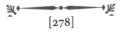

companions of prostitutes and wanderers from God's way are presented as going to, or remaining among, the Rephaim (or dead), that is, in hell. (Prov. 2:18, 9:18, 21:16) Ham's posterity was distinguished by the appearance of several families of giants.

East of Jordan were the Rephaim of Bashan, whom Chedorlaomer smote at Ashtarothkirnaim. Og, King of Bashan, who gave battle, and was entirely routed, and his kingdom seized by Moses, appears to have been the last one of them. Og's iron bedstead was 15 feet 4½ inches in length, and was long after preserved in Rabbah of the Ammonites. (Deut. 3:11) The Emims and Zamzummims were a *gigantic* people that were cut off by the Moabites and Ammonites, and their land seized by them. (Deut. 2:9-21) About the same time, there lived a number of giants around Hebron, Debir, and Anab, and in other hill-countries of Canaan. The most notable family seems to have been the *Anakim* (children of Anak), of whom Arba the father, Anak the son, and his three sons, Ahiman, Sheshai, and Talmai, were the most well known. These giants were a terror to the Hebrew spies; but Joshua, Caleb, and Othniel cut them off. (Num. 13:21-33; Josh. 11:21, 14:15, 15:13-16) Samuel Bochart thinks that part of these *Beneanach* fled north to Tyre, and gave the country its name *Phoenicia*. It is more certain that there still remained giants in Gaza, Gath, and Ashdod; but whether these were of a Canaanitish or Philistine origin, we do not know. (Josh. 11:22)

In David's time, we find a family of giants at Gath: Goliath, Suph (or Sipai), Ishbi-benob, Lahmi, and another one who had six fingers on each hand and as many toes on each foot. All these were cut off at the hand of David and his servants in several battles. (2 Sam. 21:16, 18, 20, 22; 1 Chron. 20:4, 6, 8) After this, we hear no more of giants in Canaan. Not only the Scripture, but almost every ancient writer, such as Homer, Herodotus, Diodorus, Pliny, Plutarch, Virgil, Ovid, etc., inform us of giants in the early ages, though, basing on crude facts, they usually exaggerated their height and fame.

GIDEON

The son of Joash, from the western half-tribe of Manasseh, and city of Ophrah. After the Midianites and their allies had, from about BC 1252-1245, greatly oppressed the Hebrews, eating up their crops and seizing their cattle, the Hebrews cried to the Lord. By his prophet, he reproached them for their ungrateful abuse of former deliverances,

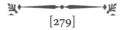

but appeared to Gideon as he was threshing wheat in a secret place, and assured him that however lowly he and family were, he would deliver Israel from their present servitude. To confirm his faith in this, with a touch of his rod, he caused fire to come out of the rock and consume the slain kid and unleavened cakes, all moistened with broth, which Gideon, at his command, had put on them. When the Lord disappeared, Gideon was terribly apprehensive of immediate death as he had seen an angel, but was assured by God that he was in no danger. He immediately built an altar to the Lord and called it *Jehovah Shalom*, that is, *the Lord shall perfect* or *send peace*. That very night, God directed him to cut down the grove and demolish the altar which his neighbours had erected for Baal, and build an altar to God on the rock where the miraculous fire had devoured his provision, and offer one of his father's bullocks on it. With the assistance of ten of his father's servants, he punctually executed these orders. Enraged at this, his fellow-citizens demanded his life; but Joash his father protested that it ill-became the covenant people of God to plead for Baal; and that it was more reasonable that everyone who did it would be slain. If Baal was truly a God, he ought to exert his power in punishing the one who had broken down his altar; and he called his son *Jerubbaal*, that is, *Let Baal contend with him.* Understanding that the Midianites, to the number of almost 200,000, had crossed the Jordan on the west, and were encamped in the valley of Jezreel at no great distance, Gideon, filled with the Spirit of God, sounded a trumpet, and assembled his friends the Abiezrites. By messengers, he required the tribes of Manasseh, Asher, Zebulun, and Naphtali, to follow him in attacking the Midianites. He quickly got together an army of 32,000 men. By a double sign, of bedewing a fleece of wool while the adjacent ground was dry, and again, bedewing the ground while the fleece was dry, the Lord condescended to quieten his doubtful mind.

Thus, assured of victory, Gideon marched his forces directly toward the Midianites. At the well of Harod, his faith was put to a double test. God ordered him to warn his army that everybody who was in the least timid should return home: 22,000 departed and 10,000 remained. That it might be more evident that the victory was wholly of God, he was further ordered to cause all his people drink out of the river without using any vessel. At this test, only 300 lapped the water, putting their hands to their mouths with it, as the Arabs sup their milk, broth, soup, etc., though not their water. Only these were retained, and all the rest sent home. These 300 he ordered to provide food for some days, and each a trumpet and a lamp concealed in an empty pitcher. We hear nothing of arms. In the night, Gideon, directed by God, went into the Midianitish camp, along with Phurah his servant. There, he heard someone tell his fellow of his dream, that a barley cake rolling the hill had overturned their tent; which dream the other explained as Gideon overthrowing the Midianites. Encouraged by this, Gideon hastened back to his men, and, ordering them to imitate himself, they, in three companies, attacked the camp of Midian on different sides. Gideon, all of a sudden, shouted, *The sword of the Lord and of Gideon!* Then, breaking his pitcher, he threw it and the lamp on the ground, and blew his trumpet. Immediately, all his 300 men did the same.

Filled with terror, the Midianites fled, and, taking their friends for foes in the dark, they killed each another. The Manassites, Asherites, and Napthalites, pursued the fugitives. Excited by Gideon's messengers, the Ephraimites took the fords of Jordan and slew Oreb and Zeeb, two of the Midianitish kings. One hundred and twenty thousand Midianites were killed; 15,000 still remained in a body, and got over Jordan with Zeba and Zalmunna their kings. Gideon pursued them at their heels. His men being faint, he asked the elders of Penuel and Succoth, as he passed, to give them some food; but they, reckoning him a fool to pursue the Midianites with only a handful of men, refused his troops refreshment. He overtook the Midianites at Karkor, near the country of Ammon; there, he took the kings prisoner, and cut their army to pieces. On his return west, he chastised the two cities for their barbarity and insult. With thorns and briers, he tore the flesh of the princes of Succoth; he killed the chief men of Penuel, and demolished their tower. After finding that Zeba and Zalmunna had murdered some of his friends or relations at Mount Tabor, he ordered his son Jethur to kill them; but the young man was so afraid that he did it himself. With mild words he pacified the proud Ephraimites, who complained that he had not more early invited their assistance. The Hebrews offered him and his posterity the government of their nation; but he piously declined it, and told them that the Lord was their rightful Sovereign alone. At his request, they gave him the earrings of their prey, which amounted to 1700 shekels of gold (£2380 sterling), with other ornaments. Of these, Gideon made an ephod and placed it in Ophrah. Whether he imagined that his being ordered to offer sacrifice constituted him a priest, or if he intended to consult God by this ephod, or if he merely intended it as a memorial of his victory, we do not know; but it proved an occasion of idolatry to Israel, and of ruin to his family. After judging Israel 40 years, he died in BC 1206, leaving behind him 70 sons, all of whom were vilely murdered by his bastard son Abimelech. (Judg. 6-8)

Gideon (KJV = *Gedeon*) is presented as a great man of faith in Hebrews 11:32.

Was not our Redeemer prefigured by Gideon? How mean his lowly condition, but express, solemn, and seasonable the call to his work, and miraculous its confirmation! How important and necessary his work of our salvation! With what burning zeal he offered his sacrifice, overthrew idolatry, and restored the true love and worship of God! By a few weak and unarmed preachers sounding the gospel trumpet, and displaying its light and fire from their earthen vessels, he foils sin, Satan, and the world, and their numerous agents. How kindly he invites us to share with him in his victories! How mildly he pacifies his unreasonable friends! And what terrible vengeance he inflicts on his despisers in Judah and Rome, and will on all those who deny his poor people supply in their time of need?

GILEAD
(1) The son of Machin, and grandson of Manasseh. His sons were, Jezor, Helek, Asriel, Shechem, Shemida, and Hepher, by whom he had a numerous posterity settled beyond the Jordan. (Num. 26:29-31, 32:40)

(2) The father of Jephthah, who also had a numerous family, and might be a descendant of the former. (Judg. 11:1-2)

GOD
Properly describes a Being of infinite perfection. Of the two Hebrew names so translated, *El* means the *strong One*, and *Eloah* the *worshipful One*. Perhaps it is so often used in the plural *Elohim* to hint at the Trinity of Persons; and Patrick Hutchison translates the word, the *Persons in covenant*. He is also called Lord, Jehovah, Jah, etc. We cannot seriously consider the nature of our own soul and body, or the things around us, or events that happen; we cannot attend to the dictates of our conscience concerning good or evil, and how it accuses

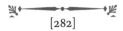

or excuses us with respect to our conduct; we cannot consider the universal harmony of all nations, however different in interest, or form of devotion, under this subject, without being persuaded of some self-existent and absolutely eternal, almighty, benevolent, but wise and just Being, who has created, and supports and governs, all things. But in our present corrupt condition, we must have recourse to the Bible for a clear and proper knowledge of him. There, we find that there is *one* God, the Creator of all things. (Deut. 6:4; Ps. 36:10; Jer. 10:10-11; John 17:3; 1 Cor. 8:6; 1 Tim. 2:5, 6:15)

God's divine attributes

He is an *eternal Spirit.* (Deut. 33:27; Ps. 90:2; John 4:24; 1 Tim. 6:16; Heb. 11:27) He is *infinite*, everywhere present, incomprehensible in excellence (1 Kings 8:27; Job 11:7; Ps. 8:1, 139:6-10; Eccles. 3:11, 8:17; Jer. 23:24; Rom. 11:33; 1 Tim. 6:16), and is unchangeable. (Exod. 3:14; Mal. 3:6; James 1:17) He *knows all things* past, present, or future, and is *infinitely wise* to purpose and order things to their proper ends. (1 Sam. 2:3; Job 9:4, 36:4, 42:2; Ps. 146:5, 129:2; Isa. 42:9, 41:22-26, 46:10, 48:3, 40:13-14; Jer. 32:19; Acts 15:18; 1 Tim. 1:17) He is *almighty*, able to do everything not base or sinful. (Gen. 17:1, 18:14; 1 Chron. 29:11-12; Job 9:4, etc; Ps. 145:5; Jer. 32:17, 27; Rev. 19:6) He is perfectly *holy* (Exod. 15:11; 1 Sam. 2:2; Ps. 145:17; Isa. 6:3, 43:15, 57:15; Rev. 15:4), perfectly *good*, kind, merciful, gracious (Exod. 34:6-7; Ps. 52:1, 145:9; Matt. 5:48, 19:11; James 1:7; 1 John 4:8), and perfectly *just, true*, sincere, and faithful. (Num. 23:19; Deut. 7:9, 32:4; 1 Sam. 15:29; 2 Sam. 7:28; Ps. 136:6, 129:4, 119:137, 97:2, 119:4; Acts 10:34-35; Rom. 2:6; Titus 1:2; Rev. 15:2) According to his fixed and eternal purpose, he has created, and, by his providence upholds and governs, all his creatures, and all their actions, good or bad. (Gen. 1:1, 20; Job 12:10, chs. 37, 39; Ps. 33:6, 36:6, 104, 107, 136:25, 145-147; Prov. 16:33; Isa. 46:10; Amos 3:6, 4:7; Matt. 10:29-30; Acts 2:23, 4:27-28, 15:18, 14:17, 17:28; Rom. 9:17-23; Eph. 1:11; Heb. 11:3)

The Father

The Bible reveals to us that this one God, necessarily in and of his own infinite, but simple and undivided essence, subsists in three distinct Persons, the Father, Son, and Holy Spirit, the same in substance, and equal in all divine power and glory. (Gen. 1:26, 3:22, 11:7; Ps. 33:6, 45:7; Isa. 6:3, 61:1-2, 63:7-9; Matt. 3:16-17, 28:19; John 14:16; Rom. 1:4;

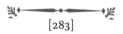

1 Cor. 12:4-6; 2 Cor. 13:14; Gal 4:6; 2 Thess. 3:5; Heb. 9:14; 1 Pet. 1:3; 1 John 5:7; Rev. 1:4-5) Concerning the Father, we are informed that he is the true God. (John 17:3; Eph. 1:3) From eternity, he begot his only Son (Ps. 2:7), consulted with him, foreordained and set him up as our Surety and Mediator, and entered into covenant with him before the foundation of the world. (Prov. 8:22-31; Isa. 49:6-9, 50:7-11; Acts 2:23; Peter 1:20) He promised, sent, and afterwards brought him into the world (Jer. 31:22; Zech. 2:8-10; Luke 1:35), where he gave him commission, and furnished him for his work. (Isa. 11:2-3, 61:1-2; Matt. 3:16-17; John 1:32-33, 4:34, 10:18, 20:21; Col. 1:19) There, he stood by him in care, love, power, and providence, during the whole course of his humiliation. (Isa. 49:2, 8, 62:1-7) He spoke through him, did mighty works by him, and bore witness to him. (John 5:19-22; Heb. 1:1) He gave him up to death, and raised him from the dead (Acts 2:23-24; Rom. 8:32; 1 Pet. 1:21), when he crowned him with glory and honour, exalted him to his right hand, gave to him as Mediator all power, authority, and judgement in heaven and on earth, and made him Head over all things to his Church. (Matt. 28:18; John 5:22, 17:5; Acts 2:32-33; Phil. 2:9-10; Eph. 1:20-22; Heb. 2:9) He promised, and sent the Holy Spirit, who proceeded from him, to anoint Jesus Christ and his prophets, Apostles, and people. (Ps. 45:7; Joel 2:28; Luke 24:49; John 3:34, 14:26, 15:26) He predestined the elect to holiness and happiness. (Rom. 7:28-30; Eph. 1:4-5) It was he who proposed the covenant and terms of their salvation. (Prov. 8:20-30; Isa. 53:10-12; Zech. 6:13; Heb. 2:10) Having sent his Son, and accepted his reconciling righteousness in their place, he shows him to them, draws them to him, and reconciles them to himself. (Jer. 31:32-34; Matt. 11:25; John 6:44; 2 Cor. 5:18-21; Gal 1:16) Furthermore, he adopts, enlivens, and sanctifies them (Rom. 8:11; Gal 4:6; Titus 3:5-6), and, by the Holy Spirit, he confirms and comforts them, and, in summary, brings them to glory. (John 10:28, 7:11, 14:16-17; 2 Cor. 1:21-22; Eph. 3:20-21; 2 Thess. 2:17; Heb. 2:10; Rev. 7:7)

The Son of God

Concerning the Son, we are informed that he is, from all eternity, begotten by the Father in a way no creature is. (Ps. 2:7; John 1:14; Rom. 8:3, 32) He is equal with him as a Person (Zech. 13:7; Phil. 2:6-7), and is One with him in essence. (John 10:30; 1 John 5:7) We find names and titles proper only to God ascribed to him, as *Jehovah* (Isa. 6:1, 9-10,

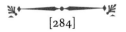

41:3, 45:23-25; Jer. 23:6, 33:16; Luke 1:76; John 12:40-41; Rom. 14:10-12), and in hundreds of other places where mention is made of the Lord speaking to prophets or others under the Old Testament. He is called *God* (Matt. 1:23; John 1:1-2; 21:28; 1 Tim. 3:16; 2 Pet. 1:1), the *true God* (1 John 5:20-21), the *great and mighty God* (Isa. 9:6; Titus 2:13), the *only wise God* (Rom. 16:27; 1 Tim. 1:16-17; Jude vv. 24-25), the *God of glory* (Acts 7:2), the *only God* (Isa. 45:15-23; Rom. 14:11). He is called *God blessed forever* (Rom. 9:5), the *God of Abraham, Isaac, and Jacob* (Exod. 3:6; Hosea 12:3-5; Acts 7:30-32), the *Lord of hosts* (2 Sam. 6:2; Ps. 118:22; Isa. 8:13-14, 54:5; Matt. 21:42; 2 Cor. 11:2; 1 Pet. 2:6-8), *King of kings, and Lord of lords* (1 Tim. 6:14-15, Rev. 17:14, 19:13-16), and the *first* and the *last.* (Isa. 41:4, 44:6; Rev. 1:17-18, 2:8)

Divine attributes are ascribed to him: *omniscience* (Matt. 12:25; John 21:17, 2:24-25; Col. 2:3; Rev. 2:23), *omnipresence* (Matt. 18:20, 28:20; John 1:18, 3:13; Col. 1:17; Heb. 1:3), *almighty power (omnipotence)* (Phil. 3:21; Rev. 1:8, 11, 17-18, 22:12-20), *eternity* (Prov. 8:23; Micah 5:2; John 1:1, 13:56; Heb. 7:3; Rev. 1:11, 17), *unchangeableness.* (Heb. 1:12, 13:8) Divine works of creation, providence, and redemption, are ascribed to him. (John 1:1-2; Acts 20:28; 1 Cor. 8:6; Eph. 3:9; Col. 1:16-17; Heb. 1:3) He is presented as the object of religious worship without limitation, as in baptism, faith, prayer, praise, and vows. (Matt. 28:19; John 5:23, 14:1, 20:28; Acts 7:5, 9; Heb. 1:6; Phil. 2:9-11)

Though, as Son, this second Person is equal with the Father, yet, in his human nature, and as appointed to be the Mediator, Surety, Prophet, Priest, and King of his people, he is his Father's inferior and servant. (Isa. 41:3, 42:13, 43:1; Mark 13:32; John 5:18-19, 14:28, 20:17; 2 Cor. 11:31; Phil. 1:6) As Mediator, he is chosen by God, and consents to the covenant of our redemption, undertaking to pay our debt to the Law of God. (Ps. 40:6-8; Isa. 42:1; Jer. 30:21) He fulfils the condition of the covenant in his state of humiliation (Isa. 42:21; Matt. 3:15; Luke 24:26), he administers the fullness of blessings purchased by his death, and he is the Husband, Friend, Shepherd, Physician, and All-in-all to his people. (Ps. 68:18; Col. 3:11) See Christ and Covenant.

To execute the offices that the Father had invested in him, the Son assumed our nature into a personal, uncompounded, and indissoluble union with his divine Person, and is God and Man in two distinct natures and one Person forever. (Isa. 9:6; John 1:14; 1 Tim. 3:16) This union of his divine and human natures was necessary to his being

Mediator, that he might be a middle-man, at once closely related to both God and men, equally careful for the true interests of both, and qualified to do what tended to bring both to agreement; necessary also to his being a Redeemer, that he might have the right of Redemption, and be qualified to give a proper price of sufficient value for, and have sufficient power to bring about, our redemption, necessary to his being a Surety, and Priest, that, *as God*, he might lawfully undertake, being absolute master of himself, to fully secure the payment of our debt, might do the world no injury by his voluntary death, might willingly bear all that Law and justice could lay upon or require at his hands, and add infinite value to his obedience and offering, and might know exactly every particular person, and his circumstances, for whom he died, and, by his own power, conquer death, coming from prison and from judgement. As man, the Law could take hold of him, that he might obey and suffer, that he might pay our debt in the same kind that we owe, and that, in his payment, of it he might have the fellow-feeling of our infirmities, and set us a pattern of holy obedience and patient suffering. As our Intercessor, he, by his divine power, was able to remove from his sacrificing state to that of his honorary intercession, that he might, with confidence, appear before God, and sit with him on his throne, and that he might know all the necessities and believing requests of his people, and might have that in his intercession which is sufficient to counterbalance all our weakness and unworthiness. *As man*, he has the ability to present our nature, and intercede for us, as one having a fellow-feeling of our infirmities (Heb. 4:14-16), necessary for his prophetic office.

As God, he might, in every age, be equally present with all his disciples, might at once have a comprehensive view of the whole of divine truth, that there can be full certainty of the authority, fullness, and infallibility of his revelations, and that he might employ the Holy Spirit, and render his instructions really effective in our heart; and, as man, might teach us, in a way adapted to our weakness, exemplifying the truths he taught, and subsequent teaching of them, in his own Person and life. This was necessary for his kingly office, that he *being God*, his subjects might be reduced under no lower head in their recovered state than in their creation-state; that he might equally defend and rule every one of them; that he might resist all the opposing power and policy of hell and earth, and be Head over all things to his

Church, and be capable of supplying all her needs at the right time and in a proper manner; that his power might be proper for conquering, changing, ruling, and comforting the hearts of his people, and that he might be capable of calling the world to an account for their treatment of him and his chosen people. And that, *as man*, his heart might be toward his brothers in condescending and tender regard, and that he might, by his example, enforce obedience to that Law, by which he, as a visible Judge, will quickly state the endless condition of both angels and men. His manhood renders every relation of his near and delightful, and his Godhead secures the everlasting comfort and infinite efficacy of his work. His manhood rendered his humiliation and exaltation possible, real, and exemplary, and his Godhead rendered his humiliation infinitely deep, meritorious, and dignified with rays of divine brightness, and renders his exaltation high, qualifying him to bear and manage it rightly.

As God is one with our Redeemer in his divine nature, in perfection, will, affection, and dignified dominion, he is *with him* in mutual operation, in support and in favour of, and in intimate fellowship with, our Mediator. He is *in him* in respect of delight, residence, and accessibility to men, and, *in him*, is the sense that every apparently opposite perfection, name, declaration, or work of God is delightfully united. In his Person and work, as God-man, is the infinity, eternity, unchangeableness, independency, subsistence in three distinct Persons, with the life, wisdom, power, holiness, justice, goodness, majesty, and inexpressible glory of God, brightly discovered in a way both saving and satisfying to sinful men. (John 5:19, 10:31, and ch. 14; 2 Cor. 4:6) Christ in his Person as God-man and office is the foundation of the counsels and works of God, the centre in which they unite, the great means of their fulfilment, the great scope and end of them, the chief glory of them, attracting the heart of God to them. (Col. 1:17-18) He is the foundation, the centre, the repository, the glory, and the exact source of the saving power of revealed truth. Nor can we perceive or find profit in them but in beholding and maintaining fellowship with him in his Person and office. All the blessings of grace and glory are lodged in his Person as our Mediator, and are had only by union with him: such as election, the giving of the Holy Spirit, righteousness, justification, a New Covenant interest in God as a friend, children, and possessors of regeneration, sanctification, comfort, preservation in grace, a happy death, and eternal glory. (Eph. 1:3-4 etc.) All our fellowship with the Father in his love, and with the Holy Spirit in his influence, is through our fellowship with Jesus in his personal beauty, purchasing righteousness, and purchased grace. No saving grace stands unconnected with his Person and office as God-man. Saving knowledge perceives the truths of God in relation to his Law, his covenants, and his gospel, and in relation to sin, righteousness, and judgement, holiness, happiness, or misery, as these are manifested in Jesus Christ, his Person, his suffering, or his work. (1 Cor. 1:30, ch. 2)

Faith is persuaded of divine truths as *yea and amen* in him, receiving and sticking close to his Person, possessing righteousness in, and deriving holiness and comfort from, his Person, as it presents the soul, and all its needs and service to God through him. (Gal 2:20) Hope has Christ in his death, and promises of the New Testament in his blood as its ground. Christ in the heart is the actuator and pledge of the thing hoped for; and Christ in his glory, and all the fullness of God in him, is its expected object. (Col. 1:27; 1 Tim. 1:1) Holy love is kindled by his redeeming *love shed abroad in the heart* (Rom. 5:5), and by views of the loveliness of his Person; and is primarily fixed on his Person, so that God is loved through him. Righteousness, grace, and comfort, holiness of life, Scripture, ordinances, providences, and saints, are loved in connection with his Person. (2 Cor. 5:14) Repentance holds the view of his Person suffering for us as the great demonstration of the love of God, and of the evil of sin, as its chief motives. His imputed righteousness sets us free from the strength of sin; and in him God is seen to be merciful and gracious, worthy of being our intimate friend, sovereign Lord, and everlasting portion. (Zech. 12:10) Christ's Person and office as Mediator are the motive and chief means of all gospel worship, and the sole cause of its acceptance with God; and, in his divine nature, he is the object of it, equally with the Father and the Holy Spirit. (Eph. 2:18) With respect to our walking with God in all holy obedience, he is the way in which we walk together with God. All reconciliation with God, all knowledge of him, all harmony of design with him, all skill, strength, and confidence necessary for this walk, and all acceptance of it, are in and from his Person. (John 14:6; Col. 3:17; Heb. 10:19-22) Our perseverance in our gracious state, nature, or course, relates to his Person; righteousness, as of his infinite value, secures an everlasting reward for us. His intercession, as infinitely prevalent, secures our grace and glory. The love and power by which he embraces and holds us firm is infinite. The unalterable and eternal vivacity of his Person is the immediate spring of our endless life. (John 14:19) In his Person, he laid down the price; in his Person he, by intercession, prepares glory for us. In his Person, he establishes our title to it. The beholding and the enjoying of his Person is a foretaste of it here; and the being with, and beholding of his Person, and God in him, is the whole sum of our everlasting happiness. (John 17:24)

The Holy Spirit

Concerning the Holy Spirit, we are informed that he proceeds from the Father and the Son. (John 15:26; Gal 4:5-6) He is called *Jehovah*. (Exod. 17:7; Isa. 6:9; Jer. 31:31-34; Acts 28:25; Heb. 3:7-9, 10:15-16) He is called *God* (Acts 5:4; 1 Cor. 3:16, 6:19), and *Lord*. (2 Cor. 3:17; 2 Thess. 3:5) Divine perfections are ascribed to him, such as *omniscience* (Isa. 40:13-14; 1 Cor. 2:10-11; 1 John 2:20), *omnipresence* (Ps. 139:7; Rom. 8:26-27; Eph. 2:17-18), *omnipotence* (almighty power) (Luke 1:35; 1 Cor. 12:11), *eternity* (Heb. 9:14), as also the *divine works* of creation and providence (Gen. 1:2; Job 26:13; Ps. 33:6, 104:30), of miracles, of the anointing of Christ, and of converting, sanctifying, and comforting his people. (Isa. 61:1; John 16:13-14; Titus 3:5; Heb. 2:4) *Divine worship* of him is permitted and commanded: such as baptism in his name (Matt. 28:19), and prayer, praise, or solemn appeals to him. (Isa. 6:3, 9; Matt. 9:38; Acts 13:2, 20:28; Rom. 9:1; 2 Cor. 13:14; Rev. 1:4)

That he is a Person, not a mere powerful energy, is plain from his being described clearly in Scripture as *understanding* (1 Cor. 2:10), *willing* (1 Cor. 12:11), *speaking, sending* messengers (Isa. 6:8; Acts 8:29, 10:19-20, 13:1-4; 1 Tim. 4:1); as *pleading* (Rom. 8:26), as *being grieved* (Isa. 63:10; Eph. 4:30), as *teaching* and *reminding* people (John 14:26), as *testifying* (John 15:26), and as *reproving*, and *executing* a commission from God. (John 16:8-14)

The Holy Spirit, in order of operation, finished the creation work. He qualified men with uncommon strength of body, and with distinguished gifts of wisdom and understanding. He inspired men with a certain knowledge of the mind and will of God; and, sometimes, he made people prophets to whom he never communicated saving grace. He effected miracles innumerable. But his work on our Saviour, and in the souls of his people, is, in a particular way, worthy of our consideration.

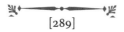

He framed the body of our Redeemer, and created his soul in a state of union with his divine Person. (Luke 1:34-35) He sanctified his manhood in its formation with all the grace it was then capable of (Isa. 11:2-3; John 3:34), and increased his grace in proportion to the growth of his human faculties. (Luke 2:40, 47, 52) At his baptism, he conferred on him those extraordinary gifts that qualified him for his public ministry. (Isa. 61:1-3; Matt. 3:16-17; John 3:34, 6:27) He led him into the wilderness to endure temptation, and enabled him to resist it. (Luke 4:1-14) He made Christ's human nature the vital instrument of many miracles. (Matt. 12:28-32; Acts 2:22) He urged him to, and supported him in, proper dispositions amid his suffering work. (Heb. 9:14) He preserved his dead body from corruption; and, in his resurrection, he united his soul and body together. (Rom. 8:11; Eph. 1:17-19; 1 Tim. 3:16; 1 Pet. 3:18) He filled his human nature with such glory and joy that suits his now exalted state (Ps. 45:7); and, in summary, after his Ascension, he bore witness to his Messiahship by the many miraculous gifts and operations displayed in his followers, and by the powerful spread of his teaching. (John 15:26, 16:7-14; Acts 5:23; 2 Cor. 10:4-5; Heb. 2:4)

In his operations on the elect, he often prepares their souls by a strong conviction of sin, and illumination in the knowledge of Christ. (Matt. 13:20-21, 32; John 16:9-10; Rom. 8:15; Heb. 6:4) In conviction, he impresses the Law of God on their consciences, fixes their thoughts upon it, and, on their lack of conformity to it, he impresses a sense of sin in their hearts so that they become filled with fear and shame. (Acts 2:37; Rom. 7:9) In regeneration, he, attending the Word of the gospel with almighty influence, opens their understanding to discern the truth, and, by means of enlightening truth, conveys Jesus and his righteousness, and himself, into their soul. He conveys heart-renewing grace from Jesus into their nature, which, as an abiding habit or vital principle, produces good works. (Deut. 30:6; Ps. 110:9; Ezek. 36:26; Rom. 8:2; 1 Cor. 6:11; 2 Cor. 4:6, 5:17; Eph. 1:17-18, 4:23; Col. 2:11, 3:10; Heb. 10:20; 1 John 5:20, 17:13) Having thus formed the habit of faith in them, he urges and enables them actively to embrace Christ, who has already taken possession of their hearts. (Phil. 1:29) In justification, he causes their consciences to condemn them, and applies Jesus as their righteousness to their consciences, and indicates the passing away of the sentence founded upon it. (1 Cor. 6:11) With respect to adoption, he brings them into the family of God, and, by his personal

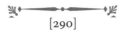

indwelling and influence, enables them to discern and believe the fatherly love of God to them, and to behave towards him as children. He witnesses with their spirit that they are heirs of God, and joint-heirs with Christ. (Rom. 8:16; Gal 4:6) In the work of sanctification, he shines on the truths of the gospel, and gives us an understanding to perceive them more and more (Ps. 119:18; Luke 24:25; 1 Cor. 2:4; 1 John 2:20, 27). Thus, by producing spiritual knowledge and wisdom, he removes pride, error, prejudice, idleness, and such like. In this, he not only discloses to them their polluted condition, and the beauty and reasonableness of holiness, but, by the views of Christ's glory, the impression of his righteousness on their conscience, and, with the shedding abroad of his love in their hearts, new supplies of grace are conveyed; and what is conveyed urges to action. Hence, they watch and struggle against sin, and grow in faith, humility, repentance, and other graces. (1 Cor. 2:10-11, 6:11; 2 Cor. 3:18; Gal 5:22-26; Phil. 4:19, 2:13; Titus 3:5-6)

He particularly promotes every grace. He shows the ground of faith and hope, and enables them to fix upon it. (Ps. 119:49) By showing a crucified Saviour and a merciful Father through the Word of the gospel, he disposes to repentance. (Isa. 55:7; Zech. 12:10) By discovering the loveliness and love of Jesus, and of God in him, and impressing them upon the heart, he makes men love him. (Rom. 5:5; 1 John 4:19) In prayer, he impresses us with a sense of our need. He encourages us to pray, basing our prayers on the relations, promises, and former deeds of God. He directs what to ask, and enables us to request it in faith and fervency, and to wait for an answer. (Rom. 8:26-27) In self-examination, he illumines the marks of grace laid down in Scripture, brings our grace or sinfulness into view, and enables our conscience to draw correct conclusions. (Rom. 8:16) He comforts the saints by shining on those truths that relate to God's relation and promises to them, or his works towards them, by impressing these on their consciences, enabling them to apply them earnestly, and by restraining Satan, the world, and our lusts, from spoiling our comfort. With respect to eternal happiness, he is the seal that sets apart the saints for it, and he prepares them for that day. (Eph. 4:30) By his presence and influence, he is the seal happiness (2 Cor. 1:21-22; Eph. 1:13-14), and he is the immediate bestower of all that fullness of holiness and glory they will possess in full in the heavenly state. (John 6:14, 14:16; Rev. 22:1)

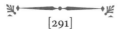

A true knowledge of God

No doubt Adam, in his state of innocence, had this property of the divine nature, its essential subsistence in three Persons, revealed to him, that he might worship the true God in conformity with his nature. Some knowledge of it is absolutely necessary for our salvation; nor can we have any proper conception of the method of our redemption without it. (John 16:7-14, 17:3) No doubt, all the Three have their distinct work in the creation of all things, in the preservation of the world, and every creature in it, and in the effecting, permitting, and ruling of everything - miraculous or natural - that takes place in the world, from the beginning to the end, and throughout eternity to come. But, in many cases, our weakness disqualifies us from knowing their respective influence. God is the *God of glory*, grace, mercy, patience, peace, comfort, salvation, etc., as he is infinitely glorious in his perfections, counsels, and works. He is full of, and marvellously exercises, mercy and patience towards creatures sinful and miserable, and he provides and bestows peace, comfort, and salvation on his people. (Ps. 59:10, 68:19; Acts 7:2; Rom. 15:33; 2 Cor. 1:3; 1 Pet. 5:10) He is the *God of hope*, as he is its object, from whom, and in whom, we expect every good thing. (Rom. 15:13) He is the *living and true God*: he possesses an infinite fullness of life in himself, and gives to his creatures whatever life they enjoy, when he alone is really possessed of infinite perfection or Godhead. (1 Thess. 1:9) He is the *God of gods*, superior to angels, governors, and whatever may be esteemed or adored as God. (Ezra 5:11) He is the *God of Christ*: he formed his manhood, appointed him to his mediatorial office, and assists in, and rewards, his work. (John 20:17; Eph. 1:3) He is the *God* of all men: in creation he formed, by providence he preserves and actuates, and therefore has a right to govern all things. He is the *God* of Church members by his Word, separating them from the world, giving them his ordinances, and in their professed dedication of themselves to his service. He is the *God* of saints by instating (investing) them in the covenant, and giving himself to them as their all-in-all, and by their solemn and hearty dedication of themselves to him. (Num. 32:16; Jer. 31:31)

He is the God of Abraham, Isaac, and Jacob, and of Israel, as he entered into a covenant of special friendship with them, and gave himself to be their portion, ruler - civil and sacred - and their last end. God very often, particularly in giving laws, makes a grant of himself to men as their God, to show how much he delights to bestow himself freely on men as their portion, and to show that all our obedience must be founded upon our taking him freely as our God in Christ. (Exod. 3:6, 24:10) Sometimes, to express the dignity or excellence of things, they are presented as *of God*; hence Moses is said to be *exceedingly fair* before *God*. (Acts 7:20) Stately cedars are called *trees of the Lord*. (Ps. 104:16) *A very great trembling* is called a trembling of God. (1 Sam. 14:15) To assist our weak minds in conceiving God, and to keep them always impressed with his presence and nature, affections innumerable belonging to creatures, especially men, are ascribed to God, to understand which, we must always remember he is a most pure Spirit, and that these affections must represent what, in his spiritual nature, or his work, corresponds with them. Thus as *eyes* in men are instrumental in discerning objects, and in demonstrating love, pity, pleasure, or anger, we must consider them when ascribed to God as meaning his knowledge, wisdom, favour, or wrath. As *hands* are the instruments of action, of kind support, affectionate embracing, or giving angry blows, these ascribed to God must speak of his power, and the kind or wrathful exercise of it.

Angels are called *gods* because of their excellent nature, and their declaring God's mind, and executing his work as his deputies; and they are required to worship Christ when the heathen idols are destroyed. (Ps. 97:7; Heb. 1:6) Magistrates are called *gods*; they ought specially to resemble God in wisdom and justice, and, as his deputies, rule over others. (Exod. 22:28; Ps. 82:1, 6; John 10:34) Moses is called a *god* because he was God's deputy in delivering the Israelites. (Exod. 4:16, 7:1) Satan is called *the god of this world*; he is believed, obeyed, and adored under various forms by most of its inhabitants. (2 Cor. 4:4) Idols are called *gods* because they are adored, worshipped, and trusted in by their followers. (1 Kings 11:33) They are *strange*, or *other gods*; the Hebrews were not originally in covenant with them (Deut. 32:16; Judg. 2:12), and the most pious among them, out of detestation, declined pronouncing their names, and hence substituted *Bosheth*, or *Besheth*, that, is, *shame*, instead of *Baal*, when they named some people. Thus for Eshbaal, Meribaal, and Jerubbaal, they pronounced them Ishbosheth, Mephibosheth, and Jerubbesheth, sometimes calling them Elilim, *nothings*, or *not gods*, and often Gilulim, *rolling excrement*. (Ezek. 30:13, etc) Men's

belly is their *god* when they are over-careful to provide for, and please, it. (Phil. 3:19)

GOG and MAGOG

Gog may signify the governor, and Magog, when joined to it, may mean the people. Magog was the second son of Japheth, and gave his name to his seed. His posterity seem to have populated Tartary, a large country on the north of Asia, and taking in part of Europe, reaching in length from west to east about 5000 miles, and in breadth from north to south about 2700 miles, most of which at present belongs to what we call the Russian Empire.

The ancient Tartars called themselves Mogli, or Magogli, or Mungli, or Mungugli, the children of Magog. A Tartar Empire in the East Indies is called the Mogul Empire, and the country Mogulistan, or the country of the Moguls. A tribe of eastern Tartars is still called Mungls or Moungals. Many names of places in ancient Tartary retain vestiges of Gog and Magog. The Arabian geographer calls North Tartary (now Siberia) the land of Giug or Magiug, and says it is separated by dreaded mountains from the rest of the world. I suppose he means the Verchaturian Hills, which, for most of the year, are often covered with snow several feet deep. Perhaps, too, Mount Caucasus was originally Goghasen, the *fortress of Gog*, and the Palus Meotis, on the north of the Euxine Sea (Black Sea), Magotis. These descendants of Magog, under the various names of Scythians, Goths, Huns, Tartars, Moguls, and Turks, have produced a terrible work in the earth.

About BC 604, the Scythians made a terrible incursion into western Asia, overrunning it till the King of Egypt, by presents and flattery, diverted them from entering his kingdom. Vast numbers of them remained in Media for about 28 years, till most of them, at least their chiefs, were massacred. Much about the same time, they seem to have conquered part of China. About BC 504, they carried on a war with Darius Hystaspes. About BC 334, they poured the utmost contempt on Alexander the Great. Some time before our Saviour's birth, the Dacians began to ravage the northeast part of the Roman Empire, but were reduced by Trajan about AD 110. The Sarmatians began their ravages on Germany, etc., about AD 69, and were reduced partly by the Huns about AD 450, and the rest by the Goths about AD 500. The Alans began their ravage of Media about AD 70, and of Europe in

AD 120, and at last settled in Spain about AD 409. After the Vandals, who began in AD 166, had ravaged from Germany to the west of Spain, they crossed the Mediterranean Sea and established a powerful kingdom on the north of Africa; and, issuing from there, they ravaged Sicily, and, in 455, took and pillaged Rome. But, about 536, they were reduced by the Emperor Justinian, if not before. About AD 269, the Gepidae began their ravages, and about AD 572 were reduced by the Lombards, a branch of themselves, who began their ravages about AD 500, and about 68 years later, established a kingdom in Italy, which was reduced by Charles the Great in AD 774. About AD 85, the Suevi began their ravages, settled in Spain 409, and were reduced by the Goths in AD 585. About AD 215, or maybe earlier, the Getae (or Goths) began their ravages. In AD 410, they took Rome, and, about the same time, settled in Italy, Spain, etc. About AD 250, the Franks began their ravage, and, in about 420, settled in Gaul, now called France. About 275, the Burgundi began their ravages, and were reduced by the Franks about 534. The Heruli began their ravage about 256, and ruined the Roman Empire in 476; but within a hundred years, they were reduced by Justinian and the Goths. Whether the Saxons, who made such terrible wars in Germany, and partly entered Britain and murdered the inhabitants, settled in their place, and were altogether of a Tartar origin, we do not know. From AD 376-660, the Huns committed terrible ravages, and, at last, settled in Hungary. About the same time, another tribe of them fearfully harassed the kingdom of Persia. From about 585-1395, the Bulgars often repeated their ravages on the eastern part of the Roman Empire, till, at last, they were reduced by the Ottoman Turks. While these savage hordes left their native countries almost desolate, with a series of murders, they rendered the whole of western Europe a perfect shambles of bloodshed and a comparative desert, and introduced their own language, feudal system, inhuman diversions, trials, etc.

About AD 1000, Mahmud, with a number of Tartars, established the Empire of the Gaznevides in East India, which, for some ages continued powerful and flourishing. Toward the decline of the Empire of the Arabs (or Saracens), great numbers of Turks poured into Armenia, Persia, and Mesopotamia. In the latter part of the 11th century, the Seljukian Turks raised four kingdoms near the Euphrates: namely, Baghdad in 1055, Damascus and Aleppo in 1079, and Iconium in 1080.

But that of Baghdad, founded by Tangrolipix (or Tongrul Beg), and extending over Persia, was the most famous. The mutual controversies of these kingdoms, and the marches and wars of the Europeans for the recovery of Canaan from the Mahometans, hindered them from extending their power in the 12th and 13th centuries. About 1260, Genghis Khan and his sons, and their eastern Tartars, from small beginnings, overran and conquered most of Asia, and eastern Europe, as far as the borders of Germany, and erected three powerful Empires: that of China and Persia in Asia, and Kipjack in Europe, besides lesser sovereignties in India, etc. But none of these continued more than nine or ten successions in any degree of glory. About these times, the Turkmen, whose posterity still abounds in Persia and Turkey, and live in tents covered with white cloth, and feed numerous flocks and herds like the Bedouin Arabs, established a kingdom in Armenia, which, for some ages, was notable, and, just before its ruin, was very powerful. To shun the ravaging Tartars, Solomon Shah, one of the Gaz, or baser Turks, attempted, with his three sons, to pass the Euphrates to the west, but was drowned, and his two elder sons returned and submitted to the enemy. Ortogrul the younger, with his three sons, Condoz, Sarubani, and Othman, some time later, passed the river, and, having obtained a settlement on the west of Armenia from the Sultan of Iconium, numbers of the subjects of the four Turkish kingdoms joined him, by whose assistance he gained several victories over the straggling Tartars, and over the Christians. These Turks, now called Ottomans, began their ravages on the Christians on the west of the Euphrates about 1281, or, according to others, in 1302. They gradually increased to prodigious numbers, especially of horsemen, sometimes to nearly a million at once. Their livery and colours were of blue, scarlet, or yellow. They were terribly desperate, furious, cruel, and bloody; and monstrous were their firearms, which they used early in besieging cities. For 391 or 396 years, in prophetic style, *a year, a month, a day, and a hour*, for the most part, they exceedingly prevailed, especially against the Christians, and made themselves masters of the western parts of Asia, the northern parts of Africa, and the southeastern parts of Europe, with many of the islands of the Mediterranean Sea; and, by their murder and oppression, they rendered these once fertile and populous countries, for the most part, a comparative desert. Instead of thousands of dense cities in their extensive Empire, only

Constantinople in Europe, Smyrna, Baghdad, Aleppo, and Scanderoon (at the northeastern corner of the Mediterranean Sea) in Asia, and Cairo in Egypt deserve careful notice.

Since 1672, they made no new conquests; and since the peace of Carlowitz in 1698, they did not attempt it much. At about the beginning of the millennium, tidings from the north and east, perhaps of Russian or Persian invasions, will give them great uneasiness. Scarcely will the Jews resettle in Canaan, when, as we expect, the Turks, assisted by the Russians, or other Tartar allies, and by the Persians, Arabs, and Africans, will attempt to dislodge them. But, by internal arguments, and the signal vengeance of God, they will perish in their attempt, and leave their carcases to be buried, and their spoils to be enjoyed by the Jews. About the end of the millennium, they and their partisans, or men of similar temper, will make a terrible effort against the Church, but will perish miserably in the attempt.

About AD 1400, Tamberlane, with a great army of Tartars, overran western Asia, and was a terrible scourge to the Ottoman Turks. He founded the two Empires of Persia and Mogulistan, the last of which is governed by his descendants to this day. About AD 1640, the eastern Tartars, in the time of civil war, made themselves masters of China, and continue so still, so that the descendants of Magog have almost all Asia, and much of Europe, in their hands at present. Many of these Tartars have already been turned to the Lord; and, in the millennium, we hope their conversion will be much more widespread. (Gen. 9:27; Isa. 43:6; Dan. 11:10-44; Ezek. 38-39; Zech. 6:7; Rev. 9:12-21, 20:7-10)

GOLIATH

A famous giant of Gath, whose height was 6 cubits and a span (11 feet 4 inches). His brazen helmet weighed about 15 pounds (avoirdupois); his target (or collar) fixed between his shoulders to defend his neck, about 30 pounds; his spear was about 26 feet long, and its head about 38 pounds; his sword 4 pounds; the greaves on his legs 30 pounds; and his coat of mail 156 pounds; and so the whole armour weighed 273 pounds. At Ephes-dammim, and for 40 days, he went out from the camp of the Philistines and haughtily defied the Hebrews to produce a man that dare engage him in single combat. He offered to lay the subjection of the one nation to the other on the victory in such a duel. The Hebrews were terrified at the very sight of him, but David, coming to the camp, dared to attack him with a staff, a sling, and a few small stones. With disdain, Goliath cursed him by his idols, and bid him come on, and he would give his flesh to the fowls of the air. Meanwhile, David slung a stone, which penetrated the hole made for the giant's eye, or while he was tossing up his forehead, leaving it bare in contempt of his puny antagonist. It sank into his head, and brought him to the ground flat on his face. David then ran up to him, and, with the giant's own sword, cut off his head. Perhaps, on the occasion of this victory, David composed the 9th and 144th Psalms. (1 Sam. 17) Four of the giant's brothers were afterwards slain by David's warriors. (2 Sam. 21, and 2 Chron. 20)

GOMER

The oldest son of Japheth. He was, no doubt, the father of the Gomerians, Gomares, Cimmerians or Cimbri, who, in ancient days, inhabited Galatia, Phrygia, etc; and here, in the name Ascanius, the Ascanian Bay, and the Askanian or Euxine Sea (Black Sea), we find traces of his son Askenaz. After they had dwelt for some time around Phrygia and Georgia, either near the east end of the Euxine Sea (Black Sea), or by crossing the Hellespont, they penetrated into Europe and populated the countries now called Poland, Hungary, Germany, Switzerland, France, Spain, Portugal, and Britain, if not also part of Scandinavia. The Welsh in England still call themselves Cymri, Cymro, or Comari; nor do the old Scots or Irish appear to be of a different origin.

These Gomerians were distinguished into the tribes of Celtæ (Gauls), Belgæ (German and Celtic tribes that inhabited the Rhine estuary, the Low Countries and north-east France), Germans, Sacæ (Scythians), Titans, etc., and, according to Paul Yves Pezron, very early, about the time of Isaac, and afterwards, composed a large and flourishing Empire whose kings were Man (or Maneus), Acmon, Uranus, Saturn, Jupiter, and Theutat (Mercury), who introduced trade among them. After him, the Empire was broken into pieces, but the Gauls who inhabited Switzerland and France were long a terror to the Romans, and sometimes even made terrible inroads into Greece and Asia. At last, the conquests of the Romans, and descendants of Magog, swallowed up most of the Gomerians; but it seems a part of them will assist the Turks in opposing the Jews about the beginning of the millennium. (Gen. 10:2-3; 1 Chron. 1:5-6; Ezek. 38:6)

(2) GOMER. See Hosea

A former prostitute, wife of Hosea the prophet, and mother of the prophet's two children. (Hosea 1:3)

H

THE BOOK OF HABAKKUK

This prophet is said to have come from the tribe of Simeon. He prophesied during the reign of Manasseh, or, rather, was contemporary with Jeremiah. (Hab. 1:1, 3:1)

In his first chapter, he foretells the destruction of Judea, and the countries around, by the Chaldeans. In the second chapter, he foretells the overthrow of the Chaldeans for their oppression and murder of others, and encourages the Jews to wait patiently for it. In the third chapter, in a most lofty manner, he celebrates God's former appearances to Israel: in bringing them through the Red Sea, in giving his Law to them, and in casting out the Canaanites before them. To him was revealed the doctrine of justification by faith. (2:4) The transgressions of the people are delineated in 2:5-20. Habakkuk then prays for the revival of true religion (3:1-2) He professes his terrible apprehension at the Chaldean invasion, and begs that the Lord would at least mitigate the stroke. He concludes by rejoicing in the God of his salvation. (3:17-19)

HADAD

Three kings of Edom bore this name. The last was the son of that king whom David conquered. His friends carried him off from the destructive ravage of Joab, and committed him to the protection of Pharaoh, King of Egypt. When he grew up, Pharaoh gave him Tahpenes his sister as wife, who bore him a son called Genubath. Informed of King David's death, he had a strong desire to return to his native country and recover his kingdom. With reluctance, Pharaoh consented to part with him. He set up as king in some remote corner of Idumea, or perhaps Pharaoh obtained Solomon's permission for him to govern Edom as his deputy. It

is certain that, towards the end of Solomon's reign, he did what mischief he could to the Hebrews. (1 Kings 11:14-25; 1 Chron. 1:46-51)

HADADEZER, HADAREZER

This son of Rehob was a powerful king in Zobah in Syria, and appears to have been very troublesome to his neighbours, particularly to Toi (or Tou), King of Hamath. David, intending to extend the boundaries of the Hebrew dominion to the Euphrates as God had promised, he defeated Hadadezer's host, and took 20,000 of them prisoners, together with 700 horses and 1000 chariots. The Syrians of Damascus came to Hadadezer's assistance, but were defeated with the loss of 22,000. David ordered the arms of the Syrians, with a prodigious spoil, particularly an immense store of brass that he discovered in the cities of Betan (or Tibbath), and Berothai (or Chun), to be transported to Jerusalem. Glad of the ruin of his rival, Toi sent Hadoram (or Joram) his son, with his grateful compliments, and with large presents, to King David. About seven years later, Hadadezer, and three other Syrian princes, assisted the Ammonites. Joab and Abishai gave them a terrible defeat. Hadadezer, intent on resistance, or ruin on the Hebrews, drew together a large body of Syrians from the east of the Euphrates. These, the Hebrews routed at Helam, a place somewhere southeast of Syria (if they knew it by that name), and killed 40,000 of them under Shobach (or Shopach) their general. From then on, all the kingdoms' tributary to Hadadezer became David's servants, and no longer assisted the Ammonites. (2 Sam. 8, 10; 1 Chron. 18-19)

HADORAM. See Hadadezer and Rehoboam

(1) The son of Tou, King of Hamath, sent by his father to congratulate David on his victory over Hadadezer, King of Syria. (1 Chron. 18:10; also called *Joram* in 2 Sam. 8:10)

(2) The fifth son of Joktan, founder of an Arab tribe. (Gen. 10:27; 1 Chron. 1:21)

(3) One who was over the tribute. He was stoned by the Israelites after they revolted from Rehoboam (2 Chron. 10:18). Also called Adoram (2 Sam. 20:24) and Adoniram (1 Kings 4:6)

HAGAR. See Ishmael, Arabia

An Egyptian handmaid of Abraham's wife Sarah. Perhaps he was presented with her by Pharaoh. When Sarah found herself more

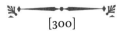

and more unlikely to conceive the promised offspring, she advised Abraham to take Hagar to bed as his concubine. Hagar had no sooner conceived than she began to despise her barren mistress. On Sarah's advice, Abraham encouraged her to do with Hagar whatever she pleased. Hagar was badly used, and fled away, intending to return home to Egypt. The Lord appeared to her in the wilderness of Shur, directed her to return to her mistress and humble herself under her hand, and told her she would have a son called *Ishmael*, whose numerous posterity would dwell in the presence of, or on the south of, Abraham's other posterity, and be remarkable for constant wildness and freedom. Deeply affected with this vision, she called the name of the adjacent well *Beer-lahai-roi*, meaning, *the well of him that liveth and seeth me*; so, all obedient, she returned and submitted herself to Sarah. About 16-17 years later, her son Ishmael, having shown some hatred or contempt for young Isaac, Sarah begged Abraham to expel him and his mother from the family. After God had directed Abraham, and assured him that he would greatly multiply Ishmael's descendants into twelve different tribes, Abraham sent off Hagar and her son with a small portion of bread and a bottle of water. Thus Abraham was chastised for taking her to his bed, and she for her haughtiness. Perhaps Abraham intended to send more provisions after her, but she never got it. Going towards Egypt, she lost her way in the wilderness of Beersheba. Her water failed, and her son became faint. Unwilling to see him breathe his last, she left him under a tree whose shadow might refresh him, and withdrew to the distance of a bowshot, and sat down and wept. The Lord called to her from heaven, comforted her, and showed her a well of water for their refreshment. After they had drunk to their satisfaction, she filled her bottle, and they went on till they took up residence in the desert of Paran, where she arranged one of her country-women as wife for her son. (Gen. 16, 21)

She and Mount Sinai, which perhaps was connected with her seed, became an emblem of the covenant of works and ceremonial law, to which all that now hold fast in opposition to Christ are slaves of Satan and outcasts from the family of God, as we see verified in the present state of the Jews. (Gal 4:24) See also *Bondwoman* in Genesis 21:10, 12-13; Galatians 4:23, 30-31. At least some of her descendants were called Hagarites, or Hagarenes. In the days of King Saul, the Reubenites and Gadites attacked the Hagarites that were living on their borders, and, cutting off their army, seized their territory east of Gilead. The Hagarenes assisted the Ammonites and Moabites against Jehoshaphat, and were cut off miserably. About the time of Jeroboam the second, or soon after, the Reubenites and Gadites, with 44,000, defeated the Hagarites, who were then governed by Jetur, Nephish, and Nodab, and took 100,000 of them prisoner, with an immense booty of flocks and herds. (1 Chron. 5; Ps. 83)

THE BOOK OF HAGGAI

One of three Jewish prophets that flourished after the Captivity. He was probably born in Chaldea; and, in the sixth month of the second year of Darius Hystaspes, he began his public work of prophesying, about 17 years after the return from Babylon. He, together with Zechariah, mightily excited and encouraged their brothers to finish the building of the Temple. He complained how wrong it was for the Temple to lie in ruins while their own houses were so fine, and their neglect of God's house and honour had provoked him to damage their outward enjoyments. He assured them that, after terrible convulsions of the nations, the Messiah would appear in the flesh, teach in the courts of the second Temple, and render it more glorious than the first. (Ezra 5:1-2; Hag. 1-2; Ezra 6:14; Hag. 1:1, 3, 12-13, 2:1, 10, 13-14, 20)

HAM

The youngest son of Noah, who mocked at his father's naked shame, and had his descendants cursed on that account. He had four sons: Cush, Mizraim, Phut, and Canaan. His posterity populated Africa, and part of west Asia. Generally, they have been most wicked and miserable, and few of them have so far enjoyed the light of the gospel. From him, the land of Egypt was called Chemia (or the land of Ham). There was another place on the east of Jordan called Ham; but whether it was Rabbah, which Stephanus of Byzantium calls Amana, or Hamath, the city of Tou, which the Targum calls Hemta, I do not know. (Gen. 14:5) Part of Ham's race dwelt, of old, on the southern borders of the tribe of Simeon. (1 Chron. 4:40)

HAMAN

The son of Hamemedatha, a descendant of Agag the Amalekite. When he was promoted by Ahasuerus, and made prime minister of the Persian Empire, and all the servants of the court were ordered to bow to him, everyone but Mordecai the Jew obeyed. Haman thought it below him to revenge this affront on Mordecai alone; he resolved to cut off the whole nation of the Jews in the Persian Empire. He cast lots for the luckiest day to accomplish his design. The lot, directed by God, fell on the 13th day of the 12th month; and so the execution was put back almost a whole year that Providence might gradually counteract it.

Meanwhile, Haman represented the Jews to King Ahasuerus as a nuisance and burden to the kingdom on account of their different laws and customs, and begged that they might be utterly exterminated, and he would pay 10,000 talents of silver to the exchequer as a full balance for the loss of their tribute. Ahasuerus replied that he would freely allow him to exterminate that people. Haman immediately despatched letters in the king's name to all the provinces of the Empire to massacre the Jews among them on the day appointed, and to take their wealth for a reward. He rejoiced greatly in his success and wealth, and the more so as Queen Esther had invited him alone, along with the king, to her banquet, but complained that it galled his spirit to see Mordecai the Jew sitting at the King's gate. Zerish his wife, and other friends, advised him to immediately erect a gallows, and get the king's permission to hang Mordecai on it. A gallows was erected about 75 or 90 feet high, and he went in next morning to ask the king to hang Mordecai on it. But the king forestalled his request by ordering him to clothe Mordecai in the royal apparel, and, as his page, lead his horse through the city of Shushan, and proclaim that he was one of the king's chief favourites.

Stung with grief, he hastened home as soon as his task was finished, and told his wife and his friends what had happened. They told him that this exaltation of Mordecai was a sad omen of the fatal consequences of his project against the Jews. That very day, Esther accused him as the intended murderer of her and her nation, and begged the king to interpose for their lives. Ahasuerus, having gone out in a rage, Haman fell at the queen's feet to implore her to intercede for his life. When the king returned suddenly, he accused him of attempting to stain the honour of his bed. Glad of Haman's downfall, the servants covered his face, and the chamberlain told the king that Haman had prepared a gallows to hang Mordecai on, the preserver of the king's life. Ahasuerus ordered him to be hanged on it directly. Not long after, his ten sons shared the same fate. (Esther 3:5-6, chs. 7, 9) See also in the book of Esther: 3:1, 2, 4-8, 10-12, 15, 4:7, 5:4-5, 8-12, 14, 6:4-7, 10-14, 7:1, 6-10, 8:1-3, 5, 7, 9:10, 12, 24.

HAMATH

Canaan had a son of this name who was the father of the Hamathites. (Gen. 10:18; 1 Chron. 1:16), and from whom it is possible the places called Hamath or Hammath, derived their name.

HAMONAH

The name Ezekiel gave to a city, and *Hamongog* the name he assigned to a valley, indicating that many of the nation of Gog will be killed in various places in Canaan. (Ezek. 39:11, 15-16)

HANNAH

Her husband Elkanah was a Levite from Mount Ephraim, 17th in descent from Kohath, the son of Levi. He had two wives, Hannah and Peninnah. The former was extremely pious, and the darling of her husband, but the latter had children, and often scolded Hannah for her lack of them. As Elkanah and his whole family attended one of the solemn feasts at Shiloh, he, at the feast, and from the share of his sacrifices, gave Peninnah and her children their various portions; but, to Hannah, he gave the best part of the peace offering that fell to his share, or the best part of the Passover lamb. At these entertainments, it was Peninnah's common practice to reproach Hannah for her barrenness. Hannah at last took it so badly that she could eat nothing. To comfort her, Elkanah told her that his distinguished regard for her was better than ten children. After eating a little, Hannah retired to the court of the Tabernacle, prayed with great fervour for a child, and vowed to surrender him as a Nazarite for life to the service of God. Eli the high priest, observing her lips move, but not hearing her words, scolded her for being drunk. She told him her case, and he desired that the Lord might grant her request. Divinely impressed that God would grant it, she went home cheerfully. She had scarcely returned to Ramah, her hometown, when she conceived, and, in due time, bore a son, and called him *Samuel* because she had *asked* him of, and *lent* him to, the Lord. After she had weaned him when he was about three

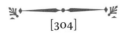

years old, she carried him to Shiloh, and, with a thank offering of three bullocks, an ephah of flour, and a bottle of wine, she presented him before the Lord, and put him under Eli's tuition, proposing that, as she had obtained him by prayer, so she was giving him up for life to the service of God. On this occasion, she composed an elegant hymn, celebrating the holiness, greatness, wisdom, power, and mercy of God. (1 Sam. 2:1-10) At an after feast, as she gave Eli a coat for her son, he blessed her, and wished her more children. After Samuel, she had three other sons and two daughters. (1 Sam. 2:20-21)

HANUN

The son and successor of Nahash, king of the Ammonites. Persuaded by evil counsellors, he abused David's ambassadors, sent to him with compliments of condolence after his father's death, as if they had come to spy out the country where it might be most easily attacked. He ordered that they have their beards shaved, and their clothes cut off from their middle. He immediately thought how badly this would be taken, and prepared for a war with the Hebrews. Once and again, he procured an assistant army from the Syrians: but, when all his forces were defeated in various battles, and the Syrians gave up, his whole kingdom was taken, and Rabbath, his capital, after a siege of some months, was destroyed. His crown, weighing, or worth, a talent of gold, and all that he had, was seized by David. It is probable that he himself was slain, and his brother Shobi, who brought food to David at Mahanaim, was appointed deputy-governor of the kingdom under David. (2 Sam. 10-12 and 17:27-29)

HARAN

(1) The oldest son of Terah, brother of Abraham, and father of Lot, with two daughters, Milcah and Iscah. As he died young, it seems his two brothers married his two daughters: Abraham, Iscah (or Sarah), and Nahor, Milcah. (Gen. 11:26-29, 31-32, 27:43) Out of respect to Haran's memory, it is probable that his father called the place of their future abode Haran, Hara, or Charran. (Gen. 27:32; Acts 7:2, 4) Here, Terah died, and Jacob lived with his uncle Laban. (Gen. 27:45, and ch. 39) It seems to have been situated between the rivers Chebar and Euphrates, considerably north of the place where they meet. Its people carried on a trade with the Tyrians. (Ezek. 27:23) Near this place, Marcus Licinius

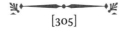

Crassus the Roman general, and almost all his army, were cut off by the Parthians in 53 BC.

(2) The son of Caleb of Judah by his concubine Ephah. (1 Chron. 2:46)

(3) A son of Shimei, of the tribe of Gershon. (1 Chron. 23:9)

HAVILAH

The second son of Cush, and grandchild of Ham. It is probable that he and his posterity populated and gave their name to the land of Havilah, on the northwest of the Persian Gulf, and which was the eastern border of the Ishmaelites and Amalekites. (Gen. 10:7) The posterity of Joktan was probably the Chaloteans (or Avalites) that lived near the Sabeans on the Avaltic Bay, south of the former Havilah. (Gen. 10:29) Augustine Calmet and Adrian Reland assert that Havilah was Colchis on the east of the Euxine Sea (Black Sea); and it is true that there was fine gold there in the earliest ages, which the inhabitants gathered in sheepskins with the wool on, as it ran down the rivers when swollen. Hence probably sprang the fable of the golden fleece. But as we have already rejected their situation of Eden, as well as Augustine Calmet's view of Ophir, we cannot admit this of Havilah.

HAZAEL

It is probable that he was the Syrian general after Naaman, who gave up his post rather than lead armies against the Israelites. Elijah had been divinely ordered to anoint him king over Syria. Elisha, about eleven years after Elijah's translation, went north to Syria. Benhadad the king, being sick, sent Hazael to the prophet to ask if he would recover. Elisha replied that, though his disease was not mortal, he would never recover. He also, with tears, told Hazael that he foresaw the horrible barbarities he would perpetrate on the Israelites. Hazael replied that he had neither power nor inclination to do those horrible things. Elisha told him that he would become king of Syria, and then do them. Hazael returned to his master, and said he would certainly recover; but, next day, he stifled him with a wet cloth, and, by his influence in the army, seized the throne. Almost immediately, when Jehu gave up the siege or care of Ramoth-gilead to establish himself on the throne of Israel, Hazael took the opportunity to ravage almost all the country of Reuben, Gad, and Manasseh, beyond the Jordan. He burnt their cities

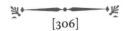

with fire, dashed their children to pieces, and ripped up their women with child. (2 Kings 8, 10) After the death of Jehu, he ravaged the kingdom of the ten tribes west of the Jordan, and reduced the country almost to a desert. (2 Kings 13:3, 22, 24-25) About the 44th year of his reign, he took Gath from the Philistines, and marched to lay siege to Jerusalem; but Joash diverted him with large presents. The very next year, a small army of Syrians invaded Judah, defeated Joash's mighty host, slew his princes, and carried off great spoil. (2 Kings 12:17-18; 2 Chron. 24:23-25) After Hazael had reigned about 50 years, he was succeeded by his son Benhadad, about BC 834.

HEATHEN. See Gentiles
Savage, and without religion. Possibly from *heath dwellers*.

HEBER, EBER
The son of Shelah, and great-grandchild of Shem. He had two sons, Peleg and Joktan, whose posterity afterwards populated Mesopotamia, and westward of it, and part of Arabia Felix. (Gen. 10:21, 24-30; 11:14-26; 1 Chron. 1:18-42) *The children of Eber*, afflicted by ships from Chittim, may refer to the Mesopotamians severely afflicted by the Greeks under Alexander and his successors, and the Jews harassed by the Romans under Pompey, Vespasian, Titus, Trajan, Adrian, etc. (Num. 24:24)

HEBREWS. See Israel

Origins
Abraham, Isaac, Jacob, and his descendants, were called *Hebrews*. We cannot believe they received this name only from Heber, for why should this branch bear his name rather than any other of his family, unless they retained his religion? Nor is Abraham ever called a *Hebrew* till he passed the Euphrates to the west. Did they not, then, rather receive it from their passing over, or coming from beyond, this river?

A *Hebrew of the Hebrews* was someone descended from Hebrew parents, both father and mother. (Phil. 3:5) Sometimes, only those Jews were called Hebrews who spoke the Hebrew language, in contrast with the Jews, who only spoke Greek. (Acts 6:1) God promised to Abraham that he would make his seed extremely numerous. It was a long time, however, before the promised seed made an appearance with the birth of Isaac. Abraham's seed by Ishmael, and by the sons of Keturah, indeed increased mightily, but neither these, nor the posterity of Esau, were the promised offspring. In Jacob's twelve sons, the nation first began to increase, and, in later years, were called *Israel* (or *Jacob*) from their progenitor. In still later times, they were called *Jews*, those of them that came under the name of Judah in the south. In roughly 210 or 215 years, they increased in Egypt from the original 70 to between two and three million men, women, and children. While Joseph lived, who preserved the Egyptian nation during a time of terrible famine, they were kindly regarded by the Egyptian monarchs; but, at a later time, they were terribly oppressed. From a suspicion that they might, in process of time, become too strong for the native Egyptians, they were condemned to labour in a most slavish and burdensome manner. The more they were oppressed, the more they multiplied, and that in abundance. The midwives and others were therefore ordered to murder every male infant at the time of birth, but the midwives made excuses to avoid this horrible task. (Exod. 1:15-19) Everyone was therefore ordered to kill the Hebrew male children wherever they could be found; the females, they intended to absorb into Egyptian society. After they had been so miserably oppressed for about a hundred years, and on the very day that completed the 430th year from God's first promise of a seed to Abraham, and about 400 years after the birth of Isaac, God, by terrible plagues on the Egyptians, obliged them to let the Hebrews go under the direction of Moses and Aaron. As the Hebrews' due wages had been denied them, God, the supreme Judge and Proprietor of all, ordered them to ask for a vast number of precious things from the Egyptians, and carry them away. Thus they departed peaceably, and with great wealth, and without so much as one of their number weak or sickly, attended by a mixed multitude of heathen to serve them, and who, later, became a snare to them. (Gen. 15, 17, 22; Exod. 1-13; Neh. 9; Acts chapter 7)

The wilderness wanderings

God directed the Hebrews to march by a pillar of cloud, which, by day, was dark, screening them from the heat, and, by night, was fiery, giving them light. He directed them not to take the quick way to Canaan, lest their early encounters with the Philistines might tempt them to return to Egypt, but he caused them to march towards the southeast, and into

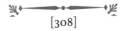

the straits of Pihahiroth, where there were mountains on either side, with the Red Sea before them. Pharaoh, expecting them to be trapped, pursued them with a great army to bring them back. The Lord opened a passage through the Red Sea for the Hebrews, but the Egyptians, attempting to follow them, were drowned. The Hebrews now found themselves in a dry and barren desert; nor did they bring along provision for the journey. God supplied them with water from a flinty rock, and with manna from heaven. Moreover, he surfeited them on quails in the desert of Sin (Exod. 16:13, and later, Num. 11:31-34) By means of Moses' prayers and Joshua's bravery he enabled them to rout the Amalekites that savagely fell on their rear.

Having appointed officers of thousands, hundreds, fifties, and tens, over them, they marched south along the eastern side of the gulf of the Red Sea where they came to Mount Sinai, arriving 50 days after their departure from Egypt. There, God, in a most tremendous way, and from the midst of a terrible fire on the top of the Mount, and after the most fearful thundering, avowed them as his special people, intimated to them his laws, and confirmed the authority of Moses as their leader. While Moses delayed in the Mount, they so far lost the impression of everything they had seen and heard and constructed and worshipped a golden calf. This was destroyed, and 3000 of the leading idolaters were cut off by the sword of the zealous Levites. God, at the intercession of Moses, spared the people, and renewed to them the tablets of his Law, then his Tabernacle was erected among them, Aaron and his sons were consecrated to the priesthood, and vast numbers of further ceremonies concerning offerings, purifications, and festivals were prescribed. The number of their fighting men was taken, and they were made into four great divisions, three tribes in each; and the manner of their marching and encampment was appointed. The Tabernacle was dedicated by the oblations (thank offerings) of their chief princes on 12 separate days, and the Levites were consecrated to their sacred service in place of the Hebrews' first-born children. After they had come out of Egypt, the Passover was again observed in the first month of the second year.

Entering the Promised Land

After lingering about a year at the foot of Sinai, they then marched north, loathed the manna, and were punished with a month's eating

of flesh till a plague broke out among them. About this time, 70 or 72 elders were appointed over them. They quickly arrived on the southern border of Canaan at Kadesh-barnea. For their rash believing the report of the ten wicked spies, and their contempt of the Promised Land, God would have entirely destroyed them had not Moses' prayers prevailed. They were actually condemned to wander in the desert for a full 40 years till that whole generation (except Caleb and Joshua) had been cut off by death. During this period, God frequently punished them for their repeated rebellions, murmurings, or loathing of the manna. The Canaanites made terrible havoc of them at Hormah when they attempted to enter Canaan contrary to the will of God. More than 14,000 of them perished over the matter of Korah, for their murmuring at his, and his accomplices' death. Many were bitten by fiery serpents. Twenty-four thousand were cut off for their idolatry and prostitution with the Midianitish women. But God's marvellous favours still continued. His cloudy pillar led and protected them, his manna from heaven supplied them with food, the streams issuing from the rock at Meribah followed their camp for about 39 years whether their way was ascending or not, and their clothes never grew old. At Kadesh and at Beer, God supplied them anew with water. The intended curse of Balaam was turned into a blessing in their favour.

During this period, the cloud led them from Kadesh-barnea, on the south of Canaan, back to Ezion-geber, which is on the northeast of Sinai, and then back to the southern border of Canaan. This journey, though no more than a few hundred miles, took them about 38 years, and it is likely that they marched here and there, so it is impossible to pretend an accurate account of their journey. Nor were they yet allowed to enter the Promised Land, but were led along the southern border of Idumea by a way extremely rough and tiring. At last, they marched to the northeast, till they came to the head of the River Arnon, and turned west to the River Jordan. While they lingered in these quarters, they took possession of the two powerful kingdoms of Sihon and Og on the east of Canaan, and made a terrible slaughter of the Midianites for enticing them into prostitution and idolatry. After crossing the Jordan, which miraculously divided under Joshua their general and successor of Moses, and, solemnly dedicating themselves to the Lord by circumcision, they celebrated the Passover. After a war of six years, they conquered 31 kingdoms. On the 7th year, the land was divided, and the Tabernacle of God set up among them at Shiloh; and, not long after, they solemnly dedicated themselves to the Lord. Under the name of each tribe, it is apparent how exactly their stations in Canaan, and their respective fates, corresponded with the prophetic benedictions of Jacob and Moses.

The Promised Land

On their entrance into Canaan, and to give the Hebrews a horror of idolatry, God ordered them to cut off every idolatrous Canaanite. They, however, through sinful pity or apathy, spared vast numbers of them, who enticed them to wickedness, and were sometimes God's rod to punish them. For many ages, the Hebrews scarcely enjoyed a blink of outward prosperity, but relapsed into idolatry, worshipping Baalim, and Ashtaroth, etc. Micah and the Danites introduced this blasphemy not long after Joshua's death. (Judg. 17-18) About this time, the sexual licence of the men of Gibeah occasioned a war of the eleven tribes against their brothers of Benjamin. To punish the tribes for their wickedness, and their neglecting to consult the mind of the Lord first, they, though more than fourteen to one, were twice routed by the Benjamites, and 40,000 of them were slain. In the third rally, all the Benjamites were slain except 600 of them. Heartily vexed at the loss of a tribe, the other Hebrews provided wives for these 600, at the expense of slaying most of the inhabitants of Jabesh-gilead, and of breaking their oath in the affair of the daughters of Shiloh. (Judg. 1-2, 17-21). Their relapses into idolatry also brought upon them repeated returns of slavery from the heathen among or around them.

The Judges

From BC 1413-1406, they were greatly oppressed by Cushan-rishathaim, but were delivered by Othniel; and from BC 1343 to 1325, by Eglon, King of Moab, from which they were delivered by Ehud. Soon after, they were delivered from the ravages of the Philistines by Shamgar. From BC 1305 to 1285, they were oppressed by Jabin, King of the Canaanites, but were delivered by Deborah and Barak. From 1252 to 1245, they were attacked by the Midianites, but were delivered by Gideon, whose son Abimelech was a scourge to Israel. From 1205 to 1187, they were attacked by the Ammonites on the east, and by the Philistines on the west; but Jephthah rescued them from the Ammonites. From BC 1155 to 1115, they were oppressed by the Philistines, who were harassed by

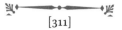

Samson, and routed by Samuel after the death of Eli. During this last oppression, the Hebrews were almost ruined. The ark was taken, and, for perhaps 110 or 130 years afterwards, it was without a settled abode. (Judg. 1-21 and 1 Sam. 1-7) The servitude of Cushan-rishathaim began in BC 1404, that of the Moabites in 1356, that of the Canaanites in 1257, that of the Midianites in 1197, that of the Ammonites in 1150, just after the death of Gideon, exactly 300 years after the death of Moses (Judg. 11:26), and that of the Philistines in 1132.

The Kings

When the Hebrews had been governed by Judges, divinely raised up for about 340 years after the death of Joshua, they took a fancy to having a king like the nations around them, with Saul as their first sovereign. Under his reign of about 20 to 40 years, they had almost perpetual struggles with the Ammonites, Moabites, and Philistines; and, at his death, the nation was left on the brink of ruin by the Philistines. After a seven-year struggle between the eleven tribes that remained loyal to Ishbosheth, the son of Saul, and the tribe of Judah, which turned themselves into a kingdom under David, David became sole monarch of Israel. Under him, the Hebrews subdued their neighbours the Philistines, Edomites, Moabites, Ammonites, and Syrians, and took possession of the whole domain that was promised them, from the border of Egypt to the banks of the Euphrates. Under Solomon, they had almost no war, but employed themselves in building, sea-trade, and other things grand and pompous. It is plain, however, that they hated the taxes that Solomon laid on them at the end of his reign. To punish his, and their, idolatry, during the latter part of his reign, Rezon the Syrian, and Hadad the Edomite, harassed them a little.

Division into two kingdoms

After Solomon's death, ten of the Hebrew tribes formed the northern kingdom of Israel (or Ephraim) for themselves under Jeroboam the son of Nebat, in opposition to the kingdom of Judah and Benjamin, ruled by the family of David. This division, that happened about BC 975, and in the 100th or 120th year of their kingdom, tended not a little to the harm of both parties in their mutual contests. The kingdom of Israel (Ephraim), or the ten tribes, had never so much as one pious king; and often the royal families were destroyed, and others took their place.

Idolatry, particularly in the worship of the golden calves of Bethel and Dan, was always their established religion, and brought miseries unnumbered on their heads. The kingdom of Judah had wicked and pious sovereigns in turn; but their frequent relapses into idolatry often brought in terrible distress for the country. To punish the kingdom of Judah (or, the Jews) for their apostasy, God delivered them into the hands of Shishak, King of Egypt, who ravaged the countryside, but appears to have done no harm to Jeroboam's kingdom, as maybe he was in league with him. There was almost perpetual war between Jeroboam and Rehoboam, and Abijah his son. In one battle, Jeroboam had 500,000 of his forces cut off by the army of Abijah, which was only half of his own. From BC 955 to 889, the kingdom of Judah mostly followed the true God, reformed from her corruptions, and had considerable prosperity and success against her enemies: Ethiopians, Edomites, Moabites, etc. Jehoshaphat raised an army of 1,160,000 men. Meanwhile, the Israelites, under Nadab, Baasha, Elah, Omri, Ahab, Ahaziah, and Jehoram, fell mostly into a most wretched condition, especially with Ahab's introduction of the worship of Baal, and by various famines and repeated wars with the Philistines and Syrians, and civil broils (arguments) between Omri and Tibni.

Not only did the kingdom of Israel, but also the kingdom of Judah, caused the royal families to join in marriage, but they made other alliances with the wicked house of Ahab, and were brought to the very brink of ruin after the death of Jehoshaphat. Nor, indeed, did his successors, Jehoram and Ahaziah, deserve a better fate. From BC 884 to 772, Jehu and his posterity governed the kingdom of Israel. The worship of Baal was abolished, but the idolatry of the calves went on. To punish them, the kingdom was terribly ravaged, and the people were murdered, by the Syrians during the reign of Jehu, and especially of Jehoahaz his son. But Jehoash, and Jeroboam (the second) his son, reduced the Syrians, and made the kingdom of the ten tribes more glorious than it had ever been. At the beginning of this period, and for six years, Athaliah tyrannised over Judah. After her death, religion was a while promoted under Joash by means of his uncle Jehoiada, the High Priest, but they quickly relapsed into idolatry; and, during the reigns of Joash, Amaziah, Uzziah, as well as of Jotham, numbers sacrificed in high places, but in the name of the Lord their God. Nor did the kingdom of Judah recover its grandeur till the reign of Uzziah.

During the reigns of Zachariah, Shallum, Menahem, and Pekahiah, the kingdom of the ten tribes was reduced to a most wretched condition by their internal broils, murder of sovereigns, and Assyrian ravages. Under Pekah, they recovered part of their grandeur, but, after he was murdered by Hoshea, a civil war of nine years seems to have happened, at the end of which, Hoshea found himself master of the crown. Under Jotham, the kingdom of Judah was moderately happy, but, under Ahaz, they relapsed into idolatry, and were terribly harassed by the Philistines, Syrians, and by the ten tribes under Pekah. About BC 724, the kings of the Hebrews were better than they had ever been since the division of the kingdom. Hezekiah, King of Judah, was an eminent reformer, and Hoshea was less wicked than his predecessors; but the abounding wickedness of both kingdoms was ripening them for ruin.

Disaster for Israel and Judah

Ignorance, stupidity, idolatry, rebellion against God, and apostasy from his way, came about with a forgetfulness of him, ingratitude for his mercies, derision of his threats, the changing of his ordinances, profane swearing, violation of sacred vows, magical arts, hypocrisy, and stiff-necked impudence in wickedness, violation of the Sabbath, a mingling of themselves with the heathen, sinful alliances with the Syrians, Assyrians, and Egyptians, and a dependence on them for help. Then pride, a lack of natural affection among families, or between the kingdoms of Israel and Judah, universal corruption of princes, judges, priests, and prophets, murder, drunkenness, luxury, prostitution, covetousness, fraud, oppression, the perverting of justice, and falsehood, were to be found everywhere. Provoked by Hoshea for entering into an alliance with So, King of Egypt, Shalmaneser, King of Assyria, invaded the kingdom of the ten tribes, furiously besieged and took their cities, murdered most of the people, ripped up the women with child, dashed infants to pieces, and carried almost all the rest captive to Hara, Halah, and Haber, by the River Gozan, and to the cities of the Medes on the northeast of the Assyrian Empire, and brought in the Samaritans as immigrants. Thus the kingdom came to its end 254 years after its erection. Sennacherib, King of Assyria, contrary to treaty, invaded the kingdom of Judah, and brought that hypocritical nation to the brink of ruin. Hezekiah's piety, and Isaiah's prayers, became a means of preventing it, but, under his son Manasseh, the Jews abandoned themselves to the most horrible blasphemies. As God's punishment, Esarhaddon, King of Assyria, about the 22nd year of Manasseh's reign, invaded Judea, reduced the kingdom, and carried Manasseh prisoner to Babylon. He also transported the remains of the Israelites to Media and countries adjacent. What has become of them since, whether they went east with the Tartars, and partly passed over into America, or how far they mixed with the Jews, when carried to Babylon, we do not know.

Manasseh repented, and the Lord brought him back to his kingdom, where he promoted the reformation of his subjects during the rest of his reign; but his son Amon defaced all, and made matters as wicked as ever. His son Josiah promoted reformation mightily, and brought it to such a pitch that had never been seen since the reigns of David and Solomon. But the people were mostly hypocritical in this, and the Lord never forgave the nation the murders and other wickedness of Manasseh, leading to external punishment. After Josiah was slain by Pharaohnecho, King of Egypt, the kingdom of Judah returned to her idolatry and other wickedness; and nothing of above-mentioned sins did they fail to indulge in. God gave them up to servitude, first to the Egyptians, and then to the Chaldeans. The fate of their kings, Jehoahaz, Jehoiakim, Jehoiachin, and Zedekiah, was an unhappy one, and so was the case of their subjects during the 22 years of their reigns. It is shocking to think what famine, pestilence, and murder by the Chaldeans came among them.

The Captivity and Exile

Provoked by Zedekiah's treachery, Nebuchadnezzar furiously invaded the kingdom, sacked and burnt the cities, and murdered so many that, of a kingdom once consisting of about six million people under Jehoshaphat, no more than a few thousand were left. The few that remained after the murder of Gedaliah fled into Egypt, making the Chaldeans suspect them of the murder, and this brought their fury against the Jewish nation. Thus the kingdom of Judah was ruined in BC 588, about 388 years after its division from that of the ten tribes. In the 70th year after the Captivity, in the 4th year of Jehoiakim, and the 52nd from the destruction of the city, the Jews, according to the edict of Cyrus, King of Persia, who had overturned the Empire of Chaldeans, returned to their own country under the direction of Sheshbazzar (or

Zerubbabel), grandson of King Jehoiachin, and Joshua the High Priest and others, to the number of 42,360, with 7337 servants of heathen origin. But as the particulars mentioned by Ezra amount to only 29,818, and those by Nehemiah to 31,031, it seems the extra of about 12,000 was of the remains of the ten tribes. The lists of Ezra and Nehemiah are different in many respects, but one might be the list of those who put forward their names to return, and the other the list of those that actually returned. Vast numbers of the Jews who had settled well, preferred their own worldly advantage to their religion, and remained in Babylon.

The return from Babylon

After their return from Babylon, the Jews, under the direction of Zerubbabel, Joshua, Ezra, and Nehemiah, rebuilt the Temple and city of Jerusalem, put away their foreign wives, and solemnly renewed their covenant with God. Vast numbers were turned to the Lord, though many still gave themselves over to despise the worship of God, and rebel against his Law.

After the return, the Jews retained a constant aversion to idolatry, which they rightly believed was the chief cause of their ejection from the land. But many corruptions still took place, such as selfishness, marriage with foreign wives, rash divorce of lawful wives, contempt of God's worship, secular work on the Sabbath, and favouritism and scandalous living among their priests. The year of Jubilee, and perhaps that of release, was scarcely ever punctually observed. Nor were their troubles few. The Temple lacked the ancient ark, cherubim, Shekinah, pot of manna, and the rod that budded. The gift of prophecy ceased after the death of Haggai, Zechariah, and Malachi. Tatnai, Shethar-boznai, Rehum, etc., greatly opposed the rebuilding of the Temple. Sanballat, Tobiah, and Geshem no less maliciously opposed the repair of the walls of Jerusalem. About BC 514 or 458, they escaped the genocide devised by Haman. About 351, Darius Ochus King of Persia, who is, by some, thought to be the husband of Esther and master of Haman, ravaged part of Judea, took Jericho by force, and carried off a great number of prisoners, part of which he sent into Egypt, and the rest he transported to Hyrcania on the south of the Caspian Sea.

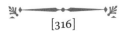

The Greek occupation

When Alexander the Great was in Canaan, about BC 334, he was at first provoked by their adherence to the Persians; but if we believe Flavius Josephus, their solemn submission, with the High Priest at their head, entirely pacified him. He caused a great number of victims to be offered for his success to the God whom they worshipped. He confirmed to them all their privileges; and, having built Alexandria, he settled vast numbers of them there, endowed with the same privileges as his own Macedonians. About 14 years later, Ptolemy Lagus, the Greek King of Egypt, to revenge their fidelity to Laomedon his rival, furiously ravaged Judea, took Jerusalem, and carried 100,000 Jews prisoners to Egypt. But he treated them so kindly, and even assigned them places of power and trust, that many of their countrymen followed them of their own accord.

It seems that about eight years later, he transported another company of Jews to Egypt, and everywhere gave them equal privileges, as Alexander had done. About the same time, Seleucus Nicator, having built more than 30 new cities in Asia, 16 of which were called Antioch, nine Seleucia, six Laodicea, settled in them as many Jews as he could, they being reckoned most faithful to their friendly sovereigns, and bestowed on them the same privileges they had at Alexandria. Nor did Antiochus Theos, his grandson, favour them less. Ptolemy Philadelphus of Egypt, about 284, at his own expense, bought the freedom of all the Jewish slaves in Egypt, and, it is said, he or his son procured a translation of their Bible for the use of his famous Alexandrian library. Ptolemy Euergetes offered a vast number of victims at Jerusalem for his victories over the Syro-Grecians, and was extremely kind to Joseph and other Jews. Ptolemy Philopater, having defeated Antiochus the Great, offered a great number of victims at Jerusalem; but, provoked by the priests for hindering him from entering their Holy of Holies, and at the fuss he stirred up in attempting it, he issued forth murderous decrees against all the Jews in his dominions. But the beasts, prepared to devour them in Egypt, turned on and destroyed the heathen that attended the entertainment.

The abominable Antiochus Epiphanes

Soon after, Antiochus the Great invaded Judea, and the Jews readily revolted to his side. To reward them, he repaired their Temple at his

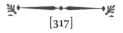

own expense, and assigned 20,000 pieces of silver, 1400 measures of wheat, and 375 of salt, for its service, and confirmed all the privileges that had been ratified to them by Alexander. The dispersed Jews that had settled at Jerusalem, he exempted from tribute for three years. Those who were slaves to his subjects, he ordered to be set free; but Scopas quickly reduced Judea, and set up an Egyptian garrison in Jerusalem. Under Philometer, Onias, about BC 154, built a temple at On (or Heliopolis) in Egypt, after the model of that at Jerusalem, and Dositheus took to himself almost the whole management of the Egyptian state. About BC 176, Heliodorus, on his master Seleucus' orders, attempted to pillage the Temple, but an angel frightened him. Soon after Antiochus Epiphanes came to the Syrian throne, the Jews felt in full the effects of his fury and madness. Because Onias the High Priest refused to comply with some imitations of heathen religion, he turned him out, and sold the office to his brother Jason for 350 talents of silver. Soon after, he took it away from him, and sold it to Menelaus, a third brother, for 650 talents of silver. About BC 170, a report being spread that Antiochus had been killed during his Egyptian expedition, an attempt was made to turn out Menelaus, and retake the high priesthood. Enraged at this, and with the Jews for rejoicing at the news of his death, and for the peculiar form of their worship, Antiochus, on his return from Egypt, forced his way into Jerusalem, murdered 40,000, and sold as many more for slaves to the heathen around, and carried off a great part of the sacred furniture, with about 1800 talents of gold and silver that be found in the treasury, and appointed two of his most savage friends, Philip the Phrygian, and Andronicus, to govern Judea and Samaria as his deputies. About two years later, enraged at the Romans for checking his designs against Egypt, on his return, he ordered the troops to pillage the cities of Judea, murder the men, and sell the women and children into slavery. On a Sabbath day, his general, Appollonius, craftily entered Jerusalem, killed many, and carried off 10,000 prisoners. Antiochus built a fort adjacent to the Temple, from where his garrison might fall on the people as they came to worship in the courts. The Temple was soon afterwards dedicated to Jupiter Olympius, an idol of Greece, and his statue was erected on the altar of burnt offering. For 2300 mornings and evenings, or three and a half years and about two months, the daily sacrifice was stopped, and the Temple made a shambles of murder, a sty of prostitution, and of all kinds of depravity. Those Jews that refused to eat swine's flesh, and

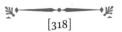

comply with idolatry, were exposed to all the horrors of persecution, torture and death.

The Maccabees

While Eleazar, the widow, and her seven sons, and others, bravely suffered martyrdom, and others with ardour taught their brothers the evils of idolatrous compliance, Mattathias the priest, with his sons, chiefly Judas, Jonathan, and Simon, who were called the Maccabees, fought bravely for their religion and liberties. After a variety of lesser advantages, Judas, who succeeded his father about BC 164, gave Nicanor and the king's troops a terrible defeat, regained the Temple, repaired and purified it, dedicated it anew, restored the daily worship of God, and repaired Jerusalem, which was now almost a ruinous heap. After four more years, and with a small handful of troops, he proved a terrible scourge to the Syrians and other heathen around: the Edomites, Arabs, etc. He was slain, and Jonathan his brother succeeded him as High Priest and general. He and his brother Simon, who succeeded him, wisely and bravely promoted the welfare of their church and state, and were both vilely murdered. Hyrcanus, Simon's son, succeeded him in BC 135. At first, he procured a peace with the Syrians, and, soon after, entirely threw off their yoke. He subdued Idumea, and forced the inhabitants to be circumcised and accept the Jewish religion. He reduced the Samaritans, and demolished their temple at Gerizim, and Samaria their capital. After the short reign of Aristobulus, his oldest son, his son Alexander Janneus succeeded him in BC 105. He reduced the Philistines, and obliged them to accept circumcision; he also reduced the countries of Moab, Ammon, Gilead, and part of Arabia. Only under these three reigns was the Jewish nation independent after the Captivity. His widow governed nine years with great wisdom and prudence. After her death, the nation was almost ruined with civil broils (arguments) raised by the Pharisees, who hated Alexander for his cruelties, and their opposers.

The coming of the Romans

In BC 65, Aristobulus invited the Romans to assist him against Hyrcanus his older brother. They, turning his enemy, quickly reduced the country, took Jerusalem by force, and Pompey and a number of his officers pushed their way into the sanctuary, if not the Holy of Holies, to view its furniture. About nine years later, Crassus, the Roman

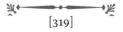

general, to obtain money for his mad Parthian expedition, pillaged the Temple of everything valuable, to the worth of 8000 talents of gold and silver. After Judea had, for more than 30 years, been a scene of ravage and bloodshed, and during 24 of which, had been oppressed by the Romans, Herod the Great, assisted by Anthony the Roman Triumvir, with much struggling and barbarous murder, got himself installed in the kingdom. Finding that neither force nor flattery would make his reign easy, about 20 years before our Saviour's birth, and with the Jews' consent, he began to rebuild the Temple. In three and a half years, the main parts were finished, and the rest not till eight years more, if ever.

The coming of the Messiah

About this time, the Jews everywhere had high hopes of the appearance of the Messiah to free them from their bondage, and to bring their nation to the summit of temporal glory. The Messiah (or Christ), and his forerunner John the Baptist, actually appeared. Both were born about BC 3, which is three years before our common calendar. Instigated by the fear of losing his throne, Herod sought to murder Christ in his infancy. When Jesus assumed his public character, and after his resurrection, many of the Jews believed in him, but mostly of the poorer sort. For the most part, offended with the spiritual nature of his office, his pure and self-debasing doctrine, his mean appearance and sorry retinue that were reproached and persecuted, the Jews, at last, got him betrayed and crucified between two thieves, as if he had been a notable criminal, and wished his blood on themselves and their children. Despite the miraculous outpouring of the Holy Spirit, and the many miracles that resulted from this event, most of the Jews everywhere poured contempt on the gospel of Christ, raged at the conversion of the Gentiles, and everywhere stirred up persecution against the Apostles and other Christian preachers, as in Judea, in Pisidia, at Iconium and Lystra, Thessalonica, Berea, Corinth, etc. The Jewish rejection of Christ was wisely ordered of God: it fulfilled the ancient prophecies, and it demonstrated that the report of Jesus' Messiahship was far from being supported with worldly influence; and, by this means, the Jews came to be standing monuments of the truth, amid almost every nation under heaven.

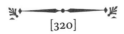

The Jews in the first century

The sceptre had now wholly departed from Judah. About 27 years before Christ's death, Judea was reduced to a province. Nor does it appear that afterwards they had any power of life and death lodged in their hands, for the murder of Stephen appears to have been effected by an outraged mob. At least, it is plain that, after the conversion of Cornelius the Gentile to Jesus, they had not the least vestige of civil power, but were entirely subject to the Romans. After our Saviour's Ascension, their misery gradually increased. Some false prophets, such as Judas and Theudas, had already risen; now their number was greatly multiplied. Simon Magus, Dositheus the Samaritan, and the Egyptian who led 4000 men into the wilderness, were of this sort. Under Felix's government, pretended messiahs were so numerous that sometimes one of them was arrested every day. Caligula would have vented his rage on the Jews for refusing to worship his statue if Herod had not soothed him, or death prevented him. At Caesarea, 20,000 Jews were killed by the Syrians in their mutual broils, and the rest were expelled from the city. In revenge, the Jews murdered a vast number of Syrians in Syria and Canaan, and were, in no small numbers, murdered in return. At Damascus, 10,000 unarmed Jews were killed, and, at Bethshan, the heathen inhabitants caused their Jewish neighbours to assist them against their brothers, and then murdered 13,000 of these erstwhile assistants. At Alexandria, the Jews murdered many of the heathen, and were murdered in their turn, to about 50,000. The Jews of Perea warred with their heathen neighbours of Philadelphia over territorial boundaries.

Both Jews and Galileans made war on the Samaritans who had murdered some Galileans on their way to a solemn feast at Jerusalem. War, too, often raged in the Empire between the different pretenders to the throne. Various earthquakes occurred in Italy, Asia Minor, Canaan, and the Mediterranean islands. A terrible famine oppressed the whole Roman Empire. The gospel was preached in most parts of the Roman Empire, and various persecutions were raised by the Jews, and by Nero, against true believers. Various strange tokens took place. A star, shaped like a sword, hung over Jerusalem for a whole year. At the 9th hour of the night, during the feast of Tabernacles, a light as bright as noon shone for half an hour on the Temple and places adjacent. About the same time, a cow, led in to be sacrificed (it is said), brought forth a lamb in the Court of the Temple. The eastern gate of the Temple, completely of solid brass, and which 20 men could scarcely shut, though fastened with strong bolts, opened of its own accord, and could only be shut again with great difficulty. Before sunset, armies were seen in the air, as if fighting and besieging cities. During the night at Pentecost, the priests in the Temple heard a noise, and a voice, as of a multitude, crying: "Let us go hence." For about seven and a half years, beginning four years before the war broke out, a country fellow called Jesus, especially at their solemn feasts, ran up and down the streets of Jerusalem crying in a woeful manner, "A voice from the four winds: Woe to Jerusalem, woe to the city, and to the people, and to the temple!" and, at last, as he added, "Woe to myself!" he was struck dead by a stone from a sling. Not even the utmost scourging or torture could restrain him from his crying out.

About AD 67, Cestius Gallus, the Roman governor of Syria, laid siege to Jerusalem; but most unaccountably raised it, and was pursued at the heels by some of the Jewish rebels. The Christians, just as Jesus had warned, took this opportunity to leave the city, and the country west of the of Jordan, and retired to Pella, a place on the east of Jordan. Soon after, the Romans under Vespasian, whom God had marvellously advanced to the Empire, invaded the country from the northeast, and furiously besieged and took the cities of Galilee, Chorazin, Bethsaida, Capernaum, etc, where Christ had been especially rejected, and sometimes murdered almost all the inhabitants. Everywhere, the Jews resisted even unto madness, and sometimes killed themselves rather than yield even to the most compassionate generals of Rome. While the Romans destroyed them in large numbers, the zealots of the Jewish nation, with enraged madness, fought against one another. At Jerusalem, the scene was most wretched of all. At the Passover, when there could be two or three million people in the city, the Romans surrounded it with troops, trenches, and walls, that none might escape. The three different factions within murdered one another, and sometimes united to make a desperate, but unsuccessful, sally on the Romans. They even murdered the inhabitants in sport, testing out the sharpness of their swords. At last, Eleazar's party was treacherously massacred by their brothers. Titus, one of the most merciful generals that ever breathed, did all in his power to persuade them to surrender to their advantage, but, mad on their own ruin, they scorned every proposal. The multitudes of unburied carcasses corrupted the air and produced a pestilence. The famine hastened on their destruction of one another. Magazines failed, people fed on one another, and even ladies boiled their suckling infants and ate them. After a siege of six months, the city was taken. Provoked by their obstinacy, the Romans murdered almost every Jew they met with. Titus was bent on saving the Temple, but a false prophet, having persuaded 6000 Jews to take shelter in it, all of whom were burnt or murdered there, a Roman soldier set it on fire with a brand he threw in; nor could all the authority of Titus make his troops, who highly regarded him, attempt to extinguish the flames. The outcries of the Jews, when they saw it on fire, were almost infernal. The whole city, except three towers and a small part of the wall, was razed to the ground. Turnus Rufus, a Roman commander, ploughed up the foundations of the Temple, and other places in the city, and the soldiers dug up the rubbish in quest of money or like precious things, and, it seems, ripped up some Jews to procure the gold they had swallowed. Titus wept as he beheld the ruins, and bitterly cursed the obstinate wretches that had forced him to destroy it. Soon after, the forts of Herodian and Macheron were taken, and the garrison at Masada killed themselves rather than surrender. In Jerusalem alone, we hear of 1,100,000 that perished by the sword, famine, and pestilence. Titus too, crucified some of them before the walls, all around the city, till he had no more wood to erect crosses. In other places, we hear of 250,000 that were cut off. About 97,000 were taken prisoner, many of whom were sent to Egypt by ship to labour as slaves. Some were sent to Syria to be exposed in shows, or devoured by wild beasts, or sold as slaves. All the family of David that could be found were cut off, and that of Herod was extinguished not long after. Every Jew in the Empire was required to pay the yearly half-shekel of soul-ransom money, which they usually paid to their Temple, for the maintenance of the idolatrous capitol at Rome.

2nd – 5th centuries

Great numbers of Jews still remained in almost every part of the Roman Empire. About 50 years later, they brought extra ruin on their own heads. In Styrene, Egypt, Cyprus, and Mesopotamia, they murdered about 500,000 of the Roman subjects, heathen and Christian. With terrible bloodshed, and with no small difficulty, the conquering

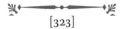

Trajan in about AD 119 reduced them. About AD 130, the Emperor Elia Adrian sent a colony of Romans to rebuild Jerusalem, and called it Elia after himself, and prohibited the Jews from circumcising their children. Barcocaba, one of those thievish banditti that had infested Canaan for about a hundred years, pretending that he was the Messiah, raised a Jewish army of 200,000, and murdered all the heathen and Christians that came in their way. About AD 134, Adrian's forces defeated him in battle, and, after a siege of three years, took Bitter his capital; after which 50 of his fortifications quickly surrendered. In this terrible war, it is said that about 600,000 Jews were slain by the sword, besides those who perished by famine and pestilence. It is said that the rivers were highly swollen with blood, and the sea, into which they ran, was marked for several miles with it. In this war, they had about 50 strong castles taken, and 985 of their best towns demolished. For some time, the Emperor caused annual fairs to be held for the sale of captive Jews, and transported those who once lived in Canaan to Egypt, and everywhere loaded with taxes those who followed the Jewish religion. Adrian built a city on Mount Calvary, and erected a marble statue of a swine over the gate that led to Bethlehem. No Jew was allowed to enter the city, or to look at it at a distance, under pain of death. Constantine further enlarged this city. His troops repressed the Jews' attempt to seize it. Many of them had their ears cut off; and, being marked in their bodies as rebels, they were dispersed throughout the Empire as vagabond slaves. About AD 360, the Jews, encouraged by Julian, Constantine's nephew, and now Emperor, bent on giving Jesus the lie, began to rebuild their city and Temple. They had scarcely begun to lay one stone on another in building the Temple, when a terrible earthquake, and flames of fire issuing from the earth, killed the workmen, and scattered their materials. Soon after, when Julian was dying, the Edict of Adrian was revived against them, and Roman guards prohibited their approach to the city. Not till the 7th century dared they so much as creep over the rubbish to bewail it without bribing the Roman guards.

However basely the Jews comply with the delusions of the countries where they are scattered, they have been exposed to the most outrageous abuse. At the end of the second century, Niger the usurper persecuted them because of their adherence to Severus the Emperor; and, for a while, Severus harassed them on the basis of Adrian's Edict. In the third century, Sapor, King of Persia, furiously harassed and murdered them; and much about the same time, Manes, one of them, founded the sect of the Manichees, who believed that there were two Gods, a good one and a bad one. Dioclesian intended to persecute them; but, by huge sums of money, they appeased his fury. In the 4th century, the council of Elvira in Spain prohibited Christians from eating with them. Constantine the Great prohibited them from retaining any Christians as slaves, and obliged them to undergo their share in public service, such as the military, etc. It is even said that he forced multitudes of them to eat swine's flesh or be murdered. Offended with their insult of the Christians in Egypt, and their insurrection in Palestine, Constans, his son, terribly chastened them, revived every harsh edict against them, and condemned to death any that had Christians either as wives or servants.

Encouraged by the Emperor Theodosius' prohibition on pulling down their synagogues, they became very insolent about the beginning of the 5th century. They crucified the image of Haman, and sometimes a Christian, in derision of our Saviour. In Egypt, they insulted the Christians on the Lord's Day. Provoked by this, the Christians in Macedonia, Dacia, Chalcis, Syria, and Egypt fell on them, and killed prodigious numbers of them, especially in Alexandria. In the island of Minorca, vast numbers of them were forced to turn Christian, or hide themselves in dens or caves. About AD 432, one Moses of Crete, pretending that he, as their Messiah, would lead them safely through the sea to Canaan, a vast number threw themselves into the deep from a precipice and were drowned. Just after, many of them, for the sake of the gifts given to new converts, were baptized at Constantinople.

6th – 7th centuries

In the 6th century, Cavades, and the two Chosroes kings, terribly harassed them; but the latter Chosroes were afterwards reconciled to them, and gratified their malice with the murder of about 90,000 Christians at the taking of Jerusalem in AD 614. About 530, the Emperor Justinian prohibited them from making wills, or appearing as witnesses against Christians, and prohibited those in Africa from exercising their religion. Soon after, one Julian of Canaan set himself up as Messiah. He and his followers did infinite mischief to the Christians; but, in the end, 20,000 of them were slain, and as many taken and sold as slaves. Just after that, numbers of Jews were executed for instigating a revolt at Caesarea. And, to revenge their assistance of the Goths at the siege of Naples, the Greek general Belisarius and his troops killed as many of them as they could find, men or women. In AD 602, they were severely punished for their horrible massacre of the Christians at Antioch. Soon after, Heraclius the Emperor banished them from Jerusalem. Multitudes in Spain and France were forced to become Christians; and the Councils of Toledo encouraged their sovereigns to oblige them to do so. About AD 700, when Erica, King of Spain, complained that the Jews of Spain had conspired with those of Africa against him, the Council of Toledo ordered that they should all be enslaved, and their children taken away from them and educated in the Christian religion. In France, a variety of edicts were made against them; Chimeric, Dagobert, and other kings, ordered that those who refused baptism should be banished. In this century, too, numbers of them in the east imagined Mahomet was the Messiah, and one of them assisted him in compiling his Koran.

8th - 9th centuries

In these centuries, the misery of the Jews continued. In the east, Caliph Zayd permitted his subjects to abuse them. About AD 760, Jaafar the Imam ordered that those that embraced Mahomedism should alone be their parents' heirs. About 841, Caliph Wathek persecuted them because some of their number had embezzled his revenues; and he fined those who refused to embrace Mahomedism. Motawakhel his successor deprived them of all honour and trust; and, marking them with infamy, caused them to wear leather belts, and ride without stirrups on asses and mules. Such marks of contemptuous distinction are still to be seen in the east, and have been imitated by other princes. Many of his successors persecuted them in a way still more severe. While the Emperor Leo Isaurus, the image-opposer, heartily hated them, the promoters of image-worship obliged the Jews to comply, and to curse themselves with the curse of Gehazi if they did not do so from the heart. In France and Spain, the people badly insulted them. Probably provoked at this, they invited the Normans into France, and betrayed Bourdeaux and other places into their hands. About AD 724, one Serenus of Spain set himself up as the Messiah. Multitudes followed him, and went so far as to take possession of Canaan. The

Christians seized what they left in their absence. About 831, another in the east pretended to be Moses risen from the dead, and raised a great number of followers.

The Middle Ages

In the 10-12th centuries, their miseries increased even further, partly through their own divisions, and partly by the persecutions they underwent. About AD 1037, we find about 900,000 of them living near Babylon, if we may believe their own notable traveller; and yet, about two years later, all their academies there, if not also their schools, were ruined. About AD 1020, Hakem, the founder of the Drusian religion, for a while persecuted them in Egypt. Besides the common miseries they sustained in the east by the Turkish and sacred war, it is shocking to think how many of them, in the eight Crusades, and in this or the two following centuries, were murdered in Germany, Hungary, Asia Minor. Wherever they could find them, as they marched to recover Canaan from the Mahometans, a great number of Jewish parents murdered their own children that these Crusaders might not get them baptised. The bloody contention between the Moors and Spaniards might have procured them some peace in Spain had not their own mutual broils (arguments) made them miserable. In France, many of them were burnt, others were banished, and others had their goods confiscated by order of King Philip; and those who offered to sell their effects and remove could get no one to buy them. About AD 1020, they were banished from England, but afterwards they returned, and had some respite. However, for their attending the coronation of King Richard I, the mob fell on, and murdered, a great many of them. This popular fury was prohibited by law, but it still raged during 1189-1190, in London and elsewhere. Richard had scarcely gone off to his sacred war, when the populace rose and murdered many of them, intending not to leave one alive in the country. About AD 1100, some of them got into the city of York, and thought to defend themselves there. A furious siege obliged them to offer to ransom their lives with money. This being refused, they first killed their wives and children, and then, retiring to the palace, burnt it over themselves. Between 1137 and 1200, there appeared nine or ten pretended Messiahs: two in France, and two in the northwest of Africa. There was one, David of Moravia, who pretended he could make himself invisible at pleasure, and one near

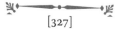

the Euphrates, who had been cured of leprosy, then El David, and two others in Persia. Most of these did a great deal of mischief to those of their nation in the places where they lived.

Nor in the 13th and 14th centuries was their condition one bit better. In Egypt, Canaan, and Syria, the Crusaders still harassed and murdered them, till they were expelled from these places. The rise of the Mamlukes turned to their misery in Egypt. Provoked by their mad running after pretended Messiahs, Caliph Nasser scarcely left any of them alive in his dominions of Mesopotamia, etc. In Persia, the Tartars murdered any they found. In Spain, Ferdinand persecuted them furiously. About 1260, the populace of Aragon badly harassed them. Henry III of Castile, and his son John, persecuted them; and, in the reign of the latter, prodigious numbers were murdered. About 1349, a terrible massacre at Toledo forced many of them to kill themselves or change their religion. After such barbaric murders, in AD 1253, they were banished from France. In 1275, they were recalled; but, in 1300, King Philip banished them, that he might enrich himself with their wealth. In 1312, they obtained re-admission for a great sum of money; but, in 1320 and 1330, the Crusades of the fanatic shepherds, who wasted the south of France, terribly massacred them wherever they could find them; and, besides, 15,000 were murdered on another occasion. In 1358, they were finally banished from France; since which, few of them entered that country. After oft-repeated harassments from both kings and people, and six former banishments founded on causes mostly pretended, King Edward, in 1291, expelled them from England, to the number of 160,000. He permitted them to carry their effects and money over to France with them, where, in his own dominions, he confiscated everything to his own use, so that most of them died in need. Despite dissimulation and false swearing, we read little else concerning those in Germany but of repeated murders and insurrections, and of terrible acts of revenge by the Christians. In Italy, they had most respite; yet they underwent some persecution at Naples. Pope John XXII, pretending that they had affronted the holy cross, ordered their banishment from his territories; but recalled his Edict for the sake of 100,000 florins. In this period, two false Messiahs appeared in Spain: one Zechariah about 1258, and one called Moses, in 1290.

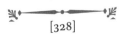

In the 15th - 17th centuries, their misery continued. In Turkey, we know of no persecution that they suffered, but what the common tyranny of the government, and their own frauds, brought on their heads. Only in Egypt did the population molest them. Nor would the people of Athens and Salome in Greece allow them to settle among them. In Persia, they were terribly treated, especially by the two Shah Abbas. From 1663 to 1666, the murder of them was so universal, that only a few escaped to Turkey.

In Portugal and Spain, they were miserably handled. About AD 1420, Vincent half converted 200,000 of them to Popery. The infernal Inquisition was appointed to make their conversion sincere and complete. About 1492, six or eight hundred thousand Jews were banished from Spain. Partly by drowning in their passage to Africa, and partly by harsh treatment, most of them were cut off, and many of their bodies lay in the fields till the wild beasts devoured them. The African Mahometans shut their gates against the poor remainder, and many were obliged to sell their children to the Moors as slaves to obtain food for the support of their lives. In Spain and Portugal, thousands of Jews became Papists in appearance, and even monks and bishops, and yet continued heartily in their own religion, and educated their children in it. If we depend on Orobio's account, we may suppose there are 16,000 or 20,000 such, even at present. About 1412, 16,000 Jews were forced to profess Popery at Naples. About 1472, they were barbarously massacred in the dominions of Venice. Nowhere in Popish countries are they better used than in the Pope's own territory, for which, no doubt, their purse must be emptied. In Germany, they experienced plenty of hardship. In Saxony and elsewhere, they were loaded with taxes. They were banished from Bohemia, Bavaria, Cologne, Nuremberg, Augsburg, and Vienna. They were terribly massacred in Moravia, and plundered in Bonn and Bamberg. Between 1520 and 1560, three false Messiahs appeared in Europe: two of whom Charles V, Emperor of Germany, burnt to death, and the other was imprisoned for life. About 1666, Zabbathai Tzevi, a pretended Messiah, made a great noise in Syria, Palestine, and the countries about; but, at last, to save his life, he turned Mahometan at Constantinople. About 1682, Mordecai, a Jew of Germany, professed himself the Messiah, and would have been punished in Italy, had he not escaped to Poland.

The Reformation

Thus they continued, scattered, despised, persecuted, and enslaved, among almost all nations, not mixing with any in the common way, but remaining as a body, keeping to themselves. While they are standing-witnesses to the dreadful guilt of Christ's death, and the truth of his divine predictions, they continue obstinate rejecters of Jesus; and, contrary to all means, harsh or otherwise, they improve their ancient ceremonies and covenant relation to God as a means of hardening themselves in their unbelief. About AD 1650, 300 rabbis, and a multitude of other Jews, assembled in the plain of Ageda in Hungary, and had a serious dispute whether the Messiah had come, and whether Jesus of Nazareth was the one? Many seemed in a fair way to believe this truth, but the Popish doctors present, by their mad extolling of papal power, and the worship of the Virgin Mary and other saints, prevented it, and strengthened prejudice of the Jews against the Christian faith. At present (the late 1700's), their number is computed to be three million: one million residing in the Turkish Empire, 300,000 in Persia, China, India on the east and west of the Ganges, or Tartary, and 1,700,000 in the rest of Europe and Africa, and in America. Except in Portugal and Spain, their present condition is generally tolerable. In Holland, Poland, and at Frankfurt and Hamburg, they have plenty of liberty. They often, but in vain, attempted to obtain naturalisation in England, or other nations among whom they are scattered.

The conversion of the Jews

We suppose the offspring of Judah, together with the remains of the ten tribes, will, by the power of God, and to the great joy and advantage of the Gentiles, be converted to the Christian faith. It seems that they will assist the opposers of antichrist at Armageddon, and greatly rejoice in his ruin. At their settlement in Canaan, their country will be crowded with followers. The Turks, and their allies, will try to dispossess them, but will perish in their attempt. Thenceforward, the twelve Hebrew tribes will, in the greatest harmony, peace, piety, and order, reside in their country till the end of the millennium. (Dan. 12; Deut. 32:36-43; Hosea 3:5; Isa. 60, 65:17-25, 49:11-26, 11:6-16, ch. 12; Ps. 149; Ezek. 36-48; Zech. 14; Rom. 11; Rev. 19)

Some Hebrews that received the gospel in the apostolic age retained a strange affection for their Mosaic ceremonies. To cure them of this,

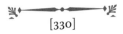

Paul wrote them an excellent Epistle (to the Hebrews), where he shows the dignity of Jesus Christ above angels, and above Moses and Aaron, explaining many of the leading types, and, from their imperfection, clearly concludes the necessity of their abolition. To these, he adds a number of exhortations relating to the Christian duties: of boldly approaching God through Christ, a careful attendance on gospel ordinances, patience under trouble, perseverance in holiness, a vigorous exercise of faith in every circumstance (whose power he illustrates in many instances), and points to activity, zeal, and reverence in holy living, and also to hospitality, contentment, submission to Christian teachers, and almsgiving, etc. The Latin churches of late have had access to study this Epistle more than those of the Greeks, and have embraced it as canonical. But none, except the Arians, who hated it for its clear proof of the divinity of Christ, ever denied its divine inspiration. The similarity of a variety of phrases to those in Paul's other Epistles, the similar order of doctrine and duty, the mention of the author's bonds in Italy, and of Timothy as his companion, all point to him. Peter assures us that Paul wrote a letter to the Hebrews in which some things, relative to the destruction of their nation, and hard to understand (2 Pet. 3:15-16), were inserted, in which be probably had in view Hebrews 10:25-31. Peter directed two epistles to these Hebrews, and James, John and Jude, wrote one each.

Israel and the New Israel

In all these things, were not the Hebrews emblems of the chosen people, the true Israel of God, the chosen children of Jesus Christ? By what miracles of grace are they brought from their spiritual bondage, protected by, and washed in, his blood and by his Spirit, and then, to the harm of their enemies and the joy of their souls, consecrated to the service of God! How solemnly, and often with terror, they receive the Law from his mouth! But how frequent their sins, their idolising of creatures, and their murmuring against the provision and lot assigned them by God! How fearfully were they chastised for their sin! After ravishing enjoyments, as if on the frontiers of heaven, how often are they turned back almost to the terrors of the broken Law, and their Egyptian slavery! How often the earth swallows up their cares! The fiery judgements of God, and the poison of the old serpent, prey upon them, and their troublesome ways make their life a burden! How often their worldly relatives harass, tempt, and seek to destroy them! But, nevertheless, how constant and oft-repeated are God's favours to them! Jesus is their food indeed, and their drink indeed. (John 6:55) Jesus, their director and protector, never leaves them or forsakes them. (Heb. 13:5) Nor do the unwasting robes of his righteousness and grace fail them.

At last, when the mixed multitude and rebels of indwelling corruptions are purged from among them, they often, amid fearful struggles with Satan and their own lusts, pass safely through the swelling Jordan of death, are made faultless before God (Jude v. 24), and take possession of the kingdom prepared for them from the foundation of the world. (Matt. 25:34) Indeed, with what terrible tossing of mind, what impression of the fiery Law, and through what horrible provocations on their side, and wonders of mercy on God's side, and often through a number of gracious-like attainments afterwards lost, are they brought into their New Covenant state! Was not this fate of the Hebrews typical of that of the New Testament Church? His New Covenant Church was brought out of Egypt by miracles and wonders in the apostolic age, through a howling waste desert of persecution from dragons and fiery serpents. Through what a multitude of sins, troubles, and mercies did she arrive on the border of rest under Constantine the Great, about AD 312! Under contempt of her spiritual ordinances and privileges, how driven back and plagued she is under antichrist's reign! How consumed by fiery troubles and persecutions, and mortally bitten by heretics: the Arians, Pelagians, and others! At the Reformation, she again retouched the borders of promised happiness, and God opened anew for her wells of living water in the preaching of the gospel, but now she compasses the land of Edom, where our souls are much discouraged on the way. Nor do I expect our entrance into the millennial state till the mixed multitude of worldly and unspiritual professors is purged from among us.

The true Israel

The saints are called the Israel of God, *Israelites indeed* (John 1:47), and *Jews inwardly*. (Gal 3:7) They, like the ancient Hebrews, are God's chosen and special people, whom he wonderfully preserves and provides for. They have his Law written in their hearts, they love him with their soul, and they serve him under the inward influences of his grace. (John 1:47; Rom. 2:29; Gal 4:16)

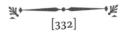

HEMAN
(1) Heman, Zimri, Ethan, Calcol, and Darda or Dara, were the sons of Zerah, the son of Judah, and were the sons of Mahol. Perhaps one was their grandfather, and the other their father. Or Zerah and Mahol may be different names for the same person. They were famous for their wisdom. (1 Chron. 2:6; 1 Kings 4:31)

(2) Heman the son of Joel, and grandson of Shemuel, and a chief singer in the reign of King David. He had 14 sons: Bukkiah, Mattaniah, Uzziel, Shebuel or Shubael, Jerimoth, Hananiah, Hanani, Eliathah, Giddalti, Romantiezer, Joshbekashah, Malothi, Hothir, and Mahazioth. Their families constituted 14 classes of the sacred musicians. (1 Chron. 6:33; 15:17, 19, 25:1-6) Which of these two Hemans (or, if any of them) was the composer of the 88th Psalm, we do not know.

HEPHZIBAH, *my delight is in her*
The name of Hezekiah's queen: and is a title given to the Church meaning that the Lord delights in her. (Only found in 2 Kings 21:1 and Isa. 62:4)

THE HERODS
(1) HEROD THE GREAT
The son of Antipater and Cypros, and brother of Phasael, Joseph and Pheroras, and a sister called Salome. His father was, some say, to have been a Jew, by others, an Idumean turned Jew. Others think he was a heathen, guardian of Apollo's temple at Askelon, taken prisoner by Idumean scouts, and afterwards became a Jewish proselyte. Herod was born about 70 years before our Saviour. When he was 15, or perhaps 25 years, of age, and with his father's and Hyrcanus the High Priest's consent, he was given the government of Galilee. With great prudence and valour, he cleared the country of the thieving bandits who swarmed in it, and arrested Hezekiah their leader. In this, he gained the esteem of Sextus, Governor of Syria. But the Jews, jealous of Antipater's authority and his sons, instigated Hyrcanus the High Priest to cite Herod to appear before their Sanhedrin to answer for his conduct. Herod came, accompanied by his chosen troops. His judges were so terrified, that none of them dare speak, except Sameas who laid the blame for Herod's misconduct on Hyrcanus, and the judges for permitting him to assume too much power. Hyrcanus, however,

observing that the judges, though afraid to speak, were disposed to condemn him, deferred bringing the matter to sentence that day, and advised Herod to make good his escape in the night. He retired to Sextus, Governor of Syria, and was entrusted by him with the government of Hollow Syria. To revenge his late affront, he marched an army to besiege Jerusalem; but his father and brother Phasael prevented him. In BC 41, when Mark Anthony was at Daphne, near Antioch in Syria, a hundred principal Jews brought accusations against Herod and his brother Phasael; but Hyrcanus, the High Priest, who had promised Herod Mariamne his grandchild in marriage, being asked his mind, presented the two brothers as better qualified to govern the Jewish state than their opposers. Hereupon, Anthony made Herod and his brother tetrarchs, and would have killed 15 of their principal adversaries, had not Herod petitioned for their life.

Not long after, Antigonus, the son of Aristobulus, invited the Parthians to come to his assistance, and obliged Herod to flee the country. He had not been long in Rome, when Anthony and Augustus got the Senate to declare him King of Judea, and Antigonus an enemy to the Romans. Returning to Judea, and assisted by Sosius the Roman deputy in Syria, after about three years of war, he took Jerusalem, and acted as king. He was disqualified to hold the double office of High Priest and King, as the Maccabees had for some ages past. He therefore made Ananel priest, but quickly turned him out to make way for Aristobulus, the brother of his wife Mariamne, to whom the high priesthood more rightly belonged. But the Jews, loving him too well, Herod, about a year later, caused him to be drowned in a bath. After the ruin of Anthony, Herod was obliged to implore the clemency of Augustus. He met the Emperor at Rhodes, and frankly told him that he had done all that he could for Anthony his benefactor, and was now ready to do the same for him if he allowed him his favour, and allowed him to keep his kingdom. Charmed with his open frankness, Augustus granted him his desire. His kingdom was now pretty quiet, but he was plagued with family disorders. He passionately loved Mariamne, but she, disgusted with the murder of her brother, heartily hated him. His mother and sister persuaded him, in his fury, to murder Mariamne. He had scarcely done it, when he was almost killed with grief. Recovering, he ordered Mariamne's mother to be killed, as she had too easily credited the report spread about his death.

To divert his tormented mind, he applied himself to building, and to instituting public sports. To ingratiate himself with the Jews, he rebuilt their Temple, and rendered it very stately and glorious. He sent his two sons by Mariamne, Aristobulus and Alexander, to be educated at Rome. Soon after their return, he married them off: Aristobulus to Bernice, the daughter of Salome his sister, and Alexander to Glaphyra, the daughter of Archelaus, King of Cappadocia. Herod's preference of Antipater, whose mother was but of mean birth, exasperated both his sons against him. By means of Augustus, and afterwards of Archelaus of Cappadocia, a reconciliation was twice effected between him and them; but Salome and Antipater never rested till they got him to murder them. Having got rid of his brothers, Antipater next resolved to rid himself of his father. To hide his hand in the conspiracy, he retired to Rome; but, the plot being discovered, he was imprisoned upon his return, and Augustus informed of his treachery.

Herod was in a languishing way when the wisemen informed him that the Messiah was born. He was exceedingly troubled, and the principal Jews, afraid of new wars, were troubled along with him. Finding out the place of his birth, he decided to murder him while only an infant, and, under pretence of a desire to worship him, asked the wisemen to bring him back word where and how he might know him. An angel ordered the wisemen to go home without returning to Herod. Provoked by this disappointment, he ordered his soldiers to murder every child under two years old in Bethlehem, or near it, that he might make sure of killing the Messiah among them. Some young men, hearing a rumour that Herod was dead, pulled down the golden eagle that he, in honour of the Romans, had erected over the principal portal of the temple. For this, he ordered 40 to be burnt alive. His ailment still increased; his hunger was insatiable, his bowels were ulcerated, his legs swelled, his private parts rotted and bred worms. His whole body was covered with an intolerable itch. To prevent the Jews rejoicing at his death, he convened all the great men of the kingdom and shut them up in the circus at Jericho (where he then was), and, with tears, constrained his sister Salome, and Alexas, to see them put to death the moment he expired. They no doubt promised, but did not execute this horrible act. In his agony, Herod attempted to plunge a knife into his own belly, but Achiab, his cousin, prevented him. The outcry on this occasion made the family believe he was dead. In his prison, Antipater heard

of it, and begged his keepers to allow him to escape. They informed his father, who ordered him to be killed immediately, about BC 2. Five days later Herod died, having lived about 70 years, and reigned for about 37 of them. He had eight or ten wives and 15 children. He left his kingdom to Archelaus, the worst; Gaulonitis got Trachonitis and Batanea, Philip got Galilee, and Herod Antipas Perea. (Matt. 2:1, 3, 7, 12-13, 15-16; Luke 3:1)

(2) HEROD ANTIPAS was promised the kingdom of Judea in his father's first will, but he altered it, and gave him only the tetrarchy of Galilee and Perea. In this, Augustus the Roman Emperor confirmed him. With great care and labour, he adorned and fortified the principal places of his dominions. He drew on himself an unfortunate war with the Arabs by divorcing the daughter of Aretas their king, that be might have Herodias, the wife of Philip his brother, who was still alive. For this incestuous marriage, John the Baptist reproved him. On that account, he imprisoned the Baptist, and would have killed him had he not feared an insurrection of the people in his favour. One day, as Herod and his lords were celebrating the festival of his birth, Salome, the daughter of Herodias, so pleased Herod in her dancing with her pretty airs, that he swore he would give her anything she asked. Instructed by her spiteful mother, she asked for the head of John the Baptist. To show regard to his oath, and to the lords that feasted with him, Herod, with great reluctance, ordered John to be beheaded in the prison, and his head delivered to Salome on a charger.

When Pilate sent our Saviour to Herod, the king ridiculed him, dressed him up in mock regalia, and returned him to Pilate. About AD 39, Herodias, growing jealous of her brother Agrippa, who was now deputy king of Judea, incited her husband to solicit that dignity at Rome. Informed of this, Herod Agrippa accused Herod of Galilee to the Emperor as an accomplice in Sedans' conspiracy against Tiberius, and of correspondence with the Parthians; and, as evidence, he alleged that Herod had in his arsenal arms for 70,000 men. Herod could not deny that he had the arms, and so was instantly banished to Lyons in France, where he and Herodias died miserably in exile. It is said that the pretty dancer, Salome, falling through the ice, sliced her head off. (Matt. 14:1, 3, 6; Mark 6:14, 16-18, 20-22; Luke 3:4)

(3) HEROD AGRIPPA was the son of Aristobulus, grandson of Herod the Great, and brother of Herodias. His grandfather sent him

early to Rome to pay court to Tiberius. Herod quickly won the affection of the famous Drusus, at whose death he was obliged to leave Rome quite plunged in debt. When he returned, Tiberius ordered him to pay his debts and be gone. Antonia the Empress lent him the money to clear his creditors; and, after that, be recovered the favour of Tiberius. Soon after, Tiberius, hearing that Herod wished him dead, and that Caligula might reign in his place, threw him into jail. When Caligula came to be Emperor, he freed Herod, gave him a chain of gold and a royal diadem, and appointed him King of Batanea and Trachonitis, and afterwards of Abilene. When Caligula attempted to erect his own statue for adoration in the Jewish Temple, and the Jews refused, Herod was in great danger between the two; but, in a long letter, he prevailed on the Emperor to desist. Herod, being at Rome when Claudius was made Emperor by the army, contributed not a little to establish his dignity. To reward his services, Claudius made him deputy-king of all Judea and Chalcis. Returning home, he governed his dominions much to the satisfaction of his people. About AD 44, or perhaps 49, he caused the murder of James, the son of Zebedee. Observing the Jews were pleased with this, he apprehended Peter, intending to murder him also for their further gratification; but providence defeated him. After the Passover Feast, he retired to Caesarea to celebrate some games in honour of Claudius. There, the inhabitants of Tyre and Sidon, who had offended him, after making Blastus his chamberlain their friend, sent their deputies to beg his favour. As he gave audience to the deputies, he appeared dressed in a robe tissued with silver, to which the rising sun, shining on it, gave a marvellous brilliance. As he spoke to the Phoenician deputies, some of his parasites cried out, "It is the voice of a god, not of a man!" He received this blasphemous flattery with pleasure. To punish him, an angel smote him directly with a most tormenting disease in his bowels, and he was eaten up by vermin after he had reigned seven or ten years, and had fathered Agrippa, Berenice, Drusilla, and Mariamne. (Acts 12:1, 6, 11, 19-21)

HETH

The second son of Canaan. (Gen. 10:15) His offspring were called the Hittites. They dwelt in the southern part of the Promised Land, near Hebron. From Ephron, who was one of them, Abraham bought his cave of Machpelah. (Gen. 23:10) In the days of Joshua, it seems that

part of them fled south and dwelt in the country where the Canaanites of Bethel built Luz. (Judg. 1:26) Two of David's mighties were Hittites, namely, Uriah and Abimelech. (1 Sam. 26:6; 2 Sam. 11:3, 6, 17, 21, 24) Those of the Hittites that remained, Solomon put under tribute; but he later married some of their idolatrous women. (1 Kings 11:1; 2 Chron. 8:7) It seems that about BC 894, the Hittites, either in Arabia or Canaan, had kings of their own. (2 Kings 7:6)

HERETIC(K)

Someone who holds to a fundamental error. He is to be rejected, and cast out of the Church if he remains obstinate after a first and second admonition; and he is self-condemned, as he publishes what is plainly wicked and contrary to his own profession. (Only found in Titus 3:10) Heretics are the false prophets and teachers that Christ and his Apostles foretold would come. They will forsake the faith themselves, and seduce others into error. (Matt. 15:24; 2 Pet. 1:1, 3:5)

HERODIANS. See Sect

Only found in Matthew 22:16 and Mark 3:6, 12:13.

HEZEKIAH. See Sennacherib

He was born when his father Ahaz was only about 11 years of age, and so was 25 at his father's death in the 36th year of his age. He succeeded him in BC 726. His idolatrous father, having left the nation plunged into a kind of heathenism, Hezekiah, with great vigour, applied himself to reform it. In the first month of the first year of his reign, he caused the main doors of the Temple to be opened and repaired. He ordered the priests and Levites to purify it and prepare it for sacrifice. This done, he and his princes solemnised the dedication with a succession of offerings. As the Temple could not be purified to observe the Passover in the first month, or the priesthood cleansed, they agreed to observe it in the second month. Hezekiah invited those of the ten tribes that remained in their country to join with him there. Some ridiculed his pious invitation, but others complied with it. This Passover was observed with more solemnity than usual for many ages before. They continued the feast of unleavened bread for 14 days instead of seven. Many indeed were not properly prepared, but Hezekiah prayed for forgiveness for their rashness in approaching God. Now, and

afterwards, Hezekiah and his people broke down the idolatrous altars and images in his own dominions, and in those of Hoshea, who, being better than his predecessors, took no offence at his subjects returning to the Lord. Hezekiah also established proper methods for procuring the priests and Levites, and their proper maintenance. Cononiah and Shimei, two brothers, with ten subordinate officers of the tribe of Levi, and Korah, with six under him, were appointed to oversee this affair.

Encouraging himself in the Lord, Hezekiah shook off the Assyrian yoke, which his father had wickedly taken upon himself, and refused to pay them the accustomed tribute. He invaded the country of the Philistines, who had lately ravaged Judea, and reduced them under his yoke. He fortified Jerusalem, and filled his magazines with armour. In the 14th year of his reign, Sennacherib, king of Assyria, invaded his kingdom and took most of his fenced cities. Hezekiah, after fortifying Jerusalem, and bringing the southern stream of the Gihon into the city, and finding that the kings of Ethiopia and Egypt were timid in coming to his assistance, begged conditions of peace from the Assyrians. Sennacherib demanded 300 talents of silver and 30 of gold (in all, about £351,000) as the condition of his leaving the country. To raise this sum, Hezekiah was obliged to exhaust his treasures, and pull off the golden plates that he had just put on the doors of the Temple.

No sooner had Sennacherib received the money, the loss of which he saw disqualified Hezekiah for war, than he sent three of his principal officers from Lachish to demand Hezekiah's immediate surrender of his capital. Hezekiah sent Eliakim, Shebna, and Joah to converse with them outside the city. Rabshakeh, the main Assyrian messenger, praised the power of his master as if neither God nor man could deliver out of his hand. He cried to the Hebrews on the wall that, if they would not surrender themselves, he would quickly force them to live on their own excrement during the terrible siege, and that, if they surrendered themselves quickly, he would place them in a fine country, as agreeable as their own. Shocked by these blasphemies, Hezekiah's messengers gave no reply, but tore their clothes, and reported the whole matter to their master. He begged Isaiah the prophet to intercede with God on behalf of the city, and was assured that the Assyrian army would quickly be ruined, and their king flee home in a hasty manner, and there perish by the sword. When Sennacherib departed from Lachish to give battle to Tirhakah, King of Ethiopia who came to assist Hezekiah, he sent Hezekiah a most blasphemous and insulting letter. This Hezekiah spread before the Lord in the court of the Temple, and begged the Lord to deliver him from this insolent enemy. The Lord, through Isaiah, assured him that he had heard, and would quickly answer his prayer; that Sennacherib would never besiege Jerusalem, nor so much as shoot an arrow at it. That very night, the whole Assyrian army was almost ruined by an angel. While Sennacherib was ravaging the kingdom, Hezekiah fell dangerously ill of an ulcer. God, through the prophet Isaiah, ordered him to make his account with death, and put his affairs in order. Hezekiah, observing that he had no child to be the Messiah's progenitor, or govern the broken state of his kingdom, and perhaps being in no proper frame for dying, wept sorely, and begged that the Lord would not cut him down in the midst of his days, as had often happened with idolatrous kings. God, by Isaiah, assured him that his prayers were heard; that in three days he would be able to walk to the Temple, and would live 15 more years. Meanwhile, he ordered him to apply a lump of dry figs to the boil, in order to assist in his miraculous recovery, and told him that the city would not be delivered into the hand of the Assyrians. For a sign of the certainty of these events, the sun, at Hezekiah's choice, went back ten degrees on the sundial of King Ahaz.

After his recovery, Hezekiah composed a hymn of thanksgiving, and a narrative of his frame of mind during his trouble. He, however, grew proud of the miracles done in his favour, and was not properly thankful to God. When Merodach Baladan, the son of Baladan, King of Babylon, sent messengers to congratulate him on his recovery, and obtain information concerning the ruin of the Assyrian host, and the retrograde motion of the sun, and perhaps to make an alliance against the weakened Assyrian Empire, Hezekiah vainly showed them everything valuable and rare in his treasures. His pride brought upon himself and his subjects wrath from the Lord, who, through Isaiah, assured him that his wealth would be carried to Babylon, and his offspring serve there as eunuchs in the palace. Hezekiah confessed the threats were just, but wished that peace and truth might continue all his time. Some of his servants copied out several of Solomon's proverbs, and joined them with the rest. After he had lived 54 years, and reigned 29 years, he died, and was succeeded by Manasseh, a boy of twelve. (2 Kings 18-20; 2 Chron. 29-32; Prov. 25:1; Isa. 36-39)

HIRAM, or HURAM

(1) A king of Tyre, the son of Abibal. When David came to the Hebrew throne, Hiram sent messengers to congratulate him, and sent him cedars and artificers to build him a palace. (2 Sam. 5:11-12) He, or his son of the same name, congratulated Solomon on his accession to the crown. He furnished him with timber, stone, and artificers for his famous structures, namely, the Temple, his own palace, etc., and lent him 120 talents of gold (or £1,657,000). He assisted him in establishing his trade to Ophir. He was displeased with the 20 cities of Galilee that Solomon gave him. (1 Kings 5:1-2,7-8, 10-12, 9:11-12, 14, 27; 2 Chron. 8:18) Dius and Menander, two secular historians, say that Hiram and Solomon corresponded by letters, and tried to puzzle one another with hard questions.

(2) A famous artificer. His father is called a *Tyrian*, perhaps merely because he dwelt for some time at Tyre, but he might have been from the tribe of Naphtali, for his mother was a widow of Naphtali, and a daughter of Dan, a native of the city of Dan, or descended from the tribe of Dan. He is presented as the *father* of King Hiram and Solomon, either because he was their director in their skilful works, or perhaps his surname was *Abi* or *Ab*, which means *father*. He was a most skilful artificer in designing and executing the most skilful workmanship of brass, copper, or other metals. He made the brazen pillars, the sea, the lavers, and the basins, etc., of the Temple. (1 Kings 7:13, 40, 45; 2 Chron. 2:3, 11-13)

HOBAB

The son of Jethro, and brother-in-law of Moses. As the Hebrews were about to leave Mount Sinai, Hobab came to visit Moses, and, at his entreaty, went along with Israel as a subordinate guide to direct them to find fuel, etc. Some scholars suggest that the Kenites were his descendants. He is mentioned only twice, in Numbers 10:29 and Judges 4:11.

HOPHNI. See Eli

One of Eli's two sons. See 1 Sam. 1:3, 2:34, 4:4, 11, 17.

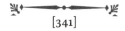

HORI, HORITES or HORIM

Hori was a son of Lotan. (Gen. 36:22). His descendants were probably an ancient people that lived near Mount Seir. At least one of that name was a chief man among them. They were governed of old by dukes: namely, Seir, Lotan, Shobal, Zibeon, Anah, Dishon, Ezer, and Dishan. Chedorlaomer ravaged their country. Some think that they also had eight kings in succession before they were expelled by, or coalesced with, the Edomites. (Gen. 14, 36; 1 Chron. 1) *Horam* often means *nobles.* (1 Kings 21:8, 11) Perhaps the Greek *Heros* (or *hero)* comes from Horim as *Anax* came from the king of Anak.

HOSEA

The son of Beeri, and a prophet of the Lord. In Greek, he is called *Osee.* (Only found once in Rom. 9:25) In the course of his work, he, under the direction of God, either parabolically or literally represented the story of, or rather married, one Gomer, the daughter of Diblaim, who had once been a prostitute, and had become penitent, or rather had an irreproachable character when she got married. (Only found in Hosea 1:1-2) Afterwards, she went back to prostitution, but, in the end, became penitent, and faithful to his bed. Hosea had by her two sons: Jezreel and Lo-ammi, and a daughter called Lo-ruhamah. By these names was signified that God would quickly avenge on Jehu's family the blood he had shed in *Jezreel*, and would cast off the ten tribes from being his *people*, and no more have mercy on them for many generations. After this, he predicted that they would be *Ammi, his people*, and *Ruhamah, obtainers of mercy.* After the death of Gomer, he bought another woman that had been a prostitute, or perhaps redeemed Gomer herself still alive, for little more than 34 shillings and almost two bushels of barley (1 bushel = a little more than 2,219⅓ cubic inches or 36⅓ litres); by which he figured out the marriage relationship between God and the ten tribes, and that they had become very contemptible in his sight, and would shortly be cast off, never to be received back in the millennium. He sharply charged the Hebrews with murders, idolatries, uncleanness, oppression, perversion of justice, reliance on the Assyrians, etc. He interjected a variety of calls to repentance and reformation. His style is very curt, and, to us who know so little of ancient customs, it is rather obscure. He is the only prophet of Israel who has left his

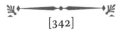

prophecies in writing. Hope is discovered in 2:14-23, 6:1-3, 11:10-11, and chapter 14.

HOSHEA

The son of Elah. After murdering Pekah his master, and after a struggle of eight or nine years of civil war, he became king of Israel, and was less wicked than any of his predecessors, allowing those of his subjects who desired to worship the Lord at Jerusalem. He had scarcely settled on his throne, when he concerted measures with So, King of Egypt, to throw off the Assyrian yoke, under which his kingdom had so long groaned. Informed of this, Shalmaneser, King of Assyria, invaded the country of the ten tribes, and, after three or four years, took all their fenced cities, reduced Samaria and others to ruin, killed Hoshea, ripped up the women with child, dashed infants to pieces, and carried most of the survivors to the territories of his eastern Empire. (2 Kings 15:30, 17:1, 3-4, 6; Hosea 1-13; Amos 2-9)

HULDAH. See Josiah.

A prophetess. (Found only in 2 Kings 22:14, and 2 Chron. 34:22)

HUR

The son of Caleb, and grandson of Hezron; perhaps the husband of Miriam, and grandfather of Bezaleel. He and Aaron held up Moses' hands at Rephidim during the engagement with the Amalekites; and they governed the people when he was on Mount Sinai. (Exod. 17:10, 12, 24:14; 1 Chron. 2:19-20, 50)

HUSHAI

The Archite, David's trusted friend, who, hearing of his flight before Absalom, met him with dust upon his head, and his clothes torn. At David's advice, he returned, and pretended to comply with Absalom, at least uttered words that were taken to indicate friendship. By humorous and flattering advice, he prevailed on Absalom and his party to defer their pursuit of David for some days; and so, contrary to the advice of Ahithophel, their cause was ruined. He, also, communicated proper intelligence to David. (2 Sam. 15-16) Probably Baanah, Solomon's deputy-governor in the tribe of Asher, was his son. (1 Kings 4:16)

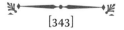

HYMENEUS
Probably a native of Ephesus. For a while, he professed the Christian faith, and seemed a real believer, but he fell into grievous errors, and perhaps abominable practices. On this account, Paul excommunicated him from the Church, delivering him and Alexander to Satan. Several years later, we find him and Philetus affirming that there was no other resurrection than that from sin to grace, through faith in baptism. (Found only in 1 Tim. 1:20; 2 Tim. 2:17)

I

I
When it refers to God, it expresses his dignity and uniqueness (Isa. 43:11, 44:6), his power (Gen. 17:1), his self-existence, and his unchangeableness (Exod. 3:14), or the certainty of his promises and threats. (Exod. 6:1-8; Num. 14:35) Referring to men, it expresses their pride (Isa. 14:13-14, 47:8-9), the certainty of what they say (Gal 5:2), and their readiness to do their duty (Micah 3:8; Matt. 21:29-30). The word I is used 8853 times in the Bible

IBZAN
Of the tribe of Judah, he succeeded Jephthah, about BC 1181 or 1126, and judged Israel seven years. He had 30 sons, and as many daughters, all of whom he married off in his own lifetime. He was buried in Bethlehem, and was succeeded by Elon. (Judg. 12:8-10)

ICHABOD. *The glory has departed.* See Eli
The posthumous son of Phinehas, one of Eli's sons. Only found in 1 Sam. 4:21.

ISAAC
The son of Abraham by Sarah, so called to mark the *laughter* and *gladness* occasioned by his birth. His mother, though 90 years old, suckled him herself. He was only young when he was badly abused by Ishmael. When Isaac was about 25, or perhaps 33, years of age, his father was ordered to offer him as a burnt offering. Isaac himself carried the wood for burning his body. When the knife was just about to be plunged into his throat, the execution was divinely stopped, and

a ram provided in his place. When Isaac was about 40 years old, his father, by means of Eliezer, provided him with Rebekah from Syria as his wife. Isaac met her in the field as she came, and lodged her in his mother's tent, who was now dead. Rebekah continued to be long barren, but Isaac, by prayer, got her pregnant in the 20th year of their marriage, and Rebekah bore twins that struggled in her womb. Upon inquiry, the Lord informed her that the two children in her womb would be very different in temperament, that the nations springing from them would be very different in their fate, and that the older would serve the younger. Her two children were called Esau and Jacob, of whom the first was the darling of his father, and the latter of his mother. (Gen. 21-24, 26)

After Isaac had become heir to Abraham, a famine occurred in Canaan. He retired to Gerer where Abimelech was king, on his way towards Egypt; but God prohibited him from going down there, and established his covenant with him and his seed. Fearing that the Philistines of Gerer might kill him for the sake of his beautiful wife, Rebekah agreed to pretend that she was Isaac's sister. From his window, Abimelech, observing Isaac being familiar with Rebekah, something not right between brother and sister, he called him, and reproved him for pretending that she was his sister, and thus laying a snare that would involve his kingdom in guilt. All his subjects were charged to beware of harming Isaac or Rebekah. Isaac had fine crops, and his flocks multiplied greatly. He opened the wells which his father had dug, and which the Philistines had stopped. Finding Abimelech weary of him, Isaac retired eastward to the valley of Gerer. Here, his servants dug wells. For two of them, the Philistines strove, and pretended that the water was theirs. Isaac called the one *Esek*, that is, *contention*, and the other *Sitnah*, that is, *hatred*. For a third, they stopped striving, and he called it *Rehoboth*, as a memorial that the Lord had *made room* for him. Weary of strife, he retired eastward to Beersheba where God again renewed his promise and covenant with him. Abimelech, dreading the increase of his wealth, came to make an alliance with him. When he was about 100 years old, he and Rebekah were mightily grieved with the conduct of Esau in his marriage to two Canaanite women. (Gen. 26)

When he was about 137 years of age, his sight failed him greatly. Supposing his death to be at hand, he desired his darling Esau to bring him some savoury venison, that he might eat it, and give him his tenderest blessing before his decease. Rebekah, overhearing, sent Jacob to the fold to bring her home some flesh, from which she prepared savoury meat for Isaac. Then she caused Jacob, whom she had dressed as much like Esau as she could, to carry the food to his father, and pretend that he was Esau. He complied with her sinful directions on how to obtain the promised blessing. His father suspected, and felt him; but he constantly asserted that he was Esau. Isaac then blessed Jacob with a fruitful land, and dominion over all his brothers. Jacob had scarcely gone off, when Esau came in with his venison, and demanded his father's blessing. Finding that Jacob had deceived him, Isaac trembled to think how the providence of God was at work. Strongly, he inclined to recall the blessing of Jacob, but he could not. At Esau's bitter entreaties, he blessed him to an inferior degree. Finding that Jacob's life was in danger from Esau, whom he had tricked out of his birthright and blessing, Isaac and Rebekah agreed to send him to Mesopotamia, and charged him to beware of marrying a Canaanitess. About 43 years later, and 10 years before Jacob went down to Egypt, Isaac died, and was honourably interred by Jacob and Esau in the cave of Machpelah. Here too Rebekah was buried. (Gen. 27-28, 35:27-29)

Was not this patriarch a distinguished type of our Saviour? How often promised, how earnestly desired, how long expected, and how supernatural his birth! What joy it gave to angels and men! And, in his name, is the whole joy and consolation of Israel wrapped up. He is the only begotten Son of Jehovah, and the darling of his heart, but at the expense of their own rejection by the church of God. How hated, mocked, persecuted, and murdered by his Jewish brothers! In his doctrine and work, how he re-dug the wells of his Father's love! And how opposed by Jews and Gentiles in this enterprise! With what cheerfulness he assumed and carried our guilt, bore his cross, and laid down his life a sacrifice for us! How willingly he went with his Father into inconceivable scenes of woe! Oh the numerous seed, and the unbounded blessings for those that are the reward of his work! And how firmly the New Covenant was ratified in his death! Having risen from the dead, and having a Church, a spouse, chiefly of Gentiles, allotted to him by his Father, how quickly his blood and his prayers produced a multitude of spiritual seed! For a while, what a struggle between the Jewish and Gentile church! At last, the Jews, like Esau, rejected their birthright, and, forfeiting the blessing, were cast out,

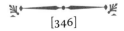

while the Gentiles, his younger seed, became the highly favoured but much afflicted people of God.

ISAIAH, or ESAIAS

A prophet, the son of Amoz; and it is said, but without any probable evidence, that he was the cousin of King Uzziah, in the latter end of whose reign he began his predictions. Perhaps the first five chapters were uttered before the death of that king. In the year of Uzziah's death, he had a glorious vision of our Redeemer, attended and praised by seraphic angels and ministers. All self-abased, he bewailed his own loathsomeness; but a seraph touched his mouth with a burning coal from the altar, intimating that his pollution was purged away. Readily, he offered himself to the prophetic work, and was informed, that his preaching would bring about the hardening and ruin of his hearers till the Assyrians had rendered the land almost wholly desolate. When Ahaz and his people were put into the utmost consternation by the ravages of Pekah and Rezin, Isaiah told Ahaz that he had no reason to be afraid of these kings as the ruin of them and their kingdoms was at hand. When Ahaz refused to ask a sign for the preservation of his kingdom, God gave him the sign of the Messiah proceeding from the Jewish royal family as an infallible security for it. Pointing to Shearjashub, his child in his arms, he told Ahaz that, before that child came to the years of discretion, both Syria and the ten tribes would be told that the Assyrians would lay the land of Judah almost desolate, and ruin the kingdom of Israel. Isaiah had another son, whom the Lord ordered to be called *Maher-shalal-hash-baz*, that is, *in hastening to the spoil, make haste to the prey.* He assured the Jews, in the front of witnesses, that before that child would he able to cry, *My father or mother*, the kingdoms of Syria and Samaria would be ruined by the Assyrians; and not long after, Judah would be brought to the brink of ruin. (Chapters 1-8) When Hezekiah was severely distressed by his bodily illness, and by the Assyrian invasion, Isaiah prayed for him, and directed and comforted him; but afterwards he prophesied that, for his vanity, his seed would be eunuchs in the palace of Babylon. While Sargon's army besieged Ashdod, Isaiah, by going barefoot, and with scant clothing, for three years, prefigured the distressed condition of the Egyptians and Ethiopians, and for three years under the Assyrian yoke. (Isa. 26-30) Despite Isaiah's excellent qualifications for his work,

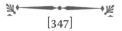

and his faithful discharge of it, his success was small. (Isa. 49:1-5) After he had prophesied 45, or rather 60 years, he was killed, perhaps sawn asunder (see Heb. 11:37), or died a natural death, at the beginning of Manasseh's reign.

Isaiah's separate history of King Uzziah's reign was not divinely inspired, and is now lost. (2 Chron. 26:22) His inspired prophecy remains. The first part of it consists chiefly of declarations of sins, and threatenings of judgements. The last 27 chapters, together with chapters 4, 11-12, 25, 33, and 35 consist chiefly of promises. In chapters 1-3 and 5, the general scope is set out to represent the ingratitude, unfruitfulness in good works, idolatry, profaneness, pride of women, oppression, drunkenness, perverting of judgement, etc., among the Hebrews, and to predict their terrible miseries under the Assyrians, Chaldeans or Romans. This too is the scope of chapters 7:17, 25, and 8, 9, 22, 24, 27:7, 11, and chapters 28-29, 30:1, 17, 32:1, 3, 59 and 66. In chapters 7:5, 9, 8:3, 9:4-21, and 17, he predicted the ruin of Syria, and of the kingdom of the ten tribes, and the calamities of the Philistines (14:29-31), of Moab (chs. 15, 16, and 25:10), of the Egyptians and Ethiopians (chs. 18-20), of the Arabians (chs. 21:11-12 and 34), of Tyre (chapter 23), of the Assyrians before Jerusalem (chs. 10, 14:24-27, 17:12-13, 27:1, 30:27-33, 31:4-9, chs. 37-38), and of the Chaldeans (chs. 13-14, 21:1-10, 43:14, 45:1-4, 46:1-2, 11, and ch. 43).

Amid these denunciations of wrath, we have many pleasant promises of the redemption and glorious kingdom of the Messiah. (1:18, 25, 27, 2:1-5, 4:2-6, 7:14, 8:14, 9:6-7, chs. 11-12, 25-26, 28:16, and ch. 30, etc) From chapter 40 to the end, the deliverance of the Jews from Babylon, and the vanity of idols, are often occasionally hinted; but its chief scope was to foretell the incarnation, sufferings, and glory of the Messiah, the erection of the gospel Church among the Gentiles, the rejection of the Jews, and their future restoration. The style of this prophet is sublime to the highest degree, and his views are extremely evangelical. Thus Isaiah is often considered to be the evangelical prophet, often quoted by Jesus.

ISHBOSHETH, or ESHBAAL

The son and successor of King Saul. In the 40th year of his life, Abner made him king in the place of his father over all the Hebrew tribes except that of Judah, which was faithful to David. He reigned two years fairly peaceably; but Abner's forwardness brought on a war between the party of Ishbosheth and the subjects of David; but it never seemed to go beyond small skirmishes. Abner, taking offence at Ishbosheth's accusing him of an intrigue with Rizpah, the concubine of Saul, deserted him, and began to set afoot the interest of David. But he was murdered by Joab. Informed of this, Ishbosheth lost all courage; and, as he took his noontide sleep, Baanah and Rechab, his captains, and perhaps kinsmen, murdered him, brought his head to David, and were rewarded with the ignominious loss of their own life. Ishbosheth's head was decently interred in the sepulchre of Abner. Thus fell the royal dignity of the house of Saul about 7 years into the reign of David.

ISHMAEL

(1) The son of Abraham by Hagar. When about 18 years of age, he sported too roughly with Isaac, a child of four or five. On this account, he and his mother were expelled from the family. After almost dying of thirst on his way to Egypt, and miraculously refreshed, he and his mother took up their residence in the wilderness of Paran, and lived by shooting venison. He married an Egyptian at his mother's direction. According to the divine predictions to his father and mother, he had 12 sons: Nebaioth, Kedar, Adbeel, Mibsam, Mishma, Dumah, Massa, Hadad, Tema, Jetur, Naphish, and Kedemah, who became parents and princes of twelve Arabian tribes. He also had a daughter called Mahalath (or Bashemath) who became the wife of Esau her cousin. His posterity took up residence between Havilah and Shur in Arabia the Stony, and in part of Arabia Deserta, and were called Ishmaelites, Hagarenes, and, in the latter times, Saracens. See Arabia. After Ishmael had lived 130 years, he died among his friends, the offspring of Keturah, etc. (Gen. 21, 25)

(2) The son of Nethaniah, being one of the royal family of Judah. He was sent by Baalis, King of the Ammonites, to murder Gedaliah, the deputy of Nebuchadnezzar over the Jews that were left in Canaan. After he had ungratefully murdered that good man, so averse to suspect his wicked designs, and a number of Jews and Chaldeans along with him, he murdered another 70 whom he met with - all except ten - who begged him to spare them, so that they might disclose to him their hidden treasures. The rest of the Jews present, women and children, he carried captive, and marched towards his country of Ammon where

he had dwelt for some time. But Johanan the son of Kareah, and other warriors, returning to Mizpeh, and finding what he had done, pursued him, and recovered his captives and spoil. But he himself, and eight of his band, escaped safely to the Ammonites. (Jer. 40-41)

ISRAEL. See Hebrews, Jacob

ISSACHAR, *hire*
The fifth son of Jacob by Leah. The name *Issachar* was given him because the occasion of his conception was purchased by some mandrakes that Leah gave to Rachel. He had four sons: Tola, Phurah (or Phut), Job (or Jashub), and Shimron. When this tribe came out of Egypt, they amounted to 54,400, under the government of Nathaneel the son of Zuar. Their spy to view the Promised Land was Igal, the son of Joseph, and their agent to divide it was Paltiel, the son of Azzan. They were stationed in front of the Tabernacle in the camp of Judah, and increased in the wilderness to 64,300. (Gen. 30:14-18, 46:13; Num. 1:8, 29, 10:14-15, 13:7, 26:23-25, 34:26) They had their lot in one of the most fertile places in Canaan, between the Zebulunites on the north, and the western Manassites on the south. They were extremely laborious and wealthy, ready, like the obedient ass, to bear the heaviest burden of labour or tribute. Nor did they forget to invite one another to the worship of God. (Gen. 49:14, 15; Deut. 33:18-19) Tola the Judge, and Baasha, the King of Israel, were the most notable of this tribe. Their princes were very active in the overthrow of Jabin's army by Barak. (Judg. 5:15) Two hundred of the principal men, who had the rest at their direction, attended David's coronation, and brought much provision with them. Under his reign, Omri, the son of Michael, was their deputy-governor; and their number able to draw sword was 143,600. (1 Chron. 7:1-6, 12:30, 40, 27:18) Many of this tribe attended Hezekiah's solemn Passover. (2 Chron. 30:18)

ITHAMAR
The fourth son of Aaron. Never but in Eli's family was the high priesthood vested in his family. But his descendants constituted eight of the orders of the priests. (1 Chron. 24:1-6)

J

JABEZ

He appears to have been a descendant of Judah by Ashur. His mother bore him with much *pain* and *sorrow*, which was the origin of his name. His notable religion, authority, and seed, rendered him more honourable than his brothers. With distinguished fervour, he begged that God would truly and specially bless him, enlarge his family and inheritance, assist and direct him in every undertaking, and preserve him from everything sinful and dangerous. God particularly granted his request. (1 Chron. 4:5-10)

JABIN

(1) A king of Hazor in the northern parts of Canaan, the most powerful of all the sovereigns in those quarters. Struck with the rapidity of Joshua's conquests, he engaged all the kings on the north of Canaan, particularly the kings of Madon, Jobab, Shimron, Achshaph, etc., to assist him. Their whole forces made their rendezvous at the waters of Merom to attack the Hebrews; but the Lord delivered them into Joshua's hand, who entirely defeated them, pursued their fugitives as far as Great Zidon, to the northwest, and Mezrephothmaim on the east. He then marched back to Hazor, burnt it, and killed Jabin its king. (Josh. 11)

(2) Jabin, King of Hazor, and perhaps the great-grandchild of the former, was a very powerful monarch, had 900 chariots armed with iron scythes, and an army under Sisera his general, and 997,000 men according to Philo Byblius. After he had for 20 years, from about BC 1305-1285, or 1257-1237, mightily oppressed the Hebrews, his army was routed by Deborah and Barak, and, it is probable, by a terrible storm of rain that made the River Kishon sweep away large numbers of them. Sisera, the general, fled away on foot, and was kindly received by Jael, the wife of Heber the Kenite. His fatigue caused him to fall into a deep sleep, so Jael, divinely instigated against this murderer of the Hebrews, killed him by driving a nail through his head, and afterwards showed him to Barak. (Judg. 4-5)

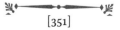

JACOB, ISRAEL

The younger son of Isaac and Rebekah, born BC 1836 or 1831, along with his twin Esau. In the womb, they struggled with one another, and the Lord informed their mother that she was with twins, both of which would become nations, but of a very different temperament, state, and condition; but the older would serve the younger. In their birth, the latter took hold of his brother's heel, and for that reason was called *Jacob*, the *heeler*, or *supplanter*.

The deceiving of Isaac

When he grew up, Jacob was of a quiet and peaceable nature, and stayed much at home with his mother, while his brother was of a restless nature, passionately fond of hunting. He bought the birthright of his brother for a meal of coarse pottage (lentil soup). By presenting some savoury meat, which his mother had prepared, to his dim-sighted father, and pretending he was Esau, he obtained the principal blessing of a fertile land, well watered, and of dominion over his brother. Enraged at this, Esau resolved to murder him. Rebekah his mother, who had advised him, informed of this, advised Jacob to retire to Mesopotamia to her brother Laban's family, and stay there till Esau's fury had cooled down. Afterwards, she communicated the matter to Isaac, and told him what an insupportable burden it would be to her if Jacob should marry a Canaanitish woman. Isaac sent for Jacob, gave him his blessing, and charged him to go to Padanaram, and there marry one of the daughters of Laban his uncle.

Jacob's dream at Bethel

Jacob departed quietly from Beersheba. After sunset, probably on the second day of his journey, he came to a place called Luz, on account of the many *almonds* or *hazelnuts* that grew there. Here, he lay down to rest all night under the open sky, with a stone under his head for a pillow. Here, in his dream, he saw a ladder, whose foot stood on the earth, and its top reached into heaven, the angels of God ascending and descending on its rungs. Above the top of it stood the Lord God, who assured him he was the God of his fathers, Abraham and Isaac, and would give him and his seed the land of Canaan for their inheritance, rendering them numerous as the sand by the seashore, and making all nations blessed through him and his seed. This ladder represented the providence of God, administered by angels and managed by God, as a God in covenant, and Jesus Christ as the wonder and Lord of angels, and our Mediator between God and man, and the way of access to him, sprung from Jacob in his humanity, but, in his divine nature, the Lord from heaven, and the means of all blessings from God to sinful men. Awakened from his sleep, Jacob was deeply struck with the reverential impression of the divine greatness, took the stone which he had for his pillow, erected it as a monument, poured oil on the top of it, and called the name of the place Bethel, or *the house of God*, and promised that, since God had promised to protect him, and provide for him, and bring him back to Canaan, he would serve him, give him the tithes of all he acquired, and, at his return, make Bethel a place of solemn worship. (Gen. 25, 27-28)

Laban of Haran

Encouraged by this vision, he hastened to Haran where Laban his uncle lived. Near to the place, some shepherds informed him where Laban dwelt, and that his family was well, and that Rachel his daughter was just coming to water her flock. At her coming up, he kindly greeted her, helped her to water her flock, and told her that he was the son of Rebekah, her aunt. She quickly informed her father, and he came and conducted Jacob to his house. When Jacob had continued there for about a month, Laban proposed to give him wages. Jacob offered seven years service for Rachel his younger, but most beautiful, daughter, and, with great cheerfulness, he fulfilled his engagement from the great love that he bore her. When the marriage-night came, as a providential punishment to Jacob for deceiving his dim-eyed father, Laban conducted Leah, his older daughter, whose beauty was far inferior, to Jacob's bed instead of Rachel. Next morning, the trick was discovered, and Jacob warmly reproved his uncle about it. Laban pretended that it was contrary to the custom of their country to marry the younger daughter first; but showing himself a greedy wretch, told him he might have Rachel too for seven years more service. This Jacob agreed to. Of his two wives, Jacob much preferred Rachel; but God favoured Leah with children: Reuben, Simeon, Levi, and Judah; and, it seems, with a thankful heart, while Rachel was barren. Vexed at this Rachel begged that Jacob would make her conceive or else she would die of grief, or by some violent means. With indignation at her

rashness, he told her he was not God to bestow or withhold the fruit of the womb at his pleasure. She next ordered Bilhah, her maid, whom her father had given her, to take her place in her husband's bed, that by her she might have children to bring up as her own. By this means, Jacob had two sons: the one Rachel called Dan, as if she hoped God would *judge* her, and avenge her lack of children on her sister, the other she called Naphtali, as if with great *wrestling* she had prevailed against her sister. In imitation, Leah put her maid Zilpah into Jacob's bed, and she bore him two sons, Gad and Asher, by whose names, Leah intended to hint her expectation that a *troop* of children was coming, and that the daughters would call her *blessed*. Soon after, Leah, with her son Reuben's mandrakes, hired her husband for Rachel's night to sleep in her bed, and, in consequence, bore Issachar; and not long after, she bore Zebulun, and a daughter called Dinah. Nor was it long when the Lord pitied Rachel and gave her a son, whom she called Joseph, in the hope that she would have another son *added* to him.

The return of Jacob and his family to Canaan

When Jacob's fourteen years' service for his two wives were over, he begged that Laban, his father-in-law, would permit him to return to his country with his family along with him, that he might provide for himself. Sensible of the advantage of his service, Laban offered him what wages he pleased if he would stay. To mark his dependance on the providence of God, Jacob proposed that all the spotted cattle and brown sheep afterwards produced should be his hire. Laban, expecting that these would not be many, readily consented. To prevent all disputes, and hinder as much as possible the future product of spotted cattle and brown sheep, all of these kinds were removed to the distance of three days' journey, and entrusted to the care of Laban's sons; and the rest were committed to the oversight of Jacob. Instigated by a vision, Jacob laid speckled, spotted, and ring-streaked rods of poplar, etc., in the watering-troughs, about the time when the stronger cattle mated and conceived. These, striking their imagination as they drunk, made them conceive spotted offspring; but he did not put them in when the weaker cattle conceived. By this means, all the stronger cattle became Jacob's, and his flocks and herds were greatly increased. Laban, therefore, frequently changed the terms of his hire; but whatever was allotted to Jacob greatly increased. Laban, too, caused Jacob to bear the loss of whatever went missing of his flocks or herds. After Jacob had served another six years with great labour and fidelity, Laban and his sons became very surly towards him, pretending that he had made himself rich at their expense. Meanwhile, God, in a dream, ordered him to return to Canaan. Resolving to do so, perhaps when he was shearing his own sheep, and at a distance from those of Laban, he, acquainted his wives with the change of their father's attitude towards him, and that he intended to return to Canaan. They, being aware of their father's bad behaviour, were glad to part with him. So Jacob, his wives and children, and servants, and flocks, moved off towards Canaan, and Rachel carried with her some of her father's idols. On the third day, Laban, informed of their departure, pursued them in no small fury; but God, in a dream, charged him to beware of giving Jacob so much as an injurious word. On the seventh day, he overtook them on the Mountain of Gilead. Some sharp words were exchanged, and Laban heavily complained that they had carried off his gods. Jacob asked him to rummage in all his stores, and, if his gods were found with anyone, let that person be put to death. Laban searched with the utmost care, but Rachel, having taken the idols, and put them into the camel's furniture, sat on them, pretending, that her frequent bleeding hindered her in rising. Nothing of Laban's being found, he and Jacob made a solemn covenant of perpetual friendship, in testimony to which they reared a heap of stones, which Jacob called *Galeed*, or *Gilead*, and Laban *Jegarsahadutha*, both of which meant *the heap of witness* (Gen.31:47). After Jacob had offered sacrifice, and entertained his friends, Laban and his company affectionately parted, and returned to Padanaram, while Jacob and his family went forward to Canaan. (Gen. 29-31)

The brook Jabbok

When Jacob advanced to the ford of Jabbok, God showed him that he was guarded with angels on every side, both from Laban and Esau. Therefore, Jacob called the name of the place *Mahanaim*, or the *double camp*. Fearing the remains of Esau's resentment, he sent messengers to inform him of his return, and to supplicate his favour. Jacob, informed by his messengers that Esau was coming to meet him with 400 men, justly suspected his intentions were murderous, and sent off before him a large present of 220 goats, 220 sheep, 30 milk-camels with their

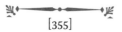

colts, 40 cows, 10 bulls, 20 she-asses and 10 foals. These, he divided into five droves, and ordered the drivers of each to tell Esau, as they met him, that it was a present for him. By this means, he hoped to appease his brother's anger. Meanwhile, he spent the whole night in solemn prayer. Our Redeemer appeared to him in the form of a man, and, to check him for attempting to detain him by force, touched the hollow of his thigh till it shrank, and made him always after that go limping. To commemorate this, his posterity never eat the similar sinew in animals. But, by weeping and supplication, and the appearance of God, he obtained a change of his name to *Israel*, because, as a *prince*, he had wrestled with *God*, and had *prevailed*, and obtained a solemn blessing on himself and his seed.

Having crossed the Jabbok, he divided his family into three divisions, that, if Esau murdered the foremost, the others might flee. The two handmaids, and their children, went first, Leah and her own next, and Rachel and Joseph last, that she might have the best opportunity to get away if there was danger. According to Jacob's directions, they all, in the humblest manner, did obeisance to Esau. Moved partly by this deportment, but chiefly by the providence of God, Esau met Jacob with most tender affection, and generously refused his present because he had great wealth already. However, Jacob urged him because, said he, "I have everything, and have had the great happiness to meet you in kindness and love." Esau offered to go with him on his journey to Mount Seir; but Jacob, not over fond of his company, begged him not to trouble himself, as the flocks and little ones could only make progress very slowly. After Esau's departure, Jacob, coming to the spot where Succoth was afterwards built, erected a house for himself, and booths for his cattle. Not long after, he crossed the Jordan westward, and, coming to Shalem, he bought a piece of ground from Hamor, the father of Shechem, for a hundred pieces of silver (probably shekels), and thus a little more than £11. Here, be erected an altar, and called it *El-Elohe-Israel*, showing that it was sacred to the *mighty* and *worshipful* God of Israel. (Gen. 32, 33:3)

The rape of Dinah

He had not dwelt here long, when Dinah, his daughter, a handsome girl of about 14 years of age, at some celebration or similar occasion, went to see the young women of the country. Shechem, the son of Hamer,

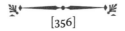

and prince of the city of Shechem, captivated with her beauty, took her and raped her. He and his father begged her in marriage for him, and offered them any price they pleased to obtain her. Jacob waited till his sons came home. They deceitfully proposed that the Shechemites should all be circumcised as the only terms of obtaining Dinah. This they proposed as a means of rendering them incapable of defending themselves, horribly abusing the seal of God's covenant to promote their murderous intentions. Dreading nothing, Hamor and Shechem, by hinting to their people how it would gain them the wealth of Jacob's family, persuaded them to undergo the operation. On the third day, when they were at their sorest, Simeon and Levi, and perhaps a number of servants, entered the city, and murdered the inhabitants; and the other sons of Jacob, coming up, seized on the spoil. This they did to revenge Shechem's seizing their sister as if she was a prostitute. Dreading the resentment of the Canaanites around, and directed of God to go up to Bethel and dwell there, Jacob, remembering his vow that he had made as he went to Padanaram, ordered his family to purify themselves, and to put away their strange gods, for several of his servants were heathen people. They, and no doubt Rachel among them, delivered up their idols to him, and he hid them under an oak. Protected of God by a dread seizing the Canaanites around, he and his family came safely to Bethel. There, he offered sacrifices to God, where God appeared to him and renewed his former blessing. Soon after, Jacob moved south to Hebron to visit Isaac, his father. Meanwhile, Deborah his mother's nurse died, to the no small grief of the family. Rachel too, who had said she would die if she got not children, died in childbirth of her second son, whom she, in her last agonies, called Benoni, the *son of my sorrow*, but his father called him Benjamin, *son of the right hand*. She was buried near Bethlehem. Not long after, Reuben committed incest with Bilhah, his father's concubine. Jacob had hardly dwelt three years with Isaac his father when Joseph was carried off from him; and for 22 years bewailed his loss, imagining that some wild beast had devoured him. About twelve years later, Isaac died, and was buried by Jacob and Esau. It seems, the two brothers were inclined to live together, but the vast number of their herds and flocks would not allow it. Therefore, Esau retired to Seir, leaving Jacob in the south of Canaan. Meanwhile, he had his share of affliction from the disorders in the family of Judah. (Gen. 35-38)

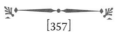

The discovery of Joseph in Egypt

About nine years after the death of Isaac, Jacob, distressed by a famine, sent his ten oldest sons to Egypt to buy corn for their subsistence. On their return, he was shocked to find that each man's money had been returned in his sack; but, furthermore, Simeon was detained as a prisoner, and the governor of Egypt had demanded a sight of Benjamin, his favourite, and, as he thought, the only surviving son of his beloved Rachel. Pinching famine, and the repeated entreaties of his children, particularly of Reuben and Judah, obliged him to let Benjamin go with the rest on their second journey to Egypt, not without angry hints that all these things were against him, and that he was bereaved of his children. On their return, he discovered that Joseph was still alive, and was governor of Egypt, and that he had sent for him and his family to come there to live. With great joy, he left the plain of Mamre near Hebron and moved on towards Egypt. At Beersheba, he offered sacrifices to the Lord, and the Lord encouraged him to go down into Egypt, and assured him that his seed would return to Canaan at the time fixed by the promise, and that there, Joseph would attend him in his last moments and close his eyes. He, and 66 of his offspring, with eight wives, went down into Egypt where there were already Joseph and his two sons. Informed by Judah, who went before the rest, Joseph met him with the utmost expression of tender affection. Jacob was presented by him to Pharaoh. He wished that monarch all true happiness, and informed him that he had lived 130 years, chiefly in troubles.

Jacob's troubles

Let us learn the fruit of unbrotherly conduct, and of obtaining blessings by unhallowed means. Jacob and his family lived about 17 years in Egypt, when he fell into his last sickness. Joseph, whom, a little before, he had made to swear that he would bury him in Canaan, with his two sons, Manasseh and Ephraim, came to visit him. He informed them of God's blessing him at Luz (or Bethel). He blessed Joseph, assuring him that his sons would form two distinct tribes of the Hebrew nation, but that of Ephraim should be the most numerous and honoured. He assured him God would bring all his posterity back to Canaan in due time, and assigned to Joseph's seed a piece of ground near Shechem, which he had first bought, and afterwards recovered by force out of the hand of the Amorites. After this, he convened his twelve sons, gave them his last benediction, and foretold what would befall their families in future ages. Reuben, Simeon, and Levi, he reproached for their sinful conduct, and predicted how God would chastise them in the fate of their seed. He especially commended Judah and Joseph, and foretold the future glory of their families. He foretold the coming of Christ, and the gathering of the Gentiles to him. Amidst the blessing of his children, he expressed his strong desire of the Messiah's incarnation, and of his own full enjoyment of God. After charging his sons to bury him in the cave of Machpelah, where Abraham, Sarah, Isaac, Rebekah, and Leah had been buried, he laid himself down on his bed, and breathed his last, about BC 1688 or 1684, in the 147th of his life. After his body was embalmed, and a solemn mourning of 70 days performed for him in Egypt, Joseph and his brothers, with the chief men of Egypt, accompanied his corpse to its interment in Canaan. At the threshing-floor of Atad, they stopped, and had a second mourning of seven days, on account of which the Canaanites called the spot Abel Ephraim, the *mourning of the Egyptians.* He was interred in the cave of Machpelah. (Gen. 42-50) His descendants, as well as himself, are called *Jacob*, or *Israel.* A well that he used, and perhaps sank, near Shechem, is called his well. (Deut. 10:22; Josh. 23:4; Ps. 105:10-23; Hosea 12; John 4:12; Acts 7:11-16)

Was not our Redeemer, who is called Jacob and Israel, prefigured by this patriarch? How long expected, earnestly desired, and supernatural his birth! How divinely was he chosen to be the father of the saved nations of elect men! How he took the first Adam by the heel, fulfilling the covenant that he had broken! How he supplanted and overthrew sin and Satan! By what red and bloody sufferings he purchased the mediatorial heirship of all things! What inestimable and irreversible blessings he obtained by offering himself to God in the likeness of sinful flesh! How fearfully was he exposed to trouble from Jewish brothers, from Satan the father of his bride, and from his offended Father! How sad his earthly exile! How hard his service! How numerous his sorrows! How unsettled his lot among men! But how notable his plainness and integrity! What love he bears to his mother and spouse, the Church! How faithful in his work! How prevalent his intercession! How glorious his reward! Having finished his work, and blessed his disciples, he retired to his rest in the heavenly Canaan. What a multitude of spiritual seed is springing up from the twelve Apostles, those patriarchal fathers of the gospel Church! (Ps. 24:6; Isa. 49:3)

JADDUA, or JADDUS

The son of Jonathan, and High Priest of the Jews. He officiated a considerable time after the Captivity. (Only found in Neh. 10:21, 12:11, 22) He is thought to be the Jaddus who lived in the time of Alexander the Great. Josephus says that Alexander, when besieging Tyre, demanded some assistance. Jaddus begged to be excused as he had sworn fidelity to Darius the Persian. Highly provoked, Alexander vowed revenge. After the taking of Tyre, he marched towards Jerusalem. After the people had exercised themselves in fasting and prayer, Jaddus and his fellow priests, directed by God, met Alexander in their sacred robes. Struck with the appearance of the High Priest, he, instead of reproaching him, fell at his feet and told Parmenio his general that such a form had appeared to him in Macedonia, and promised him the Empire of the world; and, at the High Priest's request, eased the Jews of their tribute. But, as none of Alexander's historians mention this matter, it is possibly a Jewish fable.

JAEL. See Jabin, Sisera

The woman of the nail fame. See Judg. 4:17-18, 21-22, 5:6, 24.

JAH. See Jehovah

Found only in Ps. 68:4.

JAIR, JAIRUS

(1) The son of Segub, the son of Hezron, of the tribe of Judah. Through his grandmother, the daughter of Machir the Manassite, he fell heir to an estate east of Jordan, and conquered the whole country of Argob, as far as the borders of Geshuri and Maachathi. (Num. 32:40-41; 1 Chron. 2:21-23)

(2) A Judge of Israel, who succeeded Tola in BC 1209 or 1147, and governed 22 years. He was a Gileadite, probably of Manasseh. He had 30 sons, who rode on 30 ass-colts, and were lords of 30 towns called *Havothjair*, or the towns of Jair. (Judg. 10:3-5)

(3) Jar or Jairus, a chief ruler of the synagogue at Capernaum. His daughter falling dangerously ill, he begged that Jesus would come, lay

his hands on her, and cure her. On their way to the house, some from it met him and told him it was needless to trouble our Saviour as his daughter was dead. Jesus bid him not to fear, but only believe. When they entered the house, they found the mourners prepared to follow the corpse to the grave, and making a noise. Jesus told them to be silent, as the maid was not to be given up for dead. They laughed at him. To punish their mockery of him, he put them out of the door. When no more but her father and mother and three of his disciples were present, he took her by the hand, and commanded her to arise. She did so, and Jesus ordered them to give her something to eat. (Matt. 9:18-26; Mark 5:21-43; Luke 8:41-56)

JAMES the Great (or Elder), and **JOHN** the Evangelist
The sons of Zebedee and Salome were originally fishermen of Bethsaida in Galilee, and left everything at our Saviour's call to follow him. (Matt. 4:21) Both were constituted Apostles, and both were witnesses of Jesus' transfiguration. (Matt. 10:2, 17:2) Both begged his permission to call down fire from heaven on the Samaritans who refused to receive him; and, on this account, as well as for their bold preaching, were called *Boanerges* (from Aramaic), the *sons of thunder*. He checked their furious zeal, and told them that they did not know what unreasonable tempers they had. (Luke 9:54) Our Saviour's special honour of them, and regard for them, occasioned their mother's begging that they might be made chief ministers of state in his temporal kingdom. After they had professed their ability to undergo sufferings along with him, he told them that suffer they must, but his Father was the One who had the disposal of eminent places in his kingdom. (Matt. 20:20-24; Mark 10:35-45) They witnessed his agony in the garden. (Matt. 26:37) After our Saviour's resurrection, it seems that they, for a while, returned to their business of fishing. (John 21:2-3) About AD 42 or 44, if not 49, James was arrested and murdered by Herod (Acts 3:1), and is now the pretended patron of Spain. Whether his brother John was the bridegroom at Cana of Galilee we do not know; but he was our Saviour's beloved disciple. To him, as Jesus sat next him on the couch at the Passover, he intimated who would be the traitor. It is believed that be went up to the High Priest's hall, and, being known to the servants, introduced Peter; but perhaps that disciple might be Nicodemus, or Joseph of Arimathea. (John 18:15-16) At our Saviour's dying direction,

John took home the blessed Virgin to his house, and provided for her. At the Galilean Sea, he introduced our Saviour to Peter on the sea shore. (John 19:25-27, 21:1-7) After dinner, with our Saviour there, Peter asked him what would become of John? Jesus replied that it was none of his business, although he would live to his coming. This expression, fondly mistaken, made many primitive Christians imagine that John would never die; but himself and other histories contradict this ill-founded fancy. (John 21:18-25) For a time, he shared along with Peter in preaching, working miracles, and enduring persecution from the Jews at Jerusalem; and at Samaria they conferred the Holy Spirit by the laying on of hands. (Acts 3-5, 8)

JOHN

About AD 51, John continued as a notable pillar in the Christian church in Judea. (Gal 2:7) It is said that afterwards he preached the Gospel to the Parthians and Indians; but it is more evident that he preached some time in Asia Minor. In Domitian's persecution, about AD 95, it is said that he was cast into a caldron of boiling oil, and, coming out unhurt, vigorous, and clean, was banished to Patmos, to be starved to death. Under the Emperor Nerva, he was recalled from exile, and, returning to Ephesus, preached the gospel there till he died, about 90 or 100 years old. He appears to have had a most kindly and affectionate nature; and yet, it is said, he leaped out of the bath whenever he understood that Cerinthus, who denied the divinity of our Saviour, was present; so great was his zeal. In his old age, he wrote three Epistles, one to Jewish Christians in general, another to a notable lady, and a third to one Gaius. The scope was to inculcate brotherly love, holy living, self-examination, and a cautious shunning of false teachers, particularly those who denied the incarnation and true Godhead of our Saviour. He wrote a history of Jesus' life, containing a great many things not found in the other three Evangelists, chiefly a number of excellent discourses. It was mainly designed to prove our Saviour's divinity. In the isle of Patmos, he had various revelations and visions. From Jesus' mouth, he wrote seven epistles to the Asian churches; and, in his book of Revelation, under the visions of seals opened, trumpets sounded, and vials poured out, etc., he exhibited the whole state of the Christian Church to the end of the world. From the sublimity of his revelations, and his vindication of our Saviour's

divinity, he came to be called *John the Divine* (theologian). The book of his travels, and of his acts, and of the Virgin Mary's death and assumption to heaven, and the creed ascribed to him, are just forged documents.

JAMES THE LESS

Called the brother of our Lord. He was the son of Cleophas, by Mary, the sister of the blessed Virgin. For the admirable holiness of his life, he was surnamed *the Just*. Our Saviour appeared to him on his own after his resurrection. (1 Cor. 15:7) About three years after Paul's conversion, he was at Jerusalem, and was considered a pillar or notable supporter of the church there. (Gal 1:19) About 14 years later, he was present at the apostolic council; and, speaking among the last, he gave his sentiment that as God, according to the ancient promises, had called a church from among the Gentiles to himself, it was not proper to burden them with Jewish ceremonies so hard to be borne, but merely to require them, for the sake of edification in the present circumstances, to refrain from eating things strangled, or blood, and to abstain from fornication and meat offered to idols. To this, all those present agreed. About nine years after that, he wrote an Epistle to the Jewish believers, where he sharply reproved those who pretended to faith without good works, indulging themselves in instability, bad behaviour, partiality, criticism, covetousness, oppression, vain swearing, etc. About AD 63, when Festus was dead, and Albinus had not come to succeed him, the Jews, being greatly enraged at the success of the gospel, it is said that Ananus, son of Annas, ordered James to ascend one of the galleries of the Temple, and inform the people that they had, without foundation, believed Jesus of Nazareth to be the Messiah. He got up, and cried with a loud voice that Jesus was the Son of God, and would quickly appear in the clouds to judge the world. Many glorified God, and believed, but the Pharisees threw him over the battlement. He was badly bruised, but got up on his knees, and prayed for his murderers, amid a shower of stones that they cast at him, till someone beat out his brains with a fuller's club. To the death of this just man, some Jews blame the ruin of their nation. The Talmud ascribes a variety of miracles to James, the disciple of Jesus (there called the Carpenter).

JANNES and JAMBRES

Called by Pliny Jamne and Jotape, and by some Jewish writers, Johanne and Mamre, they were two principal magicians of Egypt who withstood Moses in aping some of his miracles, like the changing of their rods into serpents, turning water into blood, and producing frogs. (Exod. 7-8; 2 Tim. 3:8) Jonathan, the Chaldee paraphrast (paraphraser) wrongly says they were Balaam's sons, and went with him when be spoke to Balak.

JAPHETH

The oldest son of Noah, born BC 2448. (Gen. 5:32, 10:21) To reward his kind and modest covering of his father's nakedness as he lay drunk, his father blessed him, saying that God would enlarge and prosper him, and make him dwell in the tents of Shem, and render the offspring of Canaan his servants. His posterity was prodigiously numerous. He had seven sons: Gomer, Magog, Madai, Javan, Tubal, Meshech, and Tiras. Their descendants populated the northern half of Asia, almost all the Mediterranean isles, all Europe, and, I suppose, most of America. How the Greeks and Romans seized the original residence of the descendants of Shem in Syria, Palestine, Mesopotamia, Assyria, Persia, etc., and how the Scythian, Tartars, Turks, or Moguls, the descendants of Gog and Magog, made themselves masters of southern Asia, may be seen under their articles. How the Dutch, English, Portuguese, Spaniards and Danes, seized the islands or other settlements in Southern Asia and its adjacent parts, is notorious. I know no country of note originally belonging to the offspring of Shem (part of Arabia excepted) that has not, or is not now, claimed to be possessed by the offspring of Japheth. God has persuaded many of them to become his special people, when the Jewish descendants of Shem are cast off. How the Canaanites in Canaan, Phoenicia, North Africa, Bæotia, Heraclea, Arcadia, or Italy, have been enslaved by Japheth's Grecian, Roman, Vandal, or Turkish descendants, is pointed out in that article. (Gen. 9:27) As Japheth (or, Japetus) was the father of the Greeks, no wonder he appears so often in their ancient fables!

JASHOBEAM

The Hachmonite (or Tachmonite), the same as Adino the Eznite. It seems he sat on a kind of a throne at the head of David's mighty men.

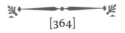

In one instance, he attacked 800, and in another 300, and cut them off to a man; or, he routed 800, slew 300 of them, and his followers slew the other 500. He, with Eleazer and Shammah, broke through the army of the Philistines and brought their master water from the well in Bethlehem. (2 Sam. 23:8, 16-17; 1 Chron. 11:11, 18, 19) I suppose that it was he who commanded the royal guard of 24,000 for the first month. (1 Chron. 27:2) That he was a descendant of Benjamin by Koreh, I dare not affirm. (1 Chron. 12: 6)

JAVAN

The father of the Greeks was Javan, the fourth son of Japheth. His sons were Elisha, Tarshish, Chittim, and Dodanim. His posterity was anciently called Jaones or Jones. They first seem to have settled on the west of Asia Minor, where part of them still continued, and to which others, in later times, returned from Greece, and formed Greek states in Asia Minor of their various tribes: Ionians, Æolians, and Dorians. In very early times, numbers of them passed into Europe, perhaps by crossing the Hellespont, and settled in Greece. Some Phoenicians, Egyptians, and perhaps others, driven out of their own countries, came later and settled among them. Despite a great many internal wars, they multiplied greatly, and spread into almost every island and coast of the Mediterranean Sea. Some of them took up their residence in the east of Italy, others at Marseilles in the south of France, and some of them settled in Cyrene and Egypt in Africa.

JEDUTHUN. See Ethan

JEHOAHAZ

(1) The same as Ahaziah, grandson of Jehoshaphat.

(2) The son of Jehu, who wickedly followed the pattern of Jeroboam the son of Nebat. To punish his and his people's wickedness, God gave them up to the fury of Hazael the Syrian, who reduced the ten tribes to such a degree that Jehoahaz had only 10 chariots, 50 horsemen, and 10,000 footmen, left him in his army. After he had reigned 17 years (BC 856-839), he died, and Jehoash, who had been installed two years earlier, became sole king. (2 Kings 13:30; 1 Chron. 3:17-18) *Jechonias* in Matthew 1:11 seems to signify Jehoiakim.

(3) Jehoahaz (or Shallum) the son of Josiah. He was not the oldest, but the people judged him fittest to govern at that critical juncture when Pharaohnecho had just killed his father; and it seems, to prevent disputes about his right, they solemnly anointed him. He had reigned just three months when Pharaoh, returning from Carchemish a conqueror, ordered him to attend him at Riblath, stripped him of his royalty, and carried him a prisoner to Egypt where be died, and placed Jehoiakim his elder brother, who perhaps was then a prisoner in Pharaoh's army, king in his place. (2 Kings 27:30-32; 1 Chron. 3:15; 2 Chron. 36:1-4; Jer. 22:11)

JEHOASH. See Joash

JEHOIACHIN, CONIAH, or JECONIAH

The son of Jehoiakim, and grandson of Josiah. It seems that his father installed him when he was only eight years of age; and, after his father's death in BC 600, he, at 18, succeeded to the sole government. After a short and wicked reign of three months and ten days, Nebuchadnezzar, King of Babylon, came up and besieged Jerusalem. Jehoiachin, with Nehushta his mother, and his wives, princes, and servants, surrendered themselves, and, with the principal artificers, judges, and warriors, to the number of 18,000, and the treasures, and part of the vessels of the Temple, were carried to Babylon. (2 Kings 24:6-16; 2 Chron. 36:8-10; Jer. 22:24, 28) After 37 years' imprisonment in Chaldea, Evilmerodach released him, and raised him to considerable dignity. (2 Kings 25:27-30; Jer. 31-34) Jeremiah was divinely ordered to write him *childless*; but either that related only to his having no children sitting on the throne of Judah, or he had adopted a variety of children (for we find Salathiel, Malchiram, Pedaiah, Shenazar, Jecamiah, Hoshama, and Nebdabiah, mentioned as his children). (1 Chron. 3:7-18; Jer. 22:24-30) *Jechonias* in Matthew 1:11 seems to signify Jehoiakim.

JEHOIADA. See Joash

JEHOIAKIM

The oldest son of Josiah. When Pharaohnecho killed Josiah, he perhaps took Eliakim prisoner. On his return home, he made him king instead of Jehoahaz, changed his name to Jehoiakim, and laid

him under a tribute of £39,693. This money Jehoiakim exacted from his subjects, according to their ability. At 25 years of age, he began his reign, and sat on the throne 11 years. He wickedly oppressed his subjects to procure money to build himself a palace; but he kept back part of the hire of his workmen, abandoned himself to inhumanity and avarice (Jer. 22:18-24), and hated the prophets who warned him or his people to repent of their wickedness, or threatened the judgements of God against him. Urijah, one of them, fled for his life into Egypt; but Jehoiakim sent Elnathan, the son of Achbor, possibly his father-in-law, along with a troop, to bring him back, and murdered him, and cast his corpse into the graves of the common people. (Jer. 26:20-23) In the fourth year of his reign, he had a copy of Jeremiah's predictions brought before him by Elishama the Scribe, Delaiah, the son of Shemaiah, Elnathan, the son of Achbor, Gemariah the son of Shaphan, Michaiah his son, and Zedekiah the son of Hananiah. Jehudi, who perhaps was a scribe, had just read three or four leaves, when Jehoiakim, despite the intercession of Elnathan, Delaiah, and Gemariah, cut the roll with a penknife, threw it into the fire, and sent Jerahmeel the son of Hammelech, Seraiah the son of Azriel, and Shelemiah, the son of Abdeel, to arrest Jeremiah and Baruch. But the Lord, knowing his murderous intentions, kept them out of his hands. This only drew down new curses on his head. Nebuchadnezzar, having routed the army of Pharaoh at Carchemish, pursued his victory, and rendered himself master of Canaan and part of Phoenicia. Jehoiakim was taken prisoner in Jerusalem and put in chains to be carried to Babylon; but on his submission to the conqueror's terms, was restored to his kingdom. After he had continued three years as a peaceful tributary, he thought of shaking off the yoke. Nebuchadnezzar detached a part of his army against him, the rest being, it seems, employed in the siege of Nineveh. These, with bands of Syrians, Moabites, and Ammonites, terribly harassed the kingdom of Judah. After four years, Nebuchadnezzar, having taken Nineveh, came in person. Jehoiakim was taken prisoner, put to death, and his body cast into a common sewer in the manner of the unburied carcase of an ass. (2 Kings 24; 2 Chron. 36; Jer. 22:18-19, 36:30) Perhaps Jehoiakim is taken for the brother of Jehoiakim (namely Zedekiah), or the yokes were made under Jehoiakim, but not sent till Zedekiah was king. (Jer. 27:1)

JEHONADAB. See Jonadab
See 2 Kings 10:15, 23.

JEHORAM. See Joram

JEHOSHAPHAT

The son of Asa, King of Judah, by Azubab the daughter of Shilhi. At 35 years of age, he succeeded his father in BC 914, and reigned 25 years. To strengthen himself against the kingdom of the ten tribes, he placed strong garrisons in all the cities of Judah, and in those cities that his father had taken from the Israelites. The more his riches and honour increased, the more his heart was lifted up in the ways of the Lord. In the third year of his reign, he ordered Benhail, Obadiah, Zechariah, Nethaneel, and Michaiah, princes, with Elishama and Jehoram, priests, and Shemaiah, Nethaniah, Zebadiah, Asahel, Shemiramoth, Jehonathan, Adonijah, Tobijah, and Tobadonijah, Levites, to go through the cities of Judah, and teach the people the Law of the Lord. To reward his zeal, God made his neighbours revere him. The Philistines and Arabs brought him large presents of flocks or money; while, besides his garrisons, he had an enrolled militia of 1,060,000, under his generals Adnah, Jehohanan, Amasai, Eliada, and Jehozabad. (2 Chron. 17) Unhappily, he joined in affinity with the wicked Ahab, and married his son Jehoram to Athaliah, the daughter of Ahab. This occasioned his being at Samaria and assisting Ahab to retake Ramothgilead from the Syrians; in which war, by the treacherous artifice of Ahab, he would have lost his life by the Syrian forces had not God, at his request, moved them to leave him. On his return to Jerusalem, Jehu, the son of Hanani, a prophet, rebuked him sharply for assisting Ahab, a notable idolater, and assured him that wrath from the Lord hung over his family and kingdom on that account. Taking this faithful admonition in good part, Jehoshaphat applied himself with the utmost earnestness to establish the best civil and religious order in his kingdom. The Sodomites, but not the high places, were removed.

Scarcely was this finished, when he was informed that a powerful alliance of Edomites, Ishmaelites, Hagarenes, Giblites, Moabites, Ammonites, Amalekites, Philistines, Tyrians, and Ashurites, had formed against him, and that the army of Moabites, Ammonites, and Edomites, had advanced to Engedi, a place about 38 miles southeast of Jerusalem.

Fearing that the time of threatened judgement was at hand, he and his people at Jerusalem observed a solemn fast to implore the protection of heaven, and himself prayed as the mouthpiece of the multitude in the new court of the Temple. His prayers were heard. Jahaziel, a prophet, divinely assured him of an easy and miraculous victory near the rock Ziz, and on the east of the wilderness of Jeruel. The very next day, as the Hebrew singers before the army began to praise the Lord, God struck his enemies with such a frenzy that they murdered one another. First, the Edomites, who took a treacherous, and perhaps a principal, hand in this alliance formed to root out the Israelites from under heaven, were destroyed. Jehoshaphat and his people had no occasion to fight, but the gathering of the spoil took them up to three days. The fourth day they observed in solemn thanksgiving to God in the valley called (from that event) the *Valley of Berachah* (Blessing). A few months later, Jehoshaphat joined his fleet bound for Tarshish with that of the impious Ahaziah, elder son of Ahab. According to the prediction of Eliezer, the son of Dodavah of Maresha, the fleet was dashed to pieces by a storm before Ezion-geber. Not very long after, Jehoshaphat and his deputy, the King of Edom, marched with the wicked Jehoram, second son of Ahab, against the Moabites, and would have perished with thirst had not Elisha procured them a miraculous supply of water. Jehoshaphat was only just dead when the vengeance of God, occasioned by his alliance with the family of Ahab, in the time of his son Jehoram, and grandson Ahaziah, almost quite destroyed his family, and reduced his kingdom to the most wretched condition. (1 Kings 22; 2 Kings 3; 1 Chron. 18-20; Ps. 83)

The *Valley of Jehoshaphat* was either the same as the Valley of Berachah, or a valley between Jerusalem and the Mount of Olives; or perhaps that mentioned by Joel signifies no more than the valley or place where the Lord will judge and punish them. (Found only in Joel 3:2, 12)

JEHOVAH, JAH, and I AM

I am that I am; or, *will be what I will be*: the incommunicable name of God, signifying his absolute independence, self-existence, eternity, and being, the cause of existence to all creatures. This name seems not to have been much used in the primitive ages. It is not compounded with any of their names, nor is it found in the speeches of Job or his friends. Yet when God says that by his name *Jehovah* he was not known to Abraham, Isaac, and Jacob, it means that they had not

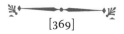

seen it effectively displayed in his giving a being to, or fulfilling, his promises. (Exod. 6:3) This name, often rendered *Lord* in our Bibles, is printed in capital letters to distinguish it from Lord, signifying a governor. It is often joined in sacred inscriptions with other words such as *Jehovah-jireh*, the Lord will see, or provide, *Jehovah-nissi*, the Lord is my banner, *Jehovah-shalom*, the Lord will perfect, or send peace, and *Jehovah-shammah*, the Lord is there. It is also compounded with other words in a multitude of names, as in those beginning with *Jeho*, and many of those in *Jo*, and in those ending with *-iah*. Whenever the name Jehovah is given to an angel, it means that he is the Angel of the Covenant, that is, the Son of God. Nor is it given to the church (in Jer. 33:16), for the words would be better rendered, "He who shall call her, is the Lord our Righteousness"; or, "He shall be called by her, the Lord our Righteousness". The modern Jews superstitiously decline pronouncing the name Jehovah. *Jevo, Jao, Jahoh, Jaou, Jaod,* and even the *Juha* of the Moors, seem to be just different pronunciations of Jehovah.

JEHU
(1) A prophet that rebuked Baasha and Jehoshaphat. (1 Kings 16:1-7; 2 Chron. 19:1-2)

(2) The son of Jehoshaphat, and grandson of Nimshi, captain of the army to Joram King of Israel. In consequence of a divine appointment given to Elijah, about eleven years after his master's translation, Elisha sent a young prophet to anoint him to be King of Israel as he commanded the army at Ramoth-gilead in Jehoram's absence. A young prophet called him aside from his fellow-officers, carried him into a private chamber, anointed him with oil in the name of the Lord, and told him he would cut off the whole house of Ahab. The prophet immediately fled away, that he might not be known. Jehu informed his fellows what had happened, and they acknowledged him king. After giving orders that none should stir from the camp to carry the news, Jehu posted off in his chariot to surprise Joram at Jezreel. Informed of his approach, Joram sent someone to meet him, and asked if all was well in the army. At Jehu's orders, the messenger joined the company. A second messenger came up, and did the same. Understanding by the furious driving of the chariot that it was likely to be Jehu his general, Joram, and Ahaziah King of Judah, who had come to visit him, set off

in their chariots to meet him. Joram asked Jehu if everything in the army was well, and at peace. Jehu told him he need expect no peace while the idolatries and witchcrafts of Jezebel his mother were so many. Joram cried to Ahaziah that certainly a plot was laid for their life, and he fled off. But Jehu killed him with an arrow shot after him, and ordered Bidkar to throw his dead body into the field of Naboth. By his orders too, Ahaziah was pursued, and slain.

As Jehu rode through Jezreel, Jezebel, with her face painted, looking out of a window, she asked him if Zimri, who slew his master, had much prosperity? Jehu, looking up, asked if anybody within favoured him, and two or three eunuchs looked out. At his orders, they immediately threw Jezebel out of the window. The horses trod her to death, and, in a few minutes, the dogs ate up her whole body except some large bones, which Jehu ordered to be interred. Having killed all that pertained to Ahab in Jezreel, he ordered the nobles of Samaria to send him the heads of the 70 children of Ahab that had been committed to their care. Next day, he went to Samaria, and, having met 42 of the near relations of Ahaziah King of Judah coming to visit Joram and his Queen, he ordered them to be killed on the spot. Going a little farther, he met with Jonadab, the son of Rechab, and, finding him hearty in his interest, took him into his chariot and bid him come and see his zeal for the Lord. Whenever he came to Samaria, he slew all that remained of the family of Ahab. Under pretence of honouring Baal with a very solemn festival, he ordered all the priests of Baal in the kingdom to attend in his temple, without one worshipper of the Hebrew God among them. They did so. He ordered his guards to fall on them in the temple, and kill them to a man. He broke down the image of Baal, demolished his temple, and turned it into a place for the easing of nature.

To reward Jehu's labour in cutting off the idolatrous family of Ahab, and in destroying Baal, God promised him and his seed, to the fourth generation, the crown of the ten tribes; but, offended with the ambition and resentment that influenced his conduct, he threatened to revenge the blood of Ahab's family on his seed. As Jehu persisted in the worship of the golden calves, and in other wickedness, God permitted Hazael, King of Syria, to terribly ravage his territories. After a reign of 28 years, Jehu died in BC 856. (2 Kings 9-10; Hosea 1:4)

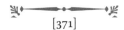

JEMUEL, or NEMUEL
The son of Simeon. (Gen. 46:10; 1 Chron. 4:24)

JEPHTHAH
He succeeded Jair in judging the Hebrews. He was the son of one Gilead (not the son of Machir) by a prostitute, a native of eastern Mizpeh beyond the Jordan. When his father's lawful children expelled him from the family, he retired to the land of Tob, and commanded a gang of robbers. The Hebrews, on the east of Jordan, having long been oppressed by the Ammonites, and knowing his valour, begged him to be their captain and lead them against the enemy. He reproached them for their expulsion of him from his father's house; but, on their repeated entreaties, he offered to be their leader if they would submit to him as their chief after the war came to an end. They gave him their oath that they would. After his instalment, without success he protested to the king of the Ammonites on the unjustness of his pretension to the land of Gilead, and presented the case that neither Balak, nor any other, for about 300 years, made any such claim; that as the Israelites claimed no territory but what had been given them by God, he would refer the matter to a divine decision by the sword unless the Ammonites gave up their groundless claim. As the haughty Ammonite despised these just reproofs, Jephthah, animated by God, raised an army of the Hebrews on the east of Jordan.

As he prepared for battle, he rashly vowed that, if the Lord gave him success, he would devote, or sacrifice, whatever came out his house to meet him. A battle was fought, and Jephthah, being conqueror, ravaged the country of Ammon. On his return home, his only daughter, with timbrels and dances, was the first to meet him from his house. At the sight of her, Jephthah cried out that he was ruined. On hearing the matter, his daughter consented that he should do to her according to his vow. She only begged that he would give her two months to go up and down on the mountains, along with her companions, and weep for her virginity. After she had done with this mourning, she returned to her father, who did to her according to his vow; but whether he offered her in sacrifice, or only devoted her to perpetual virginity, is not agreed.

Those who maintain the latter observe how unlawful such a sacrifice would have been, that neither he nor the priest were ignorant

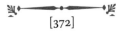

that he might have redeemed her at perhaps no more than ten pieces of silver; that she did not bewail her death, but her virginity, which would have occasioned the end of her father's family; and that the word, relative to the yearly custom of the Hebrew girls, which we render *lament*, means to talk with, and so implies that Jephthah's daughter was in life. Those on the other side, and to which I am chiefly inclined, agree that the idea of sacrifice was abominable, but remark that the Law allowed for the redemption of nothing devoted under the form of a curse; that in Jephthah's age, idolatry, and ignorance greatly prevailed; that Jephthah's way of life promised small acquaintance with the Law; that, about this time, the high-priesthood was transmitted from the family of Eleazar to that of Ithamar, which probably came about by some horrible crime; that vows of perpetual virginity are matters of a far later date; that if there had been no more in it but perpetual virginity, Jephthah had little occasion for such agony of mind, and the tearing of his clothes at the sight of his daughter. The plain tendency of the whole passage is to persuade us that she was sacrificed. Not long after this, the story of one Iphigenia (or the daughter of Jephthah) being sacrificed by her father, was spread through no small part of the east, though a different scene was fixed for it. Be it as it will, let us believe that he acted in the sincerity of his heart; and remember that, in his trophies of faith, the apostle gives us grounds to hope that Jephthah was a real saint. (Judg. 11:32; Heb. 11:32) Whatever risk and loss this victory over the Ammonites cost Jephthah, the haughty Ephraimites were so dreadfully ungrateful as to march over the Jordan in a body, and threaten to burn down his house on him for fighting without their agreement! He told them that he had invited them to a share in the war, but they did not come. They continued their insults, and called the Gileadites a pack of vagabonds, obliged to flee their country, and settle on the east of Jordan. Enraged at this, Jephthah and his friends attacked them by force, and cut off 42,000 of them. He judged Israel six years, and died about BC 1181 or 1126.

JEREMIAH

The son of Hilkiah, a priest, probably of the race of Ithamar, and a native of Anathoth.

His early call

As God very early called him to the prophetic work, he begged to be
excused because of his youth. But God promised to be with him, and
make him as bold as if he were a brazen wall, in opposition to the
wicked princes and people of Judah. He began his work in the 13th year
of Josiah. The first part of his prophecy consists chiefly of a mixture of
attacks on the sins of the Jews, and of alarming threatenings of heavy
judgements, and of some calls to repentance, and complaints of his
own afflictions. Sometimes, the mind of God was represented to him
in figures and emblems. By the visionary emblem of an *almond branch*,
and a *boiling pot* with its face towards the north, God presented the
view that ruinous calamities would quickly come from Chaldea
on the Jewish nation. By the marring of a *girdle* on the bank of the
Euphrates was meant the ruinous condition of the Jews in Chaldea. By
the emblem of a *potter* making his vessels is figured God's sovereign
power to form or destroy the nations at his pleasure. By the *breaking
of a vessel on the wheel* is meant the unprofitable state of the Jewish
nation in Chaldea. (Jer. 1, 13, 18-19) Perhaps a great part of what we
find in the first nineteen chapters was pronounced before Josiah had
carried his reformation to perfection; or, during it, there might remain
great obstinacy in sinning, and an inward adhering to their idols. It
was also, perhaps, during this period of Josiah's reign, that his fellow-
citizens of Anathoth sought to murder him, and were threatened with
ruinous vengeance on account of it. Or rather, a great part of these
prophecies relate to the time of Jehoahaz and Jehoiakim.

His prophecies of doom

When, about the beginning of the reign of Jehoiakim, he foretold that
Judah and Jerusalem would be rendered a desolation, Pashur, the son
of Immer the priest, chief governor of the Temple, arrested him, and
put him in the stocks in the gate of Benjamin. Jeremiah assured him
that he would be terribly punished in his person, and he and his family
would be carried along with other Jews into a wretched captivity. He
complained of the slanders that were put about on account of him,
and cursed the day of his birth. (Chapters 19-20) He warned the Jews
to repent of their wicked ways if they wished to prevent their ruin.
The priests and false prophets attempted to stir up the princes to put
him to death, but the people and princes opposed it, and observed

that Micah had predicted the desolation of Jerusalem, and the ruin of the Temple, and yet King Hezekiah did him no harm, and he and his people turned to the Lord, and the judgements did not happen. Not long after, Jeremiah predicted the calamities that would come upon the Egyptians, Philistines, Phoenicians, Edomites, Arabians, Moabites, Ammonites, Syrians, and Persians, by the hand of Nebuchadnezzar. (Chapters 25, 46, 49) It was, perhaps, about this time that he made yokes of wood to be sent by the ambassadors of these nations to their respective masters as a token of their servitude to Nebuchadnezzar, and his son and his son's son, though he did not send them off till the reign of Zedekiah. (27:1) During the fourth year of Jehoiakim, under the emblem of a cup passed around to these nations, and to the Jews, Medea, and, after all, to the Chaldeans, he predicted terrible and astonishing calamities to come on them. (Chapter 25) In the 9th month of this year, he caused Baruch to write out a copy of all the prophecies he had uttered, and read them before the people on a fast-day appointed by the King, in order to urge them to repentance. Micaiah, a young prince, informed his father Gemariah, Delaiah, and other princes, and they sent Jehudi to fetch Baruch and the roll. Baruch read it to them, and they were greatly affected. They advised Baruch and Jeremiah to hide themselves while they informed the King of these predictions. Scarcely had the King heard a few leaves read when he cut and burnt the roll, and sought for Jeremiah and Baruch to put them to death; but the Lord kept them hidden. At the direction of God, Jeremiah caused Baruch to write out a new roll, added to it several threatenings not in the former, and added predictions of Jehoiakim's unhappy death. (Chapter 36) It was also during the reign of Jehoiakim that, by testing the Rechabites with the drinking of wine, he figuratively showed the unreasonable nature of the Jews' rebellion against the commands of their divine Father, and predicted a happy reward to the Rechabites for their obedience to their earthly parents. (Chapter 35) Towards the end of this reign, he pronounced judgement on Jehoiakim for his pride, oppression, and other wickedness, and, soon after, on Jehoiachin, and the rulers of church and state in Judah. (Chapters 22-23)

The yokes

At the beginning of Zedekiah's reign, he delivered the yokes (signs of slavery) to the ambassadors of the various nations concerned, to be

sent to their masters. To represent the hastening ruin and slavery of the Jews, he himself wore a yoke and chain around his own neck, and advised Zedekiah to submit to bondage as the means of escaping ruin. Hananiah, the son of Azur of Gibeon, a false prophet, broke this yoke, and told the people present in the court of the Temple that thus the Lord would, in two years, break or finish the bondage of the nations to the Chaldeans. Jeremiah ironically wished it might be as he said, but hinted that there was little ground to expect it, and, soon after, told Hananiah that his uttering falsehood in the name of the Lord would be punished with death that very year; which accordingly happened. (Chapters 27-28) About this time, he had his vision of two *baskets of figs*, one very good, and the other very bad, by which was meant the piety and happiness of many that had been carried captive to Babylon along with Jehoiachin, and the wickedness and ruin of those who remained in Jerusalem. (Chapter 24) Soon after, he sent a letter to the captives in Babylon advising them to cultivate fields, build houses, and pray for the peace of the country, as they might expect 70 years' residence in Babylon, at the end of which they would be delivered. He pronounced terrible judgements of burning to death by the Chaldeans on Ahab, the son of Kolaiah, and Zedekiah the son of Maaseiah, two false prophets. This letter, he sent by the hand of Elasah the son of Shaphan, and Gemariah the son of Hilkiah, whom Zedekiah sent, probably with his tribute, to Nebuchadnezzar.

Jeremiah put in the stocks

On account of this letter, Shemaiah, a Nehelamite, or *dreamer*, informed Zephaniah the son of Maaseiah the priest at Jerusalem, desiring him to put Jeremiah in the stocks as a madman. This letter was read to Jeremiah, and he predicted the ruin of Shemaiah and his family. (Chapter 29) Twice, this same Zephaniah was sent by Zedekiah to Jeremiah to beg his prayers for the kingdom, as it was in danger from the Chaldeans. But be assured the King that the city and nation would be destroyed for their wickedness. (Chapters 31, 37) This happened about the ninth year of Zedekiah. His warnings had such an effect that Zedekiah and his people covenanted to leave off their oppressive detention of their servants; but they had scarcely dismissed them when they forced them back. On which account, Jeremiah predicted God's giving the sword a commission to destroy them. (Chapter 34) When the

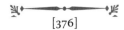

Chaldeans raised the siege of Jerusalem to go and fight the Egyptians, Jeremiah assured the Jews they need expect no real advantage from the Egyptians, and that the Chaldeans would take Jerusalem, and burn it with fire.

Jeremiah thrown into prison

Meanwhile, Jeremiah intended to leave the city. Urijah, the son of Shelemiah, arrested him as though he intended to surrender himself to the Chaldeans. The princes threw him into the dungeon. Being sent for, he told Zedekiah he would fall into the hands of the King of Babylon, and begged that he might not be returned to his dungeon as he had given no offence. He was allowed to continue in the court of the prison. But Shephatiah the son of Mattan, and Gedaliah the son of Pashur, and two other princes, offended at his faithful predictions, begged Zedekiah to put him to death. Zedekiah bade them do with him as they pleased. They threw him into a dungeon whose bottom was a deep mire into which Jeremiah sank; but Ebedmelech soon after procured his liberty from this, and he was returned to the court of the prison, and had food allocated to him every day. For this, he predicted Ebedmelech's preservation. He told Zedekiah that his surrendering himself to the Chaldeans would save him and his capital; but if he did not do this, it would be destroyed, and he himself would be taken and shamefully treated. (Chapters 37-38)

The potter's field

It was during, or about, the time of his imprisonment, that he foretold the happy return of the Jews from their mournful captivity, and bought a field from his cousin Hanameel, and laid up the deeds in an earthen vessel as a token that he believed his seed would return and possess it. (Chapters 30-32) The prophecy relative to the purchase of the potter's field for 30 pieces of silver, found in Zechariah 11, is ascribed to Jeremiah. (Matt. 27:9) Perhaps Jeremiah might have uttered that prediction, but Matthew does not say that he wrote it; or it might again have been uttered, and written by Zechariah; or, as Jeremiah stood in the forefront of the prophetic writings, the Jews might call the whole book by his name, as they did the books of Moses by their first word; or, as the ancient Greek copies were often full of contractions, when *zou*

was altered into *jou*. Indeed, what a great affair it is to suppose Jeremiah an addition of the transcribers, as well as Cainan! (Luke 3:36)

Jeremiah died in Egypt

When Jerusalem was taken, he was set free; and Nebuzaradan was extremely careful to give him a choice, either to go to Chaldea and be well provided for, or remain in Canaan with Gedaliah. He chose to stay with Gedaliah. After that prince was basely murdered, Johanan, the son of Kareah, and his followers, wanted Jeremiah to consult the Lord whether they should go to Egypt or not. In God's name, he charged them with cheating, and warned them not to go to Egypt. But they pretended that not the Lord, but Baruch, had directed him to say these things, and forced him along with them into Egypt. There, without success, he rebuked their idolatry, and threatened them with ruin from the hand of the Chaldeans. (15:10-14, chs. 39-44) After prophesying more than 40 years, he died; but where, or in what way, we do not know.

The book of Lamentations

Besides his book of prophecies, the last chapter of which was added by some other hand, Jeremiah composed *Lamentations*. Those that he composed on the occasion of Josiah's death we suppose are lost, and those that remain are what he composed on the destruction of Jerusalem. They consist of five chapters. In the first two, he bewails the miseries of the siege; in the third, his own particular afflictions; in the fourth, the ruin of the Temple and city, and the miseries of all ranks, kings, princes, Nazarites, etc., and he pronounces ruin on the Edomites for their cruelty; in the fifth, he further deplores the misery of his nation, and prays for her deliverance. He emphasises subjects mournful and ruinous, but has, here and there, the clearest displays of free grace, as we find in his prophecy in chapters 3, 23, 30-33. His writing is extraordinarily plain. His style is not a little enlivened with figures, and is tender and moving to our admiration. His *Lamentations* and part of his prophecy (such as 4:19-26, 9:1, etc) are astonishingly and deeply moving. A wise discerner would think that every letter was written with a tear, every word with the sound of a broken heart, and the writer a man of sorrows, who hardly ever breathed but in sighs, or spoke only in groans.

JEROBOAM

(1) The son of Nebat and Zeruah, of Zereda in the tribe of Ephraim. Solomon, observing him as a bold and enterprising youth, appointed him to levy the tax from the tribes of Ephraim and Manasseh. Ahijah the prophet having found him, tore his garment into 12 pieces, and gave Jeroboam 10 of them, as God would make him king over 10 of the Hebrew tribes. Without waiting for Solomon's death, he began to prepare the people for revolt. Informed of this, Solomon sought to arrest him, but he fled into Egypt, whose King, Shishak, was disgusted with Solomon. Provoked with the foolish answer of Rehoboam to their petition for the redress of their burdens, ten of the tribes revolted, and set up Jeroboam, who had just returned from Egypt, as their king. To awe his subjects into proper subjection, he fortified Shechem, where he was proclaimed King, and rebuilt Penuel. God had promised to establish the kingdom to him and his seed on condition they walked in the ways of King David. Instead of regarding these terms, and fearing that the frequent attendance of his subjects at Jerusalem for the worship of God might issue in their resubmission to the family of David, he formed two golden calves, placing the one at Bethel, in the south part of his kingdom, and the other at Dan on the north, and ordered his subjects not to burden themselves with travelling to Jerusalem, but to worship the God who had brought them out of the land of Egypt as represented by these calves. He built high places, and made priests from the lowest of the people, regardless whether they were Levites or not. He appointed a solemn feast on the 15th day of the eighth month, which was a month after the Feast of Tabernacles.

When he had assembled the people to begin the worship of his idols, he went up to the altar at Bethel to offer sacrifices on it. A prophet from Judah (but not Iddo, who lived a considerable time later), cried out that, at some future time, one Josiah, a descendant of David, would pollute that altar, burning on it the bones of the idolatrous priests that were serving at it; in token of this, it should now be broken, and the ashes poured out. Jeroboam stretched out his hand and ordered his arrest; but his hand immediately became so withered that he could not draw it in. The altar was broken, and the ashes were poured upon the ground. At Jeroboam's request, the prophet, by prayer, obtained the healing of his arm, but refused his dinner and present, as the Lord, in token of his detestation of the place, had forbidden him to eat or drink there, or return by the way he had come. But, by the villainous pretensions of a false prophet, he was brought back, and trapped into eating and drinking. To punish his disobedience, a lion soon after met him and killed him, but did not touch his donkey. None of these alarming events in the least reformed Jeroboam. He went on to force his subjects to follow his idols, and so established that idolatry which at last ruined the nation. Nor did providence refrain from punishing him. His best subjects forsook his dominions and retired to the kingdom of Judah. He experienced almost constant wars with the family of David, Rehoboam, and Abijah, in which he had 500,000 of his subjects cut off in one battle. His only pious son Abijah fell sick. Fearing to go himself, and unwilling to be an example of consulting the prophets of the Lord, be sent his wife in disguise to consult Ahijah if he would recover. She received an awful denunciation of death on her child, tending to the ruin of the whole family. Jeroboam died after a reign of 22 years. His son Nadab succeeded him, and, in the second year of his reign, was murdered by Baasha at the siege of Gibbethon, and the whole family was destroyed in a most inhuman manner, and their carcases left to be eaten by dogs and wild beasts. (1 Kings 11:26-40, chs. 12, 15; 2 Chron. 10, 13)

(2) JEROBOAM THE SECOND, the son of Jonah, and great-grandson of Jehu, began his reign about BC 825, and reigned 41 years. He followed the former Jeroboam in his idolatrous worship of the calves. The Lord, however, by him, according to the predictions of the prophet Jonah, brought the kingdom of the ten tribes to its greatest splendour. All the countries on the east of Jordan he reduced. It appears from the writings of Hosea and Amos that idleness, effeminacy, pride, oppression, injustice, idolatry, and luxury, greatly prevailed in his reign. Nor was it long after death before the Lord, according to the predictions of Amos, that his family was cut off with the sword. It was 23 years after his death before his son Zachariah could get himself settled on the throne; and, in six months, he and the whole family of Jehu were murdered. (2 Kings 14-15; Hosea 1:4, etc; Amos 7, etc)

JERUBBAAL, or JERUBBESHETH
Other names for Gideon.

JESSE
The son of Obed, and grandson of Boaz. His sons were Eliab, Abinadab, Shimea, Nethaneel, Raddai, Ozem, and David. His daughters were

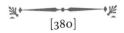

Zeruaiah the mother of Job, Abishai, and Asahel, and Abigail the mother of Amasa. (1 Chron. 3:13-16) Out of his family came the most and best of the Hebrew kings, and even the Messiah. (1 Sam. 16; 1 Chron. 3; Isa. 11) By reason of his extreme old age, he was incapable of attending David in his exile, David put him and his wife under the protection of the King of Moab. It is said that the Moabites murdered them, and so drew David's anger on themselves. (1 Sam. 22:3-4; 2 Sam. 8)

JESUS. See Joshua the son of Nun, Christ, God

JETHRO
Either the son of, or the same as, Reuel, a descendant of Abraham, and priest of Midian. From his sacrificing, when he came to visit Moses at the foot of Sinai, it is probable that the true worship of God remained in his family. He had a son called Hobab, and seven daughters, one of whom, Zipporah by name, married Moses. It is probable that he continued with the Hebrews after he had got a set of new officers established among them, till they were departing from Sinai, and then left Hobab with Moses. (Exod. 2, 18; Num. 10)

JEZEBEL
The daughter of Ethbaal, King of Zidon, and wife of King Ahab. She used witchcraft; and after her husband's death, if not before, she turned a prostitute and idolater. She was so mad on idolatry that she maintained, at her own expense, 400 priests of the groves sacred to Ashtaroth, while her husband maintained 450 for Baal. She urged her husband to murder the prophets of God wherever they could be found. Enraged at Elijah for the slaughter of 450 idolatrous priests of Baal, she vowed to kill him, but his flight prevented her. In the most villainous manner, she murdered Naboth, and procured his vineyard for Ahab. (1 Kings 16, 18-19, 21) At last, according to the prediction of Elijah, she was thrown out of a window by the wall of Jezreel, and trodden to death by horses. Immediately, the dogs ate up her body, so that nothing remained to be buried but her skull, her feet, and the palms of her hands. (2 Kings 9:30-37)

The name Jezebel has often been used as a proverb to signify any woman excessively cruel, wicked, or given to idolatry. In this sense, perhaps, it is applied to that wicked woman in the church of Thyatira,

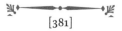

who so diligently seduced people to commit fornication, and eat things sacrificed to idols. (Rev. 2:20)

JOAB

The son of Zeruiah, brother of Abishai and Asahel, the nephew and general of King David, who was a faithful and valiant commander, but imperious, cruel, and revengeful. No doubt, he accompanied his uncle in his exile under Saul. At Gibeon, he sinfully complied with Abner's proposal of a combat between twelve on each side of David's and Ishbosheth's men. That very day, he defeated the troops under Abner, but lost Asahel his brother. To revenge his death, he afterwards treacherously murdered Abner; nor dared David punish him for so doing, as he and his brother Abishai had the troops so much at their beck and call. By first entering the city of Jerusalem, and driving back the Jebusite guards, he procured himself the office of commander to all the Hebrew troops. Chiefly under his direction of the army, the Moabites, Philistines, Edomites, Syrians, and Ammonites, were made tributaries to Israel. At David's direction, he basely promoted the murder of Uriah. By his direction, the widow of Tekoah secured Absalom's return from exile. He afterwards secured his admission to court, but was his hearty opposer when he rebelled against his father, and, contrary to David's orders, killed him as he hung by his hair in an oak tree. He wisely, but harshly, reproved David for his excessive and ill-timed sorrow for Absalom's death, and his neglect of the brave warriors who had routed the rebellious host. The killing of Absalom, and his harsh usage, David resented by demoting him from his generalship, and putting Amasa, his cousin as the commander of Absalom's host in his place. Joab, however, accompanied his brother Abishai's troop as volunteer, in the pursuit of Sheba the son of Bichri, who had raised a new rebellion. He quickly murdered Amasa, when he came up, and resumed his command. He pursued, and quickly procured the head of Sheba, and put down his rebellion. He wisely protested against David's numbering of the people, but was obliged to execute that task; and in ten months, performed the greater part of it. (2 Sam. 2-3, 5, 8-12, 14, 18-20, 24)

When, through old age, David concerned himself little in the government of the kingdom, Joab and Abiathar, contrary to their master's known intentions, thought to set up Adonijah to be his

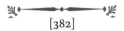

successor. The attempt miscarried, and tended to increase David's disgust of Joab. On his deathbed, he requested Solomon to punish him for the murder of Abner and Amasa. Sometime after David's death, Joab, hearing that Adonijah had been executed by Solomon's orders, fled to the horns of the brazen altar at Gibeon for refuge. Solomon sent Benaiah, now general of the host, to demand him to quit his place of protection. Joab refused, and said he would die on the spot. Solomon ordered him to be killed where he was. This being done, he was buried in his own house in the wilderness. (1 Kings 1-2)

JOASH, or JEHOASH

(1) The son of Ahaziah, King of Judah. Jehosheba, his aunt, the wife of Jehoiada the High Priest, preserved him from the murderous designs of Athaliah, his grandmother, when he was just a year old, and kept him hidden six years in a chamber belonging to the Temple. When he was seven years of age, Jehoiada entered into a solemn covenant with Azariah the son of Jeroham, Ishmael the son of Jehohanan, Azariah the son of Obed, Maaseiah the son of Adaiah, and Elishaphat the son of Zichri, to set up young Joash as their sovereign and dethrone the wicked Athaliah. After preparing matters in the kingdom, and, bringing the Levites, and such others as they could trust, to Jerusalem, they crowned him in the court of the Temple with great solemnity.

Alarmed by the acclamations, Athaliah ran to the court, but was quickly carried out and slain. Joash and his subjects covenanted with the Lord to serve him only, and with one another. No sooner was Joash placed in the palace, than the people pulled down the statue of Baal and demolished his temple, and slew Mattan his priest; but the high places were not removed. Jehoiada, then, as tutor to Joash, set on foot the repairs of the Temple; but it was so slowly done that, in the 23rd year of Joash, it had scarcely begun. Urged by Joash, Jehoiada set about it effectively by voluntary collections. While Jehoiada lived, Joash zealously promoted reformation; but no sooner was that High Priest in his grave, than Joash listened to his wicked courtiers. The worship of God was neglected, and idolatry prevailed. Zechariah the priest, the son of Jehoiada, faithfully warned the people of their sin and danger. By order of Joash his ungrateful cousin, he was stoned to death between the porch and the altar. This martyr, when dying, assured them that his death would be divinely revenged. His prediction quickly came to

JOB

pass. Hazael invaded the kingdom; but, with a large sum of money, Joash redeemed his capital from plunder. About a year later, a small host of Syrians ravaged the country, defeated the huge army of Joash, pillaged his capital, and murdered his princes. After heaping upon himself ignominy and disgrace, they left him; but his own servants, soon after, murdered him in his own bed in the 41st year of his reign, in BC 888. He was buried in the royal city, but not in the sepulchres of the kings. (2 Kings 11-12; 2 Chron. 23-24)

(2) The son of Jehoahaz, and grandson of Jehu. After a reign of two years, in conjunction with his father, he reigned fourteen more alone over the kingdom of Israel. He imitated the wickedness of Jeroboam the son of Nebat, and perhaps honoured him with the name of his son. By Joash, God delivered the Israelites from their Syrian oppressors. With no small concern, he visited the prophet Elisha in his dying moments, and from him had the prediction of a triple victory over the Syrians. Joash had not long routed the Syrians, and recovered the cities they had taken from Israel, when Amaziah, King of Judah, provoked him to war; but Joash defeated him, pillaged his capital, returned to Samaria in triumph, and died in BC 825. (2 Kings 13; 2 Chron. 24)

JOB

A notable inhabitant of the land of Uz, east of Gilead. An addition to the Septuagint version of his book, as well as Philo, Aristeas, and Polyhistor, and a great many of the fathers, identified him with *Jobab*, one of the ancient kings of Edom, third in descent from Esau. But it is more probable that he was a descendant of Nahor, by Huz, his oldest son, as Elihu was by Buz his second. Dr. John Owen thinks that Job was contemporary with Abraham. But how then could Eliphaz, a descendant of Esau, have been his aged friend? Some place him as late as the times of Ezekiel. But how then have we no allusion in his book to the passage of the Hebrews through the Red Sea, or their entrance into Canaan, though there is to the deluge, and to the burning of Sodom and Gomorrah with fire and brimstone? This renders it probable that his affliction was before the Hebrews' departure from Egypt, though perhaps a great part of his 140 years' life afterwards might be posterior to it. This is confirmed by the consideration of Eliphaz, his aged friend, who spoke first, his being a Temanite, and consequently at least a great grandchild of Esau. Some have pretended that the whole book of Job is just dramatic fiction, and that no such person ever existed. But God's mention of him as a righteous man, together with Noah and Daniel, and James' testimony to his patience and happy end, sufficiently refute that idea. (Ezek. 14; James 5:11)

At first, Job was in a very prosperous condition. He had seven sons and three daughters, and they lived in the utmost harmony and affluence. He had a very large number of flocks, herds, and servants, and was the greatest man in that country. His piety and integrity were distinguished; his clearness from idolatry and unchastity, his hatred of pride and injustice were remarkable. Not only did he regulate his own personal practices, but took care in the piety of his children. When his sons held their annual feasts, perhaps on their respective birthdays, he always rose early next morning, and, with prayer, offered up sacrifices for them, fearing they might have sinned, cursed, or despised or forsaken God in their hearts. (Job 1-5, 29, 31)

On a certain day, when the angelic or human sons of God were assembled together before God, Satan presented himself among them. In a way we do not understand, God questioned the fiend about where he had been busy, and if he had considered, or set his heart against, his servant Job, so distinguished for piety and goodness. Satan replied that Job was just a mercenary hypocrite who served God to obtain and preserve his rare wealth; but if he was sharply, or even a little, afflicted, be would curse his Maker with contempt, and bid adieu to his service. For the manifestation and exercise of Job's grace, Satan was permitted to ruin all he had, but was limited from touching his person. He immediately vented his malice against Job, and stirred up the thieving Sabeans to fall on his cattle. These they drove away, and his servants were murdered. He next caused fire from heaven to fall on his flocks and burn them up, and the servants that looked after them. Next, he made the savage Chaldeans fall on the camels and murder the servants who attended to them. Much about the same time, while the ten children were feasting in the house of the oldest brother, he raised a terrible storm that buried them all in the ruins of the house. In each of the disasters, there was just one person preserved to bring the news back to Job. Scarcely had one finished his sad story, when another came up with his. With grave composure, Job heard all; and, at last, to mark his grief, he tore his clothes and shaved the hair off his

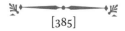

head. With resignation to the whole, he blessed God, who had given him children and wealth, and had taken them away. (Job 1:21)

Not long after, Satan presented himself again before God as before, and was asked where he had been. Had he observed how piously Job had behaved himself under his heavy afflictions, which had not been merited by any particular wickedness? Satan suggested that there was very little in Job's being content to lose his children and wealth, when his person was untouched, but alleged that if that were touched, he would curse God with contempt, and give up his service. For further exposure and testing of Job's peace, Satan was permitted to do all that he could against his body, but he must spare his life. He immediately infected his body all over with the most loathsome boils. Job laid himself down on a dunghill, and, with a potsherd, scraped off the rotting pus that ran from his boils. In a fretful tone, his wife bid him curse God and put an end to his life. He replied that this was quite absurd, as it is necessary for us to receive affliction out of God's hand as willingly as the most agreeable outward favours. (Job 2) His friends, hearing of his disaster, came to visit him. The chief ones were Eliphaz the Temanite, Bildad the Shuhite, Zophar the Naamathite, with a young man named Elihu. When they saw him at a distance, they could scarcely believe it was he. When they came near, they could not speak to him for seven days; they were so shocked at his trouble, and saw him so affected with his pain. At last, Job's patience was overcome, and he cursed the day of his birth, wishing that either he had never been born, or had been cut off shortly by death.

This started a conference between him and his friends. Eliphaz and Bildad took three different turns in the conversation, and Zophar two. To add to his trouble, they insisted that God never punishes men with uncommon strokes except for uncommon sins. They insisted that certainly he was a wicked hypocrite since he had been so mightily punished. They intermingled a great many excellent hints concerning God, and advice to duty. He answered them all in their turn. He maintained that he was no hypocrite, but a true fearer of God, and that distinguished afflictions in this world were often the lot of the godly, although eternal punishment in hell was reserved only for the wicked. By his reasoning, and his solemn protestation of his integrity, he reduced them to silence. Elihu then spoke, and, admitting Job to be a saint, he sharply reproved him for his unguarded speeches, and his desire to justify himself at the expense of God's divine honour. His discourse convicted Job. God, in a solemn speech, declared his power and sovereignty in the works of nature, particularly with respect to the earth, the sea, air, stars, lions, goats, hinds, wild asses, unicorn, ostriches, horses, hawks, eagles, and the behemoth and leviathan, and, by a series of important questions, he convinced Job of his ignorance and vileness to a great degree. Job no sooner repented of his mistakes, than God reproved his three friends for their misrepresentation of his providence, and commanded them to offer sacrifice, and to desire Job to pray for their forgiveness. (Job 42)

At that, Job was relieved of his distress. His friends came to him on every side, and each gave him presents of money. It was not long before his riches were double what they had been, and he had as many children as before. These were not doubled, as the former were not lost, but had gone to the eternal state. To his three daughters, the most beautiful in the country, he gave the names Jemima (dove), Keziah (cassia), and Kerenhappuch (beautifier), signifying that his prosperity, happiness, and glory had been recovered. After this, Job lived 140 years, and saw his posterity to the fourth generation.

Who the writer was of our inspired account of Job, whether Job, or Elihu, or Moses, or some other, we do not know for certain. Chapters 3:1 to 42:6 are generally written in a kind of poetic style; but the peculiar rules of the metre are not easy to describe. The style is, for the most part, extremely sublime, and the figures bold and striking to an uncommon degree. The poetic part of it is, perhaps, in the very language of the Arabs in the days of Job. The frequent allusions in it to things that we are unacquainted with, makes a number of passages in it not too easy for us to understand. Though the historical account of Job is inspired, we must not, therefore, conclude, that every sentence narrated in it is so too. From God's finding no fault with Elihu, it seems, that what he said was divinely sustained as true. From God's finding fault with Job and his friends for their speeches, it is plain we must not look on them as the standard of our faith and practice, but only in as far as they are supported by other scriptures. Only Job's sentiments with respect to the outward providences of God, making no distinction as to men's states, is divinely approved.

Was not Job a type of our blessed Redeemer? How infinitely rich and righteous he was! Yet, for our sake, he became poor. (2 Cor. 8:9) How quickly reduced to depths of abasement! How stupendous the trouble he suffered from God, from Satan, from men both good and bad! How tempted, reproached, afflicted! But how marvellous his resignation and patience, how timely and necessary his sacrifice! How undeserved and powerful his intercession! How illustrious the glory and honour, and his numerous family among the Gentiles that succeeded his poverty and suffering!

Extra note
Concerning the words found in Job 9:33, we find *Daysman*. Regarding Job 19:25-37, we find *Redeemer*. In these two passages, we have Job's belief in the intercessory work of Christ, his redemption, and the resurrection of his body after death.

JOEL
The son of Pethuel was one of the lesser prophets. As he makes no mention of the ten tribes, it seems that he prophesied after their Captivity, in the time of Hezekiah or Manasseh. He presents a fearful famine, occasioned by severe drought, and by destructive vermin. (1:4) He directs fasting and prayer as the means of deliverance. (2:12-13) He foretells the deliverance from famine (2:25), and the outpouring of the Holy Spirit on multitudes in the apostolic age. (2:28-31; Acts 2:16-21) He predicts the ruin of the Philistines and Phoenicians (3:4), and perhaps of the Assyrian army in the Valley of Jehoshaphat. (3:11-14) He concludes with promises of deliverance to the Jews in the latter days. (3:20-21)

JOHANAN
The son of Kareah, with his brother Jonathan, and Seraiah, and Jezaniah, and some other captains that had fled off in small bodies, came to Gedaliah at western Mizpah, and, with an oath, he promised them safety if they would continue subject to the Chaldeans. They informed Gedaliah of Ishmael's intended murder of him. After it was over, and they had pursued Ishmael and recovered the captives he had carried off, they retired to Chimham, which is by Bethlehem. Then they asked Jeremiah to ask direction from God whether they should go to Egypt or not. As they were determined to go there at any rate, they disregarded his warnings against it and pretended that not God,

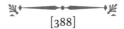

but Baruch, the son of Neriah had prompted him to speak, so that he might deliver them up to the enraged Chaldeans. As Jeremiah had told them of their deception, now it came into the open. Johanan, and his fellow-captains, carried away all the people left in the land, Jeremiah not excepted, into Egypt where, in about 14 years, they came to a miserable end in the Chaldean invasion. (Jer. 40-44)

JOHN THE BAPTIST

The celebrated forerunner of our Saviour, and the *"Elijah"* of the New Testament. He was the son of Zacharias, the agèd priest and the long barren Elizabeth. His birth and work were predicted by the angel Gabriel; and his unbelieving father's dumbness while he was in the womb was a miraculous token of its fulfilment. Being conceived six months before our Saviour, he leapt in his mother's womb at the greeting of the blessed Virgin, now with child of our Saviour. At his birth, his parents were extremely glad; and his father soon after had his tongue loosed, and predicted his and our Saviour's appearance and work. From his infancy, he was endowed with the Holy Spirit in an extraordinary way. Throughout his whole life, he was a Nazarite, drinking neither wine nor strong drink. After spending his earliest years in his father's house, he retired to the desert, where he lived on locusts and wild honey, and was occupied in meditation and prayer. His garments were of camel hair, and he wore a leather girdle. About AD 28, he began to publish the approach of the Messiah, and called the people to repent because the kingdom of God (the New Testament dispensation of the gospel) was at hand. He assured them that their circumstances were very critical; and, if they did not speedily repent, the axe of God's judgements would certainly cut them off. Those who professed their repentance, and made confession of their sins, he baptised with water, charging them to believe on the Messiah who would be immediately revealed, and would endow them with the Holy Spirit, and grant them the forgiveness of their sins. He commanded them to behave well in their various stations. Many joined with him as his disciples, and assisted him in calling the people to repentance. Such was his virtue and fame that many of the Jews suspected he might be the Messiah. He assured them he was not, and, by divine direction, informed them that he on whom they would see the Holy Spirit descend and remain was the Messiah.

Jesus came, and asked for baptism. John, discerning his true character, tried to excuse himself as unfit for the office. But when Jesus hinted that it was necessary for his fulfilment of all righteousness, he complied. To the messengers sent by the priests and rulers to ask what he pretended to be, he replied that he was neither the Messiah, nor the ancient Elijah, nor an old prophet risen from the dead, but a poor unsubstantial voice in the wilderness, calling them to prepare for the Messiah, and to remove every hindrance to their receiving him. Next day, John pointed out Jesus to the crowds, and, soon after, to two of his disciples, as *the Lamb of God, that taketh away the sin of the world.* (Matt. 3; Luke 1; John 1) Not long after, when John was baptising at Aenon, near Salem, where there were a number of small rivulets, some of his disciples informed him that Jesus had begun to baptise by his disciples, and was likely to be followed by the whole country. He replied that he had no honour except what had been freely given him by God; that as Christ was the divine Bridegroom of the Church, he was glad to have his own honour veiled and diminished, that that of Jesus might increase and shine forth, and that as Jesus was a divine Person, endowed with an immeasurable fullness of the Holy Spirit, and ruler over all, they could not escape the vengeance of God if they did not believe in him. (John 3:23-36)

He was, for a while, revered and heard by Herod, the tetrarch of Galilee; but having reproved that wicked man for marrying his brother's wife, he was imprisoned in the Castle of Machaerus. From there, he sent two of his disciples to ask Jesus if he was the true Messiah, or if they should look for another. Perhaps his imprisonment, which set him aside from his work, made his faith stagger, or, perhaps they were sent for their own confirmation of the faith. Jesus bade them go and tell John what miracles they saw performed, and what tidings of salvation they heard preached to the poor. (Matt. 11) Soon after, to gratify the malice of Herodias, and reward her daughter's fine dancing, John's head was cut off, and delivered as a present to the damsel. His disciples, with Herod's permission, carried off his body and buried it. He died about a year before our Saviour.

Jesus assures us that John was no inconstant believer or preacher, no *reed shaken with the wind*, but one of the greatest men that had ever been seen in the world; and yet there was none in heaven but is more holy and perfect than he, and no believer in the New Testament

Church but has clearer views of the method of salvation, and better tidings to tell, than he; for Jesus has died for our offences, and is raised again for our justification. (Rom. 5:25) As John's life was very austere, the wicked Pharisees said that he had a devil, but were afraid openly to express those sentiments. (Matt. 11, 14)

JOHN THE EVANGELIST. See James son of Zebedee

JONAH, JONAS
The son of Amittai, a prophet of Gathhepher in Galilee. Some Jews believed he was the widow of Sarepta's son, raised to life by Elijah, but the distance of time makes it almost impossible. Nor is it more certain that he was the son of the Shunamite restored to life by Elisha, or the young prophet who anointed Jehu. It is certain that he predicted that God would restore to the Hebrews the cities that the Syrians had taken from them during the reigns of Ahab, Jehoram, Jehu, and Jehoahaz. (2 Kings 14:25) God ordered this prophet to go to Nineveh and warn the inhabitants of their approaching destruction. Fearing that the merciful Lord might not punish them if they repented, and so seemingly tarnish his honour, Jonah shipped himself off at Joppa for Tarshish (whether in Cilicia, Africa, or Spain, is uncertain), that, being out of the Promised Land, the spirit of prophecy might stop driving him. A storm quickly pursued the ship where he was. The heathen mariners awoke him, and told him to call on his God for deliverance. Lots being cast to discern for whose sake the storm rose, the lot fell on Jonah. With shame, he confessed his guilt to the mariners. He wanted them to throw him into the sea that the storm might be stopped. At last, with reluctance, they were obliged to do so, and the storm ceased immediately. A large fish swallowed up Jonah, and kept him safe in its belly for three days. There, he earnestly prayed to the Lord, and, at God's command, the fish vomited him alive on the dry land; but whether on the eastern end of the Syrian Sea near Scanderoon, we do not know, though this is most probable.

His orders to warn the Ninevites of their approaching destruction were immediately renewed. All obedient, he hastened to that vast city. He had not travelled in it more than a day's journey denouncing their ruin, when the king, whom we cannot suppose to be Pul, but one about 50 or 60 years earlier, and all his people, devoted themselves to

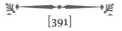

solemn fasting and prayer. As a result, God did not visit his vengeance upon them, which had been conditionally threatened. Displeased with the divine mercy, Jonah angrily wished to die rather than live and see his prediction unfulfilled.

While he was sitting outside the city waiting for his desired view of Nineveh's ruin, God caused a gourd to quickly spring up and overshadow him from the scorching heat of the sun. But next day, a worm having bitten its root, it withered suddenly. The scorching sun and blasting wind vehemently beat on Jonah so that he fainted, and angrily wished to die, and solemnly told God himself that he was right to ask. The Lord bid him think that if he had pity on the short-lived gourd, was there not far more reason for his and their Maker to pity the penitent inhabitants of Nineveh, where there were more than 120,000 infants and many herds of cattle. (Read Jonah 1-4)

Did not the fate of this prophet typify our Saviour's being cast into the raging sea of divine wrath; his lying a part of three days in the grave; his glorious resurrection from the dead; and the effective publication of the gospel to many sinners for their everlasting salvation that followed? (also 2 Kings 14:25; Matt. 12:39-41; Luke 11:29-30, 32 = *Jonas*)

JONATHAN

(1) The son of Gershom, and perhaps grandson of Moses. After he had officiated for some time as idol-priest to Micah at the yearly rate of his food, a suit of clothes, and not quite £1.25, pretending to consult his idol, he assured the Danites that their undertaking at Laish would prosper. Afterwards, he went along with 600 Danites, and he and his posterity became priests to that idol at Dan till the captivity of the land. (Judg. 17-18)

(2) The son of Saul, who was a prince, pious, and of distinguished valour. When the Philistines invaded, and quite terrified the whole Hebrew nation, near Michmash, where stood the rocks Seneh, Jonathan and his armour-bearer, taking it as a divine sign when the Philistines bade them come up to them on the rock where the garrison was posted, climbed up on their hands and feet and slew 20 men within about half an acre of ground. Seeing this setback, the Philistines were put into the utmost confusion. Saul and his frightened troops, observing it, pursued them. Not hearing his father's rash sentence of death against the man who should stop the pursuit till night, and not

take food, Jonathan, by tasting a little honey on the top of his staff as it dropped in a wood, brought himself into the utmost danger. But the people boldly told his father that they would not allow his innocent son, by whom the Lord had brought such a great deliverance, to be unjustly murdered. (2 Sam. 14)

After David had killed Goliath, Jonathan felt the strongest affection for him. He presented him with his robe, his bow, and a belt. He vindicated his character before his angry father, and faithfully informed David of the danger he was in, even though he knew he was to be king in his place, after his father died. During David's exile, Jonathan once and again resorted to him, and initiated a covenant of mutual friendship between them. He even encouraged him to hope for the Hebrew throne at his own expense. Some years later, to the great grief of David, Jonathan was slain with his father at Gilboa. David tenderly bewailed his death, and showed the most affectionate kindness to his son Mephibosheth. (1 Sam. 19-20, 2 Sam. 1, 9)

JORAM, or JEHORAM

(1) The son of Jehoshaphat, and son-in-law of King Ahab. Prompted by Athaliah his wife, he became exceptionally wicked. His father made him his partner in the kingdom about BC 895, and five years later he began to reign on his own. He murdered his brothers, Azariah, Jebiel, Zechariah, Michael, and Shephatiah, whom their father had endowed with rich presents, and appointed governors of fenced cities. In idolatry and other wickedness, he took Ahab as his pattern. To punish his impiety, the Edomites revolted and harassed the kingdom of Judah. Though he defeated them, yet they continued their revolt. About the same time, Libnah, a city of the priests, shook off his government. Letters written by Elijah reproached him with his wickedness, and pronounced fearful judgements against him and his family. These threats were fulfilled. The Philistines and Arabians ravaged his kingdom, plundered his palace, carried captive all his wives and children except Ahaziah the youngest who succeeded him, and soon after, with almost all his family, he came to a miserable end. Jehoram was seized with a terrible disease, from which, after two years, his bowels fell out, and he died. His subjects refused him the ordinary honours of their deceased sovereigns. They neither burnt any

spices for him, nor interred him in the royal sepulchres. (2 Kings 1:17, 8:16-25; 2 Chron. 21)

(2) The son of Ahab, who succeeded his older brother Ahaziah in BC 902. While Jehoram of Judah introduced the worship of Baal into his kingdom, this Jehoram of Israel removed the statues of Baal that his father had erected. Having Jehoshaphat of Judah and the Edomites as his allies, he marched to reduce Mesha, King of the revolting Moabites. In their march around the south of the Dead Sea, they almost perished for lack of water. After a sharp reproach, and ironically bidding Jehoram to go and apply for relief to the prophets of his father and mother, Elisha procured a miraculous supply of water without either wind or rain.

The Moabites, mistaking this water reddened with the beams of the rising sun for the blood of the allies, furiously hastened to the spot, and were mostly cut down. When Benhadad sent Naaman to be healed of his leprosy, Jehoram tore his clothes, reckoning that it was done to pick a quarrel with him; but Elisha removed his fears. The Syrian invaders often laid snares for his life, but Elisha exposed them, and the effect was prevented. When the Syrians besieged Samaria, till women ate their own children, Jehoram intended to murder Elisha because he did not deliver the city from its misery; but that was prevented, and Jehoram desperately concluded it was needless to expect or wait for deliverance from God. Jehoram sometimes took pleasure in hearing Gehazi relate the miracles of Elisha his master, and readily restored to the Shunamite her whole inheritance, because Elisha had brought her son to life. After the Lord had miraculously terrified the Syrians, and made them run out of the Hebrew kingdom, Joram, it seems, took Ramothgilead out of their hands. At least, he laid siege to it; but, being wounded, he went home to Jezreel to be healed of his wounds. Nor was he long there, for Jehu came and murdered him, and cast his dead body into the field or vineyard of Naboth the Jezreelite, whose murder God had threatened to avenge on the family of Ahab, and which Jehu destroyed at the same time he killed Joram his master, about BC 884. (2 Kings 2:17, chs. 3, 5-6, 8-10; 2 Chron. 22)

JOSEPH

(1) The son of Jacob and Rachel, who was born in Mesopotamia in BC 1745. Very early, God favoured him with a prophetic dream of the eleven sheaves of his brothers doing obeisance to his sheaf, and

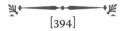

of the sun, moon, and eleven stars showing reverence to him. These emblems meant that all his father's family would be under his rule. On account of his piety, and for the sake of Rachel his mother, Jacob was extremely fond of him, and made him a multicoloured coat, such as young princes then wore. Joseph, too, informed him of some wickedness his brothers, the sons of Bilhah and Zilpah, had been guilty of. For these reasons, his brothers heartily hated him. When he was seventeen years of age, his father, who generally kept him at home, sent him to see where his brothers were feeding their flocks, and find out how they were in their circumstances. Going to Shechem, and from there to Dothan, he carefully sought them out. At the first sight of him, they resolved to murder him and tell their father that some ravenous beast had devoured him. They took him and stripped him. His most moving appeals and outcries made no impression on most of them, but Reuben, who detested the murder, begged them to throw him into a dry pit. From this, he intended to pull him out secretly, that he might escape back to his father. As he worked out how to do this, some Ishmaelitish and Midianitish merchants passed by that way carrying spices and gum from Mount Gilead to the land of Egypt. At the sight of them, Joseph's nine brothers immediately decided to sell him as a slave. His price was 20 pieces of silver (about £2.30). His coat of many colours they dipped in the blood of a kid, and carried it to their father as something they had found, and asked him to think whether it was Joseph's or not. He knew the coat, and was overwhelmed with grief for the loss of his son, whom he believed to have been devoured by some wild beast. (Gen. 30, 37)

The Arabian merchants sold him to Potiphar, the captain of the royal guard of the Egyptian King. Joseph's good behaviour quickly gained him the esteem of his master, and he made him his steward. Meanwhile, his mistress conceived a lustful passion for him, but he resisted her advances. When she, one day, begged him with the greatest earnestness, he replied that it would be the highest ingratitude to his kind master, who had given him so much power, and the most horrible wickedness against God. Unmoved, she caught hold of his garment to force him to comply. He fled away, leaving his coat in her hand. Enraged at this disappointment, she raised a terrible outcry, pretending to the servants and to her husband, when he came home, that Joseph had attempted to rape her, and, when she cried out, had run off leaving his garment in her hand. Potiphar believed his wife, and threw Joseph into prison.

Here, his virtuous behaviour gained him the favour of his keeper, if not also recovered the favour of Potiphar. The other prisoners were entrusted to his care. The King's butler and baker were prisoners at that time. Each of them dreamed a dream: the butler, that he saw a vine of three branches, and pressed the grapes, and gave the wine into Pharaoh's hand. This, Joseph told them, signified that in three days he would be restored to his office. The baker dreamed that he had three baskets full of baked cakes on his head, to which the birds came and ate. This, Joseph told him, meant that in three days he would be beheaded. Both interpretations were verified by the events that followed; but the butler, contrary to Joseph's request, neglected to exert himself, when restored to his office, to beg for Joseph's liberty. (Gen. 40)

Joseph had languished about three years in prison, when Pharaoh had a dream of seven fat cows devoured by seven lean cows; and afterwards, of seven good ears of corn consumed by seven ears empty and withered. While Pharaoh was uneasy that no one could explain his dreams, the butler remembered the story of Joseph's interpreting his and the baker's according to the truth, and told Pharaoh about him. Pharaoh ordered him directly from prison. Joseph, after shaving himself, and changing his clothes, presented himself before Pharaoh. Scarcely had Pharaoh related his dream, when Joseph told him that both the dreams signified that there would soon be seven years of great plenty, succeeded by as many of terrible famine. He also advised that it would be proper to appoint someone of skill and wisdom to collect into the granaries a fifth part of the crop during the seven years of plenty, that there might be a reserve of food in the years of famine. This advice was readily accepted, and Joseph himself was made master of the stores, and second governor in all the land of Egypt. He was gorgeously dressed. His name was called *Zaphnath-paaneah*, which, in the Old Egyptian tongue, meant *the Saviour of the world*, but, in the Hebrew, could be rendered *the revealer of secrets*. He was married to Asenath, the daughter of Potipherah, priest or prince of On, and by her had two sons, Manasseh and Ephraim. During the years of plenty, Joseph, with the utmost prudence and activity, bought, with Pharaoh's money, great quantities of corn, and stored it up in public granaries.

The neighbouring nations that had laid up little or nothing soon felt the pressure of famine, and came to buy corn in Egypt. Jacob sent his ten sons among with the rest, but he kept Benjamin at home lest some mischief come to him. Joseph knew his brothers, but they did not recognise him. Waiting for the operation of divine providence, he still concealed his case; and now, to awaken his brothers' conscience, he spoke roughly to them, and charged them with being spies, come to see how the country could be most easily conquered. After inquiring into their family circumstances, he dismissed them on the condition that Benjamin, their younger brother, would come along with them next time. To secure this, he detained Simeon, who, perhaps, had been most cruel to him, as a prisoner and hostage for the fetching up of Benjamin. On this, their consciences terribly stung them for their cruelty to Joseph. To test their honesty, he caused each man's money to be returned secretly in their sacks. Next year, Jacob, with great reluctance, sent Benjamin along with the rest; and they brought the returned money, with more for their new load.

Finding his brother Benjamin with them, Joseph prepared them a feast. When they came to the steward, they told him of the return of their money in their sacks. He told them that God had given them treasure in their sacks, for their money had been paid under his reckoning. When they were called into Joseph's house, they were mightily afraid, and bowed before him with the greatest reverence. He asked them of the welfare of their father, and if Benjamin was their younger brother; then Simeon was released. They dined at a separate table from the Egyptians, and, to their surprise, Joseph placed them at the table according to their age, not in the confused way of the Arabs, but in the polite manner now used by the Persians. To test his brother's self-control, and mark his special love for them, he ordered a fivefold meal for Benjamin. His brothers were quite astonished at these things. Next morning, their sacks were filled with corn, and Joseph's silver cup was, by his orders, secretly put into Benjamin's.

They had just gone out of the city, when Joseph sent his steward after them to reprove them for their ungrateful stealing of his silver cup from which he used to drink. Their sacks were searched, and the cup was found in Benjamin's. Shocked at that, they returned to Joseph, and surrendered themselves to his mercy to make slaves of them all. Joseph refused to enslave them, except Benjamin, in whose sack the cup had been found. Judah, in a most prudent and affectionate manner, begged Joseph to take him as a slave instead of Benjamin, as his father could not possibly live bereaved of his favourite son, and he himself could not bear to witness the anguish of his father if they returned without Benjamin. Overcome with affection, Joseph ordered the Egyptians to leave his presence; and then, with a plentiful flow of tears, he told his brothers that he was Joseph their brother, whom they had sold, and he kindly encouraged them not to fear, as God had sent him here for their preservation. He ordered them to go happily home and bring their father and all they had, down to Egypt, as the famine would continue another five years. He sent wagons along with them to bring his father's family and furniture. At the news of Joseph's being alive and governor of Egypt, Jacob fainted. But when he saw the wagons, he revived, and went off on his journey. Joseph met his father on the northeast frontier of Egypt, and great were their transports of mutual affection and gladness. Joseph presented his father to Pharaoh, and, at his direction, placed his father and brothers in the land of Goshen so that their return to Canaan might be made easy.

The famine still increased, and Joseph, by the sale of corn, drew all the money of Egypt into the King' exchequer. When money ran out, he gave the Egyptians corn for their flocks and herds. These exhausted, he sold them corn for their lands and persons. Thus all the Egyptians became, in a way, the property of their King; and they paid him yearly a fifth part of their crop as the proprietor of their land. Only neither the priests nor their lands were purchased, as they had their maintenance from the state. When Jacob died, about 17 years later, Joseph and his sons were remarkably blessed by him. The blessing implied that his posterity by Manasseh, and especially by Ephraim, would be remarkably numerous and honoured.

When his father died, Joseph burst into tears; and, according to his oath, buried him with great solemnity in the cave of Machpelah. After his return from the interment, his brothers, as in their father's name, and by messengers, begged him to forgive them what injury they had done him when they decided to murder him, and in selling him into slavery. Joseph wept, and replied that they had nothing but kindness to expect from him, as God had ordered their evil plotting for the preservation of multitudes. After Joseph had lived 110 years, he sickened. He assured his brothers that God would bring up their posterity from Egypt, and made them swear that they would carry his bones to Canaan along with them. After his death in BC 1635, his body was put into a coffin, but remained in Egypt 144 years till the Hebrews carried it out with them. In the time of Joshua, it was buried near Shechem in the very spot that Jacob, by his blessing, had assigned him. The Egyptians, to this day, ascribe almost everything grand and wise to Joseph. (Gen. 39-50; Exod. 13:19; Josh. 24:32)

Was not this patriarch a notable type of our adored Saviour? How certain a pledge was he that God would *add* to the Church, and add blessings to men! What a distinguished darling of his heavenly Father! How precious and only beloved in the sight of his mother the Church! How beautiful the robe of his humanity, adorned with every grace! How abundantly blessed of his father! And how delightfully God is in and with him! What an affectionate brother he is, dealing roughly with us to humble and prove us, and do us good at our final end! How heart-melting his discovery of himself! And how richly he makes us share the treasures of his house! What a dexterous, faithful, and successful servant! What an illuminated prophet, who foretold his own future honours, and the future happiness or miseries of men! How notable a resister of temptations from Satan and an idolatrous and sexually abandoned world! How numerous and heavy his sufferings! How hated, reviled, sold, falsely accused, condemned, crucified, and for three days imprisoned in the grave! How patient he was under the pressure! How attentive to the hand of God in all things! How ready to forgive those who injured him, and render them good for evil! To what amazing glory he entered through suffering! How blessed his marriage with the gospel-Church! How numerous his spiritual seed with ten thousands of Gentiles, and thousands of Judah!

(2) JOSEPH the carpenter was probably dead before our Saviour began his public ministry, as we never hear of him at the marriage of Cana or anywhere else; and Christ, when dying, recommended his mother to the care of John. (Matt. 1-2; etc) See Christ.

(3) JOSEPH OF ARIMATHEA, a secret disciple of our Saviour's, and a Jewish senator, who would not consent to the deeds of the Sanhedrin in condemning and crucifying Christ. He begged his body from Pilate, and he and Nicodemus, now more open followers of Jesus than previously, honourably interred it in Joseph's new sepulchre.

(Matt. 27:6; John 19:38-41) It does not appear that he attended the Sanhedrin any more after our Lord's crucifixion.

(4) JOSEPH, or JOSES, the brother of James the Less, and son of Cleophas, who is, perhaps, the same as Barsabbas. (Matt. 13:55, 27:36; Mark 15:40)

JOSHUA

(1) Or *Jesus*, a descendant of Ephraim, born BC 1544. (Acts 7:45; Heb. 4:8) His first name was Hoshea, but to mark him out that he would make Israel *safe* and *happy*, he was called *Jehoshua*, or *Joshua*. He was a notable servant or agent of Moses. At Moses' direction, he engaged and routed the Amalekites, and was divinely informed of God's perpetual indignation against that people. When Moses was on the Mount, Joshua stayed somewhere on the side of it, and came down with him. His residence was near the Tabernacle. Zealous for Moses' honour, he was for prohibiting Eldad and Medad to prophesy. He was one of the spies that searched the Promised Land. (Exod. 17, 24, 32:1-33:12; Num. 11:28-29, chs. 13-14) A little before Moses' death, Joshua was solemnly installed in the government of the Hebrew nation; and such honour was, by Moses, put upon him, which tended to make them revere and obey him. (Num. 27:18-23; Deut. 3:21, 31:14-23)

After Moses' death, God directed and encouraged Joshua to take on him the government of the Hebrews, and promised to give him his continued presence and support. Joshua warned the Reubenites, Gadites, and eastern Manassites, who were settled by Moses, to prepare for crossing the Jordan and conquering Canaan, along with their brothers. Spies were sent to view Jericho. These, by means of Rahab, were preserved and returned safe, though no small search had been made for them. They reported that the Canaanites were in the utmost consternation for fear of the Hebrew invasion. At this time, the Jordan overflowed its banks; but, as soon as the feet of the priests, who bore the ark of the Lord, going at the distance of 2000 cubits (or 3648 feet) in front of the host, touched the brim of the waters of the Jordan, they parted. Those above stood like a mountain, and those below ran off into the Dead Sea, leaving an empty space of about six miles for the Hebrew tribes to pass over. The priests, with the ark, stayed in the middle of the channel till all had passed over. To commemorate this event, Joshua erected 12 large stones at the very spot where the ark

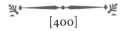

had stood; and taking 12 other stones from the mid-channel of the river, erected them on the bank. Some days later, he ordered all that had been born for the last 38 years to be circumcised, fully assured of God's protecting them, when sore, from their foes. Next, the Passover was celebrated. On the morning after, they began to eat the old corn of Canaan, and the manna fell no more around their tents. Soon after, the Son of God appeared to Joshua as a glorious man with a drawn sword, and told him he had come as chief commander of the Hebrew troops in their approaching wars. Joshua fell on his face, and reverently put off his shoes. (Josh. 1-5)

Directed by God, Joshua made his troops encircle Jericho seven days, and seven times on the seventh, with the ark carried before them, and some sounding of the rams' horns. When they had finished the 13th circuit, they gave a great shout, and the walls of Jericho all around fell flat on the ground. None but Rahab and her family were saved. The metal found there was devoted to the service of God, but everything else to ruin; and a curse was pronounced against any re-builder of the city. Achan, however, coveted and took part of the spoil. Advised by some, Joshua, to ease his troops, sent no more than 3000 to attack Ai. To punish Achan's theft, they were repulsed, and 36 were slain. This extremely grieved Joshua, as he thought it would make the Canaanites triumph over God and his people. After solemn prayer, he was informed of the cause, and the sacrilege was punished by the death of Achan and his family. Next, the Lord ordered the whole Hebrew army to attack Ai, and to use stratagems beside. This being taken, Joshua and the Hebrews seem to have marched north to Ebal and Gerizim. On Ebal, they erected stones, and plastered them over, and wrote on them plainly a copy of the Mosaic laws, or rather an abridgment, or perhaps no more than the blessings and curses in Deuteronomy chapters 27-28. An altar of rough stones was raised, and when the burnt offerings and peace offerings were finished, the people feasted on the flesh of the last with joy and gladness that they were the people of God. The priests then went down to the Valley of Moreh between the two hills, and, with a loud voice, read the blessings and curses. Six of the tribes, descended from free-women, with their wives and strangers among them, stood on Gerizim and echoed AMEN to the blessings. Six of the tribes, four of which were descended from bond-women, and one of Reuben who had lost his birthright, with their wives and strangers, stood on Mount Ebal and echoed their AMEN to the curses as they were read. After this solemn dedication of themselves to God's service, the Hebrews returned to Gilgal. (Deut. 37; Josh. 6-8) Next, Joshua and the princes entered into an alliance with the Gibeonites; and, being convinced of his mistake, he devoted that people to the slavish part of the service of God. Enraged that the Gibeonites had made peace with Joshua, Adonizedek, and four of his neighbouring princes, entered into an agreement to destroy them. Informed of it, Joshua marched to their assistance, and routed the five kings. In their flight, hailstones killed many of them; and, at Joshua's request, the sun and moon stood still for a whole day to give him light to pursue the fugitive Canaanites, and those that assisted them. A little before sunset, Joshua ordered these five kings to be brought out of the cave of Makkedah, where he had shut them up; and, after causing his captains to trample on their necks, he hanged them there. Joshua proceeded to burn their cities, and slay the inhabitants, all over the southern part of the Promised Land. Perhaps it was some years later that he routed Jabin and his allies, and made himself master of the northern parts of the country.

After employing his troops for six years in the conquest of Canaan, he began to divide it among the Hebrew tribes. Caleb, and after him his brothers of Judah, and next the tribe of Ephraim and the western Manassites had their shares assigned them. After this, the Tabernacle was fixed at Shiloh, and the tribes of Benjamin, Simeon, Zebulun, Issachar, Asher, Naphtali, and Dan, received their part, three other cities of refuge were appointed, and the Reubenites, Gadites, and eastern Manassites were dismissed to go to their homes. After Joshua had governed the Hebrews 17, or perhaps 25, years, finding his end approaching, he assembled the Hebrews, rehearsed to them what God had done for them, and made them renew their solemn engagements to worship and serve him. He died aged 110, and was buried at Timnath-serah. (Josh. 9-24) Probably, he himself wrote the book that records his transactions. The Samaritans have another book of Joshua, different from ours, consisting of 47 chapters, bringing down the history till about 100 years after our Saviour's death, and is filled with fables most childish and trifling.

Was not Joshua a distinguished type of our Redeemer? He was trained up under Moses' broken Law; God solemnly called and fitted him for his office; nor did be ever fail or forsake him. How pregnant his name

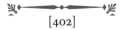

with *salvation*! Through what jordans of trouble he brings his Church into their gospel state, and her true members into their gracious state! How he circumcises their hearts, feasts them on his flesh and blood, powerfully intercedes for them, miraculously conquers their foes, and enables them to tread on their necks! He purchases and prepares for them the heavenly inheritance, and puts them into possession of it; and, by bringing them into the covenant, he causes them to serve the Lord after his own example. How ready he is to receive returning sinners from among the Gentiles; nor, till his victories are over, will the luminaries of heaven, or of the Church, withdraw their shining!

(2) JESHUA, the son of Jozadak (or Josedech), was High Priest of the Jews when they returned from Babylon. He assisted Zerubbabel in the rebuilding of the Temple. Zechariah saw Joshua as standing before the Lord in filthy garments, and Satan standing at his right hand to accuse and resist him. But the Angel Jehovah rebuked the devil, and clothed Joshua in pure raiment. Not long after, Zechariah was directed to make a golden crown for him. Did he not prefigure Jesus, as the High Priest, erector and Saviour of his Church, who, though once burdened with our iniquities, and in the likeness of sinful flesh, is now glorious in his apparel, and crowned with many crowns! (Ezra 4:3; Hag. 1:1-2; Zech. 3, 6)

JOSIAH

The son of Amon, and King of Judah, began his reign in the 8th year of his age, in BC 641. In the 8th year of his reign, he began to be noted for his piety and zeal. In the 12th year, he began to purge Jerusalem and Judah from idols, and burnt the deceased priests' bones on the altars of the false gods they had served. As the Assyrians had no more power to protect their whole territories, or perhaps had given him the inspection of them, he extended his power over the country of the ten tribes, and destroyed the idols and monuments of their false worship. The altar of Bethel he quite demolished, and burnt dead men's bones on it; but he spared the bones of the prophet who had foretold its ruin. Having destroyed the monuments of idolatry, he repaired the Temple of the Lord. As they were repairing the Temple, Hilkiah the High Priest found a copy of the Law of Moses (perhaps the original one) that had been put into the side of the ark. Informed of this book by Shaphan the Scribe, Josiah, who, it seems, had been formerly little acquainted with it, having heard a part of it read, was extremely affected that the divine laws had been so broken, and such fearful judgements incurred. After tearing his clothes for grief, he sent Hilkiah, Ahikam, Achbor, Shaphan, and Asaiah, to Huldah the prophetess, wife of Shallum the keeper of the wardrobe, to consult her what was to be done.

She assured his messengers that what was threatened would be fulfilled; but, on account of Josiah's piety and grief for the wickedness that had prevailed, the stroke would be delayed, and he would be interred in his grave before the ruinous calamities were begun. Finding by this book of the Law what a shameful neglect there had been of the three solemn feasts, he ordered his subjects to celebrate the Passover with such solemnity and exactness as had not been done since the days of Samuel. Not long before, if not afterwards, he convened the elders of Judah, and, without using any force, caused his subjects to renew their solemn covenant with God. He gave orders to destroy the soothsayers and Sodomites out of the land, and to pull down every scrap of superstition and idolatry in Judah and Jerusalem. To pollute the Valley of Hinnom, where Molech, and perhaps other idols, had been worshipped, he filled it with dead men's bones, and broke down the statues. Josiah went on in his reformation, and, while he lived, he continued as a prominent God-fearer. But it appears from the prophecies of Jeremiah and Zephaniah that most of his subjects turned to the Lord, but only in pretence. After he had four sons, Jehoiakim, Jehoahaz, Zedekiah, and Johanan, three of whom succeeded him to the throne, and had lived 39 years, and reigned 31 of them, Pharaohnecho, King of Egypt, marched his forces that way. Josiah, either being in league with Nabopolassar, King of Babylon, or with the Assyrians, raised an army to stop him. In the battle, he was slain, to the excessive loss and grief of his subjects. He died at peace with God and his conscience, and in a war in which his nation was not concerned. Jeremiah composed lamentations over his death; and his army at Hadadrimmon, in the Valley of Megiddo, bewailed his death in a most sorrowful manner. (1 Kings 13:2; 2 Kings 22-23; 2 Chron. 34-35; Zech. 12:11)

JOTHAM

(1) The youngest son of Gideon, who escaped while his 70 brothers were killed by Abimelech their bastard brother. By a parable of *olives*,

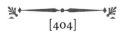

figs, and vines refusing to reign over the trees, while the *bramble* consented, which he declared with a loud voice from the top of an adjacent mount, he hinted to the men of Shechem that since, while his father and worthy brothers refused to reign over Israel, they had made the worst and basest their king, they might expect that he and they should quickly turn out mutual plagues to each another. After he had finished this parable, he fled away to Beer and concealed himself, and probably lived to see his parable fulfilled. (Judg. 9)

(2) JOTHAM, or JOATHAM (Matt. 1:9), the son and successor of Uzziah, King of Judah. When his father became leprous, for some years, Jotham ruled as his viceroy. In the 25th year of his age, he commenced as sole governor in BC 758. On the whole, he did what pleased the Lord, but permitted the people to continue sacrificing in the high places. He built the great gate of the Temple, fortified part of the wall of Jerusalem, built castles in mountains and forests, reduced the revolting Ammonites, and brought them under tribute. But, at the end of his reign, his kingdom was harassed by the Syrians under Rezin and the Israelites under Pekah. After he had reigned 16 years, he died, and was succeeded by Ahaz; and so the twentieth year from the beginning of his reign was the fourth of Ahaz. (2 Kings 15:30-38; 2 Chron. 27)

JUDAH, JUDAS

The fourth son of Jacob by Leah. His name reveals that his mother *praised* the Lord for giving her children. When about 14 years of age, he contracted a great familiarity with Hirah, a Canaanite of Adullam; in consequence, he married Shuah, a Canaanitess, by whom he had three sons: Er, Onan, and Shelah. Judah married Er, when very young, to Tamar, a Canaanitess. For some horrible wickedness, the Lord cut him off by an untimely death. According to the then custom of the east, Judah made Onan her husband that he might raise up seed to his brother. Onan, knowing that his seed would not be reckoned as his children, in his abominable way, he ejaculated, prevented his wife getting pregnant. For this, the Lord cut him off by death. Instead of giving Tamar to Shelah, his third son, in marriage, Judah put her off with empty promises. This disgusted her at him. Hearing that he was to pass that way to shear his sheep, she dressed herself as a prostitute, and sat by the wayside till he passed by, and fell into her trap. For the price of her services, he promised her a kid, and gave his staff and bracelets as a pledge. Immediately after, he sent the kid by his friend Hirah; but she could not be found, and the men of the place told him that there was no prostitute among them. Not long after, Judah heard that Tamar was pregnant, and was for burning her quickly; but the exhibition of his bracelets and staff made him quite ashamed, and he acknowledged his fault in tempting her to what she had done in not giving her Shelah for her husband. She soon bore him Pharez and Zarah. (Gen. 38)

It was Judah that urged the selling of Joseph to the Arabian merchants rather than kill him. (Gen. 37:26-27) Later, he solemnly promised to return Benjamin safe to his father if he permitted him to go with them to Egypt. In a most moving speech, he pleaded the cause of Benjamin when charged with stealing Joseph's cup by offering himself as a slave for him, which melted the heart of Joseph. (Gen. 44) In his last benediction, Jacob declared Judah superior to his brothers, and predicted he would be father of the Messiah, and allotted him a land abounding in vines. Events proved the prediction true. Judah's tribe, by his three sons, Shelah, Pharez, and Zarah, increased greatly. At their coming out of Egypt, their fighting men amounted to 74,600 under Nahshon, the son of Amminadab. In the wilderness, they increased to 76,500. Their spy to view, and agent to divide, the Promised Land, was Caleb, the son of Jephunneh. They, with the tribes of Issachar and Zebulun, marched in the first division through the wilderness. (Num. 1:10, chs. 13, 26, 34) They had the first, the most southerly, and, by far, the largest portion on the west of the Jordan. Soon after their settlement, instigated by Caleb, they were the most active in expelling the Canaanites from their territory. They marched as first of the Hebrew tribes against the wicked Gibeathites. (Josh. 15; Judg. 1:1-10, 20:18) Othniel, the first Judge and deliverer of Israel, was from this tribe. (Judg. 3) In Saul's war with Nahash, the men of Judah in his army were only 30,000, and of the other tribes, 300,000. In his war with Amalek, no more than 10,000 of this tribe assisted him, though the other tribes provided him with 200,000. Whether the Philistines had greatly reduced the tribe of Judah, or what else was the cause of this disproportion on these occasions, we do not know. After Saul's death, the Hebrew kings began to come from the tribe of Judah and family of

David. Nor did the government ever depart from them till the Messiah appeared. (Gen. 49:10; 1 Sam. 11:8, 15:4)

Judah's posterity is often called *Jews* (after his name). Bethlehem is called the City of Judah (or Bethlehem-Judah); it was the native place of David their King. (2 Chron. 25:28) But there was another city called Judah on the southeast corner of the portion of Naphtali; but whether on the east or west side of Jordan, we cannot positively determine. (Josh. 19:34)

JUDAS ISCARIOT

Why he was called *Iscariot*, whether because he was *Ish-kerioth* (an inhabitant of Kerioth), or because be was *Ishscariota* (the one who held the bag), or *Ishcarat* (the one that cuts off), or *Ishshakrat* (the one who gives a reward or bribe), I do not know. Our Saviour chose him to be one of his disciples, and gave him the charge of whatever money or provision he carried about with him. There is no evidence that his religious appearance, or his preaching, or miracles, were inferior to those of his fellow-Apostles; but covetousness reigned in his heart. Highly provoked that Mary had spent so much oil in anointing our Saviour's head, and that he justified her conduct, he decided in revenge to betray him. He agreed with the chief priests and elders to deliver him into their hands for more than £3. He returned and ate the Passover with his Master and fellow-disciples. At the supper of bitter herbs, Jesus, to gratify John, and reveal his own divine omniscience (knowing all things), he pointed him out as the traitor. Filled with rage, he went straight to the chief priests, and brought a band of men to arrest his Master. He led them to the garden where Jesus used to retire for his devotions. By a kiss of our Saviour, he gave them the signal whom they should arrest. No sooner had be seen his Master condemned by the Jewish Council than his conscience tormented him. He brought back the 30 pieces of silver, and confessed that he had betrayed his innocent Master. When the Jewish rulers told him that that was none of their business, he had only himself to blame, he threw down the money, and, as they thought the price of blood not proper for the treasury, they, as agents of Judas, gave it for the Potter's field to bury strangers in. Meanwhile, Judas hanged himself, and the rope or the tree breaking, his body burst open, and his bowels gushed out. Some think the word we render *hanged* means that he was *choked with grief*, and that in the extremity of his agony he fell on his face and burst open. (Matt. 26-27; Acts 1:16-20, 25)

JUDAS, or JUDE

The same as *Thaddeus Lebbeus*, the son of Cleophas, and brother of James the Less, and the cousin and Apostle of our Lord. (Matt. 10:3) At the Last Supper, he asked Jesus how he would reveal himself to his people and not to the world? (John 14:22) It is said that he was married, had two grandchildren who became martyrs for the Christian faith, and that, having preached at Edessa, and in Mesopotamia, Judea, Samaria, Idumea, and chiefly in Persia and Armenia, he died in Libya. But it is more certain that, to refute the Gnostics and other heretics, he wrote an Epistle to the scattered Jews. His references to the second Epistle of Peter, and to Paul's second Epistle to Timothy, proves it probable that it was written after AD 66. From the character of saints, and the various judgements of God on sinning angels and men, past or future, and from the odious character of seducers, he urges them to a constant zeal for truth, and a continued practice of holiness. His quoting a saying of Enoch (not the book that goes by this name), and a passage concerning the body of Moses, have made some rashly question the authenticity of his Epistle.

JULIUS. See Paul

A centurion of Augustus' band. Into his hands, Festus committed Paul, to convey him prisoner to Rome. He showed a great respect for that Apostle. (Acts 27)

JUNIA

An early convert to the Christian faith, and well-known among the Apostles. But whether this person to whom Paul sends his salutation was a man or a woman, possibly the wife of Andronicus, I cannot determine. (Rom. 16:7)

JUPITER

The great god of the heathen. Perhaps the name was derived from Jao, Jeve, or *Jehovah*, and *pater* = father. It is certain that the Jupiters among the Latins, and the Zeuses among the Greeks, were as common as the Baals in the east. Three Jupiters were exceptionally famous: the

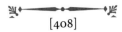

son of Æther, the son of Coelus, but chiefly the son of Saturn. His father was said to have been King of Crete about the time of Moses, or perhaps 300 years later, and to have endeavoured the destruction of all his children. When Jupiter, who was secretly brought up, came to a man's age, he stripped his father of his kingdom, and appears to have been one of the most adulterous and otherwise unclean wretches that ever breathed. The heathen, however, believed he had the government of heaven and earth, and that he gave to his brother Neptune the government of the sea, and to Pluto the government of hell. See Noah. The Jews appear to have known nothing of Jupiter or Zeus till the time of Alexander the Great. Antiochus Epiphanes placed a statue of Jupiter Olympius in the Temple in Jerusalem, another of Jupiter, the defender of strangers, in the Samaritan temple at Gerizim. On account of his gravity and majestic countenance, Barnabas was taken for Jupiter at Lystra. (Acts 14:11-13)

K

KEDAR

A son of Ishmael, and father of the Kedarenes, who resided in the southern parts of Arabia the Desert, usually in tents, but sometimes in villages, and whose glory and wealth chiefly consisted in their flocks and herds. (Song 1:5; Isa. 42:11, 21:16-17) It seems that David lay low here during the persecution of Saul. (Ps. 120:5), but it is more certain that the offspring of Kedar traded with the ancient Tyrians in sheep and goats (Ezek. 27:21), and that they were terribly harassed by the Assyrians and Chaldeans in their turn. (Isa. 21:17; Jer. 49:28)

KETURAH. See Abraham

The second wife of Abraham. (Mentioned in Gen. 25:1, 4; 1 Chron. 1:32-33) With Abraham, she became the mother of Zimran, Jokshan, Medan, Midian, Ishbak and Shuah.

KOHATH

The second son of Levi, and father of Amram, Izhar, Hebron, and Uzziel. From him, by Aaron the son of Amram, sprang the Hebrew priests. The rest of his family, at their departure from Egypt, were 8600

males, 2750 of which were fit for service. Under Elizaphan the son of Uzziel, they pitched on the south side of the Tabernacle, and they marched after the host of Reuben. Their business was to carry on their shoulders the ark, and other sacred utensils of the Tabernacle, but they were not, under pain of death, allowed to look at any of these, except perhaps the brazen laver. (Exod. 6:16-25; Num. 3-4, 10:21) Besides the thirteen cities of the priests, the Kohathites had, from the Ephraimites the following: Shechem, Gezer, Kibzaim, or Jokneam, and Beth-horon; from the Danites, Eltekeh, Gibbethon, Aijalon, and Gathrimmon; from the western Manassites, Taanach and Gathrimmon, which either were the same, or afterwards exchanged for, Aner and Ibleam (Josh. 21:5, 20-26; 1 Chron. 6:66-70) In the days of David, Shebuel, Rehabiah, Jeriah, and Micah, were the chiefs of the Kohathites; and Shebuel and Rehabiah, descendants of Moses, had charge of the sacred treasures. 4400 of the descendants of Hebron, and various Izharites, were officers on the east and west of Jordan in affairs civil and sacred. (1 Chron. 23:6, 12-20, 26:23-32)

KORAH, KORE, CORE

The cousin of Moses, son of Izhar, and father of Assir, Elkanah, and Abiasaph. Envying the authority of Moses and Aaron, Korah, together with Dathan and Abiram, sons of Eliab, and On the son of Peleth, chief men of the Reubenites, with 250 other chiefs of the congregation, formed a party against them. On deserted them, but the rest stuck together in a body. They haughtily upbraided Moses and Aaron as taking too much upon them, since the whole congregation were sacred to God. Moses replied that they were too arrogant to find fault with the prescriptions of God, and that tomorrow the Lord would show whom he allowed to officiate in the priesthood. He advised Korah and his 250 accomplices to appear with their censers full of incense on that occasion, to stand trial. They did so, and put sacred fire into their censers. They also convened a great body of the people to criticise Moses and Aaron, or at least to witness God's acceptance of their incense. From a bright cloud hovering over the Tabernacle, God ordered Moses and Aaron to separate themselves from the assembly that he might destroy them in an instant. Moses and Aaron begged that he would not destroy the whole congregation for the sin of a few that had stirred them up. The Lord granted their request, and directed them to order the congregation

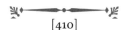

to flee as fast as they could from the tents of Korah, Dathan, and Abiram. They had scarcely retired, when the earth, according to Moses' prediction, opened her mouth and swallowed them up alive, and all their tents and families. Meanwhile, a fire from God consumed the 250 men that offered incense along with Korah.

It seems the sons of Korah detested their father's arrogance, and were probably miraculously preserved, and continued in their sacred office. Their descendants were Samuel, Heman, and others - sacred musicians in the time of David; and to them were dedicated eleven of the Psalms (namely: 42, 44-49, 84, 85, 87, 88), delivered to be set to music. (Exod. 6:21, 24; Num. 16, 26:9, 11; 1 Chron. 25) Some of them were porters in the Temple (chapter 26).

L

LABAN. See Eliezer and Jacob
The son of Bethuel, the brother of Rebekah, and father of Leah and Rachel. He appears to have been a very active man, and to have had a great deal of power in his father's lifetime. But he was an idolater, and a most covetous and deceitful wretch. (Gen. 31-46)

LAMECH
(1) A descendant of Cain by Methusael. He is reckoned the first that ever had more than one wife, his wives being Adah and Zillah. One day with a solemn air, he told them that he had slain, or could slay, a man after wounding him, and a young man to his harm; and that if Cain should be avenged seven-fold, Lamech should be seventy times seven-fold. The meaning of this speech is not agreed on. Some think that, in his blindness, he slew Cain, who was hiding in a bush, mistaking him for a wild beast, and afterwards slew his own son Tubalcain for directing him to shoot at that bush. Others think he had slain two godly persons; and that the name of his son Tubalcain referred to his daring resolution to defy the vengeance of heaven, and bring back Cain to his native soil. Perhaps rather, he meant no more but to threaten his unruly wives with some dreadful mischief if they were not duly submissive, boasting that he would slay a man, even supposing he were wounded and threatening, and that if the murderer of Cain, who

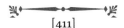

killed his brother, was to be seven-fold punished of God, they might expect that the murderer of Lamech, who had killed nobody, should be seventy times more punished.

By Adah, Lamech had two sons: Jabal, who first invented dwelling in tents, and roving about with herds of cattle, and Jubal, who was the first inventor of music on harps and organs. By Zillah, he had Tubalcain, the first inventor of foundry and smith-work, and is supposed to be the Vulcan (or god of smiths among the heathen), and a daughter called Naamah, or the *comely one*, who is perhaps the most ancient Venus of the pagans. (Gen. 4:18-24)

(2) Lamech the son of Methuselah, and father of Noah, who lived 777 years, and died five years before the Flood. (Gen. 5:25-31; 1 Chron. 1:3; Luke 3:36)

LAZARUS

(1) The name of the poor man in Christ's parable. He is presented as covered with ulcers, and as laid at a rich man's gate, and, in vain, begging for some of the crumbs that fell from the rich man's table, and having his sores licked by the dogs; in summary, as dying, and carried by angels into the heavenly state. According to the parable, soon after, the rich man died and was buried; but his soul being tormented in hell, and seeing Abraham and Lazarus afar off in glory, he begged Abraham to send Lazarus to dip his finger in water and cool the tip of his tongue. Abraham told him to remember that Lazarus, in his lifetime, had been afflicted, but was now comforted; and that he himself had enjoyed his prosperity, but was now tormented; and he was told that there was no passing from the heavenly state to the infernal regions. The rich man then begged him to send Lazarus to his five brothers to warn them to flee from the wrath to come; but this was also refused, as a certain one's return from the dead would be no more effective in convincing them than the inspired writings that they had. In this parable, perhaps, our Saviour partly alludes to some real event. It shows the danger and ruin of those who, amid wealth and prosperity, they contemn (despise): the indigent (neighbours), the afflicted, and the pious. Perhaps, too, it hints at the tremendous ruin that fell upon the Jewish rulers and people for despising Jesus, while he, after much suffering and contempt, and amid multitudes of

angels, ascended to heaven, never more to appear in the world till the end of time. (Only found in Luke 16:19-31)

(2) Together with his sisters Martha and Mary, Lazarus lived in Bethany. Jesus sometimes lodged in their house. One time when he was there, Martha, the elder sister, was extremely careful to have him handsomely entertained. She complained to him that Mary, who anxiously attended his instructions, was not assisting her in preparing the dinner. Jesus told her that she was too attentive to unnecessary things, while the one thing, of securing eternal salvation, was alone absolutely needful, and that Mary had chosen the best part of an interest in, and fellowship with, God, which would never be taken from her. (Luke 10:38-42) Not many months before our Saviour's death, Lazarus fell dangerously sick. His sisters sent to Jesus, who was then beyond the Jordan, to come with all expedition to cure him. Upon hearing this, Jesus told his disciples that the sickness would not shut up Lazarus into the state of the dead but tend to be a notable illustration of the glory of God. That the intended miracle might be more impressive, Jesus stayed two days longer where he was, till Lazarus was actually dead.

When he told the disciples that their friend Lazarus slept, he meant in death; and that he went to wake him up. Thomas, imagining that he spoke of common sleep, replied that if Lazarus had fallen into a sound sleep, it was a good sign that the chief danger of the fever was over. Jesus then told them plainly that Lazarus was actually dead. On the fourth day after Lazarus' death, when he had been buried for some time, Jesus came to Bethany. Martha, hearing that he was at hand, met him, and, unmindful of his omnipotent power, suggested that had he been present, her brother would not have died. Jesus told her that her brother would be raised from the dead. She told him that she knew he would be raised at the last day. Jesus said to her that, as he himself was the resurrection and the life, he could raise him when he pleased; and upon Jesus' asking if she believed this, she replied that she believed he was the Christ, the Son of the living God. Martha went in and informed Mary that Jesus, the Master, had come, and was calling for her. Mary went out, and the Jews imagined she was going to her brother's grave to weep. Mary met our Saviour all in tears, fell at his feet, and said that if he had been present, her brother would not have died. When he saw what grief she and the Jews who came with her were oppressed with, and thought what miseries sin had subjected men to, he affectionately groaned in himself, and asked where Lazarus was buried. The Jews present, observing him weep, said, *Behold how he loved him*, and added, Could not this man, who opened the eyes of the blind, have prevented his friend's death?

After coming to the grave, he ordered them to remove the stone from its mouth. This, Martha was averse to, and objected that now her brother's smell would be very offensive as he had been dead four days. Jesus told her to believe, and she would quickly see a display of the glorious power of God. After thanking his Father for always hearing him, he commanded Lazarus to come forth. The dead body immediately rose up alive, and Jesus ordered those present to take off his grave clothes so that he might be able to walk. This notable miracle, done almost at the gates of Jerusalem, so enraged the Jewish rulers that they resolved to murder both Jesus and Lazarus, that the report of it might be stopped. Six days before his crucifixion, Jesus lodged again in the house of Lazarus. Lazarus sat at the table, Martha served, and Mary, to the great vexation of Judas, anointed our Saviour's head. Jesus vindicated her conduct, and told his disciples that this deed of hers would, to her honour, be related through the whole world. (Matt. 26:6-13; Mark 14:3-9; John 11, 12:1-7)

LEAH. See Jacob

Jacob's first wife. (Gen. 29:16-17, 23-25, 30-32, 30:9, 11, 13-14, 16-20, 31:4, 14, 33:1-2, 7, 34:1, 35:23, 46:15, 18, 49:31; Ruth 4:11.)

LEVI

The third son of Jacob by Leah, born about BC 1750. He assisted Simeon in murdering the Shechemites, and, for that reason, had his father's dying denunciation that his seed would be scattered among the Hebrew tribes in Canaan. (Gen. 34:25-43, 49:5-7) He had three sons, Gershon, Kohath, and Merari, and a daughter called Jochebed. He himself died, aged 137 years, but his three sons produced three different families. At their return from Egypt, the tribe of Levi was by far the least of all the Hebrews, consisting of only 22,273 males above a month old. The Levites faithfully cut off their idolatrous friends for their worshipping of the golden calf. God rewarded their zeal, making them his sacred ministers. Aaron and his male descendants were chosen to be priests.

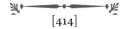

The rest of the tribe was made a kind of inferior agent in holy things. After five years of probation, they were to enter their service at 30 years of age, and leave it at 50, and no more than 8560 were fit for service. In their consecration, they were sprinkled with the holy water of separation, they shaved off their hair, and washed their clothes. They brought two bullocks to the door of the Tabernacle. The firstborn Israelites, or some in their name, laid their hands on them to indicate their resigning to them their station in the public worship of God. The Levites then laid their hands on two young bullocks, and the one was offered for a burnt offering and the other for a sin offering. To signify their being dedicated to the service of the God of all the ends of the earth, they were made to walk to and fro before the Tabernacle; and thus entered on their work, which, in the wilderness, was to carry the things pertaining to the Tabernacle. In that, and after ages, they took care of the Tabernacle, Temple, and its furniture, taught the people, and assisted the priests. They had no sacred clothing, but, though the tribe of Levi was only about a 40th of the people, they had 48 cities, with suburbs assigned for their dwelling, and received about 1/5th of the Hebrew incomes. (Exod. 6, 32:26-29; Num. 3-4, 8, 10, 18)

Did not these Levites prefigure Jesus? From the earliest ages of eternity, he was chosen to his work, and from the earliest ages of time, he was promised. Early was he circumcised and initiated; and, at twelve years of age, be began his service in the Temple. Divinely was our place in Law, and our sins were transferred upon him. Solemn was he, in his birth, and in his unction at his baptism, set apart for his work of obedience and ministry in holy things. At 30 years of age, he entered on his public service, and, having wasted his body, till, it seems, he looked like a man of 50 years, he retired by death, resurrection, and ascension, to his eternal rest. He is the great burden-bearer of his Church, who bears all his people's sins, and their persons and cares. He supports the whole frame and government of the Church, honours his Father to the highest, teaches, governs, and saves his people, and, as a reward, is crowned with glory and honour. Terrible is the curse that falls on those who continue to deny him his dues. Did not these Levites represent gospel ministers, who, being chosen for their work by God and his people, are to enter on it in a solemn manner, sanctified by the blood of the Lamb, and by his purifying Spirit; and who spend and are spent in the service of the Church, bearing Christ's name before the Gentiles,

teaching and ruling the people, and assisting the saints? These spiritual priests, in their sacred work, are to be duly provided with subsistence, and, at the end, are to have their faithful service rewarded with endless honours and happiness.

Do they not resemble the saints, who are early enrolled in the Lamb's book of life, and, in due time, are solemnly set apart for the holy service of God, to care for, and, in their stations, instruct, and promote order; and after they have finished their course, retire to their everlasting rest to enjoy the fullness of God? (Isa. 46:21) When Joshua divided Canaan among the Hebrew tribes, he gave the Levites no inheritance, as they were to live on sacred offerings. But they had 48 cities scattered among the other tribes, with a field of 3000 cubits around for pasture and gardens. Six of these cities were cities of refuge, and others of them were retained by the Canaanites. Their tithes too, and other dues, were not well paid, as often as not religion fell into a languishing condition. (Josh. 20-21; Judg. 1; Neh. 13) Soon after, a vagrant Levite helped Micah and the Danites of Laish to introduce idolatry, and his descendants were, for many ages, priests to that idol. Another, by the affair of his concubine abused at Gibeah, brought about the death of 40,000 Israelites, and of the whole tribe of Benjamin, except 600, and all the inhabitants of Jabeshgilead, except 401 virgins. (Judg. 17-21) Eli and Samuel, both Levites, were judges of Israel. (1 Sam. 1-8) 8,300 Levites attended David's coronation; and, in his days, they began to enter on their service at 25 years of age. And there were of them fit for service, 38,000, of which 24,000 were appointed to officiate in the service of the Tabernacle or Temple, 6000 of them as judges, 4000 as porters, and 4000 as sacred musicians. The officiating Levites, as well as the priests and singers - if not also the porters - were divided into 24 classes, and had their turns of service assigned them by lot. (1 Chron. 12-13, 26)

When Jeroboam, the son of Nebat, established his idolatrous worship of the golden calf, many of the Levites left his kingdom and retired to the kingdom of Judah. Jehoshaphat dispersed them throughout his dominions, along with some of his princes, to teach the people. Those of Libnah revolted from King Jehoram. Under the direction of Jehoiada, the Levites, being furnished with arms, greatly assisted in establishing Joash on the throne. In Hezekiah's time, they were more enthusiastic for promoting reformation than

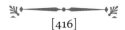

the priests, when a few of the priests sanctified themselves, and the Levites assisted in slaughtering the burnt offerings. Under Josiah, they directed the repairs of the Temple, and zealously assisted at the solemn Passover. (2 Chron. 11:12-13, ch. 19, 21:10, 23, 29, 31, 34, 35) A considerable number of them returned from Babylon, some along with Zerubbabel, others with Ezra, and 1760 priests and 212 Levites dwelt at Jerusalem. (1 Chron. 9:18; Ezra 2:40-42, 70, 8:18-19) Ten of them, under Ezra's direction, put away their foreign wives. (Ezra 10:23-24) Under Nehemiah, they assisted at his solemn fast in reading the Law (Neh. 8:7, 9:4-5), and seventeen of them subscribed to his covenant for reformation. (Chapter 10) About this time, or not long after, Nehemiah ordered their tithes to be punctually given them, as the withholding of them had obliged them to desert the service of the Temple, and take up civil employment. (Neh. 13:10-13) After our Saviour's death, we find the tribe of Levi in the utmost disorder. The high priesthood was disposed of to the highest bidder, the Levites were allowed by Agrippa to wear the sacerdotal robes of the common priests, and the porters to become singers.

LORUHAMAH, *not obtaining mercy*
Ruhamah means *having obtained mercy.* (Only found in Hosea 1:6, 8)

LOT
The son of Haran, nephew of Abraham, and, as we suppose, brother of Sarah. After the death of his father, he lived and travelled with Abraham. After their return from Egypt, the number of their flocks, and the strife of their herdsmen, obliged them to separate. On Abraham's humble and peaceful offer, Lot too proudly took his choice, preferring himself to his uncle. Charmed with the fertile appearance of the country about Sodom, he, perhaps without consulting his Maker, chose that for his place to live. His pride and carnal-mindedness were severely punished. The wicked behaviour of the Sodomites made his life a continual burden to him. Nor had he been long there, when he, if not also the most of what he had, was taken captive by Chedorlaomer. He was recovered by Abraham; and had it not been for Abraham's intercession with God on his behalf, about 16 years after, he would have perished in the overthrow of Sodom.

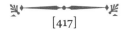

On the evening before that fatal event, two of the angels, who had just feasted with Abraham, appeared as travellers to Lot at the gate of Sodom. Lot humbly begged them to lodge in his house. At first, to test his hospitality, they spoke as if they were inclined to lodge all night in the street. But, on his further entreaty, they entered his house and supped with him in a way we do not understand. Supper had scarce finished when many of the men of the city came and demanded from Lot the two strangers, that they might abuse them in a manner shocking to chastity. Lot, in his confusion, begged them rather to take his two virgin daughters than so horribly abuse the strangers who had committed themselves to his protection. They reproached him as a saucy impertinent fellow who, though but lately come to live among them, would act the part of a judge, and dictate to them who were natives of the place. And they threatened to use him worse than they had intended to do with the strangers. At this, they furiously rushed forward to break open the door that Lot had shut behind him. The angels pulled Lot in and bolted the door, and smote the Sodomites about it with such severe blindness and stupidity that they could not find it; and, being wearied with groping, they at last went home. Meanwhile, the angels informed Lot of their intentions to destroy Sodom and the cities adjacent for their wickedness, and warned him and all his relations to leave the place immediately. He sent and warned his sons-in-law, and begged them to flee; but they contemned (despised) his message. About break of day, Lot, his wife, and his two unmarried daughters, unwilling to leave their property, or waiting for the other daughters, continued to put off the time.

The angels took them by the hand, and hastened them out of their house and from the city. Leaving them, they warned them to run with all their might to a neighbouring mountain; and that they should be consumed if they so much as looked back. At Lot's intercession, who was afraid of the wild beasts of the mountain, the angels, directed by God, promised to spare Zoar, the least of the five cities marked for ruin, as a place of refuge to him and his family. Through worldly affection of her country and wealth, or a vain curiosity to see the vengeance of God, Lot's wife looked behind her. The flames of divine vengeance seized her immediately, and transformed her into a statue of petrified salt, thus making her a standing monument to the danger of unbelief, disobedience, love for the world, apostasy from, and disobedience to,

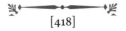

God. How long this pillar continued, we do not know. Flavius Josephus says it remained in his time, which was nearly 2000 years after it was formed. Irenaeus and Quintus Septimius Florens Tertullian say that it was still standing about AD 200. Benjamin of Tudela, the Jewish traveller, suggests that it was standing nearly 1000 years later, which would make its duration more than 3000 years. Some modern travellers pretend to have seen it; but their telling seems so fabulous, and differs so widely, that we cannot credit it. It is certain that Henry Maundrell, Thomas Shaw, and Thomson, and other travellers of known truthfulness, do not pretend that there are now the least remains of this notable salt statue.

Shocked by the death of his wife and the ruin of his country, Lot was afraid to stay in Zoar; so he and his daughters retired to an adjacent mountain. Lot's daughters, whom he had just offered as prostitutes to the unclean Sodomites, decoyed him into drunkenness and incest. Anxious of posterity, and perhaps desirous to be mother of the Messiah, and fearing there was never a man left on the earth besides their father, or at least none to whom they could have access, they resolved to have children by him. On two different nights, they intoxicated him with wine, and lay with him, one after the other. They became pregnant by him. The oldest daughter impudently called her son *Moab* to mark that he was begotten by her father. The younger called her son *Benammi* (*the son of my people).* From these two sprang the Moabites and Ammonites, on whom the curse of heaven remarkably lay. (Gen. 11:31, 13-14, 19; Luke 17:32; 2 Pet. 2:6-8) Some think Baalpeor, the immodest deity worshipped by the Ammonites, and Moabites, was a representation of Lot in his shameful drunkenness and incest.

LUCIFER
A *brilliant* star whose name was used for the King of Babylon, and referred to his glory. The passage is often used to describe the fall of Satan from heaven. Found only in Isaiah 14:12.

LUKE or LUCAS
The Evangelist. A native of Antioch in Syria, and a physician as to his business. Whether he was a Jew or Gentile, or whether he was the same as Lucius the kinsman of Paul (Rom. 16:21), or whether he was converted by Paul at Antioch, or met him first at Troas, we do not

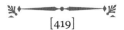

know. His mention of himself as Paul's companion began at Troas; and, after that, he often mentions himself as going along with him. (The *we* passages. Compare also Acts 16 with Col. 4:14; Philem. verse 23; 2 Tim. 4:11) Luke wrote the history of Christ's life, and the history of the Acts of the Apostles, and dedicated them both to one *Theophilus*, who, it seems, was one of his godly friends. In his history of Christ, he relates a great many circumstances of his, and his harbinger, John Baptist's birth and private life, which are not mentioned by Matthew and Mark, who are generally, though uncertainly, thought to have written their gospels before him. He also records a variety of incidents and parables of Jesus' public life omitted by them. Nor is his order always the same with theirs, the reason of which is, either that Jesus repeated or reacted similar things on different occasions, or that the Holy Spirit, in these histories, doth not always intend to inform us of the order, but of the facts that were really done. In his Acts of the Apostles, Luke principally gives us the history of Paul, whom he so much attended. Nothing in the New Testament is purer Greek than the language of Luke, and it is admirably adapted to history.

LYDIA

A woman who had been born in Thyatira but was a seller of purple dye or purple silks in Philippi. Whether she was a Jewess or Gentile we know not; but she and her family, being converted to, and baptized in, the Christian faith, Paul, upon her entreaty, stayed in her house. (Only found in Acts 16:14-15, 40)

M

MAACHAH

(1) The son of Nahor by his concubine Reumah. (Gen. 22:24) Some believe him to be the father of the Makæti in Arabia the Happy, and imagine the city Maca near the straits of Ormus on the east; or Mocha on the south coast may have been called by his name. I rather think he was the father of the Maachathites that inhabited a small tract on the east of the springs of Jordan, called Maachah, or Maachathi, or Bethmaach, as this country was not far distant from Nahor's country of Padanaram; and hereabouts the rest of Nahor's posterity dwelt.

It was, perhaps, regard for kindred that made the Hebrews spare the Maachathites and Geshurites. (Deut. 3:14; Josh. 12:5) As the Maachathites assisted the Ammonites against David, he, no doubt, subdued their country. (2 Sam. 10:8-9)

(2) Maachah, or Michaiah. She was called the daughter of Abishalom, and of Uriel, which were perhaps different names for the same person; or she might be the daughter of Uriel who married Tamar, the daughter of Absalom. She was the wife of Rehoboam, and grandmother of King Asa. As she was a notable idolater, and perhaps debased herself to be the priestess of the obscene idol Priapus, Asa stripped her of what authority she had, broke to pieces her idol, stamped it under foot, and burnt it at the brook Kidron. (1 Kings 15:2; 2 Chron. 13:2, 15:16)

MACHIR

(1) The son of Manasseh, grandson of Joseph, and head of the family of the Machirites. His sons were Gilead, Peresh, and Sheresh. He also had a daughter married to one Hermon, of the tribe of Judah, who bore Segub, the father of *Jair*, who had 23 cities in the land of Gilead, and took Geshuri, Aram, etc., from the ancient inhabitants. (Num. 26:29; 1 Chron. 2:21-23, 7:14-17) Not to Machir himself, but to his seed, Moses gave the land of Gilead. (Num. 32:39-40) Some of them appear to have commanded in the Hebrew army under Deborah and Barak. (Judg. 5:14)

(2) A son of Ammiel of Lo-debar (2 Sam. 9:4-5) who supplied David with provisions during Absolom's rebellion. (2 Sam. 17:27)

MADAI

The third son of Japheth. (Gen. 10:2) Some believe he was the father of the Macedonians, and observe that Æmathia, the ancient name of Macedonia, is the same as Ai, or Aia, Madai, the island country or land of Madai.

In Macedonia, there was an ancient king called Medus or Madai; and near it was a tribe called Mædi, or Madi. The name of Media some derive from Medea, a famous sorceress that lived in Colchis near the southwest corner of it, about the time of Asa. But, as Macedonia is too remote for a son of Japheth to go to, and as Media, both in name and situation, answers so well for Madai, we cannot but reckon him the father of the Medea. Media, now called Aiderbeitzon, is a very mountainous country, on the southwest of the Caspian Sea, east of

Armenia, north of Persia, and west of Parthia and Hyrcania. Its main cities in ancient times were Ecbatan, Rages, etc.

The Medes were subdued by Pul (or Tiglathpileser), King of Assyria; and, into Media, Shalmaneser carried his Jewish and Syrian captives. As the Medes were excellent warriors, part of them, of the city or country of Kir, assisted Sennacherib in his invasion of Judea. (Isa. 22:6) After Sennacherib's army was destroyed at Jerusalem, the Medes shook off the Assyrian yoke. Arbaces seems to have begun the work. About the 20th year of Hezekiah, BC 706, or perhaps three years sooner, Dejoces, or Arphaxad, by fair means, got himself settled on the throne. After building Ecbatan, he invaded Assyria, but Esarhaddon gave him a terrible defeat in the plain of Ragau. His son Phraortes (whom some think Arphaxad) succeeded him in BC 656. He subdued the neighbouring nations of Upper Asia, and invaded Assyria, but was slain at the siege of Nineveh. Cyaxares his son succeeded him in BC 634. He conquered Persia; and, to avenge his father's death, and the ruin of Ecbatan the capital of Media, he invaded Assyria, and laid siege to Nineveh. An invasion of the Tartars under Madyes (or Oguz-Khan) diverted him. They remained 28 years in Media. After the Medes had massacred the Tartars, and a peace had been made with the Lydians who, in a war of five years, attempted to revenge the murder of the Tartars, Cyaxares and Nebuchadnezzar joined forces and besieged Nineveh. They took and razed it about BC 601; and then Nebuchadnezzar marched against, and reduced, Hollow-Syria, Judea, and most of Phoenicia. Cyaxares reduced Armenia, Pontus, and Cappadocia; and he and Nebuchadnezzar conquered Persia. About BC 595, Astyages (or Ahasuerus) his son succeeded him. His sister Amyhite was the wife of Nebuchadnezzar, his daughter Nitocris was married to Evilmerodach the son of Nebuchadnezzar, and Mandane to Cambyses the father of Cyrus. His son Cyaxares (or Darius) succeeded him in BC 660. After a war of 20 years, and a terrible murder of the people, he, assisted by Cyrus his son-in-law and nephew, made himself master of Babylon, and the whole Empire of Chaldea. (Isa. 21:2, 14:17-18; Jer. 51:11, 27-28; Dan. 5:31, ch. 6, 9:1) Cyrus, through his wife, fell heir to the Median kingdom, and united it with that of Persia in BC 534 or 536.

MAGOG. See Gog

(Gen. 10:2; 1 Chron. 1:5; Ezek. 38:2, 39:6; Rev. 20:8)

MALACHI

The 12th (and last) of the Minor Prophets. (Mal. 1:1)

In vain, it has been pretended that he was Zerubbabel, Ezra, Mordecai, or Nehemiah. None of these were ever called prophets, nor had they any cause to change their name. Nor is it more certain that he was of the tribe of Zebulun, and a native of the city of Sepphoris near Nazareth, and died young. It is plain that he prophesied after the building of the second Temple, and, we suppose, about BC 397, sixteen years after the death of Nehemiah.

THE BOOK OF MALACHI

After mentioning the distinguished favours of God to Jacob and his seed, above what had been shown to Esau, whose land was by that time consigned to barrenness and drought, he reproved the Jews for their ungrateful and unbecoming behaviour towards their God. He hinted that the Gentiles would be called to the Church in their place. He charged the Jews with profanation and weariness of the worship of God, and with offering him sacrifices blemished and corrupt. (Chapter 1) He reproves the priests' neglect of instructing the people, their marriage of strange wives, and their frequent and groundless divorces. (Chapter 2) After informing them of the Messiah's near approach to test and refine them to purpose, he rebukes the Jews for their sacrilege and blasphemy, and declares the Lord's distinguished regard for those who feared him, and, in a time of general corruption, walked in his way. (Chapter 3) He concluded with a prediction of terrible judgements on those Jews and others that would reject the incarnate Messiah, and of special mercy on those who will believe in him; and adds a hint of John the Baptist's mission to prepare the Jewish nation to receive the Messiah. (Chapter 4)

MAMRE

The brother of Aner and Eshcol. These Amorites assisted Abraham against Chedorlaomer. (Gen. 14:13, 24) Mamre gave his name to a plain near Hebron where he lived. Some think that, instead of the plain of Mamre, we should read the *oak of Mamre*. Salminius Hermias Sozomen, Church historian, says that this oak was standing about 300 years after our Saviour's death about six miles from Hebron, and was greatly honoured by pilgrimages to it, and annual feasts there. He adds that near it was Abraham's well, much resorted to by both heathen and Christian people alike for the sake of devotion or trade. (Gen. 13:18, 23:17, 19)

MANASSEH

(1) The oldest son of Joseph, but, according as Jacob his grandfather had predicted, his tribe was less numerous and honoured than that of Ephraim, his younger brother. (Gen. 41:50-51, ch. 48) Manasseh seems to have had only two sons, Ashriel and Machir. When the Manassites came out of Egypt, their fighting men amounted to only 32,200, under the command of Gamaliel the son of Pedahzur, but in the wilderness they increased to 52,700. (1 Chron. 7:14; Num. 1:30-31, 35, 26:28-34) They pitched in the camp of Ephraim, and marched next after that tribe. (Num. 2, 10) Their spy to search the Promised Land was Gaddi, the son of Susi, and their prince to divide it, was Hanniel, the son of Ephod. (Num. 13:11, 34:23) One half of this tribe received their inheritance on the east and northeast of the Sea of Tiberias, the other half received their inheritance on the west of Jordan, on the north of the tribe of Ephraim. (Num. 32:33-42; Josh. 14:29-31, chs. 16, 23) Though Joshua advised the western Manassites to enlarge their territory by expelling the Canaanites, yet they allowed them to remain in Bethshan, Taanach, Dor, Ibleam, and Megiddo. (Judg. 1:27) Four of the Hebrew judges - Gideon, Abimelech, Jair, and Jephthah - together with Barzillai and Elijah the prophet, were from this tribe. Adnah, Jozabad, Jediael, Michael, Josabad, Elihu, and Zilthai, valiant captains of this tribe, joined with David as he retired from the host of the Philistines near Gilboa, and helped him against the Amalekites, who had smitten Ziklag. About 18,000 of the western Manassites, and many of the eastern, were at his coronation as king over Israel. (1 Chron. 12:19-21, 31, 37) The whole tribe revolted from the family of David along with the other nine; but many of them, in the reign of Asa, left their country and dwelt in the kingdom of Judah that they might enjoy the pure worship of God. (2 Chron. 15:9) After the death of Pekah, there seems to have been a civil war between this tribe and that of Ephraim. (Isa. 9:21) A part of the Manassites that remained in the land joined in king Hezekiah's solemn Passover, and their country was purged of idols by him and Josiah. (2 Chron. 30-31, 34) Part of this tribe returned to Canaan, and dwelt in Jerusalem after the Captivity. (1 Chron. 9:3)

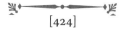

(2) The son of Hezekiah, by his wife Hephzibah. At the age of 12 years, he succeeded his father in the kingdom of Judah, and reigned 55 years. He was impious to an uncommon degree. He rebuilt the high places which his father had destroyed, he re-established the worship of Baal, and planted graves in honour of his idols. He worshipped the sun, moon, and stars, and reared to them altars in the court of the Temple. One of his idols he set up in the Temple itself, and he burnt one of his sons in a sacrifice to Molech. He had familiar communication with devils, and practised sorcery and witchcraft. By causing his subjects to follow these impious courses, be rendered them more wicked than even the Canaanites had been. By murdering those who refused compliance, or warned him of his danger, he made the streets of Jerusalem run with innocent blood; and it is said he sawed the prophet Isaiah in two with a wooden saw. About the 22nd year of his reign, Esarhaddon, King of Assyria and Babylon, invaded his kingdom, routed his troops, caught him hidden among thorns, and carried him prisoner to Babylon. In his affliction, God gave him grace to repent of his wickedness. He was restored to his throne, perhaps by Saosduchin the successor of Esarhaddon. After his return to Judea, he abolished many of the vestiges of his former idolatry; but the high places were permitted to continue. He fortified Jerusalem, and added a kind of new city on the west side. He put garrisons into all the fenced cities of Judah. He died BC 643, and was buried in his own garden, leaving his son Amon as his successor. A larger history of his life was written by Hozai, or the seers, but it is now lost. (2 Kings 21; 2 Chron. 33) God forgave him his sin with respect to the eternal punishment; but the temporal punishment of the Jewish nation for their compliance with idolatry was never forgiven. (Only mentioned in Jer. 15:4)

MANOAH
The father of Samson. See Samson. (Judg. 13:2, 8-9, 11-13, 15-17, 19-22, 16:31.)

JOHN MARK, or MARCUS
The son of Mary, in whose house Peter found the Christians praying together for his deliverance from prison (Acts 12:12), and the cousin of Barnabas. Mark accompanied Paul and Barnabas as far as Perga in Asia Minor; but, finding they intended to carry the gospel into Pamphylia

and places adjacent, he deserted them and returned to Jerusalem. After the Synod was held at Jerusalem, Paul and Barnabas, having preached for some time in Antioch of Syria, resolved to visit the places in the north where they had formerly preached. Barnabas intended to take his cousin with them; but as Paul was against taking one with them who had formerly deserted the work in these quarters, Barnabas and Mark went to Cyprus by themselves. Mark was afterwards reconciled to Paul, and was very useful to him at Rome, and, along with him, salutes the Colossians and Philemon. (Act 15:37, 39; Col. 4:10; Philem. verse 24) It seems Paul afterwards sent him into Asia, for he wanted Timothy to bring himself back to Rome, and where he would prove to be a useful minister. (2 Tim. 4:11) When Peter wrote his first Epistle, Mark was with him in Chaldea. It is said, that he afterwards preached in Egypt and Cyrene, and that the Alexandrians, seizing him in the pulpit, bound and dragged him through the streets that day, and the day after, till he died. Augustine Calmet and some others will have John Mark a different person from the evangelist, but I can see no force in their reasoning. In his Gospel, Mark begins with the preaching of John Baptist. He often, as it were, abridges Matthew, but adds several items that further illustrate the subject. He relates several miracles omitted by Matthew, such as the cure of the demoniac (chapter 1), of a deaf man of Decapolis, and a blind man of Bethsaida. (Chapters 7-8) In what Matthew has from chapters 4:12 to 14:13, Mark does not generally follow his order, but that of Luke and John.

MARY

(1) MARY the virgin mother of our Lord. She was the daughter of Eli, or Joachim, of the royal, but then debased, family of David. That she vowed perpetual virginity, and remained always a virgin, has no proof but the idle fancies of men. It is certain she lived at Nazareth, and was betrothed to Joseph of the same place and family. The Angel Gabriel appeared to her, and hailed her as one highly favoured of the Lord, as she would quickly conceive and bear the Messiah. She asked how that could be, as she had had no relations with a man. Gabriel told her that the marvellous impression of the Holy Spirit should make her conceive, as nothing was impossible with God. Mary believed; and, soon after, finding that she had conceived, she went to Hebron, which was about 90 miles south of Nazareth, to visit her cousin Elizabeth, who was near

her time with John the Baptist. No sooner had Elizabeth heard Mary's voice, than her babe leaped in her womb for joy. After speaking about their miraculous pregnancies, Elizabeth, under inspiration, uttered one song of praise, and Mary another even more exalted and rapturous. On Mary's return, she was at the point of being privately divorced, but an angel prevented it. (Matt. 1:18-25; Luke 1:26-58) An edict of the Roman Emperor caused Joseph and Mary to go to Bethlehem at the time she was to bring forth her divine child. What Simeon and Anna said of him at their sight of him, Mary laid up in her mind, and deeply pondered in her heart; as she did also what Jesus said to her when she found him disputing in the Temple at 12 years of age. (Luke 2) About 18 years later, she too rashly hinted to him at the marriage of Cana in Galilee that he should miraculously supply them with wine. (John 2:3, 5) Sometime after, she sought to speak with him. (Mark 3:20) Joseph it seems being dead, our Saviour affectionately observing her from his cross, recommended her to the care of the Apostle John, who provided for her till her death. (John 19:25-27) After our Saviour's resurrection, she no doubt saw him. After his Ascension, she attended the prayer meetings of the disciples. (Acts 1:14) The dispute among the Papists whether she was tainted with original sin has generated plenty of pretended miracles, and a prodigious number of volumes.

(2) MARY the wife of Cleophas, and mother of James, Jude, Joses, Simeon, and Salome their sister, is supposed to have been the sister of the virgin, and so her children are presented as the brothers of our Lord. (Matt. 13:55, 27:56; Mark 6:5, 15:40-41; Luke 24:10; John 19:25) She early believed in our Saviour, attended his preaching, and ministered to him for his support. At a distance, she, with grief, witnessed his crucifixion. (Mark 15:40-41) She was present at his burial, and prepared spices for embalming his dead body. (Luke 23:56)

(3) MARY MAGDALENE. She seems to have been an inhabitant of Magdala; and it is hinted by some that she was a plaiter of hair for the prostitutes and vain women of her city. It is certain that she was possessed of seven devils that Jesus cast out. I suppose she was the scandalous sinner who, in the house of Simon the Pharisee, washed our Saviour's feet with her tears and wiped them with her hair, and kissed and anointed him with precious ointment. Simon thought Jesus' admission of her to such familiarity, similar to that of an affectionate daughter towards their father, seemed evidence that

he did not know her true character, or was not sufficiently strict in his practice. Jesus, knowing his thoughts, uttered a parable about two debtors, to whom their creditors had forgiven very different accounts, and Simon was asked which of the two would love him most? Simon replied that he thought it would be the debtor to whom the greatest sum had been forgiven. Jesus approved his judgement, and, after observing how far superior this woman's kindness was to that of Simon, who had neither saluted him with a kiss, nor given him water for his feet, or oil for his head, hinted that her great love was evidence that her many transgressions were forgiven. Just then, he declared to the woman that that was so. As some murmured within themselves that Jesus took upon himself to forgive sins, he said to her, *Thy faith hath saved thee.* Soon after, she is mentioned as one of his ministering attendants. (Luke 7:36-50, 8:1-3) She accompanied him on his last journey from Galilee to Jerusalem, sorrowfully witnessed his crucifixion, and assisted in preparing spices for his embalmment. (Luke 23:55-56; John 19:25) Early on the 3rd day, she, and Mary the wife of Cleophas, went to his sepulchre; but, missing his body, an angel informed them that he had risen. As they were going to inform the disciples, Mary Magdalene returned and stood weeping at the grave. There, Jesus met her. She supposed he was the gardener, and asked him if he knew what had become of the dead body, that she might take care of it. With his known air of speech, Jesus called her by her name. Knowing him immediately, she cried out in a rapture of joy, *Rabboni,* which means, *My great Master!* falling at his feet to embrace them. But he bade her desist, and go inform his disciples he had risen. As he went and overtook the other Mary, and other women, he appeared to them. They held him by the feet and worshipped him, but were directed to go and inform his Apostles and followers and particularly Peter that he had risen. They did as he directed, but their information was not easily believed. (Matt. 28:9-10; John 20:1-18)

(4) MARY OF BETHANY. See Martha, Lazarus, Peter
See Luke 10:39, 42; John 11:1-2, 19-20, 28, 31-32, 45; 12:3, 20:1, 11, 16, 18.

(5) MARY, MOTHER OF JOHN MARK
See Acts 12:12.

(6) A Roman Christian lady. See Romans 16:6.

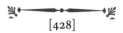

MATTHEW, or LEVI

The son of Alpheus. We suppose he was different from Cleophas, and was a Galilean by birth, a Jew by religion, and a publican by office. His ordinary residence was at Capernaum, and he had his house for gathering his toll or tax on the side of the Sea of Tiberias. Jesus called him to be one of his Apostles. He obeyed directly without taking time to settle his affairs. At his request, Jesus, perhaps some time after, was entertained at his house, along with some other publicans. As the Pharisees reproved him for eating with publicans, and other similar notorious sinners, he told them that it was sin-sick souls that needed the divine Physician, and that God loved mercy more than sacrifice and all pretensions to strictness. He told them that he had come into the world not to have fellowship with those without sin, but to call sinners to repentance. (Matt. 9:9-13; Mark 2:14-17) Hugo Grotius thinks that Matthew and Levi were two different people: the former the clerk or servant, and the latter the master. Whether Matthew suffered martyrdom in Persia, or died in Abyssinia after he had preached there, we do not know.

It is said that he began to write his gospel about AD 41; but in what language is the subject of controversy. There was very early a copy of it in Hebrew or Syriac, to which the judaising pretenders to Christianity made so many additions of their own that it was generally condemned. As early as Origen's time, it was despised; and Epiphanius reckons it spurious. The Hebrew copies published by Munster and Tillet are only modern translations from the Latin or Greek. It is certain a Greek copy of this gospel existed in the apostolic age; and, not long after, it was translated into Latin. We cannot therefore agree with the sentiment of the Christian fathers who thought the original was in Hebrew; for might it not be as easily translated from Greek into Hebrew, as from Hebrew into Greek? About AD 184, a Greek copy of it was found in the East Indies, which, it is supposed, was carried there by Bartholomew. In AD 488, a Greek copy was found at Cyprus, which was inscribed on hard wood, and was supposed to have been most ancient. Moreover, if Matthew had written in Hebrew, why did he give us the literal interpretation of Hebrew names, such as Emmanuel, etc. Matthew has exhibited to us the royal descent of our Saviour, and the obvious parts of his conduct and sufferings. His order is sometimes different from that of the other Evangelists, as the Holy Spirit did not intend to exhibit the facts in their order of time, but in the truth of their performance. He is serious without formal stiffness, plain with dignity, copious and full in his descriptions of our Lord's divine discourses and wonderful works. Whatever other works were once ascribed to him, everybody capable of judging believes now they are all forgeries.

MATTHIAS

A disciple of Jesus Christ, perhaps one of the Seventy. After our Saviour's Ascension, Peter proposed that one who had been a constant witness of his marvellous sufferings and conduct, should be chosen to take the place of Judas, who, after betraying his Lord, had hanged himself. The disciples chose Barsabbas and Matthias for the candidates. As the office was extraordinary, and perhaps the votes equal, the final determination, which of the two should be the apostle, was left to the decision of God by lot. After prayer, the lots were cast, and it fell upon Matthias. He was therefore numbered with the eleven Apostles. He is only named once, in Acts 1:15-26. It is probable he preached the gospel somewhere in the east; but whether he died a violent or natural death, we do not know.

MELCHIZEDEK, or MELCHISEDEC

King of Salem, and priest of the Most High God. Who he was has produced much dispute. Some have him to be Christ, or the Holy Spirit; but Paul distinguishes between him and our Saviour, and says he was only *made like unto the Son of God*. Both Moses and Paul present him as a mere man who reigned at Salem in Canaan. But what sort of man he was, is as little agreed. The Jews and Samaritans have him to be Shem, their ancestor. The Arabians have him to be the grandson of Shem on the father's side, and the great grandson of Japheth by his mother's, and pretend to give us the names of his ancestors. Pierre Jurieu believes he is Ham. Dr. John Owen would have him to be a descendant of Japheth, and a pledge of the offspring of Japheth's becoming the principal Church of God. But how a descendant of Japheth came to be King of the Canaanites, we do not know. Why may we not rather with "Suidas" suppose him a descendant of Ham, sprung from a cursed family, and ruling over subjects cursed in their progenitor? Would this not make him very a good comparison with Jesus Christ?

But what all this inquiry after a genealogy, which God has concealed, and to render him a distinguished type of our Saviour, has brought him before us as if dropped from heaven, and after his work returning back there? His blessing of Abraham, the great heir of promise, and receiving tithes from him, marks him superior to Levi and Aaron, who were then in his loins. When Abraham returned from the rout of Chedorlaomer and his allies, Melchizedek met him in the Valley of Shaveh, afterwards called the King's Dale, and tendered to him a present of bread and wine for the refreshment of himself and his wearied troops. He also blessed Abraham, and thanked God for giving him the victory. Abraham acknowledged him priest of the Most High God, and gave him a tenth part of the spoil. (Gen. 14:17-20; Heb. 7:1-21) Jesus is *a priest after the order of Melchizedek*; as God, he was without beginning, and without a mother. As man, his origin was miraculous, without a father. He was installed in his office only by God, and is thus superior to all the Aaronic and ransomed priests. He communicates all blessings to them, and ought to receive from them proper glory and honour. He, with his flesh that is meat indeed, and his blood that is drink indeed, refreshes his people when liable to faint in their spiritual warfare. He has no successor, but is possessed of an unchangeable priesthood (Ps. 110:4; Heb. 5:6, 10, 6:20, 7:1-11)

MENAHEM

The son of Gadi, who seems to have been general to Zachariah, the son of Jeroboam the second. No sooner had he heard that his master was murdered by Shallum, the son of Jabesh, in Samaria, than he marched from Tirzah, and cut off Shallum, and seized the crown for himself. Provoked that the citizens of Tiphsah did not readily acknowledge him and open their gates to him, he murdered most of the people, ripped up the women with child, and dashed the infants to pieces. Pul, the King of Assyria, soon after invaded his kingdom; but, with a thousand talents of silver (just over £342, 187), Menahem gained his friendship. This money Menahem exacted from his people at the rate of 50 shekels from all those who were able to bear it. After a reign of ten years, Menahem died in BC 1663, and Pekahiah his son, after a reign of two years, was murdered by Pekah. (2 Kings 15:14-26)

MEPHIBOSHETH

(1) A son of King Saul by his concubine Rizpah. (2 Sam. 21:8-9)

(2) Mephibosheth, the son of Jonathan, and grandchild of Saul. When his father and friends were killed at the battle of Gilboa, his nurse was struck with such terror at the news that she let Mephibosheth fall. This rendered him ever after lame in both of his feet. (2 Sam. 4) In his childhood, he was secretly brought up in the family of one Machir of Lodebar, in the land of Gilead. When David was established on the throne of Israel, and had avenged himself of the Philistines and Moabites, he examined Ziba, who had been one of Saul's principal servants, whether any of the house of Saul yet lived, that he might show them kindness for the sake of Jonathan. Ziba told him of Mephibosheth. With great earnestness, David sent and brought him to his house, and told him he must eat bread continually at his table. Mephibosheth accepted the favour with the utmost humility and gratitude. David ordered Ziba, and his family of 15 sons and 20 servants, to cultivate for Mephibosheth and his child Micah the whole inheritance of Saul. (2 Sam. 9)

Some years later, when Absalom's rebellion forced David to quit his capital, Mephibosheth asked Ziba to saddle him his ass that he might ride off with his benefactor, as he could not walk on foot. Ziba, instead of obeying him, resolved to trick him out of his whole estate. He went after David with a present of two ass-loads of provision, and told him that Mephibosheth waited at Jerusalem in hopes that the Hebrews, who were in arms against David, would now restore him to the throne of his grandfather and uncle. At this, David too rashly made a grant of all Mephibosheth's estate to this villainous servant. When, after the defeat of Absalom, David returned to Jerusalem, Mephibosheth met him in deep mourning, his feet never washed, nor his beard trimmed, since David had gone off from his capital. David asked him why he had not gone along with him. Mephibosheth told him how Ziba his servant had deceived him, and had slandered him; but added that David might do with him as he pleased; and that since, while his father's whole family were all obnoxious to death at his hand, he had made him his table companion, and he had no reason to complain of the disposal of his lands to Ziba. Nor was it proper the king should trouble himself to provide for him. David told him he needed to say no more, as he ordered him and Ziba to share the land between them in equal portions. Mephibosheth replied that he was content that Ziba should take it all, as the king had safely returned to his throne. By his son Micah, whose sons were Pithon, Melech, Tahrea, and Ahaz, he had a numerous posterity. (2 Sam. 16:1-4, 19:24-40; 1 Chron. 8:34-40)

MERARI

The third son of Levi, and father of Mahli and Mushi. When the Hebrews came out of Egypt, the Merarite males, from a month old and upward, numbered 6200; and those fit for service (between 30 and 50 years of age) were 3200. Their duty was to bear in their wagons, and to fix the pillars, bars, and boards of the Tabernacle. They went first of all, as Levites in their march through the wilderness, that the pillars might be set up, and boards fastened, before the hangings came forward to be laid on them, as these last were spread before the sacred furniture came up. (Num. 3:33-37, 4:29-45) Some of his posterity became sacred porters. (1 Chron. 26:10, 19) Their cities were: Jokneam, Kartah, Dimnah, Nahalal, Bezer, Kedemoth, Jahazah, Mephaath, Ramothgilead, Mahanaim, Heshbon, Jazer. (Josh. 21:34-40; 1 Chron. 6:63, 77-81)

MERCURIUS (Mercury)

The son of Jupiter and Maia, he was one of the fabulous deities of the heathen, and messenger to the rest. His Greek name *Hermes* meant that he was the interpreter of their will. He was worshipped as the god of learning, eloquence, and trade, and was famous for lying and deceit. Perhaps he was an ancient king of the Gauls. Or what if he was the Egyptian philosopher Hermes Trismegistus, or the very great interpreter worshipped after his death? Or what if the exploits of Mercury be but those of Moses and Aaron, quite overlaid with fable? At Lystra, Paul was taken for Mercury because of his fine manner of speaking. (Only found in Acts 14:8-12) See also Hermes in Romans 16:40.

MERODACH, or BERODACH BALADAN

The son of Baladan, King of Babylon. About BC 712, he sent messengers to congratulate Hezekiah on his miraculous recovery, the deliverance of his capital from the Assyrians, to enquire into these facts and the retrograde motion of the sun, and perhaps to form an alliance against the now reduced Assyrians. (2 Kings 20:12; Isa. 39:1-2) It seems that Merodach was a great king, and was worshipped after his death in Babylon.

When Cyrus took that city, Merodach's image was broken into pieces. (The name is found only in Jer. 50:2) Nebuchadnezzar, it seems, expected that his son would be another great Merodach, but he turned out to be a fool, so was called *Evilmerodach*, or foolish Merodach.

MESHA

The King of Moab. After the death of Ahab, he revolted from the yoke of the ten tribes, and refused his yearly tribute of 100,000 lambs and as many rams with the wool. Provoked by this, Joram, King of Israel, assisted by the Jews and Edomites, invaded his kingdom and routed his army before they could put themselves into battle-array. Mesha shut himself up in Ar, his capital, and, finding that he could not decoy the King of Edom, nor break through his troops whom he reckoned the weakest of the besiegers, filled with rage against the Israelites, he took his oldest son and heir to the crown, and offered him as a burnt-sacrifice on the wall, as the last and most effective means of procuring the favour and assistance of his idol-god. The enemy, seeing this token of his desperation, went home with their booty. Whether it was this outrageous king who afterward invaded the land of Edom, and having apprehended its king, whether dead or alive, burnt his body in lime, is not altogether certain. (2 Kings 2-3; Amos 2:1)

MESHECH

The sixth son of Japheth. We suppose him to be the father of the Moscheni, who inhabited the Moschic mountains on the northeast of Cappadocia, and that the Muscovites are partly his descendants. Before the Chaldean conquests, the Moscheni traded with the Tyrians in vessels of brass and in slaves. But whether they brought them by land, or whether the Tyrians sailed up to the Euxine (or Black Sea), and got them there, we do not know. (Ezek. 27:13) The *Meshech, Tubal,* and their multitude, whose graves were round about their prince, we suppose were those Scythians that were massacred in Media about the end of Josiah's reign, or perhaps also the Gauls and Scythians cut off by the kings of Lydia. (Ezek. 32:26) Meshech's posterity will assist the Turks against the Jews at the beginning of the millennium, but will perish in their attempt. (Ezek. 38:2-3, 39:1)

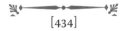

MESSIAH. See Christ

Also *Messias* (KJV, New Testament, John 1:41, 4:25). Only found in Daniel 9:25-26.

MICAH

(1) An Ephraimite from Mount Ephraim near Shiloh, the son of a rich, but superstitious widow. Micah stole from her 1100 shekels of silver, or just over £125. She pronounced the heaviest curses against the thief who had stolen her money. Afraid of her curses, or unwilling to have her living in so bad a temper, Micah told her that he had taken her money, or had recovered it. Overjoyed with the news of her money, she blessed him, and bade him keep it for himself. He, however, restored it. She told him it had been dedicated to the service of God, to make images using it for their family worship. The images, one graven and another molten, were made, and also an ephod for their idolatrous priest. Micah placed them in a chamber, and consecrated one of his sons to be that priest. As Jonathan the son of Gershom, the son of Manasseh or Moses, a vagrant Levite, passed that way, Micah imagined it would be more lucky to have him his priest, and more effective in procuring the blessing of heaven on the family. He hired him at the low rate of his food, a suit of clothes, and ten shekels (over £1 a year). Ah, how base are unfaithful clergymen! Soon after, he gave Micah the slip, and, carrying his idols with him, went along with 600 Danites to Laish. Poor Micah, almost out of his wits with grief for the loss of his deities, assembled his neighbours, and, overtaking the Danites, complained that they had made him wretched beyond words by carrying off his gods! They were so far from pitying him that they threatened his life unless he quickly made off with his attendants. (Judg. 17-18)

(2) The Morasthite, or inhabitant of Moresheth, near Gath, one of the minor prophets who was contemporary with Isaiah, and had a somewhat similar style, and even some of his expressions. (Isa. 1:1, 2:1-4, 41:15; Micah 1:1, 4:1-4, 13) He continued prophesying about 50 years during the reigns of Jotham, Ahaz, and Hezekiah, and seems to have had his full share of contempt and affliction. (Micah 1:1, 7:1-10) In the first three chapters of his prophecy, he protested against the wickedness of the ten tribes, but chiefly of the rulers, priests, and false prophets of Judah. He foretold the Assyrian invasion, and the destruction of the city and Temple of Jerusalem by the Chaldeans and

Romans. In the 4th and 5th chapters, he foretold their deliverance from the Assyrian and Chaldean Captivity, and their later flourishing state, but chiefly the birth of the Messiah, his spread of the gospel, and his spiritual conquest of the nations, and the spiritual peace and prosperity of the New Testament Church. In the last two chapters, he reproved Israel and Judah for their ingratitude, their oppression, fraud, lying, and continued observance of the idolatrous laws of Omri and Ahab, and for their lack of natural affection, their treachery, and their mocking of the pious. He predicted the Assyrian ravages and ruin, remarked on the astonishing mercy and faithfulness of God, and concluded with a prediction of God's re-establishment of the Jews as in the days of old. (Jer. 26:18; Micah 1:1)

MICAIAH

The son of Imlah, an Ephraimite, a faithful prophet who used to reprove Ahab very openly for his wickedness. Whether it was he who foretold to Ahab his repeated victories over the Syrians, we do not know; but we suppose it was he who, in disguise, met Ahab as he returned from Aphek to Samaria. He had just before, in the name of the Lord, desired his neighbour to kill him. His neighbour declined; and, as the prophet declared, a lion soon after met him and killed him. The prophet bade another who came by to smite him. The fellow did so, and wounded him. The prophet then, looking like a wounded soldier, covered himself with ash, as one come from a hot battle. When Ahab came up, he, in his disguise, called out to him, and stopped him. By a parable, he said that, having been in the battle, someone had committed to him a prisoner to be kept under pain of death, or forfeiting a talent of silver; and that while he was busy in other matters, the prisoner had escaped. Ahab told him that he must stand by the agreement, and pay the penalty. The prophet immediately took off his disguise, and Ahab recognised him. He told Ahab that, since he had allowed Benhadad to escape with life and honour, a vile blasphemer whom God had providentially delivered into his hands, his life, and that of his subjects, should be substituted for that of Benhadad and his people. (1 Kings 20) When Ahab intended to take Ramothgilead from the Syrians, he, not willingly, but to gratify Jehoshaphat his ally, sent for Micaiah, who, he said, always prophesied evil concerning him, to consult him whether he should go and besiege Ramothgilead or not.

As Micaiah was introduced in the king's presence, some courtiers told him how the prophets of Baal had unanimously assured the king of success in the war, and begged that he would do so too. He told them he would say what the Lord directed him.

When he came into Ahab's presence, and asked questions about the affair, with an ironical air, he bid him go up to Ramothgilead, and expect that the Lord would deliver it into his hand. Ahab, observing his ridiculous way of speaking, commanded him by God to tell him nothing but the truth. Micaiah then seriously told him that, in a vision, he had seen the army of Israel returning from the war without a king at their head, and presented it to him that God had permitted Satan, as a lying spirit, to enter into his prophets of Baal that they might entice him to go up and fall at Ramothgilead. Zedekiah, the son of Chenaanah, who had made himself horns of iron, and had told Ahab that with these he should push the Syrians till he had consumed them, smote Micaiah on the cheek, and asked him, which way the Spirit of the Lord had come from him to speak with him. Micaiah replied that he would know that, when, for fear of the Syrians, he would run into an inner chamber to hide himself. Ahab then ordered Micaiah to be carried to the prison of Samaria, and there be put on bread and water till he returned in peace. Micaiah took all the assembly to witness that if ever Ahab returned safe, he should be seen as a false prophet. But the event fully justified his prediction. (1 Kings 22:7-28)

MICHAEL

(1) The archangel, but at least sometimes signifies Jesus Christ. He is the person *who is as God*, and that is what his name signifies. Against him and his angels, his ministers and his followers, the devil, the heathen Empire of Rome, and their agents, fought by way of reproach, laws, persecutions, etc. (Rev. 12:7) He is the great Prince of the Jewish nation who, in the millennium, will recover them from their present misery, and raise the dead. (Dan. 12:1-3) But, perhaps, when Michael is called *one of the chief princes*, that is, one of the principal angels, or is said to dispute with the devil about the body of Moses, but dare not (that is, he thought it beneath his dignity to bring a reproving accusation against the devil), but rebuked him in the name of the Lord, this may signify a created angel. (Dan. 10:13, 21; Jude v. 9)

(2) The father of Sethur the spy, who represented Asher. (Num. 13:13)

(3) A principle Gadite in Bashan. (1 Chron. 5:13-14)

(4) A Gershonite Levite. (1 Chron. 6:40)

(5) A chief of the tribe of Issachar. (1 Chron. 7:3)

(6) A Benjamite. (1 Chron. 8:16)

(7) A Manassite, captain of thousands, who joined David at Ziklag. (1 Chron. 12:20)

(8) The father of King Omri. (1 Chron. 27:18)

(9) One of the sons of King Jehoshaphat, murdered by his brother Jehoram. (2 Chron. 21:2, 4)

MICHAL

A daughter of Saul. Her father, after his deceitful disposal of Merab, her older sister, to Adriel the Meholathite, when she ought to have been given to David, when he was informed that Michal had a strong affection for David, promised her to him in marriage. But in order to ruin him, he required a hundred foreskins of the Philistines as her dowry. Two hundred were given, and Michal was married. Not long after, her father plotting to murder David in her house, she got wind of it, and let him down from a window in the night, and begged him to escape for his life. To divert her father's messengers, she put an image and teraphim, which it seems she kept for her private idolatries, and laid it on the bed with a pillow of goats' hair for a bolster, and pretended it was David lying sick. When, next morning, new messengers came to arrest David, sick as he was thought, the bed was searched, and the trick discovered. Michal pretended to her father that David had threatened to kill her if she did not assist him in making his escape. (1 Sam. 19:11-17) Not many years later, when David was in a state of exile, Saul married Michal to Phalti (or Phaltiel), the son of Laish, a Benjamite of Gallim. (1 Sam. 25:44) When, about eight or nine years later, Abner proposed to make David king of all Israel, David required the restoration of Michal his wife as one of the preliminaries for any such treaty. Ishbosheth, her brother, sent her at David's demand. Phalti, her last, but adulterous, husband, to whom perhaps she had children, came with her weeping, till they came to Bahurim where Abner ordered him back. Her reproving David when he joyfully attended the ark to Jerusalem, as too base for one of his station, was divinely punished

with her perpetual barrenness. But, it seems, she took and educated the five children that her sister Merab bore to Adriel; or Michal could have been the sister of Michal. (2 Sam. 3:12-16, 6:16-23, 21:8-9)

MIDIAN

The fourth son of Abraham by Keturah, and father of the Midianites, who lived in the land of Midian. (Gen. 25:2, 4) In Scripture, two different places are presented as the land of Midian, one near the northeastern point of the Red Sea, where Abulfeda of Damascus places the city of Midian (or Madian), and where Jethro dwelt. These western or southern Midianites were also called Cushites because they dwelt in the country originally pertaining to Cush. They retained the true religion, when it seems to have been lost by the eastern or northern Midianites. (Exod. 2; Num. 12:1) The northern Midianites lived on the east of the Dead Sea, and were neighbours to the Moabites. The Midianites consisted of five main tribes: the descendants of Ephah, Epher, Hanoch, Abidah, and Eldaah, each of which seem to have had their own kings. Very early, the Midianites applied themselves to trade, particularly to Egypt, in spices, balm, and such like. Some of them were involved in the buying and selling of Joseph into Egypt. It seems, some ages after, they had a war with the Edomites under King Hadad. (Gen. 25:2, 4, 37:28, 36, 36:35) The Midianites were greatly alarmed at the Hebrews' passage through the Red Sea, and the marvellous appearances on Sinai and in the wilderness. (Hab. 3:7) Possibly most of the southern Midianites removed from the Red Sea on that occasion, and settled with their brothers on the borders of Moab. It seems that Sihon had conquered their country, for their five kings were called dukes of Sihon. (Josh. 13:21) Some of the elders of Midian accompanied those of Moab to bring Balaam to curse Israel. On his advice, many of the Midianite women poured themselves into the Hebrew camp, which was at Abelshittim on their northern border, and seduced the Hebrews into prostitution and idolatry. This brought a plague from the Lord upon the Hebrews, in which 24,000 were cut off. To revenge this, the Lord directed Moses to send 12,000 Hebrews into the country of Midian and cut off everybody they could find, virgins excepted. The Hebrews did so, and killed Evi, Rekem, Zur, Hur, and Reba, kings of Midian, together with Balaam, and many more. They burned their cities, and carried off a rich booty of 32,000 virgins,

675,000 sheep, 72,000 cows, and 61,000 asses, which were equally divided between the 12,000 warriors and the rest of the Hebrews. The 50th part of the congregation's half, and the 500th part of the warriors' half, were assigned to the Lord. (Num. 22, 25, 31; Josh. 13)

Some ages after, the Midianites that had escaped this destruction were greatly increased, and, for seven years, grievously oppressed the Hebrews, but were at last miraculously routed by Gideon. Their kings Oreb and Zeeb, Zebah and Zalmunna, with about 135,000, fell by the sword. (Judg. 6-8; Isa. 9:4, 10:26; Ps. 83:9-12) The small remains of the Midianites seem to have been incorporated with the Moabites and Arabians. Some of their descendants, or the inhabitants of their country, embraced the Christian faith in the apostolic age, and will do so in the millennium. (Isa. 10:6)

MILCOM. See Molech
The god of the Ammonites. See 1 Kings 11:5, 33; 2 Kings 23:13.

MILLO
A notable person, or a place near Shechem, whose family, or inhabitants, assisted the Shechemites in making Abimelech king; and were ruined by him as it turned out. (Judg. 9:6, 20)

MIRIAM
(1) The sister of Moses, who, at the desire of Pharaoh's daughter, called his own mother to nurse him. It is said that she was married to Hur. She was called "the prophetess" (Exod. 15:20). She took the lead among the Hebrew women in their song of triumph after the passage of the Red Sea. For her reproving Moses, she was smitten with a leprosy, but was cured by his prayers. She died and was buried at Kadesh in BC 1452. (Exod. 2, 15:20-22; Num. 20:1, 27)

(2) A descendant of Judah. (1 Chron. 4:17)

MIZRAIM
The son of Ham, and father of Ludim, Anamim, Lebabim, Naphtuhim, Pathrusim, and Caslubim, from which last sprang the Philistines and Caphtorim. These descendants of his, and the tribes called from their names, had no doubt their original residence in Egypt; but some of them moved towards the west, and, as Caslubim seems to have dwelt

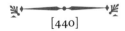

in the east of Egypt, his posterity partly settled in the southwest of Canaan. Some learned men have imagined that these names ending in *im* (a plural termination in the Hebrew) must mean tribes, not particular persons; but we do not have sufficient reasons for supporting this inference. (Gen. 10:6, 13, 14) The Arabs still call Egypt *Mesr*; and they called *Memphis* by its name, and now call grand Cairo, *Mesr*, from Mizraim.

MOAB. See Ruth

The son of Lot, sadly, by his oldest daughter, was born about the same time as Isaac in BC 1896. He and his posterity dwelt in the land called by his name, east of the Dead Sea, and around the River Arnon, with the Ammonites on the northeast, and the Midianites on the southwest, of them. They expelled the Emim, and seized their country. They had not been long a nation when they became idolaters, and worshipped Chemosh and Baalpeor. (Num. 21:29, 25:1, 3) Sihon, King of the Amorites, took from them all their territory north of the river Amon. Not long after, Balak the son of Zipper was King of Moab. In vain, he hired Balaam to curse the Hebrews who encamped on his borders. (Num. 21-24) To revenge this, no Moabite or Ammonite was allowed to enter the Hebrew congregation of the Lord up to the 10th generation. (Deut. 23:3-6) About BC 1343, the Moabites under Eglon reduced the Hebrews under their yoke, and greatly oppressed them for 18 years. But Ehud killed their king, and his troops killed 10,000 of the most valiant Moabites, and recovered for the Hebrews their liberty. (Judg. 3)

Some time later, Elimelech and Naomi, on account of a famine, left Canaan, and lived in the land of Moab. His sons Mahlon and Chilion married two Moabitish women, some say of the royal family. (Ruth 1) Saul successfully waged war with the Moabites. (1 Sam. 14:47) When David was persecuted by Saul, he fled to the land of Moab, from whence Ruth, his great-grandmother, had come, and gave up his parents to the protection of the King of Moab. (1 Sam. 22:3-4) Provoked with the Moabites, perhaps for the murder of his parents, about 12 years later, David terribly ravaged their country, and reduced them to the basest slavery. Those that he took prisoner, at least from the soldiery, he caused to lie or stand close together, and, measuring them with lines, to mark them for death or life, he killed half, if not two-thirds of them. (2 Sam. 8:1-2; Ps. 60:8) For about 150 years, they continued subject to Israel, and Saraph a Jew was one of their governors, and Ithmah a Moabite was one of David's mighties. (1 Chron. 4:22, 11:46) Solomon married some Moabitish women, and established the worship of their idol Chemosh at Jerusalem. (1 Kings 11:1, 7, 33) After the division of the Hebrew kingdom, the Moabites fell to the share of the ten tribes, as their territories were contiguous with the Reubenites. But after the death of Ahab, Mesha, their king, a notable shipmaster refused to pay his tribute. This led to a terrible defeat of the Moabites by Joram, King of Israel, and his allies, and a furious ravage of their country. (2 Kings 3) Not long after, or perhaps before, they entered into an alliance with the Edomites, Amalekites, Ishmaelites, Philistines, Ammonites, Hagarenes, Ashurites, Gebalites, and Tyrians, to destroy the whole race of Israel; but their army that came against Jehoshaphat was miraculously destroyed. (2 Chron. 20; Ps. 83) Sometime after, the Moabites seem to have invaded the land of Edom and burnt the bones of their king in lime. (Amos 2:1) About the time of Elisha's death, straggling bands of the Moabites ravaged the country of the ten tribes. (2 Kings 13:20) During the decline of the kingdom of the ten tribes, or after their Captivity by Tiglathpileser, the Moabites seized on a great part of what pertained to the Reubenites, if not more, of the land of Gilead. The Assyrians, under Shalmaneser, ravaged their country, and rendered it almost desolate. (Isa. 15-16, 25:12; Amos 2:1-2) They, however, recovered from this shock, and again became a flourishing nation. Their principal cities were: Nebo, Kirjathaim, Kir, Misgab, Hesbon, Madmen, Horonaim, Ar, Dibon, Aroer, Diblath, or Bethdiblathaim, Helon, Jahazah, Mephaath, Bethgamut, Bethmeon, Kerioth, Bozrah, Medeba, Elealeh, Jazer, and Sibmah, most of which had once belonged to the Hebrews.

It seems they early sided with the Chaldeans, and bands of them harassed the Jews under Jehoiakim. But as they formed an alliance with Zedekiah to shake off the Chaldean yoke, Nebuchadnezzar, about four or five years later, who came to destroy Jerusalem, invaded their country, and reduced it to almost a desert, and carried multitudes of them captive into his eastern dominions. (2 Kings 24:2; Jer. 48:9, 26, 25:21; Ezek. 25; Zeph. 2:8) I find no evidence that they ever much recovered this overthrow. Some of their women were married to the Jews who had come back to their own land, and were put away under Nehemiah's orders. (Neh. 13:23) The poor remnants of them were subject to the Persians and Greeks in turn, and to the Jews under Alexander, Janneus, and Herod, and finally to the Romans. Long ago, their name was lost, as they were joined with the Jews or Arabians, and their country is almost quite desolate, not properly subject to the Turks, but to the wild Arabs of Hejaz. (Zeph. 2:8-10; Isa. 25:10, 11:14; Dan. 11:41) But in Isaiah 25:10, *Moab* may be understood as the enemies of the Church in general.

MOLECH, MOLOCH, MILCOM, MALCHAM

The principal idol of the Ammonites. He had the face of an ox, and his hands were stretched out, as if ready to receive presents. He was hollow within, and there the fire was placed to heat the image, that it might burn the offerings. There were seven different apartments for receiving the different offerings: of meal, turtles, ewes, rams, calves, oxen, and children. It is said that the unhappy parent, who offered his child to Molech, put him into the burning arms of the idol, where he expired in terrible pain, and while drums were beaten to drown his cries. Whatever talk there is of causing children to pass between two fires in honour of this idol, it is pretty plain that the actual burning of them in sacrifice is intended. (Ps. 106:37; Ezek. 16:20, 23:37, 39) The sacrificed child was burnt in order to obtain a blessing on the rest of the family. That Molech was derived from the Egyptians, and is the same as Rephan, Remphan, Chiun, or Serapis, and worshipped under the form of a bull, and with the Annamelech and Adrammelech, to which the inhabitants of Sepharvaim burnt their children, we believe is true. But whether he was the same as Saturn, to whom human sacrifices were offered, or Mercury, or Mars, or Venus, or Mithras, or the sun, we cannot now determine. It is certain that Molech was very early worshipped among the Ammonites; and perhaps it was the crown of Molech, not of the Ammonitish king, that David took at Rabbah, and which weighed a talent. (2 Sam. 12:30)

God very early prohibited the worship of Molech among his people. (Lev. 18:21, 20:2-5) They, however, were often guilty of it. They carried the tabernacle of their Molech in the worship of the golden calf, which was a kind of representation of the Egyptian Serapis. (Acts 7:43) Solomon built a temple to Molech on the Mount of Olives. (1 Kings 11:7) Ahaz,

Manasseh, and other Jews, burnt their children in honour to this idol, particularly in Tophet. (2 Kings 16:3, 21:3-4, Jer. 19:5-6)

MORDECAI

The son of Jair, grandson of Kish, and descendant of the family of Saul. He was carried to Babylon, along with Jehoiachin, King of Judah, when he was very young. If he was one of the chiefs who conducted the Jews from Babylon to Judea, he must have returned to Shushan in Persia. When Esther his cousin, whom he had trained up, was married to Ahasuerus, Mordecai waited at the palace gate that he might have information concerning her from time to time. Here, having got information of Bigthan and Terish's intention to murder the King, he informed Esther of it. The traitors were hanged, and it was marked in the annals of the kingdom that Mordecai had given the information against them. When Haman was made Prime Minister of Persia, all the servants were ordered to bow the knee to him as he passed by. Mordecai, conceiving this an approach towards divine honour, or reckoning it sinful to revere an Amalekite, declined. Scorning to punish Mordecai alone, Haman obtained a royal edict for a universal massacre of the Jewish nation. Informed of this, Mordecai told Esther, and earnestly begged her to interpose with the king for the life of her people. When she agreed, Mordecai caused all the Jews in Shushan to fast three days for success from God at her attempt. (Neh. 7:7; Esther 2:5 to the end of chapter 4)

Meanwhile, providence directed to be read to Ahasuerus one night, as he could not sleep, that part of the royal annals that mentioned Mordecai's discovery of the treacherous eunuchs. Ahasuerus, finding that he had received no reward, asked Haman, who had just come to obtain the king's permission to hang Mordecai on his lofty gallows, what should be done to honour the king's great favourite? As Haman imagined it could be none other than himself, he proposed the highest honours he could think of. According to the tenor of his own proposal, he was ordered to clothe Mordecai in the king's ordinary robes, set him on the King's own horse, and lead the horse with Mordecai on it through all the city of Shushan, and proclaim before him, *Thus shall it be done to the man whom the King delighteth to honour.* In a similar manner, proselytes to the Mahometan religion are carried through the streets at their conversion. No way inflated with these extraordinary honours, Mordecai returned to the King's gate; but Haman being hanged that very day, he was advanced to his office. After he and Esther had, by letters to the various provinces, stopped the massacre of their nation, he, for some time, continued to discharge his high trust with great faithfulness and usefulness. (Esther 6-10)

MOSES

His birth and upbringing

The brother of Aaron and Miriam, and, younger than either, was born BC 1571. Before his birth, Pharaoh, King of Egypt, had issued orders to murder every male infant of the Hebrews. His parents, however, seeing something about him that they reckoned spoke of his future greatness, they hid him three months. When they could hide him no longer, his mother Jochebed made an ark of bulrushes, and, having pitched it that it might draw no water, she put Moses in it, and floated it near the banks of the Nile where the princes and other noble Egyptians used to walk. He had not lain long in this condition when Pharaoh's daughter, Thermoses, coming to wash herself, or some of her linen, observed the ark, and caused one of her maids to fetch it; and opening it, found the child. Moved with the beauty and weeping of the babe, and knowing it to be one of the Hebrew children, she resolved to bring it up for herself as a child of her own. Miriam, his sister, a girl of perhaps 10 or 12 years of age, who was waiting nearby, asked leave to call a nurse. Being permitted, she called Jochebed his mother. Pharaoh's daughter called him *Mosheh* because she *drew* him out of the water.

She took care to have him instructed in all the sciences then known in Egypt. In his earliest years, Jochebed and Amram, no doubt, took care to instruct him in the Hebrew language, and in the principles of the true religion, and in the knowledge of the promises that God had made concerning Israel. Affected by these, and endowed with the grace of God, he, when grown up, refused to be called the son of Pharaoh's daughter, and chose rather to suffer affliction with the people of God, than enjoy the short-lived pleasures of sin. (Heb. 11:25) Trusting in the invisible God, and encouraged by the hope of an everlasting reward, he did not fear the anger of the Egyptian King, nor whatever ridicule, threatening, or persecution he had to endure. It is hardly to our purpose to relate the perhaps fabulous story of his successful expedition against the Ethiopians, who, about this time, emigrated from Arabia to Abyssinia, south of Egypt, at the head of the Egyptian forces. It is certain that, being 40 years of age, and divinely instructed that he was to be the deliverer of Israel, he went to visit his brothers at their hard labour. Observing an Egyptian cruelly abusing a Hebrew, and about to murder him, he hastened to them, assisted the Hebrew, and killed the Egyptian, hiding his body in the sand. Next day, he observed two Hebrews in dispute, and begged the faulty person not to hurt his brother. The fellow saucily replied, *Who made you a ruler or judge over us? Will you kill me as you did the Egyptian yesterday?*

His flight to Midian

Finding that news of his slaughter of the Egyptian was known, he fled into the country of Midian on the Red Sea. Sitting down by a well, the seven daughters of Jethro came up to it with their flocks. They had just filled the troughs with the water they had drawn when some barbarous fellows came up, and would have given the water to their flocks. Moses assisted the girls, and drove away the rough shepherds. Jethro had no sooner heard of his kindness to his daughters than he ordered him to be called in and get refreshment. Moses hired himself to feed Jethro's flock, and received his daughter Zipporah in marriage, by whom he had two sons. The first he called *Gershon*, to denote his being a *stranger* in that place, the other he called *Eliezer* to denote that his *God was his help.* (Exod. 2; Acts 7:20-29; Heb. 11:24-26) About the beginning of BC 1491, the King of Egypt, by whose daughter or sister Moses had been educated, died; but the bondage of the Hebrews still continued under their new tyrant.

The burning bush

As Moses one day led his flocks near the north or west side of Sinai, the Lord appeared to him in a bush that burned, but was not consumed. Moses, astonished, went near to see the miracle. The Lord spoke to him out of the bush, and bid him put off his shoes before he came any nearer, as the spot was sacred to the honour of God. He declared himself the God of Abraham, Isaac, and Jacob; and that, from regard to his promise, and the groans of his oppressed people, he now intended to deliver them and bring them into Canaan with him as the instrument. Moses began to excuse himself, as if the Hebrews would

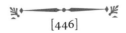

not believe that he had a mission. God promised him his presence, and bid him tell the Hebrews that the great I AM, who is Being itself, and gives being to his creatures, and fulfils every promise, had sent him to inform them of their approaching deliverance; and he assured him that they would believe him. He ordered him to go to Pharaoh, and, in God's name, demand that he let the Hebrews go three days' journey into the Arabian Desert to offer a solemn sacrifice to their God.

Meanwhile, he told him that Pharaoh would not grant this small request till he, and his country, would be almost ruined by fearful plagues. Moses still excused himself, so God encouraged him with a fourfold sign. His rod was turned into a serpent, to signify what plagues it would bring on the Egyptians. It was turned back into a rod to mark how useful it would prove for the support of the Hebrews. To show how easily God would weaken the power of the Egyptians, and strengthen the Israelites, Moses' hand, being put into his bosom, became leprous, white as snow; and again returned into his bosom, it became sound as the other. These miracles he was ordered to repeat before the Hebrews for the confirmation of his mission; and, if necessary, to add the taking of water out of the river, and turning it into blood. Moses pretended that he had not a ready utterance in his speech, and begged to be excused, wishing that the Lord would send some other person. Provoked at his unbelief, God told him that he would qualify him with speech; and that Aaron, who was just coming to meet him, would be his assistant and spokesman.

His return to Egypt

Moses, at last persuaded, went and obtained leave of his father-in-law to go and visit his brothers in Egypt. He took his wife and children along with him. As they were in an inn by the way, an angel threatened to slay Moses, it is supposed, on account of his neglect to circumcise his child (or children). To prevent his death, Zipporah took a sharp stone, cut off her child's foreskin, cast it at the feet, either of her husband or of the child, and said that now she had preserved his life by bloodshed, and he or his son was now her bloody bridegroom. Zipporah and her children returned to her father, and Moses pursued his course into Egypt, and was met by Aaron his brother. They told the Hebrews what God had said, and showed them the signs, so that the people believed and were glad. (Exod. 3-4)

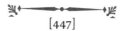

Moses and Aaron then went into Pharaoh, and, in the name of the God of the Hebrews, demanded his permission for the people to go three days' journey into the Arabian Desert to serve their God. He replied that he neither knew, nor would pay the least regard to, the Hebrew God, nor allow them to stir a foot out of his dominions. He increased their misery by requiring them to provide straw for themselves, and yet fulfil the daily tally of their bricks. He thought hard labour would put religion out of their heads. Beaten by the Egyptian taskmasters for not fulfilling what was impossible for them, the Hebrews complained to Pharaoh; but he gave them no hopes of relief, and told them that their idleness had filled their heads with hopeless religion. The Hebrews bitterly reflected on Moses and Aaron as the cause of this additional misery. Moses cried to the Lord, and was answered that Pharaoh would not let them go till terrible plagues on his land should force him to it. God assured him that he was JEHOVAH, a promise-keeping God, and would speedily deliver the Hebrews and bring them to Canaan. Moses told this to the Hebrews, but their severe servitude made them disregard what he said. Moses and Aaron again demanded Pharaoh's permission for the people to go into the desert. To verify their commission, Aaron flung down his rod, and it became a serpent. The magicians of Egypt were brought to confront this miracle, for they cast down their rods, and they became serpents, at least in appearance. Whether Satan indiscernibly slipped away their rods, and put serpents in their place, or whether he himself activated the rods, or only deceived the eyes of the spectators, it is certain that Aaron's rod swallowed up theirs as a mark of superior authority and influence.

Just after this, the Lord, through Moses, smote the Egyptians with ten plagues within the space of less than a month. About the 18th day of Adar, the waters of the Nile, where so many Hebrew children had been drowned, were turned into blood, and so continued for seven days. About the 25th day, the river produced such swarms of frogs as spread through the country, and, entering into houses and everywhere, were a terrible nuisance. These two plagues the magicians tried to imitate, but with no success. The plague of lice happened about the 27th, and that of flies on the 29th day of Adar. On the second day of Abib, there happened a grievous murrain (distemper) among their cattle; on the third and fourth, the plague of boils; on the fifth, the plague of hail, thunder, and lightning; on the eighth, that of locusts and grasshoppers; on the tenth, eleventh, and twelfth, that of deep darkness; on the fourteenth, the death of their first-born. None of these affected the Hebrews. By the sprinkling of the blood of the Passover lambs on their doorposts and upper lintels, they had their families protected from the destroying angel. (Exod. 5-12; Deut. 4:34, 11:3, Heb. 11:23-29) While some of these plagues continued, Pharaoh seemed willing to let the Hebrews go; but, whenever they started moving, be became as obstinate as ever, or refused to let their flocks go with them, and of these Moses refused to leave so much as one. But when the firstborn were slain, Pharaoh's servants urged him to dismiss the Hebrews.

The Exodus

The Hebrews, having begun their departure from Egypt in great haste, and having carried along with them a good part of the wealth of the Egyptians, took their journey to the southeast. Pharaoh and his people repented their letting them go, and a mighty army pursued them, almost overtaking them on the west of the Red Sea. The Hebrews murmured against Moses for bringing them out of Egypt. Moses prayed to the Lord for a sign. At God's direction, he stretched his rod over the Red Sea, which was perhaps about 18 miles broad, and it parted in two, giving the Hebrews an easy passage. By taking off the wheels of their chariots, and darkening their way, the Lord hindered the march of the Egyptians. When the Hebrews had all got over, and the Egyptians were all in the channel, at God's direction, Moses stretched his rod to the sea, and, moved by a strong wind, it suddenly returned, and drowned the whole Egyptian army. On the east side of the sea, Moses and the men, and Miriam and the women of Israel, sang a song of praise for their miraculous deliverance.

Directing their course to the southeast, the Hebrews went three days without water; and, when they found some in Marah, it was so bitter they could not drink it. They murmured against Moses, as if he had brought them into the wilderness to kill them with thirst. Moses cried to God for relief, and he showed him a tree, perhaps, according to Beshalach (Chapters 13-17, Section XVI), the bitter Ardiphne, which he cast into the waters, and they became sweet. Marching on, they came to Elim, where there were 12 fountains of excellent water, and 70 palm trees. On the 15th day of the second month, which was the 31st from their departure, they came to the wilderness of Sin. Their food was quite exhausted, so now they complained that Moses had brought them into the wilderness to kill them with hunger. Moses cried out to the Lord. That very night, a large flock of quails fell around their tents; and, next morning, the manna, which continued with them 40 years, began to appear. When they came to Rephidim, Moses, under God's direction, smote a rock with his rod, and, from there, issued water, whose streams seem to have followed them for about 39 years. Here, chiefly by Moses' intercession, and by his holding up the rod of God in his hand, the Amalekites were defeated. To commemorate the victory, Moses reared an altar, and called it *Jehovah-nissi*, that is, the *Lord is my banner*. While they stayed here, Jethro brought Moses his wife and children. To ease him of his great burden in judging the people, he advised him to appoint heads of thousands, hundreds, fifties and tens, and let them judge all the lesser causes. This measure, being approved by God, it was immediately put into execution. (Exod. 13-18; Deut. 11:4; Josh. 24:5-7; Neh. 9:9-15; Ps. 78:11-29, 105:26-43, 106:7-14, 135:8-9, 136:11-15)

The giving of the Law at Sinai

On the first day of the third sacred month, the Hebrews came to Sinai. On this Mount, God told Moses that the Hebrews would serve him. When Moses first ascended the Mount, God told him his intention of entering into a covenant with the people. When Moses told the people, they professed their readiness to do whatsoever the Lord commanded them. When Moses returned to the Mount, and represented their ready agreement with the divine will, God ordered him down to direct the people to sanctify themselves, and wash their clothes, as, on the third day, God would descend on the mountain, and enter into covenant with them. After they had purified themselves, fiery flames on the top of the Mount, and terrible claps of thunder, made all the congregation, Moses not excepted, to tremble and quake; and all the country about shook, and was illuminated. Boundaries were fixed along the Mount, that neither man nor beast might touch it; and all were forbidden to gaze, when curious to behold any corporeal similitude of God amid the fire. With an audible voice, that all Israel might hear, God proclaimed the covenant relationship between himself and them, and the ten summary precepts of the moral law in a way adapted to every particular person. The terrible thunders so frightened the Hebrew assembly that they begged that

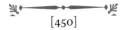

the Lord would speak his mind only to Moses, and let Moses declare it to them. Moses returned to the Mount, and there received a variety of political and ceremonial laws. Descending, he erected 12 pillars for the twelve tribes, and offered by the hands of some young men burnt offerings and peace offerings on an altar erected of rough stones. Half of the blood he sprinkled on the altar; with the other half, he sprinkled the books on which he had written the laws he had received, and the people. After which, he and Aaron, and his sons, and 70 of the elders of Israel, went a little way up the Mount, and feasted before the symbols of the presence of God. Thus was the covenant solemnly ratified. (Exod. 19-24; Deut. 4-5)

Leaving Aaron and Hur, and the 70 elders to govern the people, Moses, taking Joshua along with him at least part of his way, went up to the Mount, where they continued without any food for the space of 40 days. God gave Moses directions concerning the formation of the ark, altars, veils, curtains, lampstand, and other things pertaining to the Tabernacle, and concerning the priests' garments and their consecration, and concerning burnt offerings, incense, and perfume, and concerning the Sabbath. He ordered Bezaleel and Aholiab to frame the work of the Tabernacle. After giving him the two tablets of stone, probably of marble, where the Ten Commandments had been divinely inscribed, he bid him go down hastily, as the Hebrews had already broken their promise, and were worshipping a golden calf. He offered to make Moses' family increase into a great nation if he would leave off interceding for his guilty brothers. Moses fell on his face before the Lord, and begged him not to destroy them, as they were his covenant people. When he came down from the Mount, and observed their idolatry, his holy zeal was so excited that he threw down the tablets of the Law, and broke them to pieces before them as a token of their breaking God's covenant, and exposing themselves to be broken in his wrath. He took their idol calf and reduced it to powder, and caused the idolaters to drink water mixed with the dust as a token that their guilt should be punished. After sharply rebuking Aaron his brother for his hand in their sin, he placed himself at the door of a tent, which he erected outside the camp, and bid all that detested this idolatry to come to him. Three thousand Levites quickly joined him. These, he ordered to go through the camp and slay every man his friend or near kinsman who had been active in the idolatry.

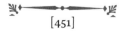

After telling the people the greatness of their sin, he returned to the Mount, and fasted and prayed for the space of 40 days. He begged that if God would not forgive the Hebrews' sin, he himself might be blotted out of the book of providential preservation, and not live to see them ruined, or have the honour of his family established on their ruin. God replied that he would only cut off from life in that quarrel those who had offended; that though they could not expect him to go with them, he would send his angel to guide them in the way. The Hebrews were extremely grieved to hear of God's refusal to go with them, but Moses continued his intercession till God promised his presence, and gave him a special manifestation of his mercy, goodness, and justice. Then Moses begged God to glorify the exceeding riches of his grace in going up with them, who were a most rebellious and stiff-necked people. After hewing two new tablets of stone, Moses returned again to the Mount, and, having continued there 40 days, came down with the moral law divinely inscribed on the tablets. His face shone with the reflection of the divine glory. When he came to know it, he covered his face with a veil that the Hebrews might converse with him. (Exod. 25-34; Deut. 9-10) The Tabernacle was now to be reared by a voluntary contribution. The people brought materials till Moses had to stop them. Every male paid half a shekel as the ransom-money of his soul. After six months' work, the Tabernacle was finished, everything exactly according to the direction of God through Moses. After divine directions were given concerning the various offerings, Aaron and his sons were consecrated to the priestly service, and then a number of other ceremonial laws were, by God, uttered. See Leviticus. An account of the Hebrews was then taken, and all were directed in their station and march, and their princes offered their oblations for the dedication of the Tabernacle. After this, the Levites were consecrated, and a second Passover was kept. Now Hobab, the brother-in-law of Moses, who had perhaps been with them about ten months, intended to return home; but Moses begged him to go along with them and receive his share of the blessings that awaited them. (Exod. 35-40; Lev. 1-27; Num. 1-10)

The giving of the Manna

Scarcely had the Hebrews departed from Sinai, when they (mostly the mixed multitude) fell to murmuring at the manna, and longed for flesh.

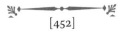

A burning pestilence began in the outside of the camp, which made the spot receive the name of *Taberah* (or *burning*). It was stopped by Moses' prayer; but the murmuring was not. Moses himself became irritated, and doubted how God could give them a month's flesh, as he had promised, and complained that he himself could not govern so unruly a mob; and that it was unreasonable to require him to do so as he was not their natural parent. To ease him, God ordered 70 or 72 elders to be added for his assistance; and by the outpouring of a prophetic spirit on them, the men were marked out and qualified for their work. Soon after, quails were brought in such plenty that the Hebrews ate them for a whole month, till the flesh, cursed of God to them, came out at their nostrils, and occasioned a pestilence that cut off many of them. Thus the place was called Kibroth-Hataavah, the *graves of lust*. At Hazeroth, Aaron and Miriam quarrelled with Moses, as if he now managed matters on the advice of his wife Zipporah, and had not consulted them in the affairs of the elders. Miriam was smitten with leprosy to punish her insolence; but, at Moses' request, the Lord healed it after a few days. When they came to Kadesh-Barnea, on the southern border of Canaan, Moses, urged by the people, and permitted by God, sent twelve spies to view the land of Canaan. After they had spent 40 days in this search, and had gone to the northern borders, they returned, and two of them (perhaps Caleb and Joshua) brought a large bunch of grapes carried on a rod between them, to show the fertility of the land. All the spies acknowledged this, but ten of them maintained that the situation was not good, and the cities and people were so strong that they could not hope to conquer it. Caleb and Joshua, with great concern, declared that as the land was very good, so, with God's assistance, they could as easily conquer the inhabitants as a man eats his food. The congregation, agreeing with the ten, were on the point of stoning the two last, and called to be immediately led back into Egypt. Provoked by their outrageous contempt of his Promised Land, God would have destroyed them on the spot, had not Moses interceded for them. He pronounced that none of them able to bear arms, except Caleb and Joshua, would ever enter it; but they would wander in the wilderness till the end of 40 years, and all the rest were consumed by death; only their children would enter it. To confirm this threat, the ten spies, who had brought about this uproar, were struck dead on the spot. Contrary to God's declaration, and Moses' prohibition,

the congregation now set themselves furiously to invade Canaan, and immediately attempted it; but the Amalekites and Canaanites easily drove them back with considerable loss. The Hebrews continued a long time at Kadesh-Barnea; but whether the affair of Korah, and of Aaron's budding rod, and his making atonement for the congregation at Moses' orders, or the giving of the laws relative to meat offerings, breach of Sabbath, Levites' portion, and red heifers, happened here, we do not know. (Num. 12-19)

The wilderness wanderings

After the Hebrews had long encamped at Kadesh, under God's direction, they moved south by 17 different marches, many of which might have been here and there to Eziongeber on the eastern gulf of the Red Sea. They then returned to Kadesh-Barnea by much the same route. Here, after the death of Miriam, their water failed again. The people complained, and God bid Moses address himself to a rock in that place. Neither Moses nor Aaron showed a proper confidence in God, and Moses, with an angry address to the Hebrews, struck the rock instead of speaking to it. For this offence, both of them were excluded from the Promised Land. The Hebrews were not yet allowed to enter Canaan, but were ordered to take a long circuit eastward. From Kadesh, Moses sent to the King of Edom, and begged a free passage through his territories, which was at first refused, but, it seems, was afterwards permitted. Soon after Aaron's death in Mount Hor, the Hebrews were harassed by Arad, King of Hormah; but they quickly prevailed against him. Fiery serpents, too, bit them for despising the manna; but they were miraculously healed by looking at a brazen serpent lifted up on a pole. God did not permit Moses to attack the Moabites or Ammonites; but when they came to the borders of eastern Canaan ruled by Sihon and Og, these kings came against the Israelites in battle. Their troops were routed, killed, and their country seized. After winding to the west for some time, the Hebrews encamped at Shittim, on the east of the Jordan. Here, Balaam attempted in vain to curse them. Here, the Midianitish women seduced many of them into prostituton and idolatry. Moses ordered 1000 of the idolaters to be put to death, and a plague cut off 23,000 more. Moses then numbered the people, and found that none of those capable of war when they came out of Egypt, except Caleb and Joshua, were alive. Here too,

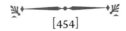

Moses received some new laws concerning offerings, feasts, vows, the marriage of daughters falling heirs to their father, and cities of refuge. He punished the Midianites with almost utter extinction, divided the territories he had taken from the Amorites among the tribes of Reuben, Gad, and part of Manasseh, on condition that they should go over the Jordan and assist their brothers to conquer the rest of Canaan. He also appointed three of their cities for refuge. God pointed out to him the borders of Canaan, west of Jordan, and directed that Eleazer the High Priest, and Joshua who had already been marked out as his successor, and ten princes pertaining to the tribes concerned, should divide it according to the proportion of the tribes and their families. (Num. 20-36)

Moses' death

The eleventh month of the 40th year of the Hebrew travels had now begun. Moses, finding that no intercession could gain God's permission for him to enter the Promised Land, and knowing that his end drew near, he preached to the Hebrews a summary of what God had done for them, and a number of the laws he had given them, with some additional ones, and caused them to renew their solemn covenant with God. He set before them the many blessings that would attend their obedience, and curses that would follow on their wickedness. He left a written copy of his Law to be placed at the side of the ark, and ordered the reading of it to the people at their public meetings, especially on the year of release. After giving Joshua a solemn charge with respect to his behaviour, he composed an elegant hymn that spoke of the excellence of God, and their duty to him, and their danger if they apostatised from him. He then blessed the tribes of Israel, but excluding that of Simeon, the chief compliers with Midianitish prostitution and idolatry. He concluded with a lofty commendation of God as the source of their happiness. This finished, he went up to the top of Pisgah where God strengthened his eyes to have a clear view of the whole of western Canaan. His natural strength was in no way abated, but, perhaps in a trance of wonder at the goodness of God, he breathed out his last. To mark the future divine burial of his ceremonies, and to hinder the Hebrews from idolising his relics, the Lord buried him in a valley hard by Bethpeor; but his grave could never be found. Satan, it seems, wanted to discover his body; but Michael the archangel prevented

it, and solemnly charged Satan to give up in his attempt. Moses and Elijah appeared to our Saviour on the holy mount: and if Moses then resumed his natural body, we can hardly forbear thinking he must now wear it as glorified in heaven. (Deut. 1-34; Matt. 17:1-6) Besides the five books ascribed to him, Moses also wrote the 90th Psalm. It has been thought that those five books were not written by him; but, as the Holy Spirit always ascribes them to him, and sometimes calls them by his name, this pretence is absurd. (Josh. 8:34; 1 Kings 2:3; 2 Chron. 23:18, 25:4, 34:14; Luke 16:29) The Jews, too, have unanimously ascribed them to him as their penman, and so have several of the heathen. In the character of Moses, everything is opposite to that of an impostor. His narratives are faithful and disinterested. He is everywhere the reverse of flattery; his miracles were done before multitudes, and in things in which they could not he deceived. Despite his loading them with ceremonies, and representing them in a shameful light, the Jews extol him almost as a deity. The Mahometans extol him as next to Jesus and Mahomet. Numbers of the ancient heathen spread his renown; and much of what they ascribe to their god Bacchus is perhaps just the history of Moses blended with fable.

Was not Moses a distinguished type of our Saviour? What a proper, indeed, divine child was he! But how early and often exposed to danger! To what exile, reproach, contradiction of sinners, and murder was he exposed! But how divinely supported in his numerous trials! How amiable his qualities, his contempt of the pleasures, honour, and wealth of this world! How great his compassion toward his injurious brothers, his amazing meekness, his notable faithfulness, boldness, prudence, and zeal! How solemn and particular his call to his work, and by what multitudes of miracles in favour of his people, and by what ruin on his Jewish, antichristian, and other enemies, is it confirmed! How extensive his office! What a marvellous deliverer is he, who frees us from the worse than Egyptian tyranny of sin, Satan, the world, heathenism, and popery can send! What a marvellous provider of spiritual food, hidden manna, and living water, and unwasting robes of righteousness for his people! What a glorious leader, who opens a safe passage through every difficulty, and, by power and prayer, subdues every enemy, and brings his people not merely to the border, but to the enjoyment of their promised rest! Nor can murmuring, unbelief, or other base behaviour, make him leave them or forsake them. What a renowned Mediator between God and men, with whom God entered into covenant, and who confirms the New Covenant by the shedding and sprinkling of his blood! He had his Father's Law written on the tablets of his heart, fulfilled it as a covenant for us, and gives it to us as a rule. He did not only fast and pray, but died for a rebellious and stiff-necked race, and is our infallible security against our experiencing the breach of God's promise, and for our everlasting enjoyment of his presence.

What an enlightened and incomparable Prophet is he who knows the whole mind of God, and can teach us to profit! He is the brightness of his Father's glory, but we behold his countenance as veiled with our nature, and so can have familiar fellowship with him. What a glorious Priest, who sheds and sprinkles his blood on the altar to satisfy his Father on the book of the Law thus fulfilling it, and, on the people, purging their consciences from dead works to serve the living God, and who sends all the ministers of the Church, and consecrates all the saints, these spiritual priests, to the service of God! He is King in Jeshurun among his upright ones (Deut. 32:15, 33:5, 26), his true Israel, and settles the whole frame, and every ordinance of his Church, and has the whole government of it committed to him. Voluntary was his death; his grave was divinely assigned him, but in it he saw no corruption, and with him was buried the Law of Moses, and the sins of his people.

MOTHER. See Father

N

NAAMAN

(1) A son and grandson of Benjamin. (Gen. 46:21; Num. 26:40)

(2) The general of the army of Benhadad, King of Syria. He was highly esteemed by his master because he had saved Syria from ruin, probably in the battle where Ahab gave Benhadad his last defeat, or at the siege of Ramothgilead where Ahab was slain. But he was severely afflicted with leprosy. A Hebrew captive, who served in his family, happened to say to her mistress that, if Naaman would apply to Elisha, the prophet in Israel, he would quickly cure him. At this hint, Naaman

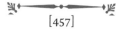

resolved to put it to the test; and Benhadad, imagining that Jehoram, King of Israel, had the prophets under his direction, wrote him a letter to see that he got his general cured of his distemper. Elisha soon eased Jehoram of his perplexity by bidding him send Naaman to him, and the power of the God of Israel would be seen in his cure. Naaman, with his chariots and train, presented himself at the door of Elisha. That Elisha might maintain a due distance from lepers, and might mortify Naaman's pride, and show that the cure was wholly of God, he only sent him out orders to go and wash himself seven times in the Jordan. He was angry that Elisha paid so little regard for him, and that he would not come out to pray for him, or stroke his body, to cure him.

Naaman intended to pour contempt on his orders; and even more so, when he thought Abana and Pharphar, rivers of Damascus, were preferable to all the rivers of Israel. His servants begged him to think how cheerfully he would have done or undergone the most difficult operation to get rid of his disease, had the prophet commanded it; so why should he then stick at a thing so very simple and easy? Naaman was persuaded, and, in conformity to the sevenfold sprinkling of the leper, washed himself seven times in the Jordan, and was perfectly cured. He returned to Elisha, and offered him a present; but it was not accepted. He then professed his faith in the God of Israel as the only true God, and craved two mules' burden of Israelitish earth to build an altar for sacrificing to him alone; and asked forgiveness for bowing himself down in the house of Rimmon, the idol of Syria, as he accompanied his master to the temple. Elisha granted him his desired quantity of earth, and bid him go in peace. Some imagine that he asked indulgence in future idolatry, which he thought his office of supporting the king obliged him to act; but it is, perhaps, as well to understand the text of forgiveness of what he had done; for it may be read, *When my master went to the house of Rimmon, he leaned on my hand, and I bowed down myself in the house of Rimmon*; the Lord pardon thy servant concerning this thing.

Naaman went off very joyfully; but Gehazi, Elisha's servant, displeased with his master for refusing his presents, soon overtook him. Naaman humbly alighted from his chariot and asked him what was his desire. He falsely told him that two young prophets from Mount Ephraim had just come to his master in great want, each needing a suit of clothes and some money. Naaman was so touched with gratitude that be never once considered how unlikely it was that Elisha would ask a talent of silver for two young scholars, and he urged Gehazi to take two talents instead of one, which was worth over £684, and sent his servants to carry them as far as Gehazi would permit. Whenever Gehazi had laid this present up as secretly as he could, he presented himself before Elisha, who asked him where he had been. He denied that he had been anywhere out of the way. Elisha told him that by the discoveries of God's Spirit he saw him when Naaman turned back to meet him, and added, "You, at this season, so very improper, intend to buy fields, vineyards, and olive yards, with the money you got; but, to punish your covetousness, falsehood, and treachery, the leprosy of Naaman will come on you and your posterity." We suppose Naaman soon after either died, or quitted his post in the Syrian army, that he might not lead it against the Hebrews, and Hazael became general in his place. (2 Kings 5; Luke 4:27)

Extra note
The remarkable conduct of Naaman, and the language he uses as recorded in 2 Kings 5:8-15, affords a striking example of man's natural dislike of the gospel. Many, like Naaman, would have gone away in a rage at the simplicity of the gospel, which, so far from flattering man's pride, or directing him to any labour in or of himself by which his leprosy of sin might he cleansed, a gospel that simply says, "*Go wash and be clean*". In other words, "*Preach the gospel to every creature*" (Mark 16:15), and declares to them that the fountain in the house of David stands open for cleansing. (Zech. 13:1) "*He that believeth and is baptised shall be saved; but he that believeth not shall be damned.*" (Mark 16:16)

NABAL

A rich, but very bad and uncouth man, of the tribe of Judah, and of the race of Caleb. He had numerous flocks, which had their pasture around south Carmel, near Maon. David, in his exile, lay low in the neighbouring wilderness of Paran. He and his men not only did no harm to Nabal's flocks, but protected them from the Arabs and from wild beasts, and assisted the herdsmen in everything they could. When Nabal held his shearing feast, David, in the most polite way, sent to desire a present of what part of the provision he pleased. Nabal, in the very harsh and surly manner, told David's messengers that he knew better than to give his servant provision to a contemptible fellow who had run away from his master, and to his partisans. Informed of this rudeness, David rashly resolved immediately to put Nabal, and all that he had, to the sword, as a means of deterring others from treating him in the same way. Abigail, by her wise behaviour, disarmed David's rage and won his affection. As soon as Nabal her husband was sober, she told him into what danger his conduct had brought himself and family. The poor creature was so terrified that he fell sick, and, ten days later, died as stupidly as he had lived. Not long after, Abigail was married to David. (1 Sam. 25)

NABOTH
An Israelite of the city of Jezreel. He had a fine garden hard by Ahab's palace, which Ahab required him either to sell to him, or to exchange for another. Naboth, attentive to the divine Law, which prohibited the alienation of inheritances without need, or to sell them irredeemably, refused to sell or exchange the inheritance of his fathers. Ahab, having taken the refusal extremely badly, Jezebel, his wife, bade him make himself easy, and she would get him the vineyard. She wrote letters in Ahab's name, and sealed them with his ring, requiring the magistrates of Jezreel to hold a fast, or, perhaps rather, a general court, and to get two or three wretched fellows to bear false witness against Naboth, that he had blasphemed God and the King, and thus condemn, and put him, to death. The corrupt magistrates directly executed her orders. Naboth was stoned to death as a blasphemer, and Ahab took possession of the vineyard; but the vengeance of heaven pursued him and his family for the covetousness, hypocrisy, perjury, and murder committed in this affair. (1 Kings 21; 2 Kings 9:21-26)

NADAB. See Aaron, Jeroboam
The oldest of Aaron's four sons. (Exod. 6:23, 24:1, 9, 28:1; Lev. 10:1; Num. 3:2, 4, 26:60-61; 1 Kings 14:20, 15:25, 27, 31; 1 Chron. 2:28, 30, 6:3, 8:30, 9:36, 24:1-2.)

NAHASH. See Ammon, Jabesh
King of the Ammonites in Saul's day. See 1 Sam. 11:1-2, 12:12; 2 Sam. 10:2, 17:25, 27; 1 Chronicles 19:1-2.

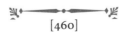

NAHOR

The son of Terah, grandson of another Nahor, and brother of Abraham. He fixed his residence at Haran in Mesopotamia, which was sometimes called by his name. He married Milcah, the daughter of his brother Haran, who was already dead. By her, he had eight sons: Huz or Uz, the father of the Husites, on the west of the Euphrates, in the land of Uz, Buz, the father of the Buzites, of whom Elihu was descended, Kemuel, the father of the Camilites, and the Arameans or Syrians, Chesed, the father of at least one tribe of the Chaldeans, Hazo, whom some carry into Persia, and make the father of the Hazoye, or Huzæans in Chusistan, or the Chosseans, Pildash, whom Dr. Hyde seems fond of making the father of the Persians, Jidlaph, and Bethuel, the father of Laban and Rebekah. By a concubine called Reumah, Nahor had four other sons: Tebah, Gaham, Thahash, and Maachah.

NAHUM

A prophet of the city of Elkosh, or Elkoshai, in Galilee. (His name is only found in Nahum 1:1) As he speaks of the Assyrian ravages of Egypt, and the destruction of No, as a thing past, and represents the Assyrian king as imagining an evil thing against the Lord, it is probable he prophesied just as either Sennacherib or Esarhaddon was returning from the ravage of Egypt, with an intention to destroy the kingdom of Judah. (Nahum 1:9, 11, 3:8-10)

After a lofty description of God, the great subject of his short prophecy is the ruin of Nineveh and the Assyrian Empire. This, he describes in a way so pathetic and picturesque, and yet so plain, as cannot be exceeded by the greatest masters of oratory. Had Herodotus written his history of the Assyrians, or had it come into our hands, with what pleasure we would have seen the exact fulfilment of these predictions.

NAME

Properly, that by which a person or thing is called, to distinguish it from another. A great many of the names of persons and places mentioned in Scripture were founded on, and express, some particular reason. Those that begin or end in EL, or begin with JE, JEHO, or end in IAH, bear a relation to God. As many people and things had different names, it is no wonder we find them sometimes called by one

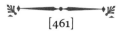

name, and sometimes by another. So Moses' father-in-law was called Reuel and Jethro, Isaac's younger son, Jacob and Israel, Jehoshaphat's grandson, Jehoahaz, Ahaziah, and Azariah, etc. Some letters too, especially the vowel **E** for **A**, etc., are altered in the spelling of the same name, as *Gashmu* or *Geshem*, *Achan* or *Achar*, etc. It is still common for the Arabs to change their names at any remarkable change of their condition.

Name, when ascribed to God or Christ, comprehends whatever he makes himself known by.

The name of God means:

(1) Himself. (Ps. 29:2, 34:3, 61:5)

(2) His titles. (Exod. 3:13-14, 6:3)

(3) His attributes or properties. (Exod. 33:19, 34:6-7)

(4) His Word. (Ps. 5:11; Acts 9:15)

(5) His worship and service. (1 Kings 5:5; Mal. 1:6)

(6) His will and purpose concerning our salvation, and his grace and mercy there displayed. (Ps. 22:22; John 17:6, 26)

(7) His power, help and assistance. (1 Sam. 17:45; Ps. 20:1, 7)

(8) His wisdom, power, and goodness displayed in his works of creation and providence. (Ps 8:1, 9)

(9) His authority, commission. (Micah 5:4)

(10) His honour, glory, and renown. (Ps. 76:1)

The name of Christ means:

(1) Himself, what he really is: Wonderful, mighty God, God with us. (Isa. 7:14, 9:6)

(2) His titles as Saviour, Prophet, Priest, King etc. (Matt. 1:21; Rev. 19:14)

(3) His authority and commission. (Matt. 7:22; Acts 4:7)

(4) His Word and gospel, and the profession of it. (Matt. 10:22, 19:29; Acts 9:15; Rev. 2:13)

(5) His exaltation to the highest honour, power and glory, as our Mediator. (Phil. 2:9-10)

The name of men means:

(1) That particular designation by which they are usually called.

(2) The persons themselves. (Luke 10:20 = *names*; Rev. 3:4, 11:11)

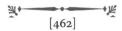

(3) Reputation, good or evil. (Deut. 22:14; Prov. 22:1)

(4) Honour, glory renown. (Deut. 26:19; 2 Chron. 26:8, 15; Zeph. 3:20)

(5) Memory or remembrance. (Deut. 29:20)

(6) Posterity, which keeps up one's name or renown. (Deut. 25:7; Isa. 66:22)

God's *name* is in Christ; his nature and authority are in him. He has sent him to be our Redeemer, and, by the execution of his office is his honour chiefly exalted. (Exod. 23:21) To be baptised *in the name* of the Father, Son, and Holy Spirit, or of Jesus, is to be baptised by warrant and authority, into the profession, faith, and obedience, of these divine Persons as one God. (Matt. 28:19; Acts 19:5) To trust or believe in the *name of God* or *Christ* is to credit his word, and rely on his perfections, titles, and relations, as the certain ground of our receiving all blessings and salvation from him. (John 3:18) To *name the name of Christ* is to profess openly that we are his, and to regard his honour and service. (2 Tim. 2:19) The new name that Christ gives, and writes on his people, is the *redeemed of the Lord, the righteousness of God in him*, etc., which answers to their new covenant state, and their new nature. And in heaven their character is made gloriously to appear. (Rev. 2:17) This is better than of sons and daughters, as it is more honourable to be the children of God and spouse of Christ than to be parents of sinful men. (Isa. 56:4-5) God's changing the *name of his Church* means his changing her condition from distress and grief to happiness and joy. (Isa. 62:3-4) The saints pray, and do all *in the name of Christ*, when they do it by faith in his promise, in obedience to his command, and with a total dependence on his righteousness and intercession for acceptance. (John 14:13; Col. 3:17) To *take the name of God in vain* is to make an unholy and irreverent use of anything in which he makes himself known, whether titles, attributes, ordinances, words, or works, and particularly by ignorant, rash, irreverent, and false swearing. (Exod. 20:7) The Hebrews were forbidden to mention the *names* of the heathen idols, except when it was necessary to warn against them, or mark detestation of them (Exod. 23:15), and so a thing *not named* is what is not mentioned with pleasure, or what is scarcely known or heard of, or is not practised, but abhorred. (1 Cor. 5:1 and Eph. 5:3)

To know someone by name is to have a special favour towards, and familiarity with, someone. (Exod. 33:12) To give names to people or animals implies dominion over them. (Gen. 2:19) To *have a name to live, and yet be dead*, is to have a profession and appearance of saintship, and yet be under the reign of spiritual death. (Rev. 3:1) The *names of the 12 tribes of Israel, being on the 12 gates of the New Jerusalem* means that the Jews will be brought into the Church in the millennium, and all the elect enter into the church here and the heavenly glory hereafter. (Rev. 21:14) The *names of the 12 Apostles being in the 12 foundations* means that it is Jesus, as presented in the doctrine of the 12 Apostles, that is the foundation of the Church, and of our everlasting happiness. (Rev. 21:14) To have the *mark, name, or number* of the name of antichrist is to believe, profess, and practise according to the errors, idolatry, and superstition of the Church of Rome. It is *names of blasphemy*, the doctrines of the pope's supremacy, and of men's perfecting Christ's sacrifice, with their offerings and good works, etc., that are a reproach to Christ and his Father. (Rev. 13:1, 17)

NAOMI

Together with her husband Elimelech, she retired to the country of Moab on account of a famine that happened in Canaan. There, their two sons Mahlon and Chilion married two Moabitish girls, Orpah and Ruth. They had been about ten years in the country of Moab, when Elimelech and his sons died, without leaving any issue. Naomi resolved to return to her country, and her daughters-in-law were intent on going with her. She told them what difficulties they might expect in doing so, and begged them to return home; and added that she was grieved on account of their affliction. At last, Orpah was prevailed upon to return, but Ruth continued resolute to go with her and to embrace the Jewish religion.

When they arrived at Bethlehem, the place of Naomi's former abode, the people crowded about them; and some in pity, and others perhaps in contempt, asked if this was Naomi. She begged them not to call her *Naomi (my pleasant one)*, but *Marah*, because the Lord had dealt very *bitterly* with her, insomuch that, having gone off full, with a husband, children, and some wealth, she had returned a poor destitute widow. It being the harvest season, Ruth went out to glean, and providence conducted her to the field of Boaz, a near relative of her deceased husband. Informed who she was, he commended her for her kindness to her mother-in-law, and bade her continue gleaning on his field, and take her food with his reapers, who, on his orders, let fall handfuls of the corn for her use. Ruth most humbly and discreetly thanked him for his kindness to a poor stranger. Informed of all this at night, Naomi told Ruth that Boaz was their near relative. When harvest was ended, and Boaz one night watched his corn on the threshing floor, Naomi directed Ruth to go and lie down at his feet, and bid him cast his skirt over her (or marry her), as he was her near relative. The known modesty of both turned away all suspicion of improper conduct. When Boaz awoke, he observed a woman at his feet, and asked who she was. She told him, and begged him to spread his skirt over her as a token of his after marrying her. Boaz blessed her for so closely adhering to the Hebrew Law in the affair of her marriage; and, in the morning, he sent her home loaded with corn for herself and Naomi, promising that he would speedily effect her marriage either with himself, or with a nearer kinsman.

Naomi, hearing of this, assured Ruth that Boaz would, without fail, be as good as his word. It was scarcely daylight, when Boaz convened the elders of the city at the gate, and called Elimelech's nearest relative to declare whether he would redeem the inheritance of Elimelech, and marry Ruth, the widow of Chilion, or not. The relative, after his offering to redeem the inheritance, took back his word, and bid Boaz do it; and, by plucking off his shoe, he resigned his right to Boaz. At the same time, Boaz married Ruth, and soon after had by her a son called *Obed*, in the hope he would be a *servant* of the Lord, and would be serviceable to his family. The neighbours greatly congratulated Naomi as having now got an heir, and a restorer of her old age. With great tenderness, she nursed the child. (Read entirely Ruth 1-4) Who wrote the short history of Ruth, whether Samuel or not, is not quite certain. The ancient fathers considered it as an appendix to Judges. This affair happened about the time of Deborah.

NAPHTALI, NEPHTHALIM

The sixth son of Jacob, and by Bilhah the handmaid of Rachel. His sons were Jahzeel, Guni, Jezer, and Shillem, all of them parents of a numerous offspring. In his blessing of Naphtali, Jacob said, *Naphtali is a hind let loose, he giveth goodly words.* This might express the activity and courtesy of that tribe, or the activity of Jesus and his Apostles, who resided much in the territories of that tribe in their preaching of the glad tidings of salvation to lost sinners. But some prefer the translation of the seventy, which passage reads, *Naphtali is a tree shot out, bringing forth goodly branches*; and so would refer to the fertility and increase of that tribe; but neither do the Hebrew accents countenance this reading, nor is it different from the blessing of Joseph in the very next verse. When this tribe came out of Egypt, it consisted of 53,400 fighting men, under the command of Ahira, the son of Enan; but they decreased in the wilderness to 45,400. They encamped on the north of the Tabernacle, and marched in the rear of the Hebrew host, in the camp of Dan. Their spy to search Canaan was Nahbi, the son of Vophsi, and their agent to divide it was Pedahel, the son of Ammihud. Their inheritance was *the Sea, and the south*, along the south of Lebanon, and the west of the Sea of Merom and Tiberias, and was extremely fertile. (Gen. 46:24, 49:21; Num. 1:15, 41, 43, 2:25, 30, 10:27, 13:14, 26:48-52, 34:28; Deut. 33:23; Josh. 19:32-39) But they permitted the Canaanites to retain Bethanath and Bethshemesh, two of their cities, on condition they paid them tribute. (Judg. 1:33)

Under Barak their general, they and the Zebulunites fought with distinguished bravery against the army of Jabin the younger, and, at the desire of Gideon, they pursued the Midianites. (Judg. 4:6, 10, 5:18, 7:23) A thousand of their captains, with 37,000 of their troops, assisted at David's coronation, and brought great quantities of provision with them. (1 Chron. 12:34, 40) We find no one of distinguished note among them, except Barak, and Hiram the artificer. Instigated by Asa, Benhadad the elder, King of Syria, terribly ravaged the land of Naphtali; and what it suffered in after invasions by the Syrians we are not told. (1 Kings 15:20) The Naphtalites were many, but most of them were carried away captive by Tiglathpileser, King of Assyria. (2 Kings 15:29) Josiah purged their country from idols. Our Saviour and his disciples, during his public ministry, much resided and preached in the land of Naphtali. (Isa. 9:1, fulfilled in Matt. 4:13, 15 = *Nephthalim*)

NARCISSUS

If he was the wicked but famous freedman of the Emperor Claudius, he was dead before Paul wrote his Epistle to the Romans; but the Christians of his family are saluted. (Found only in Rom. 16:11)

NATHAN

A famous prophet, and confidante of King David. Not long after David's advancement to the throne of Israel, he intended to build a Temple for the Lord. Nathan, without waiting for divine direction, encouraged him to do it; but soon after, was directed of God to forbid him, and tell him that that work was divinely allotted to his son and successor. Some years later, when David had taken Bathsheba, and murdered her husband, Nathan, directed by God, reproved him. He told him a parable of a man who had a great many flocks and herds of his own, and yet, when his friend came to visit him, by force, he took from a poor neighbour his only lamb, which was very dear to him, to make a feast for his friend. With great indignation, David replied that such a person should be obliged to restore fourfold to the poor man, and then be put to death. Nathan told him that he himself was guilty of the crime, for God had made him ruler over the whole Hebrew nation, and had providentially put into his power all the wives and concubines of Saul, and was about to bestow on him other favours. Yet he had taken Bathsheba, the only wife of Uriah, and had murdered him. On which account, Nathan told him, he and his family should be severely punished with loose sexual behaviour and death.

David was so well-pleased with the plainness of Nathan's rebuke, that, it seems, he named one of Bathsheba's sons after him. When Adonijah attempted to settle himself on the throne, Nathan, and Bathsheba by his direction, prevented it, and he and Benaiah, and others, were immediately appointed to crown Solomon. (2 Sam. 7, 12; 1 Kings 1) Nathan and Gad wrote the history of David, probably the second book of Samuel, and the last part of the first. He and Abijah wrote the history of Solomon (1 Chron. 29:29; 2 Chron. 9:27); but whether this Nathan was the father of Azariah and Zabud, who were officers of considerable dignity under Solomon, we do not know. (1 Kings 4:5)

NATHANAEL. See Bartholemew
One of Christ's Apostles. See John 1:45-49, 21:2.

NAZARITES
Those devoted to the special service of God for a week, a month, a year, or for life. Some of them dedicated themselves; and some, like Samson

and John Baptist, were expressly claimed by God. During their vow, they were never to cut their hair, or drink any wine or strong drink; and it was extremely wicked to offer them any. (Amos 2:11-12) Nor were they to attend a funeral, or enter a house defiled by the dead. If they accidentally contracted any defilement, or in any way broke their vow, they had the time and duty of Nazariteship to begin again. They shaved off all their hair on the seventh day, and offered to the Lord two turtledoves or pigeons, the one for a sin offering and the other for a burnt offering, and a lamb for a trespass offering. When their vow was finished, Nazarites presented themselves at the door of the Tabernacle or Temple with a he-lamb for a burnt offering, a she-lamb for a sin-offering, and a ram for a peace offering, with their respective meat offerings and drink offerings, and a basket full of cakes of unleavened bread, and wafers anointed with oil. After these were offered, the Nazarite shaved his hair at the door of the sanctuary, and burnt it under the pot in which the flesh of his peace offering was boiled. The priest then put into his hand the roasted shoulder of the ram of peace offering, with a cake and wafer of unleavened bread. These, he returned to the priest, who waved them to and fro, dedicating them to the all-present God of all the ends of the earth; and so the vow was over. As the oblations at the breach of the vow atoned for the same, the offerings at the finish of it were designed to expiate the unknown breaches of it, and to render God thanks for enabling him to fulfil it so well. (Num. 6) Those like Samuel, Samson, and John the Baptist, were dedicated for life, and had no occasion for these offerings. Those who lived out of Canaan cut their hair in the places where the days of their vow were finished, but deferred the offerings till they got to the sanctuary. So Paul shaved off his hair at Cenchrea, but deferred his offering till he came to Jerusalem. (Acts 18:18, 21:23-24) Some, who had not opportunity to perform the duties of the Nazarite themselves, contributed to bear the expenses of those who had taken the vow.

Were not these Nazarites typical of Jesus Christ? Altogether holy, he was solemnly dedicated to the service of God. Never was he defiled with worldly comforts and pleasures, nor intoxicated with sinful lusts or earthly cares. Never was he defiled by special affection towards his nearest and dearest, nor polluted by his gracious connections with men, in whom spiritual death or deadness do their work. Instead of hair, his graces and good works increased more and more, and his people, rooted in him, grow up and flourish in God's Holy Place. Never did he break his vow, but finished it in giving himself as an all-comprehensive offering for us; and, in his resurrection, he laid aside every token of continued subjection to an angry God or broken Law, and purges and inflames the hearts of his people by his bleeding love. Were not these Nazarites emblems of ministers and saints who, denying themselves, and mortifying the deeds of the body, consecrate themselves to God, renouncing this world and the pleasures of sin. And, by every breach of their vow through inadvertent fellowship with dead works, ought they not to be excited to apply Jesus' atonement to their conscience, and, after they have done that, to trust only in his all-comprehending sacrifice of himself?

NEBAIOTH

The oldest son of Ishmael, the father of the Nabatheans, who appear to have been one of the most civilised tribes of the Arabians, and the most friendly to the Jews, and part of whom were converted to Christ. (Gen. 25:13; Isa. 60:7)

NEBO (or Anambo)

An idol of the Chaldeans. Perhaps they borrowed him from the Moabites, who had a hill called Nebo, and a city near it of the same name, about eight miles south of Heshbon, and which was taken by both the Assyrians and Chaldeans. (Deut. 34:1; Num. 32:38; Isa. 15:2, 46:1; Jer. 48:1, 22) Or Nebo the idol (Isa. 15:2, 46:1) might be the same as Chemosh, or as Beltis the Queen of Belis, and so might represent the moon. The Seventy translators call this idol Dagon, and Augustine Calmet has it to be Bel. But we suppose both these opinions are groundless. It is certain that Nebo is, by Isaiah, represented as different from Bel, and that the name is compounded with many Chaldean names, such as Nabonassar, Nabocolassar, Nabopolassar, Nebuchadnezzar, Nebuzaradan, Nebushashan, etc.

NEBUCHADNEZZAR, NEBUCHADREZZAR (Nabopolassar)

The most famous king of Babylon. When Pharaohnecho had taken Carchemish, a city on the Euphrates, the Phoenicians, and part of the Syrians, revolted from the Chaldeans, who, it seems, had just before reduced them. Nabopolassar, being then stricken in years, sent

Nebuchadnezzar his son with an army to recover them. He gained a complete victory over the Egyptians at Carchemish, retook the place, and put the garrison to the sword. Then, with an army of 180,000 foot, 120,000 horses, and 10,000 chariots (according to Eupolemus), he ravaged Phoenicia and Canaan, took Jerusalem, and bound Jehoiakim, the tributary of the Egyptians, in chains, to carry him to Babylon; but afterwards he allowed him to retain his kingdom as a vassal of the Chaldeans. He carried to Babylon Daniel, Hananiah, Mishael, and Azariah, and others of the princes of Judah. To the above four young men, he gave new names, indicating a connection with his idol gods, calling them Belteshazzar, Shadrach, Meshach, and Abednego. These, and other young captives, he trained up in all the learning of the Chaldeans that they might serve in court. (2 Kings 24; Dan. 1)

About BC 605, his father died, leaving him sole king of Babylon. In the second year of his reign, he had a surprising dream, but entirely forgot it. He assembled his diviners, and charged them to tell him his dream, and its meaning. They told him that, though they could interpret dreams, yet none but the gods could tell a man what he had dreamed, and that no king had ever demanded any such thing from his diviners. Being outrageously provoked, he ordered Arioch, the captain of his guard, to put every wiseman of Babylon to death. Daniel, however, obtained leave to tell the king his dream, and its meaning. He was so satisfied with the account and interpretation that he fell on his face before Daniel, as if an inferior deity, and ordered an offering of spices to be presented to him, and acknowledged his God, the God of gods, and Lord of kings. He made Daniel chief of the wisemen, and governor of the province of Babylon, and made Shadrach, Meshach, and Abednego, subordinate governors in the same place. (Dan. 2)

Meanwhile, a peace being concluded between the Medes and Lydians by the mediation of Nebuchadnezzar, and of Syennesis, King of Cilicia, Cyaxares, King of Media gave his daughter Amyite in marriage to Nebuchadnezzar; and they two marched their troops against Nineveh and levelled it to the ground. Some of Nebuchadnezzar's troops had already ravaged Judea, but, the Assyrian war being finished, he sent his army into that country and laid it waste far and wide. Soon after, he, upon what provocation we do not know, marched his army against Jehoiachin; but that young monarch, with his whole family, surrendered themselves to his mercy, and were made prisoners and carried into

Babylon. He carried off a part of the sacred furniture of the Temple, and many captives. The Moabites, Ammonites, and Phoenicians, together with the Egyptians, encouraged Zedekiah, King of Judah, to revolt from the Chaldeans. Nebuchadnezzar, with great fury, marched to chastise them. On the southeast of Syria, he was in doubt whether to begin with the Ammonites or the Jews. He referred the matter to the decision of divination, and the divination directed him first to march against the Jews. This war took up nearly two years. He himself retired to Riblah, and left his generals, Nebuzaradan, Nergalsharezer, Shamgarnebo, Sarsechim, Rabsaris, and Rabmag, to carry it on. After raising the siege of Jerusalem to march against the Egyptians, they returned to it, and took the city, leaving the poor of the land under the charge of Gedaliah, a prince who had early surrendered himself. According to Nebuchadnezzar's express orders, they took special care of Jeremiah, but the prisoners of distinction, which were carried to him at Riblah, Seraiah and Zephaniah, the two principal priests, Zedekiah's children and general, and 68 others, were all put to death. Zedekiah had his eyes put out, and was carried captive to Babylon. (2 Kings 24-25; 2 Chron. 36; Jer. 6-40, 53; Ezek. 21:19-24) It was perhaps at this time, about the 20th year of his reign, that he, with the gold he had amassed in his western expedition, erected the monstrous image to his god Belus in the plain of Dura, in the province of Babylon. It was at least 90 feet high, and 9 feet broad. Having convened his princes, governors, captains, judges, and other officers under him, for the dedication of this idol, he issued a proclamation that whenever the concert of music by cornet, flute, harp, sackbut, psaltery, dulcimer, etc., should begin to play, everybody must fall down on his knees or face, and adore this monstrous image, under pain of being cast into a fiery furnace. Daniel either was absent, or, for fear of his great power, was not informed; but Shadrach, Meshach, and Abednego, were accused of refusing to worship the idol. Nebuchadnezzar called them before him and interrogated them if it was so. They told him they would not worship his image, and were confident their God was able to deliver them from his burning fiery furnace. Infuriated with rage, he ordered the furnace to be heated to a sevenfold degree, and them to be cast into it bound. The flames seized on those that threw them in, and burnt them to ashes. The Son of God, appearing in human shape in the midst of the fire, caused it to burn their bonds, but not so much as to singe their clothes or a hair of their head, and walked with them up and down the furnace. Nebuchadnezzar, observing this, told his people around, and called to Shadrach, Meshach, and Abednego to come out of the furnace. They were quite unhurt, with not so much as the smell of fire about them. Nebuchadnezzar extolled the power of the Hebrew God, and ordered that whoever should speak reproachfully of him should be put to death, and his house made a dunghill; and he promoted these three Hebrews to higher government in the province of Babylon. (Dan. 9:3)

About the 22nd year of his reign, he marched his troops into Phoenicia, and laid siege to Tyre. Meanwhile, by detached parties, he reduced Ammonites, Moabites, Edomites, and northern Arabians; and Nebuzaradan carried off 745 Jews, whom he found in their land. After he had besieged Tyre 13 years, till his army was almost ruined with fatigue, and, at the end, obtained nothing but a deserted place (the inhabitants having transported themselves and their effects to a neighbouring island) and ashes, he reduced the city to ashes, and cast the rubbish into the adjacent sea. With fury, he then marched against the Egyptians who had supplied the Tyrians during the siege; and, after ravaging their country, and murdering the inhabitants, and particularly the Jews who had fled there after the murder of Gedaliah his deputy, he and his army returned to Babylon loaded with rich spoil. He also subdued Persia; and Media was in a kind of subjection. But when this happened, we do not know. (Jer. 25, 27, 43-49; Isa. 23; Ezek. 25-27, 35)

By this time, in the 35th year of his reign, his astonishing structures at Babylon were almost finished. He dreamed of a tall and flourishing tree laden with fruit, and a place of refuge for birds and beasts unnumbered, and yet, all of a sudden, orders given by an angel to hew it down, shake off its leaves and fruit, but to fasten its root in the earth as if with a band of iron and brass for seven years, that it might be wet with the dew of heaven, and have its portion with the beasts of the field. None of his diviners could interpret it, so Daniel came, and, being encouraged by the king to tell him the interpretation, be what it may, he told him that it meant that for seven years, he would be reduced to the condition of a beast, and driven from the society of men; and, after his acknowledgment of the divine supremacy, he would be restored to his throne. Daniel entreated him to break off from his sinful and unjust courses, and show mercy to the poor, captives, or others. Regardless of Daniel's admonition, Nebuchadnezzar continued as proud as ever. One day, as he walked on the top of his palace, perhaps in his hanging gardens, and looked on his august city, he said, either to himself or some companions, "Is not this great Babylon, that I have built for my metropolis, and by the might of my power, and for the honour of my majesty?" A voice from heaven replied that he should immediately be driven from human society and reduced to the condition of a brute beast. He was immediately struck with some strange disease, of a kind we call lycanthropy, under which a person fancies himself a dog, cat, etc., and howls, bites, and eats in their manner, and shuns human society. Nebuchadnezzar fancied he was an ox, and imitated the manner of one. No doubt, his astonished friends bound him as a madman; but he escaped out of their hands, fled to the fields, and there lived seven years on the grass, and went naked till his hair grew like eagles' feathers, and his nails like birds' claws. At the end of seven years, God restored him the use of his reason. He humbled himself, glorified God, and ordered an account of his dream and its fulfilment to be published to all his subjects. It is said that, after he was restored to his government, he cast his son Evilmerodach into prison, perhaps that in which Jehoiachin had lain about 36 years, either for the follies he had been guilty of during his father's disability, or to secure the peace of the kingdom. (Dan. 4) About a year later, Nebuchadnezzar died in the 43rd or 44th year of his reign. It is said that, just before his death, he, seized with some supernatural impression, got up to the top of his palace, and cried to the Babylonians that a mule, assisted by a Mede (that is Cyrus), whose father was a Persian and his mother a Mede, assisted by his uncle Darius the Mede, would ruin their Empire, and reduce them to slavery.

NEBUZARADAN. See Nebuchadnezzar
See 2 Kings 25:8, 11, 20; Jer. 39:9-11, 13, 40:1, 41:10, 43:6, 52:12, 15-16, 26, 30.

NEHEMIAH
The son of Hachaliah. He was possibly of the royal family of David. Perhaps his being the royal cupbearer in the Persian court, and his succeeding Zerubbabel in the government of the Jews, tends to confirm this opinion. About BC 446 or 444, ninety years after their

return from Chaldea, he was informed by Hanani that Jerusalem still remained in rubbish, and was a reproach or object of derision to all the nations around. Deeply affected with this narrative, Nehemiah fasted, and prayed that the Lord would prosper his intention to ask the king's permission to go and rebuild it. He indeed attended to the bearing of the royal cup, but his face marked him sad and dejected. King Artaxerxes, observing it, asked him the cause, probably suspecting he had some bad design in hand. Nehemiah was afraid, but lifting up his heart to God, he presented his grief to the King, as the Queen (some say Esther) sat by him. Upon his request, Artaxerxes, in the 20th year of his reign, empowered him to go and rebuild the walls of Jerusalem. He gave him letters of safe conveyance to the governors of the west of the Euphrates, and one to Asaph the keeper of the forest of Lebanon, ordering him to furnish Nehemiah with timber, and every other thing necessary for the repair of Jerusalem, and for Nehemiah's own house.

Arrived at Jerusalem with the king's commission, he and his servant went round the wall of the city in the night, and found it wholly in ruins. At this, he assembled the chief men among the Jews, informed them of his powers and intention, and encouraged them to begin the work. They readily agreed to his proposal, and different pieces of the wall were assigned to various principal men. Thirty-two of these, together with the companies of the priests, Levites, Nethinim, and the goldsmiths and merchants, exerted themselves in this good work. Some repaired over against their own house, and some, as the inhabitants of Tekoah, Gibeon, and Mizpeh, generously repaired a part of it, though they lived in other cities. Sanballat the Horonite, and Tobiah the Ammonite, originally a servant, but now a governor, and Gashmu the Arabian, were extremely vexed to hear of Nehemiah's arrival to help and encourage the Jews, and to see the repairs of the wall of Jerusalem carried on with so much ardour. They first scoffed at the Jews and their work; but seeing it go on, they and their countrymen made several attempts to surprise and murder the Jews as they worked. To frustrate their intentions, Nehemiah placed a guard on the outside of the builders, and caused every builder to keep his sword by his side as he built. They never put off their clothes, either day or night, except for washing, and the trumpeter went along with Nehemiah, ready to sound the alarm in case of danger. Finding that they could do nothing by open violence, Sanballat and Tobiah had recourse to stratagem. Tobiah, having married the daughter of Shechaniah, a prince of Judah, had a powerful part of the Jews in his interest. These, with the Jews that lived in the country around, did what they could to dispirit Nehemiah and his friends, as if it were impossible to withstand so many enemies who would, of a sudden, attack them from every quarter. Sanballat and his companions wrote four letters, inviting Nehemiah to a friendly conference in the plain of Ono, but they caused a party to lie in wait to murder him by the way. He returned them the answer that the great and important work that he was about, requiring his constant attendance, meant that he could not come. Sanballat then wrote him an open letter, indicating that a report was abroad, and was affirmed by Gashmu, a man of credit and influence, that he and the Jews were rebuilding Jerusalem with a design to revolt, and that he had paid the prophets to stir up the people to choose him as their king; and that, as King Artaxerxes could not fail to hear this report, it was necessary that they should consult together how to refute it. Nehemiah, conscious of his innocence, trusting in his God, and persuaded of the king's favour, returned no other answer but that the whole report was false, and had been forged by Sanballat himself. Sanballat and Tobiah then bribed the prophet Shemaiah and the prophetess Noadiah to endeavour the murder of Nehemiah and the hindrance of the work. Shemaiah shut himself up in his chamber, as if habitually given to meditation, fasting, and prayer. This imposed on Nehemiah a little, and made him think he was remarkably pious, and a real friend. One time, as Nehemiah was in his house, he told him that he would be slain that very night, unless they two should shut themselves up in a secret place of the Temple. Nehemiah replied that it was quite improper that he, whose conduct was so innocent, and his presence and bold influence so necessary, should hide himself anywhere. Thus, despite all that Sanballat, Tobiah, Geshem, and their party of treacherous Jews could do, the wall was finished in 52 days after they began to repair it. Almost a year after, it was dedicated with solemn sacrifices and thanksgiving. (Neh. 1-4, 6, 12:27-43)

Meanwhile, Nehemiah applied himself to rectify disorders. He curbed the inhumanity of the nobles and rich men, who retained the lands of their poor brothers in mortgage, and held their children in slavery. To show himself a distinguished pattern of generosity, he never demanded the salary prescribed him by the Persian King, but maintained his family on the product of his own fields, and on the salary he received as the king's cupbearer. He settled the genealogies by an old register that he found. The feasts of Trumpets and of Tabernacles were observed with more exactness than had ever been done since the time of Joshua, the son of Nun; and Ezra, assisted by 13 others, on both occasions, read and explained the book of the Law to the people. Immediately after, he caused the Jews who had married heathen women to put them away. After solemn fasting and confession of sins, they renewed their covenant with God, and solemnly vowed obedience to his Law. They particularly vowed to marry no heathen women, to buy no goods on the Sabbath, to observe the year of release, give their firstfruits and firstlings to the Levites with more exactness than had been done for some time past, and dedicated the third part of a shekel extraordinary every year for the service of the Temple. 22 priests, 17 Levites, and 44 chief men of the people subscribed to this covenant, and all the rest of the people who understood it declared their adherence. As Jerusalem was poorly inhabited, the tenth man was chosen by lot to dwell in it, and Nehemiah blessed those who offered themselves willingly to dwell there. The charge of the city was given to Hanani, the brother of Nehemiah, and to Hanani the son of Zerubbabel, one eminently faithful and pious; and a guard was placed at every gate to prevent the enemies from entering. The order of the Levites, priests, singers, and porters, was rectified and established. (Neh. 5, 7-12)

After Nehemiah had governed the Jews 12 years, he returned to King Artaxerxes, and, after some stay in Persia, returned to Judea. The Jews, contrary to their covenant, had married strange wives, and profaned the Sabbath by bearing burdens, and buying fish and other wares from the Syrians. They had withheld the dues of the Levites, and obliged them to desert the service of the Temple. All these disorders, partly by reproof for convincing them of their sinfulness, and partly by force, Nehemiah quickly rectified. Tobiah had fixed his residence at Jerusalem, and Manasseh, the grandson of Eliashib the High Priest, who had married the daughter of Sanballat, had procured him a lodging in the Court of the Temple. Nehemiah drove Tobiah from his lodging, threw out his furniture, and banished Manasseh the priest from the city. Sanballat, his father-in-law, obtaining the consent not of Alexander, as Josephus says, but of Darius Nothus, built a temple for him on Mount Gerizim, where he, and perhaps his descendants, officiated as priests to the Samaritans. After Nehemiah had governed the Jewish state about 36 years, he died.

Probably, he wrote his own history, for, as he died about BC 409, Jaddua, who officiated as High Priest when Alexander passed that way in BC 334, might be a boy of 10 or 12 years of age. (Neh. 12:11) As from Ezra's commission to rectify the affairs of Judea, to the year in which Nehemiah is here supposed to have died, is 49 years, this may correspond to the seven weeks of Daniel, in which the city and wall of Jerusalem was built in troubled times. (Dan. 9:25)

The *Nehemiah* that returned from Babylon with Zerubbabel (Ezra 2:2)was a different man from him who is the subject of this article, as he had occasion to see the ruins of Jerusalem, and could scarcely have been below 110 years of age, and so not very proper for a cupbearer in the 20th year of Artaxerxes.

NERO

An infamous Emperor of Rome, who ruled from AD 54 to 67 or 68. He is mentioned only in the closing words of 2 Timothy 4:22 in the KJV. In the first part of his reign, he behaved with some decency and justice, pretending to copy Augustus. At the end of it, he turned into one of the most tyrannical wretches that ever breathed. He murdered his mother, and almost all his friends, and principal subjects. He mightily encouraged stage-plays, and everything sexual and foolish. About AD 65, he caused to be burnt the city of Rome, and sang one of his poems in full view of the flames. To appease the Senate, he transferred the blame on to the innocent Christians. Many of them were apprehended; some were sewn up in the skins of wild beasts and torn to pieces by dogs, others were crucified, others were burned in Nero's gardens as nocturnal illuminations to the city, while he, with great pleasure, beheld the spectacle from his window. Perhaps he was the more enraged that some of his own family, and, it is said, one of his darling concubines, were turned to the Lord: *All the saints salute you, chiefly they that are of Caesar's household.* (Phil. 4:22) In this persecution, perhaps most of the Apostles were cut off. After his tyranny and murder had rendered him quite intolerable, the Senate declared him an enemy of the state; and he, in despair, fled. Being

sought for to be killed, he murdered himself with the assistance of Epaphroditus, his freedman.

NICODEMUS

A follower of Jesus Christ. He was a Jewish Pharisee and a ruler among his people. At first, though he held our Saviour in some esteem, yet he was ashamed to profess it, and so came to him by night for instruction. When he had complimented our Saviour with some honorary titles, and as an excellent teacher, and hinted his desire to learn something, Jesus told him he could not become a true member of his Church unless he was born again, and his nature wholly renewed. Grossly ignorant of regeneration, and of the Old Testament oracles relative to it, Nicodemus asked how one could re-enter into his mother's womb and be born again? Jesus replied that if he was a teacher in Israel, how did he not know about these things? He told him that the new birth he spoke of was effected by the Spirit, and that if he could not believe what was so often experienced on earth, how would he receive information concerning heavenly and eternal things, known only to the Son of man, presently in heaven as to his divine nature, while his human nature was on earth? He informed him that, as the brazen serpent was lifted up in the wilderness for the general means of cure to the serpent-bitten Hebrews, so he himself would be quickly lifted up on the cross and in the gospel, for the salvation of all the ends of the earth. God, in infinite kindness, had given him to be the Saviour of the world, so that whoever believed on him, should not perish but have everlasting life; and whoever did not believe, should be damned. He added that the reason why many did not believe his instructions was because their deeds were evil, and ready to be exposed by his light. (John 3:1-21)

After this conference, we hope Nicodemus became a real disciple of Jesus Christ, and attended his ministry as he had opportunity. When afterwards he sat in the Sanhedrin, and heard the members raging at their officers for not arresting our Saviour, and deriding the people who believed on him as ignorant and accursed, he asked if it was according to the law, which they pretended to know so well, to condemn a man before they heard him? These furious bigots asked Nicodemus if he too was a Galilean? They told him to read his Bible, and he would find that no prophet ever came out of Galilee. Poor ignorant ones! Both Jonah and Nahum came from there. When our Saviour was crucified,

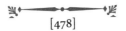

Nicodemus still more openly avowed himself a Christian, and assisted Joseph of Arimathea to inter the sacred corpse. (John 7:45-52, 19:39-40) It is said that when the other members of the Sanhedrin heard of Nicodemus' baptism, they deposed him from his office as senator, and excommunicated him from their synagogue. But Gamaliel, his cousin, took him to his country house, where he lived the rest of his time, and was honourably buried near to Stephen the deacon. A spurious gospel, called by some, *The Acts of Pilate*, is ascribed to Nicodemus, but it is plainly a forgery.

NICOLAS

One of the first seven deacons. He was a native of Antioch, a proselyte to the Jewish religion, and lately a convert to the Christian faith. He was much distinguished for holiness and zeal. (Only found in Acts 6:5) Whether by some unwise or sinful conduct, he gave any occasion to the rise of the abandoned sect of the *Nicolaitans* (Rev. 2:6, 15), or whether they, knowing his fame for sanctity, screened themselves under his name, or whether the Nicolas that founded that sect was a different person, is not agreed. Perhaps this sect was a part of, or the very same as the Gnostics. It is said that they used their women in common, reckoned adultery, and the use of meats offered to idols, indifferent things. They imputed their wickedness to God as the cause; they held a multitude of fables concerning the generation of angels and the creation of the world by subordinate powers. They had a considerable influence in Asia for a time. At Ephesus they were detested, but at Pergamos and Thyatira they were sinfully tolerated by the Christians. (Rev. 2) It does not appear that they continued long under the name of Nicolaitans; but perhaps, in reality, they continued under the name of Cainites.

NIMROD

The son of Cush. He was a mighty hunter before the Lord; and, either rendering himself useful by the killing of wild beasts, or by violently oppressing his neighbours, he procured himself a kingdom. He first set up as king in Babylon, and then extended his dominion to Erech, Accad, and Calneh, in the land of Shinar. He was no doubt a mighty promoter of the building of Babel, and, it seems, his tyranny obliged Ashur, the son of Shem, to leave the country and retire eastwards to the other side of the Hiddekel (or Tigris). There is no proper evidence that Nimrod was the Ninus who founded Nineveh, though he may be one of the Beluses concerned in the building of Babylon. Part of his history dressed up in fable is contained in the Grecian history of Bacchus. (Gen. 10:8-11)

NOAH, NOE *Rest*

(1) The son of Lamech who was descended from Seth. He was the ninth in descent from Adam, and, it seems, the *eighth preacher of righteousness.* (2 Pet. 2:5) At his birth, his father Lamech expressed his hope that he would be a great comfort to him and his family, and so gave him a name meaning *rest* and *comfort.* In his time, wickedness universally prevailed. Noah not only walked piously himself, but he admonished his neighbours to do the same. To reward his strict piety, amid so many temptations to the contrary, God preserved him and his family from the universal deluge. To effect this, at God's direction, he built an ark sufficient to accommodate him, and a sample of all the animals that could not live in the water. Perhaps he spent 120 years in building it, so that the corrupt antediluvians might have more time to repent of their sins before the Flood came. In BC 2348, and when Noah was 600 years of age, he, his wife, and his three sons, Shem, Ham, and Japheth, and their wives, and seven pairs of all clean animals, male and female, and two pairs of unclean animals, entered the ark, and were shut up in it by the Lord.

When Noah, almost a year later, found that the waters had greatly decreased, he sent out a raven to see if the earth was dry. It lived on floating carrion, and never returned to him. He next sent a dove, which, finding no dry place to rest on, returned, and Noah put out his hand and brought her into the ark. After seven days, he sent her out a second time, and she returned with a fresh olive leaf in her mouth. When he sent her out a third time, she did not return. After he and his family, and the other animals, had remained a year and ten days in the ark, they came out. Noah offered a sacrifice of thanksgiving for his preservation, and the Lord accepted it and promised that no wickedness of men would ever again provoke him to destroy the earth or its animals, or deny the regular return of the seasons. The Lord also charged Noah and his sons to multiply and replenish the earth. He allowed them to eat the flesh of clean animals, providing they did not eat them with the blood, or raw, in the manner of beasts, or having the

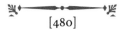

blood running through the flesh He ordered that every murderer of men should be put to death. To mark the establishment of his covenant for the preservation of the world, he promised to set his rainbow in the cloud in wet weather as a token that the waters would no more cover the earth.

Soon after the Flood, Noah commenced as a husbandman, and cultivated the vine; and, it seems, insensible of the intoxicating virtue of wine, he partook of it till he was drunk, and lay uncovered in his tent. Ham, his younger son, perhaps informed by Canaan, went and saw him in this condition, and, in a sporting manner, told his two brothers about it. They took a cloak, and, going backwards so that they might not see their father's shame, spread it over him. When Noah awoke, and was quite sober, he, understanding the behaviour of his sons, and, inspired of God, pronounced a curse of servitude upon the posterity of Ham, chiefly the descendants of Canaan. These he predicted would be slaves to the offspring of the two brothers who had covered him, and he would be oppressed by the Hebrews, Assyrians, Chaldeans, Persians, Saracens, and by the Greeks, Romans, Vandals, and Turks. That of Shem's posterity would be early and long the peculiar church of God, and those from which the Messiah would proceed. The posterity of Japheth would be exceedingly numerous, and, at last, seize on the territories of Shem, and enter into a state of church fellowship with God.

At last, Noah died, aged 950 years, a little before the birth of Abraham. Whether Noah consented to the building of Babel, or whether, before his death, he assigned to his three sons their different shares of the then known world, we do not know; nor, after perusal of the arguments on both sides, dare we say. But after the building of Babel, he might have removed east into China, and been their Fohi (founder) of that kingdom, though we cannot apprehend the arguments of Samuel Shuckford and others in favour of this journey to be really conclusive. It is said that Noah is the Saturn, or old god, of the heathen, and that Ham is their Jupiter, god of heaven, and Japheth their Neptune, or god of the sea, and Shem, Pluto, or god of hell. Perhaps their Uranus, or Cœlus, their Ogyges, Deucalion, Janus, Proteus, Prometheus, etc., are none other than Noah dressed up in fable.

Did not this patriarch prefigure our Jesus? His name is a bed of rest, and source of consolation. Amid a crooked and perverse generation,

he was singularly upright and holy, and preached righteousness in the great congregation. (Ps. 22:25, 35:18, 40:9) Through him, how the patience of God is displayed towards men! By him, the ark of the Church is gradually reared, and in it, and chiefly in him, are his chosen few, Jews and Gentiles, saved from eternal ruin. His sweet-smelling sacrifice removes the curse and vengeance of God. With him and his seed is the New Covenant established, and on them is the true heirship of all things bestowed. As by him, the Church, the vineyard of the Lord of hosts, is planted and cultivated, and the future state of his professed seed is declared in his sacred Testaments. Those who despise him, and turn his grace into an excuse for sinning, or the infirmities of the saints into ridicule, he condemns to endless slavery and woe. Those who love his Person, and bear with the infirmities of his saints, he blesses with high advancement, and delightful fellowship with God.

(2) One of the five daughters of Zelophehad who had no sons. See Num. 26:33, 27:1, 36:11; Joshua 17:3.

O

OBADIAH

(1) One of the minor prophets whose prophecy consists of one single chapter, where he severely reproves the Edomites for their rejoicing over, and helping forward, the destruction of the Jews. He foretells their own speedy and utter ruin, and the deliverance of the Hebrews from all the places where they were, or will be, scattered. When he lived is not agreed. John Lightfoot thinks his prophecy refers to the behaviour of the Edomites at the sacking of Jerusalem by Shishak, or by the Arabians in the reign of Jehoram, or by the Syrians or Israelites in the time of Joash or Amaziah. He is generally thought to have been contemporary with Hosea, Amos, and Joel. But when we compare his predictions with those of Psalm 137, Jeremiah chapter 49, and Ezekiel chapter 25, and find how similar they are, we cannot forbear thinking, with the great James Ussher, that he prophesied within a year or two after the destruction of Jerusalem by the Chaldeans.

(2) A godly man, who was one of the governors in the family of wicked Ahab. When Jezebel sought out the Lord's prophets to have them all murdered, Obadiah hid 100 of them in two caves, and, despite

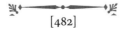

of the then famishing dearth, he fed them with bread and water. With some difficulty, Elijah persuaded him to inform Ahab that be wanted to see him. (Only found in 1 Kings 18:3-7, 16)

OBEDEDOM

The son of Jeduthun (not the sacred musician), and father of Shemaiah, Jozabad, Joah, Sacar, Nathaniel, Ammiel, Uzza, and Peulthai. When Uzza the driver was struck dead for touching the ark of the Lord on the cart, David was so terrified, that he was glad to defer bringing it to Jerusalem. As Obededom's house was nearby, they carried it there. Obededom received it kindly, and gave it a place in his house. His family not only suffered no harm, but were mightily increased in number, health, and otherwise, so that, when some years after, they were appointed porters of the Temple, they amounted to 62 able-bodied men. (1 Chr. 13:9-14, 15:18-25, 26:4, 8, 15) This Obededom is called a *Gittite* because he was a native of Gathrimmon, or stayed a while in Gath of the Philistines. (2 Sam. 6:10-12)

ODED

A prophet who reproved the Israelites, which, under Pekah, had slain 120,000 of the Jews and made 200,000 prisoners, and had done wickedly in outrageously murdering their brothers, when, for their sin, they were delivered into their hand; and that their retaining their captives for slaves would effectively draw forth the wrath of God upon themselves. Moved by his reproofs, the princes were persuaded to send home the prisoners in a kindly and affectionate manner. (2 Chron. 15:1, 8, 28:9) See Ahaz.

OG

King of Bashan. He was one of the giants. His bedstead was of iron, and was nine cubits long and four broad, which, according to our reckoning, is 16 feet and nearly five inches long, and seven feet and more than three inches broad; but Augustine Calmet makes it only 15 feet and four inches long, and six feet and ten inches broad. To relate the rabbinical fables of his living before the Flood, hanging onto the side of the ark, and receiving food from Noah during the time of it, is unworthy of this work. But it is certain that, when he heard of the overthrow of Sihon by Moses, he collected all his subjects able to bear arms to attack the Hebrews at

Edrei. His host was routed, he was killed, and his country seized; but the Ammonites sometime after carried off his iron bedstead and kept it in Rabbah, their capital, as a curiosity. (Num. 21; Deut. 3:1-14; Ps. 135:11)

OMRI

General of the forces to Elah, King of Israel. Informed, as he besieged Gibbethon, that Zimri had murdered his master and his whole family, and usurped the throne at Tirzay, he hastened there, and laid siege to the place. When Zimri found himself unable to defend the city against Omri, he, in the seventh day of his reign, burnt the palace down on himself and his family. For about four years there ensued a civil war between Omri and Tibni, the son of Ginath. At last, Tibni being dead, Omri obtained the throne, and reigned about eight years alone, and twelve in all. Having purchased a hill from one Shemer, he built a fine city on it, called it Samaria, and made it the capital of his kingdom. He was more wicked than Jeroboam, or any of his predecessors. He enacted a number of idolatrous laws, which were unfortunately too well observed many ages afterwards. He died at Samaria, BC 918, and was succeeded by Ahab. (1 Kings 16:16-30; Micah 6:16)

ONAN

A wicked, obstinate, reckless man. See Gen. 38:4, 8-9, 46:12; Num. 26:19; 1 Chronicles 2:3

ONESIMUS. See Philemon

A runaway slave. See Colossians 4:9, 18; Philemon verses 10, 25.

ONESIPHORUS

A native of Asia, perhaps of Ephesus. There, he was extremely kind to the Apostle Paul. Coming to Rome when Paul was in prison, he sought him out, and, to the utmost of his power, comforted and assisted him. Paul begged that the Lord would graciously reward him and his family at the last day. (2 Tim. 1:16-18, 4:19)

OPHIR

The son of Joktan. Whether he gave name to the country famous for gold, or where that country was, we can hardly determine. It is certain that its gold was renowned in the time of Job (Job 22:24, 28:16), and that,

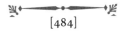

from the time of David to the time of Jehoshaphat, the Hebrews traded in it, and that Uzziah revived this trade when he made himself master of Elath, a notable port on the Red Sea. In Solomon's time, the Hebrew fleet took up to three years in their voyage to Ophir, and brought home gold, apes, peacocks, spices, ivory, ebony, and almug (sandalwood) trees. (1 Kings 9:28, 10:11, 22:48; 2 Chron. 8:18, 9:10, 26:18)

Some have located it at Urphe, an island in the Red Sea; others correctly reckoning this too near, have placed it at Sophala, or in Zanzibar, on the southeast of Africa. Others have put it somewhere near Guinea, on the west of Africa, and some at Carthage, on the north of Africa. Others have still more fancifully removed it to Peru, or some other place in America. Adrian Reland and Augustine Calmet place it in Armenia, where Ptolemy mentions Oupara or Sophara; but to what purpose the Jews should carry on a trade with Armenia by the roundabout way of the Red Sea, we cannot imagine. Nor can we believe that ships fit for coursing around Arabia could have sailed up the Tigris or Euphrates. Some have Ophir to have been somewhere in East India, either on the west of it, near Goa, or at the southeast part of it, or at Malabar, etc. Samuel Bochart, with great industry, labours to fix it at Taprobane, or Ceylon, an East Indian isle. Perhaps there was an Ophir in the south or east of Arabia Felix, whose fine gold was known to Job and David; and another more distant place in the East Indies, in Malacca, or Ceylon, and where Solomon's mariners pursued their trade, and called it Ophir because they found gold in it as good as that in Arabia. Or if there was no other than that in Arabia, the East Indians must have exported there their apes, etc.

ORNAN. See Araunah

A Jebusite living in Jerusalem. See 1 Chronicles 21:15, 18, 20-25, 28; 2 Chronicles 3:1.

OTHNIEL

The son of Kenaz of the tribe of Judah, and the first Judge of Israel. By taking Debir from the Canaanitish giants, he purchased Achsah as his wife, the daughter of Caleb his uncle. (Josh. 15:16-19) When Chushanrishathaim had oppressed Israel eight years, God stirred up Othniel to raise an army against him. With these, he routed the Mesopotamian troops, and delivered Israel; after which, the

Hebrews enjoyed rest for 40 years, or till the 40th year of their settlement. (Judg. 3:8-11)

P

PASHUR. See Jeremiah
The man that imprisoned Jeremiah. See 1 Chronicles 9:12; Ezra 2:38, 10:22; Nehemiah 7:41, 10:3, 11:12; Jeremiah 20:1-3, 6, 21:1, 38:1.

PATRIARCH
One of the principal fathers of mankind, particularly of the Jews; so Abraham, Jacob, his sons, and David, are so called. (Acts 2:29, 7:8-9; Heb. 7:4)

PAUL THE APOSTLE
Of the tribe of Benjamin, whose parents were both Hebrews. He was born in Tarsus in Cilicia, and so was, by birth, a free citizen of Rome.

Saul of Tarsus
He was at first called Saul, and never *Paul* till the conversion of Sergius Paulus. Perhaps Saul was his Hebrew name, and Paul the Roman one he used among the Gentiles, or, perhaps Sergius honoured him with his surname. His parents sent him early to Jerusalem to study the Jewish Law under the direction of Gamaliel, the most famous doctor of that age. He made great progress in his studies, and lived a blameless life. He was of the sect of the Pharisees, and was, beyond many, a strict observer of the Law of Moses. He thought it his duty, in every way he could devise, to wipe out the name of Jesus, and oppose the religion of his followers, and was zealous even to madness against them. When Stephen was murdered by the mob, he gave his hearty consent, and took care of the clothes of those who stoned him to death. He was most active in the persecution that followed. He entered the houses of the Christians, and haled them off to prison, both men and women. He entered the synagogues wherever the Christians were at any time, and caused them to be beaten with rods, compelling them to blaspheme our Saviour as the condition of their release. Not satisfied with the mischief he could do them in Jerusalem he obtained credentials

(letters) from Caiaphas, the High Priest, and the elders of the Jews, to the principal leaders at Damascus, with power to bring to Jerusalem those believing Jews that had fled there, that they might be punished. He went off breathing and threatening nothing less than cruelty and death against them.

The road to Damascus

When he and his attendants had almost finished their journey to Damascus, they were all of a sudden surrounded by a surprising light from heaven. Terrified almost out of their wits, they threw themselves on the ground. Saul alone heard our Saviour's voice, which, in a majestic manner, said to him, *Saul, Saul, why persecutest thou me?* Saul, trembling, asked him, *Who art thou, Lord?* He replied, that he was Jesus, whom he had persecuted, and added that it was very dangerous to strive against his power. In utmost consternation, Saul asked him what he would have him do? Jesus bid him rise and stand on his feet, for he had chosen him to be a notable minister and Apostle to preach his doctrines among the Gentiles for their conversion and salvation. He told him to go to Damascus, and there he would be further informed of his will. As Saul was struck blind, his companions had to lead him along the way. He had formerly accounted himself one of the best of men, and a certain heir of eternal life; now the Law of God applied to his conscience convinced him that he was a distinguished transgressor, dead in trespasses and sins, and condemned by God to endless ruin. (Rom. 7:7-9)

After he had lodged three days in the house of one Judas, without either sight or food, Ananias, a Christian preacher, was directed by God to go and enquire for him, and, by the laying on of hands, recover his sight. Saul had no sooner received his sight, when he made a solemn profession of his faith, was baptised, and afterwards was filled with the Holy Spirit. (Acts 8:1, 9:1-19, 22:1-16, 26:9-18; Rom. 7:8-13; Gal 1:13-16; Phil. 3:5-8)

After eating, and recovering his strength, regardless of whatever poverty, reproach, or persecution might await him, he began to preach the gospel in Damascus, and many were converted. Those Jews that were not, were shocked, and did not know what to think or say. To stifle the account of his conversion, and stop his usefulness, they plotted to murder him. Obtaining the governor's leave to do so, they watched the gates night and day to prevent his escape. Informed of this, his friends let him down in a basket from a window of a house built on the wall of the city. After he had preached some time in Arabia, south of Damascus, he returned to that city.

Jerusalem

In the third year of his conversion, he went up to Jerusalem to see Peter, who had begun the conversion of the Gentiles. It was not till Barnabas related the circumstances and consequences of his conversion that the disciples at Jerusalem admitted him to their society. He saw none of the Apostles at that time except Peter and James the Less; the rest, it seems, were in the country preaching the gospel. Nor did he receive any instruction from them. At Jerusalem, he preached the Christian doctrine with such evidence and zeal that the Jews could not resist, but resolved to kill him. As he was praying in the Temple, he fell into a trance when he was caught up into the third heaven, and heard things improper to be mentioned on earth. The Lord warned him to leave Jerusalem as the Jews had laid snares for his life, and go and preach among the Gentiles. Accompanied by some Christian brothers, he went down to Caesarea, and there shipped off for Tarsus. (Acts 9:19-31, 22:17-21; 2 Cor. 11:31-33, ch. 12; Gal 1:15-21)

Antioch in Syria

After he had preached around Cilicia for nearly five years, Barnabas brought him south to Antioch in Syria, where the converts to Christianity were greatly increased. After he had preached here about a whole year, he and Barnabas carried up the collection for the poor saints to Jerusalem. They had not long returned to Antioch when Simeon called Niger, Lucius, Manaen, and other preachers, directed by the Holy Spirit, sent them off to preach the gospel in other places, recommending them to the Lord by solemn fasting and prayer.

Cyprus

They went to Cyprus, and there preached everywhere in the Jewish synagogues. Sergius Paulus, the Roman governor of the island, and many others, were converted to Christ; and Barjesus the magician, who withstood them, was struck blind. From Cyprus they came to Perga in

Pamphylia, where John Mark, hearing of their intended progress to the north, left them, and returned to Antioch in Syria.

Pisidia

Paul and Barnabas then went into Pisidia. Here, on the Sabbath, as they were in a Jewish synagogue, the ruler desired them to give a word of exhortation after the reading of the Law. In a long oration, Paul rehearsed the marvellous providences of God toward the Hebrew nation, and proved that Jesus was the true Messiah, whom the prophets and John the Baptist had foretold, and called upon them to believe on his name. He was heard with rapt attention, and entreated to discourse next Sabbath on the same subject. When the day came, almost all the people of the city assembled to hear him. Offended at this great company of Gentiles, many of the Jews outrageously contradicted and blasphemed what was spoken. Paul and Barnabas told them that it was necessary, in respect of the purposes of God, that the gospel should be first preached to them, but since they had rejected it, they would now preach it to the Gentiles. The Gentiles were extremely glad to hear this, and many - those who had been elected to everlasting life - believed. But as the Jews stirred up some leading devotees of the heathen party, and raised a persecution against them, Paul and Barnabas were driven out, and shook the dust off their feet as a testimony against them. (Acts 13)

Iconium, Lystra, and Derbe

They went on to Iconium, and preached in the synagogues. Many miracles were performed, and many were turned to the Lord; but the Jews stirred up the heathen against them. Being in danger of stoning, they retired to Lystra and Derbe, cities of Lycaonia. At Lystra, having healed a man with a word who had been lame from birth, the people took them for gods in the likeness of men: Barnabas for Jupiter and Paul for Mercury. The priest of Jupiter brought oxen adorned with garlands as a sacrifice to them. Paul and Barnabas thrust themselves among the mob and told them that they were just men like themselves, and begged them to turn from these vanities and serve the only true God. With no small difficulty, they got the sacrifice stopped. Soon after, some Jews of Antioch in Pisidia, and of Iconium, came there, and stirred up the people against the Apostles. Paul was stoned, and dragged out of the city apparently dead; but as the Christians gathered about him, and no doubt prayed over him, be recovered; and, having lodged that night in the city, he set off next morning for Derbe. After preaching there for some time, they returned to Iconium and Antioch in Pisidia. In all these places, they, with prayer and fasting and the laying on of hands, ordained those presbyters (or elders) that had been chosen to that office by the church. After preaching some time in Perga and Attalia, cities of Pamphylia, they returned to Antioch in Syria, where they told what God had done by their means.

The Council of Jerusalem

After they had continued here a considerable time, the churches of Syria and Cilicia were terribly pestered with false teachers, who, pretending a commission from the Apostles and elders at Jerusalem, taught that circumcision and the observance of the ceremonial law were necessary to salvation. After much disputing, it was resolved to appeal this matter to a general decision of the Apostles and elders at Jerusalem. Paul and Barnabas were sent as commissioners from Antioch. After the Apostles and elders had met together with the deputies from Syria and Cilicia, Paul and Barnabas reviewed to them, and to the invited Christians present, what things the Lord had done by their means. The cause was then reasoned and judged. It was determined that the Gentile converts were under no moral obligation to observe the ceremonial Law; but, to avoid offending the Jewish Christians, they were required to abstain from blood, and from things strangled, and meat offered to idols, as well as from fornication. Paul, Barnabas, Barsabas, and Silas, were sent back to Antioch and the churches nearby with the letter and deed from the Council. The churches were greatly pleased with the decree, as, at once it secured for the Gentiles their liberty, and bore with the weakness of the Jewish converts. When Paul was at Jerusalem, he both publicly and privately declared what doctrines he had taught. Neither Peter, nor James, nor John, nor any other Apostle, found the least fault with this, but cordially acknowledged him as the Apostle to the Gentiles, and desired him to make collections for the poor, as he himself was inclined to do. (Acts 14-15; Gal 2:1-10)

Missionary journey to Asia Minor

When Paul and Barnabas had continued some time at Antioch of Syria, Peter came there. At first, he cheerfully ate with the believing

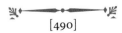

Gentiles, but when some Jewish converts soon followed him, he gave up eating with the Gentiles, and Barnabas was even tempted by him into following the same course. Paul sharply rebuked Peter for this deceit as a thing quite contrary to Christian liberty, and contrary to the late decision of their Council at Jerusalem. Paul afterwards proposed to Barnabas that they should visit the churches they had planted. Barnabas readily agreed; but, as he insisted on having Mark his cousin with them, and Paul as warmly insisted to the contrary, they parted, and Barnabas and Mark went to Cyprus, while Paul and Silas took their route northward through Syria and Cilicia.

They came again to Derbe and Lystra. Here, Paul found Timothy, and, intending to take him as his companion, he caused him to be circumcised in order to render him the more acceptable to the Jews. They travelled through Lycaonia, Phrygia, and Galatia; but the Holy Spirit forbade them to preach in Proconsular Asia. They went to Mysia, and came to Troas. Here, an angel in the clothing of a man of Macedonia appeared in a vision to Paul, and asked him to come and help their country by preaching the gospel to them.

Missionary work in Europe

They took ship at Troas, sailed to the isle of Samothracia, and, from there, to Neapolis. Soon after, they travelled on to Philippi. Here, they resorted to the riverside, where there was a place of Jewish devotion. Lydia, and her family and many others were turned to the Lord. As they went from their lodging in the house of Lydia, a maid, possessed with a spirit of divination, followed them several days, crying out that they were the *servants of the Most High God*, who showed to men the way of salvation. Detesting an outburst that tended to render them suspect as diviners, Paul, in the name of Jesus, ordered the evil spirit to leave her. Enraged at this, her masters, who had made a lot of money by her soothsaying, carried Paul and Silas before the magistrates as introducers of a new religion. They were whipped with rods, and committed to prison. About midnight, Paul and Silas were singing praises to God, when an earthquake shook the prison. All the doors burst open, and the chains of the prisoners fell off. Awakened by the noise, the jailor, seeing the doors open, supposed the prisoners had fled, and was just about to kill himself, to prevent what he knew would be worse, when Paul, with a shout, begged him to do himself no harm as all the prisoners were in their places. Having got a light, he sprang in trembling, and asked Paul and Silas concerning the way of salvation to his soul. Paul, having informed him of the Christian principles, and that the sole way of salvation was by believing in Jesus as the only Saviour, he and his whole family were baptised. He brought water, and washed the wounds of Paul and Silas, and gave them some food. In the morning, the magistrates, by their sergeants or messengers, ordered him to give Paul and Silas their liberty. Paul returned an answer that, since the magistrates had beaten and imprisoned Roman citizens uncondemned, it was proper they should come and dismiss them themselves. On hearing of their being citizens of Rome, the magistrates were not a little frightened, and came and begged their pardon, bringing them out from the prison, and asking them to leave the place, which they did, after comforting the disciples in the house of Lydia. (Acts 16)

Having passed southward through Amphipolis and Apollonia, cities of Macedonia, they came to the capital, Thessalonica. Here, Paul preached for three Sabbaths in a Jewish synagogue, and many believed; but the Jews, raising a mob, attacked the house of Jason where Paul was staying. But as neither Paul nor his brothers were found there, they dragged Jason before the magistrates, and accused him of harbouring rebels against the Emperor, and preachers of the King Jesus. After Jason had paid bail for his loyalty, he was dismissed. That very night, the Christians conducted Paul and Silas out of the place. Despite the wealth of Thessalonica, Paul was here in considerable straits for his daily bread.

He and Silas next went to Berea, where both Jews and Gentiles heard the gospel with great readiness of mind, and carefully compared what they heard with the writings of the prophets; and not a few of note believed. It was not long when the malicious Jews of Thessalonica came and raised a mob against them. Paul was obliged to withdraw, but Silas and Timothy remained behind to instruct the new converts.

Paul's guides brought him to Athens, from where he sent back word to his two companions to follow him. The excessive idolatry and vanity of this place, so famous for wisdom, was extremely grievous to Paul. He preached in the Jewish synagogues; and, on various occasions, he disputed with the Epicurean and Stoic philosophers. After no small derision, they accused him before the Court of Areopagus as an introducer of a new religion. Many empty-minded people attended his trial. In his defence, Paul observed that, among their too numerous superstitions, he had seen an altar to an unknown God, and that this unknown God, whom they ignorantly worshipped, was the Jesus whom he preached to them. He hinted how absurd it was for men that believed themselves the offspring (or children) of God, to imagine that the Deity resembled silver, gold, or any pictures or statues made by men, and that God had appointed a day for judging the world by Jesus Christ, whom he had raised from the dead. He had scarcely mentioned the resurrection, when some mocked him, and others said they would hear him again on that matter. Dionysius, however, one of the judges, and Damaris, perhaps his lady, and some others, believed. Timothy, having come up to him, and informing him of the suffering state of the Christians of Thessalonica, Paul sent him back to comfort them. (Acts 17; 1 Thess. 2)

Leaving Athens, Paul preached at Corinth with considerable success. That he might show how averse he was to the least insinuation of his seeking wealth, he lodged with Aquila and Priscilla, and worked at their business of tent-making, which, it seems, be had learned in his youth. Everyday, or at least every Sabbath, he preached in the Jewish synagogues. Numbers were converted, particularly Stephanus and his family, with Crispus and Gaius. He had not been here long, when Silas and Timothy came back, and informed him of the flourishing state of the Christians at Thessalonica. At this news, he wrote them his first Epistle. As some took occasion from it to disturb their minds, as if the Day of Judgement were at hand, he soon after wrote them his second Epistle to correct their mistakes. Assisted by Silas and Timothy, he went on with his work at Corinth. The Jews opposed him with rage and blasphemy. He shook his lap at them, and told them that their blood was on their own heads, and that now he would turn to the Gentiles. He removed his lodging to the house of one Justus, a person of some note; and, being encouraged by a vision, hearing that the Lord would support and give him mighty success in his work, he continued here about 18 months. The Jews prosecuted him before Gallio the deputy as an enemy of the Roman governor; but the deputy was too wise to give them any encouragement. Indeed, Sosthenes the ruler of their synagogue was beaten by the mob before the tribunal. At last, Paul set out for Jerusalem, intending to be there for Pentecost, when there would be crowds assembled. But before he took ship at Cenchrea, a seaport belonging to Corinth, he cut his hair, and, having finished his Nazaritic vow, Aquila and Priscilla accompanied him to Ephesus, from where he sailed to Caesarea, and then went up to Jerusalem. (Acts 18; 1 Cor. 16)

Return to Asia Minor and Europe

Returning northward, he revisited the churches of Syria, Galatia, Phrygia, and other places in Asia, confirming the disciples. Arriving at Ephesus, he found some who had been initiated into the Christian faith by Apollos, and baptised with the baptism of John. These, to the number of 12, he instructed in the truths of the gospel; and, by the laying on of hands, he conferred on them the miraculous influence of the Holy Spirit, the gift of prophecy, and of speaking in tongues. For three months, Paul preached to the Jews in their synagogues; but, finding them obstinate, he separated from them, and taught daily in the school of one Tyrannus, a Gentile, or perhaps a converted Jew who kept a kind of theology school there. Many miracles were performed; and when the linen that had touched his body was applied to the distressed, their illnesses were cured, and the devils dislodged. Many, too, who had used divination and other black arts, believed the gospel, and burnt their magical books. During the three years that Paul preached at Ephesus, he was cast to the wild beasts in the theatre, or had to do with men as outrageous as wild beasts, when Demetrius the silversmith raised the mob against him. Some time before he left Ephesus, he was informed of the sad disorders of the church of Corinth by those of the family of Chloe, and perhaps more fully by Stephanas, Fortunatus, and Achaius, who, it seems, brought him some supplies. He wrote them his first Epistle, and included the greetings of the Christians in Asia. Augustine Calmet thinks it was from here too that he wrote his Epistle to the Galatians. He had sent Timothy to Greece but, it seems he had returned, and was left at Ephesus to settle the affairs of that church. Paul, meanwhile, went off to Greece. His not meeting with Titus at Troas, whom he expected from Corinth, gave him great uneasiness; but, at last, he found him in Macedonia, and was by him informed of the good effect his first Epistle made on the Corinthians. He then wrote his second letter to that church for their comfort, establishment, and further direction, and intimated what dangers he had often been in, from Jews, pretended Christians, robbers, or the sea, and what hunger, thirst, nakedness, cold, fasting, and watching, he had suffered. How five times the Jews had beaten him to the utmost rigour of their law; twice the heathen magistrates had caused him be beaten with rods; three times be had suffered shipwreck, and, it seems, had once for a whole night and day struggled with the waves in the open sea. About this time, it is probable that he wrote his first Epistle to Timothy.

Perhaps he went westward from Macedonia, and preached the gospel in Illyricum. Returning south, he visited the faithful at Corinth, and wrote his Epistle to the Romans. Having received the collection, which those of Macedonia and Achaia had made for the poor Christians of Judea, he took his route to Jerusalem through Macedonia, where, either from Philippi or Nicopolis, he seems to have written his Epistle to Titus. Departing from Macedonia, he landed at Troas five days later. There, Sopater of Berea, Aristarchus and Secundus of Thessalonica, Timothy and Gaius of Derbe, with Tychicus and Trophimus, who were probably of Ephesus, waited till he arrived. After resting a whole week, on the Lord's Day, he dispensed the Lord's Supper to the Christians there, and preached till midnight. One Eutychus, who sat in a window, in a manner shamefully common in our times(!), and without half of his temptation, fell asleep during the sermon; and, falling from the third storey, was taken up as dead. But Paul, by a miracle, restored him to life. He taught the disciples till the break of day, and then set off on his journey. Paul's companions took ship, but he travelled on foot to Assos, and embarked with them at Mytilene. From there, he came to Miletus, and, sending for the elders of the church of Ephesus, warned them of his own suffering at Jerusalem, and of their danger from false teachers. And, having exhorted them to patience and faithfulness, he prayed with them, and, to their great grief, took his last farewell of them on earth. (Acts 19-20; Rom. 15:19-26; 1 Cor. 15:32, 16:8-9, 19; 2 Cor. 7:5-6; 11:23-28)

From Miletus, Paul sailed to Coos, then on to Rhodes, and then to Patera, and from there to Tyre. After stopping there for a week, he and his companions proceeded to Ptolemais, and, from there, to Caesarea. Here, they found Philip the deacon and evangelist. Here, too, Agabus met them, and, binding his hands and feet with Paul's belt, signified that Paul would be bound by the Jews at Jerusalem and delivered up to the Gentiles. Paul's friends tried to dissuade him from going up to Jerusalem, but could not prevail, as he told them his life was not dear to him. He desired only to finish his course with joy, and that he was ready to suffer imprisonment and death for the honour of Jesus.

In Jerusalem, and Paul's arrest

When he came to Jerusalem, the Christians joyfully welcomed him there, and the elders of the church, meeting at the house of James the Apostle, with great pleasure, heard him report on his travels and success. James told him that many of the myriads of believers in Jerusalem believed the report that as he had taught the Jews among the Gentiles to undervalue circumcision and other ceremonies, it would be right, in order to remove the offence that they had conceived, to inform them of the contrary, and to confirm their belief of his due regard for the ceremonies, and it would be fitting that he should join himself to the four men who were to offer their oblations for their finished Nazariteship. Paul, perhaps too easy in this particular matter, went up to the Temple, and signified to the priests that he and these Nazarites would, in seven days, be ready with their offerings. He had scarcely appeared in the court of the Temple with his offering, when some Jews from Asia Minor cried for help to arrest him as someone who had everywhere taught the abolition of the ceremonial law, and had brought Greeks into the temple to pollute it. He was immediately seized, and the gates of the sacred court were closed.

He would had been beaten to death had not Lysias the tribune come with his Roman guard to rescue him. All along to the Castle Antonia, the enraged mob followed him. As he entered the castle, he begged the captain to allow him a word. Lysias asked him if he could speak Greek, and whether he was the Egyptian who had infested the country with 4000 assassins? Paul replied that he was a Jew, born in the famous city of Tarsus. He was then allowed to speak to the mob. Upon his affectionately addressing them in the Hebrew language they listened the more quietly. He rehearsed to them his former rage against the Christians, his manner of conversion, and his mission to preach among the Gentiles. He had scarcely mentioned this last, when the Jews, in the most outrageous manner, cried out, that he ought not to live. To prevent a general uprising, Lysias ordered Paul into the castle, and, groundlessly supposing that he was certainly guilty of some horrible crime, he ordered him to be scourged till he confessed it. As they bound him to the pillar to be scourged, Paul asked the centurion if it was according to law to scourge a citizen of Rome without hearing his defence? The centurion ran to the tribune, and begged him to take care, as Paul was a freeman of Rome. Lysias, finding he had been born such, gave orders to loose him.

Next day, Lysias called a council of the Jewish priests and elders to have Paul carefully tried. He had scarcely begun his speech, affirming that be had always tried to live blamelessly before God and men, when Ananias ordered those who stood next to him to hit him in the mouth. Paul, directing his speech to Ananias, said that God would smite him who hypocritically pretended to judge him according to Law, and yet ordered him to be hit contrary to it. Some present asked him how he dared reprove God's High Priest? Paul replied that he did not know, or at least did not acknowledge, him to be High Priest. Looking around on the assembly, and, observing by their badges, that they consisted of an almost equal number of Pharisees and Sadducees, he cried out that he was a Pharisee, and was called in question concerning the resurrection of the dead. At this, the Pharisees took his side, and began to argue with the Sadducees. Lysias, fearing that he might be torn to pieces between the two parties, ordered him back to the castle. That very night, God encouraged Paul, and assured him that he would live, and bear witness to the truth also at Rome. Next day, more than forty of the Jews bound themselves under a terrible curse that they would neither eat nor drink till they had killed Paul; and that they might have an opportunity, the Jewish priests and rulers agreed to ask Lysias to bring him back to the council to be further examined. Informed of this plot by his sister's son, who perhaps was not a Christian, Paul procured him access to state the matter to Lysias, who, at that, next night sent off Paul to Felix the governor at Caesarea, with an account of his case, accompanied by a strong guard. (Acts 21-23)

Within five days, Ananias the High Priest, and others of the Jewish rulers, went down to Caesarea to carry on a prosecution against Paul. Tertullus their orator, one of the basest of men, after a flattering address to Felix, accused Paul as a notorious disturber of the public peace, and a profaner of the Temple. When Paul had liberty to speak, he refuted the charge, and defied them to prove anything against him, except that he professed his faith in the resurrection of the dead, and worshipped God in a Christian manner, believing everything said by the prophets. Felix put off further trial till Lysias came, and he was given fuller information; and, meanwhile he made Paul's imprisonment fairly easy, giving him complete liberty to receive visits from his friends. Some days later, Felix and Drusilla his wife sent for Paul. He discoursed to them about righteousness, self-control, and judgement, till Felix, who was extremely guilty on these points, fell to trembling, and dismissed him. As Felix expected Paul's friends to ransom him, he often sent for him, and talked with him. Having received nothing for his liberty, to please the Jews at the last, whom he had so often offended with his oppressive methods, Felix left Paul bound. Scarcely had Festus entered into his government, when the Jewish rulers accused Paul, who had now been a prisoner two years, in front of him, and, intending to have him murdered along the way, requested that he would send him up to Jerusalem for trial. Instead, Festus ordered them to come to Caesarea. They came, but could prove no criminal behaviour under Roman law. To gratify them as far as possible, Festus asked Paul if he would go up and be tried at Jerusalem. Convinced of the murderous designs of the Jews, and to forestall them, Paul appealed to Nero the Emperor who, as yet, was behaving with some moderation. After conferring with his council, Festus told Paul that he accepted his appeal, and would send him to Rome. Not long after, King Agrippa and his sister Bernice came to pay Festus a visit. Festus told them about the affair of Paul. Agrippa wanted to hear him. Paul, being required to speak for himself, and in a fine address to Agrippa, he rehearsed his case, his conversion, and his call to the ministry. When Festus, quite ignorant of these matters, said that learning had made him mad, Paul, addressing him most politely, told him that he was not mad, but spoke the words of truth with soberness. When Agrippa said that he had almost persuaded him to be a Christian, Paul, in a most handsome manner, expressed his wish that Agrippa and all present were such as himself, except as to his troubles. Agrippa gave his opinion that Paul might have been set at liberty if he had not appealed to Caesar. (Acts 24-26)

Journey by sea, and the shipwreck off Malta
Paul and other prisoners were shipped off to Rome in a ship of Adramyttium, under the care of Julius, a centurion of the Augustan

band of soldiers. Julius was very kind to Paul, and, at Sidon, allowed him to go ashore and visit his friends. After they had sailed along the coast of Phoenicia, a contrary wind obliged them to sail under the east end of Cyprus. When they came to Myra, a seaport of Lycia, they were transferred to a ship of Alexandria, bound for Rome. As the Jewish Fast of Expiation was past, and the winter begun, the weather began to be stormy; and it was with no small difficulty that they arrived at Fair Havens, on the east of Crete. Paul advised them to winter there, but others insisted they should go to Phenice, on the west of that island, where they would find a larger harbour. For some time, they sailed closely, but safely, along the south side of Crete; but, at last, a terrible storm from the east drove them onto a small island called Clauda. To prevent their being dashed on the rocks, the mariners lowered their sails, and committed themselves to the sea. After three days, they cast out part of their cargo. For fourteen days, they saw neither sun, nor moon, nor stars. Informed by God, Paul assured them that none of their lives would be lost, but only the ship. The mariners, finding by their line that the water was not very deep, judged that they were drawing near to land, and let down their boat so that they might escape in it. Paul, directed by God, desired the centurion to remain with them, as the passengers could not otherwise be preserved. The soldiers cut off the boat, and let her be driven by the sea. After they had fasted almost fourteen days, Paul begged that they would eat some food, as they might assure themselves they would not be lost, but be driven on to some island. Observing land, the mariners attempted to steer the ship into a creek. She struck aground on a neck of land, and was broken to pieces. The soldiers were advised to kill the prisoners that they might not escape; but Julius, out of regard for Paul, prevented it.

All that were in the ship, to the number of 276, some by swimming, and others on planks and broken boards, got safely to land on the isle of Malta. Here, the heathen showed them the utmost kindness. Here, a viper from among a bundle of sticks that they had gathered to warm themselves, fastened on Paul's hand. The barbarians, seeing it, concluded that certainly he was a murderer, and that, although he had escaped the sea, yet divine vengeance would not allow him to live. But when they saw Paul shake the viper off into the fire and receive no harm from it, they changed their mind, and thought him a god. Here,

Paul miraculously healed the father of Publius, the governor, of his bloody discharge, and the other diseased people on the island.

Arrival in Italy, then on to Rome

At the end of three months, they re-embarked, and arrived first at Syracuse, in the southeast of Sicily, then at Rhegium, in the south of Italy. They coasted northwards till they came to Puteoli, where they landed. After Paul had stayed here seven days with his Christian friends, he set out for Rome. The Christians of that city met him at Appii forum, and the Three Taverns: this mightily encouraged him. Whether the Jews did not prosecute their appeal, or whether it was at this time that no one assisted the Apostle to plead his cause, we do not know. It is certain that he was permitted to live two years in his own hired house, with a soldier to keep him, and to preach the gospel to those who were pleased to hear him. He sent for the principal Jews of the place, and related his case to them to prevent their being imposed on by their brothers of Judea. They told him that they had received no particular information concerning him, only that they knew the Christians were everywhere spoken against, and they would be glad to hear an account of their doctrines from himself. From morning to night, he explained to them the things concerning Jesus out of Moses and the prophets. Observing that many of then would not believe, he hinted that, according to Isaiah's prediction, they had heard the gospel, and hardened themselves through its refusal, and therefore it was sent to the Gentiles who were willing to receive it.

The final years in prison

Whether, after these two years of imprisonment at large, he was dismissed, and went to Spain or Macedonia, and afterwards returned to Rome, or whether he was kept a prisoner under close arrest, we do not know. But it is certain that his imprisonment turned out to the glory of Christ and the spread of the gospel. Several of Nero's own family were converted. Many of the Christians in Asia Minor were much alienated from him through the activities of their false teachers, Phygellus, Hermogenes, etc; yet some, out of sheer spite, became more diligent in preaching the gospel. Providence, however, provided him with friends. Onesiphorus sought him out, and ministered to him. Onesimus, a runaway thief and slave from Philemon, was converted, and became very useful to him. The Philippians sent Epaphroditus to comfort him, with some money to supply his needs. About this time, he wrote his Epistle to the Colossians and to Philemon; both of which, it seems, he sent by Onesimus. Soon after, Demas forsook him, and he wrote his Epistle to the Philippians, probably by Epaphroditus, that to the Galatians by Crescens, and that to the Ephesians, by Tychicus. Much about the same time, he wrote his second Epistle to Timothy, where he wanted him to come to Rome. After Timothy had arrived, and had been imprisoned and liberated, he wrote his Epistle to the Hebrews. At last, it is said, his preaching converted one of Nero's darling concubines. Enraged at this loss, Nero caused Paul to be beheaded. (Acts 27-28; Phil. 1:12-19, 4:22; Col. 4:14; 2 Tim. 1:15-18, 4:9, 21; Philem verses 10-14)

The zeal of Paul the Apostle

Before his conversion, he was an outrageous enemy of Christ; but after it, he was one of the most holy and humble of men, and a laborious preacher that ever breathed. Nor is his magnifying of his office and labour, in opposition to the false teachers, any evidence to the contrary, as he often refutes them upon their own pretences, and, at every proper turn, ascribes all he was, and had done in the service of Christ, to the grace of God. (1 Cor. 15:8-10, 2 Cor. 10-12; Gal 1-2)

The character and conduct of the Apostle Paul has been a subject of much controversy. Lord Edward Littleton's tract on Paul's conversion and apostleship is an excellent pamphlet, and will be read as long as any great respect for Scripture remains.

PEKAH

This son of Remaliah was general of Pekaiah, King of Israel's army. Together with Argob and Arieh, and 50 Gileadites, he murdered his master in the second year of his reign, and reigned 20 years in his place. Entering into an alliance with Rezin, King of Syria, they intended to dethrone Ahaz, and the whole family of David, and set up the son of one Tabeel to govern Judea as their tributary. To the no small offence of God, Pekah's army cut off 120,000 of Judah, and took 200,000 prisoners; but they soon returned the latter with great humanity. Instigated by Ahaz, Tiglathpileser, King of Assyria invaded the kingdom of Pekah, and murdered and carried off into captivity

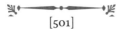

a great number of the Naphtalites, eastern Manassites, Reubenites, and Gadites. At last, Hoshea murdered Pekah, and reigned in his place. (2 Kings 15:25-37; 2 Chron. 28:6-10; Isa. 7:1-7)

PETER, CEPHAS, SIMON

The son of Jonas, and brother of Andrew, was a native of Bethsaida. His original name was *Simon*, but Jesus called him *Cephas* (or *Peter*), that is, a *stone* or *rock*, to mark his need of steadiness in his faith and practice. He married a woman of Capernaum, and had his mother-in-law cured of a fever by our Saviour. (Mark 1:29)

The fisherman is called by Christ

Invited by Andrew his brother, he went and saw Jesus, and stayed with him for a night. About a year later, Jesus found them washing their nets as they left off fishing on the Sea of Galilee. He desired the use of their boat to sit in and teach the people. After he had done so, to reward their kindness, and reveal his own power, he ordered them to cast their net into the sea for a draught. They had fished the whole night before and caught nothing, but, being obedient to our Saviour, they now caught so many fish that they loaded their own boat, and also that of James and John. Astonished at the draught, Peter begged our Saviour to depart, as he was too holy and great to stay in the company of one so sinful. Instead of fulfilling his stupid request, Jesus called Peter and Andrew, and James and John, to be his disciples. (Matt. 4; Luke 5:1-11; John 1:40-42) Peter and Andrew were the first two sent out of the Apostles, being, as is likely, the oldest. (Matt. 10:2; Luke 6:14)

Peter walking on the water

Peter, being extremely forward in his feelings, when be saw our Saviour coming walking on the sea, he requested him to meet him on the water. He had just entered the water, when, doubting his safe preservation, he cried out for Jesus to save him. Jesus preserved him, and rebuked him for the weakness of his faith. (Matt. 14:28-31) When afterwards Jesus asked his disciples if they would leave him, as many others had just done, Peter replied that they could go safely nowhere else, as he alone had the words of, and the power to give, eternal life. (John 6:66-68)

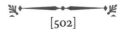

The great confession, and the Transfiguration

When, at Caesarea Philippi, Jesus asked his disciples who they believed him to be, Peter replied that they were firmly persuaded he was *Christ, the Son of the living God.* Jesus blessed him, and hinted that such knowledge and faith had been given him by the Spirit of God, and assured him that, as certainly as he was *Peter* (the rock), he would so build his church by his means, upon that very Person and truth he had confessed, and that all the gates or powers of hell would not overthrow it. He added that, to him and his fellow Apostles, and their successors in their ministry, he would give the power of founding, instructing, or governing his Church, and that whatever condemnation or absolution they should give, according to his Word, either in doctrine or discipline, it would be ratified in heaven. When Jesus, almost immediately after, foretold his sufferings, Peter rebuked him, and bid him spare himself. Jesus reproved him sharply, and told him that Satan had tempted him to say so, and that his speech savoured not of God, but of worldly indulgence. It was scarcely eight days later that Peter was admitted to witness our Saviour's transfiguration. At the sight of Moses and Elijah, he foolishly asked leave to erect three tabernacles, one for his Master, and one for each of the prophets. (Matt. 16:13-23, 17:1-4)

Paying tribute, forgiveness, rewards and persecutions

When Peter and his Master, some time later, entered Capernaum, where, it seems, they were enrolled as residents, the collectors of the Roman tribute asked him if his Master paid tribute. Jesus knowing it, ordered Peter to cast a line into the sea and open the mouth of the fish that came up first, and he would find a shekel of silver to give as tribute for the two of them. (Matt. 17:24-27) When Jesus afterwards discoursed on forgiveness of injuries, Peter asked him if it was proper to forgive any more than seven times? Jesus told him he must forgive as often as was necessary, though it amounted to seventy times seven, or 490 times in all. (Matt. 23:21-22) When our Saviour discoursed on riches hindering men from entering into the kingdom of God, Peter asked him what reward he and his fellow disciples would have, they who had left their boats, nets, and all they had in the world to follow him? Jesus replied that those who, in the commencement of his gospel Church, truly followed him from an inward principle of grace would have distinguished honour in the Church, and also at the Last Day;

and that everyone who truly followed him in the midst of persecutions would enjoy fellowship with him a hundred times better than all they could have in this world. (Matt. 19:27-30) On the Tuesday before our Saviour's passion, Peter pointed out to him how the fig tree he had cursed was so quickly withered away, and was advised to use the event as an example of faith and fervent prayer. (Matt. 21:17-22; Mark 11:11-21)

The washing of the disciples' feet

Either on that, or the Thursday evening, Peter refused to allow Jesus to wash his feet; but, being told that unless he washed him, he would have no part in him, begged to have not only his feet, but also his hands and his head, washed. Jesus told him that those who had once been washed in his blood needed no repeated justification, but only to have their daily blots of infirmity cleansed. (John 13:1-17) At the one or other of these times, Peter urged John to beg Jesus to point out which of them was to be the traitor. (John 13:24-26) He, together with Andrew, James, and John, asked Jesus when the Temple would be destroyed, and when he would return to judge the world. (Matt. 24:1-3)

The Lord's Supper

On Thursday evening, he and John, by their Master's order, found an upper room, and there prepared everything necessary for the Passover Feast. (Luke 22:8-12) When, after the sacred supper, Jesus warned his Apostles of their being offended because of him that night, Peter, with his usual rashness, promised that, although everyone should forsake his Master, he never would, but would follow him, and would rather die with him than in the least deny him. Jesus assured him that before the cock crowed twice, he would deny him thrice (three times), and that Satan desired to have permission to sift and tempt him and his fellow-disciples; but he had prayed for him, that his faith might not quite fail; and he admonished him to comfort and encourage his brothers as soon as he had recovered. (Matt. 26:31-35; Luke 22:31-34; John 13:36-38)

Peter and his sword, and his denials

When Peter, James, and John, were taken along with our Saviour into the garden to witness his bloody agony, they quickly fell asleep.

Jesus, after three different prayers, awoke them. He asked them if they could not watch with him one hour, and kindly hinted that their spirit was willing, but their flesh was weak. When he woke them as Judas approached, he ironically bid them sleep on. When Judas came with his band, Peter, being one of the two disciples that had swords, drew his and cut off the ear of Malchus, the High Priest's servant. Jesus rebuked him, and ordered him to put up his sword, otherwise it might lead to his death. Peter, at a distance, followed our Saviour to the palace of Caiaphas, and, by means of another disciple, he got access into the hall, and waited among the high priest's servants to see what was happening. A maid looked at him, and said she had certainly seen him with Jesus of Nazareth. He denied that he so much as knew him. Peter went out to the porch, and the cock crew for the first time. Soon after, another maid said to those who stood around that certainly he was one of Jesus' followers. He denied it with an oath. About an hour later, one of the company affirmed he was a disciple of Jesus, and others insisted that he certainly was, and that his very speech marked him out as a Galilean. Finally, a relation of Malchus said, "Did not I see you in the garden with him?" To give them what he thought was full evidence that he was no follower of Jesus, he began to curse and to swear that he did not so much as know such a man. At that very instant, the cock crew for the second time, and Jesus gave Peter a look. He remembered his Master's prediction of his treachery, and went out and wept bitterly; and, it is probable he continued his mourning till he heard our Saviour had risen from the dead. (Matt. 26:40-47, 69-75; John 18:10-11, 15-27)

The resurrection appearances

On the morning of the resurrection day, Peter and John, hearing that their Master's corpse had been removed from the grave, ran to see if it was so. Peter went down into the sepulchre and saw the grave clothes laid in good order, but the body was gone. Filled with perplexity, they returned to the others. When Jesus appeared to the women, he ordered them in a particular manner to inform miserable Peter that he had risen from the dead. It was not long after, that Peter had the pleasure of seeing his Master once and again at Jerusalem, along with the other Apostles. When, some time later, Peter, and some other Apostles, were fishing in the Sea of Tiberias, Jesus appeared on the shore. No sooner had Peter heard that it was their Lord than, from strong affection, he flung himself into the sea and swam to the shore. After they had dined, Jesus thrice (3 times) asked him if he loved him above every other thing? Peter did so, and at the third time with some vehemence and grief, he appealed to him that he knew he did. Jesus, just as often, charged him to feed his people, sheep, and lambs. Much about the same time, Jesus told him that he must endure bonds and imprisonment for his sake in his old age. He asked Jesus what then would become of John the beloved disciple? Jesus directed him to follow his own example, and hold fast to his cause, and leave the fate of John to the government of providence. (Mark 16:6-7; John 20:1-6, ch. 21)

The Day of Pentecost

Very soon after our Saviour's ascension, Peter proposed to the Christians at Jerusalem to elect someone else to fill the place of Judas; and Matthias was chosen. On the tenth day, when Hebrews from every corner were gathered to celebrate the Feast of Pentecost, Peter and his fellow-Apostles, endowed with the Holy Spirit, spoke in a diversity of languages to the assembly. The Jews from Parthia, Media, Persia, Mesopotamia, Judea, Cappadocia, Pontus, Proconsular Asia, Phrygia, Pamphylia, Egypt, Libya, Rome, Crete, and Arabia, heard them in the respective language of their countries. The people were astonished, but some profane scoffers said they were drunk. Peter, standing up with the Eleven, showed that not wine, but the Holy Spirit, who, according to the ancient promises, had descended on them, enabled them so to speak with tongues, and that it was a demonstration that Jesus had risen from the dead, and had gone to his Father's right hand, constituted Sovereign and sole Saviour of men. Multitudes were deeply convicted of sin, and begged the Apostles to tell them how to be saved. Peter, as the mouthpiece of the rest, directed them to believe the New Covenant promises endorsed to them and their seed, and to repent and be baptised for the forgiveness of their sins through Jesus' blood. That very day, 3000 believed, and were added to the Christian Church. (Acts 1-2)

The healing of the blind beggar

Some days later, when, Peter and John went up to the Temple about nine o'clock in the morning (which was the hour of prayer), a man who had been a cripple from birth was sitting at the Beautiful Gate of the

Temple asking alms of them. Peter told him that he had neither silver nor gold to give him; but, in the name of Jesus, he commanded him to rise and walk. The man was straightaway cured, and went along with them through the court of the Temple, leaping and praising God. He held onto Peter and John, and told the assembled multitude how they had healed him. Peter said to the admiring crowd that they had not made this man walk by their own power, but by the influence of Jesus Christ, whom they had lately murdered, and who had risen from the dead and ascended to glory. He showed them that Jesus was the promised Messiah, whom whoever rejected should certainly perish; and that God, having raised him from the dead, had sent him to them first with the offer of the gospel and the power of his Spirit to bless them in turning them from their iniquities. This sermon was blessed for the conversion of 5000.

Before the Council

About evening, the priests and Sadducees arrested Peter and John and put them in prison. Next day, they were brought before the Council, and interrogated about how they had cured the lame man. They replied that it was done by the authority and power of Christ, whom the council had lately crucified; but God had raised him from the dead. As the Council knew that Peter and John were not educated men, they were surprised at their answers. They commanded them to preach no more about Jesus, or as authorised by him. Peter and John bade them think whether it was best to disobey God, or the Council. After further threatening them, they let them go. They went to their brother Apostles and believers, and related what had happened. They all praised God, and solemnly prayed for further strength for his work. The house shook, and the Holy Spirit fell upon them in a further degree. (Acts 3-4)

Ananias and Sapphira

As the believers expected the approaching ruin of their country according to their Master's prediction, or the loss of their estates by persecution, many of them sold them, and gave the Apostles the money to be paid out for pious uses. Ananias and Sapphira his wife sold their estate, but deceitfully kept back part of the price for themselves. Peter detected the fraud. Both of them were divinely cut off by sudden

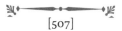

death. This tended to increase the awe and character of the Apostles. Many believed the gospel, and vast numbers of diseased people were miraculously healed. Peter and the other Apostles were imprisoned; but an angel released them, and they returned directly to preach in the courts of the Temple. Their escape surprised the Council; but they re-arrested them, and reminded them of their former charge. Peter replied that it was right for them to obey God rather than men, and told them that God had highly exalted Jesus, whom they had murdered, to be a Prince and Saviour, and had testified this by the gifts and miracles of the Holy Spirit so notorious among his followers. Provoked at this, the Council were for murdering them directly had not Gamaliel prevented them with his more sober speech. (Acts 5)

Peter and the Samaritans

After the deacons were chosen, and Stephen, one of them, murdered, and a persecution had scattered the Christian preachers, and the Samaritans had received the gospel by Philip the deacon, Peter and John went there to confer the Holy Spirit by the laying on of hands. Simon the sorcerer, who had just been baptised, offered them a sum of money for a share in their miraculous powers. Peter bid him and his money perish together, as he knew that the gifts of God could not be purchased in that way, and told him that he had no call to the ministerial work, but appeared to be in the *gall of bitterness and the bond of iniquity*, under the reigning power of his corrupt lusts. He directed him to pray to God, if perhaps the wickedness of his heart might be forgiven him. After preaching through most of Samaria, Peter and John returned to Jerusalem.

Miracles, and Cornelius the Centurion

The conversion of Paul having stopped, or at least abated, the Jewish persecution, Peter went to visit the believers in Judea, Samaria, and Galilee. At Lydda, he recovered Eneas, who had been ill of a palsy for eight years. At Joppa, he restored Tabitha to life. (Acts 8:1-25, 9:32-43) While he lodged at Joppa with one Simon a tanner, Cornelius, a Gentile Centurion, directed by God, sent messengers for him to instruct him and his friends in the way of the Lord. Meanwhile, God prepared Peter by a vision. About midday, as he was by himself on the top of the house (the roof being flat), and was very hungry, he fell into a trance in which

he saw, as it were, a great sheet full of animals, both clean and unclean, let down from heaven, and heard a voice calling him to rise, kill, and eat. He replied that he had never eaten of any unclean animals. The voice replied that it was improper to think something unclean that God had cleansed. All this was thrice (3 times) repeated, and then the sheet was apparently carried up into heaven.

He had scarcely woken from his trance, when Cornelius' messengers came to invite him to preach to these Gentiles. After hearing what had moved their master to call him, and considering the importance of his vision, he went along with them, and instructed and baptised Cornelius and his friends. The Jewish converts at Jerusalem were at first offended with his going to the Gentiles, but when they heard how Cornelius was divinely directed to call him, how he was, by his vision, directed to undervalue none whom God had regarded, and how the miraculous influences of the Holy Spirit fell on Cornelius and his friends as he preached to them, they were satisfied, and blessed God for granting to the Gentiles repentance unto life. (Acts 10, 11:1-18)

Peter set free from prison
While he continued at Jerusalem, Paul lodged with him for two weeks. (Gal 1:18) To gratify the Jews, Herod Agrippa imprisoned Peter, intending to kill him, as he had done James, the brother of John. The very night before his intended execution, and while his Christian friends were meeting in the house of Mary to pray for his deliverance, an angel came to him in the prison as he slept between two soldiers, awoke him, took off his chains, opened the prison, and conducted him to the street. He went directly to the house of Mary and knocked at the door. Rhoda, a damsel (maid), came to open the door, and on hearing his voice, ran back in a transport of joy and told the Christians that it was Peter. They did not believe her; but, imagining every good man had his guardian angel, they said it would he Peter's angel that had knocked. Peter, continuing to knock, was at last admitted, and, to their great joy, he informed them of what had happened to him.

Later travels
Whether after this he went to Pontus, Galatia, Cappadocia, Proconsular Asia, and Bithynia to the scattered Jews to which he writes in his Epistles, we do not know. It is certain that, about eight years later,

he was at Jerusalem at the Council, and there related how God, by him, had first granted the gospel to the Gentiles, and suggested that, since God had made no difference between Jews and Gentiles in his saving or extraordinary gifts, they ought to impose on them no yoke of ceremonial rites. About this time, he and James and John gave Paul the right hand of fellowship, and agreed that he should preach mainly to the Gentiles.

When Peter was travelling north, perhaps to the places mentioned above, he came to Antioch. At first, he joined in utmost fellowship with the Gentile converts; but when some sticklers for Judaism came down from Jerusalem, he drew away, and nearly induced Barnabas to follow the same course. Knowing that this encouraged the imposition of ceremonies on the new converts, Paul sharply rebuked Peter for his deceit, practically contradicting the very speech he had uttered in the Council. Peter, it seems, received this rebuke with a humble concern.

Final years and death

In his old age, it seems, Peter travelled from the south coast of the Black Sea into Mesopotamia and Chaldea, for from Babylon (not the city, but the province), where there were many Jews, he wrote his first Epistle. After many sufferings for his Master, he died; but whether by crucifixion with his head downwards or not, we cannot determine. It is said that he could never hear a cockcrow, but it revived his grief for the denial of his Master. (Acts 12, 15; Gal 2; 1 Pet. 1:1, 5:13)

Peter's two Epistles

Of the two inspired letters he wrote to the dispersed Jews, the first was designed to comfort and confirm them in the truth amid the fiery trials and temptations to which they were exposed, to direct them in their hearing of God's Word, and in their different stations, civil or religious, and to caution them against the insurrections then being whipped up by their countrymen against the Roman government. In the second letter, which was written a little before his death, perhaps about AD 66 or 68, he taught them to abound in Christian virtues, to watch against false teachers and apostasy from the truth, and to live in the holiest manner in the light of the immediate ruin of their nation, and of the Last Judgement.

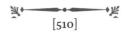

A noble majesty and rapidity of style, with a becoming freedom, is seen in his Epistles. A devout and thoughtful person can hardly read them without solemn attention and awful concern. The burning up of the earth and future judgement are so described that we can almost see the flames ascending into the midst of heaven, and feel the elements melting with fervent heat, and hear the groans of our expiring world and the crashes of nature tumbling into universal ruin. Hugo Grotius believes that this second Epistle was the work of Simon, Bishop of Jerusalem. But where were his eyes so as not to see that this was the second Epistle to the Jews by one who had been with Christ in the holy mount of transfiguration? (2 Pet. 1:18, 3:1) Nor is the style so different from that of the first as some think, except where the subject requires it.

A number of spurious tracts, such as a Gospel, Acts, Revelation, with a treatise on preaching, and another on the Last Judgement, have been falsely ascribed to Peter. The Papists pretend that he was about 24-25 years Bishop of Rome, and wrote his Epistles from there, and was there crucified under Nero. They pretend that he was possessed of a supremacy over all the other Apostles, which, from him, is conveyed to all the popes up to the present time. But it is certain that three years after Paul's conversion, he was at Jerusalem, and also when Herod died, and was there at the Council, and was at Antioch in Syria some time after, in about AD 52. There is never a word of him at Rome when Paul wrote his Epistle to the church there, and sends his salutations to many of her members; not a word of him at Rome, when Paul went there, for, at his first answer, *no man stood by him.* (2 Tim. 4:16) Not a word of him can be found in all the Epistles that Paul wrote from Rome, though people of a far inferior character are often mentioned. How possibly then could he be Bishop of Rome, unless he exercised his power underground, where no one could find him? Or suppose he had been at Rome; that no more establishes his supremacy there, than at Jerusalem, Joppa, and Antioch, where we are sure he lived for a time. Or suppose he had lived 1000 years at Rome, how does that infer that he left his office to their popes, some of whom were atheists, adulterers, Sodomites, murderers, blasphemers, and incarnate devils. And, in summary, what proof have we that he had a supremacy over the other Apostles? None at all, except that he was perhaps oldest,

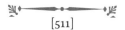

most forward by nature, and more marked with weaknesses than any of his brothers, Judas Iscariot excepted.

PHARAOH

Long a common name for the kings of Egypt, and often added to other names. Flavius Josephus says that, in the old Egyptian language, it meant *king*. It is certain that in the Arabic language it means someone that excels all the rest, and in the Hebrew, someone that is free, or is a *revenger*. It is said that the Egyptians had 60 kings of the name of Pharaoh, from Mizraim (or Menes), to the ruin of their kingdom by Cambyses or Alexander.

In Scripture we find mentioned:

(1) The Pharaoh that had his family smitten with plagues for taking Sarah, the wife of Abraham, into his palace. (Gen. 12)

(2) The Pharaoh that had the dreams foretelling the plenty and the famine of Egypt, and who exalted Joseph, and kindly settled Jacob's family in Goshen. (Gen. 41, 47)

(3) The Pharaoh that began to oppress the Hebrews with hard labour; and, finding it impossible to stop their increase in numbers, he ordered the Hebrew midwives to kill every male child at birth. And finding that they disobeyed him, he ordered all his subjects to destroy the Hebrew male infants wherever they could be found. His daughter saved and educated Moses, the Hebrew deliverer. Whether it was this Pharaoh, or his son, who sought to slay Moses after he had killed the Egyptian, we do not know. (Exod. 1-2)

(4) The Pharaoh from whom Moses demanded liberty for the Hebrews to go and serve their God, and who, after ten plagues on his kingdom, and frequent changes of mind, was obliged to let them go; and afterwards, when following them, was drowned with his army in the Red Sea. (Exod. 5-14)

(5) The Pharaoh that protected Hadad, the fugitive Edomite, and gave his wife's sister in marriage to him. Whether he was the father-in-law of the Solomon who took Gezer from the Canaanites, and gave it as a dowry with his daughter, we do not know. (1 Kings 3:1, 9:16, ch. 11)

(6) Pharaohnecho, the son of Psammitichus, who fitted out great fleets in the Mediterranean Sea, marched a great army to the Euphrates, took Carchemish, defeated Josiah on his way there, took Jehoahaz as his prisoner, and set up Jehoiakim as king of Judea on his return home.

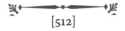

About four years later, his army at Carchemish were entirely routed, the city taken, the garrison put to the sword, and the fugitives pursued to the border of Egypt by the Chaldeans. (2 Kings 23-24; 2 Chron. 35; Jer. 46)

(7) Pharaohhophra, the grandson of the former, reigned 25 years, and was for a while reckoned one of the happiest of princes. He invaded Cyprus, and made himself master of almost all Phoenicia. Depending on his assistance, Zedekiah rebelled against the King of Babylon. Pharaoh sent an army to assist him against the Chaldeans, who were besieging his capital; but, when the Chaldeans marched to attack them, the Egyptians retreated home with all haste. About 16 years later, the Chaldeans furiously invaded his country, murdered the inhabitants, and carried off their wealth. Just before that, Pharaoh had invaded Cyrene both by sea and land, and lost the bulk of his army in that attempt. His subjects, enraged with his poor success, took arms against him, alleging that he had ruined his army in order that he might rule in a tyrannical manner. He sent Amasis, one of his generals, to crush this rebellion. Whenever Amasis began to argue with the rebels, they clapped a helmet like a crown on his head, and proclaimed him their king. Amasis then headed the rebels, and, after various battles, took King Pharaoh prisoner. He would have treated him with kindness, but the people forced him out of his hands, and strangled him. (Jer. 43:9-13, 44:30)

PHARISEES. See Sect

They were great enemies of Jesus Christ, who exposed their hypocrisies. For *Pharisee*, see Matt. 23:26; Luke 7:39, 11:37-38, 18:10-11; Acts 5:34, 23:6, 26:5; Phil 3:5; for *Pharisees*, see Matt. 3:7, 5:20, 9:11, 14, 24, 12:2, 14, 24, 38, 15:1, 12, 16:1, 5, 11-12, 19:3, 21:45, 22:15, 34, 41, 23:2, 13-15, 23, 25, 27, 29, 27:62; Mark 2:16, 18, 24, 3:6, 7:1, 3, 5, 8:11, 15, 10:2, 12:13; Luke 5:17, 21, 20, 33, 6:2, 7, 7:30, 36, 11:39,42-44, 53, 12:1, 13:31, 14:1, 3, 15:2, 16:14, 17:20, 19:39; John 1:24, 3:1, 4:1, 7:32, 45, 47-48, 8:3, 13, 9:13, 15-16, 40, 11:46-47, 57, 12:19, 42, 18:3, Acts 15:5, 23:6-8.

PHILEMON

A rich citizen of Colosse. He and his wife were converted very early to the Christian faith by Paul or Epaphras, and the Christians held their meetings in his house. His bond-slave Onesimus, having run away from him and come to Rome, was converted under Paul's ministry, and was very useful to him in his imprisonment. Paul sent him back with a letter of recommendation, insisting that Philemon should forgive him, and charge what he owed to Paul's own account. (Philem. verses 1, 25)

PHILIP

(1) The Apostle, and brother of Andrew, was a native of Bethsaida. Having been introduced by his brother to Jesus, and invited by Jesus to his lodgings, he later brought Nathaniel to him. (John 1:43-51) To test him, Jesus asked him how they could procure bread for the 5000 men (besides women and children). Philip replied that 200 pennyworth (£6. 9 shillings) of bread would not give each a scanty meal. (John 6:5-7) He and his brother introduced the Greeks to Jesus. (John 12:21-22) He, at our Saviour's Last Supper, pleaded for a sight of the Father's glory, as that would suffice. Jesus told him that, as he and his Father were mutually one, he, after seeing him by faith, had seen the Father also. (John 14:8-10) It is said that Philip preached the gospel in Upper Asia, south of the Hellespont and Euxine Sea (Black Sea), and died a martyr at Hierapolis.

(2) The second of the seven deacons. (Acts 6:5) He seems to have lived at Caesarea, on the west of Canaan. Endowed with the Holy Spirit for preaching the gospel, after the death of Stephen, he went and preached in the country of Samaria, where he performed miracles, and baptised not a few. Directed by an angel, he went to the southwest of Canaan, near Gaza. Here, he met a eunuch, treasurer to Candace, the Queen of Ethiopia, who, being a Jewish proselyte, had come to attend some of the sacred feasts. Directed by God, Philip went close to the eunuch's chariot. He was reading the 53rd chapter of Isaiah, a passage concerning our Saviour's sufferings, and his meek submission to them. Philip asked him if he understood what he was reading. The eunuch replied that he could not, without a teacher. At his invitation, Philip entered his chariot and rode along with him, and, from that passage, instructed him concerning Jesus and the Christian faith. The eunuch received his instructions with the utmost readiness and affection; and, seeing water by the wayside, asked, if he might be baptised. Philip told him he might if he believed with all his heart. He replied that he believed Jesus Christ to be the Son of God. Philip and he went out of the chariot to the water. Immediately after the baptism, the Lord carried Philip away to Azotus where he preached the gospel. He had four daughters who prophesied. (Acts 8, 21:8-9) Whether Philip afterwards went on to Tralleis, in Asia Minor, and there founded a church, we do not know.

(3) PHILIP. See Herod

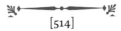

PHINEHAS

(1) The son of Eleazar, and third High Priest of the Jews. His zeal for the honour of God was very remarkable. When the Midianitish women came into the Hebrew camp to seduce them into prostitution and idolatry, Phinehas, seeing one Zimri, a prince of the Simeonites, take Cozbi, the daughter of Zur, a prince of Midian, into his tent, he followed them in, and, with a javelin, thrust them both through the belly in the very act of sexual intercourse. To reward his zeal, God immediately stopped the plague that was then raging among the Israelites, assigned the high priesthood to him and his family for many generations, and appointed him to look to the 12,000 Israelites that punished the Midianites. (Num. 25, 31; Ps. 106:30-31) He and other princes were sent to reprove the Reubenites and their brothers of Gilead concerning their erection of an altar of Ed; and, hearing their reasons, were entirely satisfied. (Josh. 22) He accompanied the army that cut off the Benjamites in the affair of Gibeah. (Judg. 20:28) He died about 1414 BC, and was succeeded by Abishua (or Abiezer), his son. See Priests.

Did he not prefigure our blessed Redeemer? How zeal for his Father's honour and his people's salvation ate him up! How he slaughtered sin, Satan, and an idolatrous world! How acceptable to God was his service! How highly rewarded, and counted for an everlasting righteousness! How it prevents a universal spread of divine wrath! Did he not establish the new covenant of peace, thus founding a perpetual priesthood for him and his seed? And in what honourable, but terrible manner, he punishes those who are unfaithful to him, or wallow in their lusts!

(2) PHINEHAS. See Eli.
A son of Eli. See 1 Sam. 1:3, 2:34; 4:4, 11, 17, 14:3; 1 Chronicles 6:4, 50, 9:20.

PHYGELLUS and HERMOGENES

Professed Christians of Asia. It is said that they were originally magicians; but it is more certain that they forsook Paul in the time of his distress and imprisonment. (Only found in 2 Tim. 1:15)

PONTIUS PILATE

Probably an Italian, and the successor of Gratus in AD 26 or 27 in the government of Judea. He was a most obstinate, passionate, covetous, cruel, and bloody wretch, tormenting even the innocent, and putting people to death without so much as a form of trial. Taking offence at some Galileans, he murdered them in the court of the Temple as they offered their sacrifices. This, as our Saviour hinted, was a prelude to the Jews being shut up in their city, and murdered when they assembled to eat the Passover. (Luke 13:1-2) Wicked as he was, his conviction of our Saviour's innocence caused him to try several ways to preserve his life. His wife, too, having sent him word to have nothing to do with condemning him, as she had a terrible dream about him, he was the more intent to save him. When the Jews accused our Saviour of calling himself the Son of God, Pilate was the more afraid, as he suspected he might be as he said. They then cried out that he would be a traitor to Caesar if he dismissed Jesus. Dreading a charge of this nature, he washed his hands, and protested that he was innocent of Jesus' death, and then condemned him to be crucified. Guided by providence, instead of an abstract of the causes of condemnation, he caused to be written on our Saviour's cross, JESUS OF NAZARETH, THE KING OF THE JEWS, which at once declared his innocence, royalty, and Messiahship; nor could all the entreaties of the Jews cause him to alter the inscription in the least. He readily allowed Joseph the dead body to give it a decent interment. He as readily allowed the Jews to seal and guard the sacred tomb; and so our Saviour's resurrection became the more notorious.

About three years later, Pilate, for his cruelty and oppression, was deposed by Vitellius, governor of Syria, and sent to Rome to give an account of his conduct. Caligula the Emperor, soon after banished him to Vienne in Gaul, where extreme poverty and distress influenced him in putting a wretched end to his own life. Justin Martyr, Tertullian, and Eusebius, and, after them, many others, inform us that it was the custom of the Roman governors in the different provinces to send copies of all their judicial acts to the Emperor; and that Pilate wrote such an account of our Saviour's miracles and death to the Emperor Tiberius that he was inclined to have him worshipped as a God. But the Senate being against this, the matter was dropped. We can scarcely believe that these authors would have published this in the midst of the heathen if it had not been true, and yet we know of no author that pretends to have seen the real *Acts of Pilate*.

POTIPHAR

An officer of Pharaoh. Some have him to be his general, or captain of his guard, others as the chief of his cooks or butchers. He bought Joseph

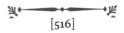

from the Midianites, and, finding everything prosper in his hand, he felt an affection for him, and committed to his care the whole management of his household affairs. But he too easily believed his sexy wife, and threw Joseph into prison. Either this, or another captain of the guard afterwards favoured Joseph. (Only found in Gen. 37:36, 39:1)

POTIPHERAH

Whether this priest, or prince of On, and father-in-law of Joseph, was the same as the above Potiphar, is hotly contested. We think he was a different person. On was about 45 miles from Zoan where Pharaoh and Potiphar dwelt. Potipherah appears to have been one of the greatest men in Egypt, which Potiphar does not seem to have been. Nor can we believe Joseph would have been fond of taking his sexy wife's daughter as his wife. (Only found in Gen. 41:45, 50, 46:20)

PRINCE OF THE POWER OF THE AIR

Satan, that distinguished fallen seraph, is called *the prince of the power of the air* (Eph. 2:2). Some think that he is so-called from his presiding over the whole family, or combination, of degenerate spirits that were permitted to divide the whole world among themselves about the time of the call of Abraham, when the greatest part of the descendants of Noah apostatised from the worship of the one true and living God. The spirit of idolatry suggested to them the propriety of assigning the government of the various departments of the material world to various real or imaginary spirits. To some, they assigned the atmosphere, and over these they imagined one mighty agent presided, to whom different nations gave different names. This agent seems to be that to whom the sacred writers allude, which, prior to the spread of the gospel, kept the inhabitants of Asia, Europe, and Africa in the chains of gross ignorance, strong prejudice, and the most absurd superstitions.

PROSELYTE

Someone who had turned from heathenism to the Jewish religion. (Acts 2:10 = *proselytes*) According to most authors, some were *only proselytes of the gate*, who, though they had renounced their heathen idolatries, had observed what the rabbis called the seven precepts of Noah, and sat under Jewish instruction, yet they were not circumcised, nor partook of the Passover. To these, the Jews admitted hope of eternal

life; and they allowed them to live in Canaan. To them, they reckoned themselves allowed to sell the flesh of animals strangled or dying of themselves. Of these kind of proselytes, we include Naaman, Cornelius, the Ethiopian eunuch, and Solomon's 153,600 servants. Others were *proselytes of righteousness*, or *of the covenant*, obliged to fulfil the whole Law of Moses. At their admission, their motives causing them to convert were examined, and they were instructed in the principles of Judaism. Next, if male, they were circumcised, and then baptised with water by plunging them into a cistern. Then they presented their offering to the Lord. Their females were also baptised before they made their offerings before God. No boys under 12 years of age, or girls under 13, were admitted without the consent of their parents, or, if these refused, without the consent of the judges of the place. After admission, children or slaves were accounted free from the authority of their parents or master. Some think that no Edomites or Egyptians could be admitted as proselytes till the third generation, and the Ammonites or Moabites not till the tenth. But we suppose this exclusion only barred them from places in civil government. (Deut. 23:1-8)

PUL

The first King of Assyria, who invaded Canaan, and, by a present of 1000 talents of silver, was prevailed upon by Menahem to withdraw his troops, and recognise the title of that wicked usurper. (2 Kings 15:19) But who he was, the learnèd are not agreed. James Ussher, Charles Rollin, Augustine Calmet, and Samuel Prideaux reckon him the father of Sardanapalis, and Simon Patrick is no less confident that he was the same as Baladan or Belesis the Chaldean. Sir Isaac Newton, and the authors of the *Universal History*, reckon him the first founder of the Assyrian Empire. His name is a pure Assyrian word without the least hint of the Chaldean idiom, and is plainly a part of the compound names of Tiglathpulassur,

R

RABBI (RAB, RABBAN, RABBON)

A title meaning *master*. It seems to have come originally from Assyria. In Sennacherib's army, we find Rabshakeh, the *master of the drinking*, or butler, and Rabsaris, the *master of the eunuchs*. In Nebuchadnezzar's court, we find *Rabmag*, the chief of the magi, and Nebuzaradan was called *Rabtebachim*, the master of the butchers, cooks, or guards. We also find in Babylon *Rabsaganim*, the *master of the governors*, and *Rabchartumim*, the master of the interpreters of dreams. (2 Kings 25:8; Jer. 39:3; Dan. 1:3, 2:48, 5:11) To keep order, Ahasuerus set a *rab* (governor) at every table of his splendid feast. (Esther 1:6) *Rab* is now regarded by the Jews as a more dignified title than rabbi, and *rabbi,* with rabbin or rabbim greater than either; and to become such, one must ascend by several degrees. The rector of their school is called *rabchacham*, the *wise master*. He who attends it in order to obtain a doctorate is called *bachur*, the *candidate*. After that, he is called *chabarierab*, the *master's companion*. At his next degree, he is called *rab, rabbi,* and *morenu* (our teacher). The *Rabchacham* decides in religious, and, frequently, in civil affairs. He conducts marriages and declares divorces. He is head of the collegians, and preaches if he has a talent for it. He reproves the unruly, and excommunicates offenders. Both in the school and synagogue, he sits in the chief seat; and, in the school, the scholars sit at his feet. When the synagogue is small, he is both preacher and judge, but when the Jews are numerous, they normally have a council for their civil matters; but if the rabbi is called before it, he usually takes the chief seat.

Our Saviour spoke out against the rabbis of his time, whether Scribes or Pharisees, as extremely proud, ambitious of titles and honorary seats, and given to impose on others vast numbers of traditions not warranted by the Word of God. (Matt. 15, 23) Since that time, God has given up the Jewish rabbis to the most astonishing folly in trifling points. They deal chiefly in idle and stupid traditions, and strange decisions on things of no consequence, except to render those who observe them ridiculous. In geography and history, they make wretched work, with inconsistencies in their dating, absurdities, and dry prose that crowd their pages. In their commentaries on the Scripture, they are uncommonly blind to what an ordinary reader might see plainly, and retail many silly stories fit to move our pity or contempt. However, the judicious Onkelos (son of Kalonymus, and nephew of the Emperor Titus), the laborious Nathan Mordecai, the famous Moses Maimonides, the two brothers Kimchi (Moses and David), Abraham ben Meir Aben Ezra, Solomon Jarchi, Jachiades,

Sephorno, Solomon Ben Melech, and some others, deserve a better assessment.

RABSHAKEH. See Sennacharib.
One of Sennacherib's messengers to Hezekiah. See 2 Kings 18:17, 19, 26-28, 37; 2 Kings 19:4, 8; Isaiah 36:2, 4, 11-13, 22, 37:4, 8.

RACHEL
An account of her beauty, of Jacob's great love for her, his eventual marriage to her, her barrenness for a time, her fretfulness under it, her putting her maid into her husband's bed for the sake of children, the angry names she gave them, her stealing of her father's idols, and her crafty concealment of them when her father searched her tent, then her handing them over to Jacob, his peculiar care in securing her and her child from the fury of Esau, her having Joseph as her firstborn son, her purchase of Reuben's mandrakes, and, at last, her dying in childbirth having Benjamin, and being buried at Zelzah, a little north of Bethlehem, all these things are dealt with in the article Jacob. The voice heard in Ramah, *Rachel weeping for her children*, and refusing to be comforted because they were not to be found in life, means that, at the Chaldean Captivity, and when the babes of Bethlehem were murdered by Herod, her daughters of the tribe of Benjamin, and their sisters of the tribe of Judah, so bitterly bewailed the loss of their children, that their weeping was heard as far as Ramah; and that if Rachel, who lay buried nearby, could have risen from her grave, she, who was so fond of children, would have joined them in their lamentations. (Jer. 31:15; Matt. 2:18)

RAHAB
A Canaanitish prostitute, or innkeeper, of Jericho. Some fancy she was only an innkeeper, and that, if she had been a prostitute, the spies would not have lodged with her, nor would Salmon have married her; but this reasoning is inconclusive. The spies might not have known her reputation when they took up their lodging, and she was mightily reformed before Salmon married her. It is certain the Hebrew word Zonah means a prostitute, and the name *Porne* in Greek, ascribed to her in James 2:25, and Paul in Hebrews 11:31, means nothing less. Inwardly touched, and converted by the Spirit of God, she kindly

lodged the messengers whom Joshua sent to spy out the city. The king, hearing of them, sent men to arrest them, but she hid them on the top of her house, and told the king's messengers that they had gone, and might be overtaken if they pursued them quickly. She then went up to the Hebrew spies and told them that she believed the Lord would deliver the country into their hand, and knew that the inhabitants were already in a panic of terror. She insisted on their oath that she and her family would be spared when Jericho was taken. They solemnly promised that everyone found in her house would be unhurt, provided her window was marked with a scarlet string. Her house being on the wall, she let them down from her window on a rope, and directed them to hide themselves three days in the adjacent mountain till the searchers for them returned. They followed her directions, and got back safely to their camp. When, a few weeks later, Jericho was taken, having marked her house according to the agreement, she and all her friends, on Joshua's orders and the care of the spies, were preserved. She joined herself to the Jewish religion, and behaved in a manner so wise and pious, that Salmon (or Selma), son of Nahshon, and prince of the children of Judah, married her, and had by her the famous Boaz. The Spirit of God highly commended her faith and good works, but never the lies she told to conceal the spies.

REBEKAH, REBECCA

Daughter of Bethuel, sister of Laban, and wife of Isaac. Her being providentially marked out for Isaac, her offer to draw water for Eliezer's camels as well as himself; her ready offer to leave her country and be Isaac's wife; her modest veiling of herself when she drew near to Isaac; her long barrenness, and, after 20 years, conceiving by means of her husband's prayer's; her consulting of, and receiving an answer from God concerning the struggling of her twins in the womb; her delivery of Esau and Jacob, and her especial love for the latter; her joining with Isaac in the pretence that she was his sister, that the Philistines of Gerar might not slay her husband for the sake of her extreme beauty; her grief at Esau's marriage with two Canaanite women; her sinful directing and assisting of Jacob to impose on Isaac in order to obtain his principal blessing; her advising Jacob to flee to Padanaram, and stay there in her brother's family till Esau's fury should be cooled; her care in preventing his marrying a Canaanitess; and, in summary, her

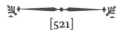

death and burial in the cave of Machpelah, have been already related in the articles Eliezer, Isaac, Jacob. (Gen. 24-28, 49:31)

RECHAB. See Baanah, and Kenites
(2 Sam. 4:2, 5-6, 9; 2 Kings 10:15, 23; 1 Chron. 2:55; Neh. 3:14; Jer. 35:6, 8, 14, 16, 19)

REDEEMER

The Hebrew *goel* (or *kinsman-redeemer*) who was also the nearest of kin, was to exert himself in favour of his destitute kinsman. If he had, through poverty, mortgaged his inheritance, the *goel* was to buy it back. If he had sold himself into slavery, the *goel* was to pay his ransom. If he was murdered, the *goel* was to avenge his blood. If he died childless, the *goel* might marry his widow, and raise up seed to him. But it does not appear that he was obliged to do this unless he was an unmarried brother. (Num. 5:8, 27:11, ch. 35; Deut. 25:1-8; Ruth 3-4)

Does not this *goel* typify Christ assuming our nature, purchasing our happiness, recovering our liberty, avenging our blood on Satan and his agents, and raising up, to our widowed nature, the seed of saints and good works? God is called a *Redeemer*, for, with mighty power and kindness, he rescued the Hebrews from their bondage and trouble, and often delivers the oppressed. He, through the blood of his Son, saves from deep slavery and woe under the broken Law, to endless glory and happiness. (Isa. 63:16) Christ is a *Redeemer*; by his righteousness, he paid the price of our redemption, and, by his intercession, he pleads for and procures it, and, by his Spirit, he applies it to our soul. (Job 19:25; Isa. 19:20)

REHOBOAM

The son and successor of Solomon, born of one Naamah, an Ammonitess, about the end of David's reign. It appears from the book of Proverbs that his father was at no small pains to teach him wisdom; but these instructions were not blessed by God to him, nor were they duly found in his father's life. When he began to reign in BC 974, he, being about 41 years of age, repaired to Shechem where the Hebrews had assembled to make him king. Instigated by Jeroboam, who had begun to raise sedition just before Solomon's death, they offered Rehoboam the sovereignty provided he would ease them of the hard

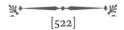

service and expensive taxes that his father had laid upon them as he carried on his building works. He took three days to deliberate on the proposal. His aged counsellors, who had served with his father in that station, advised him to give the people an easy answer, and he would soon have their loyalty. Unwilling to do so, he consulted with his young counsellors, who had been brought up with him. They advised him to tell the people that he intended to load them with far more grievous burdens, and to punish them far more severely than ever his father had done. This advice, suiting his haughty and foolish disposition, he followed. The ten tribes of Reuben, Simeon, Ephraim, Manasseh, Dan, Zebulun, Issachar, Naphtali, Gad, and Asher, provoked at this, cried out that they were under no obligation to, and had no interest in, the family of David, and so would go home and let Rehoboam and the family of David look after themselves. Upon their withdrawal in a body, Rehoboam sent Hadoram his treasurer after them to persuade them to return. Perhaps supposing him the author of their recent hardships, they stoned him to death. Rehoboam, seeing this, went off in haste to Jerusalem in his chariot, where the tribes of Judah and Benjamin acknowledged him king. Of these, he formed an army of 180,000, to reduce the ten revolting tribes by force. But Shemaiah the prophet, in God's name, dissuaded him and his army from this attempt, as it would not prosper. Rehoboam and his people then returned to their homes. To strengthen his kingdom, he fortified Bethlehem, Etam, Tekoah, Bethzur, Shocho, Adullam, Gath, Mareshah, Ziph, Adoraim, Lachish, Azekah, Zorah, Aijalon, and Hebron, and put garrisons of men, and magazines of armour and provision there. As Jeroboam, who had got himself made king by the ten tribes, cast away the true worship of God, many of the priests and Levites, and, no doubt, others, retired south to the kingdom of Judah, and strengthened it.

For three years, Rehoboam and his subjects followed the Lord, and prospered greatly, but, afterwards, abandoned themselves to every enormity. Idolatrous altars, statues, groves, and high places, were everywhere to be found, and both men and women were appointed to be public prostitutes. To punish this wickedness, God brought Shishak, King of Egypt, to ravage the land in BC 969. He pillaged the country, and carried off the treasures of the Temple and palace. Meanwhile, Shemaiah the prophet told Rehoboam and his princes that their idolatry and other wickedness had brought about these disasters.

They humbled themselves under a sense of guilt, and acknowledged the justice of God in their miseries. Shemaiah then assured them that God would not utterly forsake them, but would give them a test as to what difference there was between the hardships of serving the Lord and of serving Shishak.

When Shishak left the country, after he had held it perhaps three or four years, Rehoboam and his people, in the main, restored the worship of God; but the high places were not removed. He caused to be made brazen shields for his guard who accompanied him to the Temple, instead of the golden ones of his father's making, which Shishak had carried away. These lay in his arsenal when they were not used. After Rehoboam had reigned 17 years, he died and was buried in the city of David, leaving Abijah his son, whom he intended to have made his colleague on the throne, to be his successor. There was almost perpetual war between him and Jeroboam, the history of which, and of his life, was written by the prophets Shemaiah and Iddo; but not being intended as canonical, it has not reached our times. (1 Kings 12, 14:21-31; 2 Chron. 10-12)

REUBEN

The oldest son of Jacob by Leah, born BC 1758. When very young, he found *dudaim*, which we render *mandrakes*, in the field about the time of the wheat harvest. These, his mother sold to Rachel, who coveted them for her night with Jacob. When he was about 40 years or so, to the great grief of his father, he committed incest with his concubine; but he seems to have deeply repented of this action. Though Joseph stood fair to come between him and his father's inheritance, he did all that was in him to preserve Joseph safely, and begged the rest of his brothers not to murder him. With a view to protecting him, he persuaded them to throw him into a dry pit, and leave him to die there naturally. While he took a roundabout turn to pull him out and send him home, his brothers took him out and sold him to the Midianites. When he found him taken out, he tore his clothes, and cried out that he did not know what to do. When later, Joseph's rough usage of them brought them to a sense of their guilt over his blood, Reuben reminded them how obstinately deaf they were to all his entreaties for the preservation of his life. When his father refused to let Benjamin go back with them to Egypt, he offered to pawn the life of his two sons that he would bring him back safely. In

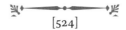

his last benediction, Jacob told him that, because of his incest, he would lose his birthright, and would never excel. (Gen. 29:32, 30:14, 35:22-23, 37:21-22, 29-30, 42:21-22, 37, 42, 49:3-4; 1 Chron. 5:1)

His sons were Hanoch, Pallu, Hezron, and Carmi, all of whom were parents of considerable families. (Num. 26:5-6) When the Reubenites came out of Egypt, their number fit for war came to 46,500 under the command of Elizur, the son of Shedeur. They, with their brothers from Simeon and Gad, formed the second division in the march of the Hebrews, and went just in front of the ark. Their spy for searching the Promised Land was Shammus the son of Zachur. Dathan, Abiram, and On, who rebelled against Moses and Aaron along with Korah, were from this tribe. In the plains of Moab, their warriors came to 43,730. When Moses seized the kingdoms of Sihon and Og, the Reubenites and Gadites, seeing how good the country was for their vast number of flocks and herds, they begged to have it as their portion. At first, Moses refused; but on their proposing to assist their brothers with all their force in the conquest of western Canaan, he granted the country to them and the half-tribe of Manasseh. There, they repaired the cities and settled their wives and children. Their warriors went over Jordan; and though perhaps they visited their families occasionally, they continued with their brothers for the most of seven years till all the tribes had got settled; after which, they were honourably dismissed. On their return home, they erected the altar of Ed, on the banks of Jordan, not for offering sacrifices or incense, but as a testimony that they were of the same Hebrew stock and religion as their brothers. The purpose of this was at first mistaken by the other tribes; and Phinehas, and a variety of the princes, were sent to question them about this matter, as they saw it as one step towards apostasy from the worship of God. But when they heard the true purpose of erecting the altar, they were satisfied. According to the predictions of Jacob and Moses, this tribe never grew great, there never being anyone notable in its history, and they were much exposed to enemies, with the Moabites on the south, the Ammonites on the east, and the Syrians from the north. (Num. 36:5-6, 1:5, 21, 10:18-21, 16, 32; Josh. 21; Deut. 33:6)

In the days of Deborah, the Reubenites were so embarrassed with internal struggles, or foreign invasions, that they could send no assistance to Barak. During the reign of Saul, they, perhaps under the command of Bela, the son of Azaz, conquered a tribe of the Hagarites on the east of Gilead, and seized their country. Of them, and their brothers the Gadites and Manassites, to the number of 120,000, attended David's coronation. In that period, the son of Zichri was their governor; and Adina, the son of Shiza, was one of David's worthies. Hazael, King of Syria, ravaged their country terribly, but it seems that afterwards, in the reign of Jeroboam the second, they and their brothers of Gilead smote the Hagarites, and took from them their country and a huge booty of flocks. Not long after, when Beerah was their prince, Tiglathpileser carried them captive into the northeastern parts of his Empire. (Judg. 5:15-16; 1 Chron. 11:42, 12:37, 27:16; 2 Kings 10:37; 1 Chron. 5:1, 3, 18)

REZIN

The last king of the ancient Syrians, perhaps a descendant of Hazael. Entering into an alliance with Pekah, King of Israel, they invaded the kingdom of Judah, which was then governed by Ahaz. Not being able to take Jerusalem, they ravaged the country, and returned home. Soon after, Rezin's army again plundered the country, and, about this time, marched to the Red Sea and took Elath, and restored it, whether to Syria or to the Edomites we are uncertain, as, in the Hebrew, *Aram* and *Edom* look similar. But it is certain that not long after, Tiglathpileser, King of Assyria, at Ahaz's desire, invaded Syria, slew Rezin, and carried his subjects captive to Media. (2 Kings 16:5-9; 2 Chron. 28; Isa. 7:1-8, 8:6)

RHODA, *a rose*. See Peter

A maid in service in the house of Mary, the mother of John Mark. Only found in Acts 12:13.

RIMMON, or REMMON

A principal idol of the Syrians, worshipped at Damascus. The name means *elevation*; but whether that idol was the *Elyon*, or *Most High*, of the Phoenicians, or the Sun, or Saturn, or Juno, or Venus, is not agreed. Perhaps he was none of all these, but Jupiter Cassius, who had a temple on the northeast of Egypt, and was portrayed with his hand stretched out. I suppose he was Caphtor, the father of Caphtorim, whose name, as well as that of Rimmon, means a *pomegranate tree*. (2 Kings 5:18)

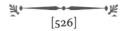

RIZPAH. See Saul
A daughter of Aiah, and one of Saul's concubines. She was the mother of Armoni and Mephibosheth. (2 Sam. 3:7, 21:8, 10-11)

ROSE
Jesus Christ is called the *Rose of Sharon*. (Song 2:1) How unbounded his beauty, delightfulness, and efficacy for the healing of our soul! The wilderness *blossoms as the rose*; through the preaching of the gospel, the Gentile world will be converted to Christ, and flourish with saints and graces. (Isa. 35:1)

S

SADDUCEES. See Sect
(Matt. 3:7, 16:1, 6, 11-12, 22:23-34; Mark 12:18; Luke 20:27; Acts 4:1, 5:17, 23:6-8)

SALMON
Husband of Rahab, and father of Boaz. (Ruth 4:20-21; Matt. 1:4-5; Luke 3:32)

SALOME
(1) The wife of Zebedee, and mother of James and John. She was one of those holy women who closely followed our Saviour, and ministered to him for his needs. She foolishly begged that her two sons might have the top posts in his earthly kingdom. She witnessed his crucifixion, brought perfumes for his dead body, and visited his grave the morning he rose from the dead. (Matt. 28:56; 21:20-22, 28:10; Mark 15:40, 16:1-2)
(2) The daughter of Herodias, but is not actually named in the New Testament. On the occasion of the birthday celebration of Herod Antipas who had married her mother Herodias, she came in and danced, and pleased Herod. (Mark 6:14-29) At her request, John the Baptist was beheaded, and his head presented to the damsel on a large dish.

SAMSON
The son of Manoah, a Danite. After his mother had been long barren, the Angel Jehovah appeared to her, and informed her that she would

have a son who would begin to deliver Israel out of the hand of the Philistines that had then begun to oppress them. He ordered her to drink no wine or strong drink during her pregnancy, nor to eat anything unclean, but to consecrate the child to God, and bring him up as a Nazarite from his infancy. But the angel refused to tell her who he was. She went and informed her husband what had happened. He prayed to the Lord that the man of God who had spoken to his wife would appear again and give further directions concerning the education of the child. The angel again appeared to the woman, and she went and informed Manoah who, along with her, hastened to the angel who repeated his former directions. Manoah and his wife begged him to stay a little till they had cooked a kid for a feast. He told them he would eat none of their meat, even though it was ready, and bade them offer their burnt offering to the Lord. They asked his name that, after the fulfilment of his predictions, they might know whom to honour as their informer. He refused, and told them that his name was *secret*, or *wonderful*. Meanwhile, Manoah offered up his kid as a meat offering on the rock beside them, and the Angel ascended up to heaven in the flames. Manoah and his wife, who, till now, had thought him a man, were seized with terror, and fell on their faces towards the ground. Manoah concluded that, since they had seen an angel, they would die; but his wife more correctly inferred that if the Lord had a mind to kill them, he would not have accepted their offering, nor given them the information concerning their son. Next year, which was about BC 1156 or 1132, Samson was born. By endowing his mind with uncommon bravery, and his body with supernatural strength, the Holy Spirit early marked him out for great exploits.

A Philistine girl and a riddle

He lived at Mahanehdan, between Zorah and Eshtaol. Going one day to Timnath, then in the hands of the Philistines, he saw a young woman whom he fancied. He requested his parents to arrange a marriage with her. They suggested that it would be more proper for him to marry a wife of his own people. As he insisted on his request, they supposed it might be an indication from God to bring about the deliverance of their nation, and, at last, they went with him to Timnath to arrange for him to marry the girl. On the way, Samson turned aside a little, and a young lion came out roaring to devour him. Without so much as a staff in his hand, he caught the furious lion, and tore him to pieces as if it had been a kid. He quickly caught up with his parents, but told them nothing of his adventure with the lion. Sometime later, as they again went to Timnath to celebrate the nuptials, Samson turned aside to see the carcass of the lion. To his surprise, he found a swarm of bees had made a hive in it. He ate part of the honey, and carried some of it to his parents; but, to indicate his continued humility, he still kept secret his killing of the lion.

When the marriage was celebrated at Timnath, 30 young men of the place accompanied him. As they began to entertain one another with puzzling riddles to be solved, Samson proposed to give them a riddle which, if they explained during the seven days of the feast, they would have thirty shirts, and as many suits of apparel; and, if not, they would give him the same. On their agreement to the proposal, he told them his riddle, which went like this: *Out of the eater came forth meat, and out of the strong came forth sweetness.* (Judg. 14:14) To no purpose, and after a long time, they tried to guess its meaning; so they urged his wife by entreaties, and even threats to burn her and her father's family if she did not get them the answer and lure the secret out of her husband. By her continued entreaties and weeping, she got it, and immediately informed her countrymen. On the 7th day, just before sunset, they asked Samson, *What is sweeter than honey? or what is stronger than a lion*? Samson replied that if they had not ploughed with his heifer (that is, dealt with his unfaithful wife), they would never have solved it. Animated by the Spirit of God, he went directly to Askelon, and, killing 30 Philistines, he gave their clothes to his 30 companions. Offended by his wife's treachery, he left her with her father and went off home with his parents. Her father, imagining that he had quite forsaken her, married her to one of the 30 young men who was there at the wedding. When Samson's anger subsided, he went back to visit her, and present her with a kid. As she had been given to another, her father denied him access to her chamber, and wanted him to marry her younger sister who was more beautiful. Bent on revenge, Samson, and some others he had employed, caught 300 foxes, for they were very numerous in that country, and, tying them together tail to tail with a firebrand between them, he let them go into the Philistines' fields of standing corn. The ripened corn caught fire and was quickly consumed. The vines, too, and olive trees were scorched or burnt. Knowing that the injury he had received from his father-in-law was the cause of his conduct, the Philistines burnt his treacherous wife and her father to death. Samson assured them that he would be further avenged on them before he ceased. He smote them hip and thigh wherever he met them, kicking them around like balls with his feet; and, after cutting off great numbers of them, he retired to the rock Etam, about eight miles or more southwest of Jerusalem.

Samson broke the cords of the Philistines

Informed of this, the Philistines invaded the territories of Judah, and demanded that their destroyer Samson should be given up to them. Three thousand Jews went up to the top of the rock and told him that the Philistines were coming to bind him and deliver him into the hands of their masters. Upon their giving him their oath that they would not kill him themselves, he allowed them to bind him. Great was the joy of the Philistines as they received him bound. But, all of a sudden, he snapped the cords with which he was bound, and, taking up the jawbone of an ass that lay at his feet, he then and there slew 1000 of the Philistines. To check his proud boasting of his victory, he suddenly almost fainted with thirst. On his humble request, the Lord opened a well in a hollow place in the rock, perhaps just under the jawbone he had just flung from him, from which he drank and quenched his thirst. To commemorate the event, the place was called *Lehi (the jawbone)*, or *Ramathlehi (the lifting up of the jawbone)*, and the fountain *Enhakkore (the well of him who cried)*.

Gaza, and Delilah

Some time later, Samson, taking a fancy to a prostitute in Gaza, lodged in her house. Informed of this, the Philistines set a watch on the gates to kill him as he went out in the morning. Having got notice of their plot, he rose about midnight, and, going off, carried with him the posts and doors of their gate to the top of the hill before Hebron, which we can hardly think could be less than 20-30 miles. Not long after, he fell in love with Delilah in the valley of Sorek. But whether he made her his wife, or only his concubine, is not very clear. The five lords or princes of the Philistines promised her 1100 shekels of silver, which, in total, amounted to almost £700, if she could discover, and deprive him of, that in which his strength lay. She did what she could to earn the bribe. Suspecting her treachery, Samson, for a while, teased her. First, be affirmed that the binding of him with green withs (twisted branches of trees) would make him as weak as any other man. Next, the binding of him with new ropes; and again, the weaving of his hair into tresses in the loom would do it. Finding that he broke the withs and ropes as easily as if threads, and went off with the web, beam and all, on his head, as soon as the Philistines, who watched in an adjacent room, were ready to arrest him, she enticed him so much with her flatteries and pleadings, that he sinfully exposed the secret, and told her that if his head were shorn, he would be as weak as any other man, as that would break his Nazarite oath, and so deprive him of the remarkable invigorating force of the Holy Spirit. She lulled him to sleep on her lap and cut off his hair. When, as usual, she woke him up with an alarm that the Philistines were ready to arrest him, he thought he would shake and bestir himself as before, but could not, as the Lord had departed from him. The Philistines, who were waiting in the next room, rushed in and arrested him, put out his eyes, and, carrying him to Gaza, put him in prison, and made him grind at their corn mill as a contemptible slave. When he had remained here for about a year, his strength returned with the growth of his hair.

Blind Samson destroyed the Temple of Dagon

While the Philistines were observing a solemn thanksgiving to their god Dagon for delivering Samson their destroyer into their hands, the lords appointed him to be brought to their temple to give them some sport. The area was capacious, and was thronged, so that not a few from the roof to the galleries could enjoy the sport. As the roof was supported by two pillars, Samson, after being sufficiently insulted, asked the boy who led him to guide him to the pillars so that he might rest on them. Having got hold of them, and being divinely appointed to lay down his life for the service of his nation and the destruction of their Philistine foes, after a short prayer, he pulled down the pillars and the temple about their ears, by which means several thousands were killed, even more than all the men he had slain in his lifetime. Thus fell Samson, after he had judged Israel 20 years, and lived to be about 38. His friends, hearing of his death, came and carried off his corpse, and buried it in the sepulchre of his ancestors. (Judg. 13-16) For all his faults, he was a real believer, as is testified by the Holy Spirit; but some imagine the passage only means that he had the faith by which he was qualified for his uncommon exploits. (Heb. 11:32-33)

Application as to type

What a mighty faith had Samson! (Heb. 11:32) Did not this Jewish hero typify our almighty Redeemer? How clear the prediction, and supernatural the manner of his birth! How solemn his separation to the service of God! How wonderfully invigorating the spiritual influences that possessed him! How early and marvellous his exploits! How he, by obedience and death, satisfied the broken Law, conquered the world, sin, death, and the devil! How sweet the provision he provided for himself and his friends! Should I not say what rest for uncountable numbers of sinful men is prepared by his victory over sin, Satan, and death! How important his parables, and known only to those who have fellowship with himself! How vilely Judas Iscariot and his countrymen betrayed him, and delivered him up to the Gentiles, that he might be crucified! His enemies rejoiced to seal him up, and watch him in his grave; but he broke their bands, and carried off the gates and bars of death, and, ascending up on high, led captivity captive. (Ps. 68:18; Eph. 4:8) All alone, he performed his great exploits. By a voluntary death in his despised manhood, and, according to his Father's will, he destroyed thousands of principalities and powers. By the despised preaching of the gospel, he conquers thousands of souls, and slays ten thousands of lusts. How dreadful his vengeance! By the Romans, like fire-branded foxes, he spread terror among his Jewish opposers and burnt up their cities. By outrageously ravaging Goths, Saracens, Tartars, Turks, etc., he resented the injuries done to his cause. And, in short, how his fiery vengeance will forever prey on the damned!

SAMUEL, or SHEMUEL

The son of Elkanah by Hannah, and the 16th in line of descent from Korah, the treacherous Levite. He was born about the same time as Samson.

Hannah's conception, and Samuel's dedication to the Lord

As his mother, after long barrenness, conceived him after earnest prayer, she devoted him to the service of God as a Nazarite from his infancy. After he was weaned, he was assigned to Eli the High Priest to bring him up in the service of the Tabernacle. When Eli, by reason of age, found it hard to officiate, and was sinfully indulgent towards his sons who profaned the service of God, the Lord, one morning, before the lamps of the Tabernacle were extinguished, called to Samuel by name as he lay in his bed very near to that of Eli. Samuel thought it was Eli, and ran hastily to ask him what he wanted. Eli bid him lie down again, for he had not called him. As this happened three times in all, Eli, at last, suspected God had spoken to Samuel, and bid him go lie down again, and if he was called again, to reply, *Speak Lord, for thy servant heareth.* (1 Sam. 3:9-10) Samuel did so when the Lord again called him, and he was told what shocking calamities would quickly come upon the Hebrews, and on the family of Eli, because be had not restrained the wickedness of his sons. At Eli's request, Samuel, not without reluctance, related all this to him. From this time on, Samuel was taken notice of as a prophet of the Lord.

Samuel's residence at Mizpeh

When Eli died, Samuel, now about 40 years of age, succeeded him as Judge of Israel. Having assembled the people, probably on the occasion of their removal of the ark from Bethshemesh to Kirjathjearim, he warned them to put away their idols and return to the Lord, and he would grant them deliverance. He dismissed them for the present, and ordered them to meet him in a body at Mizpeh, a place about 16-18 miles northwest of Jerusalem, or perhaps more easterly. There, they assembled at the appointed time; and as many of them had long - perhaps for about 20 years - bewailed the case of their country, and cried to the Lord for deliverance, they now, at a solemn fast convened by Samuel, confessed and mourned over their sins; and, instead of drink offerings of wine, he poured out water before the Lord.

Ebenezer

Meanwhile, the Philistines, dreading their intentions, marched to attack them. The Hebrews begged Samuel to pray for them. He did so, and offered a lamb as a burnt offering. God terrified the Philistines, and struck dead many of them. They fled off in the utmost consternation, the Hebrews pursuing them as far as Bethcar, recovering from them the cities they had taken away from them. Nor, after that, did the Philistines ravage the Hebrew territories any more during the government of Samuel. To commemorate this notable deliverance, he set up a stone or pillar, calling it *Ebenezer*, the *stone of help*, because there, God had helped them. For the more regular administration of

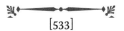

justice, Samuel, every year, took a tour from Ramah to Bethel, then on to Gilgal, and from there to Mizpeh (perhaps the one in Gilead), and then returned home to Ramah where he built an altar for his own devotions, and that of those Hebrews who flocked to him from the country around to ask his direction, or have their cases decided. (1 Sam. 1-3, 7; 1 Chron. 6:22-28)

Samuel's unworthy sons

He had two sons, Joel (or Vishni), the father of Heman the singer, and Abiah, who, in his old age, he appointed judges of the people. Unlike their father, they perverted justice and received bribes. The elders of Israel made this an excuse to ask for a king, that they might be like the nations around. Samuel hated the proposal, and consulted the Lord. Provoked by this sinful proposal, nonetheless, the Lord bid him grant the people their desire, since they were weary of divine government. But, first, to warn them what kind of tyrants that would oblige their children to serve in their wars, or drudge in their house or field, and oppress them with heavy taxes, and in other ways, he told them what to expect according to their own proposal; but persisted.

The anointing of Saul as king

About BC 1095, he was prompted by God to anoint Saul to be their king; and, afterwards, he confirmed the kingdom to him at Gilgal. On that occasion, after their peace offerings were over, Samuel solemnly challenged the assembly to accuse him, if they could, of the least injustice in his administration. They solemnly declared they could not accuse him of anything. After relating the various appearances of God in their favour while the theocracy lasted, he warned them to take heed to serve the Lord, and thus bring upon themselves special blessings. He told them that, though now it was wheat harvest when thunder or rain seldom happened, yet a storm would come that very day to testify God's displeasure at their request for a king. At Samuel's desire, the Lord sent a storm. The thunder terrified the people, and they begged forgiveness for their offence. After he had solemnly warned them against apostasy from the service of the true God, and engaged to continue his prayers for them, he dismissed them, and returned to his house, never again to act as a Judge. (1 Sam. 8-12)

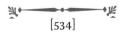

The slaying of the Amalekites; and Saul reproved

Two years later, he sharply reproved King Saul for offering sacrifice personally, and warned him of losing his kingdom. Almost 20 years later, under the direction of God, he ordered Saul to go and slay the Amalekites, and whatever belonged to them. On his return, he sharply rebuked his rebellion against God's commandment in sparing the best of the sheep, and Agag the king, the last of which Samuel hewed in pieces before the Lord. He told Saul that, for his rebellion, the Lord had rejected him, and would give the kingdom to one of his neighbours. Upon Saul's earnest desire, he honoured him before the people so far as to join in public worship with him; and then, he left him, never visiting him any more, but continuing to lament his fate. (1 Sam. 13, 15)

The anointing of David

To comfort Samuel in his grief, the Lord ordered him to anoint one of the sons of Jesse the Bethlemite to be king after Saul. To conceal the matter, and prevent Saul's murderous rage against him, he was prompted to take a heifer with him and offer it as a peace offering. The elders of the place were afraid of his coming; but he removed their fears, and told them he came in peace, calling them to prepare themselves for the sacrifice he intended to offer. He himself sanctified Jesse and his sons on that occasion. After the sacrifice, he had a secret interview with Jesse and his sons. When Eliab, the oldest, appeared before him, his stately appearance made him conclude that he was the person appointed as King. The Lord suggested to him that he was not the man, and that he did not, as men do, look on the *outward appearance, but on the heart.* The seven of Jesse's sons that were present passed before him in their turn; but the Lord suggested to him, and told Jesse, that none of them was the person appointed as King. Understanding that David, the youngest, was with the sheep, he was sent for immediately, and God directed Samuel to anoint him. It is probable that none but Jesse, David, and Samuel, knew of this anointing. After performing this, Samuel returned to Ramah where he presided over a body of young men that had devoted themselves to the special service of God. Perhaps about sixteen or seventeen years later, he died, greatly lamented, about BC 1057. (1 Sam. 16:1-13, 19:18-24, 25:1)

Samuel the first of a long line of prophets

Samuel was a notable prophet, and the first in the continued succession of prophets that ended with Malachi. He wrote in a book rules for the management of the kingdom, pointing out to the king and people their proper rights; but, it is said, some of the Hebrew kings afterwards destroyed it that they might rule as they pleased. He wrote part of the history of David, and is supposed to have written the book of Judges and Ruth. He dedicated considerable spoils to the service of God, and began to regulate the order of the priests and Levites in their sacred service. (1 Sam. 10:25; 1 Chron. 9:10, 29:29, 26:28) Though his extraordinary character, and the broken state of the church, occasioned his offering of sacrifice from time to time, yet there is no proper reason to reckon him a priest, any more than Gideon, or Elijah, or Manoah. Of the two books of Samuel, called by the Vulgate version the books of Kings, the first of which, perhaps the first 24 chapters, were written by Samuel, contains the history of about 120 years, or perhaps less. The second contains the history of David's reign, extending to 40 years. The style of these books is extremely plain, and easy for a learner.

Samuel as a type of Christ

Did not this Hebrew Judge and prophet typify the blessed Jesus? How ardently desired, and supernatural his birth! How early was he devoted to, fitted for, and employed in, the service of God! How extensive his office! At once, he was the illuminated Prophet, the extraordinary Priest, and the sovereign Judge of God's true Israel! How effectively atoning is his sacrifice, and prevalent his intercession, to preserve friendship with heaven, and obtain spiritual and other victories on earth! How marvellous his conquests of our enemies, and the restoration of the treacherously abandoned worship of his Father! How gracious his instructions, sharp his reproofs, and accurate his predictions! How by him kings reign, and princes decree justice! How sincere, generous, and just, his whole government! Yet how wickedly and dangerously were he and his Father rejected by his brothers the Jews, who looked to an earthly deliverer, and still are by worldly professors! But how broken and distressed is their case till they seek the Lord, and David their king!

SANBALLAT

A native, we think, of Hornaim, in the country of Moab. How he, with his friends Tobiah and Geshem, was vexed at Nehemiah's coming from Persia and rebuilding the wall of Jerusalem! What methods they used by fraud to destroy him! How Sanballat got a temple built for Manasseh his son-in-law may be seen in the articles on Nehemiah and the Samaritans. (Neh. 2, 3, 6)

SARAI, SARAH, SARA

(1) The wife of Abraham, who was probably the same as Iscah, the daughter of Haran, Abram's brother, and the granddaughter of Terah, but not by Abram's mother. (Gen. 11:29-31 = *Sarai*, 20:2, 14, 16, 18 = *Sarah*) She perhaps began to be called Sarai, *my mistress*, when she became the head of a family, and was called Sarah, *the lady*, after her being the *mother of a multitude* was divinely secured. (Gen. 17:15, 17, 19, 21) Her beauty endangered her chastity in Egypt. She advised Abraham to go into Hagar that she might have the promised seed by that means, and was punished by Hagar's contempt. This excited angry words with Abraham, and hard usage of Hagar. Just before the destruction of Sodom, Sarah, overhearing the Angel's promise of a son to her, laughed by way of unbelieving contempt, as if she had been too old for childbearing, and was sharply rebuked by the Angel. She added to her guilt a denial. She had just conceived, when her beauty, and her falsely affirming herself to be Abraham's sister, endangered her chastity in the court of Abimelech, King of Gerar. When she was almost 91 years old, she bore Isaac, and suckled him for three years. On the occasion of his weaning, she was provoked by Ishmael's rough usage of Isaac, and never rested till Hagar and he were expelled from the family. Not long after the intended sacrifice of Isaac, which she seems to have known nothing about till it was over, Sarah died at Hebron, aged 123 years, and was buried in the cave of Machpelah. (Gen. 12, 16, 18, 20-21, 23)

The Holy Spirit presents her as a notable believer, an eminent pattern of honouring her husband, an emblem of the covenant of grace, and the gospel dispensation. (Gal 4:22-31; Heb. 11:11; 1 Pet. 3:6)

(2) Sarah (or Sherah), the daughter of Asher. (Num. 26:46)

SARGON. See Esarhaddon

Ruler of Assyria. His name is only found in Isa. 20:1.

SATAN. See Angel, Devil

A name for the devil, revealing him as an *implacable enemy* to the honour of God and the true interest of men. He tempted our first parents in Paradise, bereaved Job of his substance and health, causing his friends to reproach him, tempted David to seduce Bathsheba, and to number the Hebrews, and caused Ahab's prophets to induce him to go to war against Ramothgilead. (Gen. 3:1-5; Job 1:2, etc; 2 Sam. 12; 1 Kings 22; 1 Chron. 21) He tempted our Saviour to distrust, to suicide, and to devil-worship, tempted Judas to betray him, Peter to deny him, and tempted Ananias and his wife to tell lies to the Apostles concerning the price of their field. (Matt. 4:1-11, 16:23; John 13:27; Luke 22:3, 31; Acts 5:3)

Long has his power been established in the world, and, by the erection of the Assyrian, Persian, Greek, and, especially, the Roman Empire, he attempted to strengthen his power against all attacks of the expected Messiah. However, God made them all contribute to the furtherance and spread of the gospel; and, by the preaching of the gospel, the working of miracles by Christ and his Apostles, and by the overturn of heathenism, his kingdom was overthrown. (Matt. 12:26; Luke 10:17-18; John 12:31, 16:11; Rev. 2:9)

Peter is called *Satan* because, in reproving Christ's intention to suffer, he did Satan's work, and under his direction. (Matt. 16:23)

SAUL

The anointing of Saul

The son of Kish, a Benjamite. Just about the time when the Hebrews so loudly insisted on a king to make them like the nations around, Kish's asses wandered astray. Saul and a servant were sent to seek them out. After they had searched a good deal without any success, the servant proposed to Saul that they should consult Samuel the seer (or prophet), who lived at no great distance, as he took him for a cunning man, who, for a trifle, would inform them. Some maidens of the place directed them to him. Samuel, who had that very day called the chief people of the corner to a sacrifice which he intended to offer, being directed by God, welcomed Saul, told him the asses were found, and hinted to him that there was a design afoot to make him the King of Israel. As Saul belonged to one of the smallest families of the least tribe of the Hebrew nation, he was surprised to hear this. At the feast of the flesh of the sacrifice,

Saul was placed at the head of the table, and had a whole shoulder served up to him to mark his distinguished honour, and his need of strength and authority. As Saul lodged with Samuel that night, they had a secret conference on the top of the house. On the morrow, as Samuel led Saul out of the place, he bid the servant pass on before them; and then, with a vial of oil, anointed Saul in the name of the Lord to be king over Israel; and, to assure him of this, he gave him a threefold token, namely, that near Rachel's grave, he would meet two men, who would inform him that the asses were found, and that in the plain of Tabor, a little distant, three men on their journey to worship the Lord at Bethel, where, it seems, there was then a high place, would make him a present of two of their loaves, and that at the hill of God, that is, where the ark then stood at Kirjathjearim, or at Gibeon, where the Tabernacle was, he would find a company of prophets, praising God; and, being seized with their spirit, he would join in that exercise.

Is Saul among the prophets?

These tokens happened, the last producing the proverb, *Is Saul, the son of Kish, among the prophets?* Almost immediately, about BC 1095 or 1097, Samuel assembled the Hebrews at Mizpeh, to receive their new king. The Lord's choice was confirmed in the casting of lots. The lot happened to fall on the tribe of Benjamin, and then on the family of Matri, then on the house of Kish, and, at last, on Saul. He had hidden himself among the baggage of the congregation, but, by the direction of God, he was found; and being presented before the people, he was found to be taller by a head than any of them. The people shouted, and wished him joy in his honours. Samuel then declared to the assembly the laws of their kingdom, and wrote them in a book. God endowed Saul with a spirit of qualification for government. The body of the people went home, but a band of men, divinely instigated, remained with him as his honorary guard. Meanwhile, some despised him as incapable of the office, but he overlooked the affront, and returned to his usual labour. (1 Sam. 9-10)

Saul's exploits in war

About a month later, the inhabitants of Jabeshgilead, being terribly distressed in a siege by Nahash the Ammonite, begged their brothers

to relieve them before the seven days of the truce were ended. When the news of their case came by their messengers to Gibeah, the people wept and cried. Saul, as he returned from his plough, being informed of the cause, hewed a yoke of his oxen to pieces, and sent these by messengers into all the parts of the Hebrew territories, charging the people to meet him and Samuel at Bezek without delay, otherwise their oxen would, in the same way, be hewed to pieces. The people, moved by God, assembled so quickly that, in five days, or perhaps less, he had an army of 30,000 men of Judah, and 300,000 from the other tribes. Crossing the Jordan, and marching all night, about the break of the seventh day, and in three bodies, they attacked the Ammonites, who expected no such thing, and cut them to pieces before the walls of Jabeshgilead.

This victory gained Saul the universal respect of his nation; and they were for killing those who had formerly despised him. Saul withstood this idea, and, soon after, had his royal authority confirmed to him by Samuel at Gilgal. When Saul had reigned about two years, he raised a standing army of 3000 men: 2000 he kept by him, and the rest were headed by Jonathan his oldest son. With these, they attempted to wrest from the Philistines the posts they had retained all along from the birth of Samson, or perhaps had lately seized at Michmash, Bethel, and Gibeah, in the very heart of the country. On the news of Jonathan's defeat of the garrison at Michmash, the Hebrews took heart, and, in great numbers, assembled at Gilgal to drive out the enemy; but they needed arms, as the Philistines had carried off most of the armour, and all the smiths, out of the country. Informed of their meeting, the Philistines, perhaps assisted by the Phoenician or Arabian shepherds now expelled from Egypt, marched a great army against them. The terrified Hebrews dispersed, and hid themselves in dens and caves, and no more than 600 remained with Saul. In his panic, Saul, without waiting a full seven days for Samuel, as he ought, on the seventh, he offered sacrifice to the Lord himself. He had just finished offering his oblation, when Samuel came up and rebuked him for his invasion of the priestly office. He told him that, for this, the Lord would transfer the royalty to another family that would act more agreeably to his mind.

Samuel, Saul, and Jonathan, with the 600 men who remained, marched from Gilgal to Gibeah, having climbed up a rock, and routed an advance garrison of the Philistines. Saul's sentinels observed it, and he, finding that Jonathan and his armour-bearer were absent, called Ahia the High Priest to consult the Lord whether he should attack the enemy. But before the priest had time to do so, Saul, hearing a great noise, and finding that the army of the Philistines were employed in killing one another, he pursued them, and the Hebrews, coming out of their caves, assisted. They pursued the enemy, killing all along as far as Aijalon on the west, and Bethel on the east. The rout would have been still more fatal had not Saul, by a rash curse, condemned to death the person who should stop the pursuit by taking the least refreshment till night, as Jonathan, who knew nothing of the curse, followed the enemy through a wood, dipped his staff in some honey that dropped from a tree, and tasted a little. At evening, when Saul's army convened, he consulted the Lord whether he should attack the camp of the Philistines by night. To punish him for commencing the pursuit without waiting for divine permission, and for his rash adjuration (solemn appeal), the Lord gave him no answer. Suspecting the wickedness of some other than himself to be the cause, he rashly devoted the criminal to death. Lots were cast to find him, and, at the second throw, Jonathan was taken. Though his excuse was good, his father told him that he must die; but the people would not allow him who had been so instrumental in their deliverance, to be slain for no crime. After this, Saul kept a standing army under Abner's cousin, and forced into it as many valiant men as he pleased; and, with considerable success, made war on the Moabites, Ammonites, Edomites, and Philistines. (1 Sam. 12-14)

About BC 1073 or 1063, Saul was divinely ordered to cut off the whole nation of the Amalekites, and all their cattle. Mustering his army at Telaim, on the south of Canaan, it consisted of 10,000 men of Judah, and 200,000 from the rest of tribes. With these, he ravaged the country of Amalek, from Shur on the west to Havilah on the east, and cut off many of the people and their cattle, but saved Agag the King, and the best of the cattle and movables. On his return, he erected a monument to his success in southern Carmel. When Samuel came to the army at Gilgal, Saul told him he had fully executed the divine orders. *What then*, asked Samuel, *means this bleating of the sheep?* Saul told him that the people had brought the best of the herds and flocks to be sacrificed to the Lord, and had spared Agag the King. Samuel told him that it was most wicked for him, who had been so divinely placed on the throne, to rebel against the Lord, and spare what he thought fit. As Saul still blamed the people for preserving the cattle for a sacrifice, Samuel told him that God regarded *obedience more than sacrifice*, and that their disobedience was as bad as witchcraft and idolatry, which it seems Saul was very zealous against, and that since he had rejected the divine commandment, God proposed to dethrone him and his family. At last, Saul confessed his sin, and entreated Samuel to go along and supplicate God for the needed forgiveness. As Samuel refused, and was for going off, Saul held his garment till it tore. *So,* said Samuel, *shall God rend the kingdom from you, and give it to one better.* Saul then begged that Samuel would at least honour him before the people that they might not despise him and rebel. Samuel complied so far as joining with him in public worship. After hewing Agag in pieces before the altar, he went off, and visited Saul no more. It was perhaps about this time that Saul murdered the Gibeonites, imagining his indiscreet zeal would atone for his indulgence in the affair of the Amalekites. (1 Sam. 15)

Saul's relations with David

About BC 1069 or 1063, Samuel anointed David to be King of Israel, when the spirit of government departed from Saul, and an evil spirit of melancholy troubled him. To alleviate his distress, he was advised to get a fine musician to divert him. David was chosen, and his music answered that end, while his good behaviour gained him Saul's affection; so he became his armour-bearer. Saul recovering, David returned to feed his flock. Some years later, when the Philistines invaded the Hebrew territories, and pitched in Ephes-dammim, while Saul and his army encamped in the valley of Elah, Goliath, having defied and terrified the Hebrews, Saul promised his oldest daughter to the man who would attack and kill him. David, coming from his flock, gained the prize; but the women in their songs at the army's return, attributing the victory chiefly to David, highly displeased Saul, who sought a proper opportunity to murder him. One day, as David was diverting his melancholy, he threw a javelin to kill him; but David avoided the stroke. With no good intention, he gave David the command of 1000 of his troops, and with no intention to bestow her, but to prompt David to rush into danger he promised him Merab, his oldest daughter, in marriage. But he actually gave her to Adriel the Meholathite, to whom, it seems, she bore five sons who were brought up by Michal, and later hanged by the Ammonites, with the exception of David. Hearing that Michal, his younger daughter, was in love with David, Saul caused some of his courtiers to inform him that he could have her for 100 foreskins of the Philistines. By these terms, he intended to render David odious to the Philistines, and to endanger his life.

David's reputation was daily increasing, and Saul decided to have him murdered at any cost. For a while, Jonathan diverted it, but Saul, in his melancholy, again attempted it. David, however, escaped to his house. There, Saul caused a body of his troops to besiege him; but Michal, who was now married, let David down by the window, and amazed her father's messengers with a pretence that he was sick, till he was out of their reach, and, by a falsehood, excused herself to her father. Hearing that David had escaped to Samuel at Najoth of Ramah, he once and again sent messengers to arrest him; but a prophetic influence seized them as soon as they came to the place. He then went there himself, but the same influence sent him prophesying, and detained him till David had time to escape. He was highly disappointed with David's absence at the feast of the new moon, as it was then that he intended to murder him, and because Jonathan excused him, he was outrageously reproached, and lost the opportunity to kill him with a javelin. (1 Sam. 18-20)

Not long after, as Saul heavily complained to his servants that none of them was so faithful as to discover David's accomplices, Doeg, his chief herdsman, an Edomite, reported that, while he had attended at the Tabernacle for some purification, he saw Ahimelech the High Priest give David and his attendants refreshment from the sacred provision, and inquire of the Lord in his favour, and give him the sword of Goliath. The innocent High Priest was sent for, and accused and condemned; and he, and 84 of his fellow priests, with all the people of Nob, and even the cattle, by Saul's orders, was murdered by Doeg. It seems he intended to murder the family of Jesse, but David carried his parents into the country of Moab. Hearing that David was in Keilah, a fortified city, he thought to take hold of him there. Soon after, on the information of the Ziphites who invited him, he pursued him with an army in the wilderness of Maon; but when he was just at his heels, an

invasion of the Philistines diverted him to other work. Soon after, he pursued David in the wilderness of Engedi, and had his skirt cut off by David in a cave. He was so moved by David's generosity in sparing his life, when it was so much in his power to take it, that he wept, and acknowledged his wickedness in seeking to murder a person so innocent. Upon a second invitation of the Ziphites, Saul again searched for David in the wilderness of Maon. A second instance of David's generous benevolence, in sparing his life when he penetrated into his camp in the night, and carried off his spear and his drinking cup, made Saul again acknowledge his innocence. Soon after, hearing that David had taken shelter among the Philistines, he gave over thoughts of getting him murdered. (1 Sam. 22-24, 26-27)

The witch of Endor

About BC 1055, the Philistines invaded his kingdom, and encamped in the very heart of it, at Shunem near Jezreel. In his distress, Saul asked counsel of God, but received no answer. According to the commandment of God, he had formerly cut off witches, wizards, and people of that kind. But now, when rejected by God, he, in disguise, applied to a witch at Endor to bring him up Samuel from the dead to show him what he should do. After plenty of spells and enchantments, she, with terror, cried out that he had deceived her, for he was Saul. Being assured that she had nothing to fear, she told him that she saw gods ascending out of the earth, and an old man covered with a mantle. Perceiving it to be Samuel, Saul bowed himself, and told the spectre on demand that he had taken this course to consult him, as he was greatly distressed by the Philistines, and God refused to give him any direction. The spectre told him that he need expect nothing comfortable, as God had departed from him, and that his kingdom would be quickly taken from him and given to David; and that the Hebrews would be routed, and himself and his sons slain, and this would happen on the next day. As this spectre was still called Samuel, and spoke like one who knew the mind of the Lord, and like Satan, who carried our Saviour to a pinnacle of the Temple, and a mountain, they think that God might as well raise a departed saint; or, as God, to punish Saul's sinful curiosity, might he not, at the time of the enchantments, cause Samuel to appear and announce Saul's ruin to him, for many think it was really Samuel who appeared.

As we have no certainty that Saul saw any apparition, some think there was no appearance at all, but merely a voice, and the form only a pretence of the witch. We cannot believe there was anything here but the devil in the likeness of Samuel. This likeness, and a pretence to be Samuel, was the reason of his being so called. Samuel had not to ascend out of the earth, as this spectre did, but to come down from heaven. It is absurd to imagine that God would raise one from the dead to answer Saul, when he refused to answer him by more usual methods, and absurd to suppose a glorified saint subject to infernal enchantments, or that God would do anything tending to honour the diabolical arts. Nothing in the history proves the spectre to be a prophet. That God would take Saul's kingdom from him, and give it to David, was publicly known. From the state of affairs, it was natural to infer that the Hebrews would be routed, and Saul and his family slain. And, besides, who knows not that God may, for holy ends, give devils hints of some future events? Indeed, the very speech of this spectre tends to prove him a devil. He never hints the sinfulness of dealing with wizards, though, for this very sin, Saul was cut off. (1 Chron. 10:12-13) He pretends that Samuel in his glorified state had been disquieted by Saul. He pretends that Saul, and his sons in general, should, the next day, be with him, whereas two of his sons, Armoni and Mephibosheth, lived long after, and were hanged by the Gibeonites, and Ishbosheth lived for several years. Nor can we believe that wicked Saul and godly Jonathan could ever be together, with this spectre, either in heaven or hell. And, in short, when we consider how long Saul remained with the witch, and had to return to his army, and that, meanwhile, David was dismissed from the camp of the Philistines, and went as far as the south border of Canaan, and routed the Philistines that had burnt Ziklag, it can hardly be believed that Saul and his sons would be slain on the following morning. It is certain that Saul fainted with terror at the spectre's speech, and could hardly be prevailed upon to take refreshment.

The shameful end of Saul
Saul then travelled all night to his troops. When the battle was fought, the Hebrews were routed, but they maintained a running fight till they came to Gilboa. There, taking the advantage of the ground, they attempted to rally, but were overpowered by the enemy. Jonathan, Abinadab, and Malchishua, Saul's sons, were slain. After Saul had

fought to the utmost, and was hard pressed by the arrows of the enemy, he begged his armour-bearer to run his sword through him and prevent his falling into the hands of his uncircumcised foes. When the armour-bearer refused, Saul fell upon his own sword, and his armour-bearer did the same. An Amalekite who was nearby, perhaps hastened Saul's death with a thrust of his sword, and brought his crown and bracelets to David. Instead of his expected reward, David ordered him to be slain as the confessed murderer of the king. Next day, the Philistines, finding Saul and his three sons among the slain, stripped off their armour, and sent it to the temple of their idol Ashtaroth. They cut off their heads, fixed them in the temple of Dagon, and hung up their bodies on the wall of Bethshan, which then belonged to the Canaanites. From there, the valiant men of Jabeshgilead took them, and buried them in a grove near their city, and mourned for their death seven days. David afterwards removed them to the sepulchre of Kish at Zelah. Meanwhile, it seems, Abner, Saul's general, and Ishbosheth his son, had fled with the small remains of the army to Mahanaim, east of Jordan, and there, Ishbosheth was made king, and reigned unhappily a few years. Many of the Hebrews left their homes, and retired beyond Jordan that they might be as far from the Philistines as possible.

A considerable time later, Mephibosheth and Armoni, the two sons of Saul by Rizpah his concubine, together with five of his grandchildren by Merab, were, on David's orders, given to the Gibeonites that they might hang them up before the Lord as an atonement for their father's murder of most of their people. It seems that they hung six months on the gallows, from March to September, when the Lord, by showers of rain, showed that Saul's murder was in this way expiated. At this time, the affectionate Rizpah waited in sackcloth at the foot of the gallows, and frightened away the birds that attempted to eat the corpses. (1 Sam. 28-31; 1 Chron. 10; 2 Sam. 1:21)

SAUL OF TARSUS. See Paul. Found only in Acts 7:58, 8:1,3, 9:1,4,8,11, 17,19,22,24,26, 11:25,30, 12:25, 13:1-2,7,9,21, 22:7,13, 26:14.

SAVIOUR
Jesus Christ is the only and all-sufficient *Saviour*; as a Surety, he undertook for, and has paid, all our debt of obedience and satisfaction to the broken covenant of works. As a Mediator and Redeemer, by

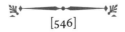

his blood and Spirit, he makes and maintains peace between God and us sinful offenders, and, by price and power, he rescues us from the slavery of the broken Law, and from sin, Satan, the world, and death. As a *Priest*, he gave himself as a sacrifice of infinite worth to atone for the guilty, and makes perpetual intercession with God on our behalf. As a *Prophet*, he delivers from ignorance, and gives true knowledge of everything important. As a *King*, he powerfully rescues us from sin and Satan, and brings us to himself. He rules, directs, and draws us by his Word and Spirit. He defends us from, and restrains and conquers, our enemies; and, in short, transports us to his heavenly mansions. (Isa. 43:11; 1 Tim. 1:15; Heb. 7:25; 2 Pet. 1:1, 11)

He is the *Saviour of the world*; he is equally suited to the case of sinful men on earth, and is, in the gospel promises, given and exhibited to them, whether they are Jews or Gentiles. (John 1:2, 3:15-16; 1 John 4:14) We are saved by the grace of God, the original cause of our salvation, and all the means of it. (Eph. 2:8) We are saved by God's Word as it exhibits and offers salvation to us; and, by it, the Holy Spirit applies salvation to our souls. (James 1:21) We are *saved by faith*, as it discerns and receives Christ and his salvation (Luke 7:50), *saved by baptism*, as by it salvation is sealed and applied to those who believe (1 Pet. 3:21), *saved* by ministers and Christians, as they publish the doctrines and offers of salvation, and warn, beseech, and excite men to receive it. (Rom. 11:14; 1 Cor. 7:16; 1 Tim. 4:16; Jude v. 23) Men are *saved as by fire* when delivered from the greatest of ruin, and when almost all their works are rejected. (1 Cor. 3:15) The righteous are *scarcely saved*; with great difficulty the Jewish Christians escaped ruin from the Romans, along with their country; and, in no small fear and at risk, the righteous escape. (1 Pet. 4:18) *Women are saved in childbearing*; amidst great danger, they are normally preserved in the birth of their children; and, though their sex introduced sin, many of them are saved eternally through the incarnation and obedience of Christ. (1 Tim. 2:15)

SCEVA

He is said to have been the chief of one of the classes of the Jewish priests. He had seven sons who, in a vagabond manner, travelled around pretending to exorcise or cast devils out of men. At Ephesus, they attempted to cast one out, and adjured (solemnly commanded) him by Jesus, whom Paul preached, to leave the possessed person. The

devil told them that he knew both Jesus and Paul, but had no respect for them. He immediately handled them so roughly by means of the possessed person as his instrument that he obliged them to flee out of the house naked and severely wounded. (Only found in Acts 19:14-16)

SCRIBE
(1) A writer who registered the affairs of a king. As few could write in ancient days, this office was very honourable, much the same as that of our Secretary of State. Shemaiah, Seraiah, and Sheva (or Savsha), were scribes to King David. (2 Sam. 8:17, 20:25) Elihoreph and Ahiah were scribes to Solomon (1 Kings 4:3), Shebna to Hezekiah, and Shaphan to Josiah. (2 Kings 19:2, 22:3, 8-10, 12)

(2) The commissary, or muster-master of an army, that enrols, calls out the names, and reviews them. (2 Kings 25:19; 2 Chron. 26:11)

(3) Someone both a writer and doctor of the Law. It seems that they transcribed the books of Scripture, and so became well-versant in it. Such scribes seem to have existed as early as the days of Deborah. (Judg. 5:14) It seems that many of them came from the tribe of Levi. (1 Chron. 23:4, 24:6; 2 Chron. 34:15, 18, 20) Jonathan, Baruch, and Ezra, were scribes. Probably, they had their education in the schools of the prophets, as we find no other schools in these times. In the time of our Saviour, the scribes were a most wicked class, perverting the Scripture, and extolling the traditions of the elders above it. (Matt. 12:28, 35, 38, ch. 23; Mark 12:32)

SEBA. See Sheba
A son of Cush. Gen. 10:7; 1 Chron. 1:9; Ps. 72:10; Isa. 43:3.

SECT
A party distinguished by some particular beliefs. Among the Jews, in the time of our Saviour, we find the Pharisees, Sadducees, Essenes, Herodians, and Kairites.

(1) It is hard to say when the PHARISEES particularly arose. Did they come from the famous Rabbi Hillel, a doctor of the Law, about 50 years before Christ? They called themselves *Pharisees* (or *Separatists*), because they distinguished themselves from others in their pretence to strictness. They were very numerous and powerful, and sometimes formidable to the kings of their nation, particularly to Hyrcanus and Jannæus, with

the last of whom their wranglings made the nation somewhat miserable. They believed in the immortality of the soul, the resurrection, and the future reward of the righteous, whom they reckoned to be only Jews. The souls of the wicked go directly to hell at their death, so their bodies will never rise again. They believed that all things, except the fear of God, were subject to fate. They, and all other sects, were looking for a Messiah to be only an earthly prince and mighty deliverer. But what mostly marked them out was their supererogatory (more than what is required or expected) attachment to the ceremonial Law, their frequent washings, fastings, and praying, their public alms-giving, their hunting for proselytes, their scrupulous tithing, their affected mode of dress, gesture, and mortified looks, and their building tombs for the prophets, to make themselves more righteous than their fathers who murdered them. They were over-scrupulous in their observance of the Sabbath, to the exclusion of good works on that day. Meanwhile, they neglected mercy, charity, justice, humility, and such like indispensable virtues. The very best of them indulged themselves in every thought and sinful indulgence that fell short of the finishing act of sin, while others, under a cloak of religion, indulged themselves in cruelty, dishonesty, and oppression even of widows. They were excessively zealous for the pretended oral Law, and the superstitious traditions of the elders, and preferred them to the oracles of God. They heartily hated and opposed our Saviour, and did all they could to entrap him when he severely rebuked them. (Matt. 5:20, 9:11, 14, 34 and chs. 15, 16:1, 6, 11-12, 23; Luke 5:30-32, 6:2, 7, 7:30, 36, 11:39, 42-44, 53, 15:2, 16:14; John 1:24, 7:32, 45, 47-48, 11:47, 57) At present, most Jews are like the Pharisees.

(2) The SADDUCEES derived their name from one Zadok (or Saddoc) who lived about 280 years before Christ. His master, Antigonus, taught that our service of God should be wholly disinterested, proceeding from pure love, without any regard to future rewards or punishments. From this, Zadok took occasion to teach that there were no rewards or punishments, nor even an after-life. The Sadducees believed that God was the only immaterial being, and that there were no created angels or spirits, and that there was no resurrection from the dead. They reckoned a man absolute master of all his actions, and that he needed no assistance to do good or avoid evil, and so were very severe judges. They rejected all traditions, and stuck to the text of their sacred books; but, like the rest of the Jews, they preferred the five books of

Moses to the rest. Some have imagined that they rejected all the sacred books except those of Moses because our Lord chose to confute them from these; but this reasoning is inconclusive. Had they done so, it is not probable that Flavius Josephus, their zealous enemy, would not have passed this over in silence. Nor could they have been admitted to the offices of High Priests and judges, as it is certain they were.

The Sadducees were generally men of the greatest luxury, choosing to live as they pleased, without fear of any future account. It is said that Hyrcanus, the royal High Priest of the Jews, threatened his subjects with death if they would not become Sadducees. His sons Aristobulus and Jannæus were not much less zealous; and during the reign of the latter, the whole Sanhedrin, except one called Simon, was said to have been composed of Sadducees. Caiaphas, and Ananias, the murderers of James the Less, were Sadducees. The Sadducees were zealous opposers of Christ and his Apostles. (Matt. 22:23-34; Acts 4:1, 5:17) At the destruction of Jerusalem, the Sadducees were much reduced. However, they made some figure in the beginning of the third century. In the sixth, Justinian the Emperor condemned them to banishment, with other severe penalties, as people impious and atheistic. In the twelfth century, Nachmanides (Rabbi Moshe ben Nachman, a Catalan rabbi, 1194-1270) and Rabbi Alpharag, were strenuous defenders of this sect. There are still some Sadducees, notably in Africa, but they seldom declare their opinions. In response to the Deists, it is not improper to observe that we never hear of one Sadducee converted to the Christian faith.

(3) The ESSENES (or *Asdanim*) appear to have been little more than a party of rigid Pharisees, living somewhat in the manner of Romish monks, and had their rise about 200 years before Christ. As they lived in solitary places, and seldom came to the Temple or public assemblies, they are never mentioned in the New Testament. They believed in the immortality of the soul, the existence of angels, and a state of future rewards and punishments; but hardly in the resurrection of the dead. They believed everything was ordered by an eternal fatalism, or chain of causes. They refused oaths, their word they reckoned to be every bit as binding. They observed the Sabbath so strictly that they would not move a vessel, and hardly ease nature. Some of them quite disallowed marriage, and the rest made little use of the marriage-bed. They fasted much, and lived on very little except simple provision. They

despised riches and fine clothing, and wore out their clothes before they changed them. They lived quietly without noise; some were given to mere contemplation while others cultivated the fields for their support. They were kind to strangers, but admitted none into their society till they had given proof of their self-control and chastity. They expelled criminals from their society, but not in the presence of fewer than a hundred. When ten of them sat together, none spoke without the leave of the other nine. They chose rather to suffer torture than to speak evil of their legislators, Moses, etc, and punished with death those who did. They inquired much into the curing of diseases, and, by means of self-control, many of them lived to a great age.

(4) The HERODIANS had a set of principles, a leaven of their own, and tempted our Saviour concerning the lawfulness of paying tribute to heathen governors. (Mark 8:15, 12:13) But what those distinguishing beliefs were is not agreed. Augustine Calmet and others think they were much the same as the Pharisees, only that they held it unlawful to give tribute to the Roman Emperor, which put them in the same camp as the Galileans or Zealots. But why should people of this stamp be called after any of the Herods, who are known to have been compliant cringers to the Romans? Others think they were flatterers of Herod the Great, as if he were the Messiah, and they say he burnt all the genealogical memoirs of the family of David that there might be no proof against his being a branch of it. Rather, with Humphrey Prideaux, we suppose that they, along with the Herods, accepted the lawfulness of the Roman government over the Jews, and that, in consequence, it was lawful for them to comply with many of the customs of the heathen Romans. If so, they were the reverse of the Zealots or Galileans.

(5) Whether the KAIRITES, or adherents to Scripture, were formed into a sect before the birth of our Saviour, and about the time of King Jannæus, or rather later, we do not know. They looked on the canonical books of the Old Testament as the only rule of their faith. They expounded Scripture by Scripture, and counted the traditions of the elders of no more than human authority, and reckoned the affairs of the oral law as mere fable. They read the Scriptures in their synagogues in the original, considering every translation as imperfect. They likewise prayed in Hebrew with great fervency, and with their face towards Jerusalem. They believed in the perfections and providence of God, and allowed a portion of his grace to be necessary to determine men's will towards the

good. They expected an earthly Messiah, and attributed the delay in his coming to the slowness of Saturn's motion, or to the sin of their nation. They condemned phylacteries, and all kinds of pictures or statues used in religion. Their practice was much the same as that of the Essenes, but less austere and rigid; and they had a profound respect for their teachers, who, for the most part, gave their instructions gratis (freely). There are just a few thousand of this sect left in Poland, Germany, etc., and they are hated by the traditionalist Jews as if almost infernal.

The Christians were called the *sect of the Nazarenes*, and were everywhere spoken against. (Acts 24:5, 28:22)

SEIR
The father of the ancient Horites. (Gen. 36:8-9, 20-21, 30)

SENNACHERIB
King of Assyria, who began to reign about BC 714, and reigned about four years attempting to extend his Empire. Informed of Hezekiah's revolt, he invaded his kingdom of Judah. Almost all the fenced cities of Judah were obliged to surrender to him. To stop his taking the rest of them, Hezekiah agreed to return to his former subjection, and paid him 300 talents of silver and 30 of gold. Contrary to agreement, Sennacherib continued the war. While he was besieging Lachish, he sent his generals Tartan, Rabsaris, and Rabshakeh with a considerable army to summon Hezekiah and the inhabitants of Jerusalem to surrender. They halted in the Fuller's Field, and, to this place, Hezekiah sent Eliakim, Shebna, and Joah, to confer with them. In the Hebrew tongue, and with the haughtiest of airs, Rabshakeh told these ambassadors that it was vain for them to expect help from Pharaoh, King of Egypt, or from God, whose altars, he said, Hezekiah had broken down, and who had ordered the Assyrians to invade the country. Eliakim and his brothers wanted him to speak to them in the Syrian language, and not in the Hebrew, lest the people assembled on the wall should know the substance of their conference. Rabshakeh then lifted up his voice the more, and told the people that, unless they surrendered themselves to his master, he would quickly, in a furious siege, oblige them to eat their own dung and drink their urine for want of other provision; but that if they surrendered, they would be allowed to dwell peaceably in the land till they were transported to another just as good.

Meanwhile, Sennacherib raised the siege of Lachish, and invaded Libnah. Receiving no return to his message by his generals, who came to him at Libnah, he wrote Hezekiah a most blasphemous letter, boasting that he would as easily subdue Jerusalem and her God as he had done other nations and their idols, and sent his messengers to rant against the God of Israel, and terrify the people into surrender. Leaving Libnah, he gave battle to Tirhakah, King of Cush (or Ethiopia), and, it seems, routed him, if not also ravaged part of Egypt. Returning, he marched almost up to the walls of Jerusalem and encamped in the Valley of Tophet on the east, but some think the northwest of the city. There, an angel of the Lord, probably with a kind of fiery pestilence, killed 185,000 of his main forces, and, we suppose, Rabshakeh among them, though it seems Tartan survived the catastrophe, and afterwards took Ashdod. (Isa. 20:1) Sennacherib hastened home with the poor remains of his army. He had not been there long when Adrammelech and Sharezer, two of his sons, whom perhaps he intended to sacrifice, killed him as he worshipped Nisroch his idol. Herodotus' bungling narrative of the ruin of Sennacherib's army near Pelusium, on the northeast of Egypt, as if by the god Vulcan's influence, swarms of rats ate all their bowstrings in the night, and so disqualified them for war, is unworthy of this work. What better could we expect him to receive from the traditions of Egyptian priests? (Isa. 30:27-33; 33, 36-37)

SERAIAH

(1) A High Priest of the Jews, son of Azariah, and father of Jozadak the father of Joshua. He was taken prisoner at Jerusalem, and was murdered at Riblah by Nebuchadnezzar, along with 70 other principal men of Judah. (Jer. 52:24-27)

(2) The son of Neriah, and brother of Baruch. He is called *Sharmenuchah*; but whether that means he was a *prince quiet* in his temper and carriage, or that he was a prince of a place called *Menuchah*, or was prince of the bedchamber, or was the king's almoner, or was the chief director of the presents that he carried from Zedekiah to Nebuchadnezzar about seven years before the destruction of the city, I do not know. Jeremiah sent along with him a copy of the prediction of Babylon, and charged him to tie a stone to it when he came to Babylon, and throw it into the Euphrates, saying, "Thus shall Babylon sink, and shall not rise again from the evil that the Lord will bring upon her." (Jer. 51:59-62)

SERAPHIM, *fiery ones*
In his vision, Isaiah saw seraphim standing above or near the Lord's throne. Each had six wings; *with twain they covered their face, with twain their feet, and with twain they did fly.* They cried, *Holy, holy, holy, is the Lord God of hosts, the whole earth is full of his glory,* till the house shook with the sound. When the prophet bewailed his guilt, one of them took a live coal off the altar, laid it on his mouth, and told him that his iniquity was purged. Did not these seraphim signify angels who are near to God, active and humble in his praise, but not capable of beholding the brightness of his glory, and who contribute to the purging and comfort of the saints? Or did they not represent ministers, humble and active in the work of the gospel, for the glory of God and the holiness and comfort of men? (Isa. 6:1-7)

SERGIUS PAULUS. See Barjesus, Paul. Found only in Acts 13:7

SERUG, or SARUCH
The son of Reu or Ragau, and father of Nahor, the grandfather of Abram. (Gen. 11:20-22) It is said that, after the Flood, he first set on foot the idolatrous worship of creatures, and maintained that those men's images that had been remarkably useful might be adored. This introduced the worship of dead men, and, in consequence, all kinds of idolatry and polytheism (the worship of many gods).

SETH, or SHETH
(1) The third son of Adam, born BC 3873, and father of Enosh. He lived for 912 years. For a long time, his posterity followed the true worship and service of God; but at last, mingling with the wicked posterity of Cain, they brought the Flood on themselves. (Gen. 4:25-26, 5:3-8, 6:1-4)
(2) A notable person or place in the land of Moab. (Num. 24:17)

SHADRACH, MESHACH, and ABEDNEGO
Originally of the princes of Judah, and, when very young, they were carried captive to Babylon, and there educated for the King's service in all the lawful wisdom of the Chaldeans. Having by prayer assisted Daniel in the relating and interpretation of the King's dream, they were made governors in the province of Babylon. (Dan. 1-3) See Daniel, Nebuchadnezzar.

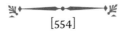

SHAHARAIM

A descendant of Benjamin, who, it seems, either sojourned in, or governed, the country of Moab. By his wives Hushim and Hodesh, he had a very numerous posterity, who distinguished themselves in the building and populating of Lod (or Lydda), Ono, and Aijalon; from the last of which, they drove out the Philistines of Gath, and, after the Captivity, lived partly in Jerusalem. (1 Chron. 8:8-28)

SHALLUM, or SHILLEM

(1) A son of Naphtali, and father of the Shillemites. (Num. 26:49; 1 Chron. 7:13)

(2) The son of Jabesh, King of Israel, who murdered King Zechariah, and almost all the family of Jehu, and, after a month, was murdered in his turn by Menahem. (2 Kings 15:10-12) See Jehoahaz

SHALMAN, or SHALMANEZER

King of Assyria and probably the same as Enemessar, we suppose to have been the son as well as the successor of Tiglathpileser. He began his reign about BC 728, and reigned 12 or 14 years. He subdued the kingdom of Israel, and obliged Hoshea their King to pay tribute. Informed, about three years later, that Hoshea had taken steps with the King of Egypt to make himself free, he marched a powerful army into the land of Israel, took and ravaged the fenced cities, and murdered the inhabitants in a most inhuman manner. After three years' siege, he took Samaria the capital, and Hoshea, and transported most of the people to Media and other eastern parts of his Empire. But if we may credit the history of Tobit, he was not unfavourable to the captives. (2 Kings 17:1-10; Hosea 10:14) Invited by the men of Gath, he commenced a war against the Tyrians, and, after besieging their capital for five years he died without taking it, and was succeeded by Sennacherib.

SHAMGAR

The son of Anath, and third Judge of Israel. The Philistines having invaded his country, he slew 600 of them with an ox goad. (Judg. 3:31)

SHAMMAH

The son of Agee the Hararite, the third of David's mightiest men. Along with Eleazar the son of Dodo, he routed the Philistines in a field of

lentils (beans), and killed a large number of them. They two, breaking through the host of the Philistines, together with Jashobeam, brought David water from the well of Bethlehem. (2 Sam. 23:11-17) Two others of David's worthies were also called Shammah, the one a Harodite, the other a Hararite. (2 Sam. 23:25, 33)

SHAPHAN, or SERAIAH
One of David's scribes. (2 Sam. 8:17; 1 Chron. 18:16)

SHEBA, or SEBA
(1) The son of Cush, who also gave his name to a country in Arabia or Abyssinia. (Gen. 10:7; Ps. 72:10; Isa. 43:3)

(2) Sheba the son of Raamah, and grandson of Cush. (Gen. 10:7)

(3) The son of Joktan. (Gen. 10:28)

(4) The son of Jokshan, and grandson of Abraham. (Gen. 25:3)

(5) The son of Bichri, who decoyed eleven of the Hebrew tribes into a revolt against King David immediately after the death of Absalom. But Joab, following him at his heels with an army, found his partisans were soon scattered, and the inhabitants of Abelbethmaachah, where he fled, cut off his head and delivered it to Joab, who then raised his siege of the place. (2 Sam. 20)

SHEBNAH
A treasurer and secretary of King Hezekiah. He was one of those who, along with Eliakim, were sent to hear Sennacherib's proposals. He was extremely proud, putting up the most sumptuous buildings. He had prepared himself a magnificent sepulchre, but, being carried into captivity either by Sennacherib or by Esarhaddon, he died in miserable exile. (2 Kings 23:18; Isa. 22:15-20)

SHECHEM, SICHEM, or SYCHEM
A son of Hamor the Canaanite, and prince of Shechem (Sychem or Sychar), who, by raping Dinah, the daughter of Jacob, and in order to have her in marriage, consented that he and all the males of his city should be circumcised, bringing about the death of himself, his father, and all the inhabitants of the city. (Gen. 34) See Jacob.

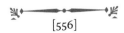

SHEM, or SEM
The second son of Noah, born BC 2446. To reward his filial duty in assisting his brother Japheth in covering his father's nakedness, he received his father's special blessing, which meant that, in his posterity, the church of God would long remain, and Canaan would be his servant; but, at the last, the posterity of Japheth would dwell in his tents. By his sons Elam, Ashur, Arphaxad, Lud, and Aram, he populated most of the southern part of Asia, and the isles adjacent. In Shem's posterity, especially the Hebrew nation, the church almost wholly continued for about 2000 years before Christ; since which, many of the posterity of Japheth have entered into it. See Canaan, and Japheth. Perhaps Shem was the Pluto or Typhon of the heathen, and, from him, the city Zama, near the head of the Tigris, seems to have got its name.

SHEMAIAH. See Rehoboam, Jeremiah, Nehemiah
There are 18 uses of this name in Scripture: 1 Kings 12:22-24; 1 Chronicles 4:37, 9:14 with Nehemiah 11:15, 9:16, 15:8, 24:6, 26:4-8; 2 Chronicles 17:8, 29:14, 31:15, 35:9; Nehemiah 3:29, 6:10, 12:34-36, 12:42; Jeremiah 26:20, 29:24-32, 36:12.

SHESHBAZAR. See Zerubbabel

SHILOH. See Judah
A name for the Messiah. Some, by a mistake of the last letter, render it *sent*, some render it *his son*, others, *he to whom it* (namely, the kingdom) *belongs*. Jean Le Clerk foolishly enough renders it *the end*, and makes the passage run thus: "*The sceptre shall not depart from Judah - till the end of it come*"; that is, it will not depart till it departs. Jacques Gousset explains it of the Messiah as a *wearied sufferer*. But as the word comes from *SHALAH*, which signifies *quietness* (Job 3:26) and *prosperity* (Ps. 122:6-7), it is most properly translated, *The prosperous Author of salvation and rest*; and the whole text might run thus: *The power of government shall not depart from Judah, nor a judge from among his descendants, till the prosperous Saviour come, and to him the gathering and obedience of the Gentiles will be.* (Gen. 49:10) The fulfilling of this prediction is evident. Nothing is more plain than that the offspring of Judah preserved their distinct existence as a tribe, together with a power of government and judging of causes,

till Jesus came in the flesh. The tribe of Judah was most numerous when coming out of Egypt. They led the van (vanguard = forefront) in the wilderness, they were divinely ordered to make the first attack on the remaining Canaanites (Judg. 1:1-2), and against the Benjamites at Gibeah (Judg. 20:13). Othniel, the first of the Judges, was from this tribe (Judg. 3:9) Long, the family of David, who also belonged to this tribe, retained the royal power. Even under the Chaldeans and Persians, Jehoiakim, Zerubbabel, and Nehemiah (all from this tribe) held superiority. (2 Kings 25; Ezra 1-6; Neh. 1-13) For about 160 years before Christ, the Maccabean priests, and the family of Herod, ruled over the Jews, both of which were, in a way, incorporated with the tribe of Judah; and, besides, the Sanhedrin of Jewish elders had much power in their hands. Not long after our Saviour's incarnation, Judea was reduced to a Roman province. Not long had the Gentiles begun to gather to, and obey, him, when the Jewish church and state were quite overturned, and the distinction of the tribes forever finished, their genealogies being lost. It is true that they pretend since to have had heads of their captivity. But where is the evidence? Or where is the nation where they have authority from their tyrannical masters to judge and determine in any important point? If they cannot produce tokens of power for the last 1700 years, the Messiah must certainly have come, and Jesus of Nazareth is that Person.

SHIMEI

The son of Gera, a Benjamite, and a relative of Saul. When David, in a most mournful condition, fled from Jerusalem for fear of Absalom, Shimei met him at Bahurim and bitterly cursed him as a murderer and wicked monster, and threw stones at him. David would not allow him to be killed for his insolence. After Absalom's death, Shimei, with 1000 men of his tribe, came with the first, particularly of the three tribes of the camp of Ephraim, to welcome David home to his capital. He confessed his crime, and begged forgiveness. Despite Abishai's plea, David gave Shimei his oath that he would spare his life and never put him to death. (2 Sam. 16:5-11, 19:16-23) But, as it was dangerous to let such an affront to the royal majesty go unpunished, David, on his deathbed, charged Solomon to do with him as he thought best. In full consistency with his father's oath, Solomon ordered Shimei, under pain of death, not to go outside the limits of Jerusalem. Shimei was content with this restriction.

About three years later, some of his slaves fled off and took shelter with Achish, King of Gath. Informed of this, Shimei went after them, and brought them back to Jerusalem. Solomon, having heard of it, called Shimei before him, and, after convicting him of his wickedness, ordered Benaiah to dispatch him with his sword. (1 Kings 2:36-46)

SHIPHRA and PUAH

Two famous midwives in the land of Goshen. But whether they were Hebrews or Egyptians, we do not know. To prevent the increase of the Israelites, Pharaoh sent for them, and commanded them to stifle at birth all the Hebrew male children. They neglected to obey his orders. He sent for them again and reproved them. They told him that the Hebrew women were not like the Egyptians, but could, and often did, bring forth their infants without help from the midwives. Possibly there might be a great deal of truth in this. But whatever falsehood was in their speech, God did not reward it. But he rewarded their fear of him, and their love for the Hebrews, and he *built them houses*; that is, he rewarded them with numerous and prosperous families. Augustine Calmet thinks it was not the houses of the midwives, but of the Hebrews, that God built up. (Exod. 1:15-19)

SHISHAK

King of Egypt, and, we suppose, brother-in-law of King Solomon. We, with Sir Isaac Newton, believe him to be the same as Sesostris, Bacchus, Osiris, and the Egyptian Hercules, and perhaps the Belus of the Chaldeans, and Mars (or Mavors) of the Thracians. Offended with Solomon, perhaps, for dishonouring his sister with his insatiable lusting after new wives, he protected Jeroboam when a fugitive in Egypt. After enlarging his kingdom into the west, perhaps to the ocean, he turned his arms against Asia with 1200 chariots of war, 60,000 horsemen, and an great company of Egyptians, Lubims, Lukiims, and Cushims. He invaded the kingdom of Judah, took Jerusalem, and carried off the riches of the palace and Temple. But he does not appear to have distressed the kingdom of Israel perhaps because Jeroboam was his ally. After ravaging Asia from the north of India to the Black Sea, he crossed over into Greece, and was there routed by Perseus; or perhaps he was rather obliged to hasten home to chastise his brother Danaus who, being left governor of Egypt, assumed the royal throne.

On his return, Danaus was forced to flee, and sailed to Greece, and was there celebrated by the names of Neptune, Python, Typhon, if not also Japetus. In his arrogance, Shishak is said to have caused his captive kings draw his chariot, till, one day, he observed one of them in his following keeping his eyes steadily fixed on the wheel; and, being asked the reason, said that he took the turning of the wheel to suggest how quickly those in high station would be brought low, and those in low stations be exalted. This speech affected Shishak, and indeed was verified in his case, for, not long after his death, his Empire fell to pieces, and the Ethiopians or Cushims became masters of Egypt. (1 Kings 14; 2 Chron. 12)

SHULAMITE
A name given to the Church to show that she pertained to Jerusalem; or rather was *reconciled* to God, is *peaceable* in disposition, and is *made perfect* through Jesus' beauty put upon her. (Song 6:13)

SIHON
King of the Amorites on the east of Jordan. About BC 1464, he invaded the kingdom of Moab, and seized a considerable part of it. About BC 1452, he refused a passage to the Hebrews through his country. Moses, therefore, attacked him in war, took his country from him, and gave it to the tribe of Reuben. (Num. 21-22; Deut. 2:26-27; Josh. 13; Ps. 136:19, 21)

SILAS, SYLVANUS, or TERTIUS
It is thought by some that he and Carpus were John the Baptist's two messengers to Jesus. (Matt. 11:2-3) He was a chief man among the early preachers, and a close attendant of Paul. He was sent along with him from Antioch to the Synod at Jerusalem, and he and Judas were sent by the Synod, along with Paul and Barnabas, to carry their decrees to the churches. (Acts 15:22) He went with Paul to Lycaonia, Phrygia, Galatia, and Macedonia; and at Philippi, he was his fellow-prisoner. (Acts 15:16) He and Timothy remained at Berea, instructing the disciples after Paul was obliged to flee. Nor does it appear they met up with each other till he came to Corinth, and, there, Silas fervently preached the gospel. (Acts 17:15; 18:5; 2 Cor. 1:19) It is likely that Silas was the brother whose praise was in all the churches, and was chosen with Paul to carry the charitable contributions to Jerusalem, and who, along with

Titus, brought Paul's second Epistle to the Corinthians. (2 Cor. 8:18-19) Being with Paul, he sent his greetings to the Thessalonians in both the Epistles directed to them. He wrote out the copy sent to the Romans, and attached his greetings. (Rom. 16:22) By him, Peter wrote his first Epistle to the dispersed Jews. (1 Pet. 5:12) He is said to have died in Macedonia; but whether by martyrdom or not, we do not know.

SIMEON

(1) The second son of Jacob was born about BC 1757. When he was about 18 years of age, he and Levi, his younger brother, contrary to treaty, murdered the people of Shechem while they were at the sorest after circumcision. (Gen. 34) After Joseph had kept all his brothers in prison for three days, he freed the rest, but retained Simeon, perhaps because he was of a most violent temper, or because he had been the most inhumane to him. (Gen. 42:17-24) On his deathbed, Jacob did not curse the people, but the rage and murder of Simeon and Levi in the case of the Shechemites, and prophesied that their combining in sin would issue in their perpetual dispersion among the rest of the Hebrew tribes. (Gen. 49:5-6) The sons of Simeon were Jemuel (or Nemuel), Gamin, Ohad, Jachin, Zoar, or Serah, and Shaul. Ohad seems to have died childless; but, by the rest, he had numerous issue. When this tribe came out of Egypt, it amounted to 59,300 men capable of war, under the command of Shelumiel the son of Zurishaddai, and marched the fifth under orders from the tribes. Shaphat, the son of Hori, was their spy to view the Promised Land, and Shemuel, the son of Ammihud, was their agent to divide it. (Gen. 46:10; Exod. 6:15; Num. 2:12-13, 13:5, ch. 25, 26:12-14, 34:20) It seems that they were implicated in the affair of Peor, as well as Zimri their chief prince, and that the 24,000 cut off in that affair were mostly from this tribe; for, at the reckoning immediately after, it had declined to 22,200. (Num. 20, 26:14-15) This, their recent wickedness, was perhaps the reason why Moses did not expressly bless them along with the other tribes. (Deut. 33) They obtained their portion out of the inheritance of Judah; and they, and the tribe of Judah, assisted one another in clearing their lot of the Canaanites. (Josh. 19:1-8; Judg. 1:1-20) The Simeonites never made any distinguished figure. We scarcely find a famous person among them; but it is said that the narrow limits of their inheritance obliged many of them to become scribes, and disperse themselves

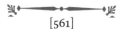

among the other tribes. At David's coronation as King of Israel, 7100 of them were present. (1 Chron. 12:25) They revolted to Jeroboam with the other nine tribes; but many of them afterwards submitted to Asa, King of Judah. (2 Chron. 11, 15:9) When Canaan was ravaged by the Assyrians, it seems a body of the Simeonites retired southward and seized the country of the Amalekites, around the western end of Mount Seir. (1 Chron. 4:39-43) Josiah purged their country of idols. (2 Chron. 34:6)

(2) An old man at Jerusalem, who was earnestly waiting for the incarnation of the Messiah. God, by his Spirit, assured him that he would not die till he had seen him. Moved by a supernatural impulse, he came to the Temple just as Mary and Joseph were presenting their divine Babe. He clasped him in his arms, and blessed God for his coming. He declared his desire of immediate death as he had seen the divine Saviour, the *light to lighten the Gentiles, and the glory of thy people Israel.* He blessed Joseph and Mary, and told them that their child was set up as an occasion of the ruin, yet as the author of the salvation, of many Israelites, and as a sign to be everywhere spoken against. He assured Mary that her heart would be pierced with grief at the sight of the maltreatment and death of her Son, and that strange discoveries would, by the gospel, be made of men's hearts. (Luke 2:25-35) It has been said by some that this Simeon was the son of the famous Hillel, and teacher of Gamaliel.

SIMON

(1) The Cyrenian, and father of Alexander and Rufus, who, it seems, were afterwards notable Christians. He is thought by some to be the same as Niger, the teacher at Antioch. (Acts 13:1) We do not know whether he was a Jew or a Gentile, but it is certain that the Jews who led Jesus to be crucified, finding him ready to sink under his cross, and meeting with Simon as he came in from the country, compelled him to bear one end of it. It is thought by some that he became Bishop of Bostra (or *Bezer*), and died a martyr for the faith.

(2) The brother (or cousin) of our Saviour, and the son of Cleophas. He is said to have been bishop of Jerusalem after the death of his brother James the Less, and, that when Trajan made strict inquiry for all those of the family of David, he was for some days terribly tortured, and then crucified in AD 107, after he had, for more than forty years,

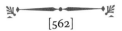

governed the church at Jerusalem, but as most of the time that city lay in mere rubbish, I know of small use for a bishop there.

(3) A Pharisee who, having invited our Saviour to be his guest, though he scarcely showed him due civility when he came, took offence at his allowing Mary Magdalene to wash and anoint his feet. But Jesus, by the parable of the two debtors, convinced him of his mistake. (Luke 7:36-50) Whether it was he whom Jesus healed of leprosy, and in whose house at Bethany Jesus supped a few days before his death, and had his head anointed by Mary, the sister of Lazarus, I do not know. (Matt. 26:6; John 12:3-5)

SIMON MAGUS

Or, the *Sorcerer*. By his enchantments, he acquired for himself great fame in his country of Samaria as some very extraordinary person. He was so affected by the doctrine and miracles of the Apostles Peter and John that he professed himself a Christian, and was baptised. Observing how they conferred the singular influence of the Holy Spirit by the laying on of hands, he offered them money for a share of their powers. Peter bid his money perish with him because he thought to purchase the free gift of God with money, and told him he had need to ask forgiveness for such wicked thoughts, as they shrewdly recognised that he was still in an unregenerate state. Struck with terror at this reply, Simon begged them to intercede with God for him, that the evils threatened him might be averted. (Acts 8:5-24) It seems that afterwards he did what he could to oppose the gospel and its preachers. He seems to have abandoned himself to the vilest sexual perversions and idolatry, and is said to have founded a sect of Gnostics that believed men would be saved by their knowledge, be their lives as vicious as they will, and believed in a vast number of Eons, or inferior gods. It is said that he made himself out to be a divine person, and the Messiah sent to the Samaritans, as Jesus of Nazareth was to the Jews; and that Helena, his concubine, was the Holy Spirit, and the pagan Minerva, Helena, etc. His followers pretended to be a kind of Christians, and yet worshipped him and her under the notion of Jupiter and Minerva. Indeed, Justin Martyr says that about AD 150, almost all the Samaritans worshipped him as their god. The senseless fable of his conflict with, and overthrow by, the Apostle Peter at Rome, is unworthy of a place here.

SIMON ZELOTES

Or the Canaanite was one of Christ's Apostles. Why he was called *Zelotes* is not hard to guess. It seems that he had been one of those Galileans, or furious bigots, who obstinately refused to pay tribute to the Romans. Perhaps his name *Canaanite* means no more than that he was such a zealot, or that he was from Cana in Galilee (Matt. 10:4; Luke 6:15) It is said that he preached the gospel in Egypt, Cyrenacia, Libya, and Mauretania, if not also in Britain. Others think he was murdered at Lunir in Persia, along with Jude.

SISERA

General of the Canaanites under King Jabin the second. After his army was quite routed by Deborah and Barak, and many of them drowned in the River Kishon to avoid discovery, Sisera fled away on foot towards Harosheth. As he passed the tent of Heber the Kenite, who was then at peace with his master, Jael, his wife, invited him into her house to hide. After she had given him some milk to refresh him, he laid himself down to sleep, and asked her to watch the door, and to deny he was there if anyone asked for him. He had scarcely fallen into a deep sleep through his excessive fatigue, when Jael, instigated by God to destroy this murderous, idolatrous and devoted Canaanite, drove a nail through his temples, and fastened his head to the ground so that he died. Barak, pursuing him, had him displayed to him in this condition. For a while, his mother and her ladies, though weary for his return, comforted themselves with the fancy that he would be taken up in dividing the spoil, chiefly the fine robes, and in receiving his share of the captive girls to satisfy his lust. (Judg. 4-5)

SO

A King of Egypt, who promised to assist Hoshea against Shalmaneser, King of Assyria, but, it seems, did not do it, at least not effectively. (2 Kings 17:4) Probably this So is the same as Sabachon the Ethiopian, who burnt to death Bocchoris, the former King of Egypt, and, after retaining the government of the country for 50 years, was succeeded by Sevechus (or Sethon), who, it seems, was priest of Vulcan, and whose prayers the Egyptians told Herodotus brought ruin on the Assyrian host.

SOLOMON

The son of King David by Bathsheba, was born about BC 1033. He was called *Solomon* to signify his *peaceful* temper and reign, and *Jedidiah*, to mark him out as the darling of the Lord. (2 Sam. 12:24-25) His father, knowing that he was to build the Temple, made great preparations for it, and trained him up with great care. As his brother Adonijah thought to usurp the throne, David, by the instigation of Bathsheba and Nathan, caused Solomon to be anointed king while he himself was still alive, which was done with great solemnity. After his father had directed him concerning the Temple, and concerning Joab and Shimei, and solemnly charged him to walk in the way of the Lord, he then blessed him and died. (1 Kings 1-2; 1 Chron. 22-23, 29; Prov. 4)

The beginning of the reign of Solomon

Solomon, who, about two years before, had married Naamah the Ammonitess, and had Rehoboam by her, was now about 18 years of age when be entered on the sole government of his kingdom. Having put Adonijah, Joab, and Shimei to death, and confined Abiathar the High Priest, for their respective crimes, he married the daughter of Pharaoh, King of Egypt, who seems to have become a Jewish proselyte, for Solomon appears not to have fallen into the idolatry of her country. To obtain divine assistance and success in his government, he and his nobles offered 1000 burnt offerings at Gibeon, where the Tabernacle then was. That night, the Lord appeared to him, and offered to grant him whatever he asked. He requested *wisdom* to qualify him for the government of so great a people. His request pleased the Lord, and he granted him such wisdom, honour, and wealth, as none before, or after him, ever possessed. Rising from sleep, he came to Jerusalem, and offered a great number of sacrifices before the ark, and then arranged a feast for his family.

Solomon's wisdom put to the test

Soon after, he had an opportunity for testing out his wisdom. Two prostitutes lived together in one house, and were brought to childbirth about the same time. One of them, killing her own child by lying on it, put it in her neighbour's bosom, and took the living child into her's. Her neighbour, on viewing the dead infant, knew it was not her's, and claimed the living one. The other no less vehemently denied the dead

baby to be her's, and claimed the living one. The case was brought before Solomon; and as parties on both sides were equally obstinate, and the matter admitted of no formal proof, Solomon, conceiving that the real mother would show a special regard for the life of her child, called for a sword that he might cut the living infant in two, and give each of the claimants a half. The pretended mother was content with that, but the other begged that the life of the babe might be preserved and given to her competitor. On this evidence of affection, Solomon knew her to be the real mother, and ordered the child to be given to her. (1 Kings 2-3)

Solomon's kingdom extended

Solomon's kingdom, which extended from the northeastern border of Egypt to the Euphrates, if not a little beyond, was altogether peaceful and affluent. He divided it into cantons under the direction of good governors, who, each in his month, provided for the subsistence of the royal family, which might number 30,000 or 40,000, indeed, the Jews said, 60,000, persons. His horses and chariots, which were many, were properly groomed. He himself exceeded all men in wisdom and knowledge. He collected or invented 3000 proverbs and 1005 songs. He sensibly explained the nature of vegetables and animals of every kind then known. His fame made all the kings around, who were generally either his tributaries or allies, send to test his wisdom. By his trade with Egypt, he imported plenty of fine horses, and a manufacture of linen. By his trade with Ophir and other places, he made gold and silver as common in Jerusalem as the stones of the street, and cedar trees as plentiful as sycamores. The fleet that he sent once in three years from Elath on the Red Sea, managed by Tyrian mariners, brought him from Ophir nearly £2,000,000. (1 Kings 4, 9:28, 10:14, 26-28; 2 Chron. 1, 9:27)

The building of the Temple

When Hiram, King of Tyre, heard that Solomon had succeeded his father, he sent him a solemn embassy to congratulate him on his accession to the throne. Solomon returned him another, requesting his assistance in building a magnificent Temple for the Lord, as his people were more skilful in cutting timber and stone. Hiram returned him word that he would cause his subjects to cut cedars in Lebanon, and

bring them to Joppa in floats. To reward this, Solomon gave Hiram, for the maintenance of his family and workmen, 20,000 measures of wheat, and as much of barley, and 20,000 baths of oil, which last was also called 20 measures (or there were 20 measures added to them for some other use). In the 4th year of his reign, in BC 1011, the Temple began to be built, and was finished in seven years. Besides the servants of Hiram, there were 153,600 Canaanites employed in this work, 70,000 of which were bearers of burdens, 80,000 diggers and cutters of stone, 3300 overseers, and 300 more a reserve to cover those officers who fell sick. All the materials were prepared at a distance, so that there was nothing to do on the spot but to join them together. Hiram, an excellent artist from Tyre, had charge of the foundry.

In the seventh month of BC 1003, the Temple was finished, and dedicated with great solemnity, Solomon, and the elders of Israel, and almost all the people, being present. After carrying in the ark, and some presents that David had left for it, and setting its various utensils and ornaments in their proper places, the Temple was filled with the cloud of the divine glory, which obliged the priests for a while to discontinue their ministrations. After prostrating himself, Solomon stood up on a high scaffold where his throne was placed, and, turning his face to the Temple in a most solemn manner, begged that God would accept and bless the house for his service, and hear the various prayers which the Jews would make towards it in their various afflictions; and that he would fulfil the promises made to David and his seed. He then turned to the people, and blessed them. As a token of acceptance, fire from heaven consumed the sacrifices on the altar, and the glory of the Lord again filled the Temple. Awed at this, the people fell on their faces and worshipped God. At this time, Solomon sacrificed 22,000 oxen, and 120,000 sheep, as peace offerings; and, as the altar of burnt offering was too small for the fat of all these, the middle of the court was consecrated to be an occasional altar. Soon after, perhaps the night following, God appeared to Solomon and assured him that he had accepted his prayers, and would grant his requests; but would bring ruin on David's family, and on Israel, and on the Temple, if they rebelled against his commandments. After 14 days spent in this dedication, and in the Feast of Tabernacles that followed it, Solomon gave the people a solemn dismissal; and they returned home, rejoicing, and praying for blessings on their king. (1 Kings 6-9; 2 Chron. 3-7)

Solomon's fame

After Solomon had finished the Temple, he built a magnificent palace for himself, another for his Egyptian queen, and a third, called the *forest of Lebanon*, where he sometimes, if not chiefly, resided. These were all finished in about 22 years. To reward Hiram for his kind assistance, Solomon made him a present of 20 cities in the land of Galilee, which, it seemed he or his father took from the Canaanites. But as the cities and soil did not please Hiram, it seems he restored them to Solomon, who repaired them and gave them to the Hebrews, and no doubt repaid Hiram his 120 talents of gold, and his friendly assistance, in some other way. He also seized on Hamathzobah, and built Tadmor and other cities in these parts. He also repaired the two Bethhorons, and Baalath, and Gezer. In carrying out these structures, Solomon allowed none of the Hebrews to work as slaves, but caused the remains of the Canaanites to be his drudges. It seems, however, that his taxes on the Hebrews, raised in order to carry on these works, severely provoked them. It appears that his annual revenue was about 666 talents of gold, besides what he had in presents from his allies and tributary kings, and what he had from merchants. It is said that Hiram, King of Tyre, and Solomon maintained a correspondence, posing hard questions to one another.

It is far more certain that the Queen of Sheba, hearing of his fame, came from the utmost part of the south to hear and see his wisdom; and, having heard his answers to her puzzling questions, and having seen the beauty and worship of the Temple, and the magnificence and order of his court, table, and attendants, she fainted with surprise, and confessed that it far exceeded all she had heard. Loaded with presents, she returned to her own country. (1 Kings 10)

The writing of books of wisdom, but a sad end to his life

Hitherto, everything in Solomon's character appeared grand and admirable, but his abominable conduct in the last part of his life has marked him out with lasting disgrace. He had 700 wives and 300 concubines, mostly heathen idolaters. In compliance with these, he forsook the Lord, and worshipped and built temples to their idols Ashtaroth, Moloch, Chemosh, and others. The Lord appeared to him, and told him that, as he had so wickedly broken his covenant, he would tear away ten of the Hebrew tribes from their subjection to his seed. Alarmed at this, Solomon repented of his sin, and it is likely about this time that he wrote his *Ecclesiastes*, where he declares all things vanity and vexation of spirit, and that he had found loose women more bitter than death; and, it this theme that is also found in his *Proverbs*, where he so earnestly warned his son against such women. His temporal punishment was not averted. Before he died, Hadad the Edomite, Rezon the Syrian, and Jeroboam the son of Nebat, began to make him uneasy. After a reign of 40 years, he died, and was succeeded by Rehoboam. The history of his reign was written by Nathan, Ahijah, and Iddo. If he wrote any more besides his Song of Songs, Proverbs, and Ecclesiastes, it was uninspired, and is now lost. (1 Kings 11)

Solomon a type of Christ

Jesus Christ is compared with *Solomon*, and was typified by that prince. (Matt. 12:42; Luke 11:31) What a darling of heaven is he! How infinitely wise and peaceful! Despite all opposition, how suddenly was he installed on his throne by the Father! And how extensive his kingdom! How justly he punishes the guilty! How wisely he judges, and how fully he enriches his people! What multitudes come to, and admire, his wisdom and glory! How he builds the temple of his Church, and consecrates her to the Lord by his unmatched sacrifice, and all-prevalent intercession! (Song 3:6, 11, 8:10)

SOSIPATER

A relative of Paul, who sent his greetings to the Roman church. (Rom. 16:21) Possibly, he is the same as Sopater of Berea who accompanied Paul part of his way from Corinth to Jerusalem. (Acts 20:4)

SOSTHENES

The chief ruler of the Jewish synagogue at Corinth. When Gallio refused to hear the Jews' accusation against Paul, the heathen Greeks severely beat Sosthenes in front of the tribunal. (Acts 18:12-17) Whether this Sosthenes was afterwards converted, and was called a brother by Paul, we do not know. (1 Cor. 1:1)

THE HOLY SPIRIT

The Third Person in the Godhead is, in particular, called the *Holy Spirit* to express his relation to the Father and Son, and because he, by spiritual methods, works spiritual qualities and feelings in us. (1 Pet. 1:2) He is called *seven Spirits* because of his perfect and diversified fullness of gifts, graces, and operations. (Rev. 1:4) He is called the *Spirit of God*; his nature is divine, and he is sent by God to perform his operations in the spiritual economy. (2 Chron. 15:1) He is the *Spirit of Christ*, as he proceeds from him as the Son of God, qualifies him, and rests on him as Mediator, and is sent by him to execute the application of our redemption. (Rom. 8:9) He is the *Spirit of promise* because he was promised to men, and he promises the New Covenant to our heart. (Eph. 1:13) He is the *Spirit of truth*; he is the *true God*, and teacheth nothing but truth. (John 14:17) He is a *holy, good, and free Spirit*; being holy and good in himself, he works holiness and goodness in us of his own sovereign will, and works in us a noble and benevolent nature. (Ps. 51:10-11, 143:10) He is a *Spirit of judgement*, wisdom, and understanding; being infinite in knowledge and wisdom himself, he qualified Christ's manhood, and qualifies his people with wisdom and understanding. (Isa. 28:16, 11:2; Eph. 1:17) He is a *Spirit of bondage and fear* when, by the application of the broken Law to men's conscience, he fills their minds with great tension and fear. (Rom. 8:15)

He is the *Spirit of adoption*, who brings us into the family of God, dwells in every one of God's children, and renders them conformed to his image. (Rom. 8:15) He is the *Spirit of life in Christ Jesus*, as, by uniting men to Christ, he bestows life on them, and, by maintaining their fellowship with Christ, he restores, increases and perfects their spiritual life. (Rom. 8:2, He is the *Spirit of power*, and *of faith*, and *of love*, and of *a sound mind*, and of *supplication*; by his almighty power, he works faith, love, and sound wisdom in the heart, and directs and enables us to pray, and wait for the answer. (Zech. 12:10; Rom. 8:27; 2 Cor. 4:13; 2 Tim. 1:7) The *love of the Spirit* is love for him, or gracious love produced by him. (Rom. 15:30) He is the *Spirit of grace* and *of glory*; as, from the fullness of Christ, he conveys to the saints their gracious endowments and glorious happiness. (Heb. 10:29; 1 Pet. 4:14) He is the Spirit of the *living creatures*, which are in the wheels, as he actuates angels and ministers, and the Church, and the world controlled by them. (Ezek. 1:20) He is said to be *sent* because he was authorised by both the Father and Son (John 16:7) to be *given*, because he was freely bestowed in his Person and gifts and graces (John 7:39) to be *poured out*, because he is carefully and plentifully bestowed (Prov. 1:23); and to *come upon*, and *fall upon*, men in respect of his beginning to act on them (Acts 1:8, 11:15), and to strive with them in opposition to their corrupt inclinations. (Gen. 6:3) Men, in their resistance of his operations, are said to *grieve, rebel against, resist, quench, do despite to, and blaspheme*, him. (Isa. 63:10; Matt. 12:31; Acts 7:15; Eph. 4:30; 1 Thess. 5:19; Heb. 10:29)

STEPHANAS, or STEPHEN

(1) Stephanas was one of the first converts to Christianity at Corinth. He and his family were baptised by Paul. (1 Cor. 1:16) He, Fortunatus, and Achaicus, came to Paul at Ephesus, probably with a letter, in answer to which Paul wrote his first Epistle to Corinth, and sent it by these people. (1 Cor. 16:17)

(2) Stephen the deacon. That he was one of our Saviour's 70 disciples, or that he was brought up at the feet of Gamaliel, is without proof. He appears to have been a foremost man among the Hellenist Jews. After he was made a deacon, being filled with the Holy Spirit, he performed many miracles. Some of the Libertine, Cyrenian, and Alexandrian Jews entered into dispute with him; but not being able to withstand his strong reasons, they suborned (bribed) witnesses to falsely charge that he had blasphemed Moses and God. They hurried him before the Sanhedrin, and charged him with reproaching the Temple and the Law, affirming that Jesus would destroy the Temple, and abolish the observance of Moses' laws. Instead of being dampened, Stephen, with a face bold and shining like an angel's, told what God had done for the Jewish nation in former times, and how they had rebelled against him; and he rebuked them for their murder of Jesus and his prophets. Filled with rage, those present gnashed their teeth at him, as if they wanted to tear him to pieces. Lifting up his eyes to heaven, he told them that he saw Jesus sitting on the right hand of God. As if shocked with blasphemy, they stopped their ears, and, with terrible outcries, dragged him out of the city and stoned him to death. Stephen expired, begging forgiveness from God for his murderers. With great demonstrations of grief, he was buried by his Christian friends. (Acts 6-7, 8:2)

STOICKS (Stoics)

A sect of heathen philosophers, taking their rise from one Zeno a Cypriot, who, being shipwrecked near Tyre, began as a philosopher.

It is said that he borrowed a great deal of his opinions from the Jewish Scriptures; but it is certain that Socrates and Plato taught much of his views earlier. From his teachings, his scholars in the Stoa (or porch) at Athens came to be called *Stoics*, or *porchers*. They generally taught that God, as a kind of soul, actuates all things; that all men have naturally inward seeds of knowledge; that it is wisdom alone that makes men happy; that pains, poverty, and such like, are only imagined evils; and that a wise man ought not to be affected by either joy or grief. In practice, they led to much severity, patience, austerity and insensibility; but some of his followers held different opinions. The Stoics were, for many ages, in vogue, especially at Athens, where some of them encountered Paul. (Acts 17:18)

T

TABITHA, or DORCAS

A Christian widow of Joppa, who much abounded in alms-deeds and other good works. Dying of some ailment, she was washed and laid on a table in preparation for her coffin. Peter was sent for, and the attending widows were all in tears as they showed him the clothes she had made for them, and told him of her other generous deeds. Peter, putting out the people, and praying over her, bid her arise. She immediately opened her eyes, and, he helping her a little, she stood up. He then called in the Christian neighbours, and presented her to them alive and well. (Acts 9:36-42)

TALMAI

A king of Geshur, to whom Absalom fled after he had killed Amnon. (2 Sam. 3:3; 13:37) His daughter Maachah was one of David's wives, and the mother of Absalom. (1 Chron. 3:2)

TAMAR. See Judah, Absalom, Amnon

(1) The daughter-in-law of Judah. (Gen. 38:6)
    (2) A daughter of David. (2 Sam. 13:1-32; 1 Chron. 3:9)
    (3) A daughter of Absalom. (2 Sam. 14:27)

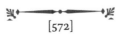

TAMMUZ

An idol, also called Adonis, Osiris, Adonosiris, and perhaps Chemosh, and Baalpeor. It is said that he was either Thamus, an ancient King of Upper Egypt, or Adonis, the son of Cyniras, an Assyrian, who founded the city of Paphos in Cyprus by his own daughter Myrrha. To cover his incestuous birth, he was brought up among the shepherds. Venus, the goddess of prostitution, fell in love with him for his beauty, on account of which, Mars her husband killed him. Venus lamented his death in a most inconsolable way. To comply with her pattern, the eastern nations of Syria, Phoenicia, etc., had a stated solemnity to bewail the ruin of the celebrated prostitute. When the rain or melting snow made the River Adonis appear reddish in colour, the women began their lamentations so loud and tender as if at the death of an only child. After they had sufficiently scourged themselves with whips, they proceeded to the sacrifices for the dead. (Ps. 106:28) Next day, pretending that he was revived and ascended to heaven, they rejoiced, and shaved their heads; and those who did not, at least at Byblus, were obliged to prostitute themselves a whole day to strangers, and consecrate their earnings to Venus. On this day, the Phoenician priests caused a letter to come into their harbour in a boat of paper-reeds, as if from Egypt, saying that the priests there had found Adonis alive. When this boat entered the harbour of Byblus, the women danced and shouted for joy like mad people. In the time of Ezekiel, the Jewish women celebrated this solemnity in all its obscene rites. (Ezek. 8:14) To this day, some vestiges of this mad revel remain at Aleppo.

TARSHISH, TARSUS

The son of Javan (Gen. 10:4), who probably founded Tarshish (Tarsus) in Cilicia, and gave his name to the country, and perhaps became the father of the Etruscans in Italy.

TARTAK

The idol of the Avites. The Jewish writers think he had the figure of an ass; but Pierre Jurieu has this idol to be the chariot of the sun, or the sun in his chariot. (2 Kings 17:31)

TARTAN. See Esarhaddon, Sennacharib
(1) One of Sennacherib's messengers to Hezekiah (2 Kings 18:17).
    (2) One of Sargon's generals (Isa. 20:1).

TEMAN, or TIMNAR

The grandson of Esau by his son Eliphaz, and father of the Temanites, of whom Eliphaz, Job's friend, was one (Job 2:11, 4:1, 15:1, 22:1), and Husham, an ancient King of Edom, another. (Gen. 26:34) We suppose that he built a city called Teman about five miles from Petra. Most, if not the whole, of the land of Edom is sometimes called *Teman*. (Jer. 49:20; Amos 1:12) The symbols of the divine presence seemed to *move from* above the land of *Teman and Paran*, to Sinai, which lay southwest of it. (Hab. 3:3)

TERAH

The son of Nahor, and father of Haran, Nahor, and Abraham. He was born in BC 2126; and, in the 130th year of his life, Abram was born to him. He and his family were idolaters; but we hope God's call of Abraham was blessed to the conversion of many in the family. It is certain that Terah went along with Abraham to Haran and died there. (Gen. 11:24-32; see also Josh. 24:2-14)

TERTIUS

The Latin name of Silas. Only found in Romans 16:22.

TERTULLUS

A famous orator among the Jews, who, by flattering Felix the wicked judge, and with plenty of falsehood, accused Paul at Caesarea. (Acts 24:1-10)

THADDEUS. See Jude

One of the Apostles (Mark 3:18), called *Lebbaeus* in Matthew 10:3, and in Luke 6:16, *Judas* the brother of James, while John 14:22, probably referring to the same person, speaks of *Judas, not Iscariot*. These different names all fit the same person, Jude or Judas, the author of the Epistle.

THEOPHILUS

A noble Christian to whom Luke directed his Gospel and the Acts of the Apostles. It seems he was a person well known for his gifts and graces, if not also for his high station. Some think that the name refers to any *lover of God*. (Luke 1:3; Acts 1:1)

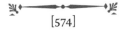

THEUDAS

Some time before our Saviour's death, he set himself up as some notable person, and was joined by about 400 men. But after he was killed, they dispersed. Perhaps he is the Judas that revolted on the occasion of Herod's death, or Flavius Josephus is wrong in his chronology, and places the Theudas he mentions as the head of a sedition too late by some years. (Acts 5:36)

THOMAS, or DIDYMUS (*the twin*)

One of our Saviour's Apostles. (Matt. 10:3; John 11:16, 20:24, 21:2) When he heard that Lazarus had died, he proposed they should all testify their affection by going to the spot, and dying along with him, or die with Christ, who endangered his life by returning to Judea. (John 11:16) Jesus, after his Last Supper, speaking of the mansions in his Father's house he was going to prepare for them, Thomas very ignorantly asked where he was going, and which way he would take? Jesus replied that he himself was *the way, the truth, and the life.* (John 14:5-6) Thomas, being absent when the other ten on the resurrection evening saw their risen Lord, and afterwards hearing of it, told them that unless he saw in Jesus' hands the prints of the nails, and put his fingers into them, and thrust his hand into the wound made by the spear in his side, he would never believe he had risen from the dead. When Jesus appeared to them next Lord's Day evening, he offered Thomas the proof of his resurrection he had mentioned. Thomas, all-captivated with such condescension, and, it seems, without making the test, cried out, *My Lord and my God!* Jesus told him that it would have been more to his honour if he had believed without any special proof. (John 20:20-29) A few days later, Thomas saw his Master again at the Sea of Galilee. (John 21) After he had stayed several years at Jerusalem, he went, so it is said, to preach among the Parthians, Medea, Hyrcanians, and Bactrians, and at last suffered martyrdom in Meliapur in the East Indies, near to which the Portuguese, about 300 years ago, found Christians of St. Thomas; indeed, some think he preached in China.

TIBERIUS

Caesar Augustus, having married Livia his mother, adopted him to be his heir in the Empire. At the beginning of his reign, Tiberius behaved himself decently, but afterwards became quite peevish (spiteful), cruel,

and oppressive. In about the sixth year, the Senate ordered all the Jews to depart from Rome or become slaves. In about the 13th year, he made Pilate governor of Judea. In the 15th year, John the Baptist began to preach. (Luke 3:1) Soon after, he took from the Jews the power of putting criminals to death. It is said that, hearing of the miracles of our Saviour, he was earnest to have him enrolled among the Roman deities, but was hindered by the Senate. He so favoured the Christians as to threaten death to those who molested them on account of their religion.

TIGLATH PILESER, or TIGLATH PILNESER

King of Assyria. Receiving the kingdom in a prosperous state after the death of his father Pul, he laboured to extend his dominions. Instigated by Ahaz, King of Judah, he invaded Syria, slew Rezin their King, plundered Damascus and other places, and carried the people captive to Kir in Media. He ravaged the Hebrew territories east of the Jordan, and carried the people captive to Habib, Haber, and Ham, on the river Gozan. He also ravaged Western Galilee, and took Ijon, Abelbethmaachah, Janoah, Kedesh, Hazor, etc., and carried the people captive into Assyria. Not content, it seems, with Ahaz's presents, and his complimentary visit of him at Damascus, he appears to have ravaged part of Judea. (2 Kings 15:29; 1 Chron. 5:26; 2 Chron. 28:20) After a reign of about 19 years, he left his throne to Shalmaneser.

TIMOTHY, or TIMOTHEUS

A notable evangelist. He was a native of Lystra in Asia Minor. His father was a Greek, but his grandmother Lois, and his mother Eunice, being pious Jewish women, trained him up from a child in the knowledge of the Scriptures. Paul circumcised him to render him more acceptable to the Jews. His bodily constitution was very weak, but his gifts and graces were eminent. (Acts 16:1; 1 Cor. 4:17; 1 Tim. 5:23; 2 Tim. 1:5, 15, 3:15) After he had been ordained a minister by Paul and the presbytery of Lystra, he became very dear to Paul for his faithfulness and piety; and so he calls him his *dear son* in the faith, his *faithful fellow-worker*, etc. (1 Cor. 4:17; 1 Tim. 1:2, 4:14; 2 Tim. 1:6)

He accompanied Paul to Macedonia, and was with him at Philippi, Thessalonica, and Berea. At Paul's request, he followed him from Berea to Athens, but was quickly sent back to confirm the Christians of Thessalonica under their persecution. (Acts 17; 1 Thess. 3:2-3) From there, he and Silas came to Paul at Corinth (Acts 18:5), and, together with him, sent their greetings to the Christians of Thessalonica. (1 Thess. 1:1; 2 Thess. 1:1) Some years later, Paul sent him and Erastus from Ephesus to Macedonia and Corinth, to confirm the Christians there. (Acts 19:21-22; 1 Cor. 4:17, 16:10) Having returned to Ephesus before Paul left the place, he was left there to settle the affairs of that infant church (1 Tim. 1:3), and there he received his first Epistle about AD 56. After ordering matters at Ephesus, he followed Paul to Macedonia, where, along with Paul, he sent his greetings to the Corinthians. (2 Cor. 1:1) Soon after, he accompanied Paul to Corinth, and from there, together with him, he sent his greetings to the Romans. (Rom. 16:21) Returning through Macedonia, he went with Paul to Asia. (Acts 20:4) There, he was called some years after by Paul to Rome in his second Epistle to him. (2 Tim. 4:9, 13) He was with Paul at Rome when he wrote his Epistles to the Philippians, Colossians, and Philemon. (Phil. 1:1; Col. 1:1) He was for a while a prisoner at Rome, but was later set at liberty. (Heb. 13:23) After which, we do not know what became of him. The two Epistles directed to him, encouraged and directed him in his feeding, and government of, the church, and warned him of the troubles that were overshadowing her.

TIRHAKAH
Or *Thearchon*, as Strabo calls him, was King of Cush; but whether that in Arabia or in Abyssinia, is not agreed. We suppose him the sovereign of Abyssinia and Egypt, and that he was defeated by Sennacherib, against whom he marched for the relief of King Hezekiah; and that at this time, to the terror of the Jews, the Ethiopians and Egyptians were taken prisoner. (2 Kings 19:19; Isa. 10:4-6)

TIRSHATHA
A name given to Zerubbabel and Nehemiah. Some think it means the *cupbearer*, but more properly it means a governor, or a commissary, appointed by the Persian King to carry his orders to a province, and see them put into execution. (Ezra 2:62; Neh. 20:1)

TITUS
A notable evangelist. Being originally a Gentile, he was never circumcised. He accompanied Paul, by whose ministry he had been

converted, from Syria to the Synod at Jerusalem. (Gal 2:1-3) Some years later, Paul sent him to Corinth where his piety, and his disinterested and zealous preaching of the gospel gained him a kindly reception. Coming from there to Paul in Macedonia, he gave him an account of the state of the Corinthian church, and was returned to them bearing a second Epistle from Paul. (2 Cor. 7:6, 15, 8:6, 16-17, 12:18) When Paul left him in Crete to settle the affairs of that church, and ordain elders in it, we are uncertain; but it is certain that, in the Epistle sent there to him, he desired him to come to him at Nicopolis, and Zenas the lawyer and Apollos with him, as soon as Tychicus and Artemas should come to take his place. (Titus 3:12-13) After this, Paul sent him into Dalmatia (2 Tim. 4:10), but it is said that he returned to Crete, and from there preached the gospel in the neighbouring islands. The Epistle sent to Titus directed him to ordain officers, to warn and censure the unruly, and to urge all ranks to act agreeably according to their Christian character.

TOBIAH. See Nehemiah

TOBIJAH. See Zachariah
See 2 Chronicles 17:8; Zechariah 6:10, 14.

TOGARMAH
The third son of Gomer, and grandson of Japheth. (Gen. 10:3) Flavius Josephus makes him the father of the Phrygians, Samuel Bochart of the Cappadocians, of whom was a tribe called Trogmi, Trocmi, or Trogmades. Others make him the father of the Turkmans in Tartary. The Armenians, too, claim to be his descendants. It is certain that his posterity traded with the Tyrians in horsemen, horses, and mules (Ezek. 27:14), and that they will assist Gog and Magog against the Hebrews at the beginning of the millennium. (Ezek. 38:6)

TOLA
(1) The oldest son of Issachar, and father of the Tolaites. (Num. 26:23)

(2) Tola the 10th judge of Israel. He was the son of Push, and grandson of Dodo, of the tribe of Issachar. He succeeded Abimelech, and judged Israel 23 years, and was buried at Shamir in Mount Ephraim in BC 1210. (Judg. 10:1)

TRYPHENA and TRYPHOSA

Two notable Christian women at Rome who, by their private instruction and generosity, mightily contributed to the success of the gospel there. (Rom. 16:12)

TUBAL

(1) The fifth son of Japheth. (Gen. 10) Flavius Josephus makes him the father of the Iberians, on the east of the Black Sea. Samuel Bochart makes him the father of the Tibarenes, on the north of Armenia the Less. And I see nothing to hinder his being the parent of both of these tribes, as their situation is not very far distant. Others, I think without ground, make him the father of the Italians, or Spaniards.

(2) TUBAL CAIN, a son of Lamech the bigamist, and the inventor of smith-work and foundery, and, it is believed, the Vulcan of gods of smiths of the heathen. (Gen. 4:22)

TYCHICUS

A notable evangelist, who accompanied Paul with the collection for the poor saints at Jerusalem. (Acts 20:4) Paul afterwards sent him to Ephesus and Colosse, with his Epistles to these churches. (Eph. 6:21-22; Col. 4:7-8; 2 Tim. 4:12) He appears to have been the successor of Titus in taking charge of the affairs of the church of Crete. (Titus 3:12)

U

URIAH, URIJAH, URIAS

(1) A Hittite, one of David's worthies, and husband of Bathsheba. Due to the taking of his wife by David, and the calling of him from the army, and endeavouring to make him drunk, and cause him to sleep with his wife in order to father a spurious child, and his resistance of these temptations, he was made the carrier of a letter leading to his murder. His death, and the vengeance of God, fell heavily upon David and his family on account of his conduct towards him, and the circumstances are related in the article David. (2 Sam. 11, 23:39)

(2) The idolatrous High Priest who, at Ahaz's direction, made an altar like another idolatrous one at Damascus, and offered sacrifices on it, instead of on the altar of the Lord. (2 Kings 16:10-12)

(3) A faithful prophet who warned the Jews of their approaching ruin, and urged them to repent of their evil ways. But Jehoiakim, hearing of this, resolved to put him to death. He fled into Egypt, but Jehoiakim sent and brought him back, and, having ordered him to be murdered, caused his corpse to be dishonourably cast into the graves of the common people. (Jer. 27:20-21)

UZ
(1) The oldest son of Aram, and grandson of Shem. (Gen. 10:23)

(2) The son of Dishan, a Horite. (Gen. 36:29)

UZZAH and AHIO
The sons of Abinadab, in whose house the ark of God long resided. At David's orders, it was conducted on a new cart from Kirjathjearim to Jerusalem. When the oxen stuck in the mud, or stumbled as they passed the threshing floor of Nachon or Chidon, Uzzah, though no priest, and perhaps not a Levite, presumed to touch the ark in order to hold it onto the cart. Offended that the ark was not carried on the shoulders of the Levites according to order, and offended with Uzzah's presuming to touch it, and perhaps also for his advice to carry it on a cart, God struck him dead on the spot, to the no small grief and terror of King David. (2 Sam. 6) Whether it was in a garden that belonged to this Uzzah that King Amon was buried, we do not know. (2 Kings 21:26)

UZZIAH, or OZIAS
See Azariah, the son of Jotham.

V

VASHTI. See Ahasuerus
A deposed queen. (Esther 1:10-12)

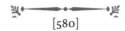

THE WORD OF GOD

Jesus Christ who, in the Chaldee paraphrast (paraphrase), and by the Apostles and others, is called the WORD. He is the express image of his Father as words are of our thoughts. He spoke for us in the council of peace; he spoke all things into being at the creation; he spoke to the ancient patriarchs and prophets; he preached the gospel in the days of his flesh; he speaks for us in his intercession; he speaks to our hearts in the day of his power; and he is the great subject matter of what is declared in Scripture. (John 1:1, 4; Rev. 19:13)

Z

ZACCHEUS

Whether *Zaccheus* was a Gentile, or, rather, a Jew, is not so certain as that he was a chief publican. As Jesus passed through Jericho, going to suffer at Jerusalem, Zaccheus had a great desire to see him. But as he was of low stature, he could not do this until he climbed a sycamore tree. When Jesus came to the spot, he bade him come down quickly as he intended to stop at his house. With great joy, Zaccheus came down, and conducted our Saviour to his house. While the Jews murmured that Jesus had gone to be the guest of a publican, Zaccheus, convinced of his sin, told him that he intended to give half of his goods to the poor, and, according to the Roman law, restore fourfold to anyone he might have wronged by false accusation. Jesus told him that, after all, he should not expect any happiness by his own repentance and good works, but merely through Christ, the salvation of God now come to his house, and sent to seek and save lost sinners. (Luke 19:1-10)

ZACHARIAH, ZACHARIAS, ZECHARIAH

(1) The son of Jeroboam the second, and the fourth descendant of Jehu. Perhaps his father left him an infant. It was about 23 years, or perhaps no more than 11 years after, that he mounted the throne, and, having

reigned six months, was murdered by Shallum the son of Jabesh, BC 772. (2 Kings 15:8-11)

(2) The son of Jehoiada the chief priest, who was, perhaps, also called Azariah. Having reproved King Joash, his cousin, for his idolatry and wickedness, that ungrateful wretch ordered him to be stoned to death in the court of the Temple. In his dying moments, he told them that the Lord would speedily avenge his death. (2 Chron. 24:20-25)

(3) The son of Jeberechiah (or Barachiah), who had understanding in the visions of God, and encouraged Uzziah in his piety, and, perhaps, withstood him when he attempted to offer incense. (2 Chron. 26:5) He was one of the faithful witnesses that attested Isaiah's writing concerning Maher-shalal-hash-baz. (Isa. 8:2)

(4) The son of Barachiah, grandson of Iddo, and 11th of the lesser prophets. He returned from Babylon with Zerubbabel; and, while yet young, he began to prophesy in the second year of Darius Hystaspes, BC 520, about two months after Haggai. These two mightily encouraged the Jews in their building of the second Temple. (Ezra 5:1)

The book of Zechariah

After Zerubbabel had exhorted the people to repentance, the Lord appeared to him as a *man on horseback, in the middle of a plot of myrtle trees, in a low place*, thereby intimating the presence of God with, and care for, his people in their distress, and also hinted to him that Jerusalem would be rebuilt. By the vision of *four horns frayed away by four carpenters*, it was hinted that God would raise up Jewish governors that should resist and harass the Ammonites, Moabites, Samaritans, and Philistines, the enemies of Judea. (Zech. 1) By the *visionary measuring of Jerusalem*, it was hinted that it would be rebuilt. And the prophet was informed that its inhabitants would be very numerous, and the Lord would marvellously protect them. (Chapter 2) By the *vision of Joshua the High Priest's preservation from Satan*, and the *change of his filthy robes for fine apparel*, and he and his fellow priests being *crowned with gold*, it was hinted the safety and glory of the priests under the second Temple. By the vision of the stone with seven eyes on it, it was hinted that the Temple would, under the care of divine providence, be finished, and Christ come in his season. (Chapter 3) By the vision of a *candlestick with seven branches, placed between two olive trees that issued oil out of themselves*, might be signified the comfort of the Jews

by means of Zerubbabel and Joshua, and the comfort of the Church by Christ and his Spirit. (Chapter 4) By a *large flying roll, written all over with curses*, was hinted the speedy and extensive vengeance of God against false swearers and thieves. The *visionary ephah filled with a woman called wickedness*, and shut in *with a heavy covering of lead*, and carried by *two winged women into the land of Shinar*, imported the speedy and terrible vengeance taken on Babylon, about four years after, by the Medes and Persians, or the terrible ruin and dispersion of the Jews, about 40 years after our Saviour's Ascension. (Chapter 5) By four chariots proceeding from between brazen mountains, and traversing the earth, was signified the fate of the Chaldean, Persian, Greek, and Roman Empires, and the fate of ministers in the various periods of the gospel Church. By an order to make crowns of silver and gold for Joshua, and for Heldai (or Helem), Tobijah, Jedaiah, and Hen, was hinted, the glory of the Jewish priesthood, and the glory of Christ as the builder of his Church. (Chapter 6) After directing the Jews concerning fasting, and inculcating a variety of moral duties, he foretells their happiness, and the vast number of their proselytes and favourites. (Chapters 7-8) He then foretells the destructive wars of Syria, Phoenicia, and the country of the Philistines, the preservation of the Jews under their Egypto-Grecian and Syro-Grecian oppressors, the birth, and injurious abuse of the Messiah, the publication and success of the gospel, the ruin of the Jewish church and state, and the conversion of the Gentiles to Christ in the Apostolic and millennial periods. (Chapters 9-14)

(5) ZACHARIAS was an ordinary priest of the course of Abia. He and his wife Elisabeth were eminently godly and blameless; but she had long been barren. About 15 months before our Saviour's birth, as Zacharias was burning incense in the Temple, the angel Gabriel appeared to him, and told him that his wife should bear him a son called John, who should be the successful harbinger of the Messiah. As the priest refused to credit the message, the angel told him that his dumbness till the event should verify the prediction. When he came out of the Temple, he could speak not at all, but made signs to the people who were praying in the court that he had seen a vision. When his turn of ministration was finished, he went home. After about nine months, his wife was happily delivered of a son. Contrary to the remonstrances of their friends, Elisabeth insisted that the child

should be named John. Zacharias, being consulted by signs, wrote that he should be so called. Hereupon, he recovered the use of his speech, and uttered a hymn of praise to God for the donation of the Messiah, whose birth was at hand. Turning himself to his babe, [he] foretold that he should, by his instructions, prepare the nation to receive the Messiah. (Luke 1)

(6) Who that *Zacharias the son of Barachias* was, who was slain between the porch of the temple and the altar, we know not exactly. Whether he was the son of Jehoiada, whose name has much the same signification as Barachiah, that is, *a blesser of the Lord*, or the son of Jeberechiah, whom perhaps Ahaz murdered between the porch and the altar, for opposing his idolatrous worship, or the prophet above mentioned (4), who was perhaps murdered in that place, or the father of the Baptist, who might have shared the same fate, perhaps about the time when his son was a public preacher, or, if it was one Zacharias the son of Baruch, whom Jesus foresaw the Jews would murder in that place a little before the last destruction of their city, is not agreed by the learned. But be who he would, the coming of all the bloodshed, from that of Abel to that of this Zacharias, upon the Jewish nation, imports that, as their rejection and murder of Christ and his apostles approved the whole of it, it should be all revenged on them. (Matt. 23:34-36; Luke 11:50-51)

ZADOK

The son of Ahitub. In his person appointed High Priest by Saul, that high office was returned to the family of Eleazar after it had continued near 120 years in the house of Eli, and the family of Ithamar. Both he and Abiathar were a kind of High Priests under the reign of King David; but it seems David chiefly consulted Zadok, as perhaps he was a prophet. Both the two, at David's desire, tarried at Jerusalem during Absalom's rebellion, and procured him proper information. (2 Sam. 15, 17) They, too, instigated the tribe of Judah to make all the haste they could to bring David home after the rebellion was suppressed, lest the other tribes should get the start of them. (2 Sam. 19:11-12) Zadok, instead of joining Adonijah, was one of those most active in the coronation of Solomon, and actually anointed him to the royalty, and came to be sole High Priest after Abiathar's confinement. (1 Kings 2:35), and was succeeded by his son Ahimaaz. Another Zadok, son of another Ahitub, was High Priest long after, and Jerusha his daughter seems to have been the wife of king Uzziah, and mother of Jotham. (1 Chron. 6:12; 2 Chron. 27:1)

ZAPHNATH. See Joseph
The name Pharaoh gave to Joseph when he raised him to the rank of prime minister. (Only found in Gen. 41:45)

ZARAH or **ZERAH**
The son of Judah by Tamar, and twin brother of Pharez. From his five sons, Ethan, Zimri, Heman, Calcol, and Dara, sprang the Zarhites, who were less numerous than the posterity of Pharez. (Gen. 38:28-29; Num. 26:20; 1 Chron. 2:6)

ZEBEDEE. See James

ZEBULUN or **ZABULON**
The sixth son of Jacob by Leah, born about BC 1748. From his three sons Sered, Elon, and Jahleel, sprang three numerous families. When this tribe came out of Egypt, their fighting men amounted to 57,400 men, commanded by Eliab the son of Elon. They increased by 3100 in the wilderness. Their spy to search Canaan was Gaddiel, the son of Sodi, and their prince to divide it was Elizaphan the son of Parnach. (Gen. 30:20, 46:11; Num. 1:9, 31, 13:10, 26:26-27, 34:25) They had their inheritance on the south of the tribes of Asher and Naphtali, and had the Sea of Galilee on the east, and the Mediterranean on the west. They enriched themselves by their fisheries, their sea trade, and the making of glass. They were very honest in their dealings, and, despite distance, were punctual attenders at the worship of God at Jerusalem. (Gen. 49:13; Deut. 33:18-20) They did not drive out the Canaanites from Kitron or Nahalol. (Judg. 1:30)

They and the Naphtalites, under Barak, were very active in routing the host of Jabin. (Judg. 4:10; 5:14, 18) They assisted Gideon against the Midianites. (Judg. 6:35) Elon, a Zebulunite, was, for ten years, Judge of Israel (Judg. 11), and 50,000 of them attended David's coronation to be king over Israel, and brought large quantities of provision. (1 Chron. 12:33, 40; Ps. 68:27) They were oppressed, and many of them carried captive to the east by Tiglathpileser. (1 Chron. 5:26) Those that remained in their country partly joined with Hezekiah in his reformation. (2 Chron. 30:11) Their country was signally blessed with the early instructions and miracles of our Saviour; and, perhaps, most of his disciples were of this tribe. (Isa. 9:1-2; Matt. 4:13, 15) Perhaps there was also a city called *Zebulun* near Accho, which is said to have been built in the form of Tyre and Sidon, and to have been taken and burnt by Cestius the Roman about AD 66. (Josh. 19:27)

ZEDEKIAH

(1) The son of Josiah, by Hamutal the daughter of Jeremiah, a prince of Libnah. When Nebuchadnezzar carried Jehoiachin prisoner to Babylon, he made Mattaniah his uncle king in his place after he had caused him to swear to be his tributary, and change his name to *Zedekiah*. He began to reign when he was 21 years of age and reigned 11 years. Contrary to many warnings of God by the prophet Jeremiah, he and his people hardened themselves in their idolatry and other impious acts. (2 Kings 24:17; 2 Chron. 36:10-16; Ezek. 17:13) In the first year of his reign, he sent Elasah the son of Shaphan, and Gemariah the son of Hilkiah, to Babylon, probably along with his tribute. With these, Jeremiah seems to have sent his letter to the captives in Babylon. (Jer. 29) About four years later, he either went himself, or, at least, sent Seraiah, the brother of Baruch, to Babylon, with whom Jeremiah sent his predictions against Babylon to be read by him, and then cast, weighed down by a stone, into the Euphrates. (Jer. 51:59-64) In the ninth year of his reign, Zedekiah, contrary to solemn treaty with Nebuchadnezzar, entered into an alliance with Pharaohhophra of Egypt, and, it seems, with the other nations around, to throw off the Chaldean yoke. Nebuchadnezzar quickly marched an army into Judea and laid siege to Jerusalem. Alarmed at this, he and his subjects dismissed their bondservants, whom they had retained longer than the law allowed, and begged that Jeremiah would pray for them. Meanwhile, when Egyptians marched an army into Canaan, Nebuchadnezzar raised the siege of Jerusalem to attack them. During this interval, the Jews forced back their servants, and drew new punishment upon their heads. Having defeated or driven back the Egyptians, Nebuchadnezzar renewed his siege of Jerusalem.

Zedekiah often consulted the prophet Jeremiah, but had not got the patience to hear, or resolve to follow, his good counsels. Jeremiah urged him to go out and throw himself on Nebuchadnezzar's mercy, and it would go well with him. For fear of derision, he declined, and it is likely

Pelatiah the prince, who, soon after, had a miserable end, dissuaded him. (Ezek. 11:13) Zedekiah, as Jeremiah had warned him, fell into great shame by his refusal to surrender. When Jerusalem was taken, he and a number of his troops fled off in the night; but the Chaldeans pursued them, and overtook them near Jericho. He was taken prisoner to Nebuchadnezzar at Riblah of Syria, who, after reproving him for his treachery, ordered his children to be murdered before his face, and then his eyes to be put out; after which he loaded him with chains, and sent him to Babylon, where, after some time, he died peaceably, and was honourably interred by his friends. (2 Kings 25; Jer. 21, 27, 32:4-7, 34, 37-39)

(2) The son of Chenaanah and the son of Maaseiah were both false prophets. See Micaiah, Ahab.

ZELOPHEHAD

The son of Hepher, of the tribe of Manasseh, who died in the wilderness, but not in any of the more notable provocations. Not long before Moses' death, his five daughters, Riblah, Tirzah, Hoglah, Milcah, and Noah (for he had no son) applied to Moses to receive an inheritance in Canaan as heirs to their father. The Lord approved their demand, with the only proviso that they married men from their own tribe. It was divinely enacted that, to prevent the portion of one tribe going into that of another, no heiress should marry out of her own tribe; or, if she did, she forfeited her inheritance. (Num. 26:33, 27, 36)

ZENAS

The only pious lawyer we read of in Scripture. Whether his learning was in the Jewish or Roman law, we do not know; but he was a notable Christian, whom, together with Apollos, Paul wanted Titus to bring with him to Nicopolis, and to take care that they were sufficiently provided for on the journey. (Titus 3:13)

ZEPHANIAH

(1) A prophet, the son of Cushi, and grandson of Gedaliah. He appears to have lived in the time of King Josiah, and, after his children were grown up, to wear robes in a foreign fashion. (Zeph. 1:1, 8) In his first and third chapters, he protested against the wickedness of the Jews; foretold their calamities and captivity, and their deliverance from it. In

the second chapter, he exhorted the Jews to repentance, and foretold the ruin of the Philistines, Moabites, Ammonites, Ethiopians, and Assyrians.

(2) The second priest (or sagan) under Seraiah the chief priest. By him, Zedekiah, more than once, consulted Jeremiah, and requested his prayers on behalf of the kingdom. (Jer. 21:1, 37:1) To him, Shemaiah directed his letter accusing Jeremiah of being a madman, and he read it to Jeremiah. (Jer. 29:24-29) When Jerusalem was taken, he and Seraiah the chief priest were carried to Riblah, and there murdered on the orders of Nebuchadnezzar. (2 Kings 25:18) Perhaps he lived too early to be the father of Hen and Josiah, the priests. (Zech. 6:10, 14)

ZERAH

(1) A son of Judah. See Zarah.

(2) A king of Cush, who, in the time of Asa, invaded the kingdom of Judah with a million footmen, and 300 chariots. But, being seized with panic, most of them were cut off. (2 Chron. 14:9-15)

ZERESH, *star of Venus*

The wife of Haman. See Esther 5:10, 14, 6:13

ZERUBBABEL, *shoot of Babylon*

The son of Shealtiel (or Salathiel), of the royal family of David. As Salathiel, who is called the son of Jehoiachin, might yet be the son of Neri, a descendant of Nathan the son of David, begotten by Jehoiachin with the widow of Neri, whom he had married, or he might have been adopted by Neri, or married the only daughter of Neri. (1 Chron. 3:17; Luke 3:27) So Zerubbabel might at once be the immediate son of Pedaiah, and the grandson of Salathiel; or Pedaiah, a younger brother, might have married Shealtiel's widow, and Zerubbabel may be the son raised up by his brother. (1 Chron. 3:19; Matt. 1:12) As Sheshbazzar is said to build the second Temple, and was prince of the Jews, it seems he was the very same as Zerubbabel, when the one is his Jewish, and the other his Chaldean, name. (Ezra 1:8, 14, 5:6; Zech. 4:5) Cyrus delivered into his hands the sacred vessels that had been carried to Babylon, to the number of 5400, and appointed him governor of the returning captives of Judah. After conducting 42,360 of them, together with 7337 servants, from Babylon to Judea, he laid the foundation of the second

Temple, and restored the worship of God by sacrifice. Despite many obstructions to the work by the Samaritans, whom the Jews refused to confer with, he and Joshua the High Priest, encouraged by Haggai and Zechariah the prophets, at last finished the Temple about 20 years after it had begun. (Ezra 1-6; Hag. 1-2; Zech. 4) He left behind seven sons: Meshullam, Hananiah, Hashubah, Ohel, Berechiah, Hasadiah, Jushabhesed, and a daughter called Shelomith. Some two of these sons, otherwise named, are Rhesa, from whom the Virgin Mary was descended, and Abiud from whom Joseph her husband sprang. (1 Chron. 3:19; Matt. 1:13; Luke 2:27)

Did not Zerubbabel prefigure our divine Saviour, who is the signet on God's right hand, and who has all things necessary for the welfare of the Church delivered into his hand; and who brings back his people from all their wanderings and captivity, and builds the temple of the Church with shoutings of *grace, grace* unto it, and carries all the glory. (Hag. 2:23)

ZIBA. See Mephibosheth
A former servant of Saul, who informed David that Mephibosheth, a son of Jonathan, was still alive. (2 Sam. 9:3)

ZILPAH. See Jacob
Concubine of Jacob, and mother of Gad and Asher. (Gen. 29:24, 30:9-13, 35:26, 37:2, 46:18)

ZIMRI
A general of Elah, the son of Baasha, King of Israel. As his master drank heartily at Tirzah, he murdered him and mounted the throne. He immediately killed the whole royal family as had been prophesied to Baasha. Hearing of this catastrophe, the royal army broke up the siege of Gibbethon, and hasted to dethrone Zimri. Finding himself incapable of defending himself, he set the palace on fire, and burnt himself and family to death after a short reign of seven days. (1 Kings 16:9-20) See Cozbi.

ZIPPORAH
The daughter of Jethro (or Reuel). Her marriage to Moses, and bearing him two sons, her accompanying him part of the way to Egypt, her

angry circumcision of her children, her return to her father's house, her coming to Moses with her father some months later, and Aaron and Miriam's jealousy of her influence over him, have been related in the article on Moses. (Exod. 2, 4, 18; Num. 12)

ZOPHAR

The Naamathite, one of Job's three uncharitable friends, who spoke twice against him. (Job 2:11, 11:20) He was forgiven through one of Job's prayers. (Job 42:7-9) Whether Naamath was the name of his ancestor or his city, we cannot determine; nor whether he was king of the Mineans, or of the Nomads (wandering Arabs).

ZUPH

A Levite, and one of Samuel's ancestors. As he was the chief of the Zuphites, he probably caused their territory to be called the land of Zuph, and their city Ramathzophin (Ramath of the Zuphites) (1 Sam. 9:5, 1:1; 1 Chron. 6:35)

AUTHORS QUOTED IN BROWN'S DICTIONARY

Aben Ezra, Abraham Ben Meir ....1092/3 - ?

Abuthnot, John 1667-1735

Alsted (Alstedius), Johann Heinrich....................................1588-1638

Aquila, Of Sinope 80-135

Artedi , Peter 1705-1735

Athenaeus, Of Naucratita ....Circa 200

Augustine, Aurelius..354-430

Bedford, Arthur 1668-1745

Bellarmine, Robert 1549-1607

Benjamin, Rabbi of Tudela...Wrote beteen 1159-1172

Ben Melech, Solomon ....15th-16th century

Bochart, Samuel..1599-1667

Boivin, Jean de Villeneuve 1663-1726

Boyle, Robert..1627-1691

Buffon, Georges 1707-1788

Bunting, Heinrich...1545-1606

Callimachus, Librarian at Alexandria ....Circa 305-240 BC

Calmet, Augustine...1672-1757

Cardan, Girolamo..1501-1576

Cato, Marcus Porcius ....95-46 BC

Caverhill, John...? - 1781

Cellarius, Solomon..1040-1105

Chandler, Edward..1668?-1750

Chardin, Sir John..1643-1713

Charleton, Walter..1619-1707

Cocceius, Johannes 1603-1669

Dale, Anthony van...1638-1708

Derham, William 1657-1735

Diodorus Siculus, Of Rome..Circa 49 BC

Dioscorides , Pedanius ....Circa 40-90

Doddridge, Philip 1702-1751

Dodwell, Henry 1641-1711

Eliezer, Rabbi (Jacob Braunschweig) ....? - 1729

Eneas, Roman and Trojan......................................?

Eratosthenes, of Cyrene ....257-194 BC

Eupolemus, Jewish historian.................................Circa 158BC

Eusebius, Bishop...260-340

Ferguson, James 1710-1776

Flamsteed, John 1646-1719

Fontenelle, Bernard le Bovier de 1657-1757

Forbes, Duncan...1685-1747

Gale, Theophilus...1628-1678

Gill, John 1697-1771

Gillespie, George 1623-1648

Gousset, Jacques...1635-1704

Gregory, John ....Circa 1650

Grotius, Hugo 1583-1645

Gussetius (Gousset), Jacobus ....Circa 1688

Halifax, William...Circa 1691

Herodotus, Greek historian in Egypt ....Circa 484-425 BC

Herschel, Dr. John 1792-1871

Hillel the Elder, Rabbi ....1st century BC

Hiller, Matthaeus 1646-1725

Hire, Gabrielle Philippe de la 1640-1718

Hottinger, Johann Conrad ....Wrote 1713-1757

Hughes, Vincent ....(1872-?)

Hutchison, Patrick...1740?-1802

Isidore, Of Seville ....560?-636

Irenaeus, Bishiop of Lyon ....Circa 130-circa 200

Jerome, Eusebius ....Circa 342-420

Jochanan (Yochanan), Rabbi bar Nappacha......................Circa 200-279

Josephus, Flavius..Circa 37-100

Judah (Yehuda), Hanasi Rabbi ....Circa AD 2nd century

Kimshi, David..1160?-1235

Kimshi, Moses..?-1190

Le Clerk, Jean 1657-1736

Leigh, Edward 1602-1671

Lemnius, Levinus 1505-1568

Leonardo, da Vinci..1452-1519

Leusden, Johannes...1624-1699

Lightfoot, John 1602-1675

Linnaeus, Karl von 1707-1778

Littleton, Lord Edward 1589-1645

Longinus, Cassius..Circa 213-273

Lowman, Moses 1680-1752

Ludolph of Saxony, Hiob 1624-1704

Maimonides, Moses..1135-1204

Macknight, James, Dr...1721-1800

Maundrell, Henry 1665-1701

Mede, Joseph 1586-1838

Menander, Of Greece ....342-291 BC

Mercator, Gerhard...1512-1594

Moebius, Georgius..Wrote 1677-1702

Mordecai, Nathan ....15th century

Newton, Isaac...1643-1727

Newton, Charles Thomas (archaeologist)................1818-1894

Nierembergius, John Eusebius..............................Circa 1600

Orellius, Johannes Conradus ....Circa 1828

Owen, John..1616-1683

Paine, Thomas 1737-1809

Pars, Adriaan..1641-1719

Patrick, Simon...1626-1707

Petavius, Dionysius 1583-1652

Pezron, Paul Yves...1639-1706

Philo, of Alexandria ....20 BC – AD 50

Pliny the Elder, Gaius Plinius Secundus 23-79

Pocock, Edward 1604-1691

Pontoppidan, Erik..1698-1764

Prideaux, Humphrey (Dean of Norwich) 1648-1724

Ptolemy (Ptolemaeus), Claudius, the geographer..........Circa 100-178

Quincy, John...? - 1722

Quintus, Curtius Rufus ....Circa AD 53

Ray, Playcard Augustin Fidèle ....Circa 1788

Reland, Adrian 1676-1718

Riccioli, Giambattista 1598-1671

Rollin, Charles 1661-1741

Rycaut, Sir Paul 1628-1700

Scaliger, Joseph Juste 1540-1609

Scheuchzer, Johann Jakob.....................................1672-1733

Selden, John...1584-1654

Shuckford, Samuel...1693/4-1754

Schultens, Albert 1686-1750

Shaw, Thomas, Dr 1694-1751

Sozomen, Salminius Hermias ....Died 447/448

Spanheim, Friedrich...1600-1649

Strabo, Of Pontus ....Circa 63 BC – AD 20

Stephanus, Of Byzantium......................................Ancient Greek historian

Sydenham, Thomas..1624-1689

Tavernier, Jean Baptiste..1605-1689

Tertullian, Quintus Septimius Florens..............................Circa 155-230

Thevenot, Jean de 1633-1667

Tournefort, Joseph Pitton de 1656-1708

Ussher, Bishop James...1581-1656

Valle de la Cerda, Luis ....Circa 1552-1606

Villalpandus, Juan Bautista....................................1552-1608

Villamont, Lord Jacques de, traveller ....Circa 1589

Vitringa, Campegius..1659-1722

Wells, Edward 1667-1727

Willoughby, Francis 1635-1672

Whiston, William 1667-1752

Witsius, Herman 1636-1708

The Systematic Theology
of John Brown of Haddington

Introduced by Joel R Beeke

John Brown (1722-1787) of Haddington was a leading Scottish minister in
the early eighteenth-century. He was
a devout Christian, a gifted preacher,
and prolific writer of theology. He
began life in obscure poverty, without advantage of wealth, position,
title, or education. Yet God favoured
him with unusual gifts and an enor-
mous capacity for hard work.

Brown taught himself Greek
while working in the fields. He became a man of deep spiritual expe-
rience with skill in preaching the doctrines of free grace and
piety. A Compendious View of Natural and Revealed Religion,
contains more than 26,000 proof texts and numerous exegetical
insights. This single volume of Reformed systematic theology is
rich in content and an indispensable tool for students, pastors,
and professors of theology.

*'It is a thrill and delight to see this excellent title reprinted and
available once again to the Christian public. It is an incredible
work, and ministers and preachers in particular, ought not to
begrudge a single penny spent on the purchase of a copy. Every
bible truth in all its relevant parts is stated and explained and
carefully laid out, with each phrase precisely crafted. At each
point, there are copious Bible references, leaving the reader in no
doubt thatwhat Brown has set before us has its roots in the Word
of God. This is a well-produced edition with clear print, and is
a pleasure to own.*

*One final comment: this volume ought to be required reading
for every candidate for the Christian ministry.'*

Bible League Quarterly

ISBN 978-1-89277-766-9

Christian Focus Publications

publishes books for all ages

Our mission statement –

STAYING FAITHFUL
In dependence upon God we seek to help make His infallible Word, the Bible, relevant. Our aim is to ensure that the Lord Jesus Christ is presented as the only hope to obtain forgiveness of sin, live a useful life and look forward to heaven with Him.

REACHING OUT
Christ's last command requires us to reach out to our world with His gospel. We seek to help fulfill that by publishing books that point people towards Jesus and help them develop a Christ-like maturity. We aim to equip all levels of readers for life, work, ministry and mission.

Books in our adult range are published in three imprints.
Christian Focus contains popular works including biographies, commentaries, basic doctrine and Christian living. Our children's books are also published in this imprint.
Mentor focuses on books written at a level suitable for Bible College and seminary students, pastors, and other serious readers. The imprint includes commentaries, doctrinal studies, examination of current issues and church history.
Christian Heritage contains classic writings from the past.

Christian Focus Publications, Ltd
Geanies House, Fearn, Ross-shire,
IV20 1TW, Scotland, United Kingdom
info@christianfocus.com
www.christianfocus.com